Appraising Economic Theories

Appraising Economic Theories

Studies in the Methodology of Research Programs

Edited by

Neil de Marchi
Professor of Economics, Duke University
Professor of the History and Methodology of Economics, University of Amsterdam

and

Mark Blaug
Professor Emeritus, University of London
Consultant Professor, University of Buckingham
Visiting Professor, University of Exeter

Edward Elgar

Published by
Edward Elgar Publishing Limited
Gower House
Croft Road
Aldershot
Hants GU11 3HR
England

Edward Elgar Publishing Company
Old Post Road
Brookfield
Vermont 05036
USA

British Library Cataloguing in Publication Data
Appraising economic theories: studies in the methodology of research programs
1. Economics.
I. De Marchi, Neil II. Blaug, Mark *1927–*
330.1

Library of Congress Cataloguing in Publication Data
Appraising economic theories: studies in the methodology of research programs/edited by Neil de Marchi and Mark Blaug.
p. cm.
Includes bibliographical references and indexes.
1. Economics–Methodology. 2. Economics–Research. I. De Marchi, Neil. II. Blaug, Mark.
HB131.A68 1991
330′.072–dc20
91–21788
CIP

ISBN 1 85278 515 2

Printed in Great Britain by
Billing & Sons Ltd, Worcester

Contents

List of Contributors viii
Acknowledgement ix

Introduction: Rethinking Lakatos 1
Neil de Marchi

PART I THE CRITERION OF EMPIRICAL PROGRESS IN ECONOMICS

A Theoretical Progress and Excess Content

1 Popper, Lakatos and Theoretical Progress in Economics 35
Jeremy Shearmur
Comment 53
Kurt Klappholz

2 The Problem of Excess Content: Economics, Novelty and a Long Popperian Tale 58
D. Wade Hands
Comment 76
Bert Hamminga
Comment 85
Uskali Mäki
Reply 91
D. Wade Hands

B Testing

3 Testing in Modern Economics: the Case of Job Search Theory 105
Jinbang Kim
Comment 132
Neil de Marchi

4 Do Economists Test Theories? – Demand Analysis and Consumption Analysis as Tests of Theories of Economic Methodology 137
Christopher L. Gilbert

Comment 169
Marjorie B. McElroy

C Empirical Hypotheses in Game Theory and Experimental Economics

5 Strategic Interactions in Economics: the Game Theoretic Alternative 179
Marina Bianchi and Hervé Moulin

6 Lakatos and Experimental Economics 197
Vernon L. Smith, Kevin A. McCabe and Stephen J. Rassenti

Comment 227
H.M. Collins

PART II PROGRAM IDENTIFICATION AND PROGRAM RIVALRY

A On Including and Excluding Lines of Enquiry

7 The Stamping Out of Process Analysis in Econometrics 237
Mary Morgan

Comment 266
Roger E. Backhouse

Reply 270
Mary Morgan

8 Stabilizing Dynamics 273
E. Roy Weintraub

Comment 291
Philip Mirowski

9 Alternative Accounts of Equilibrium Unemployment 294
Rod Cross

Comment 324
Mark Blaug

Comment 327
J.A. Kregel

B Delineating Programs

10 The Development of New Classical Macroeconomics: Lessons for Lakatos 335
Rodney Maddock

Comment 360
Alessandro Vercelli

11 Scientific Research Program or Tribe? A Joint Appraisal of Lakatos and the New Classical Macroeconomics 364
Kevin D. Hoover
Comment 395
Nancy J. Wulwick
Reply 401
Kevin D. Hoover
12 The Neo-Walrasian Research Program in Macroeconomics 403
Roger E. Backhouse
Comment 427
Maarten C.W. Janssen

C Assessing Sraffian and Austrian Economics
13 Negative and Positive Contributions: Appraising Sraffa and Lakatos 435
Ian Steedman
Comment 451
Stefano Zamagni
Comment 456
Edwin Burmeister
14 The Progress of Subjectivism 470
Don Lavoie
Comment 487
Bruce J. Caldwell

15 History and Sociology of Science and History and Methodology of Economics 492
H.M. Collins
16 Afterword 499
Mark Blaug

Bibliography 513
Name Index 557
Subject Index 563

Contributors

Roger E. Backhouse, University of Birmingham, UK.
Marina Bianchi, University of Rome.
Mark Blaug, University of Buckingham, UK; University of Exeter, UK.
Edwin Burmeister, Duke University, USA.
Bruce J. Caldwell, University of North Carolina, Greensboro, USA.
H.M. Collins, University of Bath, UK.
Rod Cross, University of Strathclyde, UK.
Christopher L. Gilbert, University of London, UK.
Bert Hamminga, University of Brabant, Tilburg, The Netherlands.
D. Wade Hands, University of Puget Sound, USA.
Kevin D. Hoover, University of California, Davis, USA.
Maarten C.W. Janssen, Erasmus University, The Netherlands.
Jinbang Kim, University of California, Riverside, USA.
Kurt Klappholz, London School of Economics, UK.
J.A. Kregel, Johns Hopkins University Bologna Center, Italy.
Don Lavoie, George Mason University, USA.
Kevin A. McCabe, University of Arizona, USA.
Marjorie B. McElroy, Duke University, USA.
Rodney Maddock, La Trobe University, Australia.
Uskali Mäki, University of Helsinki.
Neil de Marchi, Duke University, USA; University of Amsterdam, The Netherlands.
Philip Mirowski, University of Notre Dame, USA.
Mary Morgan, London School of Economics, UK.
Hervé Moulin, Duke University, USA.
Stephen J. Rassenti, University of Arizona, USA.
Jeremy Shearmur, George Mason University, USA.
Vernon L. Smith, University of Arizona, USA.
Ian Steedman, University of Manchester, UK.
Alessandro Vercelli, University of Siena, Italy.
E. Roy Weintraub, Duke University, USA.
Nancy J. Wulwick, Old Dominion University, USA.
Stefano Zamagni, University of Bologna, Italy.

Acknowledgement

The editors and contributors wish to thank the Latsis Foundation and Dr Spiro Latsis whose generous support made possible the conference held in Capri, 15-18 October 1989 as well as the preparation of this volume.

Introduction: Rethinking Lakatos

Neil de Marchi[1]

Imre Lakatos's paper, 'Falsification and the methodology of scientific research programmes', appeared in 1970, in a conference volume entitled *Criticism and the Growth of Knowledge*. An earlier version had been published in a philosophical journal, but the conference volume version is the one known to economists and happens also to be the main vehicle by which Lakatos's ideas have entered our profession. Earlier work on the development of (informal) mathematics, and various later papers on scientific progress, containing what look like serious modifications of some of his notions, have been largely ignored. For practical purposes, then, MSRP – the methodology of scientific research programs – must be considered Lakatos's main legacy to economics. The papers printed in the present volume were produced for a conference of economists, economic methodologists and historians of economics, with a leavening of philosophers and sociologists of scientific knowledge, convened to reflect on the question whether MSRP, in the light of 20 years' experience, had proved useful. Somewhat more precisely formulated, we wanted to know whether MSRP, in the hands of methodologists and especially historians of economics, had shown itself to be an appropriate framework for analysing what economics is and is not like. I take it as my task in this Introduction to give a critical overview of what has been accomplished and to indicate what remains still to be done. This will serve also as a backdrop against which to view the conference papers.

I shall ask first how economists see themselves relative to Lakatos's view of the 'good' scientist. My argument will be that economists' self-image is extraordinarily close to the ideal portrayed in MSRP. Next, I turn to what economic methodologists have enabled us to understand about the things that economists actually do. There is a three-way distinction to be drawn here. There is the unrestricted range of activities engaged in by economists; there is the narrower set of concerns singled out by Lakatosian preoccupations; and, within that narrower range, there is a difference to be attended to between what methodology has chosen for emphasis and what could be emphasized but has not. I shall argue that we have been shown, with the help of Lakatosian questions, that there are problems in reconciling economists' self-image with the reality of economic practice, but also that, even within the set of Lakatosian concerns, there is much about economic practice that has not begun to be explored. Finally I ask what historians of economics have been able to do with MSRP. Here I make a distinction between fairly mechanical applications of MSRP and what I choose to call creative applications. The so-called creative applications are so designated because they set out to explore the question, 'What is economics like?' in terms of what economists are to be observed doing, rather than the question, 'Can we obtain a reasonable fit between MSRP and economics?' The main difference is the absence of any presumption about 'fit' in the former approach, a difference that may appear subtle but seems to cause striking differences of outcome, as it does in applied econometric research. Another difference is that I count as creative exploratory uses of ideas to be found in Lakatos's overall work, not just in 'Falsification and the methodology of scientific research programmes'.

THE LAKATOSIAN SELF-IMAGE OF ECONOMISTS

Economists have taken on some Lakatosian terminology; more than in the case of Popper or Kuhn, but less than one might expect, given what I see as a very considerable overlap in perspective between Lakatos's methodology and the 'official' methodology of mainstream economics. Economists have taken from Popper not much more than the notions of falsifiable consequences and of testing to refute and to eliminate error. They seem largely unaware of and uninterested in what he wrote about situational analysis, verisimilitude, excess content, objective knowledge, discovery as an evolutionary process and a host of other subjects. Moreover, as has been widely broadcast, acceptance of the ideal of falsifiability has not led to many serious attempts at falsifying; nor have refuted hypotheses been a conspicuous cause of theory rejection among economists. Kuhn's concepts – normal and revolutionary science, exemplars, paradigms (in the broader sense of disciplinary matrices) – never gained much purchase in mainstream economic writing. But from Lakatos economists have openly adopted terms – some of them, I realize, also to be found in Popper – such as research program and 'ad hoc' stratagems (as applied to non-heuristically driven moves) and the idea of competing programs which in turn may 'progress' or 'degenerate' in terms of the 'novel facts' they do or do not predict. What is more, they seem to take these ideas and terms seriously.

As I see it, these adoptions represent something like a natural fit and signal a deeper underlying agreement about the nature and ideal practice of science. From the economist's perspective, of course, that means that he or she makes an identification with Lakatos's version of physical and mathematical science. I have in mind the following important shared elements (in which I have italicized the Lakatosian element).

1. The two – mainstream economics and the Lakatosian methodology – share Popper's Three Worlds hierarchy: a world of physical phenomena; a world of beliefs; and a world of objective, rational knowledge. *Science* (read also economics) *is rational and objective*, meaning in part that its products cannot be reduced to the observation reports that may inform them or the beliefs and social interactions associated with producing them. For the Lakatos of *Proofs and Refutations* the ascent (here just from World 2 to World 3) is illustrated by the transformation of a conjecture into a proof. For the Lakatos of MSRP a corroborated novel fact (behind which lies a theoretical novel fact) may not constitute certain knowledge, but it is on a level above the fact that certain observations guided the test conjecture in the first place, and it stands independent of the fact that certain beliefs and social conventions may have 'driven' the research. In economics, these distinctions can be illustrated by reference to statistical demand curves, which were much discussed in the 1920s and 1930s. How do you convince someone that an observation report suggesting a positive relation between prices and quantities purchased could be a (sort of) demand curve? The observations alone will not do, since they are capable of being interpreted as a supply relation. Strong conviction is also insufficient, unless it can be combined with a theory which says that there may be dominant (negative) income effects, and with evidence that these probably are present. This explanatory theory and the evidence in question are both capable of being inter-subjectively criticized and in this sense the 'knowledge' they yield is rational, objective. I suggest that this sort of thinking, which forms part of Lakatos's methodology, has such a long tradition in economics (going back at least to John Stuart Mill, who showed why inter-subjective or *common* sense-based deductive analysis is to be counted as knowledge in a way that observation reports and mere preferred beliefs are not) that it is almost instinctive to economists.

2. A second shared element of methodology is the notion that *the rationality of science* (economics) *can be seen in its progress*, where

progress is *measured by excess content*. Economists usually do not speak of excess content or even of novel facts; but they do deem it essential that a theory account for out-of-sample data, and they do seem to judge it significant that a theory explain more than its rivals. The first criterion is the same as the injunction of Lakatosians that the same fact should not be used twice (once in constructing and again in testing a theory) and the second is simply one definition of excess content.

3. For Lakatos, *rational progress also points to the way scientists actually behave*; that is, they will not be observed switching allegiance towards a theory with nothing more than in-sample 'tests' to its credit or with less explanatory power than rivals. Thus the rational progress view accounts for the best gambits of actual scientists. Economists' scepticism about data mining, their sensitivity to the problems of specification and their discomfort with black-box 'testing', which looks at predictions but leaves the structure and explanatory power of the rival theories obscure, suggests that they share much the same view of the good scientist.

4. Again, for Lakatos, *the appropriate unit for appraising rational progress (or best gambits) is the 'research program'*. The two essentials of a Lakatosian research program are its hard core and its heuristics. Economists do not in fact refer to their presuppositions as a hard core, but they adopt the notion of untouchable guiding principles which shape the dos and don'ts of coherent research strategies, and that amounts to the same thing. Moreover they wholly share the perspective that these principles are either metaphysical presuppositions or at best propositions which are an admixture of introspection or casual observation plus an a priori element (for example, agents have preferences). As to heuristics, it has been shown (Hands, 1988) that economic theorists' preferred use of the term ad hoc is as a way of making plain that rivals build their theories with the help of elements that have no internal, theoretical or programmatic justification. This is Lakatos's ad hoc_3, distinguished by him from other senses of ad hoc in order to stress the heuristic component (*Philosophical Papers, Vol. I*, p. 40, n. 7, p. 88, n. 2, p. 149 and n. 2).

5. Finally, I see a shared element in the *primary role given to theory* by Lakatos. Recall that the course of progress for him is, first, the generation of theoretical novel facts. This is to be followed, certainly, by empirical corroboration, but only intermittently and (to judge from his examples) often over a span of centuries. Thus, without challenging the notion that corroborated novel facts are the ultimate test for Lakatos, there is inevitably a temporal and numerical primacy to be accorded theoretical novelties. Recall, too, that, because experiments

and measurement are theoretically constituted, advance is in an analytical sense also inevitably theoretical: it is a matter of finding consistency between theories; the theories that enable us to make certain measurements and the theories that interpret them (ibid., pp. 44–5 and n. 2, p. 45). Thirdly, if one takes seriously Lakatos's late emendation to the definition of novel fact, that it is also novel to give a precise explanation for something already known but merely 'fortuitous' within existing theory (ibid., pp. 179, 183, 184–5, 186), then once again the primacy of theory is clear.[2] Lastly, recall that, because programs are connected sequences of theories, anomalies must not be allowed to distract a scientist from the line of inquiry dictated by the heuristics of the program. This, in practice, means a fair measure of theoretical autonomy in research. All of this is in line with the way economists function: statistical and economic theory governs the way they perceive and use numbers; the difficulties of testing mean that the primary impetus in economic research is theoretical; and economists place a relatively high value on explanations which are counter-intuitive. That in itself is a reflection of a belief in some deeper connectedness lying beneath the world of surface phenomena; a connectedness that reveals itself to the theoretician.

To summarize: I have suggested that economists (of the mainstream) share with Lakatos and Lakatosians a view of economics (science) as rational and objective; that they implicitly agree to measure rationality in the form of progress, as judged by excess content (or novelty); that there is strong conviction on both sides that reconstructions of the best gambits of economists (scientists) using the notion of (rational) progress will fit 'actual' history closely; that there is agreement that the appropriate unit of analysis for appraising the best gambits is the research program; and that the two seem to agree on the primary role of theory in the advance of science (economics).

My initial assertion (above) was that the area of agreement is so broad, and involves such key elements, that it is perhaps a little surprising that economists have not adopted more of a Lakatosian terminology. Whatever the reason for that, the common perspective remains the important thing. I am aware that many observers have expressed informed doubt about the applicability to economics of a set of ideas developed from mathematics and physics (see, for example, Hutchison, Leijonhufvud, and Hicks, all in Latsis, *Method and Appraisal in Economics*). The objections, having to do mostly with the difficulty of experimentation in economics and the non-repeating character of economic data and circumstances, are well taken; my claim is only that economists see themselves very much as Lakatosian methodology would imply. Whether it is proper that they view themselves this way is another matter. Some methodologists (Latsis, 1972, appendix; *Method and Appraisal in Economics*, p. 10; Rosenberg, 1986) have drawn attention to the tension between economists' self-image and the reality of their situation, arguing that Lakatos holds certain attractions for mainstream economists precisely because he offers a less bizarre-sounding replacement for Friedman's unrealism-of-assumptions methodology to justify their convictions in the face of falsifying evidence. Even if I am right in claiming a large overlap in perspective between Lakatosian methodology and mainstream economists' preferred self-image, the possibility that there is a reality gap means that the question whether MSRP truly applies to economics remains open.

It is an important part of the work of economic methodologists and historians of economic thought to draw attention to the reality gap, if it exists, and to define it more precisely. Often, however, it is difficult to separate out what is historical and what is methodological in work that uses Lakatos's MSRP. Hence, when I come to talk about historians' uses of Lakatos, I shall in fact be addressing elements that might also quite properly be called methodological. In the next section I confine myself as closely as possible to strictly methodological issues.

LAKATOS AND ECONOMIC METHODOLOGY

Methodologists are in the business of providing critical tools for reflecting on what it is that economists do. Economists, for their part, engage in a whole range of activities of potential interest to the methodologist: they generate hypotheses; they offer explanations; they describe tests; they invoke presuppositions; they set up idealized worlds; they estimate models; they discuss the realism of assumptions; and so on. These various activities constitute a rich field for methodological exploration. Methodologists focusing on Lakatos, however, have inevitably isolated a rather narrower set of issues. Specifically, the set of Lakatosian concerns comprises: rationality as progress; theoretical versus empirical progress; the concept of novelty; strategic coherence (positive heuristics); the unit of appraisal (research program); negative heuristics and the role of metaphysical presuppositions in theory development; and the comparability of research programs. Philosophers (Watkins, Worrall, Koertge, Musgrave, Zahar, Pera and others) have clarified some of these issues. Economic methodology in this respect has been largely derivative (a claim I do not think needs demonstrating); but it has contributed quite a lot to our understanding of just what the economists' self-image involves. It is worth listing these contributions.

1. We now know that there are considerable *difficulties in identifying novel facts and hence in measuring excess content*. Some of these are conceptual. To illustrate, if a progressive theory T_2 must always incorporate the refuted content of its predecessor and rival T_1, what conclusion do we draw if T_2 includes a prediction impossible under T_1? Presumably that T_2 cannot subsume all the unrefuted content of T_1, since that content includes the impossibility of the new fact (Bicchieri, 1989, p. 244). Moreover, if the predicted new fact is actually observed, there is surely a decrease of content (defining content as the total of all forbidden events, which, following Popper, is the way Lakatos acknowledges that he originally defined novelty: *Philosophical Papers, Vol. I*, p. 184); hence T_2 cannot represent progress (Hamminga comment, this volume). Lakatos later, as noted above, amended his definition to allow for the first exact explanation of a fact previously known but not explained (*Philosophical Papers, Vol. I*, p. 185); yet this also raises new problems about the commensurability of (say) T_1 and T_2.

   Historically, as Hands (this volume) has made clear, the whole exercise of measuring progressiveness in terms of excess content seems to derive from the idea that science aims at achieving ever 'deeper' theories, which Popper interpreted as a striving for verisimilitude or nearness to truth. Lakatos, in addition, stressed corroboration because he felt a need for 'signs' of a growing verisimilitude; otherwise excess content is just a methodological proposal without epistemological weight. Yet, as Hands also points out, verisimilitude is acknowledged by Popper and critics alike to be so problematic that it might be judged a failure, whence it follows that Lakatos was building upon sand. On a practical level, the implication is that working economists, in their own clear preference for theories of greater explanatory power, either do not know whereof they speak, or they mean something relatively straightforward that the rest of us have somehow missed (for example, a qualitative notion of verisimilitude). The last is a real possibility; all that we can confidently say is that economists cannot pretend to be 'simply following' a Lakatosian prescription.
2. Methodologists have also contributed some useful *analysis of the problems of delineating research programs* (Blaug, 'Kuhn versus Lakatos'; Remenyi, 1979; Fulton, 1984; Backhouse, this volume

and 'Lakatos and Economics'). The issues will come up again in the section(s) dealing with the work of historians of economics, so I shall say no more at this stage, except to note that here too what we may have learned is that working economists know what they mean while methodologists have been pursuing problems of their own making. We may thus urge methodologists to attend more closely to the language of economists. But economists should not assume that they can appropriate a term such as 'research program' with impunity.

3. Methodological analysis, thirdly, has given us a better appreciation of the *difficulties in applying the criterion of empirical progress in economics* (Blaug, *The Methodology of Economics*; Desai, 1981; Cross, 1982; Weintraub, 1988; Wulwick, 1989; de Marchi and Kim, 1989; Kim, 1990; Morgan, *The History of Econometric Ideas*). We now know, for example, that theories *as such* are not tested; rather predictions of theories are shaped into testable form by the deployment of various auxiliary assumptions. These auxiliary assumptions render unobservable variables measurable; they specify certain selected variables as being the ones of interest; they impose a parametric form on the relationship between the selected explanatory variables and the dependent variable; they express the relationship as one involving an error term, rendering it testable with passive observations; and so on. Most of these deployments are matters of decision, and various criteria are involved, including judgements about what is important, but also constraints such as manageability. There are rarely, if ever, unique deductive links between theory and parameter estimates. All this is common knowledge to applied econometricians, and in a sense what we have witnessed is methodologists catching up with common or 'best' practice. That is probably as it should be: methodologists bringing a critical understanding to bear on agendas set by practitioners. The fact remains that it is now a widely shared understanding that economists' 'tests', or corroborations, are at best what Lakatos refers to in 'Falsification and the methodology of scientific research programmes' as checks for inconsistency within the 'maze of theories', interpretative and explanatory, involved in shaping testable predictions (*Philosophical Papers, Vol. I*, pp. 44–5, 45 n. 2).
4. Finally, methodological concern has resulted in a more refined *appreciation of the role of various types and levels of argumentation in economic discourse* (Harvey-Phillips, 1983; Fulton, 1984; Klamer, 'Levels of Discourse'; Maddock, 1984; Glass and Johnson,

1988; Mäki, 'On the Problem of Realism' and comment, this volume).

These contributions have shown us a lot about what we cannot expect of economics as well as a lot about what it is like. Uskali Mäki has drawn this distinction recently (1990) and used it to argue a different point: that methodologists have allowed themselves to be unduly beholden to 'epistemological questions related to rational theory choice or rational theory development, formulated in a dynamic but anti-inductivist and asocial framework' (p. 79). In other words, the Popperian–Lakatosian agenda is too narrow. I agree that, while we ignore positive questions about how economists actually use metaphysics, for example, or how they actually (inductively) generate hypotheses and support their convictions, we are unlikely to arrive at any very coherent understanding of what economics is like. But here I want to suggest that a different order of criticism is worth attending to: even in the narrow context that Lakatosian methodology has reserved for itself, a lot has been neglected. Thus there has been almost no consideration by economic methodologists of the following matters within the subset of Lakatosian concerns, even though Lakatos himself in several instances gives positive hints of their importance:

- the evolution of heuristics, or the possible mutual evolution of heuristics and hard core (recall Lakatos's comment that the hard core hardens only slowly, by trial and error: *Philosophical Papers, Vol. I*, pp. 48 n. 4, and 181; and the hint that 'it is the progressing problematic frontiers of knowledge, and not its relatively solid core [unproblematic background knowledge], which gives science its scientific character': *Philosophical Papers, Vol. II*, p. 174; cf. p. 172);
- the relation between heuristics as the techniques of problem-solving (or *local* fields of concern) and program-related guidelines for modelling (or *program-wide* concerns) (recall his comment that 'progress is not even so much in the actual novel predictions . . . but in the mathematical and physical novelty of problem-solving techniques which later lead to, and form a part of, a progressive research programme': *Philosophical Papers, Vol. II*, p. 101);
- the role of empirical work in economics, given that only rarely does it have to do with testing;
- whether there is epistemic value in the discovery, and not just the deductive-testing, phase of research (why should proof analysis,

the centre of attention in *Proofs and Refutations*, and said there to be a creative enterprise, involving guesswork and intuitive leaps (1976, pp. 107 n. 1, and 142; *Philosophical Papers, Vols. I and II*, pp. 72, 79), have zero value as 'knowledge', especially considering what was just concluded about corroboration as basically a consistency check?);
- the deployment of metaphysical presuppositions by economists (here the path-breaking work by Phil Mirowski (1989) on guiding metaphors is a spectacular exception);
- how we may understand 'the acknowledged best games and the most esteemed gambits' (*Philosophical Papers, Vol. I*, p. 145) of economists in a way that gives due weight to elite and other social elements in science, *and* to the convictions of many economists that they are theorizing in a way that reflects elements which have a real existence.

Some of these neglected questions will re-emerge when we look at the work done by historians of economics interested in MSRP. Seeing them in that other context will also help to give them point; so I move at once to a consideration of the existing historical work.

LAKATOS AND HISTORY OF ECONOMICS I: SOME GAINS

Because economics is neither mathematics nor physics, Lakatos's MSRP may be a blunt instrument for finding out what economics is like. That possibility should alert the historian to beware of naive assertions of correspondence between the rational histories of those disciplines and of economics. The expectation that MSRP might nonetheless help the historian of economics is based on a belief in the potential transferability of Lakatos's categories (rational versus non-rational; empirical versus theoretical), the aptness of his unit for appraisal (the research program) and the questions he leads one to ask. What presuppositions are driving this program (hereafter RP)? Can one identify coherent strategies for modelling? Are anomalies allowed to divert the economists in this or that RP from their strategies? Are there other signs that this or that line of research is non-rational? Does one observe progressive problem shifts occurring? And so on. If these are the sort of questions that open up a field in ways that shed fresh light, the fact that they were initially developed in reconstructing histories of mathematics and physics is irrelevant.[3]

Sticking with the positive, I shall list some of what I consider to be illuminating studies that proceed using Lakatosian categories and questions. Some of these studies also go beyond Lakatos, and I shall mention that fact where appropriate. For the rest the studies generally meet two criteria: they tell us things we did not know before; and they focus attention on things that are not obvious to someone bent on a more or less mechanical application of MSRP. (The sorts of things I have in mind here are what I have just called Lakatosian concerns, but using a generous interpretation.) Those are not strong criteria; there may be other things, outside MSRP, that are more or just as worthwhile. Some of these I have mentioned in introducing the section on Lakatos and economic methodology. Here I beg the question of whether the issues chosen by the studies to be cited are the ones most needing to be worked on in order simply to report on what the creative use of Lakatos has yielded so far.[4]

(a) There have been fascinating *analyses of what might be called theoretical progress in economics*. These neglect Lakatos's criterion of empirical progress as something not striven for nor achieved by economists. Instead they concentrate on Popper's notion of problem situation, the logic of the context, and on degree of success in problem-solving as the criterion of progress. Latsis's analysis of the orthodox theory of the firm (1972, 'A research programme in economics' and 'The limitations of single-exit models'), and Wong's (1978) extended study of what he calls Samuelson's Revealed Preference Research Programme, are both excellent in this genre. They are generally regarded as falling outside the realm of strict applications of Lakatos's MSRP – though Latsis must be credited with having introduced Lakatos to economists – but precisely because so much of modern economics appears to be only remotely empirical their relevance is unquestioned.

These studies, it also bears saying, need not be viewed as un-Lakatosian. Lakatos in *Proofs and Refutations* stressed proof as the outcome of a process of problem solving and, in later writings, including 'Falsification and the methodology of scientific research programmes', he shifted the emphasis from novel facts to techniques of problem solving. Thus we read of 'heuristic techniques which provide the tools for forging ahead' (*Philosophical Papers, Vol. II*, p. 220; cf. *Philosophical Papers, Vol. I*, p. 179). Even more plainly, in reference to Newton's work – the outstanding example for Lakatos of a successful research program – we find the comment partly cited above:

> . . . progress is not even so much in the actual novel predictions which go beyond the premises . . . but in the mathematical and physical novelty of

> problem-solving techniques which later lead to, and form part of, a progressive research programme. (1978b, p. 101)

An outstanding set of illustrations of heuristics as problem solving is to be found in a recent study by Maarten Janssen, *Micro and Macro in Economics* (1990).

(b) The idea that the hard core is not carved in stone at the inception of an RP has given rise to one richly detailed study of what its author (following a hint of Lakatos, *Philosophical Papers, Vol. I*, p. 48 n. 4) calls the hardening of the hard core, in the case of proofs of existence of general competitive equilibrium (Weintraub, 'Appraising General Equilibrium Analysis' and *General Equilibrium Analysis*). Doubts have been expressed as to whether this is not explicating a bit of economics that is in fact so close to mathematics as to be indistinguishable; but *the notion that hard cores may evolve along with heuristics*, a possibility stressed by Alan Musgrave (1976), has been picked up, and pursued with intriguing results, by Birner (1990). Birner uses the distinction between idealizing and factualized models, and argues that idealizing models embody the logical presuppositions of factualized models, rather than, as is usually suggested, the latter being the empirically testable implications logically derivable from idealizing models. This yields the notion that the set of presuppositions necessary to a class of factualized models, together with a common metaphysics, is the hard core of that class of models. This treatment opens up for further exploration the view expressed by Lakatos in *Proofs and Refutations*, that finding necessary (and sufficient) conditions is a part of the creative process. It also suggests that work within a program is less a matter of guided deduction from presuppositions already firmly in place than seems often to have been assumed. Birner has shown some of the potential inherent in his approach in a detailed study of the reswitching and capital reversing debates (once again, however, an area of theoretical economics).

(c) There have been many attempts to come to terms with the difficulty of establishing *whether research programs are narrow or broad*. Because I see so much of modern economics as being analytical and technique-driven, and because of the weight I give to Lakatos's own comments on the importance of techniques, I tend to favour an interpretation which stresses the narrow idea of RP as connected sequence of models (see de Marchi, 1976). Fulton (1984) reaches a similar conclusion, but bases himself more explicitly on Lakatos's own incorporation of mathematical versions of physical laws in the hard core. This narrow, technique-defined view of RP clearly will not do, however, for most of the history of economics (O'Brien, 1976); and the whole matter of the relation of narrow to broad lines of work remains vexed (Blaug, 'Kuhn versus Lakatos' and *A Methodological Appraisal of Marxian Economics* illustrates the problems; Remenyi, 1979, offers a solution which, however, has not found much favour).

(d) A beginning has been made on the issue of *how RPs interact.* Remenyi started down this road, with his idea of a central core (neoclassical analysis) and sub-disciplinary demi-cores in modern mainstream applied economics. More recently Hendry's notion of encompassing has been viewed as a way to render comparison between programs manageable; but encompassing has been developed only for empirical (statistical) models, leaving us with unanswered Kuhnian-type questions about commensurability for more theory-based areas of inquiry. A third recent development that looks promising is the introduction of the idea that there may be guide programs (determining the issues to be addressed) and supply programs (providing the language and methods for tackling those issues). Janssen (comment in this volume, and 1992), borrowing the broad duality idea from Zandvoort (1986), has successfully applied it to modern macroeconomics.

(e) Perhaps the most intensive effort has been that devoted to the matter of *defining and identifying novel facts*. This is understandable given that Popperian or Lakatosian progress in one RP as compared with another requires a measure of excess content. Attention has been focused on novelty in the sense of unexpected (inconsistent with previous expectation or background knowledge) and hence on the novel as genuinely new and/or forbidden by the preceding or rival theory (see Lakatos, *Philosophical Papers, Vol. I*, pp. 32, 33–4, 36, 39). Hamminga (comment, this volume) offers a way of operationalizing the latter notion, but neglects other senses of novel that Lakatos stressed in his later work. These modifications were of two sorts: one was that observations may count as novel if they played no part in the design of the challenger theory; the other was that novelty may include a precise explanation for something previously known but merely 'fortuitous' within the old theory (see Lakatos, *Philosophical Papers, Vol. I*, pp. 179, 183, 184–5, 186). The first of these modifications has become known as the heuristic sense of novelty. Along with the newness/forbiddenness aspects this has been given close attention by Hands ('Second thoughts on Lakatos' and 1990). In an extended exchange between Hands and Blaug (1990, 1991; see also Ahonen, 1989, 1990), clarification has been reached as to what really was novel about Keynes's economics. But Hands remains unhappy about the restrictiveness of Lakatosian novelty, which seems not to allow place for many of what would be widely regarded as major novel contributions in economics. Moreover (I would add), the final gloss by Lakatos, incorporating as novel also the first precise explanations of known facts, has been ignored in the discussions to date, even though, as I suspect, this may be the most obviously relevant to modern economics.[5]

(f) A little work has been done directly *testing for economics the Lakatosian notion that scientists do on the whole behave rationally* (Latsis, 'A research programme in economics', on the development of theories of the firm; de Marchi, 1976, on responses to an empirical anomaly; Maddock, 1984, on why the proponents of New Classical Macroeconomics began to shift focus in the mid–1970s; Blaug, 'Second Thoughts on the Keynesian Revolution', on what exactly economists found good about Keynes's economics). But only the first of these attempts truly to meet the criteria of a test; for that demands that any historical account using Lakatosian notions not only be shown to fit the facts but to fit them better than alternative accounts, such as those which presume that scientists are guided by conventionalist, or simple falsificationist beliefs. It is odd that this rather vital requirement has been almost completely ignored (though see the useful comments by Fisher, 1986, pp. 57–64 and Vint's (1990) examination of the Thornton–Mill debate).

(g) Some outstanding historical work has been done on *problem shifts as bearers of a research strategy* (Maddock, 1984; Weintraub, 1988 and this volume). Weintraub's contribution to this volume stresses the importance of stabilizing meanings as a part of this process, a World 2 consideration of which Lakatos would not have approved; while Maddock (1984) identifies the problem shift in New Classical Economics in the mid–1970s not so much as part of a progressive change within an RP but as a tactical device to undermine rival work. Neither contribution, therefore, remains strictly within World 3; nor does the discourse analysis in Klamer ('Levels of discourse in new classical economics') which partly inspired Weintraub. These efforts none the less raise questions about the social conditions of the production of 'knowledge' – the World 2 to World 3 shift, in Lakatos's Popperian terminology – which, when based on modern pragmatic philosophy's challenge to rationality as a privileged standpoint, threaten to undermine the comfortable link in MSRP between knowledge and rationality.

(h) Finally, there are individual studies that fit into no general category but light up a particular area: Hands's (1984) discussion of crucial counter-examples in stability analysis; the gambits introduced and discussed by Vernon Smith (1989) in his exposition of experimental economics, a program which in an important sense is his own creation;

and Wulwick's (1989) discussion of how the Phillips conjecture became an empirical regularity.

LAKATOS AND HISTORY OF ECONOMICS II: DUBIOUS PROGRESS

If I have been critical even of the work that I find most constructive, the bulk of existing Lakatosian studies by historians or historian–methodologists gives much less reason to be satisfied. A summary characterization is included as an appendix (below), giving some information about the existing literature. In it I have tried to convey (1) a sense of the range of opinion that prevails about what constitutes a research program and (2) a sense of whether the proponent(s) of regarding some particular line of research as an RP also (i) give some detail about the hard core, (ii) explicitly characterize or list the positive heuristics, and (iii) assess the testable implications of the putative RP in question. I have been quite liberal in giving a 'y' for 'yes' answer ('n' stands for 'no'). This attempt at characterizing the existing literature generates several observations.

Recall the list of neglected questions from the section on Lakatos and economic methodology. On two of these, the role of the empirical, and the deployment of (metaphysical) presuppositions, most historical studies are conspicuously silent. Thus it is surprising, *firstly*, how many of the studies stick to theory without empirical assessment (y;y;n is a common pattern) even though Lakatos himself strongly stressed the empirical criterion as the ultimate check on progress; or, even more puzzling, merely suggest the existence of RPs but give little or no identifying analysis (the n;n;n and n;n;y patterns).

The neglect of empirical assessment, as has been hinted at above, may reflect, for better or worse, the nature of much work in modern economics, pretensions about testing notwithstanding. But perhaps it is also too easy simply to dismiss empirical inquiry in economics as all pretence and no substance. Economists do display serious interest in data and data preparation. Does this reflect an underlying conviction that the data, even when prepared, have their own particular 'nature' and hence too constrain what theorists can do with them? Economists also develop theories that at the very least claim to account for certain stylized facts. Why is this important to them? They also spend a lot of effort, if not in testing nevertheless in finding ways of drawing out empirical implications from specific theoretical models (see especially Kim, this volume). Why should that matter so much if no comparison between models is intended? That we have virtually no answers to these apparently fairly basic questions is itself startling.

Why too the reticence about spelling out the hard core and heuristics? My own work (1976) falls under the implied stricture. I was conscious at the time of not wanting to reduce the creative and exploratory struggle of the economists involved in developing modern trade theory to a set of mechanical applications of principles. The intuition of individuals like Heckscher, Ohlin, Samuelson and Leontief seemed to warrant a different sort of treatment, though I really did not have anything entirely satisfactory at hand. Now I would be much bolder about exhibiting the heuristic as a discovery process (see, for example, de Marchi, 1990). I also had a sense that what economists 'know' is central to their work involves a tacit component that cannot readily be codified. Yet who will deny the richness of Melvin Reder's discussion of Chicago economics (1982), which is partly achieved by using the evocative 'tight prior' to characterize just that very component? Moreover putting Lakatos to work seems to *require* clear enunciations of hard core and heuristics that can be tested against the historical record, just as Weintraub has taught us to do ('Appraising general equilibrium analysis' and *General Equilibrium Analysis)*. Or does it, in all cases?

If the hard core and heuristics evolve and mutually inform each other, as Musgrave (1976, 1989) and Birner (1988, 1990) suggest, historians looking for hard cores rather than for a process of discovery might be tempted into a misplaced concreteness. The evolution of heuristics, or the mutual evolution of hard core and heuristics, is another of the neglected areas listed above. That neglect in itself must be counted strange, given that, as we have seen, Lakatos himself came to consider more important than heuristically generated novel facts the novelty of problem-solving techniques 'which *later lead to* and *form part of*, a progressive research programme' (*Philosophical Papers, Vol. II*, p. 101; emphases added). This quotation, moreover, seems to open up the way to a more serious role for discovery than the Lakatos of Popper's 3 Worlds might have been prepared to admit, an inference reached by an entirely different route in Hands's paper below.

This is another, though related, neglected subject to which economic methodologists and historians of economics should give attention; for if testing is not as important in economics as economists' claims would imply, then perhaps it is also the case that there is (epistemic) value elsewhere than in deduced test implications alone. It may be, for instance, that such value is to be found in the arguments used to generate hypotheses; and that not all of what seems to be judged known within a line of inquiry can be subsumed under deduced test implications (see Pera, 1987, for this argument and an example from outside economics, and de Marchi, 1990, for a case in economics). If so, then there is reason to take very seriously Lakatos's late amendment to the notion of novelty: that first precise theoretical accounts of facts known but merely fortuitous are part of novel content.

A *second* observation on the existing applications of MSRP is that, in spite of the result first alluded to, it is surprising how much there is of empirical assessment without a specification of the underlying hard core or heuristics (the n;n;y and y;n;y patterns). How can one make an empirical assessment of an RP without knowing what it is that implies the testable implications? One interpretation of this feature of so much of the literature is that it betrays a commitment to the falsifiability criterion and to hypothesis testing that may be more Popperian than Lakatosian. On the other hand, possibly it also reflects a wholly Lakatosian commitment to assessing progress via empirically corroborated excess content. None the less it is clear that one cannot do justice to heuristic novelty or to novelty as the first precise account of known facts if one does not specify the hard core and heuristics.

Thirdly, I am struck by how extraordinarily familiar the whole tabulation appears. It looks like an exercise in re-naming (which is another way of putting O'Brien's point (1976) that modern economics can be assimilated all too readily to MSRP). We are given almost no explicit help in the studies themselves (though this does not emerge from the tabulation) for identifying RPs. Rather it looks as if existing, well recognized sub-disciplines and traditions have been taken and the label 'Research Program' appended. In other words, whatever economists themselves have identified as a distinct line of inquiry has been graced with the RP designation. This, incidentally, may account for the very large number of putative programs in the tabulation: historians ostensibly testing for the applicability of MSRP to economics have instead chosen simply not to omit anything. But this, of course, leaves us without really knowing how to identify an RP; and such 'applications' cannot be seen as tests of the appropriateness for economics of MSRP.

I fully accept that we must account for economists' most esteemed gambits; I question, however, whether we can expect to escape Whiggish history if we lean too heavily on working economists' own efforts to establish an identity, a history, a canon. To illustrate the point by reference to Latsis's early work: he showed the 'theory of the firm' – a conventional label – in an entirely new light by characterizing existing work as situational determinist, and existing models as 'single exit'. Bringing Lakatos (or Popper-plus-Lakatos, in this case) to economics promises to yield new insights; bringing economics to Lakatos promises little more than a series of artificially generated congruencies.

There are further consequences of the re-labelling inclination that seems to be so prevalent in the existing historical work. If one looks for research programs in traditions of inquiry that are already well defined one is also likely to suppose that the associated hard cores must be already hardened, the heuristics well understood and applied as part of normal practice. This will tend to divert one from exploring the process of emergence, or what has been discussed above as the evolution of heuristics and hard core, and tends to reduce MSRP to a stamp to be put upon existing material ('approved', 'not approved'), rather than allowing it to be an instrument for opening up the history in new and interesting ways. In addition it may lead to the abandonment of MSRP when it is discovered that there is no single way of writing the hard core or heuristics that commands universal assent or seems appropriate to all questions. This last was an inclination felt by more than one of the participants at the Capri conference, to which I now turn.[6]

THE CAPRI PAPERS

The tone of many of the papers presented at the Capri conference contrasts sharply with the mood at the first Lakatos conference, held in Nafplion, Greece, in September 1974. Then the atmosphere was one of anticipation, and most papers had something of the air of first ventures into a promising but largely unexplored territory. In Capri, by contrast, not a few participants displayed more awareness of difficulties already encountered in settling the new land, or impatience with the things that had excited the first settlers, than they did a sense of expectancy about possibilities as yet unrealized. To some extent, I have been arguing, this sense of frustration is owing to the cast of existing studies: a tendency in existing work to focus on RPs as finished products rather than as emergent entities; and a tendency to neglect certain areas of inquiry (the role of metaphysics; the role of empirical work that is not just testing; the role of problem solving and the question of how problems relate to overall programs; the role of discovery; the role of theoretical explanation in producing novelty; how best gambits can be explained using not just rational but also social elements and the epistemological commitments of scientists/economists). I have even hinted that in many of these less-travelled areas – not all – Lakatos must be viewed as a potentially useful guide, though that seems to have been forgotten, scattered undeveloped and sometimes obscure hints being no match for the confident tips and conveniently packaged tour advice that is to be found in MSRP. Having made my own biases plain, it will not be surprising if I add that I tend to see in the Capri papers hopeful signs of Lakatosian and modified Lakatosian work to be pursued in some of the hitherto neglected directions, even where the authors themselves are more ready to call it a day so far as MSRP is concerned. The reader will have to judge whether my readings are unduly optimistic.

The first session of the conference, and in fact all the chapters in Part I of this volume, are concerned in one way or another with the twin issues of how well we are served in writing the history of economics by Lakatos's insistence on measuring progress by an empirical yardstick, and by the notion of excess content.

Jeremy Shearmur takes distance from Lakatos, arguing that we are the poorer for Lakatos's having lost interest in Popper's problem analysis and theoretical progress in general. Popper gave us a way of criticizing theories from within, in terms of how well they deal with the problem situations for which they were devised. Although Lakatos spoke of theoretical progress as well as of empirical progress, he confined 'theoretical' to meaning the generation of empirical predictions, according to the hard core and positive heuristic. But theoretical problems with the hard core itself were deemed inadmissible; thus there was a narrowing of the scope of theoretical criticism and an associated loss of ability to deal with an important part of science.

Hands shows how Lakatos's notions about excess content derive from Popper. He takes note of the widely recognized deficiencies in Popper's criterion of verisimilitude and argues that, while Lakatos sensed the consequent lack of epistemological bite in Popper's methodology, he failed to fill in the gaps himself. Hands more controversially infers that there is no good reason to retain 'excess content', and perhaps none either for continuing the search for novel facts.

In his comment on Shearmur, Klappholz properly points out that there is in fact a good deal of theoretical criticism practised in economics, the alleged absence of Lakatosian warrant therefore notwithstanding. Not only this fact about economics, I would suggest, but also the fact that Lakatos eventually accepted theoretical explanation as potentially novel seem to demand a reconsideration by both authors.

The next two chapters take up the question of exactly how the empirical criterion is used in applied econometrics. We have many more complaints that economists honour the injunction to test only in the breach than we have studies of how empirical work in fact proceeds. The chapters by Kim and Gilbert are welcome additions to their number.

Kim shows how a theory is first transformed into a theoretical model, then, with the help of auxiliary assumptions, into an empirical model. He illustrates from the empirical models generated by job search theorists. His conclusion is that much of economists' effort goes into model improvement, rather than into testing as we usually understand it (three-way comparisons involving rival theories and data). He interprets this as throwing doubt on the usefulness of Lakatos's stress on corroborated theoretical progress. I read it rather as an illustration of what Lakatos may have meant when he laid emphasis upon problem-solving techniques. Ian Hacking interprets Lakatos as having 'dumped' both the logic of justification and the logic of discovery 'in favour of a global theory of objectivity that takes in many local strategies for finding out about specific domains' (1981, p. 135). For me Kim's work illustrates perfectly how crucial it is to identify the local strategies used by economists if we are to speak about their technical enterprise in a properly informed way. Clearly we also need more work on the whole range of strategies for theory development, and in this a good start has been made by Birner and by Janssen, whose *Strategies and Programmes in Capital Theory* (1990) and *Micro and Macro in Economics* (1990) form useful complements to Kim's chapter.

Gilbert's study suggests that we need to re-think our notions about testing. Demand theory seems to stress the context in which theory is used. It supplies a framework for bringing broad, underlying theoretical notions into conformity with available data so that the objects of interest – the parameters of Hicksian demand functions, or those representing cross price effects – can be measured. The underlying theory is not tested; the effort is rather one of shaping the way measurements are made. But this is a wholly Lakatosian emphasis (*Philosophical Papers, Vol. I*, pp. 44–5) and if Gilbert registers a strike against anyone it is Popper. Hypothesis testing, according to Gilbert, comes closer to describing the empirical work that is done in (macro) consumption analysis; but, even there, so many hypotheses can be drawn from the underlying theory that what is in fact tested for is the presence of assumptions which enable one (testable) implication rather than another to be derived. This is now a widely held view of what much empirical work in economics involves, and I read it as a useful addition to our knowledge of what economics is.

Bianchi and Moulin add yet another perspective. They see game theory, dealing as it does with strategic interactions, as an avenue for exploring alternative concepts of equilibrium and, even more importantly, different notions of rationality, in a way that simply is not possible within traditional neoclassical analysis. Maybe this should be regarded as core refurbishment or, as Lakatos might have viewed it, hard core 'crumbling' (*Philosophical Papers, Vol. I*, p. 49). Lakatos only hints at the 'logical and empirical' conditions under which a hard core crumbles, and it is not clear whether proliferation of conceptual entities to cover a central notion (rationality, equilibrium) qualifies. None the less it is clear that the challenge here is 'logical' rather than 'empirical', since game theory does not so much produce empirical hypotheses as define equilibrium solution concepts and then invite us to find real-world situations that match.

For this reason Smith *et al.* question whether experimental economics is usefully viewed as testing. Theory does not so completely inform experiments where strategic interactions are involved that unique links are formed between the theory and the experimental situation. Hence experiments tend to become sources of information for refining and modifying theory itself, rather than a means of testing theory.

These six chapters in Part I might be viewed as piling limitations and qualifications onto Lakatos's story about the way science progresses. I see them as forcing us also into a subtler, richer understanding of the role of theory in economics and especially of the interactions between theoretical and empirical models, and between models, measurement and testing in the ongoing process of theory development. Although several of the authors themselves seem unsure whether their work in any way needs Lakatos or bears on his approach, I would argue that it is exactly in line with the detailed study of arguments and heuristics that we must undertake in order to make sense of economists' best gambits. This I take also to be Vernon Smith's meaning in a comment made after the Capri conference (letter to Blaug, 26 October 1989): 'On almost every page of Lakatos I find articulate expressions of what I have been doing as an experimentalist for years. I never got this much out of my much earlier reading of Kuhn and Popper . . .'

Part II brings us to the issues of how we identify RPs, how they interact with each other, and how they are to be assessed. The first three chapters deal with program rivalry.

Mary Morgan compares what she refers to, somewhat hesitatingly, as two rival programs, process analysis and simultaneous equations modelling in early econometrics. Taking her chapter and reply to Backhouse's comments together, she narrates a battle for allegiance between the adherents of these alternative research strategies without becoming convinced that a Lakatosian reconstruction is the best way to do justice to the detail of the history itself. A major difficulty seems to be that no final victory was proclaimed nor defeat conceded; and in fact some version of each alternative lives on. This gives rise to the feeling that we need more distance from the events themselves before being confident that we can identify the contending hard cores adequately – in itself a very Lakatosian sentiment, as Morgan is aware (cf. *Philosophical Papers, Vol. I*, pp. 48–9).

Roy Weintraub calls into question the very notion of 'history itself', and in the process challenges Lakatos's idea that we can check our artificial histories against actual history. He reminds us that the 'facts', 'events' and inscriptions that on a simplistic view comprise the elements of histories are themselves constructions, and that there is no argument by which rational (re-)constructions can be shown to be superior to any other sort. Weintraub looks at a sequence of developments in stability analysis. On one level this might be seen as a program that progressed from the 1930s to the 1950s, incidentally elevating stability concerns at the expense of dynamics, before it suddenly degenerated. Alternatively, and perhaps with more conviction, it may be regarded as the efforts by members of a community to stabilize meanings, impose order and create knowledge by narrowing the possibilities for disagreement.

I might mention that two papers given at the conference and which strengthen Weintraub's position (the alternative just outlined) from different directions will appear separately in *History of Political Economy*. This is by arrangement with the authors, Karin Knorr-Cetina and Harry Collins. But Collins argues, in a note specially prepared for this volume, and based on some comments he made at the conference, something complementary to Weintraub's position. Science close up, while it is happening, is not orderly or assessable in Lakatosian (or other) categories of reason. It can at best be described and narratives constructed to reflect the strivings of participants. Collins also urges historians of economics to take advantage of their mental and spatial proximity to their subjects to produce such narratives rather than seek for the unattainable objectivity of a rational reconstruction done at a distance. I see no ground for exclusivity either way, and prefer to believe that multiple histories, to be set alongside one another, will almost certainly be an advance upon any single version. Weintraub's dual history surely is the best possible evidence for that view.

A third chapter in this group dealing (ostensibly) with program rivalry is Cross's account of unemployment according to the natural rate versus the hysteresis perspective. Cross asks whether there are 'reasons of good sense' for preferring one to the other. He gives a detailed description, somewhat in the multiple histories style that I have in mind, combining a discussion of negotiated meanings with an examination of differences using more traditional criteria of assessment. He seems to feel that Lakatos fails him in not providing clear and certain guidance that would issue in a rational choice. But there is a fundamental reason why this would be inappropriate, even if possible, namely that the application of Lakatos's method, as Mary Morgan reminded us, requires a considerable passage of time. Quite apart from this, I agree with Mark Blaug that the subject-matter here lends itself unusually well to the deployment of the empirical test, and much could have been gleaned from a close look at just how economists used empirical work in the course of the debate.

In the section headed 'delineating programs' three authors tackle the problems of identifying the program associated with New Classical Macroeconomics. If three authors, each knowledgeable and each using the same literature, fail to arrive at a single version of the research program supposedly responsible for generating that literature, should we conclude that the notion of RP-as-unit-of-appraisal lacks operational content? In this case the test was not rigorously applied: the authors do not follow a common method and this no doubt influenced the outcome.

Maddock focuses on Robert Lucas's research problems and strategy, and in that context two presuppositions – rational expectations and the natural rate hypothesis – stand out as belonging to the core. However Maddock is also sensitive to the likelihood that the same theoretical phenomena can be analysed in a variety of different ways, 'depending on whether they are defined as being within program A or program B: one person's hard core will be another person's protective belt'. As I interpret this, it means that the designation of an RP itself can be expected to vary with the sorts of questions and emphases that the historian imposes. That rather begs the question posed above; better, Maddock seems to have decided for a compromise outcome: no single designation of an RP can be expected, nevertheless 'as long as one starts with a clear definition of the level of program and of its core content one can apply the standard [Lakatosian] method'.

Hoover chooses a non-problem-based approach, seeking instead something more like the essence of the New Classical Economics (though I doubt whether he would agree to this blunt characterization of what he was doing). In this endeavour he feels defeated at the outset: there is no essence of New Classical Economics; yet there is New Classical economics, defined by the involvement of certain economists with 'groups of related and partly overlapping models and practices'. Shared exemplars make for family resemblances (kinships) between sequences of models and practices. Thus Hoover ends up opting for a sort of anthropologized Kuhn, and rejects MSRP: since no definite and well-patrolled borders can be defined, we cannot meet Lakatos's criteria for a scientific RP.

Backhouse concerns himself only in part with New Classical Macroeconomics. He takes on the larger task of describing a macroeconomic counterpart to Weintraub's all-embracing neo-Walrasian program in general equilibrium analysis (with its basically applied microeconomic protective belt). His approach is to transfer Weintraub's lists of hard core and heuristic propositions, making certain changes that seem necessary for the fit with macroeconomics since Keynes to be a good one. Even with the aim of deliberately introducing such changes as are needed to get the fit he wants Backhouse has to admit that there are numerous problems, some of them involving New Classical Economics (see especially 'Lakatos and Economics', which is a reflection upon his chapter for this volume). Thus the general equilibrium character of modelling is part of the positive heuristic in Weintraub's inquiry, but functions as negative heuristic for the New Classicals; and there are significant papers in the literature, written by New Classical economists, but which cannot be reconciled with certain apparently core suppositions.

All three authors struggle to reach a satisfactory characterization of the New Classical RP and end up – for somewhat distinct reasons – feeling that the effort is misplaced. But, even if they had found something satisfying, and on which they could agree, what would this have proved? The fact is that Lakatos himself seemed to accept that measurably different characterizations of the Newtonian program were in order; from which I infer that it is not the singularity of designation that makes 'research program' the appropriate unit of appraisal, but the notion of dynamically linked sequences of theories, which cohere as to research strategy (and perhaps techniques) and which share some underlying metaphysical presuppositions.

In fact there is a lot of direct evidence for such an interpretation. No reader of 'Falsification' can be unaware of the strong arguments Lakatos gives for the inevitability of our appraising, not single theories but *series* of theories, or theory changes, or problem shifts, or model variants – he uses all of these as rough equivalents. It is true that he also stresses heuristic power and the consistency (continuity) supplied by the researcher's *plan*, according to which problems are defined, anomalies foreseen and turned into examples, and so on, all in a 'preconceived' manner (see *Philosophical Papers, Vol. I*, p. 149). This might be taken as suggesting that it is possible and even usual to write down the hard core and positive heuristic of a research program in advance and with some exactness. But that would be to ignore all that Lakatos says about the articulation of our understanding of a theory ('criticism does not *assume* a fully articulated deductive structure; it creates it': ibid., p. 45 n. 4). There is nothing mechanical about that process; moreover it takes time (ibid., p. 149: 'The old rationalist dream of a mechanical, semi-mechanical or at least fast-acting method for showing up falsehood, unprovenness, meaningless rubbish or even irrational choice has to be given up. It takes a long time to appraise a research programme: Minerva's owl flies at dusk'). Again, because growth is linked to competition between theories (is not a matter of a relation between a theory and the facts), falsifications require first the emergence of a better theory, and this gives an *essentially* historical character to the business of understanding science (ibid., pp. 16–17, 27 n. 6, 35, 44–5). Giving these elements their due leads me to judge that the *prospective* element in a research program – the research 'plan' – functions for Lakatos more as a regulative device or principle than as something substantive (cf. his own remarks on 'continuity' and 'research program', ibid., pp. 32 n. 4 and 47, and n. 1 in *Philosophical Papers, Vol. II*, p. 176, where research programs themselves seem to be equated with regulative principles). For modern philosophers of biology the principle of natural selection has no empirical content but is said to function as 'an organizing principle, a principle that structures natural–selectionist explanations' (Brandon, 1990, p. 140). Similarly Lakatos's research plan idea is important for rational accounts of science history – for a methodology of the growth of knowledge (Lakatos, *Philosophical Papers, Vol. II*, p. 178 n. 3) – but should not be taken too literally.[7]

In the final section two authors address the question whether Lakatos's approach can be of help in understanding the contributions of subjectivist economics and Sraffian economics.

Ian Steedman sees Sraffian contributions as negative criticism and wrestles with the problem whether this amounts to theoretical progress and, if so, within which RP: Sraffian; marginalist; or Marxian? In the process he raises again, though in a new and special context, all the questions about broad versus narrow RPs, theoretical versus empirical progress, and so on, that have failed to receive answers in the bulk of the literature to date. Don Lavoie faces some of the same difficulties. For Austrian – better, subjectivist – economics is notoriously sceptical about the possibility of empirical work; it uses instead a criterion of explanatory adequacy; it stresses the distinctness of social inquiry from inquiry in the natural sciences; and it is quintessentially involved with ideational progress. In some ways his chapter returns us to the issues raised at the outset by Shearmur. Perhaps the main lesson to be drawn from both chapters is the one mentioned early on in this Introduction: even if we enlarge the way in which Lakatosian questions are treated – my implicit plea in response to most of the contributions in this volume – they remain a smallish subset of the sort of issues one would need to examine in order to encompass the whole range of what it is that economists do.

NOTES

1. I am grateful for stimulating comments on earlier attempts at an introduction from Craufurd Goodwin, Bob Coats, Roy Weintraub, Jack Birner, Mark Blaug, Philippe Mongin, Jinbang Kim, Maarten Janssen and Bruce Caldwell. Thanks also to Forrest Smith for his usual expert assistance in word processing.
2. After all, the emendation is not just a late switch. One finds it clearly present in 'Falsification' (i.e. in 1970). See *Philosophical Papers, Vol. I*, pp. 69–70, and compare also Lakatos's remarks on postdiction (pp. 32 and n. 3, 38–9).
3. This is not to say that metaphors may be borrowed with impunity. Mirowski (1989) has brilliantly shown what disasters can lie hidden in that assumption. It is to deny, however, his suggestion (comment below) that because Lakatos developed MSRP from mathematics and physics that any and all interest in its usefulness for historical reconstruction in economics is simply another sad manifestation of 'physics envy'.
4. Some readers may find it odd that I also do not attend directly to the philosophical and methodological objections that have been raised against Lakatos's enterprise. These are many and are by now well understood. They include:

    1. confining science to a rational and rule-dominated activity limits the applicability of the Popper–Lakatos methodology to the (western) philosophical and scientific tradition of the last couple of hundred years (Hacking, 1981), the era of the dominance of the Cartesian Syndrome (without well-defined procedures there can be no knowledge: Pera, 1989), and even then the question is begged as to why we should count as knowledge only that which is rational (Rorty, 1979; and, for an alternative perspective applied to economics, Mirowski, 1989 and comment, this volume);
    2. the need for decisions to determine the rules sets up a tension within the idea of rational progress, that is, activity in which the personal and the conventional are minimized (Pera, 1989);
    3. the same conflict strictly precludes the rules of the game from being used to advise scientists, although this self-imposed silence eviscerates the methodological project (Musgrave, 1976; Pera, 1989, for the point that methodology is internal to scientific activity, so that the two are not so easily to be kept apart);
    4. the conventional element in determining the empirical base precludes testing rational reconstructions against the 'actual' history (Hands, 1979);
    5. the refusal to deal with justification and the failure of the verisimilitude project makes Popper–Lakatos science hopelessly inefficient: if we don't know how well supported is our background knowledge we also don't know where to look when things go wrong (Hausman, 1991; see also Hands, this volume);
    6. the narrowness of the excess content (novel fact) criterion for judging progress not only causes MSRP to exclude many of the acknowledgeably best gambits of economists, but means that most of economics, indeed of all science, is irrational (Hands, 'Second thoughts on Lakatos' and 1990).

    The question whether it is proper to ignore these and other objections is related to another, more practical question, raised recently by Salanti (1990), namely, how is it that historians of economics have often felt free to construct histories guided by Lakatosian questions and categories, in the face of and with full knowledge of the philosophers' and methodologists' qualms? If I address this question I shall have indicated sufficiently why I do not devote space in the text to the objections themselves.

My proffered answer is in three parts. Firstly, issues such as those incorporated in the objections listed above are daily fare for historians, in exactly the same way as methodology is internal to the work of a scientist. It is no news to the historian to be told that it is impossible to construct a convention-free rational history; nor, of course, to hear that all histories are constructs, and the rational is but one of many possible histories; or to read that rational history fails to portray scientific practice 'truly'. One writes methodologically self-conscious history and, ideally, multiple histories for any episode, in the same spirit as a working scientist tries to be aware of the procedures he or she selects, and of the alternative procedures that might have been chosen or are in fact being used by others. This is not an instrumental defence for ignoring philosophical objections, but a pragmatic argument for proceeding anyway, dealing with the objections on the basis of the best solutions currently available.

Secondly, being aware of the problems with a strict interpretation of the Lakatosian methodology, the historian who none the less sees some value in it develops a keen eye for hints that render the strict interpretation somewhat more appealing without, however, making it so flexible as to please Humpty Dumpty. Thus I am attracted to and tend to make much of hints in Lakatos that novel fact might be interpreted as a new, rigorous explanation of something already known; that techniques for problem solving might be the real carrier of novelty; that searching for consistency among theories might better capture what is meant by heuristics than does the search for deduced test implications; and so on. In other words, as a historian I am less concerned with the strict interpretation of MSRP than I am with hints that help to make sense of what economists do and have done in the past. On the one hand, that makes me less impressed than Wade Hands by failed tests of (a narrowly-conceived) MSRP against history; but it is not out of line with Hands's own expressed interest in paying more attention to heuristic progress or exploring a role for facts that is wider than Lakatos's novel facts. The differences here are subtle. Neither Hands nor I see any point in a degenerating project in which the methodology of research programs is made to approach asymptotically the actual practice of scientists, in the same way as Lakatos's own falsificationism degenerated, according to some (Pera, 1989). But there is a large middle ground between the two extremes. On the other hand, I reject the notion that if we try to use Lakatos creatively to explore the historical materials we have implicitly abandoned the ability to appraise, which is Mark Blaug's concern. It is not the case that modifying the testing of economics against some criterion such as corroborated excess content means that we have conceded that all claims to economic knowledge are equally good. My preferred modifications run in the direction of invention (or 'discovery'), of problems and problem-solving techniques, and of a rationality that is not linked essentially, as Popper and Lakatos would have it, to methodology (see Musgrave, 1989, Pera, 1989 and de Marchi, 1990). But my own preferences are not the issue here; the point for our present context is that I, and, I think, quite a lot of other historians, tend to look sympathetically towards a richer, if broader, interpretation of Lakatos, and that means a Lakatos less subject to the strictures of philosophers and methodologists.

Thirdly, historians display a variety of choices that tend to favour Lakatos, or MSRP. Those who want to try using Lakatos tend to pre-select their episodes. This can lead to innocuous success in application, like many of the studies I criticize below. But it can also mean showing a preference for episodes in modern economics, where it simply makes more sense to adopt the elements and categories of MSRP as a way of illuminating the history. This is so for a number of reasons. For instance, much of modern economics is not directly empirical and lends itself to a discussion of heuristic or theoretical progress, whether or not this accords closely with Lakatos's requirement that ultimately we appraise by checking for corroborated novel facts. Obviously, too, technique is more important in modern economics; as is the need to attend closely to the links between theories for giving us facts and the theories we use to explain them. Salanti (1990; cf. Hands, 'Second thoughts on Lakatos') tends to see historians' willingness to use MSRP as due to the dominant influence of internal history. I think that the focus on modern economics itself may be just as much responsible (a belief, it should be obvious, which somewhat shaped the agenda for the Capri conference). Either way, we have an additional reason why historians press on in the face of methodologists' reservations.

5. Hands comes close to recognizing this sense of novel – see definition (4) in his reply to Mäki and Hamminga, below – but not as something to be found in Lakatos.
6. The reader will notice some asymmetries in the format. All papers but one are followed by one or, in a few instances, two commentaries: Bianchi and Moulin elected to integrate the commentary in a revised version of the paper. All authors were invited to reply to commentators; however, only three chose to do so.
7. There are of course heuristic imperatives in some of the metaphors or modelling strategies adopted by pioneers in a research tradition, as Mirowski's discussion of the energy/utility metaphor in neo-classical economics illustrates well (1989). In mathematical formalisms these may appear quite specific and precise (see his discussions of integrability, for example). But, such formalisms aside, the detail of the heuristic has to be explored and cannot be written down in advance.

REFERENCES

All references in the Introduction are incorporated into the Bibliography at the end of this volume.

APPENDIX: SUMMARY CHARACTERIZATION OF ENGLISH-LANGUAGE APPLICATIONS OF MSRP TO ECONOMICS, 1972–89

Note: y or n refers to presence (yes) or absence (no) of (i) an explicit characterization of the hard core; (ii) explicit characterization of the positive heuristics; and (iii) an explicit empirical assessment of a putative research program.

1 **There is one grand RP, numerous subsidiary RPs**. Three distinct versions of this view are prevalent.

(i) *Comprehensive 'neo-classical' or 'mainstream, orthodox' RP dating from Smith:* Blaug, 'Kuhn versus Lakatos': y;y;n; *The Methodology of Economics:* see subsidiary RPs under 2(i) below for details; Hutchison, 1976: n;y;n; Glass and Johnson, 1988: y;y;n.
(ii) *For modern economics there is one – neoclassical – RP:* Remenyi, 1979: y;y;n.
(iii) Weintraub calls the *single* ***modern*** *RP that drives all applied work the neo-Walrasian*, since general equilibrium analysis is at its core ('Appraising general equilibrium analysis' and *General Equilibrium Analysis:* y;y;n; 1988: y;y;y). For Remenyi, general equilibrium theory is a subsidiary RP (see 2(ii) below).

2(i) **Specific applied work in RPs subsidiary to one grand RP** (the 'neo-classical', dating from Smith).

Note that, for Weintraub, what Blaug and others regard as subsidiary RPs are instances of applied work done in the protective belt of the one encompassing neo-Walrasian RP.

Demand theory: Blaug, *The Methodology of Economics:* n;n;y; Verstegen, 1984: y;y;n.
Production theory: Blaug, *The Methodology of Economics:* n;n;y; Fulton, 1984: y;y;n.
Theory of the firm: Latsis, 1972, 'The limitations of single-exit models': y;y;n; *The Methodology of Economics:* n;n;y.
General equilibrium theory: Blaug, *The Methodology of Economics:* n;n;y; Toruño, 1988: y;y;y.
Human capital theory: Blaug, 'The empirical status of human capital theory', *The Methodology of Economics*, 1980b: y;n;y.
New economics of the family: Blaug, *The Methodology of Economics:* n;n;y.
(ii) **Sub-disciplinary (demi-core) work in the protective belt of neo-classical RP** (here subsidiary RPs are once again in view, but with more

stress on the social–disciplinary defining characteristics of specific research terrains).

Theoretical (for example, welfare economics; general equilibrium theory): Remenyi, 1979: y;y;n.
Applied or mixed theoretical/applied (for example, public finance, industrial organization, agricultural economics, economic development, regional economics, labour economics and demography: Remenyi, 1979: y;y;n); (marketing science: Leong, 1985: y;n;n).
(iii) **Work within neo-Walrasian RP**

Theoretical: development of existence proofs: Weintraub, 'Appraising general equilibrium analysis' and *General Equilibrium Analysis:* y;y;n.
Applied: Trade theory: de Marchi, 1976: n;n;y. Finance theory: Schmidt, 1982: y;y;y. New economics of the family: Weintraub, 1988: y;y;y.

3 Other largish candidate RPs

Smithian: O'Brien, 1976/1983: y;y;y.
Ricardian: O'Brien, 1976/1983: y;y;y.
Malthusian: O'Brien, 1976/1983: y;y;y; Harvey-Phillips, 1983: n;y;n.
Marxian: Blaug, 'A methodological appraisal of Marxian Economics': y;n;y; Archibald, 1979: n;n;n; Glass and Johnson, 1988: y;y;n.
Marginalist: Fisher, 1986: y;y;n.
Keynesian: Blaug, 'Kuhn versus Lakatos' and 1991: y;n;y; Weintraub, 1979 and *General Equilibrium Analysis:* n;n;n; Brown, 1981: y;y;n.
Neo-classical synthesis: Wulwick, 1987: y;y;n.
Monetarist: Blaug, *The Methodology of Economics:* n;n;y; Cross, 1982: y;y;y.
Patinkin-Clower-Leijonhufvud macro: Blaug, 'Kuhn versus Lakatos': n;n;n.
Neo-Ricardian/Sraffian: Blaug, 'Kuhn versus Lakatos': n;n;y; Weintraub, *General Equilibrium Analysis:* n;n;n; Wulwick, 1987: y;y;n.
Behavioural: Latsis, 1972 and 'The limitations of single-exit models': y;n;y; Simon, 1976: y;y;n; Weintraub, *General Equilibrium Analysis:* n;n;n.
Evolutionary: Weintraub, *General Equilibrium Analysis:* n;n;n.
New classical: Klamer, 'Levels of discourse in new classical economics': y;y;y; Maddock, 1984: y;y;y; McMahon, 1984: y;y;y; Wulwick, 1987: y;y;n.
Austrian: Rizzo, 1982: y;y;n; Langlois, 1982: y;y;n.

PART I

The Criterion of Empirical Progress in Economics

A Theoretical Progress and Excess Content

1. Popper, Lakatos and Theoretical Progress in Economics

Jeremy Shearmur*

INTRODUCTION

Neither Popper nor Lakatos has, as far as I know, written at any length on the methodology of economics. However their ideas have had an important influence.[1] In the first part of this chapter I discuss the relation between Popper and Lakatos. I suggest that Popper and Lakatos's views were closer than some believe to be the case. In addition, much of Lakatos's early work represents a fruitful development of Popper's ideas in ways that, while novel, parallel work done by Popper and others associated with him, such as Agassi and Watkins, which extends Popperian approaches beyond the empirical. I then argue, however, that one unfortunate consequence of Lakatos's later work is that within it theoretical progress – and, more generally, the appraisal of theories – is turned back into a largely empirical matter. Such appraisal is, in my view, very important; but to take it as the only way in which we can appraise theories seems to me unduly restrictive.

In the second part of the chapter, I contrast the views of Popper and of Lakatos on historiography, and suggest that Popper's pluralism is to be preferred to Lakatos's monism. Lakatos, I believe, promoted a special kind of history that both he and Popper thought needed to be written if we wished to appraise a theory into a single organizing theme for the historiography of science. I further suggest that both Popper and Lakatos were incorrect in their belief that there was an incompatibility between their concerns and the pursuit of the sociology of science – a

* This paper draws in part on 'Popper versus Lakatos on the Historiography of Economics', delivered at the History of Economics Society in Toronto, 1988. I would like to thank Neil de Marchi, Mark Blaug, Bruce Caldwell, Wade Hands, Ian Jarvie and Jagdish Hattiangadi for discussion, and also Roy Weintraub and members of the Brown Bag luncheon group at the Center for Study of Public Choice, George Mason University, for earlier discussion of some of these ideas. I would like, further, to thank my discussant at the Capri conference, Kurt Klappholz, for some important requests for clarification, and also the other participants for discussion.

view that, strangely enough, seems also to be shared by many who are attracted to the sociology of science and which I believe to have destructive consequences. In a short final section, I explore some speculative consequences of my interpretation of Popper's view of 'basic statements' as a product of inter-subjective consensus as to what is the case.

While I hope the chapter may be found provocative, it is tentative in its approach: it is merely a first try at some of these issues. My concern in thus discussing Popper's work is not to suggest that it is the only source from which we may obtain interesting ideas. Rather I wish to suggest that, if we do not read Popper through the spectacles of the later Lakatos, we may discover in his work some fresh ideas which speak in an interesting manner to our current situation.

1 POPPER, LAKATOS AND THE APPRAISAL OF THEORIES

Lakatos, in some of his later writings, put some effort into trying to distinguish between his views and those of Popper. He has been followed in this by many commentators.[2] However, as Bartley argued,[3] and as Hands has done subsequently,[4] much of substance that appeared to many people to be distinctive to Lakatos was in fact rooted in Popper's work and in the work of others who had been associated with him. In particular, Popper's own later views on what is required for the progress of science,[5] with their demand for a unifying idea, independent testability and empirical corroboration (to which latter requirement, Agassi, for example, took exception),[6] are virtually the building-blocks of Lakatos's philosophy of science.

Consider those elements of Lakatos's work which he himself presented as among his most distinctive departures from Popper. He made much of his concern with the appraisal of a series of theories as opposed to the falsification of particular claims. But this seems to me a confusion. For both Popper and Lakatos, for a theory (or, better, a system of theories and statements of initial conditions) to get into empirically-generated trouble, there has to be a falsification – one has to accept that some consequence that can be validly drawn from them is incorrect. In this sense, Lakatos needs falsifications of specific sets of premises in exactly the same sense as does Popper. They also both hold much the same view of the epistemological status of the 'basic statements' involved; although, as I shall explain later, I think that Lakatos's description of this view as a form of conventionalism is unhelpful.

Next they had much the same view of what should then be done: they believed that the theoretical system stood in need of modification. What should be modified was – in principle – a matter of conjecture. Lakatos gave a fuller account than did Popper of the heuristics of all this. To be sure, Popper often refers to the importance of metaphysics as a heuristic in the development of science, and there is his stress on a simple, unifying idea in *Conjectures and Refutations*. However there is a difference at least of emphasis here, in that Lakatos clearly had stronger hopes for the possibility of a rational heuristics than did Popper. But it might seem that, in view of the unevenness of scientific development (of which Paul Feyerabend has made so much) we would be wrong to follow Lakatos in strengthening our demands for coherence in heuristics too far. Even if a true theory for which we might eventually aim could explain things in a coherent manner, it may be the case that we cannot reach such a theory from where we currently are, and that our best move would be to put up with testable theories the underlying coherence of which we may find very puzzling.[7]

Lakatos's discussion of refutation also seems to me somewhat misleading. It was Popper's view that, for one theory to replace another, it is necessary that it should explain (and possibly correct) the previous theory's successes, that the new theory should be independently testable, and that it should pass some of these tests. In this situation, it is clear that, if we have a theory which has passed some test and which is then refuted (in the sense described above), we will hardly discard it until we have some new theory that can supersede it. For to discard it would be to discard a theory that seems genuinely informative – to have content that must be simulated by some future theory – with nothing at all. What, then, do we do with a refuted theory? Presumably, we try to see how we can improve upon it, by modifying it; by modifying some auxiliary hypothesis or statement of initial conditions; or possibly by replacing it completely. But, in the meantime, not only will we retain it (with, as it were, appendices in which we note those areas in which it seems clearly not to work) but we will still be interested in discovering those areas in which it holds up, and further areas in which it is defective, just because these are matters that will be important for the future progress of our knowledge: we will be discovering more information as to what some further, better theory must be able to cope with.

All this is suggested by what Popper has said about progress in science. It is of course the case that he has frequently written in much more simple terms about learning by conjecture and refutation; but this is perfectly understandable, as much of our actual learning is of just this simple character. It is true that, when some theory of mine is falsified, it might be a basic statement that was at fault, or some other piece of our knowledge. But in most cases I quite correctly assume that it was my speculative theory that was at fault and I try to modify or replace that.

Lakatos's most explicit departure from Popper, however, is in his emphasis on a 'hard core' of a theory being held immune to criticism through methodological decision, and in his judgement that this is desirable. That it is possible to treat of theories in this manner was clearly recognized in Popper's account of conventionalism in *The Logic of Scientific Discovery*. And Popper himself has advocated the holding immune to criticism of one element of a system of theories (for the sake of improving overall testability), in his discussion of the 'rationality principle'.[8]

It might be argued that behaviour of the kind that Lakatos favoured was, descriptively, characteristic of some fruitful periods in the development of scientific knowledge. Lakatos himself was particularly impressed by the stability of Newtonianism – although it has been questioned whether the 'hard core' of Newtonianism is quite as stable as he suggests.[9] Let us suppose that Lakatos was correct. Suppose also that we judge the period in question to have been extremely productive. Should we accept this as an argument for the acceptability of Lakatos's methodological proposal? I think we should only do so with some hesitation, just because, for at least part of this period, many Newtonians believed either that Newton's theories had been shown to be true by virtue of the fact that they had led to striking empirical confirmations, or even that they were true by convention. Thus the stability with which we are concerned may well be a product of epistemological theories which we would ourselves reject. And, if we do not ourselves accept the Newtonians' epistemological views concerning the status of important scientific theories, we should perhaps be hesitant to take their practice as a paradigm that we should uncritically emulate.

Before we make any firmer judgement about the preferability of Lakatos's views to Popper's, however, we need to look at one other issue. It concerns the development of Popper's and Lakatos's views.

The Early versus the Later Lakatos

As is well known, Lakatos's philosophical work in Britain initially focused upon issues in the philosophy of mathematics. There he combined themes from Polya's heuristics and Popper's philosophy of science in a fascinating rational reconstruction of certain developments in the history of mathematics. Lakatos's aims in this work are not easy to summarize.[10] But among other things he wished to argue that a 'Popperian' conjecture and refutation-like structure was possessed by the development of knowledge in at least some areas of the formal sciences. He also contested commonly accepted views of the status of mathematical knowledge.[11] This work of Lakatos's was most stimulating, and fruitful in many respects, not least because it offers us a way of making something of the *growth* of formal knowledge, a subject that had been widely neglected in the philosophy of mathematics. In this work – largely consisting of Lakatos's dissertation and material extracted or developed from it – Lakatos offers what may in part be interpreted as a generalization of Popper's ideas to non-empirical disciplines.

In comparing Popper and Lakatos on non-empirical theories, however, it is important to bear in mind the historical development of Popper's own views. Popper, from the time of his earliest published disputes with the logical positivists, had drawn attention to the role played by metaphysical ideas in the development of science. However, in *The Logic of Scientific Discovery*, and *The Poverty of Historicism*, Popper's own approach was typically to reinterpret metaphysical ideas in methodological terms; this offered us a way in which we could appraise them, by means of their appraisal as methodological rules.

The underlying situation here seems to have been as follows. Popper was conscious of holding metaphysical theories, notably realism. But at the time he did not have a theory as to how metaphysical theories could be rationally appraised.[12] In addition, in his *Open Society*, in the course of a critical discussion of Whitehead, he argued that it was not clear that – or how – the development of speculative metaphysical ideas could be evaluated as progressive. However he later argued that his idea of appraising theories in terms of their fruitfulness or otherwise in the solving of problems could be extended to the evaluation of non-empirical ideas in metaphysics; an argument that was developed in his *Postscript* and in material based upon it which was published during the late 1950s.[13] In fact, even in material that dates from the 1940s, Popper is to be found giving what might be called critical conjectural histories of the development of metaphysical ideas.[14] Popper has also written about the development of non-testable ideas within natural science (such as ideas about causality, the structure of matter and the interpretation of probability theory). And similar themes were discussed in a variety of interesting ways by associates of Popper's such as Agassi and Watkins. Lakatos's own 'Changes in the Problem of Inductive Logic' was itself a particularly suggestive and dynamic use of this general approach in a critical capacity in the philosophy of science.[15] (That there was nothing at issue between Popper and Lakatos over all this may be seen from Popper's use, with acknowledgement, of Lakatos's terminology of 'progressive problem shift' in his 'On the Theory of the Objective Mind'.[16]) One might, indeed, see Lakatos's own earlier work on the philosophy of mathematics as a particularly fruitful and interesting example of the same kind of view. By this I do not mean that Lakatos's work was derivative; rather that it treated of parts of mathematics in ways that were close to what Popper and others were doing in other fields at around the same time.

However, when Lakatos developed his own ideas within the philosophy of science, something strange took place. Lakatos made moves which have the unintended consequence of diminishing the significance of the very developments to which he had earlier made such important contributions. And Lakatos was, in the end, led implicitly to repudiate the idea that it was fruitful for us to make use of non-empirical forms of appraisal of theoretical ideas within science. For when Lakatos suggested that the programmatic aspects of science should be treated as 'hard cores', he placed emphasis upon *prima facie* testable theories being rendered unfalsifiable by the use of conventionalist stratagems. But – and this is the move that caused the problems – he in effect suggested that it was acceptable to disregard theoretical problems concerning this hard core so long as there was what he called 'theoretical' and empirical progress. But 'theoretical' here simply meant the making of additional empirical predictions, guided by the heuristic of the theory. That is to say, one had a narrowing of the scope of 'theoretical' criticism from the ideas which the later work of Popper and others had opened up, and to which Lakatos had contributed in such an interesting way, back to the empirical.

Lakatos was thus to return us to something akin to the ideas of the early Popper – or, indeed, to an ultra-empiricist version of them. For even in the work of the early Popper there was room for some non-empirical argument about the value of particular metaphysical ideas if treated *qua* methodological proposals. Lakatos in effect turned his back upon the important extensions of Popper's approach beyond the empirical: the very developments to which he had done so much to contribute. Thus the later Lakatos, for all his sophistication, offered us what might be called a positivistic adaptation of Popper. This, in fact, was signalled, in his earliest paper on the philosophy of economics, by Spiro Latsis, who used Lakatos's ideas to defend Friedman's instrumentalism.[17] I would therefore like to champion the later Popper and the early Lakatos against the later Lakatos. For the later Lakatos, theoretical progress in the sense of the making of greater empirical claims compatible with a theory's heuristic, and occasional empirical progress (corroboration), is all that counts.[18] Yet this move, it seems to me, is particularly one that should be resisted by the economist and the historian of economics. For in economics it will often be precisely the problem-solving abilities of a theory in the sense of its ability to furnish an explanation, along certain lines, of phenomena that are already well known to us, and counter-examples that are constructed to theoretical claims that are made on its behalf – and thus the kinds of discussion that Lakatos offered us in his *Proofs and Refutations* and 'Changes in the Problem of Inductive Logic' – rather than its ability to make empirical predictions that will be of particular importance. At the same time I certainly do not wish to suggest that Popper and Lakatos were incorrect in their suggestion that we should strive for testability.

Theoretical Progress

How can we assess theoretical progress in a way that goes beyond Lakatos's ideas about theoretical progress as making stronger and stronger empirical statements?

In addition to pointing back to Lakatos's own *Proofs and Refutations* and 'Changes in the Problem of Inductive Logic', I would like to offer a few suggestions drawn from Popper's work. His central approach to these issues – as set out, for example, in his *Conjectures and Refutations* – was to suggest that we may assess non-empirical theories *qua* solutions to problems. As I indicated earlier, one might see much of Lakatos's work on mathematics as a particularly fruitful and interesting development of this general idea, as is Larry Laudan's discussion of the role of 'conceptual problem-solving', in his *Progress and Its Problems*.[19]

More specifically there is the approach suggested in Popper's 'Philosophy and Physics'.[20] There Popper discussed the way in which Descartes, in his philosophical writings, gave us a general account of the composition of the physical world. Descartes offered us an account of the furniture of the universe and of the kind of causality that pertained to it. In addition he also suggested ways in which various phenomena with which we are already familiar might be understood in terms of his account – he offered an account of how, in principle,[21] these phenomena were to be explained. (The account was to be filled out by more empirically-oriented work that would be undertaken later.[22])

Now such general explanations play an important role in science. They may be offered explicitly, as they were by Descartes. They may be offered implicitly, by way of someone offering a detailed explanation of some specific phenomenon, and others then trying to adapt this general way of explaining things so as to deal with other phenomena. They may also be implicitly communicated to people through their education, or by many other means of which readers of Kuhn's *Structure of Scientific Revolutions* will hardly need to be reminded.

However Popper's account in 'Philosophy and Physics' is interesting because he goes on to describe the way in which Leibniz was able to criticize Descartes' account by arguing that one could not give a coherent explanation of one of the obvious features of the physical world – how hard bodies bounce off one another – in terms that were compatible with Descartes' general account of how we should explain things in physics.

The to-and-fro of such argument – the offering of a general account of how certain well-known kinds of phenomena are to be explained, and a critic then arguing that some features of these phenomena cannot be explained on the basis of our theorist's assumptions – is surely an important part of theoretical science. And the importance of such criticism should not be overlooked, not least as it can sometimes be more telling than the empirical criticism of some more detailed hypothesis. For, if a general criticism of this kind is made well, it may be devastating, and require that a major modification of the theory be undertaken. Such criticism (where it is available) may be more clear-cut than is a particular empirical criticism, in respect of which there is always the chance that something is odd about our data or with our particular assumptions about initial conditions, or that other things are going on that we have not taken adequately into account, such that the objection can be taken into account by changing some auxiliary hypothesis. Theoretical criticism may thus damage not just a particular statement of a theory but, in effect, a whole set of theories.[23]

Does such criticism occur in economics? I would suggest that it is very much the stuff of economic argument, both within and between different theoretical schools. One particularly striking example is offered in Ian Steedman's discussion of the criticism of neo-classical economics by the followers of Sraffa.[24]

But suppose that such criticism is correct. What should we conclude? Here I would suggest that Popper's ideas are again very much to the point. For, as I suggested above, we should take such criticism as a signal that the theory requires modification or replacement. But we should be unwilling to discard it – and may still continue to explore it – until we can replace it with some alternative which preserves its achievements.[25] To decide what its achievements are, however, will require that we keep a clear eye on the connection between theoretical work and real-world problems, in that we will hardly demand that a new theory preserves 'achievements' of an old theory when these are no more than the solution of puzzles internal to that theory. After all, the issue of how many angels could stand on the head of a pin was doubtless of some importance in relation to different contending schools in theology; but it is not a problem that requires solution by some later theory that denies that angels exist.

Accordingly, when Larry Laudan wrote, in his *Progress and Its Problems*, that conceptual problem solving (as opposed to empirical problem solving) 'has been largely ignored by historians and philosophers of science',[26] in my view he was incorrect. The reference here, however, to 'historians and philosophers' leads us to an important issue which, in view of Lakatos's later work, also merits discussion: the relation between the philosophy and the historiography of science.

2 PHILOSOPHY AND HISTORIOGRAPHY

Lakatos's later work has had an important influence on the historiography of economics, but, while it has led to some interesting work, it seems to me also to have some rather strange features which are illuminated if we compare his views with those of Popper. Popper's own perspective on historiography – for example, as developed in the latter parts of his *The Open Society and Its Enemies* – is pluralistic. There, in a manner that is close to Max Weber's account of the role of values in social science, Popper develops an account of historical interpretation in which different theories, concerns and perspectives can play a constitutive role in the writing of history. They serve to pick out, from the vast assemblage of socially-situated human actions and their unintended consequences, the subject-matter with which we will be concerned in the writing of particular histories.

This point is in my view significant, for the following reason. One feature in common between Popper and Lakatos is the idea that a critical examination of the historical development of a theory should play a key role in our evaluation of it. Thus, from the perspective of both Popper and of Lakatos, if we are interested in the evaluation of a theory, we must write a certain kind of history about it. This will include an account of the problems towards the solution of which it was initially directed, of the theories with which it was then competing, and of the story of how both theoretical and empirical problems were handled by its proponents. We must also compare its performance with that of competing theories.

However this is only one perspective from which history may be written, and it is, in some respects, a rather strange one. For, if our concern is with the appraisal of a theory, we will need to write an idealized history of the development of a theory and of how it relates to its competitors. Our story, while it is history of a kind, is a very distinctive kind of history; one which we need because of our *current* theoretical concerns. In *this* context, Lakatos's point about putting actual history into the footnotes is well taken;[27] clearly, if our concern is with the appraisal of a theory, we will not want to take, as weighing against the theory, the fact that its proponents at some particular point missed some option that was clearly open to them to show how a particular problem could be dealt with by the theory. Rather we are interested in the history as disclosing what the problems are against which the theory is to be appraised, what are its competitors, and how to judge its current state as compared to its earlier versions.

However Lakatos's own later views in the philosophy of science seem to have led him to regard his own ideas less as an account which, in some sense, is being brought externally to historical developments in order to evaluate them but instead as something which may be taken to be implicit within the development of science itself; at least in the moves made by a 'scientific elite'. But this has the consequence of taking us away from Popper's Weberian pluralism to something closer to Hegel's monism in historiography,[28] in which there is just one story to be told: in Lakatos's case, the story of the actual history of science as progressive in terms of Lakatos's methodological and epistemological ideas.

Now I do not think that Lakatos was incorrect in the emphasis that he placed on the importance of philosophical ideas for the writing of history.[29] Clearly a historian's views about what is possible, whether concerning the universe or concerning method, will influence strongly the kind of historical explanation that he thinks is called for. The kind of history of the Church that a Christian could write will be very different from that written by an atheist. And, similarly, what a historian of science will wish to discuss when a scientist describes as 'inductive' his discovery of some law will differ, depending on his views about the possible methods of science.

Lakatos, however, seems to me to end up confusing the legitimate influence that views of that kind may have on how the history of science is written with his more specific views about the philosophy of science, and to end up recommending, as *the* historiography of science, the writing of the kind of historical account that in his view is needed for evaluative purposes. For such purposes I think that Lakatos's views have considerable merits, although, as I have indicated earlier, I am not in full agreement with him. But what is written for the purposes of theory appraisal is a strange kind of history; and it seems to me unlikely that we will gain much by treating the activities of historical agents whose concerns and criteria differ from ours as if what they were really doing was to be explained in terms of Lakatos's ideas about methodology.

At the same time there is clearly a way in which those who are interested in current intellectual issues may recognize historical figures as being involved in a kind of activity that is familiar to them. And while, in my view, some very bad history has been written by people who assume that what historical figures were *really* concerned with was the discovery of ideas with which we are familiar, or even that ideas familiar to us are to be found implicitly lurking behind their texts, there is nevertheless a sense in which a personal familiarity with certain kinds of problem solving under theoretical constraints can be of the greatest importance in understanding the ideas of historical figures. And this, in turn, may lead to an impatience with those who, say, suggest a simple-minded 'social' reading of what, to anyone who has an eye for such things, is clearly the work of someone who is engaged in the attempt to solve difficult intellectual problems.

Indeed, while it is not quite the same as internal history in Lakatos's sense, a story can be told of the development of an intellectual discipline as a history of problem situations, of theories put forward to try to solve them, and so on. And such an approach to history may have particular attractions to those engaged in such work themselves. At the same time such an approach is clearly selective, in that it abstracts from issues of personality, institutions and power. But the writer of the 'internal' history will himself clearly have to deal with presuppositions made by his historical agents of which they were not consciously aware, and also with things of which they were ignorant. And it is certainly open to someone to suggest that, even to understand such matters, one must have recourse, directly or indirectly, to the sociology of institutions or of power relationships, or perhaps even to wider issues of political economy. And one may clearly wish to focus more upon such matters, the less one is interested in purely internal history.

While it seems to me that Popper's criticisms of the sociology of knowledge were in order if one considers the targets of his criticism, and while some of Lakatos's animadversions against sociological treatments of science are also sound, they overdraw the contrast between an approach such as theirs and an approach which is concerned with matters sociological or rhetorical. What seems to me both odd and damaging in its consequences is the agreement between Lakatos, and many of those who favour such approaches, that these views are relativistic. Some aspects of Lakatos's own work have been welcomed by some commentators, just because in some respects he seems to depart from Popper's concern with the appraisal of science on the basis of criteria that are external to it. This has been welcomed as the discarding of a piece of hubris on the part of philosophers who, in this view, had taken it upon themselves to instruct practitioners as to what they ought to be doing.

But such a judgement seems to me mistaken. First, it misconceives Popper's concern. For, while some philosophers have, to be sure, been concerned to tell us that human knowledge must be rebuilt upon new foundations provided by them, such views have been tellingly criticized, not least by Popper. For him, philosophy is not a matter of telling people what they ought to be doing, so much as explicating, and becoming involved in the critical discussion of, ideas which do, or could, guide research in particular sciences.[30] Such discussion may point out the costs and benefits of adopting one rather than the other conception of the aim of science, and how lessons that we have learned in some fields of knowledge may be of use elsewhere, too. This is an activity in which practitioners are themselves also frequently engaged (and concerning which they are likely to have various presuppositions, whether or not they are aware of them). Such activity may be seen as consensual in its aspirations and also as open-ended, as its tentative conclusions are always open to further challenge and debate. However, at any one point, we may look back from the conclusions that we are able tentatively to draw, in order to appraise and, it is hoped, to improve upon, the practice of science.

Second, to rule out such a critical perspective is to destroy the space within which principled challenges to our current practices can be explicated and argued for. It has the unintended consequence of leaving everything, including existing power relations, error and bad practice, as beyond the pale of rational scrutiny. Indeed it seems to me that sociological and rhetorical approaches to science are a natural complement to an interest in methodology and the appraisal of our theories. The espousal of relativism makes it difficult for the sociologist and the student of rhetoric to make sense of their own practice, and the rationale for their own choice of some rather than of other standards within it. It has the further consequence that work of considerable critical power becomes self-castrating. For what some of this work can do is to show us the ways in which our institutional arrangements, the forms that power takes within them, and so on, lead us to fall short, in their consequences, of what would be desirable if our concern is with the growth of knowledge – and, indeed, of many of our other ideals, to boot. But such judgements, critical comments based upon them, and above all suggestions as to how we might do things better, are avoided, just in so far as these practitioners take their relativism seriously.

Now some of those concerned with just these matters feel uneasy about making any such judgements simply because their own work has led them to be sceptical of the accounts that are often given by philosophers about the way in which knowledge claims are generated or criticized. (Compare Collins's chapter in the present volume.) But in my view this indicates precisely the need for such practitioners to involve themselves in discussion of epistemological and methodological matters, so that they can help us address the question of how we can improve upon our practices, given what they are finding out about how we are currently doing things.

Thus, if I can recapitulate briefly, my argument in this section has been that Lakatos was incorrect in recommending his (historical) ideas about how theories should be appraised as a general model for the historiography of science. Rather Popper's pluralistic approach is to be preferred. Further I have suggested that methodological appraisal and the study of the sociology and the rhetoric of science are not necessarily enemies, but, rather, may complement one another. If they are not linked, the radical edge of such studies, and the possibility of learning from them how we might do things better, are blunted.

3 THE EMPIRICAL BASIS AND TESTING

In the first section of this chapter, I suggested that Lakatos's description of Popper's account of 'basic statements' as a form of 'conventionalism' was not helpful. In this final section I elaborate upon this point and suggest that there may be something to be gained from closer attention to Popper's ideas on this topic.

While I have argued for the importance of theoretical progress in economics, I certainly do not want to diminish the importance of empirical progress, and more generally of empirical testability in the assessment of theories. However it seems to me that the radicalism implicit within Popper's theory of the empirical basis has not been properly appreciated. In my view it has some interesting consequences for the practice of empirical testing, for the way we should understand certain features of Popper's work, and also for the historiography of science.

The Inter-subjectivity of Testing and of Theoretical Argument

Popper's views on the empirical basis are put very briefly. Suffice it to say that he sees our theories as being testable against basic statements, which themselves consist of an inter-subjective consensus as to what is observable; one, however, that can in principle be called into question by anybody. But their criticisms, in turn, must themselves be subject to inter-subjective appraisal. Lakatos's description of this as a form of conventionalism seems to me unhelpful, because it draws attention away from the idea that what is agreed upon is agreed upon because those concerned take it to be true, and because it is open to renegotiation in the face of someone claiming – and being able to argue – that it is not true.

Several points about all of this are worth noting. The first is that, while Popper's account might be interpreted other than along the lines that I am suggesting here,[31] the idea at the heart of his account seems to me to be a Kantian idea of inter-subjective appraisal as a surrogate for objectivity.[32] That on the basis of which we appraise things will be a matter of inter-subjective consensus as to what can be observed – consensus, however, towards which we may have to work.

If this idea is accepted, it has important consequences for the way in which economic theories and models should be tested. For on such a view it is not enough that the proponents of some theory should run empirical tests which they consider to be appropriate. Rather the heart of a test is its inter-subjective acceptability; and this means that ideally we would have general agreement, in advance of a test being performed, as to its relevance and interest and as to the acceptability of the methods that are being used. If the results of a test are other than we expected, we may be led to question some aspect of our test procedures, or some other assumption which had, hitherto, seemed uncontentious. The argument for such revision, however, must itself again be conducted in terms which, in the last instance, will be inter-subjectively acceptable.

Of course we may be in a situation in which there are major disagreements about both theories and test methods, in which connection the running of tests upon which there is not general agreement may play an important role in the argument between the proponents of different views. And it would clearly be absurd to suspend all testing until the most recalcitrant of those with whom one was having a disagreement accepted fully one's methods. But, at the same time, it seems to me that we would gain by taking the inter-subjective character of testing seriously. Such an approach, if it were adopted, would put a premium upon discussion between those who favour different theories and forms of testing, and on the exploration and ironing out of differences of opinion before any kind of test was undertaken. In so far as theoretical discussion is cheap and testing expensive – compare the research budgets of philosophers and empirical scientists – we might also save valuable resources by adopting this suggestion!

Such an approach, however, does not necessarily require that we be able to translate everything into some language that is neutral relative to all the theories that are currently being espoused. For the proponents of one theory may be perfectly willing to work within other people's theories and assumptions, the test turning into what, in their view, would be an experimental *reductio ad absurdum* of the competing theory. For the fact that, say, all our evidence is couched in terms of the ontology of some theory does not imply that the evidence, so interpreted, must confirm the theory. Rather one of the most effective criticisms of a theory will be to let its proponent identify what, in his view, exemplifies the theory; to predict how that thing should behave; and then to observe, to his chagrin, that the object so identified does not in fact behave as his theory said that it should.

Should Popper's ideas as I have interpreted them here be accepted, they would seem to me to lead to some striking consequences. First, as Mark Blaug has argued,[33] they would lead us to be much more concerned with whether and how our theories can be tested. Second, as I have argued above, they would lead to much greater pressure for consensus with respect to the way theories are appraised, prior to testing taking place. The same, in my view, would also be the case for theoretical work: this too would be understood as argument that is couched in terms that must in principle be inter-subjectively acceptable. This view, it seems to me, would mark a difference from the kind of 'each tend their own garden' pluralism that is more usual in academic life today.

All this, I should stress, need not lead to a theoretical monism. Rather, many schools of thought could flower; but they would be pressed, if their proponents came to accept these views, to maintain an interest in and contact with the work of one another, and to have a concern for accountability in principle to people other than those who share their particular theoretical approach.

Sociology and the Empirical Basis

One other aspect of Popper's account of the 'empirical basis' that seems to me fruitful is the natural links that exist between it and the sociology of science. Rather than there being opposition between Popper's account and, say, the concerns of Collins in the present volume, it seems to me that the work of each naturally complements that of the other. For if one sees the 'empirical basis' of our knowledge as the product of inter-subjective agreement – and thus of argument and negotiation between different parties: as a social construction – then clearly one should be interested in empirical and theoretical investigations as to how all of this currently takes place.

The Popperian – or certainly this Popperian – would expect to learn from such investigations: I would hope that, through them, we would be led to develop better normative theories. But, at the same time, if we reflect on what actually takes place in the light of such normative theories, we would presumably also be led to criticisms of our current practices and institutions. In this respect it seems to me that Juergen Habermas is correct in looking back, from a concern for truth pursued through a process of inter-subjective agreement, to criticize power relations and institutions in so far as they fall short of what might best assist us in this endeavour. Such a *critical* sociology of knowledge, it seems to me, will lead us to suggest improvements in our institutions from the perspective of our pursuit of scientific knowledge. However, as I have argued elsewhere, I do not think that such investigations necessarily lead us in the direction that one might most naturally associate with Habermas himself.[34]

NOTES

1. See Neil de Marchi, 'Popper and the LSE Economists', in N. de Marchi (ed.), *The Popperian Legacy in Economics*, Cambridge University Press, 1988; S.J. Latsis (ed.), *Method and Appraisal in Economics*, Cambridge University Press, 1979; and especially Mark Blaug, *The Methodology of Economics*, Cambridge University Press, 1980.
2. I do not mean to include here John Worrall's 'The Ways in Which the Methodology of Scientific Research Programmes Improves on Popper's Methodology', in G. Radnitzky and G. Andersson (eds), *Progress and Rationality in Science*, Reidel, 1978, as he raises many interesting points of detail on which Popper and Lakatos differ. These, however, it would not be appropriate for me to discuss in the present, non-technical chapter.
3. See W.W. Bartley III's contribution to *Essays in Honor of Imre Lakatos*, Boston Studies in the Philosophy of Science, Reidel, 1976.
4. See Douglas W. Hands, 'Second Thoughts on Lakatos', *History of Political Economy*, 17, Number 1, Spring 1985, pp. 1–16.
5. See K.R. Popper, *Conjectures and Refutations*, Routledge, 1963, chapter 10, pp. 240ff, and also 'The Rationality of Scientific Revolutions' in R. Harre (ed.), *Problems of Scientific Revolution*, Oxford University Press, 1975.
6. See J. Agassi, 'Sensationalism', *Mind*, 75, 1966, pp. 1–24.
7. One obvious example is Newton's concern about action at a distance, where he

admitted hypotheses, the more fundamental character of which he could make little sense of, because of their empirical power (and despite the fact that his various attempts to explain them in ways which he could make sense of came to naught). A second concerns early moves in the theory of heat. The problem here was that it seemed almost impossible to make theoretical sense of the various phenomena which produce heat: heat could be produced by motion; it might be released as a substance changed its physical state; and, most baffling of all, it seemed at times to behave like light, so that it could even be focused through a lens-shaped piece of ice. The demand that advances in the early theory of heat should follow some single unifying idea, without loss of coherence or empirical content, is a counsel that could not, as far as I can see, be followed.

8. See K.R. Popper, 'Rationality and the Status of the Rationality Principle', in D. Miller (ed.), *Popper Selections*, Princeton University Press, 1985.
9. Compare on this Alan Musgrave's contribution to *Essays in Honor of Imre Lakatos*.
10. I still recall with amusement Lakatos's comments, after Noam Chomsky had presented a paper on his work at a departmental seminar at the LSE, in the course of which Lakatos referred to his earlier 'refutation' of Chomsky's work – which, of course, transpired to be 'Proofs and Refutations'!
11. See his 'A Renaissance of Empiricism in the Philosophy of Mathematics', in *Mathematics, Science and Epistemology*, ed. J. Worrall and G. Currie, Cambridge University Press, 1978.
12. Compare *Objective Knowledge*, Oxford University Press, 1972, p. 40, n. 9, and also the remarks on truth on p. 320.
13. Popper's *Postscript* was published in 1982–83 by Hutchinson, London as *Realism and the Aim of Science*; *The Open Universe*; and *Quantum Theory and the Schism in Physics*; see also his 'On the Status of Science and of Metaphysics', two radio talks which were published in 1958, and republished in his *Conjectures and Refutations*. Joseph Agassi's *The Gentle Art of Philosophical Polemics*, Open Court, 1988, contains many scattered remarks that would be of great interest if someone wished to reconstruct this story in more detail.
14. Compare, in this respect, the historical discussion of theories of explanation given in the paper, dating from 1948, that is reprinted as Appendix 1 to *Objective Knowledge*; Popper's discussion of the history of theories of matter in his 'Philosophy and Physics', *Atti del XII Congresso Internazionale di Filosofia*, Venice 1958, volume 2, Sansoni Editore, 1960, pp. 367–74, and also his various treatments of the ideas of the Presocratics.
15. Imre Lakatos, 'Changes in the Problem of Inductive Logic'; see his *Mathematics, Science and Epistemology*, ed. John Worrall and Gregory Currie, Cambridge University Press, 1978.
16. See *Objective Knowledge*, p. 180; the lecture dates from 1968.
17. Cp. S. Latsis, 'Situational Determinism in Economics', *British Journal for the Philosophy of Science*, 23, Number 3, 1972, especially pp. 234–42.
18. Thus, when Hands argues that emphasis on the prediction of novel facts is an odd and radical characteristic of the Popperians, I would suggest that it is in the later work of Lakatos that it is given the particular emphasis that he highlights. Compare also, however, Alan Musgrave, 'Logical versus Historical Theories of Confirmation', *British Journal for the Philosophy of Science*, 25, March 1974, pp. 1–23.
19. Larry Laudan, *Progress and Its Problems*, University of California Press, 1977.
20. See note 14, above.
21. Compare also with this Hayek's account of 'explanation of the principle' in his *Studies in Philosophy, Politics and Economics*, Routledge, 1967.
22. For a more detailed account of the interplay between the metaphysical and the empirical in Descartes' physics, see I. Sabra, *Theories of Light from Descartes to Newton*, Oldbourne, London, 1967.
23. Another line of theoretical argument that may be used to similar effect involves the critical use of thought experiments, although there we should be careful that we do

not dismiss things just because they seem to us to lead to absurdity, without investigating whether reality is, in this respect, 'absurd'. Cp. the first section of K.R. Popper, 'On the Use and Misuse of Imaginary Experiments, Especially in Quantum Theory', Appendix *ix to *The Logic of Scientific Discovery*, Hutchinson, 1959.

24. See Chapter 13 of the present volume.
25. If, however, we are in a situation comparable to that of the early theory of heat (see note 7, above), there may be no way in which our new theory can avoid so-called 'Kuhn loss'. But in that situation it would seem to me that, for the time being, we should append to our new theory a statement, in its strongest possible form, as to what was lost. This may have the consequence that we do not neglect the loss and also have the incentive to look for a new theory or theories which will be adequate to all the relevant material.
26. See Laudan, *Progress and Its Problems*, p. 45.
27. See 'The History of Science and Its Rational Reconstructions', in *The Methodology of Scientific Research Programmes*, ed. J. Worrall and G. Currie, Cambridge University Press, 1978.
28. See G.W.F. Hegel, *Lectures on the Philosophy of World History: Introduction*, tr. N.B. Nisbet, Cambridge University Press, 1975.
29. On which general issue, see also J. Agassi, *Towards an Historiography of Science*, Wesleyan University Press, 1963.
30. See, on this, Popper's discussion of conventionalism in *The Logic of Scientific Discovery*, and the 'Introduction' to *Conjectures and Refutations*.
31. See J.W.N. Watkins, *Science and Scepticism*, Princeton University Press, 1984.
32. See, on this, my 'Epistemological Limits of the State', *Political Studies*, 38, 1990, pp. 116–25 and my 'Habermas: A Critical Approach', *Critical Review*, 2, Number 1, Winter 1988, pp. 39–50.
33. See Mark Blaug, *The Methodology of Economics*, Cambridge University Press, 1980.
34. See my 'Habermas: A Critical Approach'; but for a corrective to my interpretation of Habermas's political views compare also Stephen White, *The Recent Work of Juergen Habermas*, Cambridge University Press, 1988.

COMMENT ON SHEARMUR

Kurt Klappholz

As far as *I* know, Shearmur is wrong in equating the amount of written attention Popper devoted to economics with that which Lakatos devoted to it. While the former could not avoid saying something about the methodology of economics in the *Poverty of Historicism*, and about substantive issues of economics in *The Open Society*, the latter wrote nothing about economics. Of course, as a *proportion* of his total written output, Popper wrote next to nothing about economics. Despite its title, in the present paper Shearmur follows Popper's example.

One of Shearmur's main criticisms of Lakatos is that, according to his later work, '. . . theoretical progress – and, more generally, the appraisal of theories – is turned back into a largely empirical matter. Such appraisal is . . . very important; but to take it as the only way in which we can appraise theories seems to me unduly restrictive' (p. 35). I eschew textual exegesis and do not question Shearmur's claim (p. 40) that Lakatos's ideas could be used legitimately to defend Friedman's instrumentalism, despite Lakatos's well-known opposition to the latter. In section I, instead of attempting to criticize Shearmur's very general paper, I support his argument by adding to his single example (p. 42) of successful non-empirical criticism in the recent history of economic thought. I treat 'appraisal' and 'criticism' as synonymous and must say at once that neither Shearmur's nor my view on this matter is novel in methodological writings on economics (e.g. Klappholz and Agassi, 1959), let alone in the philosophy of science. In section II, I ask whether my excursion into recent history of economic thought helps us to appraise Shearmur's comparison of Popper with Lakatos.

I

As an example of the kind of fruitful criticism he has in mind (p. 42) Shearmur refers us to Popper's account of Leibniz's criticism of Descartes, according to which Descartes could not have appreciated some logical consequences of his theory, consequences which Leibniz pointed out. Analogous criticisms have been most influential in economics and I shall now give examples of some of them which seem to me particularly *à propos* to what Shearmur calls 'our current situation'.

On page 38 Shearmur reminds us that Popper advocates the holding of the 'rationality principle' as immune from criticism. Generally economists had followed that advice long before Popper appeared on the scene. The use of the economists' version of the rationality principle led quite naturally to the development of what may be called the Pareto-hypothesis; that is, the idea that individuals will *seek* to exploit all potential gains from trade. Yet, somehow, this idea, which is at the heart of economics, seemed often to be left aside, both when economists dealt with explanations of the consequences of particular policies and when they dealt with the theory of the efficiency of a market-organized economy in general. An example of the first kind is provided by the discussion of the effects of rent control. A long, long time ago economists predicted that rent control, with security of tenure, has three effects. First, it transfers wealth from existing landlords to existing tenants; that is, it is equivalent to an inescapable capital tax on those landlords and a capital subsidy to those tenants. Second, because of this no reasonably well-informed owner of empty but potentially rentable property will let it and hence the stock of rented accommodation will at best remain constant in the short run and, in the longer run, will decline as hitherto let properties become vacant and landlords transfer them to other uses, such as owner-occupation, to escape the tax. People who wished to rent property would not find willing sellers.

These two predictions could be deduced from existing theory, but a third prediction, which was also made, could not be so deduced. That prediction was that the existing housing stock would be inefficiently distributed among its potential users and not only between owning and renting. When these predictions were first made (for some references see Klappholz, 1989) casual observation supported them and much later they were supported by more systematic investigations. Yet those who made the last prediction did not offer an explanation as to why the windfall gains and losses caused by rent control should prevent the full subsequent exploitation of gains from trade and thus the efficient allocation of the housing stock among its competing users.

Turning to the theory of the efficiency of markets, the history of its development was marked by at least two curious features, one of which is the same as that given in the above example of rent control. To summarize a long story briefly: in the last quarter of the nineteenth century Adam Smith's invisible hand conjecture had been formalized; that is, it was shown that the equilibrium of a competitive economy was characterized by optimality. However, later on, it was stressed that, when the conditions for competition were absent, market failure would result: the equilibrium of the economy would *not* be characterized by optimality. But the absence of optimality means that someone can be made better off without anyone being made worse off. As far as I am aware no participant in this discussion abandoned the assumption that individuals aim to maximize their utility. If so, why should the *inefficiency* of an imperfectly competitive economy *persist*? These questions, which were not asked for quite a long time, did not involve empirical but rather logical criticism. Yet these simple questions led to the development of what we now call the economic analysis of law and also the economic theory of politics or the theory of public choice.

The development of the theory of public choice was partly an attempt to remedy a manifest defect in the analysis of the efficiency of markets, to which I have just referred. However it was more than that and concerned the policy prescriptions which were often based on the analysis of market failure. These policy prescriptions *seemed* to follow straightforwardly from that analysis: as long as markets are competitive, there are no externalities and public goods, markets lead to efficient outcomes. If these conditions are not satisfied, then markets do not ensure efficiency and the latter can only be achieved by government action! This kind of policy prescription was advocated despite the absence of any theory of political or collective action analogous to the prevailing theory of markets and despite widespread views of the frequently pernicious effects of government actions. No wonder that the originators of the theory of public choice argued that those who advanced these kinds of policy prescriptions implicitly must have viewed democratic governments as behaving as if they were benevolent despots. This proved to be a most effective criticism; while, say, 30 years ago, much was written about market failure in textbooks and journal articles, there was little about the failure of collective, that is, political action. Today, while we remain aware of the possibility of market failure, we are equally aware of the possibility of the failure of collective action. This change was not the result of empirical criticism, as a glance at a book such as that by Buchanan and Tullock (1962) clearly shows. James Buchanan received the Nobel Prize for being one of the originators of the public choice research programme.

My examples of non-empirical criticisms, which have proved most effective in economics, obviously are not original. Moreover they are not flattering to economists. Historians of recent economic thought may well wish to reconsider to what extent these most unflattering criticisms are historically justified, although most of us can cite instances in which they are, such as Meade's advocacy, just before and after the Second World War, of regarding large economies of scale as offering a *prima facie* case for socialization (Meade, 1936, 1948).

The idea of socialized firms as a corrective for market failure was part of the basis of the theory of 'market socialism', as advocated by Lange. While this theory was incompatible with the Marxist proposition that only labour is productive, it nevertheless implied that the productivity of non-human wealth is independent of whether, for example, it is owned privately or by the state. While the development of the theory of markets was accompanied by the assumption that market activities were intimately linked to private property, the whole point of the theory of market socialism was to deny that such a linkage was necessary. This was undoubtedly a clever point which soon found expression in text-books. However, if the point had been true, it would be difficult to make sense of what is now going on in Eastern Europe.

II

I have offered examples of successful non-empirical criticisms in recent economics; successful in the sense that these criticisms have been widely accepted in the profession and have stimulated new areas of research. Assuming that my summary of these criticisms and their effects is correct, which it may not be, as I have noted, does this story shed any light on the merits of Popper's as against Lakatos's approach to the growth of knowledge? Alas, I do not think so, since neither Popper nor Lakatos would have disagreed with the criticisms, although they would probably have regretted the need for some of them to have been made. Lakatos might have been more indulgent than Popper, partly because of his theory of degenerative research programs, which implies that *even* consensus in the scientific community, not present in the cases I have discussed, gives no assurance of scientific progress, and partly because, having spent part of his life as a believing Marxist, he could, or should have been able to, empathize with people getting attached to half-baked ideas.

Although Lakatos was friendly with some economists at the LSE, he showed no interest in the subject, although in conversation he sometimes used to promise to turn his attention to it at an unspecified later date.

References

Buchanan, J.M. and Tullock, G. (1962), *The Calculus of Consent* (Ann Arbor: The University of Michigan Press).

Klappholz, K. and Agassi, J. (1959), 'Methodological Prescriptions in Economics', *Economica*, N.S. vol. 26 (February).

Klappholz K. (1989), 'Rent Control', in J. Eatwell, M. Milgate and P. Newman (eds), *Social Economics* (London: Macmillan).

Meade, J.E. (1936), *An Introduction to Economic Analysis and Policy* (Oxford: The Clarendon Press).
—— (1948), *Planning and the Price Mechanism* (London: George Allen & Unwin).

2. The Problem of Excess Content: Economics, Novelty and a Long Popperian Tale

D. Wade Hands*

INTRODUCTION

I have previously argued against using the Popperian/Lakatosian notions of excess content and novel facts as the sole criteria for theory appraisal in economics (Hands, 1985a, 1988, 1989a, 1990). It is not my intention to repeat my earlier arguments here. My current task is related but more historical. What I will do is trace the sequence of events which brought Popperian philosophy (including Lakatos) to its current position on the issues of excess content, novelty and scientific progress. My general approach will be to analyse Popper's and Lakatos's positions on these issues as an appropriate response to the particular philosophical problem situations in which they found themselves. In particular, I will argue that Popper's concept of verisimilitude played a fundamental role in the evolving problem situations of these two authors. Finally, after reconstructing this Popperian tale, I will return to economics and economic methodology. Some of the problems in contemporary economic methodology can be much better understood in the light of this reconstructed history of the Popperian and Lakatosian view.

In the first section below I will reconstruct Popper's problem situation as it pertains to the issues of content, novelty and truth. Particular attention will be given to verisimilitude and its role in Popper's position. The second section will discuss Lakatos's view and analyse his methodology of scientific research programs (MSRP) in the context of his, inherited, problem situation. The third section will consider contemporary problems in Popperian philosophy, particularly problems with the concept of verisimilitude, and relate these problems to the

* I would like to thank the participants of the Capri conference on 'Transitions in Recent Economics: Studies in Research Programmes', particularly my discussants, Bert Hamminga, Uskali Mäki, and J.N. van Ommeren, for helpful comments on an earlier draft of this chapter.

earlier discussion of Popper's problem situation. The final section will discuss economics and the relationship between these events in Popperian philosophy and recent work on economic methodology.

1 A LONG POPPERIAN TALE ABOUT CONTENT, NOVELTY AND TRUTH[1]

Popper's 1934 position in *Logik der Forschung* was purely methodological without being epistemological.[2] His falsificationist methodology of bold conjecture and severe test provided a set of rules for the game of science (rules for demarcating science from non-science, rules for correctly playing the scientific game, and a criterion for successful play or progress) without providing an ultimate aim or purpose for playing the game. Earlier philosophies of science had been explicit about the aim of science and had subordinated their rules to their stated aim. 'In Popper's philosophy this link seems to be severed. The rules of the game, the methodology, stand on their own feet; but these feet dangle in the air without philosophical support' (Lakatos, 1978, p. 154). Popper clearly recognized this lacuna in his early view and sought to fill it in his later work. 'Since publishing the *Logik der Forschung* (that is, since 1934) I have developed a more systematic treatment of the problem of scientific method: I have tried to start with some suggestions about the aims of scientific activity, and to derive most of what I have to say about the methods of science – including many comments about its history – from this suggestion' (Popper, 1983, p. 131).

Popper's main suggestion, introduced in 1959 or 1960, is that the aim of science is the 'search for truth'.[3] 'We should seek to see or discover the most urgent problems, and we should try to solve them by proposing true theories . . .' (Popper, 1973, p. 44). Popper had always preferred scientific realism and had wanted to characterize science as the search for truth, but in the early 1930s, when he was writing *LSD*, the correspondence theory of truth was in such disrepute that Popper strategically chose to 'avoid the topic' (1965, p. 223). It was not until Popper became aware of Alfred Tarski's theory that he lost his 'uneasiness concerning the notion of truth' (1973, p. 320) and formally endorsed truth as the aim of science.[4]

Actually Popper went far beyond Tarski and the Tarskian notion of truth by introducing his own concept of truthlikeness or 'verisimilitude'. Popper argued that, if science is to aim at truth, it is necessary to have a notion of approximate truth or coming nearer to the truth. His goal in introducing the concept of verisimilitude was to be able to say 'that some theory T_1 is superseded by some new theory, say T_2, because T_2 is more like the truth than T_1' (1973, p. 47). Such a concept 'allows us to say that the aim of science is truth in the sense of better approximation to truth, or greater verisimilitude' (1973, p. 57). Popper intended verisimilitude to apply to strictly false theories; it should allow us to make sense out of the notion that one theory is closer to the truth than another even if both theories are false.[5]

While an elaborate discussion of Popper's concept of verisimilitude is not required here, a brief sketch of the idea will be useful.[6] Popper's definition of verisimilitude relies fundamentally on the notion of the *content* of a statement (or conjecture or theory). The *content* of a particular statement a, is the class of all non-tautological statements which are logically entailed by a. This content class (call it A) is subdivided into the truth content (A_T): the set of all true statements which follow from A, and the falsity content (A_F): the set of all false statements which follow from a. Actually we need to be a little more careful in specifying A_F since true statements can be deduced from false ones, but these definitions of A_T and A_F capture the basic ideas of truth and falsity content.[7]

Given these notions of truth and falsity content it is rather simple to define verisimilitude or truthlikeness. A theory T_2 has more *verisimilitude* than a theory T_1 if and only if (a) their contents are comparable, and *either* (b) the truth content but not the falsity content of T_2 is greater than T_1, *or* (c) the falsity content but not the truth content of T_1 is greater than T_2. In other words, of two comparable theories, the one with more true implications (and no more false implications) or fewer false implications (and no fewer true implications) has the greater verisimilitude. This type of verisimilitude or nearness to truth became the Popperian aim of science: 'To say that the aim of science is verisimilitude has considerable advantage over the perhaps simpler formulation that the aim of science is truth' (Popper, 1973, p. 57).

So around 1960 Popper introduced the notions of truth and truthlikeness, and specified truthlikeness or verisimilitude as the aim of science. It is easy to see this move as an appropriate response to his philosophical problem situation. Popper wanted an approach which was basically realist ('the only sensible hypothesis', Popper, 1973, p. 42) while still avoiding essentialism; he perceived Tarski's notion of truth and his own concept of verisimilitude to be a solution to his problem.

> I wish to be able to say that science aims at truth in the sense of correspondence to the facts or to reality; and I also wish to say (with Einstein

> and other scientists) that relativity theory is – or so we conjecture – a better approximation to truth than is Newton's theory, just as the latter is a better approximation to the truth than is Kepler's theory. And I wish to be able to say these things without fearing that the concept of nearness to truth or verisimilitude is logically misconceived, or 'meaningless'. (Popper, 1973, p. 59)

Now, however satisfying verisimilitude might be as the aim of science, it only becomes an appropriate solution to Popper's problem situation if it does not require him to abandon the falsificationist methodology of *LSD*; not surprisingly it does not. Popper argues that verisimilitude as an aim is perfectly consistent with the falsificationist methodology of bold conjecture and severe test which he has advocated in all of his methodological writings.

For a new theory to have more verisimilitude than its comparable predecessor the new theory either needs to have more truth content or less falsity content than the theory it replaces. First consider the case where the falsity content of the two theories is the same and focus on the truth content. In this case the bolder theory, the one with the most total content, the one which says more, will have more truth content and thus more verisimilitude. In this way Popper's traditional preference for bold theories, theories which take greater risks, seems to be entirely consistent with verisimilitude as the aim of science. Now consider falsity content. For more verisimilitude we want less falsity content. Popper's methodology has always been a method of severe test and attempted refutation; it is a falsificationist method. This falsificationist method of seriously attempting to refute theories and eliminating those which fail these severe tests seems entirely consistent with the aim of finding theories with low falsity content. Popper summarizes these arguments in the following way.

> A theory is the bolder the greater its content. It is also the riskier: it is the more probable to start with that it will be false. We try to find its weak points, to refute it. If we fail to refute it, or if the refutations we find are at the same time also refutations of the weaker theory which was its predecessor, thus we have reason to suspect, or to conjecture, that the stronger theory has no greater falsity content than its weaker predecessor, and, therefore, that it has the greater degree of verisimilitude. (1973, p. 53)

So Popper argues that verisimilitude as an aim is consistent with falsificationism as a method: but this is not the end of his argument. It seems that verisimilitude as a 'solution' opens up another problem. The search for truth or truthlikeness is not enough; we need 'interesting truth' (Popper, 1965, p. 229). 'In other words, we are not simply looking for truth, we are after interesting and enlightening truth, after theories which offer solutions to interesting *problems*. If at all possible, we are after deep theories' (Popper, 1973, p. 55, emphasis in original). The search for ever deeper theories requires *more than* simple falsificationist practice: more than bold conjecture, severe test, and avoiding ad hoc defensive stratagems. The method of *LSD* is consistent with the search for truth but it is not enough. Popper says: 'I have been asked, "What more do you want?" My answer is that there are many more things I want; or rather, which I think are required by the logic of the general problem situation in which the scientist finds himself; by the task of getting nearer to the truth. I shall confine myself here to the discussion of three such requirements' (1965, p. 241).

The first of Popper's famous three requirements is that the 'new theory should proceed from some *simple, new, and powerful unifying idea*' (1965, p. 241, emphasis in original); this is the so-called 'simplicity requirement'. The second requirement is the requirement of 'independent testability'. 'That is to say, apart from explaining all the *explicanda* which the new theory was designed to explain, it must have new and testable consequences (preferably consequences of a *new kind*); it must lead to the prediction of phenomena which have not so far been observed' (1965, p. 241, emphasis in original). This second requirement is designed to eliminate ad hoc modification of a falsified theory parading as a new theory.[8]

Finally, Popper's 'third requirement', is that 'the theory should pass some new, and severe, tests' (1965, p. 292). This third requirement is the requirement of 'empirical success' and it simply says that some of the independently testable implications required by the second requirement actually gets corroborated by the empirical evidence. Popper says,

> I contend that further progress in science would become impossible if we did not reasonably often manage to meet the third requirement; thus if the progress of science is to continue, and its rationality not to decline, we need not only successful refutations, but also positive successes. We must, that is, manage reasonably often to produce theories that entail new predictions, especially predictions of new effects, new testable consequences, suggested by the new theory and never thought of before. (1965, p. 243)

Popper argues that this third requirement may 'sound strange' (1965, p. 247) because it makes the evidence which counts in the progress of science a 'partly historical idea' (1965, p. 248). Nevertheless this third requirement is indispensable to a science which seeks theories of ever-increasing verisimilitude.

Let us now recap this rather long Popperian tale. Though Popper has always been sympathetic to scientific realism, in *LSD* he advocated a falsificationist methodology without connecting it to truth.[9] Later Popper not only accepted truth as the aim of science but proposed his own theory of verisimilitude to better characterize that aim. Since verisimilitude was consistent with his falsificationist methodology, it allowed Popper to solve his earlier problem of a methodology independent of truth. But this solution raised new problems; once verisimilitude was the stated aim the methodology needed to be expanded. Since science progressed and approached truth by means of deeper and deeper theories, certain kinds of corroborations were of special significance. Corroborations of predictions which had 'never been thought of before' (or what later came to be called 'novel facts') became necessary for progress towards theories of ever greater verisimilitude. This final position became part of the inherited problem situation of Imre Lakatos, to which I now turn.

2 LAKATOS WHIFFS THE PROBLEM

The philosophical problem situation of Imre Lakatos was in part based on the above Popperian view of scientific progress and in part based on more historical influences such as Thomas Kuhn. Lakatos's response to these influences generated the Lakatosian rebellion which attacked the Popperian conventional wisdom (presented above) at two separate levels: the methodological level and the epistemological level. The former, the methodological criticism, is the best known part of Lakatos's work and it resulted in his own methodology, the methodology of scientific research programs (MSRP).[10] The second part of the attack, the epistemological criticism, is probably less well known and it resulted in Lakatos's plea to Popper for a 'whiff of inductivism'.[11]

Regarding the *methodological* issues Lakatos saw a number of problems with the Popperian conventional wisdom. Probably most important was the fact (apparent from contemporary history of science) that Popper's falsificationist methodology was at odds with the actual practice of great science. Lakatos advocated a 'quasi-empirical approach' (1978, p. 153); he argued that a methodology 'must reconstruct the acknowledgedly best games and the most esteemed gambits as "scientific"; if it fails to do so, it has to be rejected' (1978, p. 145). Lakatos, among others, argued that Popper's methodology failed in this regard. In particular, Popperian falsificationism fails because it 'stubbornly overestimates the immediate striking force of purely negative criticism' (1978, p. 148). For Lakatos, actual great science has succeeded in a sea of inconsistencies and anomalies (refutations) and any adequate methodology must recognize (and rationalize) these facts. Many parts of Lakatos's MSRP, particularly the concepts of a research 'program', the hard core, and the protective belts, were attempts to accommodate the actual history of science and avoid these perceived problems in Popper's methodology.

One methodological issue where Lakatos did *not* disagree with Popper was on the importance of predicting novel facts;[12] for Lakatos's MSRP, as for the Popperian view which he inherited,[13] progress requires novelty. On the same page (1970, p. 118) where Lakatos presents his famous definitions of 'theoretical progress' ('predicts some novel, hitherto unexpected fact') and 'empirical progress' ('this excess empirical content is also corroborated') he provided the following footnote, accentuating the importance of novelty.

> If I already know P_1: 'Swan A is white', P_w: 'All swans are white' represents no progress, because it may only lead to the discovery of such further similar facts as P_2: 'Swan B is white.' So-called 'empirical generalizations' constitute no progress. A *new* fact must be improbable or even impossible in the light of previous knowledge. (1970, p. 118h)[14]

Thus, while Lakatos's MSRP was critical of much of the Popperian methodology, one aspect, the importance of novel facts, was not only accepted, but actually emphasized more than by Popper. For Popper novel facts are a bit of an add-on, since much of the empirical burden is still carried by falsification and refutation. For Lakatos, on the other hand, who wanted to decrease (to zero) the role of negative evidence and refutation, the entire burden of scientific progress is left on the shoulders of novel facts. Lakatos's solution to his perceived methodological problem situation left him with a methodological position where 'the only observational phenomena which have *any* bearing on the assessment of a research programme are those which are "novel" ' (Gardner, 1982, p. 1).

In the realm of *epistemology*, as opposed to the realm of methodology, Lakatos is more critical of his progenitor. His criticism is based on the fact that Popper, despite his claim that verisimilitude is the aim of science, remains deeply sceptical about the certainty or guaranteed reliability of our knowledge. Popper has argued consistently that, while we may (and should) search for truth, we never know when we find it; 'even if we hit upon a true theory, we shall as a rule be merely guessing, and it may well be impossible for us to know that it *is* true' (1965, p. 225). For Popper there are 'no general criteria by which we can recognize truth' (1965, p. 226). Not only can we not recognize truth, this lack of epistemological confidence extends even to our ability to know that we are getting closer to the truth. 'My defence of the legitimacy of the idea of verisimilitude has sometimes been grossly misunderstood. In order to avoid these misunderstandings it is advisable to keep in mind my view that not only are all theories conjectural, but also all appraisals of theories, including comparisons of theories from the point of view of verisimilitude' (1973, p. 58). 'We cannot justify our theories, or the belief that they are true; nor can we justify the belief that they are near to the truth' (1983, p. 61).

Popper does believe that we have rational arguments for our theoretical preferences; we have rational reasons to suspect or conjecture that one theory has more verisimilitude, but we do not *know*. Recall the earlier quotation, where Popper was relating verisimilitude to boldness; he says, 'we have reason to suspect, or to conjecture, that the stronger theory has no greater falsity content than its weaker predecessor' (1973, p. 53): notice 'reason to suspect', not 'we know'. Later in the same paper Popper says, 'But if it passes all these tests then we may have good reason to conjecture that our theory, which as we know has greater truth content than its predecessor, may have no greater falsity content' (1973, p. 81). We 'know' about truth content because that is a logical relation, but when it comes to the question of less falsity content, required for verisimilitude, Popper says only that 'we may have good reason to conjecture that' it 'may have no greater falsity content'.

Lakatos considers this lack of epistemological bite to be a major difficulty for the Popperian position. Lakatos's argument is that merely defining the aim of science as verisimilitude is not enough; one needs to be able to identify this progress when it occurs. It is not enough to say that novel corroborations 'may be a good reason to conjecture' that we are getting closer to the truth: we need a firm connection between the two; the game of science needs a 'truly epistemological dimension' (Zahar, 1983, p. 167). Lakatos gives Popper credit for his Tarskian turn, for introducing verisimilitude and promoting it as the aim of science; it is just that Popper did not go far enough. Lakatos argues that, after Popper modified his views, it 'became possible for the first time to define progress even for a sequence of false theories: such a sequence constitutes progress, if its truth-content, or, as Popper proposed, its verisimilitude (truth-content minus falsity-content) increases. But this is not enough: we have to *recognize* progress' (Lakatos, 1978, p. 156). As Watkins characterizes the problem, 'it is one thing to have an aim for science and another to have a method by which we can, in favourable circumstances, actually pick out the hypothesis that best satisfies that aim' (1984, p. 279). For Lakatos, 'Popper has not fully exploited the possibilities opened up by his Tarskian turn' (1978, p. 159); he provided a solution in the form of his theory of verisimilitude, but then 'shrank back' (ibid.) from actually solving the epistemological problem associated with his methodology.

Lakatos's solution to this epistemological problem is a 'plea to Popper for a whiff of "inductivism" ' (ibid.). He recommends 'an inductive principle which connects realist metaphysics with methodological appraisals, verisimilitude with corroboration, which reinterprets the rules of the 'scientific game' as a-conjectural-theory about the *signs* of the *growth of knowledge*, that is, about the signs of *growing verisimilitude of our scientific theories*' (1978, p. 156, emphasis in original). Lakatos argues that, without such an inductive principle, any methodological proposals are mere conventions without epistemological bite:

> Without this principle Popper's 'corroborations' or 'refutations' and my 'progress' or 'degeneration', would remain mere honorific titles awarded in a pure game. With a *positive* solution of the problem of induction, however thin, methodological theories of demarcation can be turned from arbitrary conventions into rational metaphysics. (1978, p. 165)

In summary, Lakatos's solution was to modify Popper's methodology: play down falsification, emphasize novel facts and add both historical and heuristic dimensions to appraisal, but basically to take as given Popper's aim and his characterization of verisimilitude. On the epistemological side Lakatos was more radical: he pleaded for a 'whiff of inductivism', a positive solution to the problem of induction which would connect the purported methodological rules (his or Popper's) with verisimilitude as an aim. This brings the discussion to developments in post-verisimilitude Popperian philosophy of science.

3 THE TALE UNRAVELS

So we have heard a long Popperian tale with a Lakatosian twist on the end. Where does the story go from Lakatos? Unfortunately, beyond Lakatos, the story starts to unravel. I will not provide a complete discussion of these events, but let me at least review the previous discussion and comment on the evolution of the main parts of the story.

First, on the final question discussed above, Lakatos's plea for a whiff of inductivism, there is relatively little to say. Lakatos's proposal, however guarded his presentation, is basically a plea for a justification of the method of science in terms of the truth likeness of the theories the method produces. However recurrent such pleas have been in the history of philosophy it is doubtful whether such a justification will soon be upon us. Some neo-Popperians, Watkins (1984) in particular, argue that Lakatos's concern is legitimate but that the problem is not to be solved in Lakatos's way, by connecting corroborated appraisals to verisimilitude appraisals with an inductive principle (1984, pp. 282–8). Rather, Watkins rejects verisimilitude as the aim of science and proposes his own adequacy requirements (1984, p. 124) for any such aim. Given these broader adequacy requirements, Watkins argues that corroborations are in fact sufficient for the aim of science (1984, p. 306); this provides a possible solution to Lakatos's problem without actually responding to his 'plea'.

Clearly the most important factor in the unravelling of the later Popperian position has been the 'admitted failure' (Popper, 1983, p. xxxv) of Popper's definition of verisimilitude. This definition, which formed the backbone of Popper's methodological proposals regarding progress and novelty, has encountered a number of serious difficulties. Hacking, in a discussion of Lakatos's work, refers to verisimilitude as 'Popper's hokum' (1979, p. 387), while for Agassi it is simply 'a boo-boo' (1988, p. 473) and, for advocates of alternative non-Popperian interpretations of verisimilitude such as Oddie, Popper's work on verisimilitude has simply produced 'embarrassing results' (1986, p. 164). The recognition of these difficulties was initiated in two papers, Miller (1974) and Tichy (1974), which demonstrated that no false theory ever has more verisimilitude than any other false theory. Since being able to make sense of statements like 'Newton's theory is closer to the truth of Kepler's theory' was one of the most important reasons for the verisimilitude concept (Popper, 1973, p. 59) these initial negative results represented a serious setback for the program. Following these initial papers the critical literature has continued to such an extent that Popper now fully admits the failure of the project:

> A new definition is of interest only if it strengthens a theory. I thought that I could do this with my theory of the aims of science: the theory that science aims at truth *and* the solving of problems of explanation, that is, at theories of greater explanatory power, greater content, and greater testability. The hope further to strengthen this theory of the aims of science by the definition of verisimilitude in terms of truth and of content was, unfortunately, vain. (1983, p. xxxvi)

Now, while almost everyone admits that Popper's definition of verisimilitude has severe problems, opinions differ regarding the *importance* of these difficulties. Some, such as Zahar, consider these results to be 'a severe setback for fallibilist realism as a whole' (1983, p. 167). Others, such as Watkins (1984), discussed briefly above, simply reject verisimilitude as the aim of science and build their own neo-Popperian program without it. Popper himself, of course, does not see the difficulties of his technical/quantitative definition of verisimilitude to be at all significant. He says:

> The widely held view that scrapping this definition weakens my theory is completely baseless. I may add that I accepted the criticism of my definition within minutes of its presentation, wondering why I had not seen the mistake before; but nobody has ever shown that my theory of knowledge, which I developed at least as early as 1933 and which has been growing lustily ever since and which is much used by working scientists, is shaken in the least by this unfortunate mistaken definition, or why the idea of verisimilitude (which is not an essential part of my theory) should not be used further within my theory as an undefined concept. (1983, pp. xxxvi–xxxvii)

Such a disclaimer is relatively easy for Popper in the 1980s, since his latest turn has been towards 'critical rationalism'. This is the view, often associated with W.W. Bartley III, that rationally accepted propositions are those which have been critically discussed: that rationality simply means openness to criticism.[15]

Despite these Popperian disclaimers about the importance of verisimilitude, there are at least two places in Popperian philosophy where the problems of verisimilitude clearly have important (and negative) ramifications. Both of these places, by the way, are important in the relationship between Popperian philosophy and economic methodology. The first place where the failure of verisimilitude matters is in Popperian philosophy of social science, his so-called 'situational analysis' view of social science explanations. The second place where verisimilitude matters is in Lakatosian methodology. Let us consider Popper's philosophy of social science first.

Popper's 'situational analysis' approach to social science requires a 'rationality principle' which serves as the law in situational analysis explanations.[16] This rationality principle is 'an integral part of every, or nearly every, testable social theory' (Popper, 1985, p. 361), and yet 'the rationality principle is false' (Popper, 1985, p. 361). Assuming that the aim of science is truth, and assuming (as Popper clearly does) that there are no fundamental methodological differences between social and physical science, the falsity of the rationality principle represents a real difficulty. But the solution to the problem is easy: verisimilitude saves the day; if verisimilitude is the aim of science and if one false theory can have more verisimilitude than another false theory, then the notion of progress towards truth need not be lost when theories involve the rationality principle. 'Ultimately, the idea of verisimilitude is most important in cases where we know that we have to work with theories which are *at best* approximations – that is to say, theories of which we actually know that they cannot be true. (This is often the case in the social sciences.)' (Popper, 1965, p. 235.)

> The explanations of situational logic described here are rational, theoretical reconstructions. They are oversimplified and overschematized and consequently in general *false*. Nevertheless, they can possess a considerable truth content and they can, in the strictly logical sense, be good approximations to the truth, and better than certain other testable explanations. In this sense, the logical concept of approximation to the truth is indispensable for a social science using the method of situational analysis. (1976a, p. 103)

Notice that Popper said that verisimilitude was 'indispensable' for social science using the rationality principle.

Now consider Lakatos and the MSRP. Recall Lakatos's problem situation and how he came to advocate novel facts as the sole criterion for progress in science. Popper, in attempting to improve his basic *LSD* methodology so that it was more in agreement with verisimilitude as the aim of science (attempting to capture the notion of ever deeper theories), proposed novel facts as a particularly significant form of corroboration. Lakatos, picking up Popper's suggestion, abandoned falsificationism entirely, and elevated novel facts to the position of sole criterion for scientific progress. If Popper had never taken the Tarskian turn, never advocated verisimilitude as the aim of science, the notions of novelty and independent testability would be given only a minor role in Popperian methodology. Lakatos would have needed either to present a more traditional Popperian (that is, falsificationist) methodology, or to move entirely away from Popper, take a big whiff of inductivism, and simply rate research programs on the basis of how well they were confirmed by the evidence. As it worked out Lakatos could advocate novel facts as the sole criterion for progress in science and stay attached (however insecurely) to the Popperian tradition. But this linkage, so important to Lakatos, is, in the light of the entire Popperian story, quite thin and frail. If what is known about verisimilitude now had been known to Lakatos there is a very real possibility that the MSRP would characterize scientific progress in an entirely different way.

4 ECONOMICS: FINALLY

This Popperian tale can give us a number of important insights into contemporary economic methodology. First consider Lakatos and the MSRP. Economics has been fertile ground for application of Lakatos's MSRP. Because of Lakatos's novel fact requirement for progress, many of these economic applications have amounted to novel fact hunts. And, in particular, since there are now many different definitions of novel facts in the literature, these papers can become mired in semantic debates which provide little insight into either economics or philosophy.[17] More useful Lakatosian notions like the metaphysical hard core, the programmatic nature of scientific research, and the positive and negative heuristics, often get neglected in the rush to find novel facts. In the light of the above Popperian story, novel facts have a minor role in the overall Popperian approach to the philosophy of science; they were introduced to help forge a link between methodology and verisimilitude which now seems either futile or unnecessary (depending on how one views the final evolution of the Popperian position). If Lakatos is going to continue to play a role in economic methodology, then, in the light of the above story, we should re-evaluate the various roles of the different parts of his position.

Popperian philosophy of social science and situational analysis is another area where the developments in Popperian philosophy (particularly verisimilitude) have an impact on economic methodology. Microeconomic explanations are a special case of situational analysis using the rationality principle. Situational analysis itself is a special case of so-called 'folk psychology': explanations of behaviour in terms of the beliefs, desires and intentions of the relevant agent. Recently folk psychology (and therefore, by implication, situational analysis and microeconomics) have come under attack by philosophers who argue that intentional explanations are not legitimate scientific explanations. While most of these critics (and defenders as well) are concerned with folk psychology in general, Rosenberg (1981, 1988) has specifically indicted economics in this regard. Now the success of Popper's verisimilitude program would have provided at least a partial realist defence of such explanations (and thereby microeconomics), but, as it is, with the failure of verisimilitude, Popperians are left with only a critical-rationalism-as-a-default sort of argument in favour of situational analysis. This issue, the question of how (whether) it is possible to regard intentional explanations as valid explanations, is an important issue in the philosophy of economics. One possible defence, the one which seemed to be envisioned by Popper, has apparently collapsed with verisimilitude.

Finally there are the important questions of instrumentalism and essentialism. Let me consider instrumentalism first. Many, perhaps most, practising economists think of their work exclusively in instrumentalist terms. There does not seem to be any one single explanation for this instrumentalist preference. Some of the things which might reasonably be suggested for it are: the nature of econometrics and the ease with which it allows prediction from past trends, the demand for economic predictions from government agencies and private firms, and (possibly) the influence of Friedman's instrumentalist methodology. Of course Popper has always been an outspoken critic of instrumentalism.[18] His major criticism is that instrumentalism does not distinguish between science and mere technology; instrumentalism makes scientific theories 'nothing but computational rules' (Popper, 1983, p. 113) and, according to the instrumentalist, 'scientific theories cannot be real discoveries: they are gadgets. Science is an activity of gadget-making-glorified plumbing' (Popper, 1983, p. 122). Despite arguments such as these and a sustained anti-instrumentalist rhetoric, Popper's fallibilist philosophy of science hovers very close to instrumentalism: the empirical basis of science is accepted by convention, the methodological rules themselves are merely conventions, and all knowledge is conjectural (among other things). Verisimilitude temporarily seemed to widen the gap between Popper and instrumentalism, but the failure of the verisimilitude program has again moved them closer. In Lakatos where falsification makes no contribution to science and progress occurs only through a special type of corroboration, the instrumentalist flavour seems to be even stronger.

The fact of instrumentalist practice in economics and the anti-instrumentalism of Popperian philosophy generates a tension in Popperian economic methodology. It is clearly the case that economic methodologists *need* to make sense of instrumentalism in economics, but the dominance of Popperian ideas and the negative evaluation of instrumentalism in Popperian philosophy have focused the attention of economic methodologists away from serious consideration of this instrumentalist practice.

On the other hand, it is also true that Popperian philosophy is fundamentally anti-essentialist. Not only did the Popperian influence in economic methodology contribute to the neglect of instrumentalist practice, it also seems to have biased the discussion against essentialism. While much of contemporary economic practice may appear to be instrumentalist, the founders of modern microeconomics, Menger in particular, were committed to essentialist realism.[19] Of course the same can also be said of the Marxian tradition in economics and, on a broader (non-Popperian) definition of essentialism, maybe much of modern economics as well. It is very likely that Popper's influence has simultaneously turned our attention away from *both* how the founders of the profession perceived the discipline *and* how modern economics is practised.

None of these problems might matter too much if Popper's program of conjectural realism were on firm foundations, but it is not, and it does not appear that it will find such foundations in the near future. The failure of verisimilitude is certainly an important part of these difficulties. Lakatos's MSRP, however pregnant it might be with interesting ideas, is also unable to provide the requisite forward thrust. Economic methodology has been dominated by Popperian ideas for quite a number of years and, in the light of the entire story, that domination may have lasted quite long enough. There are still many issues in economic methodology which could benefit from the Popperian light, but in using it we should keep two points in mind: (a) the history of how that particular light came to shine the way it does; (b) there are other lights.

NOTES

1. Even before I start this tale it should be noted that many 'Popperians' will find my argument to be too much of a Lakatosian version (or possibly adulteration) of the story. In fact my story is very close to Lakatos's version but the reason is not that I am unfamiliar with the alternatives; the reason is that I think the Lakatosian version is basically correct. The story which follows seems to rationalize the value-impregnated history of Popperian philosophy much better than any of the other stories available in the literature.
2. English translation, *The Logic of Scientific Discovery* (1968): hereafter abbreviated *LSD*.
3. Popper (1965; 1973, pp. 44–84, pp. 319–35; 1976b, p. 150; 1983, pp. 24–7) for instance.
4. Popper (1965, pp. 223–6; 1968, p. 274n; 1973, pp. 319–21; 1976b, pp. 98–9).
5. Popper (1965, p. 235; 1973, pp. 56–7) and Koertge (1979, p. 234).
6. Popper's primary discussion of verisimilitude is contained in (1973) ch. 2 (esp. pp. 44–60) and ch. 9 (esp. pp. 329–35) and (1965) ch. 10 (esp. pp. 231–5) and Addenda (esp. pp. 391–402). The topic is surveyed in a number of works by other authors: Koertge (1979, esp. pp. 234–8) and Watkins (1984, esp. pp. 279–88) for example.
7. The interested reader may consult Popper (1973, pp. 48–50) for a more detailed discussion.
8. Much of the above Popperian tale could be couched in 'ad hoc' terms, that is, in terms of finding theories which are non-ad hoc. In this discussion I will try to skirt the ad hocness issue as much as possible since I have discussed the topic in detail elsewhere (Hands, 1988).

9. In fact in *LSD* (p. 276) Popper said: 'I think that it would be far from "*useful*" to identify the concept of corroboration with that of truth.' (Emphasis in original.)
10. Lakatos (1970).
11. Lakatos (1978).
12. An extensive literature has developed around Lakatos's use of 'novel fact'. Did his concept differ from Popper's? Did he have more than one concept? Can his definition of novel fact be modified so that the MSRP will be able to rationalize a greater portion of the actual history of science? I will try to avoid these controversies by simply arguing that Lakatos considered the prediction of novel facts to be necessary for progress in science, and that Lakatos's notion of novel fact was 'something' like Popper's. The interested reader who would like to pursue the question of how the term 'novel fact' is properly defined should examine some of the extensive literature on the topic (for instance, Carrier, 1988; Gardner, 1982; Musgrave, 1974; Worrall, 1978).
13. As we will see in the next section this view is not necessarily the same as the view of the most recent Popper. As my references in the last few paragraphs of the previous section indicate, the best example of the view Lakatos inherited is 'Truth, Rationality, and the Growth of Knowledge' (ch. 10 of Popper, 1965). It is probably fair to say that this paper is the best presentation of the 'middle' (verisimilitude) Popper, as opposed to the 'early/*LSD*' (don't talk about truth) Popper, or the 'final' (critical rationalist) Popper discussed briefly in the next section.
14. Later (1970, pp. 155–7), in his discussion of 'budding research programmes', Lakatos states that factual novelty may not be 'immediately ascertainable', but he never alters his view of the fundamental role of novel facts in scientific progress.
15. This is not the place to become involved in this latest Popperian turn but I cannot resist a passing comment. I fundamentally agree with Lakatos on this topic: 'the basic weakness of this position is its emptiness. There is not much point in affirming the criticizability of any position we hold without concretely specifying the forms such criticism might take' (1978, p. 144n). Also see Nola (1987).
16. Popper's best statements of this view are (1976a) and (1985). For summaries by other authors see Hands (1985b, 1989a), Koertge (1974, 1975), or Watkins (1970).
17. I may have been partially responsible for some of these debates myself (Hands, 1985a).
18. See Popper (1965, ch. 3) and (1983, pp. 112–31) for instance.
19. See Mäki (1986) and (1989).

REFERENCES

Agassi, J. (1988), *The Gentle Art of Philosophical Polemics* (LaSalle, IL: Open Court).

Carrier, M. (1988), 'On Novel Facts: A Discussion of Criteria for Non-adhocness in the Methodology of Scientific Research Programmes', *Zeitschrift für allgemeine Wissenschaftstheorie*, **19**, pp. 205–31.

Gardner, M.R. (1982), 'Predicting Novel Facts', *British Journal for the Philosophy of Science*, **33**, pp. 1–15.

Hacking, I. (1979), 'Imre Lakatos's Philosophy of Science', *British Journal for the Philosophy of Science*, **30**, pp. 381–410.

Hands, D.W. (1985a), 'Second Thoughts on Lakatos', *History of Political Economy*, **17**, pp. 1–16.

—— (1958b), 'Karl Popper and Economic Methodology', *Economics and Philosophy*, **1**, pp. 83–99.

—— (1988), 'Ad Hocness in Economics and the Popperian Tradition', in N. de Marchi (ed.), *The Popperian Legacy in Economics*, pp. 121–37 (Cambridge: Cambridge University Press).
—— (1989), 'Falsification, Situational Analysis and Scientific Research Programs: The Popperian Tradition in Economic Methodology', in N. de Marchi (ed.), *Methodological Reflection in Economics* (forthcoming).
—— (1990), 'Second Thoughts on "Second Thoughts": Reconsidering the Lakatosian Progress of *The General Theory*', *Review of Political Economy*, **2** (1), 69–81.
Koertge, N. (1974), 'On Popper's Philosophy of Social Science', in K.F. Schaffner and R.S. Cohen (eds), *PSA 1972*, pp. 195–207 (Dordrecht: D. Reidel).
—— (1975), 'Popper's Metaphysical Research Program for the Human Sciences', *Inquiry*, **19**, pp. 437–62.
—— (1979), 'The Problem of Appraising Scientific Theories', in P.D. Asquith and H.E. Kyburg, Jr (eds), *Current Research in Philosophy of Science*, pp. 228–51 (East Lansing, MI: Philosophy of Science Association).
Lakatos, I. (1970), 'Falsification and the Methodology of Scientific Research Programmes', in I. Lakatos and A. Musgrave (eds), *Criticism and the Growth of Knowledge*, pp. 91–196 (Cambridge: Cambridge University Press).
—— (1978), 'Popper on Demarcation and Induction', in J. Worrall and G. Currie (eds), *The Methodology of Scientific Research Programmes: Philosophical Papers, Vol. I*, pp. 139–67 (Cambridge: Cambridge University Press).
Mäki, U. (1986), 'Scientific Realism and Austrian Explanation', unpublished.
—— (1989), 'Mengerian Economics in Realist Perspective', paper presented at a conference on 'Carl Menger and His Legacy in Economics', Duke University, April 1989.
Miller, D.W. (1974), 'Popper's Qualitative Theory of Verisimilitude', *British Journal for the Philosophy of Science*, **25**, pp. 166–77.
Musgrave, A. (1974), 'Logical Versus Historical Theories of Confirmation', *British Journal for the Philosophy of Science*, **25**, pp. 1–23.
Nola, R. (1987), 'The Status of Popper's Theory of Scientific Method', *British Journal for the Philosophy of Science*, **38**, pp. 441–80.
Oddie, G. (1986), 'The Poverty of the Popperian Program for Truthlikeness', *Philosophy of Science*, **53**, pp. 163–78.
Popper, K.R. (1965), *Conjectures and Refutations* (New York: Harper & Row).
—— (1968), *The Logic of Scientific Discovery* (New York: Harper & Row).
—— (1973), *Objective Knowledge* (Oxford: Clarendon Press).
—— (1976a), 'The Logic of the Social Sciences', in T.W. Adorno *et al.* (eds), *The Positivist Dispute in German Sociology*, pp. 87–122 (New York: Harper & Row).
—— (1976b), *Unended Quest: An Intellectual Autobiography* (LaSalle, IL: Open Court).
—— (1983), *Realism and the Aim of Science* (Totowa, NJ: Rowman and Littlefield).
—— (1985), 'The Rationality Principle', in D. Miller (ed.), *Popper Selections*, pp. 357–65 (Princeton: Princeton University Press).
Rosenberg, A. (1981), *Sociobiology and the Preemption of Social Science* (Baltimore, MD: Johns Hopkins University Press).

—— (1988), *Philosophy of Social Science* (Boulder, CO: Westview Press).
Tichy, P. (1974), 'On Popper's Definitions of Verisimilitude', *British Journal of the Philosophy of Science*, **25**, pp. 155–60.
Watkins, J. (1970), 'Imperfect Rationality', in R. Borger and F. Cioffi (eds), *Explanation in the Behavioural Sciences*, pp. 91–121 (Cambridge: Cambridge University Press).
—— (1984), *Science and Scepticism* (Princeton, NJ: Princeton University Press).
Worrall, J. (1978), 'The Ways in Which the Methodology of Scientific Research Programmes Improves on Popper's Methodology', in G. Radnitzky and G. Anderson (eds), *Progress and Rationality in Science*, pp. 45–70 (Dordrecht: D. Reidel).
Zahar, E. (1983), 'The Popper–Lakatos Controversy in the Light of "Die Beiden Grundprobleme der Erkenntnistheorie" ', *British Journal for the Philosophy of Science*, **34**, pp. 149–71.

COMMENT ON HANDS

Bert Hamminga

Wade Hands is discouraged in the hunt for novel facts when studying economic research programs. By way of consolation, he argues that 'novelty' is, after all, not so fundamental in the history of Popper–Lakatos methodology. But when he comes to listing the useful part of the Lakatosian notions, he not only omits 'novel facts', he also omits 'content', 'excess content' and 'corroborated excess content'. So Wade Hands' discouragement goes beyond the realm of 'novelty'.

I have no difficulty in understanding this. But I wish to make some attempt to apply the 'content'-related Lakatosian concepts to economic research programs. Let me try to do so in a more precise way than has, I suspect, hitherto been done.

1 The Meaning of Excess Content

Figure 1 shows what a theory does to events. Some events are forbidden; they are inside the circle. Some are allowed, they are outside the circle. The allowed events, if we are to believe Popper and Lakatos, are uninteresting, the forbidden events are the only ones that are interesting, because, if a forbidden event occurs, your theory is falsified. The empirical content is associated with the set of forbidden events.[1]

Figure 1 Theories and events

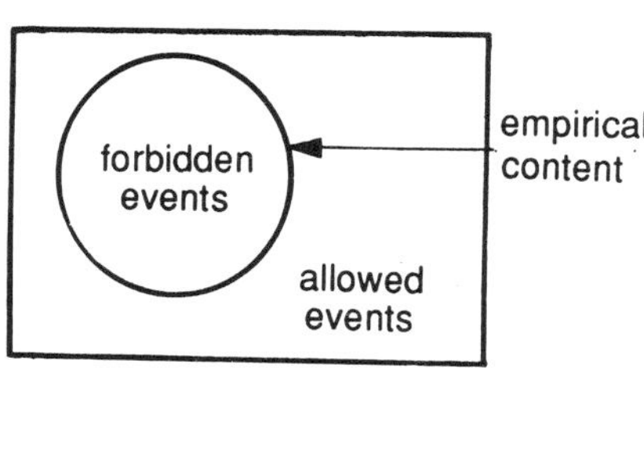

The path of degeneration is depicted by the path in Figure 2. If, after observing a falsifying event of T_1 you make a shift towards a T_2 that simply narrows down content so as to allow for the event that falsifies the old theory T_1, your research program will degenerate. This path yields ever smaller circles and ends with empty content, with not forbidding any event, with not saying anything.

Figure 2 Progress and degeneration

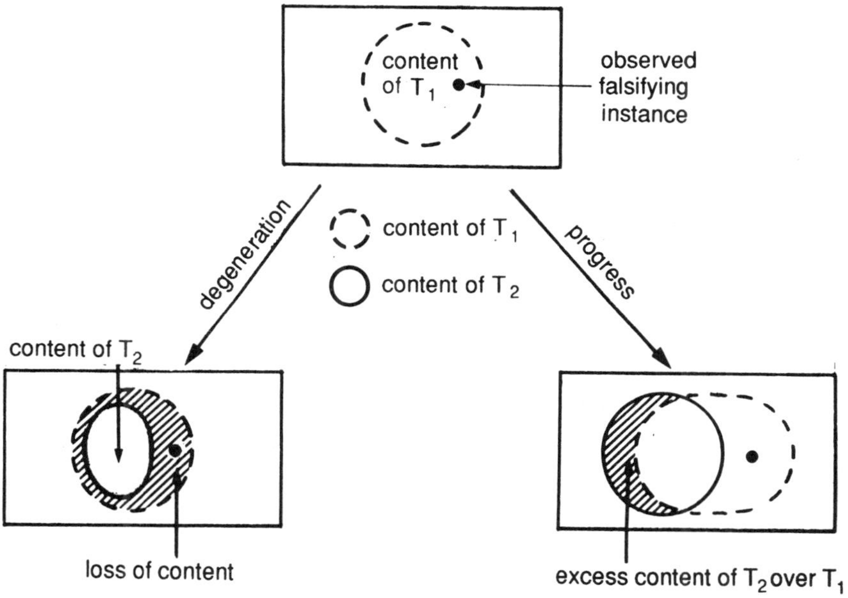

Now, whatever T_2 you choose to shift towards, some loss of content is unavoidable: the new T_2 has to allow for the observed event that falsified T_1. But a problem shift to some T_2 is 'progressive' only if, by the same stroke, T_2 forbids some events that were allowed by the old theory T_1. These events are called the *excess content* of T_2 over T_1 (shaded in the box at lower right in Figure 2).

This excess content is *corroborated* if, despite severe attempts, we fail to observe some of the events it contains (forbids). And 'corroborated excess content' means the same as 'a (discovered) *novel fact*'. According to Lakatos (please note!) the discovery of a *novel fact* is not, as in ordinary English, the novel observation of an event, but the *failure, despite severe attempts, to observe a newly forbidden event.*[2]

These are the meanings of 'content', 'excess content' (or, what is the same, 'predicted novel fact') and 'corroborated excess content' (or, what is the same, 'the discovery of a novel fact'). Let us turn to their measurement.

2 The Measurement of Excess Content

Let T_1 be the theory that Samuelson presents as an 'Illustrative tax problem' on p. 14, *Foundations of Economic Analysis* (Samuelson, 1947). T_1 consists of (1) and (2):

$$\pi := xp(x) - C(x) - tx \tag{1}$$

where π is profit, $xp(x)$ is called 'total revenue in function of output', $C(x)$ is total production cost and t is a tax rate on output.

$$\frac{\partial \pi\ (x,t)}{\partial x} = 0\ , \ \frac{\partial^2 \pi(x,t)}{\partial x^2} < 0 \tag{2}$$

Samuelson proves the following theorem:

$$T_1 \rightarrow \left(\frac{\partial x^{\text{o}}}{\partial t}\right) < 0 \tag{3}$$

Which events are forbidden by T_1, and which ones allowed? Before answering that question we have to determine the set of events *relevant* to the theory.[3] Profit is a function of x and t *only* (prices and costs are functions of x), so we have only two variables t and x, which can go up (+), remain unchanged (0), and go down (−). The list of logically possible, relevant events evidently reads as in Table 1.

The theory implies a downward effect of taxes on equilibrium output. Since there are no other variables, if taxes go up (events 1, 2, 3), equilibrium output should go down (event 3). Event 3 is allowed, events 1 and 2 are forbidden. They are in the 'content' of T_1, Lakatos and Popper would say. Similarly 4 and 6 are in the content, because t is, according to T_1, the *only* variable affecting equilibrium output. If t remains unchanged, x^{o} should remain unchanged (event 5 is allowed) and any change of x^{o} in this case (events 4 and 6) is forbidden.[4] Events 7, 8 and 9 now speak for themselves. The content of T_1, what is in the circle of Figure 1, so to speak, is the set of events 1, 2, 4, 6, 8, 9.

Kinship exists between these Popper–Lakatos ideas and Samuelson's concept of an 'operationally meaningful theorem'. Samuelson calls theorems like the right-hand side of (3) operationally meaningful

Table 1 T_1 *and 'events'*

	Set of events		*Content of* T_1	
	tax t	*equilibrium output* x^o		
1	+	+		forbidden
2	+	0		forbidden
3	+	−	allowed	
4	0	+		forbidden!
5	0	0	allowed	
6	0	−		forbidden
7	−	+	allowed	
8	−	0		forbidden
9	−	−		forbidden

because they 'could conceivably be refuted, if only under ideal conditions' (Samuelson, 1947, p. 4). That is what Popper and Lakatos mean by 'having non-empty empirical content'.

Now let us study, by way of exercise, a hypothetical falsification and subsequent shift to a new theory T_2. Suppose we observe event 4 (this is symbolized by the exclamation mark). Now, T_1 is falsified. Any new T_2 that does nothing but omit event 4 from the content would lead us into degeneration. T_2 should at least 'newly' forbid some event allowed by the old T_1! So a theory T_2, say, giving in by allowing event 4 and at the same stroke forbidding, say, event 3, that was allowed by T_1, would mean 'progress', Popper and Lakatos would say. But there is another way that is more typical and illustrative, and that is to introduce a theory T_2 that contains an additional variable that is used to *explain* why we have observed this falsifying event.

Let us consider a shift towards some theory T_2 that stops treating price as a function $p(x)$ of output, and turns p into an exogenously given variable. The additional variable p can of course go up, down and remain unchanged, and this triples our list of relevant events (Table 2).

To event 1 of Table 1 (t and x both rising) there correspond events 1, 2 and 3 of Table 2 (p going up, remaining unchanged, or going down) etc. We now have tripled the size of the boxes of Figures 1 and 2, so to speak. This does not affect the content of T_1, of course. To every one forbidden row in Table 1, there now correspond three forbidden rows in Table 2. But where do we place our exclamation mark, symbolizing

Table 2 An example of 'progress' from T_1 to T_2

		t	x^o	p	content T_1	content T_2	
	1	+	+	+	*f*		loss
1	2	+	+	0	*f*	*f*	
	3	+	+	–	*f*	*f*	
	4	+	0	+	*f*		loss
2	5	+	0	0	*f*	*f*	
	6	+	0	–	*f*	*f*	
	7	+	–	+			
3	8	+	–	0			
	9	+	–	–			
	10	0	+	+	*f*!		loss
4	11	0	+	0	*f*	*f*	
	12	0	+	–	*f*	*f*	
	13	0	0	+		*f*	gain (excess content)
5	14	0	0	0			
	15	0	0	–		*f*	gain (excess content)
	16	0	–	+	*f*	*f*	
6	17	0	–	0	*f*	*f*	
	18	0	–	–	*f*		loss
	19	–	+	+			
7	20	–	+	0			
	21	–	+	–			
	22	–	0	+	*f*	*f*	
8	23	–	0	0	*f*	*f*	
	24	–	0	–	*f*		loss
	25	–	–	+	*f*	*f*	
9	26	–	–	0	*f*	*f*	
	27	–	–	–	*f*		loss

the falsifying event? Our old falsifying event 4 in Table 1 corresponds to events 10, 11 and 12 in Table 2. Now we have to go back to our falsifying event to see what happened to prices! Suppose it is observed that they went up. So our exclamation mark should be on row 10. T_2 may still forbid events 11 and 12; they were not yet observed. But it should allow for event 10.

Now suppose we have a theory T_2 maximizing $\pi(x, t, p)$ and suppose two 'operationally meaningful' theorems can be derived:

$$T_2 \rightarrow \left(\frac{\partial x^o}{\partial t}\right) < 0 \text{ and} \left(\frac{\partial x^o}{\partial p}\right) > 0$$

That is, taxes keep having a downward effect on equilibrium output, and prices now have an upward effect. Event 1 of Table 2 is allowed by T_2, because tax and price changes work in opposite directions and T_2 does not say which effect will dominate. But events 2 and 3 of Table 2 are forbidden by T_2 as they were by T_1. Likewise we lose content by newly allowing events 4, 10, 18, 24 and 27. But we gain content too! Events 13, 14 and 15, all allowed by T_1 because they correspond to event 5 of Table 1, are not *all* allowed by T_2. With price + and tax change 0, equilibrium output should go up (event 10) and therefore event 13 is forbidden by T_2. Similarly event 15 is forbidden by T_2. These two events, 13 and 15, form the *excess content of T_2 over T_1*, symbolized by the shaded area in the box at bottom right in Figure 2.

Given a falsification of T_1 by an event of type 4, from the perspective of Table 1, that turned out to be event 10 from the new perspective of Table 2, T_2 does all that Lakatos requires of a theoretically progressive problem shift: it removes event 10 from the content, at the same stroke adding events 13 and 15.[5] The problem shift is also empirically progressive if this excess content is also 'corroborated'; that is, if, despite severe attempts, we fail to observe the events 13 and 15. 'Severe attempts' means, here, collecting observational reports on events with rising prices and no tax change (events 10, 13, 16), and *never* finding an event 13 (always finding 10, since 16 is also forbidden). *Corroboration of the excess content of T_2 over T_1 means failure to observe event 13* and, similarly, failure to observe event 15.[6]

3 Conclusion

These exercises in economic Lakatosianism should suffice to make clear what blueprint of economics it implies. *Does* economics conform the blueprint? *Should* it do so? I do not know whether it *should*, so I am happy not to be in power. But, contrary to Wade Hands, I find these purely empirical questions interesting and not entirely useless: *do successive comparative static theories in economic research programs have 'excess content', in the specific logical meaning given to this notion by Popper and Lakatos? Is some of this excess content 'corroborated'?*

Note that *any two* comparative static theories can be compared in the above manner, *no matter what variables they contain!* Simply lump all variables together to construct your table of relevant events. Note that this procedure obeys nice mathematical laws, from the realm of combinatorial theory.

My present bet for the answer is that each shift (say in the history of demand theory or in the history of the theory of international trade, job search theory and so on) involves heavy losses in 'content', very small gains, some falsification and no 'corroboration'.[7] This does not mean raising your eyebrows about economics.[8] But any outcome whatever would mean some growth of knowledge about it. And it would throw some novel light upon Lakatos. Why not do some calculation!

Notes

1. Logical note: if you scrutinize the Popper–Lakatos texts on 'content', the definitions chosen turn out to be remarkably consistent and constant over time: theories *T* are universal statements. The 'Logical content of T' (*LC(T)*) is the consequence class of *T*, that is the set of universal statements *u* described by: $LC(T) := \{u | T \rightarrow u\}$, where '$\rightarrow$' means 'logically implies'. *LC(T)* is the set symbolized by what is in the circle in the left-hand box below.

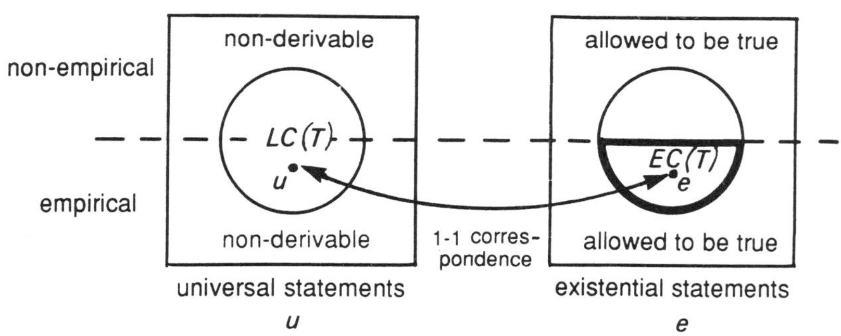

Out of the set of universal statements *u*, you can make the isomorphic set of existential statements *e* by taking, for every universal statement *u* in the left-hand box, a statement $e = \not- u$ ('$\not-$' means 'not'). The statement in the set $\{e | e = \not- u \text{ and } u \in LC(T)\}$ are those inconsistent with *T*. They are in the mirror-image circle of the right-hand box. But only part of these existential statements can be verified by observable events. This part is the 'empirical content of T' (*EC(T)*). *EC(T)* is defined as a set of existential statements *e*: $EC(T) := \{e | e \rightarrow \not- T \text{ and } 0(e)\}$, where the predicate '0' says that *e* is verifiable by observable events (though, if you believe *T*, you hope such events turn out never to occur, despite severe attempts to observe them; in other words, you hope that your *T* is, or will be, corroborated).

In the main text I only use the lower half (the empirical part) of the right-hand box, because that is where it all happens: the non-empirical upper half is methodologically irrelevant according to Popper and Lakatos, and the left-hand box is the exact mirror-image of the right-hand box, and hence superfluous. For this summary I used Popper (1934) (1963) (1972) and Lakatos (1970). The references are so numerous that I simply refer to the indexes of the books and I add that all passages use the concepts with complete consistency. My set-theoretical illustrations here are inspired by structuralism, especially Theo Kuipers's approach to verisimilitude (Kuipers, 1982, 1987).

2. Here is my evidence for this claim: for *corroboration* of T as the failure, despite severe attempts, to observe events forbidden by T, see Popper (1934), section 82 and *passim* in Popper (1934) (1963) (1972), as well as Lakatos (1970). Lakatos equates 'having excess empirical content' with the 'prediction of a novel fact' as follows: 'Let us say that . . . a series of theories is theoretically progressive (or "constitutes a theoretically progressive problemshift") if each new theory has some excess empirical content over its predecessor, that is [*sic!*], if it predicts some novel, hitherto unexpected fact' (Lakatos, 1970, p. 118). And Lakatos equates 'corroborated excess content' with 'the actual discovery of some new fact' as follows: 'Let us say that a theoretically progressive series of theories is also empirically progressive (or "constitutes an empirically progressive problemshift") if some of this excess content is also corroborated, that is [*sic!*], if each new theory leads us to the actual discovery of some new fact' (Lakatos, 1970, p. 118). These quotations are only examples. As long as we stick to the logic of the Popper–Lakatos definitions, the definition of novel fact as 'failure to observe' is crystal clear. Lakatos supplies an example of novel facts in research programs: Einstein's theory newly forbidding 'transmission of light along straight lines near large masses', and eclipse experiments actually failing to observe such linear transmission, thereby 'corroborating' Einstein's theory (Lakatos, 1970, p. 124). A large part of the 'economic applications' of Lakatos seems to have overlooked Lakatos's non-common use of 'novel fact'. This may partly have been caused by some ambiguities in Lakatos (especially 1971), where he sets out to show that his Methodology of Scientific Research Programs is itself 'progressive' in relation to older Popperian methodologies. He does so by pointing out that MSRP *allows* more types of behaviour by scientists, which, under his logical definitions, would count, not as a gain, but as *loss* of content. (See also M. Pera, 'Methodological Sophisticationism: A Degenerating Project', in Gavroglu, K. *et al.*, 1989.)
3. Structuralists call this the set of *partial potential models* (M_{pp}).
4. Some might object here that 4 and 6 may be allowed in case of violation of a *ceteris paribus* clause implicit in the theory. It is suggested that they read '*ceteris paribus* forbidden' instead of 'forbidden', and should of course do so too for events 1, 2, 8 and 9, because, if we assume that Samuelson's T_1 contains an implicit *ceteris paribus* clause *which is not claimed to hold*, we have no content whatsoever and every event is allowed.
5. Note that, if T_2, instead of T_1, was the *old* theory and if, say, event 13 had been observed, then T_1 would constitute a theoretically progressive problem shift over T_2 (T_1 has even more excess content over T_2, if we simply count events, than T_2 has over T_1)! This shows how essential 'history', that is, the observations made on specific points in time, are to MSRP.
6. If you wish to do an exercise in order to check whether you have mastered this subject, I calculated for Samuelson's famous analysis of the Keynesian system Case I (Samuelson, 1947, pp. 278–80) a set of 729 events, 454 of which are, after imposing all restrictions, in the content of the theory.
7. My bet is independent of what I wrote (1984), esp. pp. 303–14, where I dealt with some mathematical and formal econometric objections to considering 'content' as a concept relevant to economic research programs. And it is also independent of my observations (1983) on 'weakening-of-conditions related' strategies of theorizing (see, for Lakatos, esp. pp. 119–23).
8. My position here is that raising eyebrows is *never* the methodologist's job (see my (1983), pp. 1–2, 134–7 and my (1990)). Economists do it all the time, legitimately so, and methodologists should study when and why economists do it.

References

Gavroglu, K. *et al.* (1989), *Imre Lakatos and Theories of Scientific Change* (Dordrecht: Kluwer).

Hamminga, B. (1983), *Neoclassical Theory Structure and Theory Development* (New York: Springer).

—— (1984), 'Possible approaches to reduction in economic theory', in W. Balzer *et al.* (eds), *Reduction in Science*, pp. 295–317 (Dordrecht: Reidel).

—— (1990), 'Learning economic method from the invention of vintage models', in N.B. de Marchi (ed.), *Methodological Reflection in Economics* (forthcoming).

Kuipers, Th.A.F. (1982), 'Approaching Descriptive and Theoretical Truth', *Erkenntnis*, **18**, pp. 343–78.

—— (1987), 'A Structuralist Approach to Truthlikeness', in Th.A.F. Kuipers (ed.), *What is Closer to the Truth?* (Amsterdam: Rodopi).

Lakatos, I. (1970), 'Falsification and the Methodology of Scientific Research Programmes', in I. Lakatos and A. Musgrave (eds), *Criticism and the Growth of Knowledge*, pp. 91–196 (Cambridge: Cambridge University Press).

—— (1971), 'History of Science and its Rational Reconstructions', in R.C. Buck and K.S. Cohen (eds), *Boston Studies in the Philosophy of Science*, vol. 8, pp. 91–136 (Dordrecht: Reidel).

Popper, K.R. (1934), *The Logic of Scientific Discovery* (London: Hutchinson) 1959.

—— (1963), *Conjectures and Refutations* (New York: Harper Torchbooks).

—— (1972), *Objective Knowledge* (Oxford: Oxford University Press).

Samuelson, P.A. (1947), *Foundations of Economic Analysis* (Cambridge, Mass: Harvard University Press).

COMMENT ON HANDS

Uskali Mäki*

There should be no doubt that, as Wade Hands points out, the Popperian dominance in the methodology of economics in recent years has had some undesirable effects (Hands, this volume; see also Mäki, 1990a). To these belong two omissions among the objects of methodological studies, namely prevailing instrumentalist and essentialist beliefs and practices within the economics profession, both denounced by Popperian canons. As Hands further argues, the Popperian project as a realist project has encountered difficulties because of Popper's failure to provide an adequate explication of the intuitive notion of closeness to the truth (truthlikeness, verisimilitude). Two ways out of this latter impasse can be chosen. One is to proceed with the Popperian project without the idea of increasing verisimilitude as the aim of science. This is the option chosen by Watkins (1984). The other is to rebuild a realist notion of truthlikeness without the burden of Popperian methodology. Such non-Popperian explications have been provided by Niiniluoto (1987) and Oddie (1986). In the brief remarks which follow I attempt to outline an idea of how an economist with essentialist intuitions might view scientific progress as increasing truthlikeness.

Popper's *Die Logik der Forschung* (1934) was metaphysically neutral or indifferent. He admitted that he had *realist inclinations*, but this was not incorporated into his methodological system. It would seem that Popper's early followers in economics, such as the M^2T group at the London School of Economics in the late 1950s and early 1960s (see de Marchi, 1988), are true to Popper in this respect, too. The revolution they proposed was essentially a methodological revolution. After all, realism would not have been a revolutionary idea at that time at the LSE: Lionel Robbins, emperor of the former reign, was no doubt a firm realist.

Popper introduced the notion of verisimilitude in 1960, but it was never adopted by Popperian methodologists of economics. Some of them, such as Mark Blaug, declare themselves to be advocates of realism, but they have not backed up this position with the Popperian notion of verisimilitude, or with any other well-developed doctrine of truth and truthlikeness. This implies that the reasons for the downfall of Popperianism in economic methodology have nothing to do with the failure of Popper's explication of the concept of truthlikeness.

* I wish to thank Ilkka Niiniluoto for helpful comments on an earlier draft.

It is true that there is, after all, an instrumentalist flavour involved in Popperian scepticism. This may also explain the fact that, even though many economists have declared themselves advocates of Popperian methodology, they nevertheless simultaneously feel comfortable with instrumentalist beliefs and practices, with no appreciable interest in matters of truth. It is the Popperian dictum of *testing theories by their empirical implications* that seems to have played the main role in the reception of Popperian ideas by economists. And, after all, was not this dictum precisely the one that was presented as the fundamental message of the Friedman–Machlup position in the methodological discussions by economists in the 1950s and 1960s? Needless to say, the dictum itself does not imply instrumentalism. The important thing is that the notion of truth does not have any operational significance in Popperian methodology; this may also be the case in much of economics.

Popper (1963, pp. 103–5) defines *essentialism* as a doctrine which subscribes to the following three tenets:

1. Scientific theories 'describe the "essence" or "essential natures" of things' lying behind the appearances. Let us call this the semantico-ontological component of essentialism.
2. By so doing, theories provide ultimate explanations in the sense that such theories are 'neither in need nor susceptible of further explanation'. Let us call this the ultimate explanation component.
3. The truth of such theories can be finally established 'beyond any reasonable doubt'. Let us call this the certitude component.

There should be no doubt, in my view, that many economists think of the task of theory formation in terms of something like the semantico-ontological component of essentialism. They do, indeed, think that good – or the best, or the desirable – economic theories provide true descriptions of what is essential in the economy, to the exclusion of the inessentials or the appearances. The other two, both epistemological, components seem to be much less popular among economists.

It follows that very few economists subscribe to the radical essentialism defined in terms of all three, both semantic and epistemological, components. Ludwig von Mises is a famous advocate of such a radical view. Many others, even Milton Friedman in a few passages of his 1953 essay, can be interpreted as espousing a weak version of essentialism consisting of the semantic component (see Mäki, 1990b). This means that, if we follow Popper by defining 'essentialism' in his narrow way, we manage to exclude weaker and probably rather popular forms of economic essentialism from serious consideration within the Popperian framework.

To this we immediately have to add that elsewhere Popper himself subscribes to something that at least comes close to the semantico-ontological component of essentialism. In his *Realism and the Aim of Science* (1983, p. 137), he writes as follows:

> . . . although I do not think that we can ever describe, by our universal laws, an *ultimate* essence of the world, I do not doubt that we may seek to probe deeper and deeper into the structure of our world or, as we might say, into properties of the world that are more and more essential, or of greater and greater depth.

Popper even calls this view 'modified essentialism'. Again, the problem with this is that the idea of science penetrating into deeper and deeper layers of the world has no adequate connection to Popper's methodological framework.

I shall now make a few speculative remarks on how weak or modified essentialism could be connected to the notion of progress, and whether and how it is being implicitly so connected in the research practices of the economics profession. I suggest, in rather intuitive terms, that the following forms of theoretical progress may occur in science:

1. Progress occurs when a theory is formed that gives a truthlike description of the essence or an essential layer of the object under study.
2. Progress occurs when a theory is formed that gives a more truthlike description than its predecessor of the essence or one of the essential layers of the object under study.
3. Progress occurs when a theory is formed that provides a truthlike description of a deeper essential layer of the object than its predecessor.
4. Progress occurs when a theory that gives a truthlike description of the essence of an object is expanded so as to give a truthlike account of the way(s) its essence or essential layer manifests itself.
5. Progress occurs when a theory that gives a truthlike description of the essence of an object is expanded so as to give a more truthlike account of the way(s) its essence or essential layer manifests itself.

It is difficult not to conflate these five forms of progress in Popper's framework, or rather the framework does not provide adequate tools for analysing the five forms. By using a bit of imagination, we can give them Lakatosian reformulations. The first step is to suggest that there are metaphysical or ontic correlates for the elements in the theories of Lakatosian research programs. Let us call the correlate of the theoretical hard core the 'ontic core' and the correlate of the protective belt the 'ontic periphery'. On this reformulation, the hard core of a research program is a condensed statement of the allegedly essential features of the subject-matter (the ontic core), while the protective belt describes some of the relatively less essential features (in the ontic periphery), which none the less have an impact on the manifest behaviour of the objects under study. The conjunction of the hard core and the protective belt implies statements about the appearances or manifestations of the objects of the theory.

Progress in senses (1)–(3) then consists of either formulating a successful hard core or improving it or replacing it with a better one. Progress in senses (4)–(5) takes place on the belt of auxiliary statements that describe the ways in which the essential features combine with other features so as to constitute the appearances of the object under study. A major part of progress in science is of kind (5). This is the case with 'mature' science in particular (see Nowak, 1980; Krajewski, 1977). For instance, it seems obvious that progress in senses (1) and (3) has been absent in mainstream economics for a long time. An essentialist interpretation of the situation might refer to neoclassicism as a mature science that has discovered and theoretically described the ontic core of the economy and now takes as its major task the refinement and application of the theory without questioning the statements of the hard core.

One difficulty with the Popperian notion of verisimilitude is that it is not adequate for discussing all of these five forms of scientific progress. The problem is that this notion is an attempt to explicate the idea that science approaches or should approach the true description of the whole of the actual universe. However such comprehensiveness is not required for progress to occur in senses (1)–(3) in particular. When trying to describe ontic cores or essences or essential layers, one deliberately omits most facts about the actual world. Such a description is an attempted theoretical isolation of the ontic core from peripheral factors. To speak about the truthlikeness of such descriptions, the Popperian concept will not do. As Popper (1963, p. 234) says, '[v]erisimilitude is so defined that maximum verisimilitude would be achieved only by a theory which is not only true, but completely comprehensively true: if it corresponds to all facts . . .'. This is, of course, a consequence of linking the notions of verisimilitude and 'content' together so as to vindicate his falsificationist methodology: a 'completely comprehensively true' theory is also maximal in regard to logical strength.

L. Jonathan Cohen (1980) makes a distinction between verisimilitude and what he calls 'legisimilitude'. He is critical of definitions of verisimilitude in terms of truth and falsity in regard to the actual world. Science, he argues, pursues truths about laws, understood as physically necessary truths. Such necessities are defined in terms of possible worlds. As Cohen (p. 500) points out, Popper (1959, pp. 432f) elsewhere accepts this notion of natural necessity, but 'he omits to consider its implications for the doctrine of verisimilitude'. Cohen suggests that, instead of verisimilitude, or truthlikeness, science is after legisimilitude, or lawlikeness.

Close to, but not identical with, Cohen's proposal is the distinction between 'descriptive truth' and 'theoretical truth', suggested by Theo Kuipers (1982). A statement is descriptively true if it is true in the actual world; a statement is theoretically true if it is true in all physically possible worlds (p. 347). Descriptive verisimilitude is then defined as closeness or likeness to descriptive truth and theoretical verisimilitude as closeness to theoretical truth (pp. 352–7). Kuipers criticizes other writers on the topic for conflating the two kinds of truth and verisimilitude and for ignoring the fact that theoretical scientists aim at theoretical truth.

What unites Kuipers's suggestion with that of Cohen is the idea of scientific theory having natural necessities as its object. It is not altogether inconceivable to pursue truth about natural necessities in economics, as the popular use of counter-factual reasoning and the theoretical endeavours of Austrian and Marxian traditions indicate. However the idea may be unnecessarily restrictive for our purposes. Necessity is, of course, one possible attribute of essence. Some economists, however, may use essentialist terminology: 'this is the essence of the matter', 'these seem to be the essential features of the situation' and so on, without committing themselves to the notion of natural necessity. Therefore perhaps we would need a more general notion for expressing the intuitive idea of likeness to the essential truth about the economy – that is, likeness or closeness to the truth about essences or ontic cores in the economy. Labouring over an analysis of this intuitive notion is a task for another occasion, but let us suggest a name here: perhaps it could be called 'essesimilitude'. Forms (1)–(3) of scientific progress would then imply increasing essesimilitude.

No analysis of essesimilitude is currently available. It is obvious that such an analysis cannot be provided in the Popperian framework. More powerful and flexible frameworks, such as Niiniluoto's (1987), are needed.

We have found that Popper's philosophy of science contains both what he calls 'modified essentialism' and the notion of natural necessity, but that these have not been adequately incorporated into his idea of verisimilitude. The methodology of economics might find some use for a notion of truthlikeness with these essentialist ingredients.

References

Cohen, L. Jonathan (1980), 'What has science to do with truth?', *Synthese*, **45**, 489–510.

Hands, D. Wade (1991), 'The Problem of Excess Content: Economics, Novelty and a long Popperian Tale', this volume.

Krajewski, W. (1977), *Growth of Knowledge and the Correspondence Principle* (Dordrecht: Reidel).

Kuipers, Theo (1982), 'Approaching descriptive and theoretical truth', *Erkenntnis*, **18**, 343–78.

Mäki, Uskali (1990a), 'Methodology of economics: Complaints and guidelines', *Finnish Economic Papers*, **3**, pp. 77–84.

—— (1990b), 'Friedman and realism', *Research in the History of Economic Thought and Methodology*, **10**.

de Marchi, Neil (1988), 'Popper and the LSE economists', in N. de Marchi (ed.), *The Popperian Legacy in Economics* (Cambridge: Cambridge University Press).

Niiniluoto, Ilkka (1987), *Truthlikeness* (Dordrecht: Reidel).

Nowak, Leszek (1980), *The Structure of Idealization* (Dordrecht: Reidel).

Oddie, Graham (1986), *Likeness to Truth* (Dordrecht: Reidel).

Popper, Karl (1959), *The Logic of Scientific Discovery* (London: Hutchinson).

—— (1963), *Conjectures and Refutations* (London: Routledge & Kegan Paul).

—— (1983), *Realism and the Aim of Science* (London: Hutchinson).

Watkins, John (1984), *Science and Scepticism* (Princeton: Princeton University Press).

REPLY TO HAMMINGA AND MÄKI

D. Wade Hands

1 Introduction

Responding to the comments of Mäki and Hamminga places me in a rather unusual position. On the face of it my chapter is quite critical of Popperian philosophy; I trace the development of the concepts of excess content, novelty and verisimilitude and demonstrate how these concepts have contributed to certain problems in economic methodology. Despite this critical stance, here and in other recent work, my philosophical preferences remain basically within the Popperian (or maybe neo-Popperian) tradition. My two commentators, on the other hand, are in general much less sympathetic to the Popperian program. Mäki basically agrees with my evaluation of the difficulties of Popperian economic methodology, but argues for an essentialist solution. Hamminga, contrary to my view, argues that the Popperian concept of excess content *is* a useful tool for understanding theory choice in economics, but his defence of excess content is based on a very narrow definition of the concept of a novel fact. Such a narrow interpretation of the Popperian terminology is frequently the analytical philosopher's response to Popper.

Thus Mäki and Hamminga leave me in the paradoxical position of responding to the comments on my anti-Popperian chapter by defending the Popperian tradition. With respect to Mäki, my argument will be that, despite the problems discussed in my chapter, Mäki's essentialism does not really offer a more viable solution to the current problems in economic methodology than simply continuing to go forward with the (evolving) Popperian tools. With respect to Hamminga, I appreciate his economic application, but his characterization of novelty does such an injustice to the history of this important concept that I feel compelled to provide a detailed (Popperian) defence. I will respond to Mäki first, since my comments are relatively brief. My response to Hamminga, though it focuses on only a small section of his comment, is more lengthy.

2 Response to Mäki

Mäki agrees that Popper's falsificationist methodology does not 'connect up' in any systematic way with his scientific realism and that Popper's theory of verisimilitude was an (unsuccessful) attempt to provide such a 'connection'. Mäki correctly notes that Watkins's (1984) replacement of verisimilitude by a set of adequacy requirements is one attempt to provide a Popperian solution to this problem – I would also add the 'structural realism' recently proposed by Worrall (1989), and Bartley's (1984, 1987) 'comprehensively critical rationalism'[1] to this list of purported Popperian solutions. Although Mäki mentions Watkins, his concern is not really with Popperian solutions; his solution is essentialism. Mäki does argue that Popper himself advocated a weak version of essentialism in his 'modified essentialism',[2] but this, like Popper's advocacy of scientific realism, has no systematic connection with his falsificationist methodology.

Mäki's solution seems to be a Lakatosian version of essentialism. The hard core of the scientific research program 'is a condensed statement of the allegedly essential features of the subject-matter (the ontic core), while the protective belt describes some of the relatively less essential features (in the ontic periphery), which none the less have an impact on the manifest behaviour of the objects under study' (p. 88). Unlike traditional essentialism, where essential natures are posited, Mäki's own modified essentialism only seeks 'essesimilitude' – likeness to the essential truth about the economy (p. 89) rather than necessity. Progress occurs by increasing essesimilitude and these increases can come about in a number of different ways during the development of the research program.

I have at least two difficulties with Mäki's suggested solution, but my difficulties are general problems I have with essentialism and essentialism in economics, rather than problems with Mäki's own Lakatosian version or his concept of essesimilitude. Mäki's own thesis is simply too briefly presented (as is appropriate in this context) to be evaluated at this time; I will simply withhold judgement until these ideas have been developed in more detail.

My first problem with essentialism as a solution to any problem in economic methodology (or the methodology of any other science) is that essentialism is methodologically mute. Essentialism is an ontological position; it implies no particular theory about how one comes to know these posited essential natures. In fact most defences of essentialism work in the opposite direction of most methodological discussions; they argue for an ontology of essential natures by showing that any ontology devoid of such essential natures would be in conflict with the inductive practice of natural science.[3] This is just the reverse of our normal concerns in the methodology of science; normally one is not concerned about which ontological posits are consistent with scientific practice, one is concerned with knowing which scientific practice best exposes this posited necessity. It may be necessary to posit essential natures in order to proceed with empirical science (this is the source of Popper's modified essentialism) but, even if this is accepted, it only sets the stage: all of the methodological questions remain unanswered. This problem is demonstrated by Mäki's list of five ways of characterizing essentialist progress. This list, while perfectly reasonable, offers no procedures for determining when such progress has occurred; we are told where we are going, with no information about how to get there. Thus I find it hard to accept an essentialist solution to the problems in economic methodology. Essentialism does not solve the basic Popperian problem I discuss in my chapter, it just reverses it. Popper fails to connect his particular methodology with his desire for truth; essentialism fails to connect its desire for truth with any particular methodology.

Secondly, essentialism in economics must face a fundamental issue that must be faced by any type of scientific realism in economics. This is the so-called 'no miracles' argument or the 'ultimate argument' for realism. In the case of natural science the argument goes as follows:

> It would be a miracle, a coincidence on a near cosmic scale, if a theory made as many correct empirical predictions as, say, the general theory of relativity or the photon theory of light *without* what that theory says about the fundamental structure of the universe being correct or 'essentially' or 'basically' correct. But we shouldn't accept miracles, not at any rate if there is a nonmiraculous alternative. If what these theories say is going on 'behind' the phenomena is indeed true or 'approximately true' then it is no wonder that they get the phenomena right. So it is plausible to conclude that the presently accepted theories are indeed 'essentially' correct. (Worrall, 1989, p. 101)

The 'no miracles' argument is a standard argument in favour of a belief in scientific realism or, combined with essentialism, a belief that our best scientific theories are basically correct in isolating the real essential natures of the objects under investigation. The argument is simply that our best scientific theories must tell us the way things really are because there is no other way to explain their predictive success. Now such an argument may be quite compelling in the case of natural science, where the record of predictive success is beyond dispute, but can such an argument reasonably be applied to economics? Even at its best the predictive record of economics is nowhere near the predictive record of most established theories in natural science; economics is (literally) not rocket science. If the extraordinary predictive success of science is the best argument for scientific realism and that success is absent in economics, what is the argument for realism or essentialism in economics? I am not at all certain how one might answer this question, but it is an important question and I believe it is a question that needs to be answered by those arguing for essentialist realism in economics.

3 Response to Hamminga

Hamminga argues, contrary to the position I took in my paper, that continuing to search for Popperian/Lakatosian excess content and novel facts in economics is a worthwhile project. He supports this claim by defining novel facts (ostensibly in a straightforward Lakatosian way) and then providing a detailed application of his definition to Samuelson's *Foundations of Economic Analysis* (1947); this application constitutes the main body of his paper.

I would like to say right away that I do not have any real problems with Hamminga's particular application to Samuelson's *Foundations*. *Given Hamminga's definition of novelty*, what he says about Samuelson seems to be perfectly reasonable. My problem is not so much with the economic application, but rather with his definition of novelty. In fact, I do not even have a problem with his definition of novelty (it is a perfectly fine definition of novelty), *I have a problem with his saying that it is clearly Lakatos's definition of novelty*. There is no reason to start a debate among economists over what Lakatos 'really meant' by novel facts. I have spent a great amount of time with the Lakatosian literature and I have *no idea* what Lakatos 'really meant' by novel facts. Either Lakatos changed his mind between (and sometimes within) works, or he simply held more than one view simultaneously. The point is not to contest Hamminga's particular reading of Lakatos; the point is to contest anyone who has the audacity to argue that there is one 'crystal clear' (p. 83) definition of novel facts in Lakatos. There are, by my count, currently five separate definitions of novel facts in the literature, most proposed by philosophers who are active participants in the Popperian tradition. What Hamminga has proposed is H-novelty, Hamminga novelty, and it is a perfectly reasonable notion of novelty; it is also perfectly reasonable, and possibly interesting, to ask if such H-novelty can be found in Samuelson's *Foundations*. What is not perfectly reasonable is to assert that H-novelty is clearly what Lakatos meant by novelty.

Now if it were simply the issue that there is more than one reasonable way to interpret Lakatos on novel facts and Hamminga argued that his definition is the only one, then my response could be quite brief (in fact what I have already said with a few footnotes on the five kinds of novelty would suffice). But the problem is much deeper than this. The main point of my chapter was that, if economists are going to use the concepts and nomenclature from the Popperian tradition, then they (we) need some sense of the history of these concepts, some sense of the filiation of the ideas, and some sense of the problem situations of the authors involved; this is why I told the 'long Popperian tale'. This history, this context, is precisely what Hamminga avoids: either because Popperian philosophy is trivially simple if one reads carefully (the analytical philosopher's response) or because the 'real' issue is economics and we want to spend a minimal amount of time on philosophy (the economic methodologist's response). Hamminga takes a few sentences where the term 'novel fact' appears in Lakatos (1970), finds it to be a relatively simple (though 'non-common') idea that can be demonstrated with a few Venn diagrams and then rushes out to apply it to economics. This is precisely the type of trivial misapplication of Popper and Lakatos that my chapter was written to protest. As I said above, Hamminga may have an independently interesting analysis of *Foundations*, but *as* an application of, or an exercise in, the philosophy of the Popperian tradition, it is entirely at odds with my central thesis. Therefore I do not feel that it is appropriate to simply end my response with 'there is more than one way to define novel facts'; I feel it is necessary to reply by ferreting out this notion of novelty, with its history and context squarely in mind, in order to demonstrate (reinforcing the theme of my chapter) how much is lost without it.

The concept of a novel fact arises in the Popperian tradition in response to the question: when does a particular fact *support* a particular theory? When does fact *e* support theory *T*? According to the *logical approach* to confirmation, evidence *e* supports or confirms theory *T*, if *e* is empirically accepted and if *e* is a logical consequence of *T*; to use the standard ornithological example, a particular black raven confirms the theory that all ravens are black. For Popper, though (and this is the seed of the entire discussion about novelty in the Popperian tradition) confirmation is not the issue, *corroboration* is the issue, and not all confirmations are corroborations. Confirmations only count as corroborations when they are the result of a severe test and a severe test is a test where the evidence was not probable (was not expected) on the basis of the background knowledge alone.[4] But notice that by introducing background knowledge we have moved away from a logical theory of corroboration and introduced a fundamentally historical (or temporal) element into the discussion of what counts as corroborating evidence.[5] If background knowledge is everything provisionally accepted by the scientific community, then any evidence *e*, known at the time the theory was proposed, is part of the background knowledge (has a probability of 1 on the basis of the background knowledge alone) and thus cannot count as a corroboration of the theory. Therefore the only evidence which *can* count as a corroboration of a theory is a fact which was *unknown* at the time the theory was proposed: 'a fact which was already known before the theory's proposal does not support it' (Worrall, 1978, p. 46).[6] This brings us to the first, strictly temporal, view of a novel fact:[7]

(1) Strictly Temporal Novelty: A fact *e* is novel with respect to theory *T* if *e* was unknown at time *T* was proposed.

Is (1) Lakatos's view of novel facts? Well, maybe. Gardner (1982, p. 2), Worrall (1978, p. 66) and Zahar (1973, pp. 101–3) clearly say that (1) is what Lakatos (1970) means by a novel fact, but Musgrave (1974, p. 8) claims that he has 'not been able to find where Lakatos explicitly adopts the strictly temporal view'.[8] Trying to garner support for (1) directly from Lakatos (1970) leads to ambiguity. For example, if one reads 'knowledge' in, 'A new fact must be improbable or even impossible in the light of previous knowledge' (p. 118) as 'background knowledge', then the sentence seems to support (1). On the other hand, with a different reading of the word 'knowledge', this same sentence can support other views (even Hamminga's). Similar ambiguous things can be said about almost every other quote (and there are many) involving 'novel facts' or related terms in Lakatos (1970). Probably the clearest support for (1) comes from where Lakatos says, 'Bohr's theory logically implied Balmer's formula for hydrogen lines as a consequence. Was this a novel fact? One might have been tempted to deny this, since after all, Balmer's formula was well-known' (1970, p. 156).

The next definition of novelty, what Musgrave (1974, p. 12) calls the 'heuristic view', is due to Worrall (1978) and Zahar (1973).

(2) Heuristic View of Novelty: A fact *e* is novel with respect to theory *T* if *e* was not used in the construction of *T*.

Definition (2) was a conscious attempt to weaken (1); if *e* was 'unknown' it certainly could not be used in the construction of the theory, however *e* could be known and still not be used in the construction of the theory. Thus any fact that satisfies (1) will satisfy (2), but the converse does not hold. If one wants to find a great number of novel facts, and thereby reconstruct large segments of the history of science as Lakatosian progressive, then (2) is more efficient than (1). I used (2) as my standard for defining novel facts in my discussion of the Keynesian revolution (Hands, 1985, 1990) because I felt that it was the most popular definition in the Lakatosian literature and also because I wanted to be as lenient as possible on Keynesian economics: to give it the greatest chance of showing progress. There is some debate about whether (2) is the 'correct' definition of novel facts but there does not seem to be much of an exegetical debate since almost everyone agrees that (2) is a modification (or some would say improvement) of Lakatos's view of novel facts.

A third definition of novel facts is the 'background theory' view of Musgrave (1974, pp. 15–19).

(3) Background Theory View of Novelty (Musgrave): A fact *e* is novel with respect to theory *T* if *e* was not also predicted by the best existing predecessor to theory *T*.

Since empirical content in the Popperian tradition means potential falsifiers, (3) could be restated as 'the new theory should have potential falsifiers which are not also potential falsifiers of the old theory' (Musgrave, 1974, p. 16). The main difference between (3) and the earlier definitions of novelty, (1) and (2), is that (3) refers to novelty relative to a background *theory* rather than background *knowledge*. Under (3) novel facts can come from two separate sources: (a) predictions which conflict with the earlier theory (falsifiers which were not falsifiers of the earlier theory) and (b) predictions of phenomena about which the earlier theory says nothing at all. To demonstrate (3) we can use Hamminga's box diagrams; this was not possible for definitions (1) and (2) since Hamminga's diagrams are defined by what is forbidden or allowed by a particular theory, not by the (temporally variable) state of background knowledge. Applying these diagrams to definition (3) we have novel facts of type (a) from above given by nf_a and novel facts of type (b) from above given by nf_b in the box below.

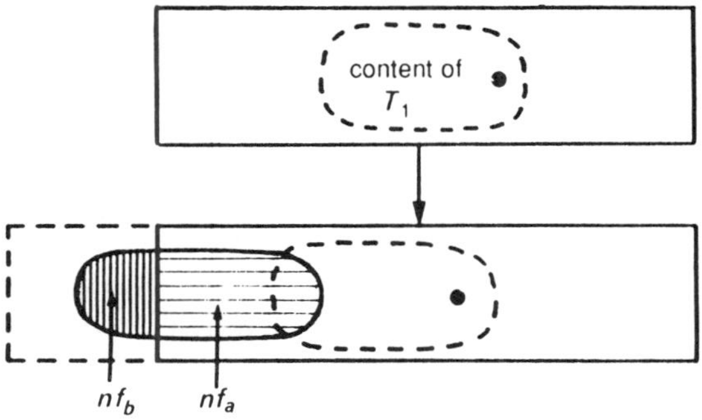

There are a few things to notice that make my diagrams different from Hamminga's. First, I indicate one potential falsifier by a dot as in Hamminga's diagrams but I do not indicate that the dot is necessarily an observed falsifying instance. This is because novel facts need not have anything to do with falsification. One gets this idea from Popper's discussion since he is concerned with non-ad hoc adjustments in the face of falsifying evidence, but there is no inherent relationship between the two; it is quite reasonable to discuss the novel facts predicted by a new theory even though its predecessor was never falsified. Second, notice that the excess content indicated by nf_b is truly 'novel'; it consists of 'predictions concerning phenomena about which the background theory predicts nothing at all' (Musgrave, 1974, p. 16). Finally, notice the similarity between the (3) definition of novelty and Hamminga's definition, 'failure, despite severe attempts, to observe a newly forbidden event' (p. 77). Hamminga's definition simply amounts to the nf_a part of Musgrave's (3) definition.

Now what about the exegetical question: is (3) what Lakatos 'really meant' by novel facts? Well, again it is not at all clear. Musgrave (1974, p. 15) certainly believes that this *is* Lakatos's view, in fact he calls it Lakatos's view.[9] The problem is that the 'Lakatos' that Musgrave cites is Lakatos (1968), not Lakatos (1970), the author of the methodology of scientific research programs. As with (1), the Lakatosian fidelity of (3) seems to be an open question.

The fourth definition of novel facts is also a 'background theory'-based definition (like (3)) rather than a 'background knowledge'-based definition (like (1) and (2)). It is due to Watkins (1984, p. 295).

(4) Background Theory View of Novelty (Watkins): A fact *e* is novel with respect to theory *T* if *e* has no counterpart among the consequences of the existing predecessors to theory *T*.

In Watkins's words, the new theory 'breaks new ground here by making a predictive assertion in an area where its predecessor is silent' (1984, p. 295). Definition (4) differs from definition (3) in that (4) is a special case of (3): the case of (b). In the earlier (3) definition the new fact must not have been an event *allowed* by the old theory; this leaves the two possibilities: (a) it was forbidden by the old theory, or (b) the old theory said nothing at all about it. In Watkins's (4) definition the new fact must not be a consequent, either allowed or forbidden, by the old theory. This means that type (4) novel facts must break 'new ground', as indicated by the area nf_b in the above diagram. According to Watkins (1984, p. 297) a theory may receive a *strong* corroboration from such novel facts; moderate and weak corroborations may come from other types of facts. Watkins does not attribute this (4) definition to Lakatos. He considers it to be his own definition and presents it as an improvement on both the 'Popperian' view (which for Watkins is (1)) and the Worrall–Zahar view (2).

The final definition of novelty (5) needs little discussion, since the author of this view, like Watkins, does not claim that his definition is 'really' what Lakatos meant but rather offers it as an improvement on the earlier definitions. This final definition is from Gardner (1982, p. 10), a definition he calls Novelty_K.

(5) Novelty_K: A fact *e* is novel with respect to theory *T* if *e* was unknown to the person who constructed theory *T* at the time theory *T* was constructed.

Gardner (1982) argues that this definition, though it may sound as if it makes novelty a person-relative affair, solves a number of the purported problems of earlier definitions, (1) and (2) in particular.[10]

So five different definitions of novelty have been presented, three Lakatosian and two 'improvements'. Hamminga's definition of novelty, H-novelty, is not exactly any of these five but it is most closely related to the (3) definition of Musgrave. In fact, in terms of the above diagram, if the Watkins definition (4) were removed from the Musgrave definition (3), the remainder would be H-novelty: the (3) definition is nf_a and nf_b, the (4) definition is nf_b alone, and H-novelty is nf_a alone. Can support for H-novelty be found in Lakatos? Of course, but then again support for (1) and (3) (and some would say (2) as well) can also be found in Lakatos. Is it interesting to see if H-novelty can be found in economics? Maybe, but not any more interesting than searching for any of the other types of novel facts (1)–(5). I have never suggested that such novel fact hunts are entirely without merit – I have certainly engaged in them myself. My point in what I have written in this volume, and to a lesser extent in Hands (1988), was simply that it is now time, if we are really interested in the Popperian tradition in economics, to take a more reflective stance. I argued that, rather than hunting for novel facts based on a particular definition or arguing over what the correct definition should be, economic methodologists should be concerned with understanding how novel facts came to play the role they did in Lakatos's methodology – similarly for the Popperian concepts of ad hocness, verisimilitude and the rationality principle. By understanding these concepts, their history and the role they have played in Popperian philosophy we can better understand their importance in economic methodology. We have tried (desperately) to 'apply' Popper and Lakatos to economics during the last 20 years and the results have not been a glorious success. For some this indicates that we should abandon the Popperian tradition entirely and seek guidance from other sources: essentialism, rhetoric, instrumentalism, the sociology of science, and so on. This is not my response. My response is not to give up, but rather to engage in a careful, reflective re-examination of the Popperian tradition. There is still room for economic 'applications' of Popperian concepts, but these applications should be careful to respect the integrity of the concepts being applied. Hamminga's 'Lakatosian' definition of novel facts does not.

Notes

1. It should be noted that, while Bartley's critical rationalism can be packaged as a solution to this Popperian problem, it is not a direct approach like that of Watkins (1984) or Worrall (1989). Rather it is a solution in the sense that one 'solution' to the problem of a poor tee-shot in golf is to play tennis.
2. Popper (1972, p. 195; 1983, p. 137). Worrall (1982, 1989) calls Popper's view 'conjectural realism', a more appropriate term for Popper's position.
3. See, for example, Fisk (1973, ch. IV).
4. Popper (1968, Appendix *ix; 1983, pp. 238–44).
5. The distinction between *logical* and *historical* (or temporal) theories confirmation is emphasized in Musgrave (1974), a paper which (rightly) remains one of the standard sources on these topics.
6. 'Facts "known to science" before a hypothesis is provided will not be able to confirm that hypothesis, since they will already be contained in background knowledge and cannot represent the results of severe tests' (Musgrave, 1974, p. 8).
7. This Popperian interest in severe tests is *only one* of many reasons why novel facts (however defined) might have a special status with respect to theory support. Another reason to favour novelty is simply the surprise power of unexpected facts. This 'anticipating nature' argument is traced through Descartes, Leibniz and Duhem by Musgrave (1974, pp. 1–3). Still another reason for their importance is that novel facts are less subject to the so-called 'paradoxes of confirmation'; temporal properties of evidence can prevent many of these paradoxes from occurring (see Lawson, 1985; Musgrave, 1974; Watkins, 1978, 1984). Finally, there seems to be 'diminishing returns' to background knowledge; each additional confirmation of the same 'kind' should count for less than a confirmation of a new (novel) kind (see Watkins, 1984, pp. 292–3); Popper, 1965, p. 240).
8. From here on I will only be concerned with Lakatos's view of novelty. Despite the fact that Hamminga claims that his definition is the view of both Popper and Lakatos, Popper is actually even less clear on the matter than Lakatos; Musgrave (1974, p. 19) finds at least three different views in Popper (1965) alone. In all fairness to Popper though, it should be noted that Popper's real concern was ad hocness (or non-ad hocness) and not novelty *per se*, thus his lack of consistency is not all that problematic. Of course the same cannot be said for Lakatos, the person responsible for what I have called 'a novel fact fetishism' (Hands, 1988, p. 135).
9. Lawson (1985, p. 405) concurs.
10. It should be noted that these five definitions are not exhaustive of the definitions in the literature; they are simply the definitions most discussed (others include Carrier, 1988; Nunan, 1984). There are also subtle differences in various presentations of the five definitions I have discussed; for example, what I present as the Worrall–Zahar definition (2) is slightly different in Zahar (1973) from what it is in Worrall (1978).

References

Bartley, W.W. III (1984), *The Retreat to Commitment*, 2nd enlarged edn (LaSalle, IL: Open Court).

—— (1987), 'Theories of Rationality', in G. Radnitzky and W.W. Bartley III (eds), *Evolutionary Epistemology, Rationality, and the Sociology of Knowledge*, pp. 205–14 (LaSalle, IL: Open Court).

Carrier, M. (1988), 'A Discussion of Criteria for Non-ad-hocness in the Methodology of Scientific Research Programmes', *Zeitschrift für allgemeine Wissenschaftstheorie*, **19**, pp. 205–31.

Fisk, M. (1973), *Nature and Necessity: An Essay in Physical Ontology* (Bloomington, IN: Indiana University Press).

Gardner, M.R. (1982), 'Predicting Novel Facts', *British Journal for the Philosophy of Science*, **33**, pp. 1–15.

Hands, D.W. (1985), 'Second Thoughts on Lakatos', *History of Political Economy*, **17**, pp. 1–16.

—— (1988), 'Ad Hocness in Economics and the Popperian Tradition', in N. de Marchi (ed.), *The Popperian Legacy in Economics*, pp. 121–37 (Cambridge: Cambridge University Press).

—— (1990), 'Second Thoughts on "Second Thoughts": Reconsidering the Lakatosian Progress of *The General Theory*', *Review of Political Economy*, **2**, pp. 69–81.

Lakatos, I. (1968), 'Changes in the Problem of Inductive Logic', in I. Lakatos (ed.), *The Problem of Inductive Logic* pp. 315–417 (Amsterdam: North Holland).

—— (1970), 'Falsification and the Methodology of Scientific Research Programmes', in I. Lakatos and A. Musgrave (eds), *Criticism and the Growth of Knowledge*, pp. 91–196 (Cambridge: Cambridge University Press).

Lawson, T. (1985), 'The Context of Prediction and the Paradox of Confirmation', *British Journal for the Philosophy of Science*, **36**, pp. 393–407.

Musgrave, A. (1974), 'Logical versus Historical Theories of Confirmation', *British Journal for the Philosophy of Science*, **25**, pp. 1–23.

Nunan, R. (1984), 'Novel Facts: Bayesian Rationality, and the History of Continental Drift', *Studies in the History and Philosophy of Science*, **15**, pp. 267–307.

Popper, K.R. (1965), *Conjectures and Refutations* (New York: Harper & Row).

—— (1968), *The Logic of Scientific Discovery* (New York: Harper & Row).

—— (1972), *Objective Knowledge* (Oxford: Oxford University Press).

—— (1983), *Realism and the Aim of Science* (Totowa, NJ: Rowman and Littlefield).

Samuelson, P.A. (1947), *Foundations of Economic Analysis* (Cambridge, Mass: Harvard University Press).

Watkins, J. (1978), 'The Popperian Approach to Scientific Knowledge', in G. Radnitzky and G. Anderson (eds), *Progress and Rationality in Science*, pp. 23–43 (Dordrecht, Holland: D. Reidel).

—— (1984), *Science and Skepticism* (Princeton, NJ: Princeton University Press).

Worrall, J. (1978), 'The Ways in Which the Methodology of Scientific Research Programmes Improves on Popper's Methodology', in G. Radnitzky and G. Anderson (eds), *Progress and Rationality in Science*, pp. 45–70 (Dordrecht, Holland: D. Reidel).

—— (1982), 'Scientific Realism and Scientific Change', *Philosophical Quarterly*, **32**, pp. 201–31.
—— (1989), 'Structural Realism: The Best of Both Worlds?', *Dialectica*, **43**, pp. 99–124.
Zahar, E. (1973), 'Why Did Einstein's Programme Supersede Lorentz's? (I)', *British Journal for the Philosophy of Science*, **24**, pp. 95–123.

B Testing

3. Testing in Modern Economics: the Case of Job Search Theory

Jinbang Kim*

1 INTRODUCTION

Many methodological and historical arguments about economics are based on differing views about what constitutes theory testing. These views are seldom explicated and often seem to be inaccurate. In fact such implicit and/or inaccurate notions of testing are an unavoidable result of the lack of careful studies on the nature of testing itself in economic applications. This paper is offered as one such study. Using job search theory as the case material, it will describe and analyse how economists actually undertake the testing of economic theories.

In particular, the Duhem–Quine thesis is one of the important ideas which motivates this work. In its weak interpretation the thesis asserts the impossibility of a direct test of an isolated theory; it is only a conjunction of theories that scientists can test. Consequently scientists can and do render a theory testable in many different ways by replacing auxiliary theories. The applicability of this thesis to economics, however, is only part of what we shall discuss. More importantly the paper will distinguish and characterize the measures which economists take in order to render economic theories testable. In particular, the empirical or methodological status of the measures will be investigated.

This inquiry then will lead to a discussion of Lakatos's methodology. Though he says that the Duhem–Quine thesis does not cause any difficulty to *his* falsificationism, I will argue that it is not the case. My contention is that 'progressive problem shifts' might be a virtue for a series of *theories*, but we do not have to seek the virtue in a series of *empirical models* in which a theory under test is embedded.

2 A SKETCH OF JOB SEARCH THEORY

Job search theory, which will provide the material of this case study,

* Thanks to Neil de Marchi and Tony Smith for helpful suggestions.

can be characterized by its initial problems, basic assumptions, primary predictions and extensions. Though the theory had been pioneered by Stigler (1962) mainly to explain the alleged fact that homogeneous workers are paid different wages, it was reformed by McCall (1970), Mortensen (1970) and Gronau (1971) to explain the existence of unemployment and changes in the duration of unemployment for individual workers.[1] In this new version of job search theory the wage dispersion is no longer a phenomenon to be explained.

The following are among the basic assumptions of job search theory. (1) An unemployed worker faces a number of prospective employers who would offer different wages to him/her. (2) The worker has only 'imperfect information' about wage offers; the worker does not know the wage which will be offered by a particular employer at a particular time, though the worker knows the probability distribution of the population from which the wage will be drawn at random.[2] (3) The worker can contact one prospective employer each time to find out the employer's offer. This search, however, might cost the worker money and time, and thus reduces the level of utility which the worker can enjoy while unemployed. (4) The worker can either accept the job offer which he has just received or reject it in order to continue searching. If he accepts the job offer he will never quit or lose the job. (5) The worker adopts a sequential search strategy; the worker will set a 'reservation wage' each time and accept a wage offer only if the wage is not lower than the reservation wage. Further the reservation wages are determined to maximize the expected lifetime utility from his wage and leisure stream discounted by a fixed rate.

Based on these assumptions, job search theory explains extended unemployment as a result of the 'rational' choice of workers who have imperfect information about wage offers. That is, taking into consideration the opportunity costs and expected benefits of further search, most unemployed workers will set their reservation wage higher than the average wage offer. Thus they will probably search more than once and continue to be unemployed. It is in this way that job search theory locates the cause of unemployment in the dispersion of wage offers and workers' imperfect information about it.

On the other hand, job search theory attributes the differences in the duration of unemployment for individual workers to two different, but related, elements. First, the theory characterizes the duration of unemployment as a random variable. Though the reservation wage is intimately related to the duration of unemployment, the worker's decision about his/her reservation wages does not amount to a decision about the *exact* duration of unemployment, but to a decision about the *probability distribution* of unemployment spells. Thus the duration of unemployment may differ between two workers who are identical in every respect. Second, the observed differences in the duration of unemployment might also be a reflection of the different characteristics of individual workers, which affect the probability distribution of unemployment spells.

Besides these causal explanations, job search theory yields more specific predictions about the effect of personal characteristics on the reservation wage and the probability distribution of unemployment spells. Let us take a look at these predictions.

The 'optimal' reservation wage ($\tilde{w}$) can be characterized as follows:

$$\frac{\tilde{w}}{1-r} = b - c + r\int v(w)dF(w) \tag{3.1}$$

where

r ≡ the discount rate,
b ≡ unemployment benefits including additional leisure,
c ≡ search costs,
$v(w)$ ≡ the value of having received an offer w and following the optimal search strategy.
$F(w)$ ≡ the probability of receiving a wage offer which is no greater than w.

We can also deduce Bellman's equation for this problem.

$$v(w') = max\left[\frac{w'}{1-r}, b - c + r\int v(w)dF(w)\right] \tag{3.2}$$

The two equations above lead to another which characterizes the reservation wage without involving the implicit value function v:

$$\tilde{w} - (b - c) = \frac{r}{1-r}\int_{\tilde{w}}^{\infty} (w - \tilde{w})dF(w) \tag{3.3}$$

This new equation can be manipulated to yield several predictions about the effect on the worker's reservation wage of personal characteristics such as unemployment benefits, search costs and wage offer distribution. For example, the reservation wage decreases if unemployment benefits decrease or search costs increase. Another prediction, which is more or less unexpected, is that a 'mean-preserving spread' of the wage offer distribution also leads to an increase in the reservation wage. In other words, the more dispersive the wage offer distribution, the higher the reservation wage.

Job search theory also implies that the duration of unemployment (D) has a geometric distribution:

$$Prob[D = d] = (1 - p)^{d-1}p \tag{3.4}$$

where p denotes the re-employment probability, or the probability of encountering an acceptable job offer in each period:

$$p = 1 - F(\tilde{w}) \tag{3.5}$$

Further, some algebraic manipulation reveals that the expected duration of unemployment is $1/p$. Given the relationship between the reservation wage and the probability distribution of unemployment spells, it is a straightforward matter to deduce that an increase in unemployment benefits or a decrease in search costs will lead to a decrease in the re-employment probability and thus an increase in the expected duration of unemployment.

But it should be noted that the above analysis is dependent upon the assumption of an infinite time horizon in a critical way. If the worker is instead assumed to understand that he will retire at the end of the Tth period, the value of having received a wage offer will be affected by the remaining time to work or search.[3] Accordingly Bellman's equation should be modified as follows:

$$v_t(w') = max\left[\frac{w'}{1-r}, b - c + r\int v_{t+1}(w)dF(w)\right] \text{for } t \leqslant T - 1$$

$$v_T(w') = max[w', b] \tag{3.2a}$$

where the subscript to the value function denotes the time that an offer is received.

In this case the reservation wage must also be derived in a different way, that is, by using a backward solution technique. But we do not have to derive the reservation wage as an explicit function of other elements to see that the assumption of a finite time horizon helps to yield a new prediction about the reservation wage. A short cut leads us to the prediction that the reservation wage is not constant over time; the worker will lower his or her reservation wage period by period. This prediction in turn implies that the re-employment probability increases over time because

$$p_t = 1 - F(\tilde{w}_t) \tag{3.5a}$$

Consequently, the probability distribution of unemployment spells can no longer be characterized by equation (3.4):

$$Prob[D = d] = \prod_{t=1}^{d-1} (1 - p_t)p_d \tag{3.4a}$$

Another interesting extension is to include on-the-job search.[4] The extension is interesting as it leads job search theory to a different phenomenon of the labour market. Now that on-the-job search is included as a possible choice of workers, the theory can deal with turnovers as well as unemployment. There then emerges a new kind of theory which specializes in explaining turnover, which is usually called job matching theory.[5]

Job search theory can be extended in several other ways as well. For instance, one can introduce uncertainty concerning the number of prospective employers which an unemployed worker contacts per period.[6] Some economists have also embedded the theory in a continuous time framework by randomizing the length of time between job offers. It is an equally reasonable assumption, though not easy to formulate, that the wage offer distribution and unemployment benefits vary over time.

Considering these extensions, we can say that job search theory has been 'progressing' at least theoretically; each extension predicts novel facts. But theoretical progression has not been the only concern of economists, who have also been involved with what Weintraub (1985) calls a 'hardening of the hard core'. For instance, Weitzman (1979) gave a justification of one of the basic assumptions by formally proving that a *sequential* search strategy is better than any other strategies in terms of expected utility. A similar improvement has long been needed of the assumption that wage offers are drawn at random from a non-degenerating distribution. Instead of *assuming* the dispersion of wage offers, economists have demanded that it should be *explained* as a market equilibrium, that is, a coordinated result of employers' and buyers' rational behaviour. This demand, however, has not been successfully met yet.

3 FROM THEORY TO EMPIRICAL MODELS

We have just seen that job search theory makes claims about the world. Yet economists would not consider the theory to be directly testable by experience. This section will explore the reason for this. We will then discuss the measures which economists take in order to render the theory testable, though a more specific and detailed discussion is deferred to the next section.

Statistical Tests and Specifications

As will be discussed shortly, job search theory has several unobservable entities, but I will pretend in this subsection that we could observe all the entities occurring in the theory. This is to show that unobservable entities are not the only source of difficulties in testing the theory.

Consider one of the predictions made by job search theory, that is, the prediction that an increase in unemployment benefits or a decrease in search costs would lead unemployed workers to raise their reservation wage. In actuality, there is a missing clause in this statement. For the prediction to be fully stated, the above proposition should be followed by a clause reading, 'in so far as all other relevant things remain unaltered', or '*ceteris paribus*'. This clause is essential, though it is not always stated explicitly. For instance, the theory implies that a worker's reservation wage might increase rather than decrease if the increase in his search costs were accompanied by an increase in the mean or variance of his wage offer distribution. The reservation wage might be affected by the third or higher moments of the wage offer distribution as well. Without the *ceteris paribus* clause, therefore, the prediction about the relationship between reservation wage and net unemployment benefits will no longer be a correct implication of the theory. In fact, almost all the predictions of economic theories include a *ceteris paribus* clause.

Such a clause does not cause much trouble in itself. Economists would have little difficulty in testing a *ceteris paribus* prediction if they were able to perform a controlled experiment in which all the *ceteris paribus* conditions were properly fulfilled. By artificially fixing all the other elements, researchers could observe the effects of only the element of concern. Such a controlled experiment, however, is seldom performed for the purpose of testing economic theories.[7] Instead almost all the tests in economics have been statistical. That is, most economic data consist of observations from a sample which is chosen at random from a population,[8] and the population is usually heterogeneous in more than one respect.[9] This is one of the difficulties encountered in testing economic theories.

To make the discussion clearer, let us return to the prediction mentioned above: an increase in net unemployment benefits would lead unemployed workers to raise their reservation wage in so far as other conditions remain unaltered. We could test this prediction if we had an opportunity to observe the behaviour of a number of unemployed workers who are homogeneous except for their net unemployment benefits. We could judge the validity of the prediction by examining points plotted on a graph of reservation wage versus net unemployment benefits. The prediction would be rejected unless the line connecting these points sloped upward. We could also increase the severity of the test if we had more than one such opportunity. But in practice we cannot have even one of them. We have to depend only on observations from a random sample, but any available sample usually consists of workers who may have wage offer distributions with differing means and variances. The discount rate and other features of the wage offer distribution might also differ for each of the workers. The data on reservation wage and search cost from any available sample, therefore, may not be directly compared with the *ceteris paribus* prediction. In the rest of this subsection we will see how economists solve this problem. Two steps can be distinguished.

First, economists typically would formulate the theory's entire implication for the reservation wage even if they wanted only to test its prediction about the relationship between reservation wage and search cost. The theory's implication can be formulated as follows: $\tilde{w} = H(b - c, r, \mu, \sigma^2, \ldots)$ where $H_1 > 0$, $H_2 > 0$, $H_3 > 0$, $H_4 > 0$ and so on. In words, a worker's reservation wage depends positively on the net unemployment benefits, the discount rate, and the mean and variance of the wage offer distribution. The reservation wage might also be affected by other elements such as higher moments of the wage offer distribution, elements which are represented by '...' in the function above. Economists, however, usually have to limit their analysis to the effect of a small number of selected elements. For this purpose, they would divide the function H into two parts; for example, $\tilde{w} = h(b - c, \mu, \sigma^2) + \varepsilon$ where ε represents the effect of all the relevant elements except those included in the function h.[10] A variable like ε is often called an error term. Of course, this error term would be identically zero if the omitted variables had no effect at all on the dependent variable. Economists sometimes make such an assumption to suppress the error term.

Second, having limited the number of explanatory variables to be explicitly considered, economists typically impose a parametric form on the relationship between the selected variables and dependent variable so that they can translate the predicted effect of the former on the latter in terms of the parameters. In particular, economists prefer to embed the job search theory's implications in a 'linear-in-parameters' equation which is easy to manipulate; for example, $\log(\tilde{w}) = \alpha_0 + \alpha_1(b - c) + \alpha_2\mu + \alpha_3\sigma^2 + \varepsilon$ where $\alpha_1 > 0$, $\alpha_2 > 0$, and $\alpha_3 > 0$. Embedded in this log-linear equation, the predictions about the reservation wage can be statistically tested.

What then do these steps amount to? And what, if any, is the justification for the steps? The first step might seem innocuous in so far as the deductive link is concerned. However the equation containing an error term is not just a reformulation of the theory's implication about the reservation wage. When economists introduce an error term to represent the effect of all the omitted variables, they usually make an auxiliary assumption that the error term is statistically independent of the selected variables. This assumption would be unacceptable if the selected and omitted variables were either related to or interacted with each other to determine the reservation wage. Economists thus often struggle to replace the assumption with a more realistic one.

It is also not unusual that, when economists introduce an error term, they make another auxiliary assumption that the error term constitutes a specific distribution, especially a parametric one such as a 'normal' distribution.[11] In fact economists often view a normal distribution as a good approximation to reality, invoking the central limit theorem to justify this view. According to the theorem, a sum of independent random variables converges to a normal distribution as the number of random variables increases to infinity.

Economists seem to have the same view about the auxiliary assumption which they make in the second step. That is, when they impose a specific form on the relationship between variables, they view the form as an approximate description of reality. Moreover they often expect the form to be a better approximation than others, though this expectation sometimes lacks any empirical or theoretical justification.

Besides the deductive link there are two other aspects of the first step worthy of note. One is that, when variables are selected for explicit consideration, it is often because the variables can be controlled or measured with comparative ease, rather than because they are believed to be most important. The other is that, when the effect of omitted variables is represented by an error term, we move from a deterministic to a probabilistic statement about the relationship between variables; observations on the selected explanatory variables no longer lead us to a precise prediction on the value of the dependent variable. In fact it is in this way that most economic theories become probabilistic before they are actually tested.

To summarize, most predictions of economic theories include a *ceteris paribus* clause. Such predictions are to be tested by observations from a random sample only after being embedded in a specific form of equation containing an error term. This embedding is in turn the combined result of a decision and auxiliary assumptions. Only a few explanatory variables are chosen for explicit consideration, while others are relegated to an error term. Then auxiliary assumptions are made about the probability distribution of the error term and the relationship between variables. I have argued that this assumed functional form or distribution is usually viewed by economists as an approximate description of reality.

Unobservables and Auxiliary Assumptions

Now let us stop pretending to be able to observe all entities occurring in job search theory. As a matter of fact, most of the entities are 'unobservable' if we apply the criteria by which economists distinguish between observables and unobservables.[12] (1) Job search theory assumes that each worker has his own rate by which he discounts his future income or utility. A person's discount rate, however, is regarded as unobservable because the *public* cannot observe it even in principle. (2) Another assumption of job search theory is that a jobless worker must spend money and time to continue searching for an acceptable job. This search cost is another 'unobservable' entity. Above all the time to be spent must undergo a *subjective* evaluation. The amount of money and time actually spent is also *practically* difficult to measure. For the same reason the unemployment benefit which includes the additional leisure is 'unobservable' as well. (3) Job search theory argues that an unemployed worker will accept a wage offer if and only if it exceeds the so-called reservation wage. Though a few economists have measured the reservation wage through the survey method,[13] most economists consider it to be one of the unobservable entities. (4) Suggesting that unemployment duration is a random variable, job search theory advises us to focus on the population from which a worker's actual duration of unemployment shall be drawn at random. This population, however, is merely conceptual. We can never measure its frequency distribution, though we can observe what is drawn at random from it. This situation is not improved by the argument that each worker has a clear idea of the probability distribution. The probability distribution is still unobservable to the *public*. The same thing can be said about the re-employment probability – a parameter which exclusively determines the probability distribution of unemployment duration. (5) The wage offer is also assumed to behave like a random variable. Though the population from which each wage offer is drawn at random might be real, it is still *impractical* to measure its frequency distribution. Further, whether economists consider the wage offer as observable or not, no observation has actually been made on the rejected wage offer as far as I know. What is currently available to economists is only the censored data, that is, the data on the accepted wage offer.

This unobservability or unavailability is another reason why economists cannot test job search theory as it is. Of course we do not have to observe all the entities occurring in the theory. For instance, no data on the re-employment probability are necessary to test the theory's prediction about the probability. As the following section will show, we can substitute observations on unemployment duration which is governed by the re-employment probability. We will also see in the next section that unobservability of the reservation wage can be solved in a similar way. But this solution does not work for all the unobservable entities. Some of them force economists to take other measures. To discuss these measures, I would introduce a re-employment probability function which has already been fully specified: $p_t = exp[\beta_0 + \beta_1 t + \beta_2(b - c) + \beta_3 r + \beta_4 \mu + \beta_5 \sigma^2]$. In this specification the error term is set to be identically zero in order to make the discussion more straightforward. Let us suppose that we are primarily interested in testing the prediction of the theory of job search with a finite time horizon that the re-employment probability decreases over time, that is, $\beta_1 < 0$. We understand that all the right-hand-side variables except t are unobservable.

One of the ways to deal with unobservable entities is to assume that such entities are irrelevant because they are *identical* for all the subjects of study. For instance, every worker in the population might be assumed to have the same discount rate and wage offer distribution. This homogeneity assumption allows us to delete the three unobservable elements from the re-employment probability function: $p_t = exp[\beta_0 + \beta_1 t + \beta_2(b - c)]$.

Economists, however, understand that the homogeneity assumption is at best an approximate description of the reality. Thus they might choose to take an alternative measure. We know that economists introduce an error term to represent the effect of minor elements, but the minor elements are not the only reason for introducing an error term. Instead of assuming away the effect of the discount rate and wage offer distribution, economists often capture their effect by an error term: $p_t = exp[\beta_0 + \beta_1 t + \beta_2(b - c) + e]$. This alternative procedure, however, is not always easy to execute, especially if we are unwilling to impose a parametric distribution on the error term.

Besides the homogeneity assumption or its alternative, economists often adopt another auxiliary assumption which relates unobservables to observables. For example, we can make the assumption that the value of additional leisure due to unemployment depends negatively on the number of dependents and positively on the household income from other sources. We can also make the assumption that a worker with a longer tenure at his/her previous job pays a higher search cost. These assumptions help us replace the net unemployment benefit with a function of observable elements: $b - c = \tau_0 + \tau_1 x_1 + \tau_2 x_2. + \tau_3 x_3$. Economists might introduce an error term at this step as well; $b - c = \tau_0 + \tau_1 x_1 + \tau_2 x_2. + \tau_3 x_3 + \tilde{e}$. Combined with the homogeneity assumption or its alternative, either equation enables us to test the prediction about the sign of β_1. The assumptions mentioned above, however, are not the only ones we can conceive of. There are many others, each of which might lead to a different relationship. In fact two economists would seldom end up with the same empirical model though both of them had started with one and the same theory.

To summarize, job search theory contains a number of unobservable entities. Though not all the entities have to be observable for the theory to be testable, economists are still forced to employ auxiliary assumptions which either suppress some of the unobservable entities or replace them with observable ones. Job search theory is not unique in this respect. Most scientific theories contain unobservable entities and can be tested only after being combined with auxiliary assumptions.

Summary and Discussion

We have examined the difficulties in testing job search theories as they are, and the steps which economists usually take in order to render the theory testable.

First of all, most available data are observations from a sample which is drawn at random from a heterogeneous population, whereas the predictions include a *ceteris paribus* clause. Because of this conflicting situation, most economic theories cannot be tested before they are augmented by an auxiliary assumption which specifies the relationship between variables. The specification is also accompanied by the introduction of an error term which represents the effect of omitted variables, and economists make another auxiliary assumption to restrict or specify the distribution of the error term. Sometimes they even assume the error term to be identically zero. I have argued that economists usually expect such an augmented model to be an *approximate* description of the reality. Approximation, of course, is not the only concern. Above all the specification should lead to a *manageable* model. That is the reason economists favour a 'linear-in-parameters' function and a parametric distribution.

Unobservable entities are another reason for our needing auxiliary assumptions to render economic theories testable. That is, economists must restrict the population heterogeneity and/or relate unobservables to observables. Instead of restricting the population heterogeneity, economists might introduce an error term which represents the effect of unobservable variables on a dependent variable. An error term can also be attached to the equation relating an unobservable variable to observable ones.

I have stated that this study was motivated by the Duhem–Quine thesis. This study, however, shows that economic theories go through a different and more complicated process to become testable than the thesis suggests. In particular, the thesis contends that we can test no theory without invoking auxiliary hypotheses to measure some of its entities. In economic applications, however, auxiliary hypotheses are used not to *measure* unobservable entities but to *relate* them to other observable ones. It is also important in rendering economic theories testable to specify the relationship between variables about which few economic theories yield a detailed description. Most economic theories must go through this step, whether they contain unobservable entities or not. The thesis also failed to pay attention to the role of an error term.

4 THREE TYPES OF EMPIRICAL JOB SEARCH MODELS

The analysis in the previous section showed that job search theory cannot be directly tested by experience, and it is a very involved procedure to embed the theory in an empirical model. The analysis, however, was general and hypothetical. We still need concrete knowledge about the procedure, which we will try to obtain in this section. In particular we will see what auxiliary assumptions are actually employed for the procedure.

Another purpose of this section is to show that a theory can be embedded in different types of empirical models and that we can often find a hierarchical relationship among these. Though a theory contains a number of propositions, only a few of them are selected when economists build an empirical model. On the other hand, one proposition of a theory is often a deduction from another in the context of the theory. The empirical models can therefore be ranked according to the logical status of the proposition(s) on which each empirical model is built.

Type I Model

The reservation wage is one of the most important entities occurring in job search theory, and the theory yields several predictions about it. For instance, the theory predicts that a worker will raise his/her reservation wage if the net unemployment benefit increases or the wage offer distribution becomes more dispersive. At the same time the theory relates this reservation wage to another entity, the worker's re-employment probability, which in turn determines the probability distribution of his/her unemployment duration. Thus the prediction about the reservation wage leads to another prediction about the re-employment probability or the probability distribution of unemployment duration. For example, an increase in the net unemployment benefit will be accompanied by a decrease in the re-employment probability and a corresponding change in the probability distribution of unemployment duration.

We have distinguished, up to now, two predictions, one of which is logically prior to the other: one about the reservation wage and the other about the re-employment probability or the probability distribution of unemployment duration. In the following subsections, we will see that each of these predictions plays a central role in building each type of empirical job search model. In this subsection, however, we will examine a different type of empirical model which implements neither prediction as a whole. Instead this empirical model incorporates only one aspect of the theory's prediction about the probability distribution of unemployment duration, that is, the distribution's mean. This type of empirical model has actually been built, by Ehrenberg and Oaxaca (1976) and Classen (1979), among others. The discussion below, however, will not be based on any particular case in detail, and will thereby be more general and consistent.

According to the basic theory of job search examined in section 2, the expected duration of unemployment is the inverse of the re-employment probability, which in turn depends on the net unemployment benefit, the discount rate and the wage offer distribution. But if the worker has a finite time horizon, the expected duration (δ) of unemployment will depend on the length of the worker's time horizon (T) as well. That is,

$$\delta = G(b - c, r, T, \mu, \sigma^2, \ldots) \tag{3.6}$$

where the dots represent such elements as the third and higher moments of the wage offer distribution.

Let our economist build a statistical model based on this under-specified relationship between unobservables. First, he must limit the number of explanatory variables by introducing an error term and/or invoking a homogeneity assumption. For instance, the economist might choose to give no explicit consideration to the mean (μ) of the wage offer distribution, maintaining that its effect is negligible. He could also drop the discount rate and the variance (σ^2) and other higher moments of the wage offer distribution, assuming that they are the same for every worker. Then

$$\delta = g(b - c, T) + u \tag{3.7}$$

where u is a random variable representing the effect of μ on δ, and g is constructed so that u is distributed around zero. For reasons which will be discussed later, however, it does not make any significant difference to assume that every worker has the same μ, and thus μ is identically zero. Thus let the first step end up with an equation with no error term.

$$\delta = g(b - c, T) \tag{3.7a}$$

The next step is to replace each unobservable variable with a function of observable variables. For example, our economist might consider the argument that a worker's search cost depends positively on the worker's previous job tenure (x_1) and negatively on the worker's education level (x_2). It is also a reasonable interpretation that the unemployment benefits consist of unemployment insurance (x_3) and additional leisure, and that the latter's value in turn is affected positively by family income from other sources (x_4) and negatively by the number of dependents (x_5). He might also assume that there is an inverse relationship between a worker's time horizon and his/her age (x_6). Of course an error term can be introduced in this step as well, though our economist, we assume, will not do this.

Then a specific form is given to both the function g and the relationships between the function's arguments and the observable variables listed above. More realistically, a specific form is given to the function which relates the dependent variable directly to the observable variables. Possibly our economist would like to embed the relationship in a log-linear equation as Ehrenberg and Oaxaca did for their work:

$$ln\delta = \alpha_0 + \alpha_1 x_1 + \alpha_2 x_2 + \ldots + \alpha_6 x_6 \qquad (3.8)$$

One apparent reason for choosing this formulation is its manageability. Moreover it is logically impossible for the unemployment duration to be less than zero. Consequently the distribution's mean can never be less than zero. This non-negativity is secured by the above equation, in which $\delta = exp(y)$.

Now that our economist has arrived at this equation, he can rephrase the predicted effect of b, c, T, and r on δ in terms of the sign of α_i's. For example, since x_3 is a part of b and b has a positive effect on δ, α_3 should be greater than zero. For another example, because of the inverse relationship between x_6 and T, the negative effect of T on δ corresponds to the positivity of α_6. It is these and other inequalities about α_i's that our economists will actually test.

The transformation is not quite finished, however. The expected duration of unemployment must be related to the unemployment duration (D) itself. We know that the ratio of a random variable to its mean such as D/δ is another random variable whose mean is one. Thus,

$$logD = log\delta + u \qquad (3.9)$$

where u is a random variable with zero mean. To combine it with the previous equation,

$$logD = \alpha_0 + \alpha_1 x_1 + \alpha_2 x_2 + \ldots + \alpha_6 x_6 + u \qquad (3.10)$$

It is this equation, with or without the exact distribution of u being specified, that our economist will actually bring to data. The α_i's can be estimated through the method of least squares.

Note that the final equation states that there is a probabilistic relationship between D and x_i's. In other words, x_i's do not determine the *exact* value of D. But the omitted variables played no role in moving from a deterministic to a probabilistic statement. Even if our economist has assumed that none of the omitted variables has an effect on δ, the final equation still has an error term on its right-hand side. The error term is introduced because of the nature of D postulated in job search theory. This is, however, an unusual case. Most economic theories are not probabilistic in nature, and the omitted variables are essential for moving from a deterministic to a probabilistic relationship between observables.

Now let us list the elements which have helped our economist arrive at the final equation and inequalities. First, they are based on the theory's implications about the expected duration of unemployment. Second, the number of explanatory variables is limited by restricting population heterogeneity. (An error term could have served the same purpose.) Third, other auxiliary assumptions are invoked to relate the unobservable variables to observable variables. Fourth, a specific form is given to the relationship between the dependent variable and the observable variables.

Type II Model

Recall that job search theory yields a prediction about the re-employment probability which determines the whole structure of the distribution of unemployment duration, not just the expected duration of unemployment. The Type II model, which we are now going to examine, is based on the theory's prediction about this more fundamental variable, that is, the re-employment probability. This type of empirical model has actually been built by Nickell (1979a, 1979b), Lancaster (1979) and Lancaster and Nickell (1980).

Let us see how the theory of job search with a finite time horizon is to be embedded in an empirical model of Type II. According to the theory, a worker's re-employment probability is not the same for each period; it increases period by period as the worker reduces his/her reservation wage each period. To put this particular prediction in an equation,

$$p_t = H(t,b - c,r,T,\mu,\sigma^2,\ldots) \quad \text{for} \quad t = 1,2,\ldots,T \qquad (3.11)$$

where the partial derivative with respect to t should be positive. Other predictions of the theory can also be expressed in terms of the sign of other partial derivatives.

Given the above equation, our economist will derive another equation containing a limited number of variables. For example, through the same process as was used to derive equation (3.7), the economist can derive the following:

$$p_t = h(t,b - c,T) + \varepsilon_t \quad \text{for} \quad t = 1,2,\ldots,T \qquad (3.12)$$

The economist, however, might prefer an equation without an error term, not only because such an equation is much easier to implement, but because the error term is not essential in preventing the final relationship between observables from being deterministic.[14]

$$p_t = h(t, b - c, T) \quad \text{for} \quad t = 1,2,\ldots,T \tag{3.12a}$$

We understand that an assumption restricting population heterogeneity and/or its effect on p_t's must be imposed to drop the error term. That is, equation (3.12a) depends on the assumption that the differences, if any, in the omitted variables such as discount rate and wage offer distribution have no effect on p_t's.

Then our economist would invoke another assumption to relate the unobservable variables, $b - c$ and T, to other observable ones, say x_i's. An example of such an assumption was discussed in the previous subsection. It was also mentioned that this step could have provided another opportunity to introduce an error term.

The next step is to specify the relationship between p_t on the one hand and t and x_i's on the other hand. Our economist might agree with Nickel (1979a, 1979b) that the following is among the reasonable forms.[15]

$$p_t = \frac{1}{1 + exp(-y)} \text{ where } y = \sum_{i=0}^{k} \beta_i x_i + \tau t \text{ and } x_0 \equiv 1 \tag{3.13}$$

One apparent merit of this formulation is that the dependent variable is allowed to vary only between zero and one. That is, the equation is a faithful reflection of the axiomatic truth that the re-employment probability must be somewhere between zero and one. Nevertheless our economist might prefer what Lancaster (1979) suggested:[16]

$$p_t = \tau t^{\tau-1} exp\left[\sum_{1=0}^{k} \beta_i x_i \right] \tag{3.13a}$$

Though it might not be straightforward to some readers, equation (3.13) or (3.13a) requires no further auxiliary assumptions to become a relationship between observables. Recall that the probability distribution of unemployment duration depends exclusively on the re-employment probability:

$$Prob[D = d] = \prod_{t=1}^{d-1} (1 - p_t)p_d \tag{3.14}$$

Intermediated by this relationship, the re-employment probability equation regulates the relationship between D and x_i's. Furthermore both equations (3.13) and (3.13a) are constructed so that all the parameters, that is, τ and β_i's, can be estimated through the method of maximum likelihood.

Now that the re-employment probability equation is embedded in a parametric form, we can express the predictions of job search models in terms of the parameters. For example, if x_i's denote the same things as they do in equation (3.8), the sign of β_i should be the opposite to that of α_i for each $i = 1,2,\ldots,6$. On the other hand, as the theory of job search with a finite time horizon predicts a monotonous increase in the re-employment probability across succeeding periods, the newly introduced parameter τ should be greater than zero in equation (3.13) or greater than one in equation (3.13a).

Let us summarize the elements involved in moving from equation (3.11) to (3.13). First, an auxiliary assumption was invoked to restrict population heterogeneity and/or its effect on p_t's. Second, another kind of auxiliary assumption helped to replace unobservables with related observables. Third, a specific form was given to the relationship between p_t's and the observables. These three elements work together with the theory's implication about the re-employment probability and distribution of unemployment duration so as to derive this type of empirical model.

Finally, it might be interesting to compare this type of empirical model with the previous one, which is based on the theory's implication about the expected duration of unemployment. To repeat, the expected duration can be deduced directly from the re-employment probability, but not vice versa. Equations (3.8) and (3.13a) illustrate this logical relationship very well. So far as a continuous time framework is concerned, the latter readily implies that

$$E[D] \equiv \delta = exp[-\Sigma(\beta_i x_i)/\tau] \tag{3.15}$$

which is of exactly the same form as that of equation (3.8). Equation (3.15) or (3.8), however, is not the only implication that we can deduce from equation (3.13a). The latter tells us about the entire probability distribution of unemployment duration, not just its first moment. Thus much information would be lost if we employed equation (3.15) instead of equation (3.13a). As an immediate result of this information loss, we could not test the prediction about the value of τ.

Type III Model

We have mentioned several times that in job search theory the reservation wage is a more fundamental variable than any others, such as the expected duration of unemployment or the re-employment probability; the implication about the latter is to be deduced from that about the former. In this subsection we will examine how the implication about this fundamental variable is transformed into an empirical model. This type of empirical model has actually been built by Kiefer and Neumann (1979a, 1979b, 1981).

According to job search theory, the reservation wage depends on the net unemployment benefit, the discount rate and the wage offer distribution. Further, if workers have a finite time horizon, the reservation wage will depend on the length of their time horizon, and will vary over time. That is,

$$\tilde{w}_t = Q(t, b - c, r, T, \mu, \sigma^2, \ldots) \tag{3.16}$$

Given this relationship, our economist would derive a testable relationship through the same steps as we discussed above. First, the economist might consider a homogeneity assumption to limit the number of explanatory variables. For example, by employing the same assumption as Kiefer and Neumann (1979a and b, 1981) did, our economist can simplify the above equation:

$$\tilde{w}_t = q(t, b - c, \mu) \tag{3.17}$$

Second, another auxiliary assumption could be used to relate the unobservable variables, $b - c$ and μ, to observable ones, say z_i's. Third, a specific form is given to the relationship between $\tilde{w}_t$ and z_i's. A linear function is among the easiest to manipulate.

$$\tilde{w}_t = \sum_{i=0}^{n} k_i z_i + \theta t \text{ where } z_0 \equiv 1 \tag{3.18}$$

An error term may be added to this equation, but without creating any significant difference.

Now that the reservation wage equation has been fully specified, the theory's prediction about it can be expressed in terms of the signs of parameters. For example, the theory of job search with a finite time horizon predicts θ to be less than zero, whereas the basic theory predicts the same parameter to be zero.[17] Nevertheless such predictions are still untestable. An obvious reason is that the left-hand-side variable, that is, the reservation wage, is not observable. Furthermore the reservation wage is not as directly related to an observable variable as the re-employment probability or expected duration of unemployment. That is, the reservation wage can be related to the distribution of unemployment duration only through the wage offer distribution. In order to render the prediction about the reservation wage testable, therefore, our economist must specify an initial condition, that is, the wage offer distribution.

Let our economist employ the same assumption that Kiefer and Neumann (1979a and b, 1981) did: wage offers are drawn from a normal distribution. Though this assumption lacks any empirical or a priori justification, it is still attractive as it renders the analysis manageable. Further our economist has already assumed that the wage offer distribution differs for each worker only in its mean, and that the mean is a function of some z_i's, say $(z_1,\ldots,z_m)$ where $m < n$.[18] The specification, therefore, can be completed by assigning a particular form to the function. A linear function is always favourable: $\mu = a_0 + a_1z_1 + a_2z_2 + \ldots + a_mz_m$. To summarize,

$$F(w) = \Phi[(w - \Sigma a_iz_i)/\sigma] \tag{3.19}$$

where Φ is the standard normal cumulative distribution function.

From equations (3.18) and (3.19) we can derive the re-employment probability as a parametric function of observables:

$$p_t = 1 - F(\tilde{w}_t) = \Phi\left[\sum_{i=0}^{m} (a_i/\sigma)z_i - \sum_{i=0}^{n} (k_i/\sigma)z_i - \theta t\right] \tag{3.20}$$

or, equivalently,

$$p_t = \Phi\left[\sum_{i=0}^{m} [(a_i - k_i)/\sigma]z_i - \sum_{j=m+1}^{n} (k_j/\sigma)z_j - \theta t\right] \tag{3.20a}$$

As we discussed in the previous subsection, this equation in turn defines the relationship between the unemployment duration (D) and z_i's, all of which are observable. Thus, given a proper set of data on D and z_i's, we can estimate the 'reduced-form' parameters such as $(a_i - k_i)/\sigma$ and (k_j/σ). Based on this estimation, we have to identify the structural variables such as a_i, k_i and k_j. (θ can be directly estimated.) If we succeed in assigning a unique value to the structural variables, we can test the theoretical model's prediction as expressed in terms of them. For instance, if k_i is to be identified, we can test the prediction about the effect of z_i on $\tilde{w}_t$.

In this case, however, the estimation of the reduced-form parameters would not lead to the identification of the structural parameters. We must invoke other information, if any, to assign a unique value to the structural variables. Consider the fact that the distribution of re-employment wages, about which we can gather reliable data, is determined exclusively by the wage offer distribution and the reservation wage. In particular, job search theory informs us that

$$f(w|d) = f(w)/[1 - F(\tilde{w}_d)] \tag{3.21}$$

where $f(w|d)$ represents the probability density that a worker's re-employment wage is w given that he is re-employed after d periods of joblessness. Further we can invoke equations (3.18) and (3.19) to generate a *specified* probability density function (pdf).

$$f(w|d) = \frac{\sigma^{-1}\phi[(w - \Sigma a_i z_i)/\sigma]}{\Phi[(\Sigma a_i z_i - \Sigma_k i z_i - \theta d)/\sigma]} \tag{3.22}$$

It is this pdf that will help solve the identification problem, but we will not discuss how it could actually be exploited.[19]

Now let us compare the Type III model with the Type II model. (1) Whereas the Type II model specifies the re-employment probability equation itself, the Type III model specifies the wage offer distribution and the reservation wage equation from which a specified re-employment probability equation is to be deduced. (2) No matter which approach is taken, it is the re-employment probability equation that is actually estimated. Accordingly, the identification problem occurs in the Type III model, but not in the Type II model. On the other hand, we might be able to solve the identification problem since the Type III model contains a specified pdf of the re-employment wage as well. (3) The Type III model offers at least a chance to estimate the effect of z_i's on $\tilde{w}_t$, but the Type II model does not. The latter enables only the effect of z_i's on p_t to be estimated, an effect which might have been caused via the wage offer distribution rather than $\tilde{w}_t$. The prediction about the effect of z_i's on $\tilde{w}_t$, therefore, could be tested more effectively in the context of the Type III model.

Finally let us list the auxiliary assumptions which were employed to build the Type III empirical model. First, an assumption was made about the initial condition; the wage offer distribution is 'normal', and its variance is the same for all workers. Second, the initial condition was further specified by the assumption that workers have the same time horizon. Third, both the reservation wage and the mean of the wage offer distribution reservation wage were assumed to be a *linear* function of some observables.

Summary and Discussion

One of the purposes of this section was to illustrate how economists might render a theoretical model testable. In particular, we have examined the auxiliary assumptions which economists could employ, explicitly or implicitly, to move from a theory to empirical models in the case of job search theory. First, an auxiliary assumption is often invoked to restrict the population heterogeneity or its effect. Economists could also introduce an error term to represent the effect of unobserved heterogeneity. Second, another auxiliary assumption is invoked, if necessary, to relate unobservable variables to observable ones. Third and last, a particular form is assigned to the relationship between relevant variables which has not been fully specified by the theory. This particular form is to be viewed as an approximation to the true, but unknown, form.

We have also seen that job search theory can be transformed into three different types of empirical models, among which there exists a hierarchical relationship. The Type I model specifies the equation whose dependent variable is the expected duration of unemployment, whereas the Type II model specifies the equation whose dependent variable is the re-employment probability. It has been noted that a particular equation of re-employment probability will yield a corresponding equation of expected unemployment duration, but the former cannot be recovered from the latter. This relationship exists between the Type II and III models, too. Instead of specifying the re-employment probability equation itself, the Type III model specifies the reservation wage equation and wage offer distribution, from which a corresponding re-employment probability equation is to be derived. Consequently each parameter of the Type I or II model could be derived as a function of one or more of the parameters of the Type II or III model, but not vice versa.

This unilateral relationship among different types of statistical models is connected to the issue of identification. In particular, though the Type III model specifies the reservation wage equation and the wage offer distribution, it is the re-employment probability equation that is to be actually estimated. Nevertheless we might still be able to identify all the structural parameters, since the model contains another estimable relationship, that is, the re-employment wage distribution, which is derived from the reservation wage equation and wage offer distribution. In fact there would be no reason to build the Type III model instead of the Type II model if we were not able to identify the former's structural parameters of interest. We could neither test the prediction about the structural parameters, nor estimate the reduced-form parameters more efficiently.

5 AN APPRAISAL OF LAKATOS'S METHODOLOGY

After examining the nature of auxiliary assumptions which economists must employ to move from a theory to an empirical model, one might be left with a doubt about the 'falsifiability' of economic theories: can we refute or confirm an economic theory based on statistical tests of a conjunction of the theory and auxiliary assumptions, especially when some of the auxiliary assumptions lack any empirical or theoretical justification? This scepticism might be fortified by the fact that an economic theory can be embedded in many different, but equally plausible or implausible, empirical models by changing auxiliary assumptions. For instance, in building the Type III model of job search, our economist would have ended up with a different empirical model if he had assumed that wage offers come from a Pareto distribution instead of a normal distribution. But what conclusion can we draw if the model based on the assumption of a normal distribution is refuted, whereas the other is confirmed?

Given that the above criticism is justified, can one still argue for 'falsificationism', a methodological view that the growth of science can be, and has been, secured by proliferation of falsifiable theories and elimination of falsified theories? In what follows in this section I will outline and appraise Lakatos's methodology, which he himself calls a 'sophisticated falsificationism', in the light of the above criticism.

The starting-point for Lakatos is the dictum by Popper that the rationality of science is to be located in its rule of acceptance and elimination. Yet Lakatos ends up with a different characterization of the rule. According to the rule, a theory is acceptable and leads to elimination of its predecessor only if the theory has excess empirical content over its predecessor and some of this excess content is corroborated. In other words, Lakatos 'sophisticates' Popper's 'naive falsificationism' by re-defining the key word: a theory is 'falsified' not by data but only by another theory which predicts novel facts with some success.

Lakatos then confronts the Duhem–Quine thesis that a theory can be tested only in a conjunction of auxiliary theories. Calling the thesis a 'trivial observation', he argues that it is innocuous so far as *his* falsificationism is concerned. His contention is that his methodology renders it redundant to decide *which* part to replace or eliminate if a complex of a theory and auxiliary hypotheses is refuted by data. 'We may try to replace *any* part and only when we have hit on an explanation of the anomaly with the help of some content-increasing change (or auxiliary hypothesis), and nature corroborates it, do we move on to eliminate the "refuted" complex'. In short, Lakatos dismisses the Duhem–Quine thesis by denying that an isolated theory must be falsifiable.

Lakatos's reply, however, is not applicable to the criticism discussed above. Above all, few economists regard it as necessary for new empirical models to contain excess empirical content in order for them to replace earlier models. Though Lakatos might see 'dishonesty' in this attitude of economists,[20] I myself find 'rationality' in it. Many economists are still interested in the truth value of an isolated theory or its predictions although they understand that a conclusive test is seldom available because of the reasons discussed above. Given this conflicting situation, economists try to enhance the credibility of their judgement, either by testing the theory in conjunction with fewer or weaker auxiliary assumptions, or by designing a more powerful test for a given conjunction. To test the theory in conjunction with many different but equally plausible sets of auxiliary assumptions is another way to reach a safe judgement. It is therefore a category mistake always to seek for content-increasing changes in a series of empirical models.

Discussing Lakatos's reaction to the Duhem–Quine problem, I have suggested my own answer to the criticism discussed above: there might be no conclusive test of a theory or series of theories, but there can be a better test of it. This answer, however, needs further elaboration, especially on the meaning of the word 'better,' which is not attempted in this chapter.

6 CONCLUDING REMARKS

I would like to conclude by making two points. First, the above analysis of testing in economics is not intended to reiterate or reinforce the argument which was once made by apriorists and lately by anti-positivists, that is, the argument that we have to give up testing economic theories. Considering the above discussed difficulties in testing economic theories, we should not be surprised that some methodologists urge economists to give up testing altogether. The awareness of the difficulties, however, seems to have led a number of competent economists to improve their empirical practices rather than give up testing altogether, and the outcome of their unyielding efforts appears, at least to me, quite impressive. I thus do not at all intend to discourage such efforts. My analysis is rather designed to help economists become more conscious of what they are doing when they move from theories to empirical models. This heightened awareness could lead economists to further improvement in their practice.

Secondly, testing is not the only purpose of building empirical models. Economists often value the 'quantification' of theories. Having embedded a theory in an empirical model, they estimate the parameters of interest to find out how *much* effect one variable has on another. In this setting, data can be said to cooperate with rather than stand in judgement on a theory. To non-Bayesians, however, the logic of this practice has not yet been explicated. More philosophical study of this issue is needed.

NOTES

1. See Kim (1988).
2. Most studies of job search do not make it clear whether the population is real or conceptual. It is surely conceptual if each prospective employer chooses the wage to offer at random from a given population. But it is often suggested that each employer will offer a fixed wage though the wage may be different from that offered by other employers. This suggestion, however, causes a logical difficulty unless there are an infinite number of prospective employers for the searching worker.
3. This case was first studied by Gronau (1971).
4. This case has been studied by Burdett (1978).
5. See Jovanovic (1979).
6. See Lippman and McCall (1976), pp. 164–6.
7. A notable exception to the paucity of controlled experiments is the research program of Vernon Smith *et al.* See his paper for the Capri conference.
8. A random sample can be defined as a sample chosen so that every possible sample with the same number of members has an equal chance of being chosen.
9. It should also be noted that the population is often not well specified. Folks (1981) provides an example: when an economist looks at GNP data for the last 30 years,

he or she might choose to regard the data as a random sample from some population, necessarily vaguely specified. This seems to have been the attitude of Haavelmo (1944), who called such data 'passive observations'.

10. ε sometimes represents measurement error as well.
11. The normal distribution was invented by De Moivre and Laplace in the eighteenth century, and was firmly established by Gauss in the early nineteenth century. The distribution was then discovered to be useful for describing frequency distributions from many varied sources.
12. As Popper and Lakatos emphasized repeatedly, there is no natural demarcation between observables and unobservables; a methodological decision cannot but enter into the demarcation.
13. For instance, Lancaster and Chesher (1983) have asked unemployed workers the following question: 'Would you tell me the lowest amount you are prepared to accept after stoppage?' Lynch (1983) has measured the reservation wage in the same way.
14. In job search theory, the relationship between unemployment duration and selected explanatory variables is already probabilistic, whether or not an error term is introduced to represent the effect of omitted variables.
15. In fact Nickell himself included t^2 as another explanatory variable: $y = \beta_0 + \Sigma\beta_i x_i + \tau_1 t + \tau_2 t^2$.
16. In fact Lancaster's equation is intended to describe the instantaneous probability of re-employment. That is, his equation is based on a continuous time model, unlike ours.
17. In fact, so far as this particular equation is concerned, the two versions of job search theory are to be distinguished only in their prediction about the parameter θ.
18. As the reservation wage depends on the wage offer distribution, anything that affects the latter's mean will affect the former as well. That is why $m < n$.
19. For example, see Kiefer and Neumann (1979a and b). Their approach, however, was criticized by Flinn and Heckman (1982).
20. Lakatos's negative view is revealed in the following statements. '[P]atched-up, unimaginative series of pedestrian "empirical" adjustments . . . are so frequent, for instance, in modern social psychology' (1984, p. 88), '[O]ne wonders whether the function of statistical techniques in the social sciences is not primarily to provide a machinery for producing phoney corroborations and thereby a semblance of "scientific progress" where, in fact, there is nothing but an increase in pseudo-intellectual garbage' (1984, pp. 88–9, n. 4).

REFERENCES

Burdett, K. (1978), 'A theory of employee search and quit rates', *American Economic Review*, **68**, 1, pp. 212–20.

Classen, K.P. (1979), 'Unemployment insurance and job search', in S.A. Lippman and J.J. McCall (eds), *Studies in the Economics of Search*, pp. 191–219 (Amsterdam: North-Holland).

Ehrenberg, R.G. and Oaxaca, R. (1976), 'Unemployment insurance, duration of unemployment and subsequent wage gain', *American Economic Review*, **66**, 5, pp. 754–66.

Folks, J.L. (1981), *Ideas of Statistics* (New York: John Wiley & Sons).

Gronau, R. (1971), 'Information and frictional unemployment', *American Economic Review*, **61**, 2, pp. 290–301.

Jovanovic, B. (1979), 'Job matching and the theory of turnover', *Journal of Political Economy*, **87**, 5, pp. 972–90.

Kiefer, N.M. and Neumann, G.R. (1979a), 'An empirical job search model with a test of the constant reservation wage hypothesis', *Journal of Political Economy*, **87**, 1, pp. 89–107.

—— (1979b), 'Estimation of wage offer distributions and reservation wage', in S.A. Lippman and J.J. McCall (eds), *Studies in the Economics of Search*, pp. 171–90 (Amsterdam: North-Holland).

—— (1981), 'Individual effects in a non-linear model: explicit treatment of heterogeneity in the empirical job search model', *Econometrica*, **49**, 4, pp. 965–79.

Kim, J. (1988), 'The development of job search theory: a methodological essay', unpublished paper, Duke University.

Lakatos, I. (1978), *Philosophical Papers, Vol. I: The Methodology of Scientific Research Programmes* (Cambridge: Cambridge University Press).

Lancaster, T. (1979), 'Econometric methods for the duration of unemployment', *Econometrica*, **47**, 4, pp. 939–56.

Lancaster, T. and Chesher, A. (1983), 'An econometric analysis of reservation wage', *Econometrica*, **49**, 4, pp. 939–56.

Lancaster, T. and Nickell, S. (1980), 'The analysis of reemployment for the unemployed', *Journal of the Royal Statistical Society*, **143**, 2, pp. 141–65.

Lippman, S.A. and McCall, J.J. (1976), 'The economics of job search: a survey, I', *Economic Inquiry*, **14**, 2, pp. 155–89.

McCall, J.J. (1970), 'Economics of information and job search', *Quarterly Journal of Economics*, **84**, 1, pp. 113–26.

Mortensen, D.T. (1970), 'A theory of wage and employment dynamics', in E.S. Phelps *et al.*, *Economic Foundation of Employment and Inflation Theory*, pp. 167–211 (New York: Norton).

Nickell, S.U. (1979a), 'Estimating the probability of leaving unemployment', *Econometrica*, **47**, 5, pp. 1247–66.

—— (1979b), 'The effect of unemployment and related benefits on the duration of unemployment', *Economic Journal*, **89**, pp. 34–49.

Popper, K.R. (1968), *The Logic of Scientific Discovery* (New York: Harper & Row).

Stigler, G.J. (1961), 'The economics of information', *Journal of Political Economy*, **69**, 3, pp. 213–25.

—— (1962), 'Information in the labor market', *Journal of Political Economy*, **70**, 5, pp. S94–S105.

Weintraub, E. Roy (1985), *General Equilibrium Analysis: Studies in Appraisal* (Cambridge: Cambridge University Press).

Weitzman, M. (1979), 'Optimal search for the best alternative', *Econometrica*, **47**, 2, pp. 641–54.

COMMENT ON KIM

Neil de Marchi

Jinbang Kim's chapter is an excellent statement of the way modern applied microeconomic research is pursued. It is exactly the sort of case study on which methodological reflection must be based if it is to be relevant to the best gambits of contemporary economists.

Kim draws a lesson from his material, however, that I wish to question. He sees it – mistakenly in my view – as undermining Lakatos's insistence that we find corroborated excess content in any theory that is to count as progressive. Economists, Kim concludes from his case study, do not always demand an increase of content in their models, far less are they exclusively or even mainly concerned with testing. Rather they try to 'improve' their models. This may involve increasing the 'power' of a test; or trying whether the same results obtain with alternative sets of auxiliary assumptions, each more or less equally plausible; or weakening or reducing the number of needed auxiliary assumptions. Since these three sorts of improvements seem unrelated to testing novel predictions, Kim concludes that Lakatos's MSRP is descriptively inappropriate to modern applied economics.

I have two comments to make on this. The first is that Kim does not persuade that his economists are all that different from Lakatos's ideal scientist. Secondly, I want to argue that Lakatos's MSRP can be given a reasonable interpretation that places it much nearer to what Kim feels describes what modern economists actually do.

Kim's criticism would bite if he provided strong grounds for our believing that (his) economists understand by the 'improvements' mentioned above something quite distinct from the Popper–Lakatos testing of excess content. But he does not do this. He suggests in fact that his economists are interested in truth. And he points out that the parametric form chosen for the empirical model version of a theory's predictions is frequently defended as being a reasonable approximation to reality. Thus we seem to be not all that distant from the regulative roles of truth and empirical 'reality' which undergird Lakatos's methodology.

What of my second claim, that MSRP can be interpreted as concerned with improvement of much the same sort as Kim sees in the practices he observes? At first sight this looks unlikely. More powerful tests and more economical ways of expressing empirical content seem to be linked to changes in the auxiliary assumption of particular models. They refer to different ways of restricting a theoretical model to produce an empirical variant of it, and to different ways of forging connections between the 'facts' and some such empirical variant. Think of adding and specifying an error term to make exact theory into something to which statistical inference may be applied; and think of the different levels of empirical model described by Kim, in each of which a different 'depth' of connection is established between the data and the unobservables crucial to the theory. These represent ingenious refinements, but what do they have to do with excess content, which is undeniably Lakatos's criterion for improvement (progressivity)?

I shall argue two related points: one, that Lakatos places a lot of emphasis on technical refinement as important to the process of inquiry, though this aspect of MSRP is typically neglected; two, and this is equally little remarked upon, though more remarkable, that he actually links progress to such refinements. For him progress occurs in the form of a succession of new *models* (1978a, p. 51) which presumably embody these refinements. It remains unclear, however, how these refinements come to fulfil his requirement that progress means an increase of content at 'each step' (ibid., p. 49).

We may distinguish three definitions of 'novel' fact in Lakatos's writings:

1. There is novelty in the sense of something unexpected, or inconsistent with previous expectation or background knowledge, hence something genuinely new and/or forbidden by the preceding or rival theory (ibid., pp. 32, 33–4, 36, 39).
2. Later it was conceded that observations might count as novel if they played no part in the design of the challenger theory. This is the heuristic sense of novelty: an anomaly may be dealt with as 'an unintended by-product', or its resolution may be 'an unexpected present' dropped into the lap of researchers busily pursuing their heuristic strategy, undistracted by the sea of anomalies through which they move (ibid., p. 185; cf. p. 149).
3. Finally, as a further gloss on the heuristic definition, the first exact account of something previously known, but existing only as a fortuitous result in the preceding theory, may count as novel (ibid., pp. 185, 186, 187).

Now (1) is heavily dependent on Popper's way of viewing the content of a theory: a theory has empirical content only in terms of potential events that it denies. Lakatos talks in these terms in his discussion of novelty in 'Falsification and the methodology of scientific research programmes'. Yet in that same paper he undermines the basis of his own argument, by insisting that even the most respected scientific theories 'may fail to forbid any observable state of affairs' (ibid., p. 17). This statement becomes a much bolder assertion just a few pages further on: 'no theory forbids a state of affairs specifiable in advance' (ibid., p. 45). Lakatos's point is that a good theorist will always be able to find an ingenious auxiliary assumption to deflect the thrust of a poor factual outcome. In the light of this argument against the Popperian sense of novelty, and in view of Lakatos's admitted preference later on for definitions (2) and (3), I focus from here on wholly on them.

Definitions (2) and (3) directly reflect the things that Lakatos represented as separating him from Popper: an insistence on heuristic rather than isolated tests; an awareness that crucial experiments are seen to be so only in retrospect, once a new theory has emerged to supply the reinterpretation that may turn false 'facts' into corroborating evidence; a shift of emphasis away from clashes between single theories and background knowledge and towards a view of scientific inquiry as marked by competition between theories (observational, to provide the 'facts', and explanatory of them); and a focus on the technical and mathematical means by which theories are improved.

References to these things are scattered throughout 'Falsification and the methodology of scientific research programmes', and Lakatos's later writings. Lack of space prevents me from giving quotations here, but I will narrow my focus at this point and at least try to justify the inferences I draw from the characterization just given.

The main thing that stands out from the list of Lakatos's claimed novelties is what we might call the primacy of theory, or what he repeatedly refers to as 'the relative autonomy of theoretical science' (ibid., pp. 52, 149). All propositions are theoretical, even those we call observational or 'factual' (ibid., p. 16). The progress of science comprises *for the most part* the struggle among competing theorists to gain ascendancy. Here is Lakatos's own description of what is *typical* in science:

> The theoretician may demand that the experimentalist specify his 'interpretative theory', and he may then replace it – to the experimentalist's annoyance – by [*sic*] a better one in the light of which his originally 'refuted' theory may receive positive appraisal. (Ibid., p. 45)

Why may we regard this as typical? Because, as Lakatos would have it, the core of background knowledge (uncontested 'facts') is simply less insistent than the claims made by theorists. He is adamant about the need to appraise theoretical shifts, and adamant that this must be done against some background knowledge (or 'ignorance'!) (see ibid., p. 46).

But this is a piecemeal and conventional business (ibid., p. 46); almost a last resort, to put a stop to what would otherwise be an unending theoretical dispute. After all, the 'facts' are only as good as our observational theories. And what scientists are about is in fact the sorting out of inconsistencies in the maze of theories being continually put forward (ibid., pp. 44–5). Hence our unit for analysis and criticism is always and inevitably 'several theories – more or less deductively organized – . . . [and] soldered together' (ibid., p. 45). We make a decision, however, to draw a line somewhere, differently at different points in time, simply because if we want to learn from experience then 'we cannot articulate and include *all* "background knowledge" . . . into our critical deductive model' (ibid., p. 46). The fact remains that observations do not generate hypotheses, theories do; and all we can appraise is theoretically-anticipated new facts. It is that which makes even learning from experience 'a normative idea' (ibid., p. 38 and n. 2).

The fact remains, too, that appraisal takes a long time (ibid., p. 149). Theoretical disputes may be protracted. Not only do we tend to postpone drawing the line as to what will count as test or background knowledge, but 'there is no falsification before the emergence of a better theory' (ibid., p. 35). And discovering the content-increasing auxiliary hypotheses needed to turn refutations into corroborating evidence requires not only ingenuity but good luck. Moreover some, even repeated, failures may be allowed (ibid., pp. 71–2). For all these reasons, theoretical progress can be verified at once, but empirical progress *cannot* (ibid., p. 49). Hence, too,

> progress is not even so much in the actual novel predictions which go beyond the premises . . . but in the mathematical and physical novelty of problem-solving techniques which later lead to, and form part of, a progressive research programme. (1978b, p. 101)

All this seems to be a long way from progress as measured exclusively by positive test outcomes or corroborated empirical excess content. Yes, we have to appraise; and yes, we choose as our criterion learning from experience. But the primacy (relative autonomy) of theory is undeniable; it is theoretical disputes that comprise much of what scientists do; and the bearers of progress are the ingenious and lucky identifications of content-increasing auxiliary hypotheses. If we ask how scientists come upon those hypotheses, it seems that Lakatos is willing to say that they stem from technical solutions to problems. Problems, in turn, are defined by the heuristic of a program (1978a, p. 111), and this heuristic comprises 'a chain of ever more complicated *models* simulating reality' (ibid., pp. 50–1). Theoretical progress is thus reflected in 'a series of new [model] variants superseding each other' as successive puzzles facing the earlier models are resolved (ibid., p. 51).

This is so far from Lakatos as falsificationist that an uninformed reader might be forgiven for confusing the Lakatos I have just described with one of Kim's modern applied microeconomists. If I have rendered such a confusion plausible I have achieved my immediate purpose. I want to end, however, by sounding the appropriate notes of caution. Firstly, I may have shown that there is evidence in Lakatos's writings that he was prepared to identify progress with model improvement; but he seems to have retained the idea that each new model must embody theoretical excess content for the sequence to be judged progressive. In other words, the 'each step' requirement stands, only it applies to successive models, not theories. I have not tried to apply this strict requirement to the models Kim discusses, but I doubt whether they would all qualify. I suspect that there is still a distinction to be drawn between refinement-type improvements and genuine content-increasing improvements. If so, Kim's reticence about MSRP is well founded, only its basis is now seen to be somewhat different from the one he first brought forward.

Secondly, the Lakatos I have sketched does not sit well with the Lakatos who strongly denies epistemic value to discovery (important though it may be to the process of science). It also remains true that Lakatos's own ultimate test of progressivity is (intermittent) corroborated excess content, which involves drawing the line and standing firm, for the moment at least, on some background knowledge. The process of inquiry seems to be one thing, appraisal another. The one belongs to (Popper's) World 2, the other to World 3. Lakatos, for all he said about the significance of problem-solving technical advance and theoretical disputes, seems not to have been able to reconcile it with his anti-inductivism.

References

Lakatos, Imre (1978a), *The Methodology of Scientific Research Programmes. Philosophical Papers*, vol. 1, ed. by John Worrall and Gregory Currie (Cambridge: Cambridge University Press).

—— (1978b), *Mathematics, Science and Epistemology. Philosophical Papers*, vol. 2 ed. by John Worrall and Gregory Currie (Cambridge: Cambridge University Press).

4. Do Economists Test Theories? – Demand Analysis and Consumption Analysis as Tests of Theories of Economic Methodology

Christopher L. Gilbert*

1 INTRODUCTION

Discussions of the methodology of empirical economics tend to assume that this entire activity may be characterized by a single methodological approach.[1] Blaug (1980, p. 262) quotes Keynes as seeing '*economics* as a branch of logic, a way of thinking' (emphasis added). And Blaug himself states in the concluding sections of his widely respected book on economic methodology, 'the central aim of *economics* is to predict and not merely to explain' (ibid., p. 262, emphasis added).

There is a danger that in discussing methodology one starts with a view of the way scientific activity is or should be carried out and then looks for examples which illustrate this view. An alternative, empiricist, approach is to start from the science and work back to the methodology. Doing this I am impressed by the diversity of our methodological approaches. In this chapter I explore part of this diverse universe by contrasting the role of theory in applied demand analysis and in applied consumption analysis.

In particular I shall be interested in the claim that in doing econometrics we are testing economic theory. There is currently a view that economists never reject theories, or at least not on the basis of econometric evidence. McCloskey (1985, p. 182) states '. . . no proposition about economic behavior has yet been overturned by econometrics . . .' and Morgan (1988) records that 'It is a commonplace criticism that econometricians never refute a model they set out to "test" in the sense that they never reject the underlying theoretical

* I have benefited from comments on earlier drafts from John Campbell, Nancy Cartwright, Neil de Marchi, Vanessa Fry and Mary Morgan; and also from participants at the Capri conference. All errors remain my responsibility.

model they have used.' Morgan suggests that theory needs to be embedded in an empirical model and that, at most, econometricians are testing these empirical models. It is true that in the first instance one is always testing an empirical model and not a theory; however, the outcomes of these tests may have some bearing on our views about the validity of the underlying theories. I discuss the role of empirical models in sections 2 and 3.

Specifically I argue that in demand analysis (sections 3–6) frequent rejection of particular models has not in any way threatened demand theory. This is in line with Morgan's claim. By contrast, in consumption analysis (sections 7 and 8) econometricians do see themselves as discriminating between alternative theories, and not simply models. Moreover the dominant theory (the Permanent Income Hypothesis) is now under serious threat. In section 9 I look for the origin of this methodological difference. Section 10 contains brief conclusions.

2 TESTING THEORY

The current consensus is that a major role of econometrics in applied economics is that of testing theory. An earlier (postwar) generation of applied economists had been content simply to posit a theory and to estimate the implied parameter values: 'If you believe my theoretical model, this is the numerical counterpart implied by the data.' Rival economists from different ideological schools could produce conflicting models, each apparently validated by the data – see my discussion of Smith and Marks in Gilbert (1986). This was widely seen as bringing applied economics into disrepute. Mayer (1980, p. 166) complained that 'All that has happened is that arm-waving has been replaced by t coefficient waving.'[2] Blaug (1980, p. 257) complained that journals 'abound' with papers which rely on 'cookbook econometrics': 'express a hypothesis in the form of an equation, estimate a variety of forms for that equation, select the best fit, discard the rest, and then adjust the theoretical argument to rationalize the hypothesis that is being tested'. Other examples will come to mind, but perhaps this view was most succinctly summarized by Leamer's (1983) invitation to take the 'con out of econometrics'.

Those worries are now largely in the past. It is generally agreed that acceptance of a theory as a valid or useful description of economic data requires not only that it provide a good statistical description of a particular sample of data, but in addition that it extend outside the sample (Blaug's prediction function – see Harvey, 1981, pp. 179–83) and also that it provide a superior description of the sample data than other alternative theories. This final requirement, referred to in the technical literature as the requirement that the theory should 'encompass' rival theories (Mizon, 1984; Mizon and Richard, 1986; Gilbert, 1989a), was in fact anticipated by Blaug (1980, p. 159):[3]

> Scientific theories can only be meaningfully assessed in terms of competing hypotheses for the simple reason that methodology provides no absolute standard to which all theories must conform: what it does provide are criteria in terms of which theories may be ranked as more or less promising.

Under the influences of a vague knowledge of Popper, Kuhn and Lakatos, together with a more secure grounding in Neyman–Pearson testing methodology and a newly acquired armoury of non-nested tests, applied economists now recognize testing theories as a major professional obligation.[4] This emphasis on falsificationist testing is not confined to economics. According to Hacking (1983, p. 244), 'Today, Popper's philosophy is rampant, and when one describes one's experiment, one says one is trying to test theories (otherwise you [*sic*] would not be funded!).'

This suggests a paradigmatic situation in which there are theories T_0, T_1, T_2,..., a sample S of data and a set N of extra-sample information. On the basis of a battery of tests the investigator concludes that a particular theory, say T_k, provides the best description of S subject to consistency with N. He therefore tentatively accepts T_k until further information or new theories oblige revision of this decision; or, alternatively, devises an 'immunizing stratagem'[5] which enables him to adhere to the previously accepted theory T_0.

This is the modern myth in applied economics. In the next section I argue that economic theory seldom relates directly to data. Instead economists are required to intermediate theory and data with empirical models. We can test empirical models but cannot directly test theories. Whether or not we may interpret these tests of models as indirectly testing theory is a more complicated question.

3 THEORETICAL AND EMPIRICAL MODELS

Morgan (1988) argues that if theory is to be usable it needs to be translated into empirical models. The distinction between theoretical and empirical models rests on three crucial differences. First, empirical models must be operational in the sense that they must be framed in terms of measurable quantities. In demand theory, for example, we observe purchases and not (in general) consumptions and so empirical demand models should in principle take into account the fact that current purchases may be intended for future consumption. Second, the *ceteris paribus* assumptions will differ between a theory and its empirical counterpart. I argue below that theories and empirical models necessarily make different simplifications. Third, empirical models are necessarily stochastic (any that are not can immediately be rejected) whereas the probabilistic revolution has yet to permeate the entirety of economic theory.

First consider measurement. Spanos (1986, pp. 15–21), who is explicit on the distinction between theoretical and empirical models, refers to this additional layer as the augmentation of the theoretical model with a measurement model. In principle one can subsume this aspect of the difference between theoretical and empirical models into a difference in *ceteris paribus* assumptions. Nevertheless it is worth maintaining it as a separate distinction since there have at various times been economists who have argued the positivist position that theory should itself relate solely to measurable quantities. Schultz (1938) flirted with this view under the influence of Bridgman (1927) – see Morgan (1989, p. 160). But the most strident advocacy of the positivist position in economics is associated with the M^2T group of LSE economists in the early 1960s and in particular with Lipsey.

Lipsey and his collaborators were strongly influenced by Friedman's essay on 'positive economics' (Friedman, 1953) and its practical implementation in his work on the consumption function (Friedman, 1957). An LSE staff seminar on 'Methodology, Measurement and Testing', which became known as the M^2T seminar met continuously from 1959 until Lipsey's departure to the University of Essex in 1963. It was natural that Popper's falsificationist approach, at least in a simplified version, would appeal to them and Lipsey records that they 'learned, and came to accept, much of Popper's views on methodology' from one of Popper's students (de Marchi, 1988).

The M^2T methodological position is set out in Archibald (1959) and Klappholz and Agassi (1959) but received its strongest statement in the introduction to the first edition of Lipsey's famous textbook (Lipsey, 1963). Positive economics, according to Lipsey, is concerned with uncovering empirical regularities, and the Phillips Curve and the theory of the consumption function formed paradigms of how this should be done. Lipsey subsequently moderated his position and it would now generally be acknowledged as extreme to move from the uncontentious statement that economic theories should relate to empirical phenomena to the positivist assertion that they must be framed solely in terms of operationally measurable objects. Once one has granted this, one has admitted the need for a measurement model.

A crucially important element of the measurement model relates to aggregation over agents. The majority of empirical studies in economics are conducted on aggregate data, whereas economic theory is now almost universally based on the decisions of individual optimizing agents. The conditions for an exact correspondence between propositions at a micro level and at the aggregate level are implausibly strong. Consequently an empirical model framed in relation to aggregate data will necessarily differ from the micro-based theory. Perhaps somewhat surprisingly, it is not clear a priori whether theory is best represented by empirical models formulated at the individual or the aggregate level – see Granger (1987, 1988) and Gilbert (1989b).

Consideration of *ceteris paribus* issues reinforces this position. Any modelling exercise must simplify by focusing on certain interactions and ignoring others. It would however be incorrect to suppose either that empirical models are more highly simplified than theoretical models or vice versa. Economic theory considers those aspects of the behaviour of firms, households and governments that can be explained within either an atomistic optimizing or a strategic framework, but it would be foolish to suppose that all societal interactions can be explained in these ways. Changing tastes and technologies are, for example, important in explaining shifts in commodity demands over long periods and in developing a theory it is often useful to simplify other aspects of the economy. Furthermore economic theories are generally timeless and independent of institutional and cultural context.

Haavelmo (1944, pp. 14–15) contrasted the experiments 'we should like to make' in relation to our theories with the 'stream of experiments Nature is steadily turning out from her own enormous laboratory'. Because economists are in general obliged to rely on these 'passive experiments' to test theories (but also more generally since experiments seldom correspond precisely with theory), econometricians are obliged to make different sets of *ceteris paribus* assumptions from those used in developing the theory. A particular dataset will reflect the totality of agents' actions in a particular institutional context and at (or over) a particular time period. The appropriate empirical model may have to combine implications from different theories; to acknowledge the possibility that implications of the theory under investigation may be blurred by failure of the theoretical *ceteris paribus* conditions; and to admit nuisance parameters to account for theoretically extraneous effects.

In those respects empirical models are more complicated than their theoretical counterparts. However they must also and inevitably simplify theory. In discussing demand analysis we shall see two important ways in which this happens. First, theory seldom implies more than general features of the form of functional relationships. The modeller will frequently wish to use linear relationships in order to preserve a relatively low level of paramaterization and to ease computation, but the choice of metric remains. Second the theoretical model may be highly parameterized in other respects. In demand theory there are in principle many more cross-price effects than can be estimated even on the largest datasets, and a major issue is how these may reasonably be simplified (see section 6). The Permanent Income Hypothesis, by contrast, is specified in terms of a very small number of parameters.

That empirical models are stochastic follows from the fact that they simplify theory, approximate functional form and neglect the large number of individually small effects that arise from individual variability and the absence of experimental control. Part of Haavelmo's probabilistic revolution (Haavelmo, 1944; see Morgan, 1989, ch. 8, and de Marchi and Gilbert, 1989, for discussion) was the now standard view that these effects could be subsumed under a probability law. Under relatively weak conditions a Law of Large Numbers will apply, ensuring normality and this forms the basis either for classical hypothesis testing or for Bayesian inference.

Econometricians frequently claim to be testing *theories*. Morgan has suggested that this claim should not be taken literally. All that is being tested is a particular empirical model. However one can concede that a theory can only be tested through the vehicle of an empirical model without granting that theories can never be tested. I shall argue that in demand analysis we are indeed only testing the appropriateness of particular empirical models, while in consumption analysis tests of empirical models are genuine tests of the underlying theory.

4 TESTING DEMAND THEORY ON AGGREGATE DATA

Demand theory and savings theory are both part of the theory of consumer behaviour. In the former, consumers allocate their budget for a particular period over different expenditure categories ('commodities'); in the latter, they allocate expenditure over time. In principle, one can develop a unified theory of inter-temporal and inter-commodity allocation (Attfield and Browning, 1985; Browning *et al.*, 1985), but this turns out not to be very useful. The practical difference between these two arms of consumer theory is that in the current period one is likely to know (at least to a good approximation) one's income and current commodity prices; whereas by contrast future incomes and prices will be subject to considerable uncertainty.

Consideration of uncertainty is therefore central to the analysis of savings behaviour but can safely be neglected in discussion of inter-commodity allocation. If we assume that consumers' utility functions are separable over time we can justify separation of the two allocation problems through a two-stage budgeting procedure (Deaton and Muellbauer, 1980a, ch. 5 and pp. 309–10) in which consumers first make an allocation of expenditure to the current period depending, if they are unconstrained, on inter-temporal relative prices; and at the second stage allocate that expenditure across commodities, looking only at current period relative prices.

Modern demand theory consists of the theory of individual demand and the theory of market demand. At the individual level one derives the demand functions of a utility-maximizing agent facing a specified budget constraint. In the standard case in which the budget constraint is linear one derives the familiar results that the Hicksian demand functions are homogeneous of degree zero in prices, and that their Hessian matrix is symmetric and negative semi-definite (implying that the compensated demand function is downward sloping). The Hicksian demand function for a particular good, say the *i*th, may be written as

$$x_i = h_i(p_1,p_2,\ldots,p_n,m/P) \tag{4.1}$$

where $p_1,p_2,\ldots,p_n$ are the prices of all the commodities considered, m is total money expenditure, which, ignoring saving, we may loosely refer to as 'income', and $P = P(p_1,p_2,\ldots,p_n)$ is a suitable (homogeneous of degree one) price index such that m/P may be interpreted as real income which we may identify with utility.[6] An obvious restriction on these functions is that they must sum to give total expenditure:

$$\sum_{i=1}^{n} p_i h_i(p,m/P) = m \tag{4.2}$$

where p is the vector of prices. Demand theory imposes three further sets of restrictions on the demand functions. First, they must be homogeneous of degree zero in prices:

$$h_i(\lambda p,.) = h_i(p,.) \text{ for all } \lambda > 0. \tag{4.3}$$

Second, the cross-price effects must be symmetric:

$$h_{ij} = \frac{\partial h_i}{\partial p_j} = \frac{\partial h_j}{\partial p_i} = h_{ji} \tag{4.4}$$

Finally, the matrix $H = (h_{ij})$ must be negative semi-definite:

$$a'Ha \leqslant 0, \text{ all } a. \tag{4.5}$$

All of these restrictions are testable given appropriate data, but, since the theory relates at this stage to the individual agent, that implies data at the individual or household level.

The theory of market demand asks what the restrictions implied by the theory at the individual level imply for the aggregate market demand functions. The most simple way in which demand models can be aggregated from an individual basis is to suppose that the economy may be conceived in terms of the decisions of a representative agent maximizing an 'as if' utility function subject to the aggregate budget constraint. This is possible if individual preferences are homothetic since it is irrelevant who, at the margin, has an additional dollar to spend. But it is possible to make a similar argument more generally if agents' utility functions take the PIGL form.[7] The most widely known demand system in this class is the Almost Ideal (AI) model (Deaton and Muellbauer, 1980b), which has the implication that the aggregated equation should contain Theil's (1967) entropy measure of income inequality.

In the light of these remarks, the surprising feature of aggregate demand studies is how well the theory does in 'explaining' data to which it does not obviously apply. The two best-known sets of tests are those conducted by Barten (1969) on Dutch data and Deaton (1974a) on UK data, both using the Rotterdam model. Deaton found that homogeneity is clearly rejected on his sample, but that imposition of symmetry conditional on homogeneity did not lead to a significant further deterioration.[8] Barten had also rejected homogeneity but did not separately test symmetry conditional on homogeneity. Deaton's estimated Hessian matrix was not negative semi-definite, but was 'nearly so'. The puzzling feature of these results is that it is the basic intra-equation postulate of homogeneity that is problematic while the inter-equation restrictions implied by rationality and which do not survive aggregation appear to do little harm.[9] Homogeneity is so central to economists' perceptions of consumer behaviour, both at an individual and an aggregate level, that it was inevitable that the profession would conclude that the simple models employed by Barten and Deaton are inadequate representations of the theory.

There are a number of possibilities. The Barten and Deaton models are not dynamic, and that this might be a problem was indicated by low Durbin–Watson statistics. Anderson and Blundell (1983, 1984) and Muellbauer and Pashardes (1988) have attempted to generalize standard demand models to allow dynamics arising respectively from adjustment costs and habit persistence. Second, it may be incorrect to condition on labour income: Attfield (1985) has shown that the standard test for homogeneity may be reinterpreted as a test for the exogeneity of income in the demand system, and this opens up the route to inclusion of the demand for leisure in the demand system (see, for example, Deaton and Muellbauer, 1980a, pp. 86–96). These two areas of modification arise from the perspective that theoretical demand models have made stronger *ceteris paribus* assumptions than can be sustained in relation to available data. Finally it may be that the failure of homogeneity arises from the omission of income distributional factors from the aggregate equations. This is an aggregation issue since income distribution would only affect individual demands if utility depends on relative consumption levels (as in Duesenberry, 1949). But, at the aggregate level, income distributional effects may interact with income and price effects obscuring parametric restrictions derived from the theoretical model (Stoker, 1986).

If one were to take seriously the view that econometricians have been testing demand theory one might see support for a Kuhnian position. The profession had a strong and universally accepted theory which nevertheless, when carefully tested, gave rise to anomalies. There was no suggestion that the theory should be discarded, and in any case there were no alternative demand theories in the wings. Instead the profession set about investigating a range of immunizing stratagems. However, in the light of the distinction between theoretical and empirical models, it seems more sensible to view this work as a groping towards a satisfactory empirical representation of a theory whose validity has not been called into question.

5 THE MICROECONOMETRICS OF DEMAND

I have already noted that demand equations estimated on aggregate time series data will not in general be directly interpretable into individuals' utility functions unless these utility functions satisfy particular and restrictive conditions. This suggests that, if one is concerned to test demand theory, one should do this on data at the level of the individual agent or household.[10] Econometricians have benefited in the 1980s from the availability of large micro (individual, household and firm) datasets and also from the technology (mathematical and computational) which allows the exploitation of these datasets. Not only does this allow the estimation and testing of demand systems on household data, but also direct comparison of the aggregated and disaggregated estimates.

In practice one finds that, if one is to adequately represent the diversity of behaviour displayed by individual households, we need to take the interactions between demographic characteristics and price and income responses in much more complicated ways than allowed by the models commonly estimated on aggregate data. Rather obviously, expenditure patterns differ between households with and without children. Furthermore, as a consequence of the much greater range of variation of incomes in cross-sectional and panel data than in aggregate time series, one needs to be much more flexible in the way one models income responses than is permitted by standard demand models. The AI model, along with the translog model of Christensen *et al.* (1975) and the Rotterdam model (Barten, 1969), may be classified as 'rank two models' (Gorman, 1981; Lau, 1982), in the sense that the coefficient matrix of the budget terms in the expenditure equations is of rank two, whereas for homothetic systems this matrix is of unit rank (see also Lewbel, 1989). (Thus, in rank one systems, budget shares are independent of income, while in rank two systems they depend linearly on incomes.) However there is now considerable evidence that restricting attention to rank two systems results in considerable distortion of the Engel functions, and that it is necessary to move to rank three systems in which budget shares depend also on quadratic terms in income (Blundell *et al.*, 1989). Their model may in principle be aggregated to give an aggregate equation which is interpretable in terms of the micro parameters, but the data requirements for this are considerable, and the complexity of the interactions implies that any representative agent interpretation of their results is highly tenuous.

Blundell *et al.* (1988, 1989)[11] estimated the AI model on both a panel of micro data and on the aggregated macro data. They found substantial biases in the estimated coefficients from the aggregate relationships in comparison with the microeconometric estimates. Furthermore, and, they suggest, as a consequence of these biases, the aggregate equations exhibited residual serial correlation and rejected the homogeneity restrictions, while the household equations were satisfactory in these respects. Similarly Stoker (1986), who estimated the Linear Expenditure System on US data, argued that neglect of distributional considerations results in coefficient biases and residual serial correlation in the aggregate estimates. These studies suggest that it is difficult to claim that elasticities estimated on aggregate data correspond in any very straightforward way to underlying micro parameters.

In section 4, I argued that at the aggregate level econometricians have not made any serious attempt to reject the homogeneity and symmetry hypotheses. The same is true on micro datasets. Blundell *et al.* (1989, p. 21) comment favourably on their non-rejection of homogeneity, 'which has proved a stumbling block for other demand studies'. They suggest that in aggregate models omitted characteristics may apparently be accounted for by dynamic adjustment or trend-like terms. The symmetry restrictions are less happy and in an earlier version of the same paper (Blundell *et al.*, 1988) they state '. . . our Minimum Chi Squared test of Symmetry Restrictions gives a value of 80·1 for 15 degrees of freedom. This might appear a large number, but on samples of this size rejections at standard significance levels are to be expected.' So, as on aggregate data, satisfaction of the homogeneity and symmetry conditions is a welcome result, but failure to satisfy them does not threaten the theory.

6 THE ROLE OF DEMAND THEORY IN APPLIED DEMAND ANALYSIS

What is the purpose or function of work on consumer demand? The student whose acquaintance with this area is confined to articles in academic journals is likely to come away with the impression that their sole purpose is detached scientific inquiry. But demand studies are also used both in the formation of public-sector tax policy (see, for example, Deaton, 1977) and in private-sector price formation and demand forecasting (see, for example, Gilbert and Jalilian, 1989). In these activities the crucial inputs from demand studies are the size of own and cross-price elasticities. Users of demand theory are therefore interested in *measurement* of parameters of interest.

It is easy to underestimate the role of measurement in economics. One reason for this is that there are no 'economic constants' in the way that there are natural constants. The parameters of our theoretical models depend on tastes, technology and other factors which will not be invariant over time or space. But in any case the applied modeller is confined to estimating the parameters of his empirical model and, as I noted in section 3, there is likely to be considerable latitude in the specification of the empirical model. Furthermore parameters estimated on aggregate data may not be directly comparable with those estimated on micro data. Because empirical models cannot be derived as logical implications of theoretical models, the link between the parameters of the theoretical model and those of empirical models is also complicated.[12] In comparing parameter estimates across models we need to examine whether the *ceteris paribus* assumptions are comparable (the own price elasticity of butter should be higher in a model which controls for the price of margarine than in a model which omits the margarine price) and also whether either model specification in any way restricts the parameter estimates.

The importance for measurement of the 'scientific' contributions to the applied demand literature is in attempting to devise a suitable empirical modelling framework to allow estimation of parameters of policy interest. 'Measurement without theory' is dangerous because it is unclear on what basis the measurements are being made, and therefore it is unclear what is being measured. Theoretical restrictions should structure but not distort our measurements. In section 4, I listed the restrictions – adding up, homogeneity, symmetry, negative definiteness – imposed by the theoretical model on the form of the demand functions. Apart from this, the theoretical model leaves the form of these functions unspecified. The first problem in moving from theory to empirical model is functional specification. Three considerations have been dominant here: ease of imposition of the symmetry condition (4.4), the requirement that the Engel curves $x_i = h_i(.,m/P)$ should be unrestrictive (see Leser, 1963) and a possible integrability requirement that the underlying utility or cost function be recoverable (Deaton and Muellbauer, 1980b).

The second respect in which the theoretical model fails to provide sufficient guidance for the empirical modeller is in structuring the cross-price effects. Ever since Hicks (1939) it has been appreciated that the demand for a particular good depends not only on income and the good's own price but also the prices of all other goods. There is a very large number of goods in a modern economy and this implies a correspondingly large number of cross-price effects. We are restricted, however, to estimating a relatively small set of parameters by limited data availability. Before the availability of powerful computers, computational burden imposed an even tighter constraint. Empirical demand models have therefore either to operate at a very high level of aggregation (so that there are not many prices to consider) or to impose restrictions on the cross-price effects additional to those implied by the theoretical model.

There has been a number of stages in this endeavour. In the pre-demand systems work, best exemplified by Schultz (1938) and Stone (1945, 1954a), the basic object of investigation was the Marshallian demand function $x_i = g_i(p,m)$ in which demand for each commodity is a function of nominal income[13] and the own price. Both authors augmented their equations with time trends and prices of other goods were taken into account through deflation of the own price. Specific consideration of competing goods appears to have been regarded as a second-order effect: in Schultz these do not appear until the two final substantive chapters of his 20-chapter book, and they are completely absent from Stone's initial study (Stone, 1945).[14]

The postwar decades saw a remarkable growth in the general equilibrium approach to economics, significantly under the influence of Hicks (1939) and Samuelson (1947). It was natural therefore that in subsequent work Stone should wish to make the role of the prices of competing goods explicit in his estimated demand functions. To this end Stone (1954a) included the prices of a small number of major substitutes and complements in each equation. However shortage of data points and computational burden (the calculations were all performed by human 'computors' using hand calculators) limited the number of additional regressors he could entertain even when he imposed values on as many of the other coefficients as was possible.[15] Furthermore for some of the equations he did not find it possible to estimate coefficients with the 'correct' sign, and this led to further reduction in the number of price variables included. Therefore, although Stone attempted to grapple with the problem of estimating demand equations within a general equilibrium framework, in retrospect it is clear that a large part of his achievement is to indicate the difficulties inherent in this program.

Modern applied demand theory begins with the Linear Expenditure System (the LES) introduced by Stone (1954b). Stone specified expenditure on each commodity group as a general linear function of total money expenditure and of the nominal prices of each expenditure category. Homogeneity (of degree one) holds by construction. He then derived the most general function of this class which exhibits symmetric cross-price effects. This gives the LES as

$$v_i = p_i x_i = p_i c_i + \beta_i \left[m - \sum_{j=1}^{n} p_j c_j \right] \qquad (4.6)$$

where the parameter c_i (which need not be positive) is sometimes interpreted as the 'committed' quantity of the commodity. The income effects β_i (which must be non-negative to ensure a negative definite substitution matrix) sum to unity. If the model distinguishes n commodity groups, it will therefore contain $2n - 1$ parameters. By contrast, the unrestricted general model contained $n^2 + n$ parameters (n income effects and n^2 price effects). Crucially the own and cross-price effects are all proportional to the income effects and it is this which gives the dramatic reduction in parameterization. Conditional upon a set of estimates for the $\{c_j\}$, (4.6) is linear in c_i and β_i and this suggests an obvious iterative procedure, no longer helpful in an era in which non-linear least squares is routine but essential at a time when calculations were carried out using desktop calculators.

The merit of the LES was that it allowed estimation of a complete set of cross-price effects in a computationally tractable manner from samples with relatively small numbers of observations. Stone is explicit on this point. 'I introduced the [Slutsky] condition, which could not be expected to hold rigorously for a community of consumers, as a plausible means of greatly reducing the number of constants to be estimated' (Gilbert, 1988, p. 27). There is no question for Stone of using the LES as a test of demand theory since he recognized that, whatever the status of the theory at the level of the individual household, aggregation considerations entail that it will not hold exactly in the aggregate. Nevertheless it may hold sufficiently well to enable the estimation of the complete set of cross-price effects.

We now know that this feature of the LES, which appeared so attractive to Stone, is far more restrictive than was initially appreciated. Imposition of the homogeneity and symmetry conditions on a general n commodity demand system reduces the number of parameters to be estimated to $(n - 1)(\frac{1}{2}n + 1)$ (Deaton and Muellbauer, 1980a). The remaining and dramatic reduction to $2n - 1$ in the LES comes from the additional and implicit assumption of additivity of the utility function which is required if symmetry is to be imposed within the apparently innocuous framework assumed by Stone, in which expenditure v is made a linear function of income (total expenditure) and the n prices. Demand systems such as the translog, Rotterdam and AI models have the full set of $(n - 1)(\frac{1}{2}n + 1)$ parameters.

Additivity of the utility function was tested by Byron (1970) on Barten's Dutch data and by Deaton (1974a) on UK data and subsequently in a large number of less important contributions. The tests performed by Byron and Deaton both gave clear rejections of additivity, a result which is maintained in other studies. The LES,[16] along with other additive models, is regarded by the profession as having been rejected. This appears to conform to the falsificationist paradigm. The hypothesis A is proposed, is rejected in a number of independent studies, and is discarded. However, if we are to accept this view, we have to be able to explain why the rejection of additivity was accepted by the profession while the rejections of symmetry and homogeneity, implied by the same studies, were apparently ignored. Equally we need to explain why Blundell *et al.* (1989) were prepared to ignore the rejection of symmetry on their micro dataset but at the same time were concerned to reject rank two specifications of the income terms in favour of rank three specifications.

One possibility would be to argue that homogeneity and symmetry are central to ('in the hard core of') the demand analysis 'research program', while additivity is peripheral. That judgement is easy *ex post*, but was perhaps less easy *ex ante*. What is required is a criterion which will enable us to identify propositions in the hard core of the research program which is independent of the profession's propensity to abandon them. One might argue that, over the past half-century, the dominant paradigm in neoclassical economics has been individual optimization within a general equilibrium context. At the individual level, homogeneity and symmetry of demand equations with a complete set of prices are direct implications of this view; but there is no implication of additivity. This story is comprehensible once one has learnt the technical language of methodological discourse, but it does seem to me to be simpler to say that homogeneity and symmetry are implications of the *theoretical* demand model, while additivity, on the one hand, and the low rank of the income coefficient matrix on the other, are features of certain *empirical* models.

The purpose of the additivity assumption was to reduce the dimensionality of demand systems to manageable proportions. However the admission that the demand for each good depends in principle on the price of all other goods does not imply that many of these effects are individually quantitatively important. One would still expect the income and the own price, together with time trends and so on, to be the most important explanatory variables and for many (policy and forecasting) purposes these will remain the parameters of interest. The cost associated with the additivity hypothesis was that it generated estimates of the cross-price effects only at the expense of distorting the own price effects. Deaton (1974b, p. 355) summarizes the effects as follows:[17]

> Convenience and ease of estimation are purchased at the cost of severe

> distortion of those effects which it is most desirable to measure accurately. On this argument, the extent to which additivity has been used in applied work seriously over-states its real usefulness.

This quotation may be paraphrased as saying that additive empirical models provide unsatisfactory representations of the theoretical model. Blundell *et al.* make the same objection to the estimated Engel functions implied by rank two demand systems. By contrast, there is no suggestion in general that imposition of either homogeneity or symmetry distort estimated elasticities.[18]

Rejection of homogeneity or symmetry are to be interpreted in this framework as specification tests on the empirical model. Since these are necessary implications of the theoretical model, any empirical model which does not have these properties cannot be said adequately to represent the theoretical model, and it is therefore unclear what the purported estimated elasticities are in fact measuring. The rejection may be because of insufficient attention to dynamics, or of failure to allow for the endogeneity of labour income, or of the imposition of too restrictive a form on the Engel curves. From an alternative standpoint these all appear under the heading of 'auxiliary assumptions', but this is unhelpful, since economic theory is not restrictive in these regards, and the applied economist's task is to find (not assume) a structure which does satisfactorily embody the theoretical restrictions. Neither is it correct to see research into empirical demand analysis as a search for immunizing stratagems to shore up empirically rejected theoretical restrictions. Demand theory is in principle rejectable but that will not become a real possibility until there is a viable alternative.

We are therefore fooling ourselves if we believe that we are testing demand theory: for different reasons, the theory cannot be expected to hold, except as a tolerable approximation, at either the aggregate or individual household level. At best, supposed tests of the theory can be interpreted as measures of the degree of approximation attained in a particular empirical model. Van Fraassen (1980, p. 74, emphasis in original) remarks: '. . . theory has a twofold role in experimentation: formulation of the questions to be answered in a systematic and compendious fashion, *and* as a guiding factor in the design of the experiments to answer those questions'. The fundamental objects of modern demand theory are the parameters of the Hicksian demand functions (in the sense that the theory is most simply and succinctly developed in terms of these objects) and the contemporary general equilibrium perspective focuses attention on the parameters representing cross-price effects. Our data arise from the passive experiments of Nature or of the designers of questionnaires. Claimed tests of demand theory should be interpreted as tests of the appropriateness of the design of these passive experiments in relation to the objective of representing theory in a usable empirical model rather like specification tests for serial correlation and so on in standard econometrics. The theory itself is not at issue, since there is no alternative and theoretically unstructured measurement is agreed to be undesirable.

7 THE PERMANENT INCOME HYPOTHESIS

The methodology which underlies work on consumption and savings contrasts starkly with that of applied demand analysis, even though they are both concerned with aspects of the household allocation decision. A major difference between the two is that there is an important stylized fact about consumption which requires explanation. This is the fact that universally (so far as I am aware) consumption is less variable than income but, in the long run, grows more or less proportionately with income. Furthermore this stylized fact is of considerable importance for the framing of macroeconomic policy since it suggests that the private sector may (partially or completely) absorb shocks to the economy, including fiscal 'shocks' administered by the government. Ever since the first criticisms of the Keynesian function, consumption theory has been oriented towards explanation of this phenomenon which has no counterpart in inter-commodity allocational behaviour.

The theory which is most widely held to have successfully reconciled these two aspects of consumers' behaviour is the Permanent Income Hypothesis (PIH). The PIH is one of a number of postwar consumption theories which posit that a household's current consumption will depend only on current wealth, current and expected future income receipts, and current and expected future interest rates (Friedman, 1957). In the standard simple PIH model, all these influences may be summarized through a single measure of 'permanent income', defined as the annuity value of current wealth and expected future receipts. The PIH implies that, once one has conditioned on permanent income, actual income should have no further effect on consumption levels. Consumption is proportional to permanent income and in the long run permanent income and actual income coincide – hence the long-run proportionality result. However variation in permanent income accounts for only a proportion of the variation of actual income, implying that the short-run variability of consumption is less than that of income. The theory has the implication that changes in taxation will only affect consumers' expenditure in so far as they are perceived to be permanent.

The purported sole dependence of consumption on permanent income is a falsifiable proposition provided one has a measure of permanent income. A conventional view is that the fact that permanent income is not directly observable implies that the PIH requires augmentation by 'auxiliary hypotheses', in particular in relation to expectations formation, and that any tests of the PIH must therefore be seen as joint tests of that theory and the auxiliary hypotheses. In the light of the distinction drawn in section 3 between theoretical and empirical models, we may paraphrase this view as saying that any empirical counterpart to the PIH must augment the theoretical model with a measurement model which operationalizes the implications of the theoretical model. One way of doing this in relation to time series data is to attempt to construct a proxy for the unobserved permanent income series. However, in many respects, more powerful tests of the theory are obtained by drawing out the variance and covariance implications of the theoretical model.

The literature on testing the PIH during the 1950s and 1960s is conveniently summarized by Mayer (1972). Considering first tests using models which exploit the covariance implications of the PIH, a number of early studies that looked at the consumption behaviour of ex-wartime prisoners who received reparations are of particular interest. Since, apparently, it is almost certain that these could not have been anticipated, the PIH implies (almost[19]) zero covariance between consumption and windfall receipts. Note that it is sufficient here that the windfalls be regarded as transitory – we do not need to know permanent income. The evidence from these studies points strongly to a higher propensity to consume out of unanticipated income than can be easily explained by the PIH.[20] Furthermore, the same conclusion was obtained in other studies (Liviatan, 1963, being the most famous) which test similar zero covariance assumptions on more conventional samples.

The bulk of the evidence assembled by Friedman himself (Friedman, 1957) relates to consumption and income variances rather than covariances. This evidence is consistent with the PIH, but it does not permit clear discrimination between the PIH and alternative hypotheses which also imply smooth consumption. However Friedman also undertook a time series regression test of the theory, and to do this he proxied permanent income as expected future income estimated by supposing that consumers form expectations adaptively, a hypothesis he took over from Cagan (1956) and which remained best practice in modelling expectations until the mid-1970s.

Friedman appreciated that a theory can only be adequately tested if compared with other theories (see section 2). It was widely recognized that the PIH and the Life Cycle hypothesis (Modigliani and Brumberg, 1955) are not mutually inconsistent. Although conceived as separate theories, both make the same move of dropping the period-by-period budget constraint implicit in the Keynesian consumption function for a longer-term budget constraint. Typically, therefore, they are now thought of as variants of the same hypothesis and it has become general to refer to them jointly as the Life Cycle–Permanent Income Hypothesis (LC–PIH). The strongest rival theory was therefore Duesenberry's (1949) habit persistence model.

The time series version of the habit persistence model related current consumption to current income and highest previous income. At the theoretical level there were major impediments to the widespread acceptance of this model. The model implies an asymmetry between upward and downward movements of income, and has a non-decaying property (a high previous level of income continues to raise consumption for an indefinite period), both of which were regarded as arbitrary (Friedman, 1957, p. 142). More generally, Duesenberry failed to provide a formal grounding of the model in optimization theory. Brown (1952) demonstrated that, if one recasts the model in a partial adjustment framework, which may be rationalized in terms of adjustment costs, Duesenberry's asymmetry disappears, and under the influence of Koyck's (1954) work on distributed lags it came to be believed that the LC–PIH and habit persistence models were operationally (nearly) indistinguishable.[21] Interestingly, when Friedman compared Duesenberry's model with his own (and also a model advocated by Mack, 1948), the habit persistence model gave the superior fit, a result which Friedman dismissed using a bogus argument about simultaneity.[22]

The success of the Permanent Income Hypothesis over these initial decades is due to the fact that, first, it could explain the central stylized facts of consumption; second, it came to subsume rival theories (life cycle, habit persistence) and third, the concept of permanent income was clearly a useful addition to the economist's intellectual toolbox. It remains true, however, that when PIH models were tested they were typically rejected. And although one could find reasons for this in terms of the auxiliary hypotheses, it seems unreasonable to suppose that it was always the auxiliary and not the main hypothesis that was in error. Many economists tended therefore to believe that the PIH provided a good general description of consumption behaviour even if it was too extreme in viewing permanent income as the only argument of the consumption function. But in any case, as indicated above, there were no serious rival theories. Thus, when Mayer (1972) concluded that the evidence favoured a 'standard income theory' in which consumption depends on both permanent and transitory income, but with a lower propensity to consume out of transitory income, this could hardly be said to add to the available explanations of consumers' behaviour. As he himself admitted (ibid., p. 352) 'the success of the standard income theory in reconciling conflicting results is a limited one if one cannot make the theory more specific than to formulate it merely as an in-between theory'.

8 THE RATIONAL EXPECTATIONS–PERMANENT INCOME HYPOTHESIS

The most substantial challenge to the LC–PIH over the past 15 years has arisen from the need to adapt the theory to accommodate the Rational Expectations Hypothesis (REH) and not directly from any conflict with evidence. The REH, due initially to Muth (1961), states that agents' expectations are identical to the mathematical expectations of the quantities in question given the agents' information sets. The theoretical attraction of the REH is that it extends optimization theory into expectations formation. In this way an atomistic optimizing explanation is offered for an aspect of economic behaviour previously modelled in an 'arbitrary' manner. The REH is seen as an improvement over adaptive expectations in the same way that the PIH was seen as an improvement over Keynes's 'fundamental psychological law'. Furthermore it is possible to argue that the REH is consistent with Friedman's view of consumption. Friedman disliked arbitrary assumptions (see Friedman, 1957, pp. 142–3) and actively embraced the atomistic optimization paradigm. His use of adaptive expectations was an innovative step towards a satisfactory theory of expectation formation, but that theory still lay well in the future. It is therefore natural that there should be a movement to integrate the REH into the LC–PIH.[23]

As with the earlier version of the theory, it is in principle possible to test the resulting Rational Expectations–Permanent Income Hypothesis (RE–PIH) either by directly constructing a proxy for permanent income, or by looking at the variance and covariance implications of the theory. In fact the literature has almost totally adopted the latter route. The seminal contribution was that of Hall (1978) who noted that under the REH consumers' forecasts of their future incomes will be unbiased and consequently there will be equal probabilities of upward and downward revisions of permanent income. This implies that permanent income and hence also consumption will be martingale processes; and thus that the (proportionate) change in consumption will have zero covariance with variables in the lagged information set.[24]

Hall's tests were broadly favourable to his representation of the RE–PIH. Following Flavin (1981) attention has tended to focus on the covariance of the change in consumption with lagged income, predicted to be zero by the Hall model. She found a significant covariance implying 'excess sensitivity' of consumption to (lagged) income.[25] The subsequent literature has become diverted into the econometric issue of the appropriate test distribution when the null hypothesis implies a unit root (see Bannerjee and Dolado, 1988, for a summary) and a clear consensus on the substantive question of excess sensitivity has therefore been slow to emerge. However it is probably now true to say that econometricians are agreed that the data does exhibit excess sensitivity (Campbell and Deaton, 1989).

Of more fundamental importance to the RE–PIH is the observation that, on reasonable assumptions about the patterns of income changes over time, the Hall (1978) model fails to yield the stylized fact that consumption is less variable than income. By focusing on the covariance of the change in consumption with variables in the lagged information set, Hall ignored the fact that the RE–PIH also has implications for the covariance of consumption and current income. Suppose, most simply, that income itself follows a random walk. This implies that the perceived change in permanent income is the same as the change in current income, and that the short- and long-run marginal propensities to consume will be the same (Beveridge and Nelson, 1981; Nickell, 1985; Deaton, 1987; Campbell and Deaton, 1989). If changes in income are positively autocorrelated, as appears to be the case, the perceived change in permanent income will exceed the rise in current income since, if there is a rise in current income, further rises will be expected in the following periods. In this case, the short-run marginal propensity to consume will exceed the long-run propensity and the model implies, incorrectly, that the variance of consumption should exceed that of income. The Hall model can only explain the stylized facts of consumption if income changes tend to reverse themselves over time. Campbell and Deaton (1989, p. 358) conclude: 'If permanent income really is smoother than measured income, there is remarkably little sign of it in the aggregate data. . . . We believe that the reason consumption is so smooth is that the permanent income theory is false . . .' The irony of this is that Friedman's original PIH was framed to explain the smoothness of consumption, but the conjunction of the PIH and the REH, a move in sympathy with Friedman's *Weltanschauung*, removes this fundamental implication.

It would be premature to state that the PIH has been rejected by the profession, and in any case there may be a tendency to cling to this theory for non-scientific reasons. Nevertheless there is now a possibility of a substantial shift in professional opinion. The theory has evolved in such a way as to become inconsistent with the phenomenon which provided its original motivation; there are major anomalies; all that is lacking is a rival theory which can account both for the smoothness of consumption and for at least some of the known anomalies. Liquidity constraints are likely to be one element of that story. Join that with the REH and one finds that the possibility that one may be constrained in the future can affect one's current unconstrained savings behaviour. This suggests a precautionary theory of saving.[26]

9 DEMAND ANALYSIS AND CONSUMPTION THEORY COMPARED

The substantive issue of the correctness or otherwise of the PIH is less relevant to the questions I have raised in this chapter than the fact that economists investigating the PIH have clearly seen themselves as attempting to reject (or possibly confirm) an entire theory and not, as I have suggested (sections 4–6) in the context of demand theory, simply a framework for representing a theory. This was true of Friedman and Liviatan, and it remains true in the more recent work which exploits the REH – see the quote from Campbell and Deaton (1989) at the end of section 8.

One might go so far as to argue that consumption theory conforms to a straightforward falsificationist paradigm. The story would be Popperian rather than Lakatosian: the PIH is a central component of postwar macroeconomics and so, if macroeconomics may be characterized as possessing a hard core of inviolable propositions, it should be one of them; yet its rejection is now openly on the cards. By contrast, applied demand analysis is, directly or indirectly, about measurement. When a demand analyst says that he or she is testing a theory he or she is to be interpreted as saying that he or she is testing the appropriateness of a proposed framework for measuring the (agreed) objects of interest. The status of the overall demand analytic framework is not called into question.

I asked in section 1 whether there is a single methodology of applied economics. Examination of these two closely related areas of the discipline suggests that any account of economic methodology that attempts to embrace both will be too general to be useful.[27] One possibility would be to stop at this point: demand analysis is unlike consumption analysis, just as economics is unlike sociology and the social sciences are unlike the physical sciences. However the possible implication that 'anything goes' may be taken as suggesting that methodologies are accidental. On the contrary, methodologies are to a large extent implicitly defined by the questions being addressed.

The central element of both demand theory and consumption theory is the view that consumers make their allocational decisions by maximizing expected utility, subject to a budget constraint. Both assume separability of the utility function over time and, in simple expositions, either separability between goods and leisure or exogenous labour supply. All of these assumptions are substantive and may therefore be incorrect, but they do not enable us to drive any wedge between the two theories. A central problem in demand theory is the large number of relative prices that are considered, whereas standard expositions of consumption theory contain only a single relative price (the interest rate, generally taken to be constant and parametric).[28] However, if there were evidence that inter-temporal substitutability were sufficiently high and the term structure of interest rate sufficiently informative, one could generalize the PIH to include inter-temporal relative prices. So it is also difficult to argue that it is the different role attributed to relative prices that generates the difference in methodological approach. Turning to income effects, it is true that the PIH assumes homotheticity. This would be a very bad assumption in relation to allocation over commodities since it would imply that all goods exhibit unit income elasticity of demand; but it is not obviously a stupid assumption in relation to allocation over time, and does not appear to be enormously contentious.

At the theoretical level, therefore, it may appear difficult to provide a reasonable account of the differences in methodological approach that I have documented in sections 4–8. However the origin of these differences is to be found not in the theories themselves but in the context in which the theories seek to explain behaviour. Both demand theory and consumption theory are building-blocks in the Walrasian general equilibrium edifice. In addition their empirical validity depends on the well-functioning of the entire system. In particular, both theories will misrepresent behaviour if there is rationing. In consumption theory, rationing takes the form of liquidity constraints, and I have noted that the possibility of being constrained in the future can affect the agent's current behaviour even if he or she is currently unconstrained. In demand theory, if a good is rationed, demand for unrationed goods will depend on the (appropriately defined) shadow price of the rationed good, so again the effects of rationing generalize across the system (Deaton and Muellbauer, 1980a, pp. 109–14).

In the developed free enterprise economies rationing of goods (with the possible exception of housing) is not a serious issue; however the question of inter-temporal rationing is more problematic. This question is discussed under the heading of 'perfect capital markets'. In a perfect capital market all agents can borrow and lend as much as they choose at the current rate of interest. It is not disputed that this assumption is unrealistic; nor that adverse selection and moral hazard considerations make the concept of a 'perfect capital market' unachievable (Stiglitz and Weiss, 1981). The question is whether market imperfections of this sort 'matter' in the explanation of (usually aggregate) behaviour. Economists with faith in the ascendancy of markets suggest that, if one can explain behaviour without invoking 'market imperfections', it is better to do this – an implicit appeal to Occam's razor. The suggestion is that casual observation of constrained behaviour gives an exaggerated impression of its importance. Others remain unconvinced.

For my present purpose it is sufficient to note that, whether or not capital market imperfections do have a major impact on savings behaviour, temporal separability of the utility function is sufficient to ensure that commodity demands conditional on total current expenditure and prices will not be affected. The difference therefore between demand theory and consumption theory is that the PIH involves an additional contextual hypothesis not required in demand modelling. This additional hypothesis cannot be derived from a theory of optimizing behaviour but rather asserts that the general optimization-based economic equilibrium is such as will ensure the preconditions for its own existence: 'if all markets exist and all agents are price takers with the result that allocations are Paretian, then consumers' inter-temporal decisions will be identical to those they would declare to the Walrasian auctioneer'. In other words, belief in the PIH requires that one believe that the optimization framework provides a characterization not only of how agents make inter-temporal allocation decisions but also how the whole of the remainder of the economy functions. This is very close to Friedman's (1953) 'as if' argument for the perfect competition model. It is not unreasonable to characterize such assertions as ideological.

The difference in empirical methodology between demand analysis and consumption analysis is seen therefore to stem from the difference in the contextual assumptions required by the two theories. Both demand theory and the theory of the consumption function simplify, as must any theory, but in demand theory the simplifications are motivated by the need to reduce the scale of the modelling enterprise, whereas in consumption theory they are motivated at least in part by a desire to generate a particular set of implications. In demand theory these simplifications are part of the empirical model, while in consumption theory they are part of the theoretical model. It follows that in testing demand theory we are testing for the appropriateness of an empirical model, and that our tests have the character of specification tests, while in consumption theory tests of the empirical model are tests of the theoretical model. This is why the PIH can be rejected while demand theory (currently) cannot. That an optimizing framework, or even a rational expectations framework, is required is not at issue in either case, so in that sense the fundamental model is never a subject of test. But the PIH is only one theory that is available within this general framework and is obtained through the assumption that a particular set of potential interactions may be ignored. The policy implications of that position are such that it will not be abandoned easily by its defenders.

Tests of consumption models therefore genuinely are tests of an underlying theory. By contrast, in the purely scientific activity of demand analysis, purported tests of theories are only tests of the extent to which different models represent the common consensual theory. Discussion of the methodology of applied economics cannot ignore the role of political economy in applied econometrics.

10 CONCLUSION

Empirical models intermediate theory and data. In the first instance, one is always testing an empirical model and not a theory. The interesting question is the implication of rejection of an empirical model for the status of the theoretical model. In demand analysis econometricians have been happy to reject additive and rank two demand systems in favour of more general alternatives, but regard satisfaction of the homogeneity and symmetry restrictions as specification tests on the empirical model. For example, rejection of additivity implies that the additive LES is an unacceptable empirical model, whereas rejection of homogeneity in a particular empirical model implies that this is an inadequate representation of the theoretical model in which homogeneity does hold. Here the theoretical model is not being tested. By contrast, when economists test particular empirical models embodying the PIH, the theoretical PIH model is at issue. It is arguable that, whether or not there are crucial experiments in the physical sciences, there will never be a 'crucial test' in econometrics, but the cumulative effect of a large number of negative tests of the RE–PIH empirical models is such as to cast doubt on the PIH itself. So the answer to the question, 'Do economists test theories?' is that in certain cases (for example, consumption analysis) we do, and in certain cases (demand analysis) we do not.

There is a reason for this difference. The homogeneity and symmetry restrictions in demand theory are, at the level of the individual agent, direct implications of individualistic optimization in the context of a free market. There is no significant rival paradigm for the description of consumers' allocations over goods in the developed market economies. By contrast, the PIH requires us to believe not only that agents make their inter-temporal allocational decisions in the same way, itself a more controversial proposition since it requires strong assumptions about choice under uncertainty, but also that the outcomes of these decisions are 'as if' capital markets were 'perfect'. Alternative theories which acknowledge liquidity constraints do not require this assumption. Since there are both strong theoretical and empirical reasons for supposing that capital markets are at least to some degree imperfect it is possible to discard the PIH without abandoning the optimization paradigm.

The comparison of demand analysis and consumption analysis therefore teaches us that whether or not a theory can be tested depends at least in part upon the character of the theory. But in view of my opening remarks on diversity, I would be wise to avoid concluding that this comparison of two closely related areas can encapsulate the whole of economic methodology.

NOTES

1. I shall not concern myself in this chapter with questions relating to the methodology of economic theory.
2. He goes on to say that this is 'a bit of an overstatement'.
3. Also, less explicitly, by Davidson *et al.* (1978).
4. This is the majority view. A vocal minority of econometricians, particularly in the United States, denies the validity of these testing procedures and prefers to look for an objective basis for inference within the necessarily subjective framework of Bayesian statistics – see e.g. Hill (1976) and Zellner (1978).
5. Popper (1972, p. 30), Blaug (1980, p. 25).
6. Since utility functions are only defined up to a monotonic transformation.
7. The Price Independent Generalized Linear class – see Deaton and Muellbauer (1980a, 1980b).
8. It is not possible to impose symmetry without homogeneity.
9. Compare Schultz (1938, p. 633) who estimated demand functions for beef and pork and found that the cross-price effects were 'in much better agreement with the theory than we had a right to expect, considering the errors in the data and the nature of

the assumptions we have been compelled to make'. The agreement was in fact less good when mutton was added. However Schultz was only able to calculate the cross-price effects from the unrestricted estimates; he was not able either to impose or to test the restrictions.

10. However there is an argument that effects which are important in the aggregate may be relatively difficult to identify on individual data – see Granger (1987, 1988). This view was anticipated by Hicks (1956, p. 55) who wrote: 'To assume the representative consumer acts like an ideal consumer is a hypothesis worth testing; to assume an actual person, the Mr. Brown or Mr. Jones who lives round the corner, does in fact act in such a way does not deserve a moment's consideration.' (Hicks uses 'ideal consumer' in the sense of the representative consumer of aggregation theory and 'representative consumer' in the sense of Quetelet's average consumer.) I discuss this issue in Gilbert (1989b).
11. The results of Blundell *et al.* (1988) are summarized in Blundell (1988).
12. This poses a major conceptual difficulty for Bayesian econometricians.
13. Not available to Schultz who used activity variables in certain equations.
14. Although the inclusion of the prices (or quantities) of competing goods was standard in American agricultural economics in the 1930s – see Morgan (1989, pp. 153–4).
15. In particular, he imposed (and tested) homogeneity and imposed (but did not test) the income elasticity from a separate household budget data study – see Gilbert (1988) for discussion.
16. Byron tested additivity within a log-linear model, and Deaton within the Rotterdam model, although he also compared his results with the LES. Strictly, therefore, the tests do not apply to the LES although Deaton's estimates for the LES were very similar to those for the rejected additive version of the Rotterdam model.
17. This is because additivity imposes near proportionality on the relationship between income and own price elasticities, whereas unrestricted estimates show no such tendency.
18. See Gilbert and Jalilian (1989) for an exception. This study involved the estimation of cross-elasticities of demand between bus and underground rail transportation in London. We found that imposition of symmetry did generate a severe distortion since unrestricted estimates clearly showed bus travel to be much more price-sensitive than rail travel, while symmetry required that the elasticities be nearly equal. We argued that this failure arose from lack of data on the price of an alternative travel mode (private automobiles).
19. The covariance would be zero if the recipients were infinitely lived, or if they valued their children's expected utility streams.
20. Kreinin (1961), Landsberger (1970); see also Bodkin (1963). There is a large literature on expenditure out of windfall receipts – see Mayer (1972, pp. 93–106) who attaches less significance to this evidence.
21. Wallis (1969, 1973). Application of the Koyck transformation to the PIH generates a moving average error which might permit discrimination. This equation depends on the adaptive expectations interpretation of the LC–PIH and adjustment cost interpretation of habit persistence, neither of which currently finds favour. Duesenberry's discussion clearly indicates that he saw utility as deriving from consumption relative both to previous consumption and to peer group consumption. This theory has been elaborated in Spinnewyn (1979, 1981) and Muellbauer and Pashardes (1988).
22. See Friedman (1957, pp. 148–50). The argument is bogus because his own model is also vulnerable to simultaneity bias. See also Mayer (1972, pp. 77–81).
23. In fact it is possible to justify adaptive expectations in terms of the REH by supposing that consumers, like econometricians, are obliged to estimate their permanent incomes using their actual income streams as data. Actual income differs randomly from permanent income. Confronted by a rise in actual income, the consumer must disentangle this into a component reflecting the probable rise in permanent income and a remainder reflecting this random error. Simple Kalman

filtering theory implies that the proportion of the change in income that should be regarded as permanent is given by the ratio of the variance of permanent income to the variance of total income (Meinhold and Singpurwalla, 1983). This story is somewhat artificial: it is as if an outside agency is deciding each consumer's permanent income which he or she has to estimate from his or her actual income. It is more straightforward to assume that consumers evaluate permanent income as the discounted value of expected future receipts given the known generating process or actual income. Sargent (1977) showed that this would be equivalent to adaptive expectations if income follows a particular and unlikely moving average process.

24. This version of the proposition differs slightly from that in Hall by taking the utility function to be negative exponential.
25. See also Muellbauer (1983) and Campbell and Mankiw (1987).
26. See Deaton (1989). To see that the precautionary theory is distinct both from simple liquidity theories and from the PIH consider a change in the expected variance of next period's income for a consumer who is unconstrained in the current period. This leaves permanent income unaffected, so neither the liquidity theory nor the PIH predicts any change in current consumption; however a precautionary saver will wish to increase his/her savings.
27. The quotation from Keynes at the start of the chapter, which may be paraphrased as 'economics is a bag of tools', is right about the microeconomic topic but, ironically, wrong about the macroeconomic topic, while Blaug's emphasis on prediction hits the second target but misses the first.
28. Models which interpret consumption as consumption of non-durables sometimes (correctly) include the relative price of durables and non-durables.

REFERENCES

Anderson, G.J. and Blundell, R.W. (1983), 'Testing restrictions in a dynamic model of consumers' expenditure', *Review of Economic Studies*, **50**, pp. 397–410.

—— (1984), 'Consumer non-durables in the U.K.: a dynamic demand system', *Economic Journal*, **94**, Supp., pp. 35–44.

Archibald, G.C. (1959), 'The state of economic science', *British Journal for the Philosophy of Science*, **10**, pp. 58–69.

Attfield, C.L.F. (1985), 'Homogeneity and endogeneity in systems of demand equations', *Journal of Econometrics*, **27**, pp. 197–209.

Attfield, C.L.F. and Browning, M.J. (1985), 'A differential demand system, rational expectations and the life cycle hypothesis', *Econometrica*, **53**, pp. 31–48.

Bannerjee, A. and Dolado, J. (1988), 'Tests of the Life Cycle–Permanent Income Hypothesis in the presence of random walks: asymptotic theory and small sample interpretations', *Oxford Economic Papers*, **40**, pp. 610–33.

Barten, A.P. (1969), 'Maximum likelihood estimation of a complete system of demand equations', *European Economic Review*, **1**, pp. 7–73.

Beveridge, S. and Nelson, C.R. (1981), 'A new approach to decomposition of economic time series data into permanent and transitory components with particular attention to measurement of the business cycle', *Journal of Monetary Economics*, **7**, pp. 151–74.

Blaug, M. (1980), *The Methodology of Economics* (Cambridge: Cambridge University Press).

Blundell, R.W. (1988), 'Consumer behaviour: theory and empirical evidence', *Economic Journal*, **98**, pp. 16–65.
Blundell, R.W., Pashardes, P. and Weber, G. (1988), 'What do we learn about consumer demand patterns from micro-data?', Institute for Fiscal Studies, Working Paper No. W88/10.
—— (1989), 'What do we learn about consumer demand patterns from micro-data?', paper given to IFS–LBS conference 'Aggregation in Economic Modelling', October 1989.
Bodkin, R. (1963), 'Windfall income and consumption: a comment', *American Economic Review*, **52**, pp. 445–7.
Bridgman, P. (1927), *The Logic of Modern Physics* (New York: Macmillan).
Brown, T.M. (1952), 'Habit persistence and lags in consumer behavior', *Econometrica*, **29**, pp. 355–71.
Browning, M.J., Deaton, A.S. and Irish, M. (1985), 'A profitable approach to labor supply and commodity demands over the life cycle', *Econometrica*, **53**, pp. 503–43.
Byron, R.P. (1970), 'A simple method for estimating demand systems under separable utility assumptions', *Review of Economic Studies*, **37**, pp. 261–74.
Cagan, P. (1956), 'The monetary dynamics of hyperinflation', in M. Friedman (ed.), *Studies in the Quantity Theory of Money* (Chicago: University of Chicago Press).
Campbell, J.Y. and Deaton, A.S. (1989), 'Why is consumption so smooth?', *Review of Economic Studies*, **56**, pp. 357–74.
Campbell, J.Y. and Mankiw, N.G. (1987), 'Permanent income, current income, and consumption', NBER Working Paper, 2436.
Christensen, L.R., Jorgenson, D.W. and Lau, L.J. (1975), 'Transcendental logarithmic utility functions', *American Economic Review*, **65**, pp. 367–83.
Davidson, J.E.H. and Hendry, D.F. (1981), 'Interpreting econometric evidence: the behaviour of consumers' expenditure in the UK', *European Economic Review*, **16**, pp. 177–92.
Deaton, A.S. (1974a), 'The analysis of consumer demand in the United Kingdom, 1900–1970', *Econometrica*, **42**, pp. 341–67.
—— (1974b), 'A reconsideration of the empirical implications of additive preferences', *Economic Journal*, **84**, pp. 338–48.
—— (1977), 'Equity, efficiency and the structure of indirect taxation', *Journal of Public Economics*, **8**, pp. 299–312.
—— (1987), 'Life-cycle models of consumption: Is the evidence consistent with the theory?', in T.F. Bewley (ed.), *Advances in Econometrics*, II (Cambridge: Cambridge University Press).
—— (1989), 'Saving and liquidity constraints', Fisher–Schultz Lecture, European Meeting of the Econometric Society, Munich, September 1989.
Deaton, A.S. and Muellbauer, J. (1980a), *Economics and Consumer Behaviour* (Cambridge: Cambridge University Press).
—— (1980b), 'An Almost Ideal Demand System', *American Economic Review*, **70**, pp. 312–32.
Duesenberry, J.S. (1949), *Income, Saving, and the Theory of Consumer Behavior* (Cambridge, Mass.: Harvard University Press).
Flavin, M. (1981), 'The adjustment of consumption to changing expectations about future income', *Journal of Political Economy*, **89**, pp. 974–1009.

Friedman, M. (1953), 'The methodology of positive economics', in M. Friedman, *Essays in Positive Economics* (Chicago: Chicago University Press).
—— (1957), *A Theory of the Consumption Function* (Princeton: Princeton University Press).
Gilbert, C.L. (1986), 'Professor Hendry's econometric methodology', *Oxford Bulletin of Economics and Statistics*, **48**, pp. 283–307.
—— (1988), 'Richard Stone and the emergence of modern econometrics', Institute of Economics and Statistics, Oxford, processed.
—— (1989a), 'LSE and the British approach to time series econometrics', *Oxford Economic Papers*, **41**, pp. 102–28.
—— (1989b), 'Economic theory and econometric models', *Economic and Social Review*, **21**, pp. 1–25.
Gilbert, C.L. and Jalilian, H. (1989), 'The demand for travel and the demand for travelcards on the London Regional Transport network', Institute of Economics and Statistics, Oxford, Applied Economics Discussion Paper 83.
Gorman, W.M. (1981), 'Some Engel curves', in A.S. Deaton (ed.), *Essays in the Theory and Measurement of Consumer Behaviour* (Cambridge: Cambridge University Press).
Granger, C.W.J. (1987), 'Implications of aggregation with common factors', *Econometric Theory*, **3**, pp. 208–22.
—— (1988), 'Aggregation of time series – a survey', Federal Bank of Minneapolis, Institute for Empirical Macroeconomics, Discussion Paper 1.
Haavelmo, T. (1944), 'The probability approach to econometrics', *Econometrica*, **12**, Supplement.
Hacking, I. (1983), *Representing and Intervening* (Cambridge: Cambridge University Press).
Hall, R.E. (1978), 'Stochastic implications of the Life Cycle–Permanent Income Hypothesis: theory and evidence', *Journal of Political Economy*, **86**, pp. 971–87.
Harvey, A.C. (1981), *The Econometric Analysis of Time Series* (Deddington: Philip Allan).
Hicks, J.R. (1939), *Value and Capital* (Oxford: Clarendon Press).
—— (1956), *A Revision of Demand Theory* (Oxford: Clarendon Press).
Hill, B.M. (1986), 'Some subjective Bayesian considerations in the selection of models', *Econometric Reviews*, **4**, pp. 191–246.
Klappholz, K. and Agassi, J. (1959), 'Methodological prescriptions in economics', *Economica*, **26**, pp. 60–74.
Koyck, L.M. (1954), *Distributed Lags and Investment Analysis* (Amsterdam: North-Holland).
Kreinin, M. (1961), 'Windfall income and consumption – additional evidence', *American Economic Review*, **51**, pp. 388–90.
Landsberger, M. (1970), 'Restitution receipts, household savings and consumption behavior in Israel', Jerusalem, Research Department, Bank of Israel.
Lau, L.J. (1982), 'A note on the fundamental theorem of exact aggregation', *Economic Letters*, **9**, pp. 119–26.
Leamer, E.E. (1983), 'Let's take the con out of econometrics', *American Economic Review*, **73**, pp. 31–43.
Leser, C.E.V. (1963), 'Forms of Engel functions', *Econometrica*, **31**, pp. 694–703.

Lewbel, A. (1989), 'A demand system rank theorem', *Econometrica*, **57**, pp. 701–6.
Lipsey, R.G. (1963), *Introduction to Positive Economics* (London: Weidenfeld & Nicolson).
Liviatan, N. (1963), 'Tests of the Permanent-Income Hypothesis based on a reinterview savings survey', in C.F. Christ *et al.*, *Measurement in Economics* (Stanford: Stanford University Press).
Mack, R.P. (1948), 'The direction of change in income and the consumption function', *Review of Economics and Statistics*, **30**, pp. 239–58.
de Marchi, N. (1988), 'Popper and the LSE economists', in N. de Marchi (ed.), *The Popperian Legacy in Economics* (Cambridge: Cambridge University Press).
de Marchi, N. and Gilbert, C.L. (1989), 'Introduction', *Oxford Economic Papers*, **41**, pp. 1–12.
Mayer, T. (1972), *Permanent Income, Wealth and Consumption* (Berkeley: University of California Press).
—— (1980), 'Economics as hard science: realistic goal or wishful thinking', *Economic Inquiry*, **18**, pp. 165–78.
McCloskey, D. (1985), *The Rhetoric of Economics* (Madison: University of Wisconsin Press).
Meinhold, R.J. and Singpurwalla, N.D. (1983), 'Understanding the Kalman Filter', *American Statistician*.
Mizon, G.E. (1984), 'The encompassing principle in econometrics', in D.F. Hendry and K.F. Wallis (eds), *Econometrics and Quantitative Economics* (Oxford: Blackwell).
Mizon, G.E. and Richard, J.-F. (1986), 'The encompassing principle and its application to non-nested hypotheses', *Econometrica*, **54**, pp. 657–78.
Modigliani, F. and Brumberg, R. (1955), 'Utility analysis and the consumption function: an interpretation of the cross-section data', in K.K. Kurihara (ed.), *Post Keynesian Economics* (London: George Allen & Unwin).
Morgan, M.S. (1988), 'Finding a satisfactory empirical model', in N. de Marchi (ed.), *The Popperian Legacy in Economics* (Cambridge: Cambridge University Press).
—— (1989), *The History of Econometric Ideas* (Cambridge: Cambridge University Press).
Muellbauer, J. (1983), 'Surprises in the consumption function', *Economic Journal*, **93**, Supplement, pp. 34–50.
Muellbauer, J. and Pashardes, P. (1988), 'Tests of dynamic specification and homogeneity in demand systems', Institute for Fiscal Studies, Discussion Paper 88/6.
Muth, J.F. (1961), 'Rational expectations and the theory of price movements', *Econometrica*, **29**, pp. 315–35.
Nickell, S.J. (1985), 'Error correction, partial adjustment and all that: an expository note', *Oxford Bulletin of Economics and Statistics*, **47**, pp. 119–31.
Popper, K. (1972), *Objective Knowledge: An Evolutionary Approach* (London: Oxford University Press).
Samuelson, P.A. (1947), *Foundations of Economic Analysis* (Cambridge, Mass.: Harvard University Press).

Sargent, T.J. (1977), 'Observations on improper methods of simulating and teaching Friedman's time-series consumption model', *International Economic Review*, **18**, pp. 445–62.

Schultz, H. (1938), *The Theory and Measurement of Demand* (Chicago: University of Chicago Press).

Spanos, A. (1986), *Statistical Foundations of Econometric Modelling* (Cambridge: Cambridge University Press).

Spinnewyn, F. (1979), 'The cost of consumption and wealth in a model with habit formation', *Economics Letters*, **2**, pp. 145–8.

—— (1981), 'Rational habit formation', *European Economic Review*, **15**, pp. 91–109.

Stiglitz, J.E. and Weiss, A. (1981), 'Credit rationing in markets with imperfect information', *American Economic Review*, **73**, pp. 393–411.

Stoker, T.M. (1986), 'Simple tests of distributional effects on macroeconomic equations', *Journal of Political Economy*, **94**, pp. 763–95.

Stone, J.R.N. (1945), 'The analysis of market demand', *Journal of the Royal Statistical Society*, **108**, pp. 286–382.

—— (1954a), *The Measurement of Consumers' Expenditure and Behaviour in the United Kingdom, 1920–38*, vol. 1 (Cambridge: Cambridge University Press).

—— (1954b), 'Linear expenditure systems and demand analysis: an application to the pattern of British demand', *Economic Journal*, **64**, pp. 511–27.

Theil, H. (1967), *Economics and Information Theory* (Amsterdam: North-Holland).

Van Fraassen, B. (1980), *The Scientific Image* (Oxford: Clarendon Press).

Wallis, K.F. (1969), 'Some recent developments in applied econometrics; dynamic models and simultaneous equation systems', *Journal of Economic Literature*, **7**, pp. 771–96.

—— (1973), *Topics in Applied Econometrics* (London: Gray-Mills).

Zellner, A. (1988), 'Bayesian analysis in econometrics', *Journal of Econometrics*, **37**, pp. 27–50.

COMMENT ON GILBERT

Marjorie B. McElroy*

Gilbert's chapter is stimulating, and his own methodology is sensible and refreshing. He starts by observing what investigators do and then works backwards to ascertain the methodology. He examines two related areas, demand systems and the permanent income hypothesis (PIH). Based on the fact that the PIH is in danger of rejection, whereas the theory underlying demand systems is not, he concludes that different methodologies are being used. I remain, however, unconvinced.

To express my views, I will use the framework of Jinbang Kim (in this volume). Underlying both demand systems and the PIH is the *fundamental general theory* that individuals are constrained optimizing agents (that is, individuals can order bundles, they prefer more to less, and so forth, and they do the best they can, given whatever constraints they face). Call this FT, for fundamental theory. This is the primordial ooze that gives rise to and defines neoclassical economics (as opposed to, say, Marxian or radical economics). In informal conversations, when a theorem or insight is called 'deep', it is because it seems to be created directly from the ooze, or helps us see the ooze better – the ooze always being there, slipping with glacial slowness, as revealed by the small lights we shine on it.

Now, just as the real world is too complex to understand in its entirety, the FT is too general to comprehend in its entirety. To use the FT, we have specific theories, the aim of which is to abstract the essence of the problem of interest and cast away all excess baggage. Call these specific theories ST's. Finally we have auxiliary assumptions and measurement rules that get us to empirical models of these specific theories. Call these empirical models EM's.

Perhaps the best illuminated part of the primordial ooze is the one period problem of maximizing (well behaved, twice differentiable) utility, subject to a linear budget constraint. The appropriate separability assumption allows us surgically to remove this problem and examine it. We all know the standard derivation of a system of demand equations therefrom, as well as the 'deep' theorem due to Samuelson (1947). This theorem states an if and only if relationship between the existence of the utility function and the symmetry (S) and negative semidefiniteness (N) of the substitution matrix. Hence, as Samuelson pointed out, S and N of the substitution matrix *exhaust* the empirical

* My thanks to Neil de Marchi for helpful conversations and comments.

content of utility theory. Homogeneity, for example, follows from the S and N of the substitution matrix.[1] Now for any demand system it is a straightforward matter to compute the substitution matrix (possibly different for every price–income combination) and to check for S and N, and hence to check whether the system could have arisen from constrained utility maximization. Samuelson showed us that the primordial ooze covers systems of demand equations and can be viewed there in the form of the S and N of the substitution matrix.

Samuelson's result sounds 'directly applicable' to real world phenomena, but let me emphasize, as I think Kim would, that there are many steps to take and additional assumptions to make before it can be applied. I view the primordial ooze as containing statements of the sort, 'If preferences can be represented by continuous, twice differentiable and well-behaved utility functions, and if preferences are time separable for the appropriately defined period of time, then the associated demand system will exhibit an S and N substitution matrix.' The ooze, however, does not contain rules for when the if part of such statements are fulfilled. Nor does it specify what or who is the appropriate consumer unit to whom we will ascribe the utility function (an individual, a family, an entire state?). Nor does it specify the objects of choice.[2] Nor does it specify how to treat consumer durables or whether or not labour supply need be endogenous. Furthermore all of these choices are constrained by the content of existing data sets which are, in turn, constrained by the costs of gathering data and the interests of the gatherers.

Suppose one has made all of the above decisions. One is still left with the choice of functional form and of embedding that functional form in a stochastic framework.[3] Historically, there have been three routes here: (1) start with a demand or expenditure system and impose on it the constraints implied by utility theory (Stone's original statement of the linear expenditure system (LES) and the Rotterdam models arose this way); (2) start with a specific functional form for utility and derive the associated demand system (Stone's LES can be derived this way from the Stone–Geary, Klein–Rubin utility function, but this method often proves intractable); (3) begin with an indirect utility function with the appropriate properties and derive the associated demand system via Roy's identity. (By approximating the indirect utility with transcendental functions, this method resulted in the flexible functional forms, including the translog approximations. More recently other series approximations have been proposed; see Gallant (1984) and Barnett *et al.* (1988).) Inherent in methods (1) and (2) are built-in restrictions on the price–quantity interactions or, equivalently, on the underlying utility function. For example, the LES rules out complements, and the corresponding utility function rules out Houthakker's specific substitution effects.[4] Inherent in method (3) is the problem that the approximation only applies at a point and may be very bad as we drift away from that point.

Now the point of reviewing these varieties of demand systems is to remind us that, as we pass from the beautiful world of abstraction and 'if . . ., then . . .' to the world of application, we quickly descend into a world involving judgements about trade-offs. Hence, when we test the symmetry (*S*) and negativity (*N*) of a substitution matrix, we are jointly testing the adequacy of some specific theory, say the LES, *along with S* and *N*. Upon rejection, we throw away the LES, not the *S* and *N*. We do this because *S* and *N* are part of the Fundamental Theory, and the LES is not. The LES is only a specific theory, shown to be not as useful an approximation as some had originally hoped. Furthermore we do not throw it away for all time and all data sets. Every graduate student still learns the LES as a standard demand system, albeit with emphasis on its limitations. Further, 20 years after it was pretty much 'rejected', one still sees it being used when investigators have inadequate data to estimate more flexible models (for example, housing studies by Hammond (1987) and daycare studies by Robins (1990)).

I would say that the LES, the Rotterdam models and so forth are all instances of STs. Likewise I would also say that the PIH, the Modigliani and Brumberg life-cycle model and so forth are also instances of STs. For the PIH this is readily documented by returning to Friedman's *A Theory of the Consumption Function*. The title itself testifies to the fact that it is one of several (or even many) possible theories. Chapter 2, 'The Implications of the Pure Theory of Consumer Behavior', is so convincing precisely because it begins in the primordial ooze with a graph of this period's versus next period's consumption – of C_1 vs C_2 (carefully pointing out that a prior maximization which enables us to define C_1 and C_2 (and that also embodies *S* and *N*!) lies elsewhere in the ooze). He shines light on the ooze to convince us that we already 'knew' about 'permanent income' and 'permanent consumption' and uses only some accounting identities and the mild restriction of quasi-concavity of utility to arrive at permanent consumption as a function of permanent income and the interest rate. He then argues that there is no a priori case that current consumption is more highly valued than future consumption or vice versa and that even the introduction of uncertainty does not give a prior reason for tipping the balance one way or the other. So he tentatively postulates homotheticity of the indifference map – making permanent consumption proportional to permanent income with the constant of proportionality depending on the interest rate and the ratio of wealth held in the form of human capital to wealth held in other forms. He takes time to point out that there are different forms of wealth, some more liquid than others, and that each may have its own interest rate, but that the biggest distinction is between human (the least liquid by far) and non-human forms. Hence for simplicity the PIH recognizes only these two types of wealth in the factor of proportionality. Friedman repeatedly makes it clear that his hypothesis is tentative and arises by starting with the ooze and layering on simplifying assumptions that he hopes will catch the essence of his specific problem while jettisoning all possible baggage short of imposing obviously ridiculous restrictions. In his words, 'we shall, therefore, tentatively accept it [the homotheticity of preferences], subject as always, of course to the possibility that empirical evidence will be discovered that turns out to be inconsistent with it and that will therefore *require complicating the hypothesis*' (emphasis added). It is clear from the way Friedman presented the PIH that he intended it as an ST, and one can attack it without making any alteration to the primordial ooze.

In concluding I would like to update this discussion of testing the PIH. A decade ago Robert Hall (1978) profoundly changed macroeconomics by suggesting that, by replacing estimation of the consumption function *per se* with estimation of optimality conditions for a representative agent, we could immunize our empirical results from the Lucas critique. There followed a flurry of estimated Euler equations for representative agents with rational expectations. Deaton (1987) showed that, when the income process has a unit root, the PIH has a hard time accounting for the observed smoothness of consumption. At a recent NBER conference, Campbell and Mankiw (1989) proposed explaining the time series data on consumption, income and interest rates by the coexistence of two types of consumers – half of income goes to consumers who obey the PIH and half goes to households who simply consume current income (rule-of-thumb households) – call their model C/M. A brief overview of the conference discussion of the Campbell and Mankiw paper follows.

In his comment, Christiano (1989) pointed to a particular representative agent model due to himself and Eichenbaum – call this model C/E. He shows that, while C/M can account for a certain statistical relation among forecastable components of consumption growth, income growth and interest rates, it does a poor job at predicting a smooth pattern of consumption. The opposite results hold for his C/E model. He conjectures that the households that consume current income are credit-constrained, that who is credit-constrained varies over time, and that it 'would be of interest to see whether such an economy, with a relatively small fraction of rule-of-thumb households and with a reasonable amount of inter-temporal substitution in consumption could account for the Campbell–Mankiw empirical regularity' (p. 232). Christiano's comment was followed by one of Robert Ando and then the following open discussion:

> Mankiw noted that Christiano's implied regressions yielded much poorer first stage regressions than those found by the authors and that interest rate mismeasurement does not matter for the results. He also questioned whether 'rule-of-thumb' consumers make Ando's inflation-adjustment to income.
>
> Bob Hall objected that Campbell and Mankiw had set up a 'straw man' version of the random walk hypothesis by not taking into account the effects of liquidity constraints. He further stated that Campbell and Mankiw had used the identifying restriction that there are no random consumption components. He argued that, if such components exist, they cause spontaneous movement in output, which would be correlated with the instruments used by Campbell and Mankiw. They do not, he argued, establish the direction of causation and yet take a strong stand on the results. In addition, Hall suggested that Campbell and Mankiw should use additional measures of rates of return.
>
> Mankiw responded that there is large variation in post-war real interest rates. Further, the authors had tried 'truly exogenous' instruments to account for taste shocks, but the results were insignificant. Theory suggests that such instruments may be poor in small samples.
>
> Kevin Murphy asked whether the estimated coefficient of zero on the interest rate was evidence of bad instrumental variables or zero inter-temporal substitution. Bill Nordhaus questioned whether there is measurement error in consumption since the theory applies to utility. Consumption ignores durables, such as housing services consumed. Further, lagged variables would not be good instruments if durables are included. Mankiw responded that, since durable goods follow a random walk, that would not affect the estimate. (p. 245)

Neither the comments nor the discussion ever broach the validity of the PIH. Christiano's comment concerns two specific theories that embody the spirit of the PIH and results in conjecturing a third. The general discussion is even farther removed from challenging the PIH – it focuses, rather, on the empirical model (measurement issues and the suitability of instrumental variables, in this case). Although the details differ, the methodology is no different from pitting one expenditure system against another and arguing over the choice of instruments for, say, endogenous labour income.

Finally I would like to point out that even Angus Deaton's (1987) paper, which is widely viewed as doing significant damage to the rational-expectations PIH, contains the following quote: 'Whatever the final verdict on rational expectations consumption functions, the distinction that they recognize between anticipated and unanticipated events is surely one that makes a great deal of sense' (p. 140). This all points to the rational-expectations PIH as being a specific model, and therefore up for rejection. But the fundamental insight underlying the rational-expectations approach (differential responses to anticipated and unanticipated events), much less the fundamental insights underlying the PIH (permanent income and permanent consumption), are not at all at issue. They are articulated in the ooze.

So what do we observe? We observe rejection of the LES and rejection of the PIH, but no rejection of anything so fundamental as *S* and *N* of the substitution matrix or of the usefulness of the notions of permanent income and the differential responses to anticipated and unanticipated events. These are now articulated in the ooze. That is, we are not upset by rejection of STs – especially as they usually get rejected only in specific contexts.[5] We do not, however, ever put anything so fundamental up for rejection as the *S* and *N* of the substitution matrix or of the rationality of (expected) wealth as a determinant of current consumption. This would be to question the existence of our primordial ooze – something we are unwilling to do unless and until a better basic medium for economic analysis is invented.

To make Gilbert's distinction between testing in the context of demand systems and in the context of the PIH, one would have to think of *S* and *N* as on a par with the PIH – namely, both would have to be STs. I heartily contend that they are not. The PIH is an ST and is on a par, not with *S* and *N*, but with, for example, the LES. Both of these are always up for rejection according to the same methodology.

Notes

1. Formally the utility axioms and the *S* and *N* of the substitution matrix are equipollent axiomatic systems – either one implies the other.
2. In practice this is a crucial issue. If one enumerates everything consumers buy over short intervals, there are many zeros (for example, consumers who bought no Pine State Cottage Cheese in October 1989, and made no trips to Capri in November 1989). With regard to labour supply, corner solutions have been a major preoccupation in the technical and applied literature. When labour income is taken as exogenous the problem is 'solved' by aggregating across goods and time (to annual purchases of dairy products and annual expenditures on vacations) – but see Lee and Pitt (1986) for exceptions. Such aggregation is at best guided by intuition relating the real world to the primordial ooze, and it is often carried out by non-economists.
3. McElroy (1981, 1988) made the error specification an integral part of the model specification and argued against the practice of 'tacking on linear error terms'.
4. $U^{ij} = 0$ where U^{ij} is the i,j^{th} element of the inverse of the Hessian.
5. Even if a consensus evolves that the PIH is 'rejected' for US data, it is hardly dangerous to predict that graduate students will study it 20 years from now and use it over their careers to illuminate particular problems.

References

Ando, Albert (1989), 'Comments' [on Campbell and Mankiw, 'Consumption, Income, and Interest Rates: Reinterpreting the Time Series Evidence'], in Olivier Jean Blanchard and Stanley Rischer (eds), *NBER Macroeconomics Annual 1989*, pp. 234–44 (Cambridge, Mass.: The MIT Press).

Barnett, William A., Geweke, John and Yue, Piyu (1988), 'Semiparametric Bayesian Estimation of the Asymptotically Ideal Model: the AIM Demand System', unpublished manuscript, University of Texas at Austin.

Campbell, John Y. and Mankiw, N. Gregory (1989), 'Consumption, Income, and Interest Rates: Reinterpreting the Time Series Evidence', in Olivier Jean Blanchard and Stanley Fischer (eds), *NBER Macroeconomics Annual 1989*, pp. 185–215 (Cambridge, Mass.: The MIT Press).

Christiano, Lawrence J. (1989), 'Comments' [on Campbell and Mankiw, 'Consumption, Income, and Interest Rates: Reinterpreting the Time Series Evidence'], in Olivier Jean Blanchard and Stanley Rischer (eds), *NBER Macroeconomics Annual 1989*, pp. 216–33 (Cambridge, Mass.: The MIT Press).

Deaton, Angus (1987), 'Life-cycle Models of Consumption: Is the Evidence Consistent with the Theory?', in Truman F. Bewley (ed.), *Advances in Econometrics: Fifth World Congress, Volume II*, pp. 121–48 (Cambridge: Cambridge University Press).

Friedman, Milton (1957), *A Theory of the Consumption Function* (Princeton: Princeton University Press).

Gallant, A. Ronald (1984), 'The Fourier Flexible Form', *American Journal of Agricultural Economics*, **66** (2), pp. 204–8.

Hall, Robert E. (1978), 'Stochastic Implications of the Life Cycle–Permanent Income Hypothesis: Theory and Evidence', *Journal of Political Economy*, **86**, pp. 971–87.

Hammond, Claire Holton (1987), *The Benefits of Subsidized Housing Programmes: An Intertemporal Approach* (Cambridge: Cambridge University Press).

Kim, Jinbang (1989), 'Testing in Modern Economics: The Case of Job Search Theory', this volume.

Lee, Lung-Fei and Pitt, Mark M. (1986), 'Microeconometric Demand Systems with Binding Nonnegativity Constraints: The Dual Approach', *Econometrica*, **54**, pp. 1237–42.

McElroy, Marjorie B. (1981), 'Duality and the Error Structure in Demand Systems', National Opinion Research Center, University of Chicago working paper, no. 81–2.

—— (1988), 'Additive General Error Models for Production, Cost, and Derived Demand or Factor Share Systems', *Journal of Political Economy*, **95**, pp. 737–55.

Modigliani, F. and R. Brumberg (1955a), 'Utility Analysis and the Consumption Function: An Interpretation of Cross-Section Data', in K.K. Kurihari (ed.), *Post Keynesian Economics* (London: George Allen & Unwin).

—— (1955b), 'Utility Analysis and Aggregate Consumption Functions: An Attempt at Integration', mimeo.

Robins, Philip K. (1990), 'Child Care Policy and Research: An Economist's Perspective', paper prepared for the Carolina Public Policy conference on The Economics of Child Care, University of North Carolina, Chapel Hill, May 1990.

Samuelson, Paul Anthony (1947), *Foundations of Economic Analysis* (Cambridge, Mass.: Harvard University Press).

C Empirical Hypotheses in Game Theory and Experimental Economics

5. Strategic Interactions in Economics: the Game Theoretic Alternative

Marina Bianchi and Hervé Moulin*

1 INTRODUCTION

A game describes a problem situation where agents interact knowing that their different moves and plans may affect each other. The configuration of the strategy space – the agents are allowed to communicate, to commit themselves to binding agreements, or, on the contrary, they display different and opposed interests, they may not communicate, and so on – characterizes the many possible problem situations of games. The solution concept of the game comprises the selection, through the strategic interaction of the agents, of that combination of strategies that maximizes agents' individual pay-offs. This solution may lead to cooperation among players, as for example in cooperative games without conflict, or it may simply ratify their opposition of interests, as in non-cooperative games with conflict. A game, particularly those in non-cooperative form, may offer more than one solution, or a solution which is not stable, or a solution which is stable but compatible with more than one strategic behaviour. The theoretical task thus becomes to clarify and discover the institutional and behavioural rules that may help to select and choose among these multiple solutions.

The introduction of a game-theoretic approach into economics has brought with it two fundamental changes. The first is that the traditional domain of analysis has been expanded to include complex situations of strategic interdependence. The complexities here include mutually incomplete information and absence of prior knowledge as to the 'mood' (loyal, aggressive, innovative, passive and so on) and hence the behavioural inclinations of the players, and these things carry the analysis far beyond such interaction as may be spawned by

* We are very grateful to Neil de Marchi for many stimulating comments and criticisms during the preparation of this paper. Further remarks by Jim Friedman are also gratefully acknowledged.

interdependence of utilities. The second involves the specification of problem situations: the institutional rules, the available strategies, according to which interaction takes place. The analysis does not proceed *in vacuo*, but the social and institutional environment is an integral part of the strategy space.

Two consequences follow from these changes. The traditional (modern: Arrow–Debreu) portrayal of economic interaction turns on the notion of mutually compatible plans, and reasons back from the corresponding equilibrium or market-clearing price vector to the conditions necessary for it to be realized. The 'agents' are anonymous, and have pre-known and, in effect, similar plans. They are also quite one-dimensional, choosing their behaviour in the face of given preferences and constraints, but having no other potential and not interacting in any real sense with other agents. To the extent that one can properly speak here of interaction, the equilibrating solution of this 'interaction' is already embedded in the way plans are structured. By contrast, in the game-theoretic approach this (impersonal, competitive, efficiency) solution becomes only one of the possible equilibria that a game can model. Many equilibrium concepts other than the core have had to be introduced in order to represent more complex interactive processes.

The second consequence is that the notion of rationality itself has had to be refined. Rationality is still the rule of behaviour of economic agents, but the outcome does not always correspond to an optimal allocation (as in the well-known Prisoner's Dilemma game). Moreover the end-solution or equilibrium of a game might be compatible with behaviours that must be deemed irrational according to the traditional analysis.

In this chapter we try to clarify further the methodological status of game theory and to delineate more precisely the changes this new tool has induced in economic theory. We begin with a brief historical review which will clarify the sense in which we may speak of progress in game theory itself. Ever since its inception the theory has been accumulating mathematical results and simultaneously has generated a host of equilibrium stories pertaining to rational individual behaviour in situations of strategic interdependency. Next we discuss the empirical content of game theory: can we test it by experimenting? We outline a few successes of practical importance and point to some difficulties in modelling 'real-life' situations as games. In the last part of the chapter we propose that the main methodological contribution of the theory is to deepen our understanding of rationality in social contexts. Specifically we argue that, because rationality becomes multifaceted and equilibrium concepts multiply accordingly, one should view game theory as a logical tool – the first rigorous one available – for classifying different kinds of rationality. As the exploration of complex interdependencies expands the domain of economic analysis and alters core concepts like equilibrium and rationality itself, one sees something like an alternative to the neo-Walrasian program emerging.

2 A HISTORICAL PERSPECTIVE

John von Neumann developed in the late 1920s (together with other eminent mathematicians such as Borel), a completely rigorous treatment of finite two-person zero-sum games. He showed that a pair of optimal strategies in such games consists simply of a saddle point and reduced the computation of those strategies to the solution of a special kind of optimization problem (namely a maximinimization). From there on the theory of two-person zero-sum games fits very well the Lakatosian framework of linear progress by successive additions of excess content. The initial existence theorem (any game with finitely many strategies has at least one saddle point in mixed strategies) was generalized under more and more weak topological assumptions. The equivalence between linear programming and the computation of optimal mixed strategies in finite games helped to spread the influence of the theorem through the applied mathematics profession. New classes of difficult games such as pursuit–evasion differential games and Nim-games were attacked and partially solved. The key to linear progress here rests on the persistence of an undisputed equilibrium concept, namely the saddle point.

The situation is radically different in the theory of non-zero sum games, where the subtle mixture of conflict and opportunities for cooperation considerably complicates the conceptual analysis. Von Neumann and Morgenstern were fully aware that economic games cannot all be modelled in the framework of two-person zero-sum games, but their attempt to discuss non-zero-sum games (through such concepts as the 'stable set', on which more below) was by and large a failure. Thus, in first approximation, we may say that the theory of non-zero-sum games was born around 1950 when John Nash invented the celebrated equilibrium concept for non-cooperative games and proposed the first axiomatic treatment of (two-person) cooperative games (Nash, 1950, 1953).

For the next 25 years or so conceptual investigation was concentrated on the intriguing puzzle of cooperation among selfish actors. If the players can freely form coalitions and sign binding agreements to share the benefits of their collusion, how will the competition among potential coalitions be resolved? Various concepts were proposed, some of them normative (the Shapley value, the nucleolus) some of them descriptive of an equilibrium scenario (core, strong equilibrium). Many more concepts were uncovered en route but never passed the test of applicability to economic theory. The most successful of the cooperative concepts, namely the core, was not discovered until the late 1950s (Gillies, 1959) but quickly attracted considerable attention as its implications for competitive exchange unfolded. Through the work of Shubik, Debreu and Scarf there emerged a very general result, known as the Edgeworth proposition, and stating that the core of an exchange economy is approximately equal to the set of its competitive equilibrium when each agent is small relative to the whole economy. This result, proved in 1963 by Debreu and Scarf, established for the first time that game theory was a useful tool for economic analysis. A great deal of mathematical effort was spent on the refinements of the Edgeworth proposition. Many more applications of the core were later developed: these include the provision of public goods and cost sharing of externalities, and the regulation of natural monopolies.

The impact of the non-cooperative equilibrium concept, the Nash equilibrium, was even more considerable. Yet we have to wait until 1975 for its first important economic application: the unification of three different early analyses of imperfect competition by Cournot, Bertrand and Hotelling. Starting with James Friedman's landmark book (Friedman, 1977) the Nash equilibrium rapidly becomes the dominant paradigm of the theory of industrial organization. This success is reinforced by the theory's increasing ability to deal with situations of mutually incomplete information (that is, where a player knows only imperfectly his opponents' preferences). Soon the framework of games of incomplete information allowed for a rigorous treatment of many important issues (research and development investments, limit pricing, reputation effects) that were not even addressed by the traditional neoclassical theory.

The mid-1970s represent a turning-point in several other dimensions. Following Brams's book (Brams, 1975) and a deep mathematical result due to the philosopher Gibbard and the economist Satterthwaite, game-theoretical methods rushed into the field of political science in general and social choice in particular. As a result, a whole new discipline, often called mathematical politics, emerges on the scene of political science: its theoretical core is a pure and simple strategic model of voting which, however, bears no relation whatsoever to neoclassical equilibrium.

Another important even in 1975 is the seminal work of Selten in refinement of the Nash equilibrium concept. The initial observation is that if a game is played over time (in several successive moves) it tends to have many Nash equilibrium strategies, some of them hardly plausible at all. Hence the need for a more precise definition of non-cooperative rationality in dynamical contexts. This idea led to an extensive fine-tuning of the Nash concept that resulted in a multiplication of equilibrium notions. Nowadays the study of games with incomplete information is structured like a catalogue of rival interpretations of non-cooperative equilibrium scenarios; each interpretation has its pet economic application but none emerges as the leading story.

3 GAME THEORY TODAY

In its most general formulation, game theory describes the behaviour of selfishly motivated agents involved in situations of mutual interdependency. Several agents pursue the maximization of their own welfare by each controlling a different parameter influencing the state of the world.

Thus defined, the scope of the theory is enormous, encompassing virtually all aspects of socioeconomic or political competition, as well as some facets of inter-species conflicts. On the other hand, the formal core of the theory, namely the mathematical objects describing a game situation, is very simple: loosely speaking there are three such objects, called respectively game in normal form, in extensive form, or in characteristic function form (the second model used to analyse non-cooperative situations, the third to analyse cooperative situations, and the first model used for both). Three models, however rich, cannot capture the whole complexity of social interactions. So game theory produces its most influential contributions by mingling with models of denser empirical content. The brief historical survey in section 2 illustrated three of the most impressive success stories of this hybridization process.

The outputs of the theory are equilibrium concepts. The number of those concepts is in steady expansion. In non-cooperative games only, every year in the last ten years we have seen at least one new notion of refinement emerge. The rate of growth, although slower, is clearly positive in cooperative games, too.

But no clear trend of progress emerges, as concepts also die out. For instance, the stable set of von Neumann and Morgenstern was the subject of active research until, in 1958, Stearns gave an example of a ten-person game without any stable set. Shortly thereafter the concept virtually disappeared from the scene of cooperative game theory. It was in effect eliminated by the disproof of the conjecture that every cooperative game has at least one stable set. Another example is the death of such concepts as the bargaining set, the kernel and the pre-kernel, once it was recognized that they were hard to compute and had 'funny' shapes. Furthermore they did not bring any significant application to economic theory.

In the non-cooperative theory the recent unitarian program proposed by Harsanyi and Selten attempted to derive a systematically unique equilibrium selection for every game in normal form. Their proposal is a very complex tracing procedure, the definition of which takes an entire book! It is now part of the game theoretic folklore but no one seriously thinks of using the concept. Instead the current consensus among game theorists appears to be that the choice of an equilibrium concept depends upon the environment of the particular model under consideration. The very notion of rationality in game situations explodes into a host of possible rationality scenarios, each supporting a different equilibrium concept. For a more detailed discussion of this point, see Moulin (1986). See also the last sections of this chapter.

Who are the game theorists today? Some of them are mathematicians, eager to test new concepts for their existence and stability properties. Given the intense production of these objects, this first group of game theorists is prospering. The mainstream game theorist, however, is not motivated by mathematical tools (no matter how high his technical skills). His goal is to understand the means and ends of existing concepts and to classify them accordingly. His main criteria are simplicity and breadth of potential applications. He is the key actor in the process of concept selection.

A well thought out classification includes a careful description of the links between categories. One of the most challenging tasks is then to resolve the contradiction between cooperative and non-cooperative concepts. Can we analyse an object that we call a game without any preconceived idea of whether its players are going to cooperate or not? Does the structure of the interdependency between actions and preferences influence in some predictable way the player's behaviour (cooperative, non-cooperative)? Although the current state of the theory does not provide a universal answer, it goes a long way towards it. For instance, the paradigm of repeated games (Aumann) can be applied to virtually any game in normal form: if there is always a tomorrow where the actors of today will again be playing the same game, then cooperation becomes non-cooperatively rational and the tension between the two kinds of behaviour disappears.

As most of the 'mainstream' game theorists (in the above sense) are employed by economics departments, business schools or political science departments, the prediction of its founding fathers ('this theory of games of strategy is the proper instrument with which to develop a theory of economic behavior', von Neumann and Morgenstern, 1943, introductory remarks) has finally been fulfilled, 50 years later.

4 EMPIRICAL CONTENT

The game theorist thus supplies a panoply of concepts describing various kinds of rational and equilibrium behaviour (say cooperative in the sense of the core, or non-cooperative in the sense of Nash). Mathematics alone, in the most optimistic case, attaches a small subset of outcomes to each of those concepts, but additional assumptions are necessary to select one of the rationality/equilibrium scenarios. In practice we lack a systematical method for testing the behavioural mood of our players: do they trust each other enough to engage in cooperative moves? Which coalitions of players are likely to form, or simply could conceivably form? Short of being able to answer those questions independently of the strategic interaction that actually occurs, we are led into the trap of unfalsifiable statements. For instance, observing the outcome of a Prisoner's Dilemma 'reveals' something of the cultural and/or psychological pattern of interaction between two particular agents. Incidentally this is one of the applications of the gigantic empirical literature on the Prisoner's Dilemma (see Rapoport and Chammak, 1965). We refer the reader to the chapter by Smith, McCabe and Rassenti in this volume, who also make the point that theory is often too unspecified to dictate precise experimental conditions.

How, then, are we going to test the empirical content of game theory? If the 'theory' tells us that outcome A will occur if the players perceive it in that way, the burden of verifiability is passed on to the psychologist or whoever has the means to detect in what mood (say cooperative or not) our players actually are. The way out of this trap, it seems to us, is to recognize that game theory is not a theory which has as output a set of refutable statements, but merely a syntax articulating the vocabulary of interdependent rationality. Game 'theory' *per se* is no more empirically verifiable than an alleged translation from English into an unspoken language. Yet its application to specific economic, political or social situations produces many testable statements. Indeed an economic model of, say, imperfect competition requires a non-cooperative analysis in view of the existence of anti-trust regulation. Or, the strategic analysis of majority voting must take place in a cooperative context, because of freedom of association. And so on.

If experiments have been few, it is easy to name specific instances where the game analysis is corroborated by strong empirical evidence and influences our view of optimal allocation mechanisms. We pick three characteristic examples.

Example 1 Vickrey's Second Price Auction

In the first price auction, every buyer submits a bid and the highest bidder wins the object and pays his own bid. In the second price auction the winner is still the highest bidder but he pays only the second highest bid. The trick is that a bidder has no incentive whatsoever to distort his bid in the second price auction: his equilibrium strategy is simply to report his reservation price (namely the dollar value of the object to him). By contrast, in the first price auction, bidders tend to underbid, and there are several conflicting strategies. Vickrey's auction deeply influences the theoretical literature on auctions.

Example 2 The Shapley Value for Sharing the Cost of Joint Production

Here the players share the cost of an indivisible service (for example, water system) exhibiting increasing returns to scale. The cost of serving any subset of those agents is given. The problem is to find a fair cost sharing. More generally a cooperative game (with transferable utility) gives a unified framework to describe any surplus-sharing problem where each coalition of agents has the opportunity to achieve a certain benefit on its own. Examples include the exchange of private goods, the production of public or private goods by a common property technology and the allocation of portfolios in a multiparty coalition. The Shapley value is an elegant formula that suggests a compromise in all such situations. It is both computationally tractable and axiomatically justifiable. Although other axiomatic solutions are available as well, the Shapley value shows the greatest potential for applications (see for example, Young, 1985).

Example 3 Approval Voting as an Alternative to Plurality Voting

In approval voting, voters name as many candidates as those they approve of, and the candidate approved most often is elected. Invented recently by Weber, Brams and Fishburn, this voting rule is an appealing alternative to the familiar plurality rule. It tends to favour moderate candidates at the expense of extremists. It is also less strategically manipulable than plurality, Borda or any other such scoring rule (Brams and Fishburn, 1978). It has been adopted by several professional societies (such as the Econometric Society).

5 DIFFICULTIES WITH RATIONALITY AND EQUILIBRIUM IN GAME THEORY

Let us go back now to the basic twist introduced by game theory, its deliberate decision to treat strategic interdependence. What exactly does this imply for the traditional central notions of rationality and equilibrium?

The key to any equilibrium concept is the rational strategy which represents a particular chosen behaviour of the players. Game theory, no less than traditional economic analysis, presupposes rationality, or individually maximizing agents. As Aumann says (1988, p. 1), 'game theory without rationality sounds like geology without rocks, or biology without life'. Nevertheless this concept has been subtly and tacitly altered in game theory. Many of the paradoxes and puzzles uncovered by the theory are linked to the assumption of rationality; for individual rationality – maximizing behaviour – seems capable of leading to solutions (equilibria) that turn out to be somewhat less than or at least other than rational, so defined. In this section we illustrate some of the main changes that game theory has brought in the traditional notions of rationality and equilibrium.

Expanding the Strategy Set

The first point to be made is that the modelling of a game of strategy requires that we specify and circumscribe the feasible moves available to each individual player.

A game in normal form is the data for each player of a set of strategies (feasible moves) and preferences (utility) over the possible outcomes (an outcome is a vector with one strategy per player).

The need to specify the exhaustive list of legal moves for each player is stressed by all theorists (for example, Harsanyi, 1977). When they run experiments, game theorists try to keep under tight control the set of moves available to each player (Roth, 1988). This is one reason why experiments often sound fairly remote from actual instances of conflict/cooperation. But this is a price to pay for discovering the true limits of the game model.

In real life, only certain 'games', in the ordinary sense, exhibit such a clear-cut pattern: chess, tennis (but not beauty contests). By contrast, in games of business or political competition, most of the skill of good players consists of inventing new moves, in creating new options. In the cooperative context, this skill is the very art of negotiation (in the sense of Raiffa, 1982); in the non-cooperative context of election campaigns, think of the war of political advertisements.

Thus one of the things that game theory has taught us is that it can be useful to expand the set of strategies, though, of course, this means changing the original game. The simplest illustration of this is the Battle of the Sexes. Here each player has two strategies, with (dollar) pay-offs as shown below. The inherent conflict between the two equilibria can

	Left	Right
	3, 2	1, 1
	1, 1	2, 3

be resolved in four different ways by expanding (or contracting) the strategy space. A single player wins by effectively ruling out one of his strategies (Schelling, 1971) or by adding the opportunity to 'burn a dollar' *ex ante* (van Damme, 1983). Alternatively a symmetrical equilibrium can be constructed if the players randomize their strategies independently (mixed strategies). Randomizing one's own choice of strategy may increase the expected gain in this two-person zero-sum situation. Finally, and more interesting from a methodological point of view, the players may pursue correlated equilibria. In these equilibria the players build a machine (or hire a referee) to coordinate their actions. The machine randomly picks an outcome (a choice of strategy for each player) and only informs each player of the strategy chosen for him. This selective distribution of information can be self-enforcing and achieve better pay-offs than any Nash equilibrium. (See Aumann, 1987 or Moulin, 1986, for simple examples.) The possibilities of coordination may expand still further if messages are sent during the game, or if the players can communicate with the referee.

Note that in these examples something different is going on than traditional theory allows for. We have here players who are no longer confined to a single equilibrium outcome, but may alter their strategy space by deliberate decision and thereby both introduce and reach a different equilibrium. The analogue of this in traditional theory would be allowing each agent to have altered preferences, caused by the fact that not only prices and incomes influence choice but also the actions of other agents. But, whereas multiple preference sets traditionally might be deemed evidence of irrationality (or chaotic preferences), here it is a natural part of rational interdependence.

The Importance of Not Playing to Win

Nor is this all. There is a sense in which one may do better by not being too deliberate a maximizer, a curious notion for traditional theory to accommodate.

Consider Axelrod's experiment (Axelrod, 1980) where computer programs play against one another a repeated Prisoner's Dilemma. Tit for Tat is the following strategy: in period 1 cooperate; in all subsequent periods, play exactly what your opponent played last period. Despite the fact that Tit for Tat was not designed as a winning strategy, it obtained the highest score among 63 programs. As Rapoport notes, 'The interesting feature of this result was that Tit for Tat did not "beat" a single program against which it was pitted'. Tit for Tat won because other programs, 'designed to beat their opponents, reduced each other's scores when pitted against each other, including themselves' (Rapoport, 1987, p. 202). This shows the inefficiency of strategies based on attempts to maximize one's own expected gains in situations where 'both cooperative and competitive strategies are possible' (ibid., 202).

Evolutive Strategies

Next consider evolutive games. In an evolutionary approach the rationality of following a strategic rule changes over time. To be precise, it depends on the prevailing decisional norm that emerges at every stage of the repeated game. The norms game invented by Axelrod (1986), for example, models the way norms grow and decay, and how norms are displaced by new ones. The players (who exist only within the computer) are given the opportunity to 'defect' – by, for example, cheating on their income tax returns. At the beginning of the game the norm against cheating has some force: low levels of boldness towards defection and high levels of vengefulness against cheaters prevail. But, as the game is repeated, the level of boldness falls: vengefulness starts to decrease, because the enforcement costs of punishing defectors rise, and boldness suddenly makes sense again. Eventually the norm collapses. Here the rationality of a norm evolves through a process of trials and errors and this is the reason for the fundamental difficulty of stabilizing a norm. The Tragedy of the Commons is a variant of the Prisoner's Dilemma where each player has a continuum of strategies. It provides another example of a form of rationality 'which takes into account the circumstance that the effectiveness of a strategy may depend crucially on how many others adopt it and the fact that a strategy initially successful may become self-defeating because its success leads others to imitate it' (Rapoport, 1987, p. 204).

Evolutive games show that no one specific optimum will necessarily emerge from the evolutionary forces at work. On the other hand, when a stable equilibrium solution can be described (for example, the evolutionary stable strategy of Maynard Smith), it does not necessarily select only one type of behaviour, but a composite, giving rise to what is called a stable 'polymorphism'.

Paradoxes of Backward Induction

Finally, in this listing of illustrations of the way rationality and equilibrium notions are affected by game theory, we turn to some quite counter-intuitive results. The most famous is the (finitely) repeated Prisoner's Dilemma where the only equilibrium strategy prescribes defection at each stage no matter how long the game is repeated. This equilibrium prescription follows an application of backward induction, but contradicts our intuition and experimental observations (of non-defection until quite close to the end of such games).

Here are two other examples, due to Megiddo (see Aumann, 1988) and Kalai. In the Megiddo game (which joins the list of Rosenthal's paradoxes, 1981; see also Rubinstein, 1989), $10.50 is lying on a table. At the outset, Alice can pick up $10 and leave 50 cents to Bob, in which case the game ends. If she does not exercise her option the amount increases tenfold, and in the next round Bob can pick up $100, leaving Alice $5. If he does not do this, again the amount is raised tenfold, and at next play Alice can pick up $1 000, leaving $50. And so on. The game ends automatically after the point when Bob may pick up $1 000 000 and leave Alice $50 000, whether he does this or not. Backward induction, once again, tells us that Alice will exercise her first option; for, with knowledge of the terminal option, Alice would prefer the previous opportunity ($100 000 for her and only $5 000 for Bob), while he, knowing this, would exercise his previous option ($10 000 for him, $500 for her) and so on back to the beginning.

In the Kalai hat game, as a hat passes from player 1 to player 100, everyone has an opportunity to put in a dollar or not. If all players do put in a dollar each will receive two. However, if at least one player fails to put in a dollar, all the money is forfeited. The rational strategy is clear: everyone puts in a dollar and wins two. But this equilibrium strategy is unlikely to be observed, because the smallest chance of a mistake by one of my successors will make me hesitate to contribute. Knowing this, my predecessors are even more reluctant to contribute.

Aumann's suggested solution to the Megiddo game is the introduction of a small breakdown in the commonality of knowledge, in effect turning the rationality problem into one of 'some kind of approximate or bounded rationality' (Aumann, 1988, p. 6). What he has in mind is common knowledge of mutual rationality, but only up to a specified level. His aim is to leave open the possibility that rational action will be taken, in the form of strategies that are more profitable than the 'pathologically pessimistic' subgame perfect equilibrium in the Megiddo game and safer than the 'unreasonably optimistic' equilibrium of the Kalai game.

6 WHERE ARE WE NOW?

The examples we have discussed briefly have pinpointed a number of problems with the traditional notions of equilibrium and rationality. But what exactly are the challenges posed by the problems and paradoxes uncovered by game theory?

Firstly, it must be observed that the problems and subtle changes in the concept of rationality are rather different from those which are commonly thought to weaken the traditional assumption of rationality in economics. In the economic theory of individual choice, the difficulties of the rationality principle are mainly of two kinds. One is the overload of knowledge and information which it is required that agents possess in order to make a rational decision (models of bounded rationality are attempts to overcome this difficulty). The second is that the assumption of rationality may be used tautologically. As the conditions under which rationality can be 'tested' are left unspecified, they can always be re-formulated in a way to 'match' the primitive assumption. Thus the concept of rationality that may result is either too strong in terms of the computational power it requires or too weak in terms of its explicative power.

In the situations described by a game-theoretic approach, things are different. Here, even if the former difficulties were solved (and they are not, as much discussion on the epistemic foundations of equilibria – what the players must know about each other's strategies and each other's rationality – shows), there still remains the problem that, in many games, as we have seen, strict rationality is not enough to select 'reasonable' outcomes. For such reasonable outcomes to become possible options, rationality, or the common knowledge of it shared by players, must be re-formulated.

A second observation is that appeals to bounded rationality, or to bits of 'irrationality', to 'trembles', to erratic perturbations in a game, and to automata (see, for example, Kreps and Wilson, 1982a and b; Kalai and Stanford, 1988), as ways of saving 'reasonableness' from strict rationality, hence as ways of discriminating among equilibria, represent tentative first steps towards a solution. Without a background theory as to how deviations from rationality work and come to take specific forms we are left without a rule as to what particular solution should prevail. If we cannot explain why a particular mistake, or a particular deviation from the equilibrium strategy occurs, our proposed 'reasonable' solutions cannot but be arbitrary.

It is worth driving this point home by referring once again to the Megiddo game. Strict rationality here tells us that play will revert to the first round. All other nodes can be reached only 'out of equilibrium'. It may seem reasonable in terms of total gains that later nodes be striven for; yet, if mutual rationality and common knowledge of it obtains strictly, then nodes other than the first will never be observed. If they happen to be reached players may offer an explanation in all sorts of terms; for example, the belief that they were in the presence of an imperfectly rational opponent, or even that they thought their fellow players were super-sophisticated and merely bluffing by seeming to 'tremble' (hesitate). (See, on all of this, Reny, 1985; Binmore, 1987 and Bicchieri, 1988.) The possibilities of rationalization are endless. Clearly stronger theoretical efforts to explain 'out of equilibrium' behaviour are needed.

Re-formulations of the concept of rationality via models of players' thinking have begun to appear. For example, in the eductive process described by Binmore (1987), which is based on a constructive rather than an axiomatic view of rationality, deviations from predicted play may be explained and justified by changing the model which proved inconsistent with observed events. Deviations therefore are not simply discarded as non-Nash equilibria, but become the signals of a more complex way of reasoning where 'trembles' or even systematic mistakes may represent the right way to play. The meaning of rationality expands in order to include learning procedures in which making systematic, or random, mistakes is a device to discover, to explore, to make plain the character of the opponent and his strategy.

Attempts have also been made to formulate some learning processes in games (Fudenberg and Kreps, 1988). In order to avoid the inconsistency of beliefs of non-Nash equilibria, a play may be modelled which explicitly involves experimentation with actions which are not currently perceived as optimal. A Nash equilibrium can be selected, even if global stability cannot generally be reached. Much remains to be done to explain in detail the formation of the strategic thinking process but these recent researches move us a few steps in the right direction.

7 A NEW PROGRAMME?

We return, finally, to the tentative suggestion made at the end of the introductory paragraphs, that in game theory something like a new program may be emerging. It is early days, and Lakatos's own writings suggest that a long passage of time may be required before we can usefully begin to apply the notions of MSRP. We are also hesitant because it is not obvious that what is happening in game theory fits very naturally the categories required by a Lakatosian view of the history of science. Nevertheless it may be instructive to ask how far this particular history fits MSRP.

Firstly, it is clear that with game theory the analysis of optimizing behaviour has taken a new turn. We have lived with this basic paradigm in economics for 200 years and more. But the crowning analytical achievement in our own time has been the proofs in the late 1950s of the existence of a market clearing vector of prices, in an economy of independent, impersonal agents. Viewed from the perspective of game theory, and with the hindsight of 30 additional years of exploration, the achievement looks somewhat less than monumental: it shows, under very strong assumptions, that a certain sense can be given to the notion of consistency of plans. There is no explanation offered as to how this consistency may be reached through real interaction among the agents. Game theory asks, why confine our interest to whether there is existence in this formal sense, postulating zero or minimal interaction, when all around us are instances of interactions, deliberately entered into and actively pursued?

By focusing expressly on strategic interaction, game theory has incorporated a host of new and interesting problem situations into the general paradigm of maximizing subject to constraints. Does that amount to a new hard core of a new program? Probably not. It might seem more like the territorial expansion undergone by traditional optimization analysis at the hands of the Chicago school, led by George Stigler and Gary Becker, in the 1960s and 1970s, with the major difference, however, that, instead of forcing problems into the shape required by the tools of that analysis, game theory allows the problems to re-shape the tools. Heuristically this might be viewed as progress, because the number of falsifiable implications of the optimization approach is thereby greatly enlarged. On the other hand, as we have remarked, game theory is a logical tool being used for cataloguing in a rigorous way the implications of rationality in interactive situations (cf. Aumann, 1988, p. 2); it does not naturally fit into the category of theories that generate testable hypotheses, because it lacks a method of testing the behavioural mood of players independently of actual experience (section 4 above). It is perhaps better thought of as showing the poverty (degeneration?) of the traditional analysis, in that game theory is what one gets if one admits strategic interaction into the analysis of optimizing bahaviour, yet game theory is unable – so far, anyway – to generate the testable propositions that most positivist defenders of the traditional analysis have implied were there.

At the same time, game theory does represent a new enterprise, because it is forcing a re-examination of the basic postulate of the optimizing approach, rationality. We have noted some of the changes this has brought. One is not stuck with outcomes that represent the best one can do within a given strategy space; that space itself may be re-drawn by the players. This looks suspiciously like saying that rational players can be thought of as changing their preferences, a troublesome thought for the traditional analysis. Nor is it clear that one should always seek to win: rationality may involve something less, or different (survival, for instance). Again we have seen that solutions are not always stable, once attained, and that those which are may involve multiple behaviours. Finally it has emerged that strict rationality may be quite unreasonable, as revealed in the paradoxes of backward induction. Efforts to find solutions to problems like these last have given rise to many modified notions of rationality. At the moment these suffer from a certain ad hocness. Indeed, since a more subtle, richer understanding of rationality via game theoretic exploration has gone along with the generation of a plethora of notions of equilibrium, part of the progress one sees in game theory might almost be said to consist in conceptual proliferation. It would be a fascinating historical and interpretative exercise to examine the production and winnowing out of equilibrium and rationality concepts, but it is not clear that the Lakatosian framework is the best fitted to help with this.

Finally what one gains from game theory is a vastly enriched understanding of optimal allocation processes and problems. Who will deny that this is a genuine gain; yet there seems to be no Lakatosian criterion to capture gain in understanding, where this does not directly issue in testable consequences.

REFERENCES

Aumann, R.J. (1987), 'Correlated Equilibrium as an Expression of Bayesian Rationality', *Econometrica*, **55**, pp. 1–18.

—— 'Preliminary Notes on Irrationality in Game Theory', IMSSS Summer Seminar on Economic Theory, Stanford.

Axelrod, R. (1980), 'The Emergence of Cooperation Among Egoists', *The American Political Science Review*, **75**, pp. 306–18.

—— (1986), 'An Evolutionary Approach to Norms', *American Political Science Review*, **80** (Dec), pp. 1095–111.

Bicchieri, C. (1988), 'Strategic Behavior and Counterfactuals', *Synthese*, **76**, pp. 135–69.

Binmore, K. (1987), 'Modeling Rational Players', *Economics and Philosophy*, Part 6, I and II.

Brams, S. (1975), *Game Theory and Politics* (London: Macmillan).

Brams, S. and Fishburn, P. (1978), 'Approval Voting', *American Political Science Review*, **72**, pp. 831–47.

van Damme, E. (1983), *Refinements of the Nash Equilibrium Concept* (Berlin: Springer Verlag).

Eatwell, J., Milgate M. and Newman, P. (eds) (1987), *The New Palgrave: A Dictionary of Economics* (London: Macmillan).

Friedman, J. (1977), *Oligopoly and the Theory of Games* (Amsterdam: North-Holland).

Fudenberg, D. and Kreps, D.M. (1988), 'A Theory of Learning, Experimentation, and Equilibrium in Games', mimeo, Stanford University.

Gillies, D. (1959), 'Solutions to General Non-Zero Sum Games', in *Contributions to the Theory of Games*, **4**, Princeton University Press.

Harsanyi, T. (1977), *Rational Behaviour and Bargaining Equilibrium in Games and Social Situations* (Cambridge: Cambridge University Press).

Kalai, E. and Stanford, W. (1988), 'Finite Rationality and Interpersonal Complexity in Repeated Games', *Econometrica*, **56**, pp. 397–410.

Kreps, D.M. (1987), 'Nash Equilibrium', in Eatwell, Milgate and Newman, *The New Palgrave*, pp. 167–77.

Kreps, D.M. and Wilson, R. (1982a), 'Reputation and Imperfect Information', *Journal of Economic Theory*, **27**, pp. 253–79.

—— (1982b), 'Sequential Equilibria', *Econometrica*, **50**, pp. 863–94.

Maynard Smith, J. (1982), *Evolution and the Theory of Games* (Cambridge: Cambridge University Press).

Moulin, H. (1986), *Game Theory for the Social Sciences*, 2nd edn (New York: New York University Press).

Nash, J. (1950), 'Equilibrium Points in N-person games', *Proceedings of the National Academy of Sciences, USA*, **36**, pp. 48–9.

—— (1953), 'Two-person Cooperative Games', *Econometrica*, **21**, pp. 129–40.
von Neumann, J. and Morgenstern, O. (1943), *Theory of Games and Economic Behavior* (Princeton: Princeton University Press).
Raiffa, H. (1982), *The Art and Science of Negotiation* (Cambridge, Mass.: Harvard University Press).
Rapoport, A. (1987), 'Prisoner's Dilemma', in Eatwell, Milgate and Newman (eds), *The New Palgrave*, pp. 199–204.
Rapoport, A. and Chammak, A. (1965), *Prisoner's Dilemma* (Wisconsin: University of Michigan Press).
Reny, P. (1985), 'Rationality, Common Knowledge and the Theory of Games', mimeo, Princeton University.
Rosenthal, R. (1981), 'Games of Perfect Information, Predatory Pricing, and the Chain Store Paradox', *Journal of Economic Theory*, **25**, pp. 92–100.
Roth, A. (1988), 'Laboratory Experiments in Economics', *The Economic Journal*, **98**, pp. 974–1032.
Rubinstein, A. (1989), 'The Electronic Mail Game: Strategic Behavior Under "Almost Common Knowledge" ', *American Economic Review*, forthcoming.
Schelling, T. (1971), *The Strategy of Conflict* (Cambridge, Mass.: Harvard University Press).
Young, H.P. (ed.) (1985), *Cost Allocation: Methods, Principles, Applications* (Amsterdam: North-Holland).

6. Lakatos and Experimental Economics

Vernon L. Smith, Kevin A. McCabe and Stephen J. Rassenti

> They [theorists] have elaborated these theories of supersymmetry, supergravity, and superstrings in a way that I think is unprecedented in the history of science for a theory that has *no experimental support whatsoever*. I've done it myself, I'm not badmouthing them . . . you do what you can, and this was the best that could be done. We just can't go on doing physics like this without support from experiment. The experimentalists do great things – discover the W and Z – and God bless them, it's wonderful. But the theory has moved to the point where these experiments are not helping. I hope that with the next generation of accelerators, we'll get out of this morass.
>
> (Steven Weinberg)

1 INTRODUCTION

This chapter is about some microeconomic experiments and results, and their relation or potential relation to theory. It is not about laboratory experimental methods in economics. But many of the participants at this conference, and readers of this volume, are unfamiliar with experimental economics thought, and its 30 or so years of development. So we shall begin with a brief discussion of the thought process which motivates an economics experiment. For more comprehensive statements of experimental methodology, see Smith (1987, 1989).

We do not go to the basement (laboratory) with the idea of reproducing the world, or a major part of it; that is better done (and it is hoped will be done) through 'field' observation. We go to the laboratory to study, under *relatively* controlled conditions, our *representations* of the world – most particularly our representations of *markets*. Markets, since Adam Smith, have been thought to underlie the nature and causes of the wealth of nations. But how, as theorists, do we represent markets? Anyone who has been to an open 'English' or progressive auction (it was used at least as far back as Babylonian times) will have noted that more and more bidders become inactive as the price is bid to higher and higher levels. Ultimately there is only one remaining bidder, whereupon the sale item is declared sold to that bidder at his/her final bid price. The most casual observer cannot help but see that revealed willingness-to-pay varies among buyers, and that more people are willing to pay a low price than pay a high price. Thus the first important element of every market is the *environment*: the preferences of individuals together with their resources, and their technology for transforming resources into items and services of value. Second, every market is characterized by an *institution* which specifies the language of the market – bids and/or offers, and their acceptance or non-acceptance – and the rules under which messages map into trades (outcomes). Finally in every market is manifest the *behaviour* of its participants which consists of their message-sending responses and interaction.

Neoclassical theories (such as supply equals demand) of markets derive predictive hypotheses concerning the relationship between observed *outcomes* and the environment; *institution-specific* theories (of which we have a growing number) predict *message* behaviour, given the environment *and* the institution(s) of exchange. When we test theory(ies) we compare observations with predictions using metrics defined on *message space*; the shorter the distance between observed messages and the predicted messages of a theory, the 'better' is the theory. Often our metrics are statistical (for example, the mean deviation per unit of standard error) and are used as essentially persuasive arithmetical exercises, since any *Lakatosian* (see section 2) improvement in theory that shortens this distance would certainly be welcome in the community of economists. If there is *any* error between theory and observation, improvement is possible and desirable whatever the statistical tests show. Possible improvements in theory include those extensions which show that the existence of error is itself predictable from infallible and imperfectly informed agents. But statistics in the sense of sampling theory is important since an experiment is a sample of one, and the cost of running experiments often precludes taking appropriately large samples.

Since we study only our representations of markets in the laboratory, we can ask, if our representations are 'wrong', will not the experimental results be irrelevant, even if conditionally right? Of course this is true, but exactly the same statement can be made about observations of markets in the field. Theory concerns the *consequences of things unseen*; the consequences of the internal processes of decision-making organisms. We have *no direct observations* in or outside the laboratory on those internal processes, only on subjects' actual decisions and/or their verbal expressions. What we study in the laboratory and in the field are the *observable traces* of these internal processes. Because these traces may be different in the laboratory than in the field, all aspects of the *empirical* question of *parallelism* between laboratory and the field are worthy of careful examination. Laboratory and field empirical studies are complements, not substitutes.

2 THE CONTRAST BETWEEN TWO CULTURES

Two recent experimental discoveries in physics illustrate the chasm between the cultures of economics and the physical sciences as each is practised: (1) the discovery of superconduction at temperatures far higher than was predictable from the prevailing (Nobel prize winning) theory of superconductivity; (2) the reported production of energy by a cold 'fusion-like nuclear' process. The phenomenon (1) has been replicated, though imperfectly, and is now part of the observational foundation of new approaches to superconductivity theory. Although (2) has not been adequately replicated, and the experimental conditions well documented, there are many reports, and lively controversy, with a tendency for chemists to be pro and physicists con, concerning the possibility of new nuclear reaction processes not previously identified or understood (Pool, 1989).

What has been the cultural reaction to these new developments in the physical science community? There have been two responses: (1) experimental laboratories the world over have rushed to confirm, replicate and/or explore the empirical boundaries of the new phenomena; (2) theoretical physicists have intensified their collective efforts to modify theory to (a) accommodate (or dispute, in the case of cold fusion) the new observations and (b) to deduce any new empirical implications of the modified theory.

Examples of such a tight coupling between the theoretical and empirical research sub-communities are – to say the least – difficult to come by in mainstream microeconomics. Although there is a controversy between physicists and chemists on whether cold fusion has been observed, and the weight of evidence currently appears to favour the physicists (Beardsley, 1989), there is no controversy that experimental measurements and replication will be the primary arbiter of which position or theory is to be accepted. Such vital, and vitalizing, clashes in professional 'tournaments' aimed at achieving consistency between theory and observation are not plainly characteristic of what the mainstream community of economists do.

These two examples, and the gap they illustrate, pose a formidable problem for the application and interpretation of the Lakatosian concept of research programs to economics. This is because it is an implicit axiom of Lakatos that we are dealing with observational sciences; sciences in which theoretical concepts are responsive to observation and data-gathering exercises are responsive to theory. We believe that, within the broad field of microeconomics, experimental economics provides many research programs that run counter to the claims stated above. We believe there are other important contrary examples, such as economic history and labour economics, but our concentration in this essay will be on experimental methods in economics.

To paraphrase Lakatos (1978), economists (scientists) do not discard theories because some, even many, tests have refuted them; neither do they accept theories because all tests have failed to falsify them. McCloskey (1983) has argued that there is a vast gulf between what economists say about what they do, and what they do. Thus, as economists, we often use the rhetoric of falsification, particularly in the conventionalist context of statistical tests, but we do not discard and/or add theories because of the results of those tests. Econometric specification searches – the process of deleting/adding variables/equations until the estimated signs of coefficients satisfy our prior notions of consistency with theory – have come under severe criticisms (Leamer, 1983; McCloskey, 1983). The work of Lakatos directly concerns and illuminates these and other issues in the context of his concept of the methodology of scientific research programs. What we learn from Lakatos that is of direct relevance to this essay can be stated briefly by summarizing what Lakatos asserts, with numerous supporting arguments and examples, to be the essential elements of an 'accepted' theory in the context of a progressive research program.

1. It accounts for some observations.
2. It has excess empirical content relative to its nearest competitor(s); that is, successful theories or research programs satisfy an opportunity cost criterion.
3. At least some of its excess empirical content is consistent with observation.
4. The predictions of the program include some novel, even 'stunning', facts that are not predicted by any of its competitors.
5. The program provides a problem-solving heuristic which enables it to digest some anomalies, anticipate others, and even transform them from falsifications into verifications by suitable development of the 'protective belt' of implementational assumptions.

6. Degenerate (non-progressive) programs are characterized by a continuing tendency for the theory to lag behind observation; that is, extensions in the theory are made primarily *ex post hoc* in response to observations falsifying the previous state of theory. But new programs are afforded a period of infant developmental grace to establish a track record. Thus consistency with all or most known facts, far from being the hallmark of received theory, can fail utterly to rescue it, as with the Ptolemaic model of the universe.

We are theoretical experimentalists, not methodologist–philosophers, and we are not competent to appraise Lakatos. In the pages to follow we provide a practitioner's perspective. What we do as theoretical experimentalists we have done, are doing, and will do as if Lakatos had never existed. This is because the *art* of the 'next step' in science (itself not a 'science') is really not part of Lakatos as we interpret him. As practitioners we can and will, in the following, suggest many points of contact between economic experimentation and the Lakatosian framework, leaving any deeper Lakatosian account of experimental methods in economics to methodologists better able to conduct such investigations.

3 LAGGING THEORY: CONTRADICTORY INFORMATION REQUIREMENTS IN THEORY AND IN EXPERIMENT FOR A NASH NON-COOPERATIVE EQUILIBRIUM

> There are two kinds of experimenters. The first kind do what theorists tell them to do . . . The second kind follow their own ideas. I am happy to eat Chinese dinners with theorists, but to spend your life doing what they tell you is a waste of time. (Sam Ting)

Informational Assumptions of Non-cooperative Equilibrium Theory

In his Nancy L. Schwartz Memorial Lecture, Sonnenschein (1983, p. 16) states: 'The weakness of the Nash equilibrium concept is that it requires each agent to know the preferences of all other agents.' The competitive equilibrium, viewed as the limit of a Nash equilibrium (NE) as the number of agents is increased without bound, has also been viewed historically as a market state that is achievable only if each agent knows the preferences of all other agents. This seems to be the prevailing view among economic (game) theorists. It is of course true that in order to calculate a NE it is necessary for the theorist *qua* experimentalist who is designing an experiment to have complete information on preferences. But this is not the same thing as saying that economic *agents* require this information. There appear to be two reasons why economic theorists have supposed that complete information is necessary for a NE: (1) historically the NE was thought to apply only to a single-decision game; consequently, without complete information, it is deemed highly unlikely that the $n \geqslant 2$ players in such a game would reach a NE; (2) it was not thought to be possible for agents to realize any equilibrium state except through common rational cognition (you see it, I see it, we both see it, we both see that we both see it; only then do we both do it) and calculation, which requires the same complete information needed by the theorist. In fact it is often suggested by theorists that, when theory fails to be confirmed in the laboratory, this is the result of a failure in '. . . their [subjects'] understanding of the situation' (Aumann, 1987, p. 462). This can be construed as coming uncomfortably close to saying that games between rational players means games between game theorists or their cognitive equivalents, although we do not suggest that this interpretation is intended. Rather the point is that 'understanding' if not defined a priori can always be invoked *ex post hoc* as a basis for the claim that a particular theory has not 'really' been tested. The more important and interesting question is whether game theory has predictive power for participants who know nothing of game theory.

The most relevant game environment for most microeconomic phenomena is one with repeated play and major elements of incomplete information. But repeated play games have tended to be limited to an investigation of the theoretical results that can be derived by replicating the single-decision *complete* information game: 'The study of supergames (where the same game is replicated repeatedly in time) was initially – and still is to a large extent – motivated by the theme that "repetition enables cooperation" ' (Mertens, 1987, p. 552).

It was Harsanyi (1967–8) who successfully generalized the Nash equilibrium solution to incomplete information games between Bayesian players, but 'Harsanyi's formulation . . . is primarily a device for thinking about incomplete information in an orderly fashion' (Aumann, 1987, p. 472), by taming the infinite regress potentially in the minds of players thinking about the beliefs about the beliefs, and so on of other players. But it is much more than this. In section 5 we provide a discussion of an experimental research program applying the Harsanyi approach, as it was anticipated by Vickrey (1961), to the analysis of the standard sealed-bid auction. As will be seen in that application, agents are assumed to have probabilistic information on each other's 'types' (value and utility parameter). But in most of the 'incomplete information' environments that have been studied experimentally, subject agents are in *complete ignorance* of each other's 'types' and pay-offs. (Of course Harsanyi models of such markets could be based on the assumption of diffuse priors.)

From this very brief sketch we shall suggest that game theory was quite unprepared for the sort of results we shall summarize below. But, as is often the case in science, concepts developed for one purpose, and/or thought to require certain conditions, have found unexpected application in situations that were not part of the original intention.

Experimental Studies of the Effect of Information on Outcomes

We shall summarize the results of experiments in four different institutions, each examined under private information, and also under complete, and in some cases, common information. The four institutions are: bilateral bargaining, Cournot oligopoly, Bertrand oligopoly and double oral auction. Private information refers to the condition in which each subject knows privately only his/her message (or decision)-contingent monetary pay-off. Siegel and Fouraker (1960) originally referred to this condition as incomplete information, but it is not necessarily incomplete information in the sense modelled formally by Harsanyi (1967–8). We will follow the common current usage for *incomplete information* and refer to the Siegel and Fouraker conditions as *private* information environments. Complete information will mean that each subject knows his/her message-contingent pay-off, and that of all other subjects. Common information will mean that, in *addition* to complete information, each subject is informed that all other subjects have complete information (for example, subjects are all given the same tables and same instructions, which are read out loud to them, or each is told that all subjects have received identical instructions and pay-off tables). Siegel and Fouraker (1960, p. 28) pioneered this important concept and called it complete–complete information as distinct from complete–incomplete information (I have information on both pay-offs, you know only your own pay-offs, and I know that you know only your own pay-offs). Subsequently game theorists (unaware of these sophisticated treatments of information by Siegel and Fouraker), following the philosopher Lewis (1969), say that common 'knowledge' exists when a set of agents all know something, all know that all know it, and so on without limit. We have eschewed this phraseology because common *knowledge* has been interpreted widely as being identical to common *expectations*, which it is not, as has been demonstrated repeatedly since

1960 in a wide variety of experiments. What can be operationalized in the laboratory is the state of common information, but what subjects 'know' in the sense of expecting (or in the sense of knowing what others will do) is a private, uncontrolled state. (For further discussion see section 4 below.) We know of no data supporting the hypothesis that common information is sufficient to induce common expectations.

Bilateral bargaining

Fouraker and Siegel (1963) report results from bilateral bargaining experiments in which the message space for a seller is a set of prices; the message space of the corresponding buyer is a set of quantities. Each buyer and seller (paired anonymously in separate cubicles) engage in a sequence of 24 transactions: three practice trials without cash pay-offs, followed by 19 trials with cash pay-offs. (There was a twentieth trial, announced as the final trial, and a special twenty-first trial; these will not be discussed here.) On each trial the seller begins by choosing price. This price is communicated to the buyer, the buyer chooses quantity, which is communicated to the seller, and the trial ends. The seller's profit, provided in the form of a price–quantity seller table, is calculated as seller revenue (the seller's price message times the buyer's quantity message) minus induced seller cost (where induced seller cost is a convex quadratic increasing function of the buyer's quantity message). The buyer's profit, provided in a price–quantity buyer table, is calculated as induced buyer revenue (where induced buyer revenue is a concave quadratic increasing function of the buyer's quantity message) minus buyer cost (the seller's price message times the buyer's quantity message). Under complete information buyers and sellers all receive the same table, and for each price–quantity pair in the table both the buyer's and the seller's profit is entered.

The median prices and quantities across all bargaining pairs on each transaction for both private and complete information are charted in Figure 6.1. Under private information convergence is relatively rapid, and is nearer to the Nash price–quantity equilibrium (or Bowley equilibrium, after Bowley who in 1922 first articulated the non-cooperative equilibrium for the first mover bilateral bargaining institution) than the bargainers' joint maximum cooperative outcome. Note that this is the classical monopoly outcome: given a price chosen by the seller, the buyer's best response is to choose the quantity that maximizes his/her profit. But this behaviour reveals the buyer's marginal value (demand) schedule after a few rounds. Consequently, by sampling and remembering which prices produced the larger profits, the median seller converges to the NE prediction. Under complete

Figure 6.1

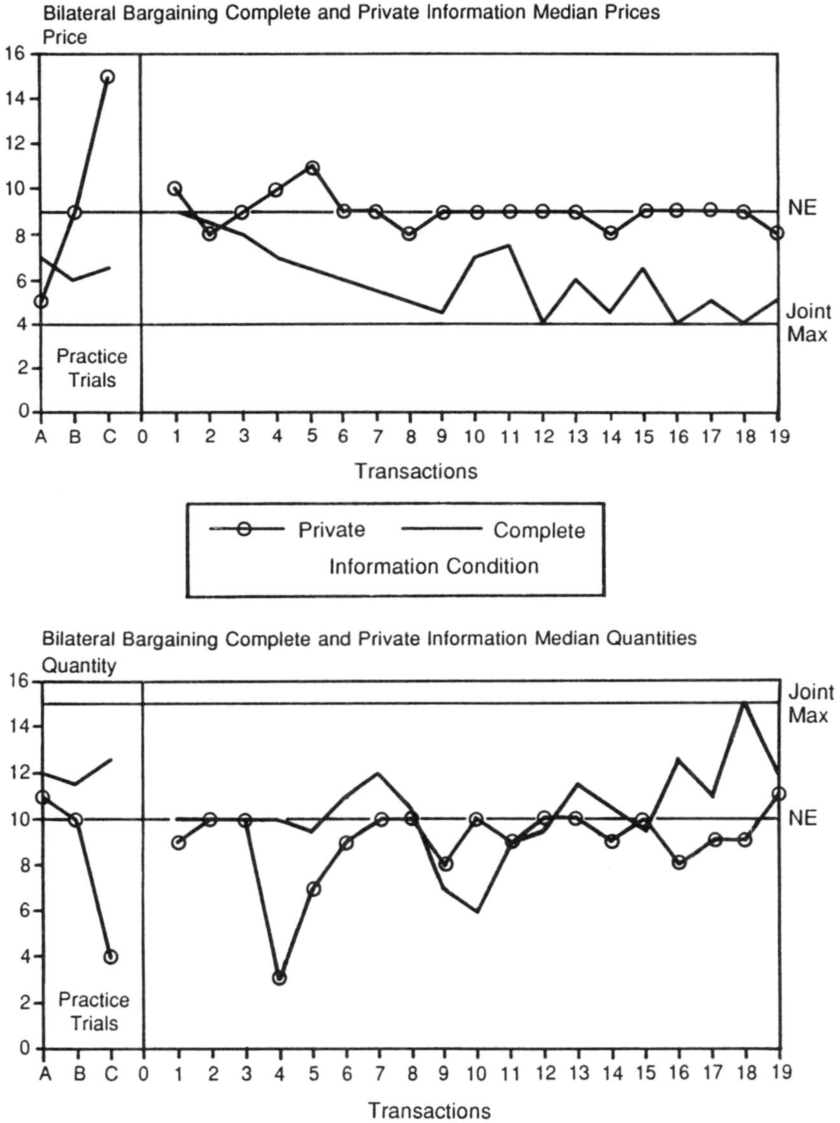

Seller chooses price,then buyer chooses quantity.
Median price and quantity shown in sequence.
(Fouraker and Siegel, *Bargaining Behavior*, 1963)

information, each bargainer can identify the more lucrative competitive equilibrium where joint profit (surplus) is largest. Although the median pair start at the Nash price–quantity equilibrium, there is a slow and erratic move away from Nash and toward the cooperative outcome. Sluggishness is to be expected since the seller must be induced by punishing strategies, or be willing to volunteer cooperative price messages, if the bargainers' joint maximizing outcome is to be achieved.

Thus bilateral bargaining under this particular repeated play, first mover (or minorant game) institution, supports the NE prediction under private information. Under complete information there is a greater tendency to the cooperative outcome. This confirms (for *finite* horizons) the 'Folk Theorem' (Aumann, 1987, p. 468; Mertens, 1987, p. 552; Weber, 1987, p. 459) prediction of cooperation in complete information repeated games (for *infinite* horizons). In both cases theory is supported under *weaker* conditions than postulated by the theory; ergo the theory is inadequate, and requires weakening of its assumptions without changing its predictions. For the cooperative case a step in the right direction might possibly be provided by Kreps, Milgrom, Roberts and Wilson (1982; also see Weber, 1987, p. 459) for the finitely repeated prisoner's dilemma game. The key assumption they introduce is that players are uncertain about the 'type' of player they face. Thus the 'type' may 'irrationally cooperate' with some probability. Then there exist equilibria (also a plethora of others) in which, with high probability, players will cooperate until near the end of the game. This is broadly consistent with the cooperative tendencies observed, although observed defections 'near the end' may be less reliably consistent with the model's predictions.

Cournot oligopoly

In the Cournot model of oligopoly the message space consists of quantities of a homogeneous product that the oligopolists can elect to place on the market. Price is then assumed to adjust immediately to a level that clears the market between a given demand function and the sum of the individual quantities produced by the oligopoly. Fouraker and Siegel (1963) tested the Cournot model, implemented with a linear demand function, and constant symmetric marginal cost, for $N = 2$, duopoly, and $N = 3$, triopoly. In the experiments demand is simulated to yield one price given the sum of outputs. Duopoly pairs and triopoly triads were run simultaneously in separate cubicles under both complete and private information. When the institution specifies that the messages be quantities of output, there are three distinct equilibrium concepts: (1) the joint maximum monopoly, or cooperative equilibrium which maximizes the total profit of the oligopolists, the NE (or Cournot equilibrium, invented by Cournot in 1838; the Cournot–Bowley equilibrium was generalized by Nash in 1951), and the competitive equilibrium, CE, where demand price equals the constant marginal cost and surplus is maximum for sellers plus buyers.

Table 6.1 lists the percentage of observations supporting each equilibrium concept on transaction 21, defined as the equilibrium transaction (transaction 22 was announced as the last to determine end effects). There were 16 duopoly pairs run under private information and 16 under complete information, while 11 triopoly triads were run under each information condition. Support for the NE is greater under private information than under complete information for both duopoly and triopoly. The tendency towards increased support for the CE with complete information is perhaps explained by the greater use of punishment strategies to retaliate when attempts to cooperate fail, or as an effort to induce cooperation. This causes second-order degeneration to the CE. Figure 6.2 plots the median quantity choice by transaction for duopolists and triopolists under both complete and private information.

Bertrand oligopoly

The message space consists of prices in Bertrand oligopoly. The product is homogeneous, all sellers have identical marginal costs, and each oligopolist has sufficient capacity to satisfy all demand. Under these highly competitive conditions the low price seller satisfies the entire market, while tied low price sellers split market sales equally. Fouraker and Siegel (1963) use demand and cost parameters such that the NE, which is identical to the CE, is at a price of 0.5 cents, and the joint

Table 6.1 Cournot oligopoly: percentage of observations supporting joint max, NE and CE on transaction 21

	Duopoly		*Triopoly*	
Equilibrium concept	*Private information*	*Complete information*	*Private information*	*Complete information*
Joint max	6.25	31.25	12.12	9.09
NE	81.25	39.06	60.61	45.45
CE	12.5	29.69	27.27	42.42

Source: Based on Fouraker and Siegel, 1963, pp. 131, 134, 140, 141.

Figure 6.2

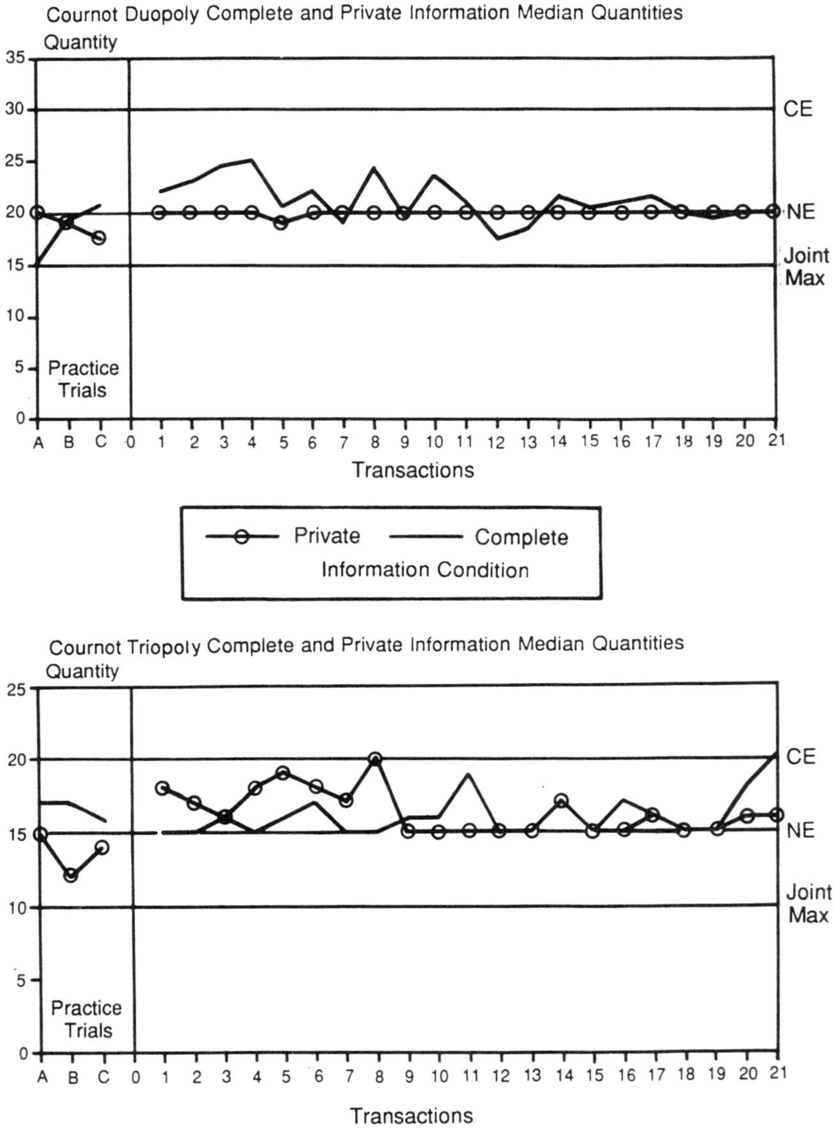

For Bertrand, the CE price equals the NE price.
(Fouraker and Siegel, *Bargaining Behavior*, 1963)

maximum occurs at 3.5 cents. Demand is simulated to yield total sales given the low prevailing price.

In the upper panel of Figure 6.3a is plotted the median low price message announced on each transaction in sequence for 17 duopoly pairs under private information and 17 under complete information. On all transactions – three practice trials, and 15 for cash rewards – the median price message under complete information exceeds that under private information. But the triopoly condition completely dominates the effect of information as is shown by the median announced price series for triopolies in the lower panel of Figure 6.3a (11 triopolies under private information and 10 under complete information). Early signals to cooperate in the practice trials, and in the first three reward trials under complete information, tend to break down. The CE prevails in four of the final five trials under both complete and private information. Such are the strong competitive forces in the Bertrand institution and cost environment. A different perspective is provided in Figure 6.3b, which plots the median *low* price among the two (three) oligopolists on each transaction. Rccall that the ruling price is the low price since that seller supplies the entire market. Two sellers (upper panel) are able to coordinate well enough to avoid the zero profit CE in 10 of 14 transactions under private information and in all 14 transactions under complete information. But triopolies quickly lock onto the CE whatever the information conditions. In the Bertrand environment and institution (posted pricing), $N = 3$ is a large number and sufficient for a CE.

Supply and demand: continuous double oral auction trading

Finally we report large-group experiments using the double oral auction rules characteristic of the organized commodity, stock index, interest rate futures and stock exchanges. These experimental markets are all oral two-sided ('double') auctions. Each trading period opens with a call for bids and offers and ends with a call for final bids, offers and contracts. This soft-close feature is characteristic of pit trading on the Chicago Mercantile Exchange and in other organized exchanges. Individuals designated as buyers (sellers) are free to announce bids to buy (offers to sell) for a single unit. In the experiments reported below, each bid or offer stands until either a new bid or offer is announced, or an acceptance occurs. If and when a bid (offer) is accepted by a seller (buyer) this becomes a binding contract between the two matched traders. Each buyer (seller) has a capacity to buy (sell) at most one unit. Trading occurs over several repeat periods for a total of four (or five) periods; each period is timed to last about 7–8 minutes.

The environment is the special case in which all buyers are assigned

Figure 6.3a

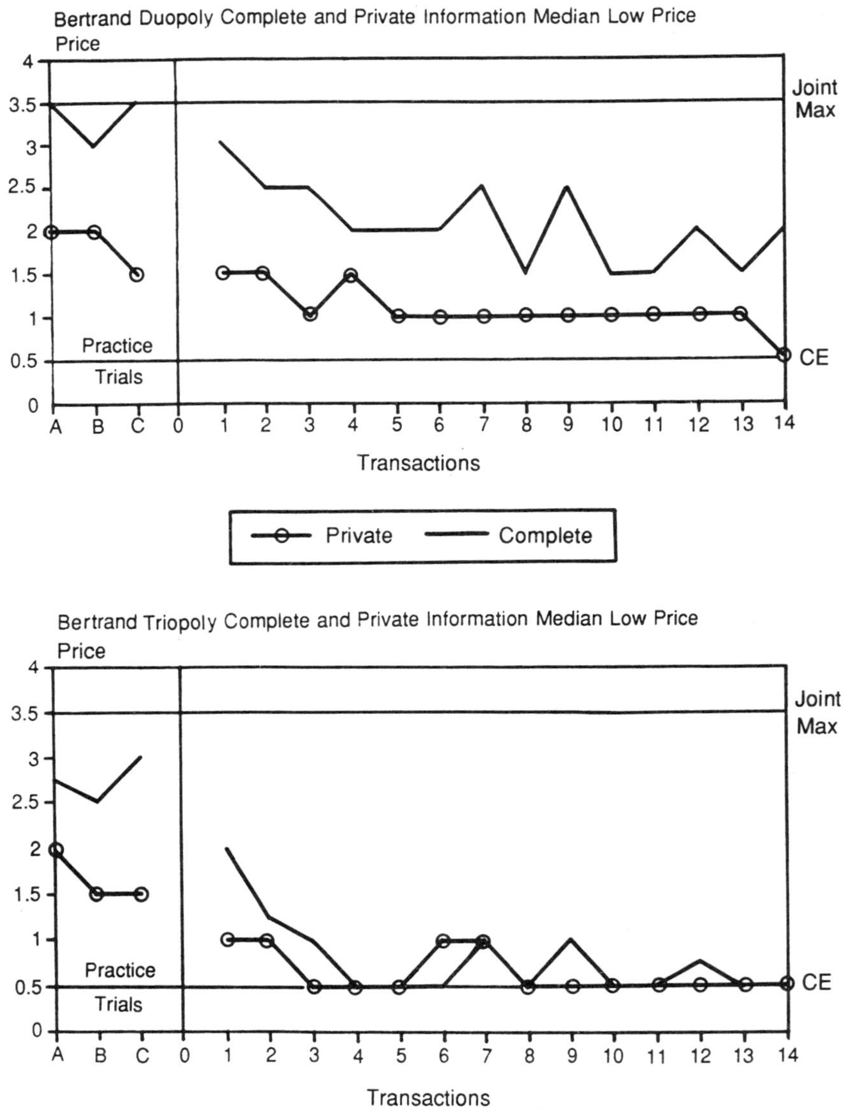

For Bertrand, the CE price equals the NE price.
(Fouraker and Siegel, *Bargaining Behavior*, 1963)

Figure 6.3b

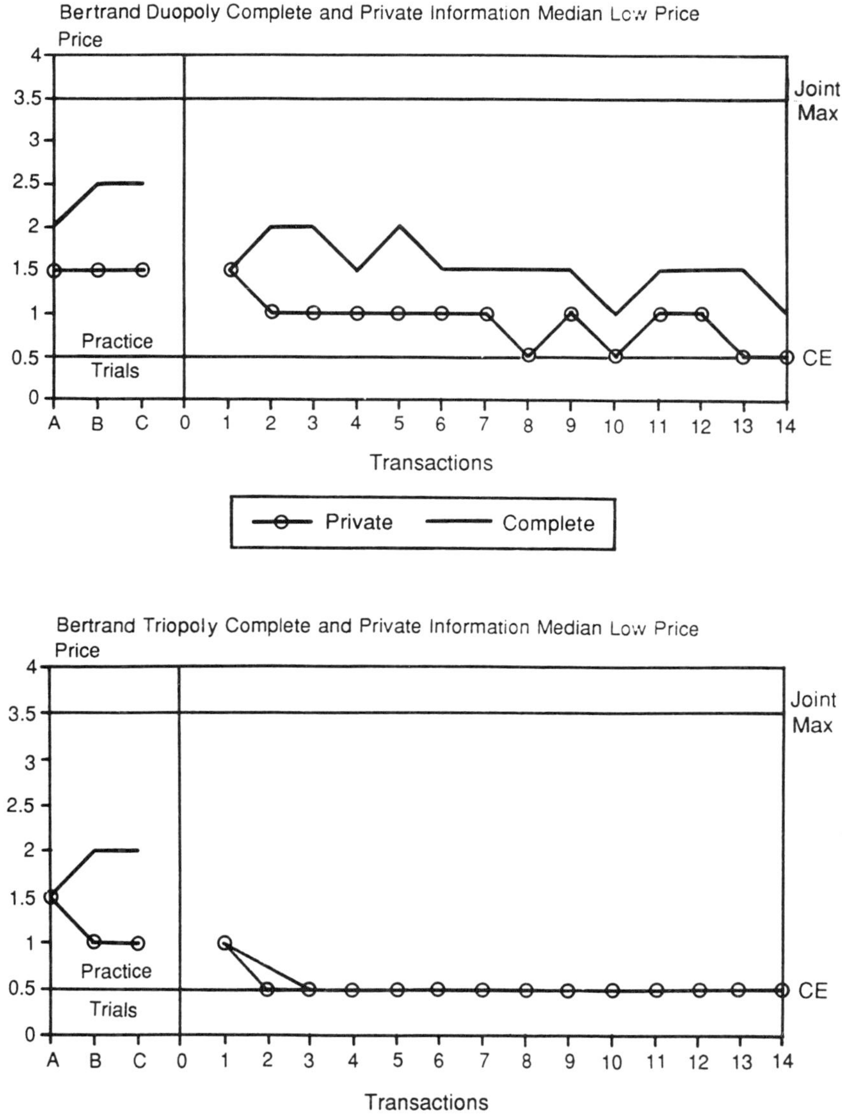

For Bertrand, the CE price equals the NE price.
(Fouraker and Siegel, *Bargaining Behavior*, 1963)

identical induced values of 420 cents, and all sellers are assigned identical induced costs of 310 cents. Each buyer receives cash earnings equal to induced value minus price paid; each seller receives cash earnings equal to sales price minus induced cost. Thus each buyer (seller) may transact up to four (or five) times – once in each trading period.

Figure 6.4 summarizes the results of eight experiments. In experiments 1–4 there were 11 buyers and 16 sellers, giving an excess supply of $e = 5$ units; in experiments 5–8 there were 11 buyers and 19 sellers, with $e = 8$ units. Experiments 1 and 2 ($e = 5$) are two replications, using different subject groups, under private information; experiments 5 and 6 ($e = 8$) are similarly two replications under private information. Experiments 3 ($e = 5$) and 7 ($e = 8$) are conducted under complete common information; that is, after the experimenter read the instructions explaining the double auction rules and the rules for calculating profit, as in the private information treatment, all subjects were told that there were 11 buyers, each with an assigned value of 420 cents and 16 (19) sellers, each with an assigned cost of 310 cents. Consequently all could see that all were being given this information. In experiment 4(8) the first two (three) trading periods are conducted under private information, followed by two periods under complete information.

In Figure 6.4 we plot median (= mean) contract prices in sequence for experiments 1 and 2 ($e = 5$, private information) and for experiments 5 and 6 ($e = 8$, private information). Comparing the results for complete with those for private information it is seen that the convergence over successive periods and contracts to the Nash–Competitive equilibrium is weaker under complete than under private information. This holds for both the 5 and 8 unit excess supply conditions. In experiment 4, where complete common information is introduced before trading opens in period 3, the declining contract price series in periods 3 and 4 shifts up relative to that in periods 1 and 2 under private information. A similar result occurs in experiment 8, where complete common information is introduced after the close of period 3 and applies in periods 4 and 5.

This section, comparing private with complete information under bargaining, Cournot and Bertrand oligopoly, and double continuous auction, is easily summarized: contrary to conventional theoretical beliefs, the non-cooperative equilibrium concept fares best in the laboratory under private information; under complete (also sometimes common) information, either the non-cooperative equilibrium is not supported (as under two-person bargaining) or its attainment is slower than under private information.

Figure 6.4

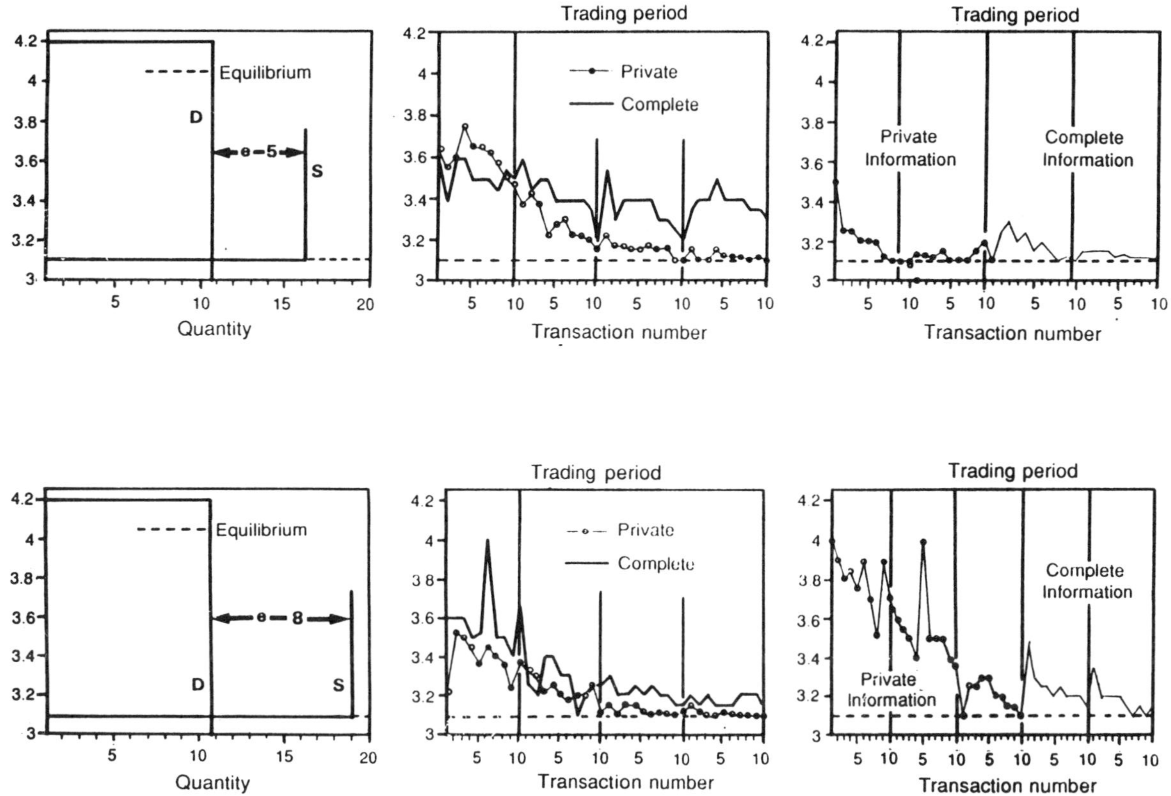

Equilibrium
D
S
e = 5
Quantity
Trading period
Private
Complete
Transaction number
Trading period
Private Information
Complete Information
Transaction number
Equilibrium
D
S
e = 8
Quantity
Trading period
Private
Complete
Transaction number
Trading period
Private Information
Complete Information
Transaction number

4 STOCK MARKET BUBBLES IN THE LABORATORY; DISTINGUISHING COMMON EXPECTATIONS FROM COMMON INFORMATION

> . . . suddenly I realized that the whole point of theoretical science was to understand what was *really happening*. It was not to please the teacher or older colleagues, but this grubby man from the basement who was reporting somebody's measurement. (Murray Gell-Mann)

Rational Expectations theory informs us that, if people have common 'priors', or expectations (Brock, 1974, 1982; Tirole, 1982), and that such expectations correspond to the fundamental or intrinsic value of the asset, then the prices of the asset cannot deviate from fundamental value, except for random white noise. Field data tests of this proposition are frustrated by the fact that the fundamental value of an asset, such as a common share, is not known with any certainty independently of the asset's exchange value. Such tests of rational expectations are indirect, and based on the behaviour of price changes relative to new information or the absence of new information. Thus Shiller (1981), using variance bounds tests, finds that stock prices tend to vary too much relative to dividends, while Kleidon (1986) shows that this is not proved because Shiller used unconditional rather than conditional measures of variance.

In the laboratory we can create an environment in which fundamental value and participant information are controlled. Game theorists assume (Aumann, 1987) that the state of common knowledge controls for the infinite regress on expectations so that common knowledge, *ipso facto*, provides common expectations. But the state of common knowledge or expectations must be distinguished from that of common information. It is the existence of the latter, not the former, that one can guarantee as part of the initial state of experimental subjects, or that might represent some particular field condition. We tell subjects what we want them to know, but the state of their expectations, or knowledge, of what actions to take depends upon how they process the information provided them. Thus the laboratory stock market experiments we summarize below provide common information on 'dividend' (fundamental) value. The research questions we discuss here are the following. (1) If subjects have common information on dividend value, is this sufficient to yield common expectations as revealed by prices that approximate dividend value? (2) If price bubbles are observed will they be eliminated with increasing subject experience? (3) Are observed price bubbles dampened by the opportunity to make short sales and/or margin purchases, by the presence of futures markets, or by regulation using price limit change rules?

The typical environment studied consists of 12 inexperienced subjects or nine subjects who are once or twice experienced. Subjects have the opportunity to trade via a computerized version of New York Stock Exchange (double auction) rules in each of 15 consecutive trading periods. At the end of each period a common 'dividend' return is realized from a probability distribution of dividends (independently and identically distributed) whose parameters are common information to all traders. Each trader is given an initial endowment of cash and shares. At the end of the experiment each subject is paid his/her initial cash endowment, plus all dividend earnings, plus all capital gains less capital losses. The declining dividend value of a share is represented by the step function shown in Figure 6.5. In this example, which illustrates the environment used for experienced subjects, the expected dividend value in each period is \$0.24. Since there are 15 dividend realizations, the dividend value of the asset in period 1 is 15 × \$0.24 = \$3.60, declines

Figure 6.5 Stock market experiment, mean price and volume by trading period

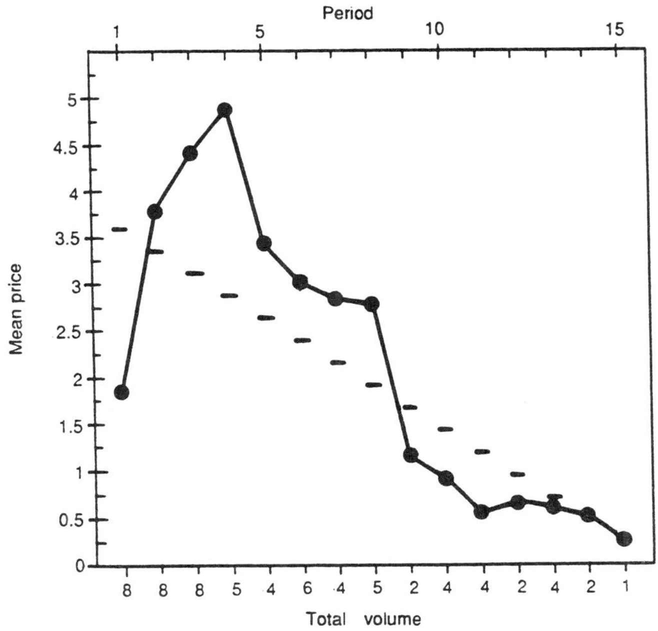

to \$3.36 in period 2 and so on to \$0.24 in the final period, as the number of realizations remaining declines from 15 to 1. All subjects are informed at the end of each period what is the next period's dividend value of a share based on the number of periods remaining. Thus the implications of subjects' dividend information is calculated for them, and updated each period.

A total of 78 experiments using this environment and a variety of treatment variations have now been reported (Smith, Suchanek and Williams, 1988; King, Smith and Williams, 1989; Porter and Smith, 1989, hereafter SSW, KSW and PS respectively). When subjects are inexperienced there is no exception to the following observation: subjects trade in high volume at prices substantially below or above dividend value until the final 1–3 periods. In the typical price bubble pattern, prices begin below, then rise above dividend value, and reach a peak somewhere between periods 9–13, then crash to near dividend value by the end of the horizon (SSW, 1988).

Once-experienced subjects tend to bubble and crash earlier than twice-experienced subjects; the former case is illustrated in Figure 6.5. The mean price in period 1 is substantially below dividend value, then rises above in period 2. The market peaks out in period 4 and crashes in two waves, falling below dividend value in period 9, then rises to dividend value in the final two periods. Total volume by period tends to be much less for experienced than for inexperienced subjects. Subjects brought back a third time who have been part of a group that participated in the same two earlier experiments, tend to trade very near declining dividend value at volumes of 0–3 units per period. These results show that common information is not sufficient to induce common expectations. Behavioural or strategic uncertainty is not eliminated by common information. But with experience subjects learn that sustainable capital gains cannot be made by selling below or buying above dividend value, although some may find such strategies profitable initially. This conclusion is reinforced by the fact that price bubbles continue to occur when the per period dividend is *certain*, and therefore all individual uncertainty must be attributable to the trading behaviour of others (PS, 1989). Learning, however, is somewhat faster where dividends are certain; the bubble tendencies of once experienced subjects is dampened relative to baseline experiments with uncertain dividends, but the data under certain and uncertain dividend structures are indistinguishable from each other when subjects are inexperienced.

These general features of laboratory stock market bubbles are not softened by endowing subjects with the right to sell short (borrowed shares) or buy on margin with borrowed funds. In fact bubbles are worse when the right to buy on margin is available, lending credence to the widespread self-imposition of margin rules by the brokerage industry.

Limit price change rules are common in commodity futures markets but not in the stock, index futures and options markets. Such rules have been widely recommended in the wake of the crash in world stock markets in October 1987. But the comparative results when limit price change rules are applied in laboratory stock markets are not encouraging (KSW, 1989). After correcting for experience, duration and turnover (as measures of bubble intensity) are not significantly affected by limit price change rules, while bubble amplitude is significantly increased. Essentially this appears to be the case because subjects perceive that the downside risk is reduced during the over-valuation phase of the price cycle. But when the bubble bursts prices tend to decline by the limit, and there are no buyers at this limit. Individual learning of these characteristics of market traders takes as long as the characteristics that must be learned when there are no limit price change rules. The latter have no overall influence in speeding up the learning process, only in changing what has to be learned.

The robust tendency of laboratory stock markets to produce bubbles is attributable to the myopic trading behaviour of subjects. Subjects are fully aware that dividend value must fall to the expected one-period dividend value in the final period: this is shown by the fact that virtually all the markets collapse to dividend value by, or before, the final period. Each hopes to ride the profit boom, but sell out in advance of the other traders. In effect, subjects fail to act according to the backward induction principle: if a share must sell for dividend value at the end, then it must do so near the end, hence in the middle, and so on to the beginning. It is by experience in three successive markets, not by backward induction logic applied to common expectations, that subjects learn this principle. Similar findings have been reported by McCabe (1989) in the context of trading using fiat money that becomes worthless in the final period of trade. Harrison and McCabe (1989) also demonstrate the same phenomena in the context of bilateral bargaining. Subjects learn to backward induct properly by alternating the playing of the subgame consisting of the last two rounds of a three-round sequential bargaining game and the playing of the full three-round game. It should be noted that the failure to backward induct is not necessarily a calculatory or logical failure but probably an expectational failure. Backward induction requires each person to expect other subjects to have intrinsic value expectations in later periods; in fact they initially do not have such expectations, so that individuals are reinforced in their failure to backward induct according to rational intrinsic value expectations. The process unwinds with experience because subjects learn what to expect from other subjects in later trading periods. This interpretation appears justified by the fact that Cox and Oaxaca (1989) have found that in wage search experiments subjects have no difficulty 'solving' the backward induction problem. But this is a game against nature in which each subject has only to anticipate his/her own behaviour at the end.

The Harrison–McCabe (1989) technique of first giving bilateral bargainers experience with later subgames before placing them in the full sequential game is exactly a presumed function of futures markets. Futures markets allow traders to play the end (and intermediate) game in advance and thus provides an institutional tool for solving the backward induction problem properly; that is, on the basis of information about market expectations. Thus the important function of futures markets may not be to forecast the 'future' so much as to provide a reading on expectations that enables the formation of common expectations.

Against this background and the results reported in SSW and KSW, Porter and Smith (1989) compared subjects' behaviour for two levels of experience with and without a futures market run simultaneously with the spot market. PS operationalize a single futures claim that expires in period 8 and trades concurrently with the spot share market for the first eight periods. Since all futures claim settlements occur at the end of period 8, futures and shares are identical claims during period 8. The objective is to get traders to focus on, and think about, a share's period 8 value during the first eight periods. It is already known that spot markets in these environments crash to dividend value towards the end. Will a futures on period 8 tend to shorten, and dampen, bubbles? The answer is yes. The presence of a futures market reduces the amplitude, duration and turnover of bubbles; the effect on amplitude is statistically significant for both inexperienced and once experienced subjects.

5 AUCTION THEORY AND BEHAVIOUR; A DIALOGUE BETWEEN THEORY AND EVIDENCE

> Science walks forward on two feet, namely theory and experiment. Sometimes it is one foot which is put forward first, sometimes the other, but continuous progress is only made by the use of both . . .
>
> (Robert Millikan)

A research program consisting of continuing interplay between experimental testing, theory modification, further testing and so on is illustrated by the experimental study of auctions. This example is particularly strong in illustrating the development of excess empirical content in theory modification.

The program was initiated by Vickrey (1961) in a classic paper introducing the profession to incentive compatibility and to important exercises in the formulation of institution-specific theory in the context of the four common forms of auctions. Eventually, Coppinger, Smith and Titus (1980) initiated an experimental program testing various predictions derivable from Vickrey's models of four different auction procedures: the English ascending bid auction, whose rules require bids to increase until the final bidder is declared the winner; the Dutch descending bid procedure, whereby the declining price is indicated on a clock until the first bidder stops the clock and wins the item; the first price sealed bid auction, wherein the highest of the submitted bids wins and pays the amount bid; and the second price sealed bid auction under which the high bidder wins and pays a price equal to the second highest bid. This study yielded data generally consistent with the predictions of English and second price auction theory, but not with those of Dutch and first price auction theory. In this chapter we confine our discussion to the theory and behaviour of the first price auction. Vickrey's analysis of bidding in the first price auction was based on the game theoretic concept of a Nash or non-cooperative equilibrium (*NE*) assuming that there are known to be $N \geqslant 2$ competing bidders for a single object. The theory was implemented by two auxiliary assumptions: (1) bidders are risk-neutral and (2) individual values for the object are distributed as a constant (rectangular) density probability function, with $v_i \in [0,1]$ where v_i is the value of the object to bidder $i = 1,2,\ldots,N$. Vickrey showed that the *NE* bid strategy was

$$b_i = \frac{(N-1)v_i}{N}, \forall_i, \text{ and } v_i \in [0,1]. \tag{6.1}$$

The experiments testing (1) assigned values to N subjects from a rectangular probability function (with replacement) repeatedly in a sequence of T auctions. The first auction data reported by Coppinger, Smith and Titus (1980) and subsequently replicated more systematically by Cox, Roberson and Smith (1982) showed a marked tendency for winning bids (prices) to be higher than is predicted by equation (6.1). Further extended replication and the analysis of all individual bids (for $N = 3,4,5,6,9$) relative to corresponding randomly assigned values

(Cox, Smith and Walker, 1988; hereafter CSW) established that the typical subject's bid relative to value was consistently higher than Vickrey's model predicted. Holt (1980) showed that, if bidders were identical but strictly risk-averse, then, as we observe, the *NE* bid would be higher than the Vickrey prediction. However the Holt model predicts identical bids for any two individuals assigned the same values. A test of the null hypothesis that the bids of the *N* individuals in an experiment are indistinguishable (that is, are samples from the same population) is rejected in 60 per cent (28 of 47) of the experiments (CSW, 1988, p. 73 and Table 3). After learning of these results theorists sometimes comment, 'Well, this is what you expect – that people have different preferences, etc.' But if this is so, why did all auction theories prior to CSW assume *identical* individuals? The rhetoric here is not consistent with the publishing behaviour of the community of theorists. Also, if observed bidding had turned out to be very noisy, one could easily have been unable to reject the hypothesis of bidder homogeneity in 100 per cent of the experimental groups.

Having rejected both the Vickrey and Holt implementations of *NE* theory it was natural to ask, 'How can the model be modified to accommodate this strong falsifying evidence?' Since there are other institutions of exchange (some examples are discussed in section 3) besides auctions for which there is support for *NE* theory, it is clear that there was no empirical basis for abandoning the Vickrey–Holt efforts to work within the *NE* framework. In fact that framework has provided a sufficiently powerful problem-solving heuristic to justify modifying only the 'protective belt' of implementational assumptions when falsifying evidence is encountered. The first modification was proposed in Cox, Roberson and Smith (1982), and is called the constant relative risk averse model (CRRAM); the second, which is a generalization of the first is the log-concave model (LCM) found in CSW (1988, pp. 62–7). Vickrey had assumed that utility for a winning bidder was $u_i = v_i - b_i$; that is, u_i is measured by the monetary surplus from bid b_i. This means that all bidders have identical preferences and that various bidder 'types' are defined only by their private valuations, v_i, $i = 1,2,\ldots,N$. Holt retained this assumption, but assumed that utility to each i was $u_i = u(v_i - b_i)$, where u is concave and identical for all i. Thus all bidders have identical risk-averse preferences. Holt's modification accounted for the very strong tendency of bidders to bid 'as if' risk-averse, but failed to account for the heterogeneous bidding behaviour observed in 60 per cent of the experiments. Cox, Roberson and Smith (1982) postulated utility of the form $u_i = u(v_i - b_i, r_i) = (v_i - b_i)^{r_i}$, $r_i \in [0,1]$ which is the log linear constant relative risk-averse utility function. Each bidder is now characterized by the preference parameter, r_i, in addition to his/her value, v_i. This implies the CRRAM bid function

$$b_i = \frac{(N-1)v_i}{N-1+r_i}, \forall_i \text{ and } v_i \leqslant \bar{v}_i; \frac{(N-1)\bar{v}_i}{N-1+r_i} = \bar{b} = \frac{N-1}{N} \quad (6.2)$$

where $\bar{b}$ is the maximum bid (corresponding to the maximum value, $v_i = 1$) that would be entered by a risk neutral bidder. When $r_i = 1$ equation (6.2) reduces to (6.1). The log-concave model (LCM) generalizes CRRAM by assuming that $u_i = u(v_i - b_i, \theta_i)$ where θ_i is an $M - 1$ vector of parameters, and log u is strictly concave in $v_i - b_i$ for each θ_i. The LCM bid function cannot be written in explicit form, but it has the properties: (1) distinct values of θ_i yield distinct *NE* bid functions; (2) values of θ_i corresponding to greater risk aversion imply higher bids.

Both CRRAM and LCM account for the qualitative features of the data summarized above. Consequently, further testing focused on the special properties of CRRAM, which makes precise predictions, compared with LCM. We summarize three such tests reported in CSW.

(A) For most subjects (62.5 per cent) one can reject the hypothesis that the individual bids are a non-linear (cubic) function of value, in favour of linearity. Most of the contrary cases are for subjects appearing in the same experiments. The latter results are consistent with LCM, since it is not optimal for *i* to bid linearly if *i* has competitors who bid non-linearly in value.

(B) The estimates of $\hat{\beta}_i$ in the regression $b_i(t) = \alpha_i + \beta_i v_i(t) + \varepsilon_i(t)$, where $t = 1,2,\ldots,T$ is the auction number, are strongly consistent with risk aversion: $\hat{\beta}_i > (N-1)/N$ for 92 per cent of 156 subjects. But the $\hat{\alpha}_i$ should not be significantly different from zero; in fact 22 per cent are, with the intercepts biased towards the negative.

(C) A unique implication of CRRAM is the following: if you multiply the profit from a winning bid ($v_i - b_i$) by any factor $\lambda > 0$, this affects only the utility scale $u_i = \lambda^{r_i}(v_i - b_i)^{r_i}$ and has no affect on the equilibrium bid function (6.2). Four experiments (CSW, 1988, pp. 80–1) were run, in which the pay-offs were tripled relative to baseline experiments. Estimates of individual $\hat{\alpha}_i$ and $\hat{\beta}_i$ where $\lambda = 1$ were found not to be significantly different from the estimates obtained when $\lambda = 3$.

The tests reported in CSW are highly consistent with CRRAM except that there are too many intercepts, $\hat{\alpha}_i$, that are significantly positive or negative. Accordingly CSW suggest a modification of CRRAM, called CRRAM*, in which it is postulated that (1) the positive intercepts, $\hat{\alpha}_i$, are due to subjective value attached to the act of winning the auction, parameterized by w_i; and (2) the negative intercepts are due to a threshold level of monetary surplus, parameterized by t_i. These assumptions lead to writing utility, $u_i = (v_i - b_i + w_i - t_i)^{r_i}$, when $v_i - b_i + w_i - t_i \geqq 0$, with $u_i < 0$ otherwise. CRRAM* predicts a positive or negative intercept depending upon whether $w_i - t_i > 0$, or $w_i - t_i < 0$. Thus CRRAM* provides an *ex post hoc* explanation of the non-zero intercepts. But does CRRAM* have testable excess empirical content over CRRAM? The answer is yes. CRRAM* predicts that, if you make a lump sum payment, w', to the winning bidder (in addition to the payment, $v_i - b_i$), this will tend to increase $\hat{\alpha}_i$ relative to a baseline with $w' = 0$. Similarly, if you deduct a lump sum charge, t', from the surplus $v_i - b_i$ paid a winning bidder, this will tend to decrease $\hat{\alpha}_i$ relative to a baseline with $t' = 0$. Although the individual w_i and t_i parameters are not observable, the introduction of payments, w', or charges, t', results in predictable shifts in the observed bid function intercepts. Note, in particular, that without the modifications indicated above, the original model provides no justification, and makes no predictions, for experiments that introduce payments or charges. In fact without CRRAM* no one would dream of doing such experiments. In this sense, CRRAM* makes 'novel' new predictions, and conforms to one of the key elements in Lakatos's concept of a progressive program. New experiments were run and reported by CSW (1988, pp. 94–6) in which lump sum payments, or charges, were introduced. Of 45 paired comparisons, 35 of the intercepts shifted in the direction predicted by CRRAM*.

Although CRRAM* is impressively consistent with most of the test observations, it is not consistent with all of them. A glaring failure is the following: CRRAM (and CRRAM*) predict that if, instead of paying the winner $v_i - b_i$ dollars (normalized on 1), you pay him/her $v_i - b_i$ chances, or unit lottery tickets, on a fixed sum of money, say $15, then the optimal bidding strategy is (1), not (2); that is, paying in lotteries that are linear in probability will have the effect of risk neutralizing the subject in lotteries. In fact subjects do not bid as if risk-neutral under lottery payments, which is in clear violation of the conjunction of CRRAM and the lottery procedure (Walker, Smith and Cox, 1990). One likely culprit in accounting for this failure is the compound lottery axiom of expected utility theory, since an added compounding of probabilities is the only new element in the test procedure.

Auction theory also illustrates Lakatos's frequent reference to the problem of induction; one does not deduce theories from facts. Theories imply observations; observations do not imply theories. One deduces *NE* bid functions, such as (6.2), by maximizing with respect to b_i the expected utility $E(u_i) = (v_i - b_i)^{r_i} G_i(b_i|N)$, where $G_i(b_i|N) = G(b_i|N)$ is the common rational expectations probability that a bid of b_i will be the highest of the N bids submitted. From the *NE* conditions one deduces that $G(b_i|N) \sim b_i^{N-1}$. Then from the first order condition, one obtains the strategy function (6.2). But note that an alternative non-expected utility criterion yields the identical strategy function: choose b_i to maximize $(v_i - b_i)G(b_i|N)^{1/r_i}$. Now the interpretation is completely different: each i maximizes expected value, but 'discounts' the objective probability $G(b_i|N)$ with the parameter $1/r_i$ to arrive at the subjective probability of winning $G_i(b_i|N) = G(b_i|N)^{1/r_i}$. Why do we not claim that this is the appropriate interpretation? The answer informs us of the *key role of theory in empirical tests*: we have no equilibrium theory justifying the existence of different probabilities, $G(b_i|N)^{1/r_i}$, for different i, but the expected utility axioms permit utility of the form $(v_i - b_i)^{r_i}$. The subjective probability interpretation of equation (6.2) is ad hoc empiricism with *no coherent theoretical basis*.

The *NE* concept provides a powerful problem-solving heuristic for the derivation of testable propositions in experimental microeconomics. In auction theory empirical consistency is obtained by adjusting the 'protective belt' of assumptions defining the 'prize' that appears in the utility function. An open question is whether similar prize modifying assumptions will account for other anomalies in expected utility theory. Since there is no end to the alternative ways of implementing the *NE* concept these successes strongly suggest the desirability of deliberate searches for implementations that resolve anomalies. General theories are born, it seems to us, when one finds common sets of implementational assumptions across widely different institutional forms.

6 LAKATOSIAN PROGRESS IS EMPIRICAL

The chapter's opening quotation from Weinberg makes it plain that in any science there can be episodes in which it is felt that theory becomes disembodied from observation. Just as surgeons have to operate to maintain their skill levels, and income, so also do theorists have to do theory. But when this happens in sciences that take it for granted that theory and observation must be coupled, the happening may be accompanied by questioning concern and guilt: 'We just can't go on doing physics like this . . .' But in the sub-community of economic theorists what is taken for granted is that theory is literature-driven; it is not driven by, nor does it in turn drive, either observations or problems of the world. This is the state of practice and even the rhetoric of economic theory. The consequences of this incompatibility between individual scholarly incentives and our professional charge is that Lakatosian progress within economics is far more limited than is deserved by the size and prominence of professional economics. A major reason for this is the fact that the most interesting phenomena on which we have solid experimental regularities are essentially intractable by the techniques of the day. With a few important exceptions the intellectual demands of modelling double auctions and other two-sided processes are just too difficult, given the state of economic theory. The same can be said for other institutions modelled as real time processes. The prospects of near-term publication being dimmed, the best and the brightest intellects work on literature-driven problems of the imagination. Of course these are *not* useless problem exercises; it is just that the *probability* of their being useful, or of the resulting techniques that are developed being useful, does not seem very high.

For all these reasons it is all too common for experimental economists to go with Sam Ting and work on problems of their own choosing; this would occur less often if theorists worked on problems of the laboratory and of the world. These will provide plenty of scope for exercising one's imagination. Good theorists need not be sidetracked into irrelevant modelling and ever-deepening game-theoretic models of complete common 'knowledge' independently of its behavioural relevance. We seem to have, in both Harsanyi and the laboratory, the essential ingredients of potential progress – for economics to walk forward on both its feet. Economic theory, after all, is concerned ultimately with what is really happening in the laboratory and in the field.

REFERENCES

Aumann, R.J. (1987), 'Game Theory', in J. Eatwell, M. Milgate and P. Newman (eds), *The New Palgrave*, vol. 2, pp. 460–79 (London: The Macmillan Press).

Beardsley, Timothy M. (1989), 'Chilling Out', *Scientific American*, September, **261**, p. 20.

Brock, William (1974), 'Money and Growth; The Case of Long-run Perfect Farsight', *International Economic Review*, October, **15**, pp. 750–70.

—— (1982), 'Asset Prices in a Production Economy', in J.J. McCall (ed.), *Economics of Information and Uncertainty*, pp. 1–43 (Chicago: University of Chicago Press).

Coppinger, Vicki, Smith, Vernon L. and Titus, Jon A. (1980), 'Incentives and Behavior in English, Dutch, and Sealed-Bid Auctions', *Economic Inquiry*, **18**, January, pp. 1–22.

Cox, James C. and Oaxaca, Ronald (1989), 'Laboratory Experiments with a Finite Horizon Job Search Model', *Journal of Risk and Uncertainty*, **2**, September, pp. 301–29.

Cox, James C., Roberson, Bruce and Smith, Vernon L. (1982), 'Theory and Behavior of Single Object Auctions', in *Research in Experimental Economics*, vol. 2, pp. 1–43 (Greenwich, CT: JAI Press).

Cox, James C., Smith, Vernon L. and Walker, James M. (1988), 'Theory and Individual Behavior of First-Price Auctions', *Journal of Risk and Uncertainty*, March, **1**, pp. 61–99.

Fouraker, L.E. and Siegel, Sidney (1963), *Bargaining Behavior* (New York: McGraw-Hill).

Harrison, Glenn and McCabe, Kevin A. (1989), 'The Role of Experience in Testing Non Cooperative Bargaining Theory in Experiments', working paper.

Harsanyi, J.C. (1967–8), 'Game With Incomplete Information Played by Bayesian Players', Parts I, II and III, *Management Science*, **14**, pp. 159–82, 320–34, 486–502.

Holt, Charles A. (1980), 'Competitive Bidding for Contracts Under Alternative Auction Procedures', *Journal of Political Economy*, **88**, pp. 433–45.

King, Ronald R., Smith, Vernon L. and Williams, Arlington W. (1989), 'The Robustness of Bubbles and Crashes in Experimental Stock Markets', Department of Economics, University of Arizona.

Kleidon, Allan W. (1986), 'Anomalies in Financial Economics: Blueprint for Change?', in R.M. Hogarth and M.W. Reder (eds), *Rational Choice* (Chicago: University of Chicago Press).

Kreps, David, Milgrom, Paul, Roberts, John and Wilson, Robert (1982), 'Rational Cooperation in the Finitely Repeated Prisoners' Dilemma', *Journal of Economic Theory*, **27**, pp. 245–52.

Lakatos, Imre (1978), *The Methodology of Scientific Research Programmes*, John Worrall and Gregory Currie (eds), vol. 1 (Cambridge: Cambridge University Press).

Leamer, Edward E. (1983), 'Let's Take the Con Out of Econometrics', *American Economic Review*, March, **73**, pp. 31–43.

Lewis, D.K. (1969), *Convention* (Cambridge, Mass.: Harvard University Press).

Marschak, Jacob (1968), 'Economics of Inquiring, Communicating, Deciding', *American Economic Review Proceedings*, May, **58**, pp. 1–18.

McCabe, Kevin A. (1989), 'Fiat Money as a Store of Value in an Experimental Market', *Journal of Economic Behavior and Organization*, **12**.

McCloskey, Donald N. (1983), 'The Rhetoric of Economics', *Journal of Economic Literature*, June, **21**, pp. 481–517.

Mertens, Jean-François (1987), 'Supergames', in J. Eatwell, M. Milgate and P. Newman (eds), *The New Palgrave*, vol. 4, pp. 551–2 (London: The Macmillan Press).

Pool, Robert (1989), 'Skepticism Grows Over Cold Fusion', *Science*, 21 April, **244**, pp. 284–5.

Porter, David and Smith, Vernon L. (1989), 'The Scope of Bubbles in Experimental Asset Markets', Department of Economics, University of Arizona.

Shiller, R.J. (1981), 'Do Stock Prices Move Too Much to be Justified by Subsequent Changes in Dividends?', *American Economic Review*, **7**, pp. 421–36.

Siegel, Sidney and Fouraker, L.E. (1960), *Bargaining and Group Decision Making* (New York: McGraw-Hill).

Smith, Vernon L. (1987), 'Experimental Methods in Economics', in J. Eatwell, M. Milgate and P. Newman (eds), *The New Palgrave*, vol. 2 (London: The Macmillan Press).

—— (1989), 'Theory, Experiment and Economics', *Journal of Economic Perspectives*, Winter.

Smith, Vernon L., Suchanek, Gerry L. and Williams, Arlington W. (1988), 'Bubbles, Crashes, and Endogenous Expectations in Experimental Markets', *Econometrica*, September, **56**, 1119–51.

Sonnenschein, Hugo (1983), *The Economics of Incentives: An Introductory Account*, Nancy L. Schwartz Memorial Lecture, Evanston: J.L. Kellogg Graduate School of Management, Northwestern University.

Tirole, Jean (1982), 'On the Possibility of Speculation Under Rational Expectations', *Econometrica*, pp. 1163–81.

Vickrey, William (1961), 'Counterspeculation, Auctions and Competitive Sealed Tenders', *Journal of Finance*, May, **16**, pp. 8–37.

Walker, James M., Smith, Vernon L. and Cox, James C. (1990), 'Inducing Risk Neutral Preferences: An Examination in a Controlled Market Environment', *Journal of Risk and Uncertainty*, **2**, September, pp. 219–35.

Weber, Robert J. (1987), 'Games with Incomplete Information', in J. Eatwell, M. Milgate and P. Newman (eds), *The New Palgrave*, vol. 2 (London: The Macmillan Press).

COMMENT ON SMITH, McCABE AND RASSENTI

H.M. Collins*

Smith, McCabe and Rassenti (SMR) start with some general comments about the relationship between theory and experiment in physics and economics and move rapidly to a description of economic experiments.[1] The chapter is meant to show that economists should do more testing of theory with empirical studies of the sort described. Not being an economist I cannot make informed technical comments on the work. What I will do is discuss, in general terms, the nature of such experiments and their relationship to experiments in physics.

What is an experiment? Looking at the comments SMR quote with approval, for them, 'experiment' includes the discovery of the W and Z particles, things done in basements by grubby men who come to the attention of theoretical physicists, and things done by Robert Millikan, most famous for the discovery of the charge on the electron. Finding the W and the Z and Millikan's discovery could be said to be a matter of careful observation rather than experiment, but we will set that aside. Experiments, let us say, include difficult observations that involve instruments or the statistical analysis of data. In economics there are many such observations, such as the discovery of the Phillips curve, as well as more manipulative experiments.[2]

Of SMR's physics examples Millikan's experiment is the best known. Millikan thought there was an irreducible unit of electrical charge. It was small. It followed that all measured charges would be made up of multiples of that unit. To prove his point he needed to measure some very small charges and show that they increased in steps; no charge should be smaller than the irreducible unit and no charge should include a fraction of a unit. What Millikan did was to observe tiny drops of oil in an electric field. By varying the electric field he was able to balance the oil drop against gravitational pull and he could work out the size of the charge on the drop. According to his experimental reports, the charge on the drops did vary in integral steps, confirming his view. Quite a lot has been written about the relationship between what Millikan said in his experimental reports and what is to be found in his notebooks. He did not report everything; he dismissed certain 'anomolous' readings. This we will take as a model experiment.[3]

Not all experimental manipulations and complex observations are

* I would like to thank John Cullis and Allister McGregor for helpful comments on the first draft of this discussion.

experiments. Consider simulations. Physicists do simulations: they might simulate the flow of electric current with flows of water or, in more recent times, with computer models. Some of the most advanced elementary particle physics involves computer simulation. Weather forecasters and bridge designers do computer simulations while boat and airplane builders do simulations with scale models. Civil defence planners do simulations of emergencies by recruiting teams of victims with pretended injuries and seeing how the emergency services respond. Army manoeuvres are simulations. Economists, of course, do simulations too. Macroeconomists, for example, build computer models of the economy, give them some starting assumptions, and run them.

Note that simulations have a lot in common with experiments. Simulations certainly *involve* a lot of experimentation and manipulation. Their outcomes are unknown in advance. They can produce surprises. What then is the difference between experiment and simulation?

At first sight the difference between a simulation and what Millikan did seems to have something to do with the fact that Millikan was doing his best to look as directly as possible at electric charges, whereas economic modellers, for example, do not look at economies at all – they look only at computers. SMR seem to imply that doing laboratory work is acting more like Millikan than typical economists – either theorists or computer modellers. They appear to be claiming that they look at the world more directly than other economists. The distance between what they see and what actually happens in the world is shorter than it is for simulators.

The trouble is that this business of looking directly at things gets complicated. Millikan did not look directly at electric charges. What he looked at were the positions of the knobs that controlled the charge on the electrostatic plates. It is quite a long journey from there to the electron; the journey goes via oil drops, air currents, gravitational pulls, microscopes, and so on. Actually that long journey was quite useful to Millikan because his 'raw data' did not support his views in quite the way he would have liked. The long journey made it possible for him to dismiss some of his 'anomolous' readings; in these cases, something must have gone wrong along the way.[4]

Once one sees that both experiment and simulation involve long journeys between reality and observation it becomes still less obvious what the difference is. I think that if there is a difference it must be to do with causal chains. One can tell a plausible story about the causal relationship between charge and the position of the knobs in the case of Millikan, whereas there is no causal relationship between the world and the results of a simulation except via the imagination of the simulator.[5] In the case of computer simulation the causal story starts not with the world but with the equations and assumptions that go into the model. From there it is the usual long journey to the observations.[6] The macroeconomic modeller does *experiments* on the effect of equations in a computer, but *simulations* in respect of the economy. The ship designer does *experiments* on scale models in order to *simulate* the performance of a full-scale ship. The civil defence coordinator does *experiments* on mock victims in order to *simulate* the effects of war.

Accepting this account of the difference between experiment and simulation, let us return to SMR's economic experiments. The following argument is not a critique of SMR's work but an attempt to establish the epistemological status of their work.[7] In philosophical terms, do SMR most resemble Millikan or the weather forecasters?

There does not seem to be a causal connection between economies and SMR's laboratory observations. If you want to tell a causal story about the relationship between the things that happen in economies and the outcome of laboratory experiments it still has to be via the experimenter's imagination. The experimenter has to imagine the relationship between economies and what happens in the lab. The economy is not to be found in the lab in the way that charge is to be found in Millikan's apparatus. The direct causal story starts with people in labs playing a game.[8]

I cannot see a lot of difference between people playing games in laboratories and computers working through programs in so far as *their causal relationships to economies* is concerned. A few people in a laboratory are not a society. They *may* act in the same way – and the whole point of simulation is an assumption that they *will* act in the same way – but they may not.[9] The same is true of all simulations. The weather may not act in the same way as a computer model;[10] bridges may not behave as earthquake simulations may have led one to believe;[11] boats and planes may not behave in the same way as scale models;[12] real injury victims and their helpers may not act in a way that they do in a mock emergency, and manoeuvres certainly are not war – war is more scary.[13]

If economics is about economies rather than the behaviour of people in laboratories, SMR are describing simulations. To reiterate, there is nothing wrong with simulations – they form a major part of many sciences, but the distinction is worth making because simulations do not have the epistemological priority that we accord to experiments. For example, simulations of one kind do not have epistemological priority over simulations of another kind in the way that experiments do.[14]

Of course I may be mistaken about the nature and object of economics. Large parts of economics are about the behaviour of idealized people and idealized markets. If these are *meant* to be idealizations of the way people interact in laboratories – so that economics is more like social psychology than sociology – then my argument falls. Under these circumstances theoretical models could be tested by *experiments* on the behaviour of people in labs. Only in that case is the causal story complete and plausible.[15]

Smith, McCabe and Rassenti describe some very interesting work. There are bad simulations and good simulations. Experience tells us that good simulations, such as scale-model testing of boats and airplanes, are often as effective as experiments themselves. We discover this from experience – for example, comparing the results of scale-model testing with the results of full-scale testing. Occasionally, as in the cases of Trident III, the weather, and the Bay Bridge in San Francisco, things go wrong. In these circumstances the epistemological priority of experiment becomes clear. Nevertheless simulations of various types will always be at the forefront of scientific research.

Notes

1. Smith V.L., McCabe, K.A. and Rassenti, S.J., 'Lakatos and Experimental Economics', this volume.
2. I have been told that a good example involved the New England negative income tax.
3. For a fascinating account see the chapter on Millikan in Holton, G., *The Scientific Imagination* (Cambridge: Cambridge University Press, 1978).
4. Some of these anomolous results were rescued briefly in the late 1970s, when the idea of free quarks made it seem that one-third and two-third charges ought to be possible. Millikan's notebooks were studied again, and it was found that he had discovered and dismissed such readings.
5. Millikan could have been entirely wrong, of course. His observations may have had nothing to do with charge. That is why we have to talk in terms of plausibility. In science, it is plausibility all the way down.

   I think I have picked up the causal chain idea from Nancy Cartwright's book *How the Laws of Physics Lie*. Cartwright, however, would not want to go along with the idea that physics is plausibility all the way down.
6. And this long journey is subject to all the Millikan-like problems that were discovered by Dewald, Thursby and Anderson (Dewald, W.G., Thursby, J.G. and Anderson, R.G., 'Replication in Empirical Economics: The *Journal of Money, Credit and Banking Project*', *American Economic Review*, **76**, 1986, pp. 587–603).
7. It seemed to be read as a criticism by many at the Capri conference.
8. The journey from there to what you observe has, of course, all the problems of experimental social psychology – such as experimenter expectancy effects. (For example, see Rosenthal, R., 'Interpersonal Expectancy Effects: The First 345 Studies', *The Behavioural and Brain Sciences*, 1978, **3**, pp. 377–415.)
9. For reasons that might lead one to think that, for example, simulated auctions are

not like real auctions, see Smith, C.W., *Auctions: The Social Construction of Value* (New York: The Free Press; Hemel Hempstead: Harvester Wheatsheaf, 1989).

10. Chaos theory shows that it probably will not.
11. As the San Francisco earthquake, which happened during the Capri conference, revealed.
12. As tests on the Trident III in the summer of 1989 showed. The Trident III failed because it was just too big and engineers had not properly simulated the hydraulic forces on such a large object travelling through water at speed.
13. You could argue that all experiments are simulations in the sense that no experiment exactly reproduces 'real' conditions. Many experiments fail in this way. But with simulations the differences are of a different order; the medium of manipulation is different – computers rather than the atmosphere itself – scale models in tanks rather than ships at sea. This difference is made clear by thinking about the causal story. Whatever weather a computer model predicts, the operator will not get wet; whatever the outcome of a mock battle the soldiers will not get killed. Compare this with the Millikan case. It is conceivable (but so implausible as to be uninteresting) that charge is integral in a Millikan oil drop apparatus but continuous in the real world. The conditions of the oil drop apparatus may be special. Irrespective of this, however, there is a chance that Millikan could do things with the charge in his apparatus that would make his hair stand on end. He could not make his hair stand on end with a computer simulation of charge however clever he was.
14. Of course, a good simulation has priority over a poor experiment, but it is not epistemological priority, it is a matter of technique.
15. I really hope, however, that economics is not social psychology. If economics is not about economies but about people in laboratories why are economists, like Sir Alan Walters, advising the government? Suffering under Friedman's economics is bad enough; I would hate to think we are suffering under Friedman's social psychology.

PART II

Program Identification and Program Rivalry

A On Including and Excluding Lines of Enquiry

7. The Stamping Out of Process Analysis in Econometrics

Mary Morgan*

1 INTRODUCTION

The first serious debate within econometrics about how to build models was sparked off by the introduction of process analysis to model the dynamics of economic activity. Econometricians trying to capture the economy in their statistical models found that adapting process analysis to their needs raised fundamental questions about the nature of economic observations and relationships, and about the way economies worked. The divisions that emerged over these issues proved sufficiently deep to cause a split within the field, even though the econometrics research program was only just fully developed at this stage, and its dimensions were still rather fluid.

2 PROCESS ANALYSIS IN THE ECONOMETRICS MOULD: TINBERGEN AND WOLD

In order to understand how process analysis migrated into econometrics and the form it took there, we need to go back to the work of Jan Tinbergen. Tinbergen was the most creative and innovative of applied econometricians working in the 1930s.[1] He formulated the first large-scale business cycle models for the economies of Holland, USA and UK. His aim in building his business cycle models was to explain how the economy moved through time, and how the relations between the variables caused these movements. He built these models by

* An earlier version of this paper was prepared for a Symposium on the History and Philosophy of Econometrics, Duke University, Department of Economics: History of Thought Program, on 19 November 1987. I am grateful to the discussants on that occasion, John Geweke and John Whittaker; to other participants, particularly Neil de Marchi and Roy Weintraub; and to John Aldrich, Jens Andvig, Roger Backhouse, Mark Blaug, Chris Gilbert, David Hendry and Duo Qin for helpful comments in seminar discussion at Oxford and Southampton, in Oslo and Capri.

synthesizing the 'sequence' or 'process' analysis of the Swedish School of macroeconomics with the 'statistical' models which had been developed in microeconometrics in the late 1920s and early 1930s.

Process or sequence analysis was a disequilibrium approach to economic analysis developed by the Stockholm school of economists in the 1930s (see Hansson, 1982). It was assumed that at each point of time the plans made by one group of people did not exactly match those made by others and thus remained in part unfulfilled: this led to disequilibrium in the aggregate outcomes. The analysis was also multi-period and dynamic, for it was the mismatching of plans in one period which led to changes and movements in the economy in the next period. Tinbergen attached these ideas to a model form, developed in the 1920s in microeconometric studies of supply and demand, known as the cobweb model. These cobweb models shared many features of sequence analysis. They were explicitly dynamic, and the supply and demand decisions taken in each period might lead to disequilibrium outcomes, equilibrium outcomes, or a tendency towards equilibrium: the actual outcomes depended on the coefficients found for the equations.

Tinbergen built his macrodynamic models in the same fashion as these cobweb models. He used discrete, time-dated variables, and each equation represented a one-way causal relationship of the expectations and actions of groups of individuals in the economy over a number of time periods. The individual equations together formed a system of equations in which each causal relationship could be related back to other or earlier causal relationships. Such models could explain how the economy moved through time, and might (depending on the parameters of the individual equations) give a cyclical pattern in the time-series solution for the economic system as a whole. By the addition of random shocks which fed through the system (following Ragnar Frisch's (1933) model design), the 'process' econometric model could also be reconciled with the observed business cycle data, which showed both jagged variability and continued irregular cycles.[2]

These notions of dynamic model building using process analysis were not fixed from the start. Tinbergen developed them gradually over the period 1935 to 1940, as he groped his way towards expressing the relationships within the macroeconomy in an econometric model, and as he defended himself against the critics of his method of causal modelling. Although his ideas developed, his aims of building models which captured the movements of the economy remained unchanged. He was not particularly interested in equilibrium positions, for the essence of process analysis, and of econometricians' understanding of economic time-series data, was that positions of rest would never be observed. Tinbergen's dynamic causal models were not a subject of essential disagreement for econometricians in the 1930s, though they proved controversial amongst economists.

Herman Wold developed the probability analysis necessary for the further analysis of such econometric models in his thesis of 1938. He was one of the earliest graduate students of Harold Cramer, who taught the ideas of the Russian school of probability theorists in a graduate course on stochastic processes at the University of Stockholm in the early 1930s (see Wold, 1982, pp. 203–4). Wold's thesis was primarily in theoretical statistics, and involved the development and application of Kolmogorov's ideas on stochastic processes to the linear regression model for stationary time-series data. The thesis quickly became a classic text in its field, and Wold continues to have a considerably greater reputation in time-series econometrics and statistics than he does within structural econometrics. Although Wold was not trained as an economist, he was well connected in this respect. In particular, he was great friends with Erik Lundberg,[3] an important figure in the development of the disequilibrium dynamics of the Stockholm School (see Hansson, 1982, Chapter 10) and discussed his work briefly in his thesis. Furthermore the main applications of his thesis were on economic data: he provided a re-analysis of Beveridge's long run of wheat prices and experimented with Mydal's cost of living index. He also discussed how his analysis could be applied to the dynamic business cycle system models with random error terms which had been developed by Frisch and Tinbergen.

Following Tinbergen, there were two lines of development of system models in the 1940s and 1950s. The one which quickly became fashionable and dominant in econometric theory discussions and adopted in the macroeconometric models of the post-war period, was that of Haavelmo, developed by the Cowles Commission. The other line, apparently less successful, was that due to Wold and developed by his Swedish associates. Both groups believed that they were following Tinbergen's lead in the way they built models and in the sort of models they built, and both referred back to his example.

3 HAAVELMO AND THE SIMULTANEOUS EQUATIONS MODEL

In the first development of Tinbergen's model form, Trygve Haavelmo (1943 and 1944) proposed a system model involving simultaneous equations as part of his advocacy of the use of probability reasoning in econometrics.[4] It is important to see the set of meanings attached to his idea of this model formulation. My insistence here might seem strange, for surely, one might argue, the simultaneous equations model is the natural system model for econometricians, for it fits the general equilibrium model of Walras, the pre-eminent system model in economics. But in the 1920s and 1930s the thinking of econometrics and mathematical economists was dominated by dynamics and business cycle analysis which, as we have seen, did not necessarily involve equilibrium ideas. Further, Haavelmo's economic ideas had been nurtured in the Scandinavian environment, and like Frisch (his Professor) and the Stockholm School of economists, he was much influenced by the work of Wicksell.

Haavelmo was careful to distinguish static relationships (in which the time sequence of observations was not relevant) from the measurement of dynamic relationships, in which the sequence of observations was important. Under the latter, each point provided a new set of conditions which influenced the choice (decision) of the next point. The influencing conditions were interpreted by Haavelmo as 'causal factors':

> This viewpoint is something that is deeply rooted in our way of reasoning about the things we observe in reality. We do not need to take the notions of cause and effect in any metaphysical sense. What we mean is simply that the individuals, firms, etc., are bound in their planning and decisions by a set of conditions that are *data* in the process of adaptation. Within the limits of these given conditions the adaptation process consists in choosing what is deemed the 'best' decision, in some sense or another. (Haavelmo, 1944, p. 22)

But then, moving on from the process analysis of the individual decisions, he was anxious to place these systems of causal relations which held within sections of the economy (individuals, firms or groups) within the context of mutual dependence systems at the level of the economy as a whole:

> In point of principle there may, perhaps, appear to be some logical difficulties involved in operating with such *one-way*, or causal relationships. In fact, modern economists have stressed very much the necessity of operating with relations of the mutual-dependence type, rather than relations of the cause–effect type. However, both types of relations have, I think, their place in economic theory; and, moreover, they are not necessarily opposed to each other, because a system of relations of the mutual-dependence type for the economy *as a whole* may be built up from *open* systems of causal relations within the various *sectors* of the economy. The causal factors (or the 'independent variables') for one section of the economy may, themselves,

> be dependent variables in another section, while here the dependent variables from the first section enter as independent variables. The essential thing is that, while for the economy as a whole everything depends upon everything else, so to speak, there are, for each individual, firm, or group, certain factors which *this* individual, firm, or group *considers as data*. The notion of causal factors is of a relative character, rather than an absolute one. (Haavelmo, 1944, p. 22)

Apart from the addition of 'mutual dependencies', Haavelmo's description of how to build up a system of relations for the model is very similar to that given by Tinbergen (for example, see his Dutch model, 1937, p. 8). Haavelmo pointed out that the mutual dependencies (the simultaneity) within the system as a whole restrict the possibilities for variation of all the relations in the system. This makes it difficult, in practice, to see how the restrictions work. In contrast, in a causal chain model, each equation restricts only the relationships which come later in the chain, so that the way the restrictions work is much clearer.

Model form and causality were important questions for Haavelmo because he was interested in structure and the autonomy of relationships. But what was new and persuasive for econometricians was the formulation and estimation of these system models as simultaneous equations. Although discussion of the simultaneous equations model took up only a small part of Haavelmo's long paper (1944), all other aspects were discussed using this model as the exemplar. Furthermore the use of such a model was popularized by two shorter papers: Haavelmo (1943) and Koopmans (1945), both of which pointed out the novelty of the estimation results. If the economy was a simultaneous system, then to measure it with probability theory would give accurate measures, but to measure it without such techniques would produce biased measures. The simultaneous equations bias was the crucial example that convinced people of the importance of adopting the probability approach for measurement and inference in econometrics (see Morgan, 1987).

The Cowles Commission group took up Haavelmo's program and their work dominated theoretical econometrics in the 1940s. They became obsessed with the simultaneous equations model form because it presented challenging new technical problems of identification, estimation and inference.[5] But their interest was in the system aspects of the model and they had comparatively little to say on dynamics or on causality in such models.

4 WOLD AND RECURSIVE CHAINS

Modelling the system of equations of the economy in a way that had implications for causal interpretation did not go unnoticed by those outside the charmed circle at Cowles. In reaction to Haavelmo's work, Bentzel and Wold (1946) restated the case for process analysis and further defined the model form appropriate to its use. They discussed the meaning and consequences of the simultaneous equations model and distinguished static or moving equilibrium system models from dynamic and disequilibrium systems, which, like Tinbergen, they approached from the point of view of sequence (or process) analysis. As we shall see, at this stage, the two groups had many beliefs in common.

Wold and Bentzel presented Haavelmo's simultaneous equations model of demand and supply, involving a joint probability distribution for price and quantity (p and q) and with disturbance variables u_{1t}, u_{2t}, as follows:

$$q_t = Ap_t + u_{1t}$$

$$p_t = Bq_t + u_{2t}$$

They described this as a moving equilibrium model obtained by imposing the constraint that supply and demand quantities were equal at each point of time. They could see no causal relations in the Haavelmo model, only stochastic relations due to their common dependence on the shift factors, evident in the reduced form equations:

$$q_t = a_1u_{1t} + a_2u_{2t}$$

$$p_t = b_1u_{1t} + b_2u_{2t}$$

The reduced form described the relationships but not, for Wold and Bentzel, in a way which led to an understanding of causes or provided an explanation of the system. This viewpoint was endorsed by Tinbergen in his brief 1947 discussion of the simultaneous equations model (see Tinbergen, 1949).

An understanding of causes could be obtained in sequence analysis on the other hand, because each relation involved current time period variables determined only by variables of past time periods or other variables independently determined elsewhere in the system. These relations fitted together to form a complete causal chain or recursive system and the path of causation could then be traced through the system. Equilibrium conditions were not imposed because the model was designed for disequilibrium analysis; and in building models for observed economic data, Wold and Bentzel considered disequilibrium, not equilibrium, was to be the guiding principle. They gave, as their alternative model for demand, a recursive system, in which each endogenous variable was determined by lagged endogenous variables, exogenous variables, or endogenous variables determined earlier in the causal chain. Their model (with the equations reordered) was:

$$s_t = b_1 p_{t-1} + b_2 l_{t-1} + u_{1t}$$

$$p_t = c_1 p_{t-1} + c_2 s_t + c_3 l_{t-l} + u_{2t}$$

$$d_t = a_1 p_t + u_{3t}$$

$$l_t = d_1 l_{t-1} + s_t - d_t + u_{4t}$$

(*Where* d and s are quantities purchased and produced, p is price and l is stocks at the period end, and u_{it} are disturbance or error terms.) As can be seen, the endogenous variables are determined in the following causal sequence: supply, price, demand, and lastly, stocks. (See Appendix I for a general description of recursive versus simultaneous model forms.)

Like Haavelmo's innovation of the simultaneous equations model, Wold's model form was also more fully defined than Tinbergen's, in two respects. First of all, Tinbergen's systems had not always been completely recursive because he did not check the causal chains as he built up the model. Consequently his Dutch model (1937) had been recursive, but his US model (1939, II) had involved some mutual dependencies. Secondly, compared with Tinbergen's informal use of Frisch's shock model (1933), Wold and Bentzel followed the probability approach in formally introducing random shocks into each equation in the causal chain. The set of equations could then be reduced to a set of stochastic linear difference equations, each containing only one of the variables in autoregressive form: the reduced form for the recursive model.[6] This was the stochastic process form of the model analysed extensively in Wold's thesis (1938) and which he believed accurately described economic time-series data.

Wold made no quarrel with Haavelmo's probability approach at this stage; and was happy to admit Haavelmo's new results on estimation bias and the implication that system estimation methods should be used on simultaneous equations models. But the corresponding advantage of Wold's model form was that the recursive model could be estimated without bias by ordinary least squares (OLS), a point already conceded by Tjalling Koopmans of the Cowles Commission. Koopmans (1945) had shown how the use of time lags in relations could produce a recursive model which he presented as a special case of the simultaneous equations model. He then went on to say, almost as an afterthought, that this enabled one to select the dependent variable on the basis of cause–effect relations and to know the path of causation through the system. Since both sides agreed that recursive models could be estimated without bias by OLS, but that the simultaneous equations model could not, the estimation issue seemed to have been settled (although it later re-emerged as a subject for argument). The only problem with the recursive model to which Bentzel and Wold did admit was that time units of observation were sometimes not short enough to reflect the decisions of agents in the process model, leaving no alternative but a Haavelmo-type model.[7]

At first sight, it looks as if Wold's disagreement with Haavelmo and the Cowles group was only a matter of different competing model forms within the same probability-based econometrics research program. But this would be a simplistic judgement for, when we delve below the surface level of model forms and their estimation, we find the protagonists are arguing about more fundamental issues: static versus dynamic models, equilibrium versus disequilibrium models, causes and how they are to be introduced and interpreted in econometric models, aggregate versus individual (or group level) variables and description versus explanation. These arguments involved the relevant economic theories as well as how to do econometrics. Although the two sides seemed close together in the mid-1940s, they drifted apart over the following 10–15 years, as these fundamental issues emerged into open debate.

5 RECURSIVE CHAINS VERSUS SIMULTANEOUS EQUATIONS: DIMENSIONS OF THE DEBATE

There were three dimensions to the debates between proponents of Haavelmo's simultaneous equations approach and Wold's recursive chain approach. These may be classified as arguments about the practical usefulness of the models; intellectual discussions about how the economic world really was and how it should be represented in models; and methodological arguments about the way to find out about the world using those models.

The Practical Level

Although Haavelmo and the Cowles Commission held the theoretical high-ground in econometrics because of their discovery of the simultaneous equations bias, it remained to be shown that the simultaneous equations model was useful as an accurate description of the economic world. Two sorts of evidence came in here: (1) the evidence of the size of the simultaneous equations bias in the parameter values from comparisons of OLS versus system methods (maximum likelihood (ML) or limited information maximum likelihood (LIML)) of estimating the same simultaneous equations model; (2) the performance of simultaneous equations versus causal chain models in their ability to match the economic data.

The original test of the bias, due to Koopmans (1945) had suggested very large biases of up to 89 per cent of the true parameter values on a demand and supply simultaneous system. But this test was on artificial data; on a macroeconomic example with real data Haavelmo (1947) found the bias to be very much smaller. OLS parameter estimates differed by less than 10 per cent from the 'system' estimates. After a number of other tests of the two methods in measurement and in prediction performance, no clear dominance for the system methods was found: in some cases, OLS did better; in others ML (or substitute methods) did better. Other tests on small samples suggested the simultaneous equations bias to be perhaps no larger than ordinary sampling bias; and others that the mean square errors of system estimates were much higher than the OLS estimates when serial correlation of the errors was present (see Orcutt and Cochrane, 1949). Where improvements in accuracy from the simultaneous methods were obtained, they seemed to be small compared to improvements possible from better models, better formulation of dynamics and more data.[8]

It was the evidence of these tests which, no doubt, prompted Wold to re-open the theoretical arguments about estimation. As we found earlier, this question seemed to have been resolved back in the 1940s when Koopmans (1945) and Bentzel and Wold (1946) had agreed that OLS could be used on a recursive chain model, but that the simultaneous equations model needed system estimation techniques. By his 1956 paper, Wold had changed his mind and begun to argue in favour of the old method, even for system estimation, on the grounds that its use required less stringent assumptions about the distributions of the variables involved and it was computationally easier (see Wold, 1956, pp. 38 and 43). Wold believed that the assumptions made about the stochastic elements (the probability distributions) in the interdependent system were unlikely to be fulfilled in observed data, leading to a large specification bias compared to the sample bias. By taking this position, Wold attacked the Cowles position on the very grounds on which they felt themselves strongest: the estimation program based on classical ideas of probability which had sprung from Haavelmo's (1944) work. Wold's position is consistent both with his more recently expressed long-standing preference for OLS[9] and with more general aspects of his methodology discussed below.

In 1958, the evidence on the performance of system estimators, on both real and artificial series, was assessed at a special symposium and published in *Econometrica* (see Christ *et al.*, 1960). These papers reflected the prevailing uncertainty on the empirical advantages of simultaneous system methods of estimation compared to simple, old-fashioned, OLS, both for accurate measurement and for accurate forecasting. In the face of these doubts, the overwhelming practical advantage lay with the computational ease of OLS and this contributed to its widespread continuation as a method of estimation for system models in the 1960s and 1970s.

The tests discussed so far compared system methods of estimation with other methods on the same simultaneous equations model. They were not tests of the model form, which was more fundamental to both positions. The Cowles group had already found to their chagrin that their early simultaneous system models of the late 1940s and 1950s often predicted no better than naive time-series models of the type discussed by Wold in 1938 (see Christ, 1951, and the comments by Friedman which followed this paper). Wold (1958) himself tested his recursive system against the simultaneous system, using a model of the watermelon market by Suits (1955). Suits's work was very much in the Tinbergenian tradition of dynamic system modelling, in which attention is paid to the dynamic properties of the system and its time-series solution path. The model itself (given in Appendix II) was a mixed Wold/Haavelmo model containing three equations: the crop supply equation depended on previous prices, but the harvest supply and the demand relations were modelled as a simultaneous system, and were estimated following the Cowles approach.

To conduct a test on the two model forms, Wold needed to build an equivalent recursive model for the watermelon market. His rationale was also Tinbergenian: each relation had to be a causal behavioural relation referring to the actions of a specific group of economic agents. His revised three-equation model (given in Appendix II) referred to the actions of producers (planting according to last year's prices, as in Suits's model), consumers (demanding according to current prices and incomes) and middlemen (fixing prices according to last year's demand and this year's crop). Each group acted autonomously, so there was no simultaneity in the model. The three equations formed a causal chain or recursive model: supply, price and demand each being determined in turn by the previous equations and by the links between the variables in the system.

Wold compared his results against Suits's original results by comparing their degrees of explanation, their parameter values for price and income elasticities of demand, their dynamic properties and, finally, tests of whether the causal chain accurately predicted prices and quantities in years of excess demand. On the whole, the causal chain/recursive model performed rather well on these criteria.[10] Wold's lower price and income elasticities seemed rather more reasonable for a low-cost food like watermelons, and these results were confirmed in his further experiments (see Wold, 1959, Section 5). Both models showed a tendency to move towards a supply–demand equilibrium, but, paradoxically, Suits's model with the imposed equilibrium restriction moved to an equilibrium much more slowly than Wold's system. (See Appendix II for a summary of the test results.) Wold thought his quicker response more natural for a product with no storage life and suggested that the solution to the paradox of Suits's slower damping factor was that the simultaneous equations model form was incorrect, causing an upward bias in the coefficient values, leading to higher elasticities and slower damping. In other words, Wold believed that Suits had a problem of mis-specification bias, due to modelling the system as simultaneous when it was really a dynamic causal chain.[11]

Wold's test was of a different type from those reported earlier on the size of the simultaneous equations bias. In those cases, the tests were made assuming the simultaneous equations model was the 'true' model of the world (the correct model specification). There, biased measurements were claimed if the 'wrong' method of measurement were used. Here Wold was claiming that the simultaneous equations model was mis-specified and this led to specification bias – the measurements were biased because the model form was wrong. Strotz (in a 'triptych' on causal models with Wold, 1960), strengthened this attack by presenting interdependent models as logically suffering from specification error. Strotz (1960) argued that an interdependent model is either an approximation to a causal model, in which case to estimate it as a system of simultaneous relationships involves a specification error; or it is a stochastic equilibrium model, in which case equilibrium occurs rarely and only by chance in observed data, also a specification error. These practical arguments about the mis-specification of simultaneous system models bring us to the much broader question tackled by these econometricians: how should the economic world be modelled?

The Intellectual Level

There were considerable intellectual (or non-technical) grounds for debate between proponents of the simultaneous equations model and the recursive chain model which centred on the nature of relationships in economics. One issue which particularly concerned Wold was causality, and its representation and interpretation in economic models. But, as remarked earlier, Wold's objections to the Cowles Commission approach embraced other worries: his disequilibrium and dynamics versus their equilibrium and statics; group level variables versus aggregate variables; and whether econometric models provided explanations or only descriptions of the economy. Most (but not all) of these elements were to be found in Bentzel and Wold's 1946 paper, discussed above. The Cowles Commission group seemed to ignore these criticisms in their two famous monographs of 1950 (Monographs 10 and 11, which were conceived and partly written in the mid-1940s). But other evidence, from letters and reports of meetings, suggests that the two groups did argue face to face.[12] The early 1950s saw the debate come back into print, even though by this time the Cowles Commission had more or less ceased work on econometrics, and the group disbanded.

The specific question of the new debate was that of causality in econometrics. In Monograph 10, the Cowles Commission had proposed a new label and definition of causal variables: they were 'predetermined' variables, which included both exogenous variables and temporally prior values of the endogenous variables. This definition matched Wold's usage of 'causal variables' in his time-dated recursive chain models; but for Cowles, the time dating of variables continued to be of importance only because of characteristics associated with the status of lagged variables as predetermined (for example, in identification), not because of their importance for modelling dynamic equation systems. The causality issue was taken seriously and discussed in greater depth by Simon in Cowles Monograph 14 (1953); this provoked a response from Wold (1954) and an interchange between the two followed (see Simon and Wold, 1955).

Simon and Wold failed to agree on certain notions about causal systems. Simon placed asymmetries and relationships at the basis of his causal orderings, not time sequences and variables as Wold had done. For Simon, time sequences often provided the basis for asymmetries, but not all time sequences implied causal orderings within a self-contained structure. Wold quarrelled with Simon's definition of asymmetric functional relations as the basis for causal ordering, since he saw these as definitions imposed on the structure without regard to the underlying economic behavioural relationships.

In other respects, Wold's ideas were rather closer to Simon's. For example, Tinbergen in his original 1930s work had argued that you needed the causal chain system model, not only for interpreting and explaining the economy, but also to see how policy changes worked through the economic system. Both Wold and Simon agreed with this: in order to know how a policy change would affect the equations in the structure, it is necessary to know the causal ordering. Simon related causal ordering both to identifiability and to autonomy, and thence to the power to intervene in the economic structure but leave the model and causal ordering intact. Wold for his part referred to Tinbergen's later work on policy targets and instruments and the need to understand the causal chain for these to work. Wold and Simon agreed, then, on both the need for causal systems and their purpose for intervention analysis and policy decisions.

Both sides had also modified their views on the causal interpretation of interdependent relationships. Simon's causal ordering can be interpreted, as was done by Wold, as providing a recursive causal ordering at the level of submatrices of the variables, rather than at the level of individual variables in the system. On the other hand, if the causal relations were very complex, a recursive chain could not be constructed. In this situation, Wold advocated the idea of linked sets of causes, causes for which several endogenous variables were conditional on the same set of predetermined variables. This notion he later termed 'vector causality' in a paper with Strotz (Strotz and Wold, 1960, pp. 421–2). It was not the same as the reduced form for Wold, because a causal interpretation was still possible, but it was a movement towards a causal interpretation of interdependency, and provided a way for Wold to make sense of Simon's block recursive systems.[13] Wold later adopted a conditional regression approach to give different causal interpretations for interdependent versus simultaneous models (see Wold, 1959 and 1960).

Despite these agreements on causality, there were several other issues on which Wold continued to hold out against Cowles views. Foremost amongst these was the issue of equilibrium. Epstein draws a sharp contrast here between the Swedish group's commitment to disequilibrium econometrics and the Cowles model which was, as he says: 'often expounded as the statistical embodiment of the Walrasian general equilibrium system' (Epstein, 1987, p. 156). Wold's group had little sympathy with such an approach, and here the most impressively argued contribution was by two of Wold's associates, Bentzel and Hansen (1954). They compared the economic meaning of recursive versus interdependent models. They worked from the basic notions of process analysis with the view that models must reflect the disequilibrium outcomes which are inherent in this approach. They claimed that, provided every single plan from all economic agents were taken into account, interdependency is ruled out and recursiveness always obtained. Ordinarily, they suggested, interdependency occurs in derived models, that is models such as the Walrasian system (which are derived from more basic behavioural and causal relationships), because of the presence of imposed equilibrium conditions (for example, consumers maximizing utility subject to given prices and incomes involves the imposition of static equilibrium conditions). But this does not mean that these underlying behavioural relationships were simultaneously determined in time; rather the derived models provide a description of the economy in which the relations only appear to be determined simultaneously. So, they argued, the interdependency that appears in static simultaneous equations models is not an argument for interdependency in dynamic models. For them, the theoretical issue was whether interdependency (simultaneity) should be a normal property of dynamic economic models. Since the disequilibrium approach to dynamics ruled out simultaneity in favour of recursivity, their answer was, emphatically, 'No'.

When it came to practical model building, Bentzel and Hansen readily admitted that interdependency arises in dynamic models because of aggregation of time periods and behavioural units and because *ex ante* observations are usually not available, only *ex post* data. This seemed to point to interdependent models which necessarily suffered from several sorts of aggregation bias, causing the sort of misspecification envisaged by Strotz (1960) (discussed above). The implications of such aggregation problems for econometric models were first considered in detail by Theil (1955).

For Wold, the insistence of the Cowles group (and those who followed in their path) of inserting equilibrium relations and conditions into their models meant that those models could not be causal models in the sense of Wold's understanding and could not therefore be used for the policy analysis purposes that he and Simon agreed upon. (Remember, Wold's accommodation with Simon did not include a causal interpretation of equilibrium models, only of 'interdependent relations'.) For Wold's group, equilibrium system models were descriptive, not explanatory; or as Wold put it, in his later paper with Strotz (1960):

> To assume that the values of the two variables determine each other makes sense only in an equilibrium system, and such a system provides no explanation of how the equilibrium comes about (of change or of causal connections among the endogenous variables of the system). (Strotz and Wold, 1960, p. 423)

Wold was particularly vehement in his arguments against the practice of 'mixed' systems: models involving both causal and equilibrium relationships. We can hear his frustration on this issue at the meeting of the Econometric Society at Uppsala in 1954. Wold, and Bentzel and Hansen, had already presented their papers (appearing as Wold (1955) and Bentzel and Hansen (1954)), when Haavelmo read his paper on 'Structural Models'. In the discussion which followed, Wold and Haavelmo had already had one interchange, when Wold intervened again:

> I wish to make two points. The first is that Professor Haavelmo has not at all tried to clear up the issues that I find obscure in the interdependent systems, issues which I have repeatedly stressed in my *Demand Analysis*, in my paper to the meeting and its oral presentation, and in the discussion at the present session. Hence the rationale of mixing causal relations with identities or equilibrium relations remains as obscure as ever, and in particular it is not clear for what purpose such mixed systems can be used in practice. (See Wold, in Hansen, 1955, p. 206)[14]

This underlying disagreement on disequilibrium versus equilibrium models cannot logically be resolved. It was a fundamental source of disagreement between the two groups about how the economic world was and how to build models to represent it.

Although Wold did not modify his views on this issue, there is some evidence that Haavelmo did; two papers in particular suggest he gained a certain sympathy with Wold's concerns, if not with his techniques. In the first, Haavelmo (1956) drew on Marschak's earlier (1942) analysis to give a mathematical definition of the difference between identities and equations and thus the extent to which each placed constraints on the values that could be taken by the variables. This analysis pointed to the greater explanatory power of equations compared to the descriptive power of identities.[15] Haavelmo's 1958a paper asked 'What can static equilibrium models tell us?' His discussion of the static equilibrium supply/demand model suggested the answer 'Not much!' He argued that, if greater explanatory power were required, then models either had to be non-equilibrium or non-static; indeed the usefulness of dynamics for learning about behaviour was one of the main points stressed in the paper. His concern for applicable theories for dynamic problems was apparent also in his 1954 study of growth models, which discussed the random shock, or stochastic, system models of the type used in the 1930s by Wold and Frisch.[16]

Haavelmo remained committed to the ideas and methods of his 1944 program, but he appeared to have become doubtful of their successful application by the late 1950s. In his 1957 Presidential Address to the Econometric Society, Haavelmo (1958b) expressed his disappointment at how little progress had been made using his approach. He believed that further progress in econometrics (meaning better, more realistic, econometric models) would come from learning more about the economy through applied work and from re-thinking basic economic theory at the level of individual behaviour, rather than from the development of more sophisticated statistical techniques. It is notable that one of his concrete suggestions for the improvement of applied models was to bring a more realistic and complex dynamics into process analysis models by estimating multiperiod time lags!

The Methodological Level

The other sources of disagreement between the two sides turned out to be methodological: about how to do econometrics. In the 1940s, there seemed to have been no disagreement on this, but in the 1950s, Wold re-defined his position in response to the things he did not like about the Cowles program. In 1956, Wold began to deny the usefulness of the particular form of the probability approach based on Fisherian ideas of sampling from experimental data which Haavelmo and the Cowles group had adapted for econometric usage, and which he (Wold) had earlier appeared to accept. He argued (1956, pp. 36–7) that the use of Fisherian methods of estimation (maximum likelihood) were of extremely doubtful validity when applied to the non-experimentally obtained data typical of economics. This was not a rejection of all probability reasoning for, as noted in section 2, Wold had earlier (1938) accepted the use of another sort of probability analysis in economics, that based on time-series analysis and associated with Russian ideas on stochastic processes, and this approach was re-stated in his econometric study of demand (with Juréen, 1953).

Wold also came to believe that the Neyman–Pearson hypothesis-testing techniques supported in Haavelmo's program were also invalid for econometrics, again because economic data were not true samples (1956, p. 39). He felt it was more important to check causal inferences against other sources of knowledge. He proposed three sorts of tests: estimating the same model on data of other periods and places;

comparing the model against a priori arguments (that is, against theory); and, most important, testing the model by prediction tests. It is not quite clear what he meant when he talked about prediction; probably he had in mind extrapolating the time paths of the variables rather than the predictions of the fitted values from the structural equations. This would be consistent with his work on demand with Juréen (1953), in which he only dealt with testing at the level of the time-series representations; and with his desire to formulate the equations into a recursive model which could then be solved for a stochastic autoregressive scheme to allow inference about the time-series behaviour of the system (see Wold, 1960, p. 445). This practice was in turn consistent with the disequilibrium dynamics of the 1930s when tests of the business cycle model took place at the level of the time-series descriptions of the causal models (see Tinbergen, 1939, and Frisch, 1933) and Wold's own book on time-series analysis (1938). For Wold, the recursive system of causal relations was for explaining and understanding the economy and for policy analysis, but the structure of the system was to be found in the time-series representation (interview with Hendry and Morgan, 1990). Structure was a characteristic revealed in the time path of the variables not, as for the Cowles group, in the constant parameters of the simultaneous relationships between variables.

The dimensions of the differences outlined here are considerable and suggest Wold's growing isolation in the 1950s from the mainstream econometric methodology dominated by the Cowles approach. Whereas it was possible to see the original Wold/Haavelmo argument of the 1940s as part of a local squabble within the econometrics research program, it begins to look increasingly as if Wold envisaged himself in a different version of that program, certainly different from the Cowles version, by the mid-1950s. What had begun as an issue of estimation technique had become an argument over what the economic world was like and what models and methods were appropriate to investigate that world. The simultaneous equations and recursive chain model forms lay at the centre of their positions: each was associated with different beliefs about the nature of the economy, about what economic observations represented, and with different levels of explanation of the economy. Furthermore the models were linked to methods, which from Wold's experience as a statistician implied a different sort of econometrics for recursive models than the structural program associated within the Cowles simultaneous equations models.

6 THE FATE OF PROCESS ANALYSIS

There was no obvious intellectual victory in the debate, yet there is no doubt that process analysis was effectively squashed out of econometrics. How did this occur?

First of all, within the econometrics community, experience of the 1940s and 1950s pointed in different directions. From the Cowles Commission viewpoint, Wold's initial objections to their model form had seemed easily dealt with and thus his continued objections merely repetitive and pointless (see Epstein's account, 1987, Chapter 5.3.1), for they could incorporate Wold's model as a special case of their simultaneous equations model. And, since the Cowles work of the 1940s had set the agenda for theoretical econometrics, econometricians of the 1950s and 1960s concentrated on developing alternative methods of estimating simultaneous equations systems. Furthermore Basmann's (1965) technical critique of Wold's work, stressing the mathematical and observational equivalence of the two model forms, seemed to be the final nail in the coffin of Wold's attempt to claim certain *technical* distinctions for his recursive model form.[17]

From Wold's point of view, the Cowles model seemed untenable, except as a solution to the problem of building models when only aggregate and annual data were available, as in most macroeconomics. Of course, this did not necessarily invalidate causal chains as such, nor their use for modelling particular markets where the required data were available. The irony was that, although the simultaneous equations *model form* was seen as a 'practical' solution, simultaneous equations *estimation* was in fact a less practical method which did not appear to result in a very dramatic improvement in the measurement of the models or knowledge of the economy. So, though Wold lost the battle over model form, his view that OLS was perfectly adequate as an estimation method, and had certain advantages over system methods, was a message which met with approval in that pre-microcomputer era (see McCarthy, 1987). As Qin points out (1989, Chapter 2.5) econometricians learnt to transform their models so that versions of least squares methods could legitimately be used and these methods continued in favour even when computing capacity increased during the 1970s.

The decisive changes which took process analysis out of econometrics were to be found not in theoretical econometrics, or in arguments about methods, but in the aspirations of econometric model builders. Modelling systems as simultaneous relations does not necessarily imply removing dynamics from economic model building; yet, somewhere between Tinbergen's macrodynamics of the 1930s and Klein's macroeconometrics of the 1950s, dynamic disequilibrium models gave way to static equilibrium models. This process may not have been entirely conscious. Strotz (1960) suggested three reasons why economists found themselves using interdependent systems to approximate causal chains: either they ignore time lags, or dynamic adjustments are replaced with equilibrium conditions, or flow variables are replaced by stock variables. Wold (1960) has a longer description of how this historical downgrading of dynamics occurred:

> Pure causal chains are completely dynamic, all relations of the system being behavioural relations, the propositions on equilibrium tendencies being implications of the model, and no equilibrium assumptions entering in the construction of the model. The residuals enter as unspecified forces that interact with the specified driving forces of the model and prevent the system from ever reaching a state of complete rest.
>
> Interdependent systems and conditional causal chains mark a drastic cut in the aspiration level of a completely dynamic approach. The introduction of equilibrium assumptions is a key device, a shortcut that refrains from obtaining the equilibrium as a deductive implication of the model. There is no objection against the shortcut as such, for it is a good thing to have models that work at different aspiration levels. It is rather that owing to their mixed static-dynamic nature the approaches are of limited scope for purposes of dynamic inference. What in particular is a serious limitation is that every equilibrium assumption is an approximation that ignores a potential driving force of the model. To assume instantaneous equilibrium between demand and supply is to ignore changes in stocks; to equilibrate savings and investments is to ignore the unplanned changes in money holdings and inventories, and so on. In reality, according to observed facts, such disequilibrium gaps are often quite considerable and to disregard them in model construction is in conflict with basic arguments in dynamic economic theory. (Wold, 1960, pp. 461–2)

Wold's 'driving forces of the model' harks back to Frisch's (1936) paper where it had been suggested that the differences between actual disequilibrium observations and the dynamic equilibrium ('normal') values might be the essential 'forces at play within the system' (Frisch, 1936, p. 105). In practice, when disequilibrium modelling was thrown out in favour of equilibrium systems, dynamics went out of the window too. This merely moves the question one step backwards: why did econometric model builders no longer aim to build dynamic models?

The changing concerns of economists and the professional organization of the economics field both contributed to the movement away from Tinbergen's dynamic models. In the 1930s, econometricians such as Tinbergen had been responsible for developing mathematical economic theory and carrying out statistical work. As professional specialization proceeded in the 1940s and 1950s, the responsibility for theory development passed to mathematical economists who were in the process of splitting off their subfield from (statistical) econometrics. The cutting off of econometrics from their theory development role seems to have led to a difference in the way econometricians like Klein used theory compared to the way in which Tinbergen had used theory. Klein, like most subsequent econometricians, presented his model building as logically prior to statistical work. His model was built to represent theory first, and be consistent with its dictates; whereas Tinbergen, in his desire to build models which could 'explain' the observed data, worked more closely to his data where the problems of disequilibrium and dynamics were much more obvious. Theory guided Tinbergen in his initial formulation of relationships, but, thereafter, he iterated between theory and data to build his model.

The theory available for econometric models had also changed in several ways by the early 1950s. First, mathematical economics became a less useful source of models for econometricians. Under the influence of Samuelson, mathematical theorists became fixed on the stability of dynamic systems rather than on the stochastic or disequilibrium dynamic analysis designed by mathematically minded econometricians of the 1930s to fit observed business cycle data.[18] (These developments form a parallel story, in a number of respects, to the changes outlined here in econometrics (see Weintraub, this volume, and 1991).) Meanwhile, at Cowles, a mathematically based general equilibrium research effort grabbed the limelight just as their statistical econometrics program began to fade (see Weintraub, 1985, Chapter 6). Secondly, the increasing dominance of Keynes's *General Theory* ideas in theoretical macroeconomics involved a move to static equilibrium models with variables in levels (see de Marchi, 1987). Though new mathematical theorizing was not easily applicable to real data in the 1950s, Keynesian-style macroeconomic theories were, and proved a strong influence on model building in econometrics.

The influence and advantages of Keynesian theory are evident in Klein's first generation of macroeconometric models. Klein had been expressly hired to re-do Tinbergen's model of the USA, using the new tools developed at Cowles. Naturally Klein paid some lip service to Tinbergen's work, but he also acknowledged a debt to theoretical discussions following Keynes's work. These discussions he credited with making it possible to 'formulate more sharply the structure of the economic system and thereby to gain added simplicity and accuracy not available to Tinbergen at the time of his work' (Cowles Commission Monograph 11, 1950, p. 1). Model simplicity was obtained because

Keynesian economics could be characterized in a very few equations involving macroeconomic aggregate variables, in contrast to Tinbergen's complicated business cycle theories and use of disaggregated business cycle variables.

Klein's equilibrium assumption also marked a complete change of direction compared to Tinbergen's disequilibrium or process approach of the 1930s. When discussing markets, Klein took it for granted that, 'Since our objective is a complete system, we must operate with the theory of general equilibrium' (Cowles Commission Monograph 11, 1950, p. 52). His model building reflected his concern with starting from equilibrium conditions rather than with trying to explain the movements of the economic variables through time. Where dynamic elements crept in, they seem to have been dampened and squashed down by equilibrium arguments, so that the resulting system of interrelated equations 'feels' static.[19] There was no discussion of time-series solutions or of dynamics and stability in the main large model and little in the small example models. This all contrasts very strongly with Tinbergen's constant reference to 'movements' and 'fluctuations' of variables, and to Wold's insistence on causal explanation, disequilibrium and time-series representations.

Klein discussed these changes openly in his second textbook on econometrics (1962); he portrayed the aftermath of the Keynesian Revolution as focusing 'attention on influencing the level of activity at any moment of time rather than the study of the whole temporal shape of the cycle'. He went on:

> *Multiplier* analysis, which shows the current effect of policy decisions on variables representing economic activity, requires a system that will show the levels of these variables at any desired point of time. In a general sense, the problems of business-cycle analysis and employment policy seem to be mutually consistent and are both studied on the basis of the same parent models. Yet . . . the two methods use the parent system in different ways and have different emphases. (Klein, 1962, p. 182)

The policy implications and analysis of Keynesian economics, as reflected in econometric model building, were concerned with short-run management of the levels of aggregate variables, in contrast to Tinbergen's desire to influence or control disaggregated variables and thus the dynamic movements of the economy in the longer run.

These developments indicate the considerable fall in the levels of explanation and analysis, and thus in policy concerns, aimed at by economists in the mid-twentieth century compared to those of the earlier 1930s, when the dynamic multiperiod analysis typical of the

Swedish School was developed and economists of all types were struggling to build dynamic trade cycle theories and models.[20] In the 1950s and 1960s, with the stability of post-war economies and the dominance of Keynesian macroeconomic analysis, business cycles went out of fashion and dynamic models of the process type disappeared from mainstream econometrics along with them.

Tinbergen's model form, based on the multiperiod idea, had been succeeded by two offspring: the simultaneous equations model for comparative static macroeconomics and Wold's recursive model form for dynamics and business cycles – ideal models for two different programs in econometrics. Given the developments in economics and econometrics of the 1940s and 1950s, it is no surprise that the econometrics handed down into the first generation of widely-used textbooks of the 1960s was dominated by models in which dynamics and causal systems were of only marginal interest. The causal model system pioneered by Tinbergen had disappeared; Wold's recursive model form, shorn of its process analysis interpretation, was relegated to a minor special case of the general simultaneous equations system.

7 POSTSCRIPT

Though process analysis, with its disequilibrium dynamics, seems to have disappeared, certain other key elements of Wold's econometric program have been revived over the last 15–20 years. With the breakdown of Keynesian macroeconomics and the revival of business cycle studies, economists have returned to the themes of 1930s dynamic business cycle analysis, particularly to Frisch's dynamic shock model. Time-series methods of econometrics, for which Wold's thesis (1938) is a reference work, have re-emerged into mainstream econometrics both in Europe and the USA.[21] Causality has again become a topic for econometric discourse; and even Wold's recursive model has been utilized for policy analysis in Sims's vector autoregressions.[22] These recent developments suggest that it would be unwise to declare Wold's research program dead and buried. Lakatos's (1978) several comments on the difficulties of recognizing births and deaths of research programs, except with the benefit of considerable hindsight, are particularly apt in this context. A longer perspective is needed to see whether these developments indicate a transformation of Wold's disequilibrium program, or a shift towards a different sort of dynamics, or a further bifurcation in the econometrics program itself.

NOTES

1. On Tinbergen's econometrics, see Morgan, 1990, ch. 4.
2. For the importance of the shock thesis in the development of econometric business cycle research, see Morgan, 1990, ch. 3.
3. This emerged in a recent interview with Wold. In fact, Wold was friendly with the Lundberg family as a whole, having worked for a while for Erik's father, Filip Lundberg.
4. I have described elsewhere (see Morgan, 1987) the introduction of the probability approach as a Kuhnian revolution in econometrics. After economists had rejected probability reasoning in the 1920s and 1930s, the view that econometric models should be formulated as probabilistic hypotheses quickly became accepted as an essential part of the way to do econometrics in the 1940s, following Haavelmo's work. See also the recent thesis by Qin, 1989, chs 1.2 and 1.3, on Haavelmo's probability ideas compared to those of Wold.
5. A detailed history of the development of the ideas of the Cowles group is given by Epstein, 1987. See Qin, 1989, chs 1.3 and 1.4, on the difference between Haavelmo's ideas and the Cowles work.
6. In Tinbergen's work, the causal chains were reduced to one autoregressive equation, the 'final form' equation, which represented the system as a whole.
7. The alternative version of this problem, very quick reaction times between cause and effect, leading to continuous-time econometric models, was recognized by Wold (1956). See Bergstrom (1988) for an historical account of this approach.
8. See Epstein, 1987 (ch. 4.4.1.1 and ch. 5.1.3.1) and Qin 1989 (pp. 201–2) for discussion (and references) of the issues raised in this paragraph.
9. Wold has always remained committed to the OLS method; see Wold 1982, p. 195.
10. Later tests on predictive ability of the two models were perhaps more favourable to Suits's model (see L'Esperance, 1964), but the shortness of the time periods used for these tests suggests the results are not very reliable.
11. One further practical example, whose details are lost, concerns the performance of the recursive model in macro-models. Footnotes in the literature (see Basmann, 1965, p. 1090) suggest that Wold built an 85-equation causal chain model for The Econometric Institute Inc. (a private consulting company). Wold claimed that this model predicted better than simultaneous equations models, but since we do not know the details or whether this was another comparative test, this claim should be treated cautiously.
12. Wold sent his 1946 paper with Bentzel to Marschak, director at Cowles. Marschak's reply (Marschak archives, Box 96/u–v) shows little recognition of the differences between their positions. He invited Wold to visit Cowles in 1947, but I found no record of such a visit in the Cowles archives. There are however several recorded interchanges at meetings: Koopmans was the discussant at Wold's presentation to the Econometric Society meeting in Washington 1947 (see Wold, 1949) and Wold commented briefly on Marschak's paper at the same meetings (see Marschak, 1949). There were also the arguments at the Econometric Society's Uppsala meeting of 1954 (see Hansen, 1955) and Klein's discussion of Wold's paper at the Royal Statistical Society (see Wold, 1956, discussion).
13. A later argument on causality appeared to hinge on the definition of causality adopted, but in fact also involved the disputed equilibrium assumption and a hidden assumption about stability (see Basmann, 1963; Strotz and Wold, 1963).
14. Wold here views identities and imposed equilibrium conditions as equally problematic. In the discussion following presentation of Wold's 1956 paper, Klein tried to set Wold straight on the question of identities.
15. I am indebted to Jens Andvig for drawing this paper to my attention and to Hali Edison for providing me with an English translation.

16. But, true to the interests of the times, he was more concerned with their stability than with their dynamics (see Weintraub, 1991).
17. Wold had already pointed out the equivalence problem (see Wold and Jurèen, 1953, ch. 12.7; Wold, 1959, pp. 410–12), but still claimed a greater operative and explanatory power for his model form.
18. The 'process' dynamic ideas of Tinbergen's era were dropped very quickly; for example, Samuelson's *Foundations* (1947) has no mention of process analysis in his discussion of dynamics. Baumol's (1951) book does contain a short chapter.
19. For example, Klein reverts to the 1920s econometricians' ideas of dynamics when he suggests that a simple time trend variable can be used to model 'dynamic elements'.
20. Tinbergen, in his survey of business cycles theories for *Econometrica* in 1935, discussed the dynamic multiperiod models of Keynes's *Treatise on Money* (particularly ch. 20) as well as the theories of Hayek and several others. By contrast, commentators of the time noted that the *General Theory* provided a static analysis (see Harrod's review (1937, pp. 85–6), of which Keynes (1973, p. 84) approved) and an equilibrium theory (see Ohlin's review (1937)). Hansson (1982, chs 11 and 12) suggests that the Stockholm School authors felt a certain sympathy with the multiperiod approach of the *Treatise*, but not with the static equilibrium approach of the *General Theory*.
21. Gilbert (1988) has suggested that the time-series legacy of the pre-Cowles work was carried on in Europe, and it may also be that process anlaysis did not entirely disappear from other national econometric modelling practices.
22. On the issue of casality, a useful collection of recent papers is Aigner and Zellner (1988). On the use of recursive form models in vector autoregressions, see Epstein, 1987, ch. 7.7.

REFERENCES

Aigner, J.A. and Zellner, A. (1988), *Journal of Econometrics*, **39**, pp. 1–234 (Special issue on 'Causality').

Basmann, R. (1963), 'The Causal Interpretation of Non-Triangular Systems of Economic Relations', *Econometrica*, **31**, pp. 439–54 and 'A Rejoinder', same volume, pp. 451–6.

—— (1965), 'A Note on the Statistical Testability of "Explicit Causal Chains" against the Class of "Interdependent" Models', *Journal of the American Statistical Association*, **60**, pp. 1080–93.

Baumol, W. (1951), *Economic Dynamics* (New York: Macmillan).

Bentzel, R. and Hansen, B. (1954), 'On Recursiveness and Interdependency in Economic Models', *Review of Economic Studies*, **22**, pp. 153–68.

Bentzel, R. and Wold, H. (1946), 'On Statistical Demand Analysis from the Viewpoint of Simultaneous Equations', *Skandinavisk Aktuarietidskrift*, **29**, pp. 95–113.

Bergstrom, A.R. (1988), 'The History of Continuous-Time Econometric Models', *Econometric Theory*, **4**, pp. 365–83.

Christ, C. (1951), 'A Test of an Econometric Model for the United States, 1921–1947', in *Conference on Business Cycles*, Universities-National Bureau Committee for Economic Research, New York: National Bureau of Economic Research, pp. 35–107; and Comments by M. Friedman, pp. 107–14.

Christ, C. *et al.* (1960), 'A Symposium on Simultaneous Equation Estimation', *Econometrica*, **28**, pp. 835–71.

Cowles Commission, Monograph 10 (1950), *Statistical Inference in Dynamic Economic Models*, ed. T.C. Koopmans (New York: Wiley).
—— Monograph 11 (1950), *Economic Fluctuations in the United States 1921–1941*, L.R. Klein (New York: Wiley).
—— Monograph 14 (1953), *Studies in Econometric Method*, ed. W.C. Hood and T.C. Koopmans (New York: Wiley).
Epstein, R. (1987), *A History of Econometrics* (Amsterdam: North-Holland).
Frisch, R. (1933), 'Propagation Problems and Impulse Problems in Dynamic Economics', in *Economic Essays in Honour of Gustav Cassel* (London: Allen & Unwin).
—— (1936), 'On the Notion of Equilibrium and Disequilibrium', *Review of Economic Studies*, **3**, pp. 100–105.
Gilbert, C. (1988), 'The Development of Econometrics in Britain since 1945', PhD thesis, Oxford.
Haavelmo, T. (1943), 'The Statistical Implications of a System of Simultaneous Equations', *Econometrica*, **11**, pp. 1–12.
—— (1944), 'The Probability Approach in Econometrics', supplement to *Econometrica*, **12**.
—— (1947), 'Methods of Measuring the Marginal Propensity to Consume', *Journal of the American Statistical Association*, **42**, pp. 105–22.
—— (1954), *A Study in the Theory of Economic Evolution* (Amsterdam: North-Holland).
—— (1956), 'Ligninger vs. Identiteter i Okonomisk Makroteori', in *25 Essays in Honour of Erik Lindahl* (Stockholm: Ekonomisk Tidskrift).
—— (1958a), 'Hva Kan Statiske Likevektsmodeller Fortelle Oss?', *Festskrift til Frederik Zeuthen* (Copenhagen: Nationalokonomisk Forening) (Supplement to *Nationalokonomisk Tidsskrift*, 96) published in English: 'What Can Static Equilibrium Models Tell Us?', *Economic Inquiry*, **12** (1974) pp. 27–34.
—— (1958b), 'The Role of the Econometrician in the Advancement of Economic Theory', *Econometrica*, **26**, pp. 351–7.
Hansen, B. (1955), 'Report of the Uppsala Meeting', *Econometrica*, **23**, pp. 198–216.
Hansson, B.A. (1982), *The Stockholm School and the Development of Dynamic Method* (London: Croom Helm).
Harrod, R.F. (1937), 'Mr Keynes and Traditional Theory', *Econometrica*, **5**, pp. 74–86.
Keynes, J.M. (1930), *Treatise on Money* (London: Macmillan).
—— (1936), *The General Theory of Employment, Interest and Money* (London: Macmillan).
—— (1973), *The Collected Works of John Maynard Keynes*, vol. XIV, ed. D. Moggridge (London: Macmillan).
Klein, L.R. (1950), *Economic Fluctuations in the United States 1921–1941*, Cowles Commission Monograph No. 11 (New York: Wiley).
—— (1962), *An Introduction to Econometrics* (New York: Prentice-Hall).
Koopmans, T.C. (1945), 'Statistical Estimation of Simultaneous Economic Relations', *Journal of the American Statistical Association*, **40**, pp. 448–66.
Lakatos, I. (1978), *Methodology of Scientific Research Programmes*, ed. J. Worrall and G. Currie (Cambridge: Cambridge University Press).
L'Esperance, W.L. (1964), 'A Case Study in Prediction: the Market for Watermelons', *Econometrica*, **32**, pp. 163–73.

McCarthy, M. (1987), 'Econometrics after the Cowles Commission Work and The Brookings Project: Successes, Mistakes and Possible New Directions', unpublished paper.

de Marchi, N. (1987), 'The Cambridge Didactic Style and Keynesian Macroeconomics', paper given at the History of Science Meeting, Raleigh, October 1987.

Marschak, J. (1942), 'Identity and Stability in Economics: A Survey', *Econometrica*, **10**, pp. 61–74.

—— (1949), 'Statistical Inference from Non-Experimental Observation: An Economic Example', *Proceedings of the International Statistical Conferences*, 1947, III (A), pp. 289–301.

Morgan, M.S. (1987), 'Statistics without Probability and Haavelmo's Revolution in Econometrics', in L. Krüger, G. Gigerenzer and M.S. Morgan (eds), *The Probabilistic Revolution Vol 2: Ideas in the Sciences* (Cambridge, Mass.: MIT Press).

—— (1990), *The History of Econometric Ideas* (Cambridge: Cambridge University Press).

Ohlin, B. (1937), 'Some Notes on the Stockholm Theory of Savings and Investment', *Economic Journal*, **47**, pp. 53–69, 221–40.

Orcutt, G.H. and Cochrane, D. (1949), 'A Sampling Study of the Merits of Autoregressive and Reduced Form Transformations in Regression Analysis', *Journal of the American Statistical Association*, **44**, pp. 356–72.

Qin, D. (1989), 'The History of Econometric Thought: The Formation of Econometrics (1930–1960)', PhD thesis, Oxford.

Samuelson, P. (1947), *The Foundations of Economic Analysis* (Cambridge, Mass.: Harvard University Press).

Simon, H.A. (1953), 'Causal Ordering and Identifiability' in W. Hood and T. Koopmans (eds), *Studies in Econometric Method*, Cowles Commission Monograph 14 (New York: Wiley).

Simon, H.A. and Wold H. (1955), 'Causality and Econometrics: Comment' and 'Causality and Econometrics: Reply', *Econometrica*, **23**, pp. 193–7.

Strotz, R.H. (1960), 'Interdependence as a Specification Error', *Econometrica*, **28**, pp. 428–42.

Strotz, R.H. and Wold, H. (1960), 'Recursive versus Nonrecursive Systems: An attempt at Synthesis', *Econometrica*, **28**, pp. 417–27.

Strotz, R.H. and Wold, H. (1963), 'The Causal Interpretability of Structural Parameters: A Reply', *Econometrica*, **31**, pp. 449–50.

Suits, D. (1955), 'An Econometric Model of the Watermelon Market', *Journal of Farm Economics*, **37**, pp. 237–51.

Theil, H. (1955), *Linear Aggregation of Economic Relations* (Amsterdam: North-Holland).

Tinbergen, J. (1935), 'Annual Survey: Suggestions on Quantitative Business Cycle Theory', *Econometrica*, **3**, pp. 241–308.

—— (1937), *An Econometric Approach to Business Cycle Problems* (Paris: Hermann & Cie).

—— (1939), *Statistical Testing of Business Cycle Theories*, vols I and II (Geneva: League of Nations).

—— (1949), 'Comments in discussion on Marschak's paper (1949)', *Proceedings of the International Statistical Conferences*, 1947, III (A), p. 299.

Weintraub, E. Roy (1985), *General Equilibrium Analysis: Studies in Appraisal* (Cambridge: Cambridge University Press).
—— (1991) *Stabilizing Dynamics* (Cambridge: Cambridge University Press).
Wold, H. (1938), *A Study in the Analysis of Stationary Time Series* (Uppsala: Almqvist & Wiksell).
—— (1949), 'Statistical Estimation of Economic Relationships', *Proceedings of the International Statistical Conferences*, 1947, V, pp. 1–22.
—— (1954), 'Causality and Econometrics', *Econometrica*, **22**, pp. 162–77.
—— (1955), 'Possibilités et Limitations des Systèmes à Chaîne Causale', *Cahiers du Séminaire d'Econométrie*, **3**, pp. 81–101.
—— (1956), 'Causal Inference from Observational Data: A Review of Ends and Means', *Journal of the Royal Statistical Society*, Series A, pp. 28–50.
—— (1958), 'A Case Study of Interdependent Versus Causal Chain Systems', *Revue de l'Institut International de Statistique*, **26**, pp. 5–25.
—— (1959), 'Ends and Means in Econometric Model Building', in U. Grenender (ed.), *Probability and Statistics: The Harald Cramer Volume* (Stockholm: Almqvist & Wiksell).
—— (1960), 'A Generalization of Causal Chain Models', *Econometrica*, **28**, pp. 443–63.
—— (1982), 'Models for Knowledge', in J. Gani (ed.), *The Making of Statisticians* (New York: Springer-Verlag).
Wold, H. and Juréen, L. (1953), *Demand Analysis* (Stockholm: Almqvist & Wiksell).

APPENDIX I

A recursive form model is one in which the matrix of endogenous variable parameters has ones on the diagonal, zeros on one side of the diagonal, and parameters in some or all of the spaces on the other side. A simultaneous equations model has parameters on both sides of the diagonal.

For the example discussed in section 4 above, Haavelmo's simultaneous equations model has the following square matrix of parameters on the endogenous variables (p and q):

$$\begin{array}{c} \\ q \\ p \end{array} \begin{array}{c} \begin{array}{cc} q & p \end{array} \\ \left[\begin{array}{cc} 1 & -A \\ -B & 1 \end{array} \right] \end{array}$$

Bentzel and Wold's recursive form model has the following triangular matrix of parameters on the endogenous variables (s, p, d and l):

$$\begin{array}{c} \\ s \\ p \\ d \\ l \end{array} \begin{array}{c} \begin{array}{cccc} s & p & d & l \end{array} \\ \left[\begin{array}{cccc} 1 & 0 & 0 & 0 \\ -c_2 & 1 & 0 & 0 \\ 0 & -a_1 & 1 & 0 \\ -1 & 0 & 1 & 1 \end{array} \right] \end{array}$$

APPENDIX II

The US watermelon market models discussed in section 5 are:

Suits's simultaneous equations (SE) model:

1. crop supply: $Q_t = a_1P_{t-1} + a_2C_{t-1} + \ldots$
2. harvest supply: $X_t = b_1(P/W)_t + b_2Q_t + \ldots$
   (or if 2) gives $X > Q$, then $X = Q$
3. demand: $P_t = c_1(Y/N)_t + c_2(X/N)_t + \ldots$

Wold's recursive chain (RC) model:

1. supply: $Q_t = a_1P_{t-1} + a_2C_{t-1} + \ldots$
2. price: $(P/L)_t = b_1[(X^*/N)_{t-1} - (Q/N)_t] + \ldots$
3. demand: $(X^*/N)_t = c_1(P/L)_t + c_2(Y/NL)_t + \ldots$
   ($X^* = X$ when $X < Q$, otherwise X^* unknown)

where Q is available watermelon crop, P is price of watermelons, C is price of cotton (the alternative crop), X is actual watermelon harvest, W is the wage rate, Y is disposable income, N is population, and L is cost of living index.

Summary of Test Results

	Suits (SE)	*Wold (RC)*
price elasticity of demand	−0.90	−0.21
income elasticity of demand	1.38	0.43
damping factor (>1 explosive tendency) (<1 equilibrium tendency)	0.62	0.21

COMMENT ON MORGAN

Roger E. Backhouse

In this chapter Mary Morgan discusses the transition between two econometric research programs which may, loosely, be termed the simultaneous equations research program (SERP), associated with Haavelmo, and the process analysis research program (PARP), associated with Wold. Though there has been, as she explains, a revival of certain aspects of Wold's program, the story is one of the SERP's victory over the PARP. Such a story seems, at least at first sight, a suitable testing-ground for Lakatos's methodology of scientific research programs (MSRP), for we want to understand why one program superseded the other. However, although her concluding section implies that these research programs have something in common with Lakatosian programs, Mary Morgan does not use Lakatos's MSRP. Two questions thus present themselves: (1) Can Lakatos's MSRP be applied to the history of econometrics, and if so how? (2) What would we gain from such an approach?

1 Applying Lakatos's MSRP to Econometrics

A research program in methods?

One of the most important questions raised by Mary Morgan's discussion is that of the sense in which it is legitimate to speak of a research program in econometric techniques. In so far as the forces moving the subject forward are internal, technical ones, it is clearly correct to identify research programs, but it is not clear that these are research programs in the Lakatosian sense. The reason is that an *essential* feature of a Lakatosian program is empirical content. To tell the story of econometrics in Lakatosian terms we need novel facts which can be either corroborated or refuted by empirical evidence. If we are to view the victory of the SERP over the PARP in Lakatosian terms, therefore, we need to search for the excess empirical content associated with the SERP.

Of what could such empirical content consist? The only candidate of which I am aware is simultaneous equation bias. Putting aside the problem that we would expect a progressive research program (and given that the program was successful we would expect it to be progressive) to produce not one, but a sequence of novel facts, there are problems with this. How could such a 'novel fact' be tested, for it is a novel statistical result, not an economic one. Simulation studies are hardly tests, for if they are set up correctly the results must conform with the theory. The hypothesis suggests that simultaneous equation bias must exist, not that it is significant when compared with specification and other errors. However any theory that predicted, for example, that simultaneous equation bias would be large relative to other errors would have to be an economic theory, not a statistical one. This suggests that we should be thinking of defining research programs in economics, not research programs in econometric techniques.

Defining research programs

Notwithstanding these remarks, the notion that there are two competing research programs does seem to explain something of what was happening in the debates between the two 'schools'. The failure of Wold's group and members of the Cowles Commission to communicate properly with each other is important. Mary Morgan's argument that they had different presuppositions and ways of tackling problems is persuasive and it is hard to resist the temptation to analyse it in terms of different hard cores and heuristics. There are good reasons, not least those given above, why we should not push Lakatosian ideas too far, or apply them too rigidly, but it might be helpful to see a more formal attempt to define hard cores and heuristics of the two research programs. Such an attempt might clear up some of the problems which emerge from this paper.

The disagreements between Wold's group and Cowles involve disagreements over several issues:

- beliefs about whether the economy should be modelled as being in equilibrium;
- beliefs about how best to fit models to the data (about efficient estimation techniques and so on);
- beliefs about the type of causation involved in economic models;
- beliefs about the nature of economic explanation and whether we are concerned to predict or to explain.

All these areas of disagreement are discussed in the paper, but we do not discover which are the fundamental ones, or how they are related to each other (if they are). The attempt to define the SERP and the PARP more formally (following Weintraub's example) might provide a way to address this issue.

2 Why Did Process Analysis Get 'Stamped Out'?

Technical econometric reasons

The main reason Mary Morgan gives is that simultaneous equation methods are appropriate where one has only discrete observations of a continuous process (or something similar). This is a very respectable reason, but how far was it a rationalization of something that people wanted to do anyway? In Keynes's *General Theory* we have both dynamic and equilibrium versions of the multiplier, but (apart from elementary teaching and a few other instances) it is the equilibrium version that has been taken up. Was this for the same reasons that process analysis was 'stamped out' from econometrics?

Neo-Walrasian economics

Mary Morgan also argues that process analysis was stamped out because of economists' interest in general equilibrium models – the 'neo-Walrasian' strategy (research program?). Is it possible that, had economists not been working in terms of general equilibrium models, econometricians would have found ways round the logical problems posed by observations being aggregated over time? Should we be considering developments in econometrics as part of the neo-Walrasian research program?

Alternative empirical research programs

An alternative viewpoint, considered by Mary Morgan above, is that these developments form part of a broader probabilistic revolution. The issue of process analysis versus simultaneous equation methods then becomes a debate between two interpretations of this broader program, rather than one between two different programs. To choose between these two interpretations it might be helpful to see the programs defined more formally.

It might also be interesting to analyse developments in terms of an 'econometric' research program, representing an approach to empirical economics that could be contrasted with, for example, that of the National Bureau of Economic Research (NBER) under Burns, Mitchell *et al.*

Rhetoric

The chapter also notes that Cowles pursued the simultaneous equation approach because it posed interesting mathematical problems. This, together with the evidence for the failure of Wold's group and Cowles to communicate effectively with each other, invites an investigation along the lines of McCloskey's analysis of the work of Muth and Samuelson.

3 What Would We Gain by Adopting a Lakatosian Perspective?

Mary Morgan writes that 'there was no obvious intellectual victory in the debate, yet there is no doubt that process analysis was effectively squashed out of econometrics' (p. 254). This raises the issue of whether there *could* have been an intellectual victory for either side. Here it is helpful to return again to Lakatos, for his work was concerned not only with empirical sciences (his MSRP) but also the history of mathematics (in *Proofs and Refutations*). With empirical sciences the criterion for intellectual victory is corroborated excess content: novel facts which are supported by empirical evidence. In *Proofs and Refutations* the argument is logical, and the criteria for progress are, on the whole, fairly clear. In the case of the debate between Wold and Cowles, neither of these applies: because of the wide range of areas of disagreement, more than simply logical argument is required, and yet empirical evidence cannot be used, for this would bring in economics, rather than simply econometric techniques.

This problem is tied up with the question of appraisal (which Mary Morgan carefully avoids, except in so far as it is implied by the sentence just quoted). If Lakatos's MSRP is correct, scientists support progressive research programs and abandon degenerating ones. It is important, therefore, that the SERP was either a progressive research program or constituted part of one, and that the PARP formed part of a degenerating program. We thus have to appraise the two programs to discover whether they were progressive or degenerating at the time when process analysis was stamped out (maybe the program, or a variant of it, is progressive now, but that is a different matter). This is something, it seems to me, that we cannot do without relating the history of econometrics to the wider history of economics. Novel facts and empirical testing can be brought in only when we consider economic ideas as well as econometric techniques. The defence of the SERP would thus be that it formed part of a much broader, progressive research program in economics (such as the neo-Walrasian research program). If one econometric research program is no better than another in enabling economists to predict novel facts, then we need to be told clearly the grounds for choosing between them. Without knowing this we are limited in what we can say about the history of econometrics.

REPLY TO BACKHOUSE

Mary Morgan

One of the unusual features about the Wold–Haavelmo history is that both of their programs were consciously laid out as research programs for the overall conduct of econometrics. This certainly seems to invite a Lakatosian analysis which, in the usual format of 'scientific research programs', might begin with a description like this:

	Wold (1956)	*Haavelmo (1944)*
hard core beliefs	economic system is a process; data are disequilibrium outcomes	economic system is a constant structure; data are simultaneously determined equilibrium outcomes
positive heuristic	build recursive chain models; use time-series probability approach; use broadly based methods of estimation and testing	build simultaneous equations models; use Fisher's classical probability approach; use distribution based methods of estimation and testing

I am wary of taking the Lakatosian analysis much further in this case, for a number of reasons. First, the detailed history in the chapter suggests that both Wold and Haavelmo to some extent changed their views over this period, which makes the fixing of their 'scientific' programs either somewhat shaky or else ahistorical. Secondly, the historical discussion of process analysis has not allowed a complete enumeration of important elements of Haavelmo's 1944 program (for example, 'autonomy' has not been fully discussed here (see Aldrich, 1989), and it is also necessary to differentiate Haavelmo's program from that of the Cowles group (see Morgan, 1990a, and Qin, 1989).

More seriously, a general problem arises: the description of any 'scientific' research program is defined by the particular interest of the historian at that particular time. My examination of process analysis has concentrated attention on model form, and this places beliefs about how the economy worked at the hard core, and methods and methodology in the positive heuristic. But if I were to characterize Haavelmo's 1944 program in comparison to the alternative 1920s/1930s program in econometrics, the hard core propositions would centre on the probability approach; that is, methods and methodology. The commentator's suggestion that I compare econometrics with the statistical empirical program of the NBER would place both beliefs about what is observable in the economy and methodological approach in the hard core, but the characterizations would differ from those offered above for the Wold–Haavelmo case.[1] All three provide valid historical descriptions, but each would lead to a different answer in any Lakatosian analysis of progress and a different deviant history would be relegated to the footnotes.

Since Lakatos's seminal work, it has been difficult to talk and write about research programs without using the paradigm of 'scientific research programs'. The benefit of Lakatos's approach is that it can be used to analyse whether economics changes 'rationally'; that is, whether it 'progresses'. But, if progress is not the issue, or if there is no progress, the description and analysis associated with 'scientific research programs' may prove a straitjacket imposing unnecessary discipline on the history. There are, after all, other ways of describing and analysing research programs. One possibility is to adopt the metaphor offered by Hoover's kinship tables (see Chapter 11). My preference would be to use this at the level of the individual, and portray the ideas (or research work) of Tinbergen and Frisch as the parent programs and those of Haavelmo and Wold as their offspring. Both offspring research programs show some traits of the parents; as the offspring grow more mature, these traits may appear stronger or less evident.

An alternative way of analysing the two econometric programs, equally consistent with the history described in this paper, was suggested to me by John Aldrich. This views the Wold and Haavelmo econometric research programs as structures consisting of a number of complementary component ideas and methods. These components could well be those recognized by Åkerman (1955), a contemporary observer (or perhaps sympathizer) in the debate, who saw a fundamental duality in the two positions as follows:

Recursive	*Simultaneous*
explanation	description
causality	interdependence
consecutive (recursive) models	simultaneous models
disequilibrium	equilibrium (T_0 and $T_{+\infty}$)
dynamics (dy/dt)	statics (undated concepts)
causal analysis	calculation models
ex post reconstruction leading to prediction	*ex ante* decisions leading to action
conditioned plans carried out by autonomous decision units	final balancing of flows

Analysis of the history would then run along the following lines. As the emphasis within Wold's and Haavelmo's programs changed, because of the weight of criticism and because of their further research experience, some components were abandoned (for example, Cowles abandoned dynamics), or modified (for example, Wold changed methods) leaving the structures strengthened and/or weighing more heavily on the remaining parts. In time Wold's structure collapsed as technical criticisms reduced the strength of certain components and the structure was required to support new pressures (for example, Keynesian models) for which it was not designed.

Both these alternatives to Lakatos offer sensitive and flexible ways of describing the two research programs, ways which offer both analytical opportunities and rational explanations of the changes involved in recent transitions in econometric ideas without doing violence to their history.

Note

1. Both these comparisons have been made (though not in Lakatosian format) in my 1987 discussion of Haavelmo's work and in Part I (particularly ch. 2) of my book (1990).

References

Åkerman, J. (1955), discussion of a paper in 'Report of Uppsala Meeting', by Bent Hansen, *Econometrica*, **23**, p. 201.

Aldrich, J. (1989), 'Autonomy', *Oxford Economic Papers*, **41**, pp. 15–34.

Morgan, M.S. (1990), 'Perspectives in the History of Econometrics', *Econometric Theory*, **6**, pp.151–64.

8. Stabilizing Dynamics

E. Roy Weintraub[1]

> Almost no one has had the courage to do a careful anthropological study of formalism. The reason for this lack of nerve is quite simple: a priori, before the study has even started, it is towards the mind and its cognitive abilities that one looks for an explanation of forms. Any study of mathematics, calculations, theories, and forms in general should do quite the contrary: first look at how the observers move in space and time, how the mobility, stability and combinability of inscriptions are enhanced, how the networks are extended, how all the informations are tied together in a cascade of re-representation, and if, by some extraordinary chance, there is something still unaccounted for, then, and only then, look for special cognitive abilities. What I propose here, as a seventh rule of method, is in effect a moratorium on cognitive explanations of science and technology.
>
> (Bruno Latour, 1987, pp. 246–7)

The usual history of stability analysis in economics, as presented in, for example, the text by Arrow and Hahn (1971), suggests that:

1. The economic analysis of the early to mid-1930s that was concerned with dynamics and dynamic problems, contained a rich and full range of argument, idea, concept and language which expressed the variety of what were called dynamical theories.
2. Simultaneously the mathematical literature had developed a full and detailed language, a formal structure, for discussing and analysing dynamical sytems.
3. The mathematical theories were, by the mid-1930s, in a form suitable for a re-casting of some of the arguments that economists had been developing.
4. From 1939 to the early 1940s Samuelson was the individual primarily responsible for linking the mathematical and economic literatures on dynamics.
5. The period from the early 1940s to the late 1950s was one in which the mathematical analysis of stability of equilibrium increasingly defined the content of economic dynamics; problems of dynamics were re-cast as problems of establishing whether a system was stable or unstable.

6. The mathematics necessary to establish stability of particular systems was increasingly known, and disseminated among mathematicians, in the 1940s and early 1950s.
7. The means of demonstrating the possibility of stable equilibria, Liapunov techniques, were increasingly available to economists by the mid-1950s.
8. Arrow and Hurwicz established the conditions under which the competitive equilibrium would be stable in the late 1950s.
9. Scarf and Gale showed that those conditions were quite strong ones, and thus stability of the competitive equilibrium was not necessarily demonstrable for any particular model.

But there are many other ways to tell the story.

1 A LAKATOSIAN RATIONAL RECONSTRUCTION

As I have elsewhere argued (Weintraub, 1985), the neo-Walrasian research program was constituted in its modern form by the early 1950s. The program had, among its hard core elements, propositions involving concern with equilibrium states of interrelated multi-agent systems. Heuristics which asked that analysts model problems as optimization problems with constraints, and outcomes as equilibrium outcomes of such problems, necessitated that equilibria of models be robust with respect to small changes in initial conditions. That is, given a model, and its equilibrium state, the model would be useful to the extent that a perturbation of its structure, defined by its parameters, would likewise lead to an equilibrium outcome. Stability analysis was precisely concerned with this issue. Thus the development of the neo-Walrasian program was aided by the development of stability theory.

As a subprogram itself, stability analysis was driven initially by the question, 'Is the competitive equilibrium stable?' This question was answered in the affirmative by Hicks, who showed that optimization and stability went hand in hand. Samuelson showed, however, that Hicksian stability was not the same notion as was required for more general systems, and Samuelson created the 'true' or mathematical definition of stability and showed its relation to the Hicksian definition. Other writers in the 1940s, individuals like Lange, Metzler, Patinkin, Allais and Yasui, pushed out the knowledge frontier as they showed in more and more detail, and with more and more clarity, the relationship between the economics of equilibrium states and the mathematical property of 'being a stable equilibrium state'. In the late 1940s and early 1950s, the mathematical community developed, and disseminated the information about the developments of mathematical techniques necessary for demonstrating that a particular model possessed a stable equilibrium state. The program came to fruition in the late 1950s when Arrow and Hurwicz proved that the competitive equilibrium was stable under a variety of economic specifications; they developed a variety of sufficient conditions for a competitive equilibrium's being stable. Shortly thereafter, however, Scarf and Gale showed that those conditions were self-limiting because other reasonable economic models could be shown to be unstable, or to possess unstable equilibria.

Developed in this way, the story I have been telling is one of a research subprogram which could be called the 'Stability Program', and which was associated with a sequence of papers and books from Hicks to Scarf. The heuristics involved searching for a model of the competitive general equilibrium system for which a stable equilibrium could be found. This subprogram was linked with the 'hardening of the hard core' of the neo-Walrasian research program, for the neo-Walrasian program required a coherent model in which the hard core propositions could be shown to be not inconsistent. Since one of the primary propositions of that hard core was the statement that outcomes are equilibrium results of optimization problems, a strong coherence check on the value and worth of the neo-Walrasian program was provided by a check of the robustness of the core propositions in the following sense: since the heuristics asked that models be developed with equilibrium states as outcomes, those states would be relatively more useful if they were robust with respect to small re-specifications of the model. Thus stability of the competitive equilibrium was sought by analysts seeking to encourage general equilibrium treatments of a variety of economic problems.

The story is then one of progress as problem gave rise to problem gave rise to problem, and anomaly or counter-example gave rise to new theorems in a sequence which seemed to end, in triumph, with the papers by Arrow and Hurwicz. The original problem of showing stability was seen to have been solved. But then, in fact, the program immediately degenerated as Scarf and Gale showed that reasonable economic models, with well-defined competitive equilibrium states, were unstable. Paraphrasing the words of a later commentator, Frank Hahn (1970), what had been achieved was no more than the compilation of a collection of anecdotes about how prices might adjust in abstract markets. Put in Lakatosian language, the stability program took shape around 1939, progressed until around 1958, and degenerated immediately thereafter.

Better, perhaps, than the language of research programs is the language of proofs and refutations which suggests that, in a sequence of papers between 1939 and 1958, the original conjecture, 'The competitive equilibrium is stable' was shaped, re-shaped, refined and re-cast by a sequence of mathematical papers which produced, eventually, a theorem. That final theorem had the form, 'If the competitive general equilibrium model of Arrow–Debreu is such that prices move in accord with excess demand *tâtonnements* and excess demand functions (1) are continuously differentiable, (2) are homogeneous of degree one in prices and income, (3) satisfy Walras's Law, and (4) possess weak gross substitutability, then the competitive equilibrium is stable.'

Moreover this theorem was shown to be but one of a variety of such attainable, but the original conjecture was shown to be false as Scarf and Gale produced models of competitive general equilibrium systems which possessed equilibria which were totally unstable. The final theorem and proof used lemma-incorporation, monster-barring, and other proof strategies discussed by Lakatos (1976) in his historical reconstruction of the proof of the Euler Conjecture.

2 DECONSTRUCTING THE RECONSTRUCTION

I have just provided an account of a large and diffuse literature, one created by many individuals in many places over a 20-year period; my rendering of the history showed the unity and wholeness and organic coherence of the work. That vision is, of course, imposed on the history by my conscious choice to 'rationally reconstruct' the history. Using the Lakatosian framework commits the storyteller to a series of choices in the writing of the history. One is forced, before setting the words to the paper, to create a 'program' which is the major actor in the story. This requires the historian to look at the material, ascertain common elements in the various texts, moves and counter-moves, and abstract from them all a linking unity. That skeleton is termed the hard core of the program, and the manoeuvres which allow theory or paper B to follow from A are termed the heuristics of the programmatic core. Thus, if one can get B from A by the rule 'Create B-like stuff from A-like stuff', then, were that to be the heuristic, certainly B follows 'Lakatos-rationally' from A.

The point, of course, is that the perspective gained from a rational reconstruction is only one perspective. Lakatos himself asked, indeed, that the 'above the line' reconstruction be compared with a 'below the line' discussion which shows how the actual events failed to conform to the rationally reconstructed story. This history was actually constructed – performed by Lakatos (1976) in his *Proofs and Refutations*. The rational reconstruction of the history of the Euler conjecture in geometry, presented in conversation between a teacher and students as a series of moves and counter-moves, was linked by footnotes to the actual history.

Since 'historical' material itself does not coerce the writer to reconstruct the activity as a sequence of rational moves by anonymous actors, such a predilection for telling the stories of sequences of 'scientific work' would appear to be a result of prior belief in the identification of science with reason itself, with a belief that progress in science can be identified and discussed in terms of increasing truthfulness. As Latour and Woolgar (1979, p. 107) point out:

> Historians, as portrayed in historical texts, can move freely in the past, possess knowledge of the future, have the ability to survey settings in which they are not (and never will be) involved, have access to actors' motives, and (rather like god) are all-knowing and all-seeing, able to judge what is good and bad. They can produce histories in which one thing is the 'sign' of another and in which disciplines and ideas 'burgeon', 'mature', or 'lie fallow'.

At the heart of the claim that rational reconstructions of scientific work are necessary to understand the work itself is a belief that Nature or Reality itself constrains the texts in such a manner that the texts can be read or re-read as a sequence of moves in which Science gets closer and closer to the Truth about Nature or Reality. In effect, then, a Lakatosian framework predisposes the historian to select the elements of the narrative to confirm the coherent progress (in terms of successor papers solving problems posed in predecessor papers) of scientific research programs. Alternatively, failing to find progress the historian establishes the counter-claim that a program degenerated because it failed to solve the problems necessary for its continued success.

I do not want to reopen, in these pages, the debate about Realism, Relativism, Pragmatism and so on which has so determined the intellectual life of the post-modern era. I have little to contribute to the big themes so clearly addressed by Rorty, Derrida, Habermas, Bordieu, Latour, Fish and others. For what it is worth, I myself am most taken with the position developed by Barbara Herrnstein Smith (1988), a position critical of both objectivism–absolutism and radical relativism.

I think, however, that *it is too little appreciated how our notions of writing histories of science, and particularly histories of economics, would have to change were we to take seriously the claim that the rational reconstruction of scientific activity, or in our case the rational reconstruction of sequences of economic writings, cannot be elicited from the texts themselves*. Put another way, we have written the history of economics from the rationalist point of view that says that we historians *discover* the true history, where that true history is one in which papers are linked to other papers in terms of their truth-claims, and theories develop to solve problems which previous theories failed to solve. Other histories, ones in which, say, Keynes's Theory of Liquidity Preference is related to his own sexual history, or in which the success of Friedman's Monetarism is related to the clarity of his prose and the power of his voice in oral argument, are ruled non-historical.

This kind of idea is not new, except in economics. Replacing 'ethnography' with 'economics' we can appreciate Clifford Geertz's (1988, pp. 140, 144) comment that:

> To argue (point out, actually, for, like aerial perspective or the Pythagorian theorem, the thing once seen cannot then be unseen) that the writing of [economics] involves telling stories, making pictures, concocting symbolisms, and deploying tropes is commonly resisted, often fiercely, because of a confusion, endemic in the West since Plato at least, of the imagined with the imaginary, the fictional with the false, making things out with making them up. The strange idea that reality has an idiom in which it prefers to be described, that its very nature demands that we talk about it without fuss – a spade is a spade, a rose is a rose – on pain of illusion, trumpery, and self-bewitchment, leads on to the even stranger idea that, if literalism is lost, so is fact. . . . [The new work based on such ideas] spells the end of certain pretensions. There are a number of these pretensions, but they all tend to come down in one way or another to an attempt to get round the un-get-roundable fact that all [economic analyses, and histories of economics] are homemade, that they are the describer's descriptions, not those of the described.

We must seek to leave 'discovery' in the history of economics in favour of interpretation, or hermeneutics:

> [Gadamer's] 'universality of hermeneutics' refers to the fact that enquiry involves tradition-bound theoretical presuppositions in the social and natural sciences. Nowadays, we are more familiar with this contention in the form of three distinctive lines of argument, all linked to the notion of interpretation: 1) The first centres around the denial of brute facts. In essence, it holds that data beyond the challenge of rival interpretations are unattainable by science. 2) The second refers to the circularity of interpretation. It implies that any interpretation of an event or text ultimately depends on yet another set of interpretations, thus leading to an infinite regress of meaning. 3) The third can perhaps best be described in terms of Wittgenstein's notion of a language game. It conceives of interpretation as a condition for the possibility of data in general, and emphasizes the interconnection and interdependency of various levels of interpretation. (Knorr-Cetina, 1981, p. 138)

What I am suggesting here is both easy to understand and hard to relate to the substantive corpus of writing in the history of economic thought. From Blaug's magisterial *Economic Theory in Retrospect* to Samuelson's (1987) 'Out of the Closet: A Program For the Whig History of Economic Science', producers and consumers of the history of economics have accustomed themselves to read the past from the present's perspective, which in economics has led to a concentration on issues of precursors, harbingers, logical slips, factual errors, misuse of evidence and all manner of past writing which illuminates the present state of economics or helps us understand what we currently believe.

What all such history-writing has in common is that it takes up the challenge of presenting the history of science, in this case economic science, as an exemplar of rationality itself.

3 SCIENCE HISTORY WITHOUT RATIONALITY

If rationality is associated with the idea that science is the exemplar of rational thought, of the growth of knowledge, then the history of science is the history of reason itself. This view was developed in the writings of the French philosopher Gaston Bachelard:

> The conceptual basis of . . . Bachelard's philosophy of science, developed in a series of books written from the 1920s through the 1950s. According to Bachelard, reason is best known by reflection on science, and science is best known by reflection on its history . . . The proof of [this latter statement] lies in the repeated refutation of a priori philosophical ideals of rationality by historical scientific developments . . . There are, then, no viable accounts of rationality except those derived from the historical developments of scientific reason. To understand reason, philosophy must 'go to the school of science' . . . The rationality that philosophy tries to discover in the history of science is no more fixed and monolithic than that history itself. (Gutting, 1988, pp. 159–60)

Bachelard's view led him to focus on the breaks that science created in mankind's experience; the re-categorization and re-conceptualization that science induces define the process which is described by the Western notion of change which has been transformed into the idea of scientific progress. For Michel Foucault, who was deeply influenced by Bachelard, this uncovering, developed in his explorations of discursive practice in an almost archeological analysis, is rooted in a similar attempt to provide a history of reason, although he concentrated on a historical period before reason could be uncovered by attention to science. Foucault did not have science, but only had practice, and description, to unpack reason's history.

Writing the history of a science like economics from a perspective other than Whiggish compilation of successes goes against the grain, not only of standard historiography, but of a larger Western tradition. Such a revisionist project threatens those who believe that an other than rational reconstruction of the history deconstructs the objective nature of the activity which the history attempts to describe. The frightened believe that rational practice must be described rationally, must be reconstructed rationally, else reason itself be subverted by description.

To see that this is not, in the memorable phrase of Barbara Herrnstein Smith, a straw herring, consider the rules for writing the history of economic thought promulgated by Don Walker (1988, pp. 101–2), in his Presidential Address to the History of Economics Society:

> First, we believe that the writings of economists should be judged on the basis of whether or not they were original . . . Second, we believe that a writer's work should be judged on the basis of whether or not it was important . . . Third, we judge economic writings in the light of modern economic knowledge [in the sense that] we use current knowledge to detect sound arguments and defective arguments . . . Fourth, we believe a writer's work should be evaluated for its logical consistency . . . Fifth, we criticize a writer for asserting that he achieved something that he did not . . . Sixth, we praise a writer if he explained reality well and criticize him if his work was unrealistic.[2]

But what, in fact, is feared, is illusory. The anxieties in the closet, or underneath the bed, of the historian of economics are private vices, not public facts. To ask how the Negishi survey article constructed a history of stability theory is not to say that Arrow and Hurwicz contributed less. To ask, and write, about the stabilizing function of mathematics on the language games played in dynamic economics is not to denigrate mathematics. To deconstruct the evolutionary metaphor rooted in the mathematics which Samuelson assimilated from A.J. Lotka and E.B. Wilson is not to deny the magnitude of Samuelson's genius.

4 STABILIZING DISCOURSE

With this in mind, I want to suggest that there is another way that the sequence of papers on dynamics and stability can be read, and that is as an attempt, by members of a particular community, to narrow the possibilities for disagreement among community members. This is unobjectionable as a reading, for it is even part of what the primary figures of the subdiscipline said they were attempting to do. What I would like to suggest, over and beyond this form of the claim, is that there were a number of other implications of this strategy which need to be uncovered if we are to understand in more detail the moves and counter-moves in the sequence.

Let us agree that there were, indeed, rampant confusions abroad in the 1930s among economists about the nature and meaning of equilibrium. At the very least there were political ramifications to claims that the economy was, or was not, in equilibrium. To argue, for instance, that the economy was inherently 'unstable' was perhaps to claim that the capitalist system was inherently unstable; capitalism's 'contradictions' would lead to a systemic economic collapse, and a move to socialism would be required for the next stage of economic development. From this perspective, concern with the nature and meaning of equilibrium, and the possibility of stability of the system's equilibrium path, would be of political importance.

Were the 1930s a time in which the system could be described unambiguously as in or out of equilibrium? I think not. In the face of the international trade collapse, and private wealth collapse, and unprecedented levels of unemployment, arguments were still being offered to suggest that the economy was finding its own natural level or suffering from a temporary adjustment to a new equilibrium position. Keynes of course was beginning to suggest, as early as his 1930 Macmillan Committee testimony, that the economy was not self-righting in the neo-classical sense (which he termed the Classical sense) and that the economy could continue in semi-permanent slump. In the language of later writers, Keynes suggested that the economy was in equilibrium, but that equilibrium was one in which unemployment was very high: equilibrium (in the sense of equality between aggregate supply and aggregate demand) could be consistent with any level of unemployment at all.

Now the neoclassical synthesis, which attempted to wed Keynesian macroeconomics to neo-Walrasian general equilibrium analysis, or to instantiate Keynesian macroeconomic theory, or significant portions of that theory, in the belts of the neo-Walrasian program, required *all* markets to be in equilibrium in order to permit the claim that the economy was in equilibrium. This led to the fundamental problem which had to be 'solved' by the neo-classical synthesis: how was one to combine market clearing in all the economy's markets with the notion that the labour market, in reporting very high levels of unemployment, was apparently not clearing?

There are a variety of responses one could make to this dilemma:

1. One could deny that the labour market was not clearing; this view would lead one to argue that the levels of unemployment were in fact equilibrium levels of employment, and that it was a voluntary choice of leisure that was revealed preferred in the labour market. In popular myth, 'those people are just too lazy to work for wages, albeit low wages. They would rather receive welfare, or unemployment, or stay on the dole, etc.' This is the kind of analysis associated with the New Classical Economics, and Robert Lucas's (1985) claim that all unemployment is best modelled as voluntary unemployment, because all observed states of the economy must be modelled as equilibrium states and so on.
2. One could argue that the labour market would clear if only some impediment or other to its clearing were not present; this view led to the notions that union demands for high wages lead to unemployment, or minimum wage laws lead to unemployment, or unemployment compensation leads to unemployment. Such a view merges into the first view if structural imbalances (like workers in West Virginia and vacant jobs in Texas) and barriers of immobility (taste for family land, costs of relocating and so on) prevent the matching of workers with jobs.
3. One could deny the sense, or observation (!), that markets do in fact clear; this view would lead one to say that the synthesis itself was perversely misguided in its interest in wedding the Keynesian Princess with the neo-Walrasian troll. This position was taken by the Post-Keynesians.
4. Finally, one could agree that markets must clear in equilibrium, and that the labour market was not in equilibrium, and that there is a tendency to equilibrium in general, but argue that the movement to equilibrium is weak, vulnerable to obstruction and on occasion subject to systematic failure. That is, the economy could be 'off' the demand or supply curves for labour, and so the normal tendency to return to equilibrium might not be present. This explanation left Keynesian unemployment in the realm of 'generalized market failure' (for example, distributional shifts, monopoly on one or both sides of the labour market, governmental interference, income effects, monetary policy failures and so on) thus ceding the theoretical ground to neo-Walrasian theory, and the realm of practical policy measures to Keynesians interested in remedying the market failures. In substance, this is the position outlined by Don Patinkin (1957) in his *Money, Interest, and Prices*, which created

the neo-classical synthesis as we understand it. In its fully historicized form, the argument was first offered to economists by Axel Leijonhufvud (1968) in his *On Keynesian Economics and the Economics of Keynes*.

To repeat, there were at least these several potential strategies available to relieve the tension between the depression levels of unemployment ('depression levels of unemployment' themselves are associated with the rhetorical shift which constituted certain workers' behaviour as 'unemployed involuntarily' and requiring action to be taken) and the theoretical perspective which held that individual behaviour, mediated by market interaction, leads to coordinated, or equilibrium, outcomes. But, of the strategies outlined above, it was the fourth one which allowed the community of economists simultaneously to preserve the theory and the phenomenon.

The neo-classical synthesis allowed there to be both a general equilibrium and unemployment in the labour market: the synthesis could allow there to be an equilibrium which was not easily, or simply, attained. What was needed to effect this result was simply the idea that there were two kinds of equilibria – easily attainable ones and others not easily attained. This disjunction permitted, encouraged even, the distinction between stable and unstable equilibria, and thus it created the concern with conditions under which the competitive equilibrium would or would not be stable.

This set of observations makes sense of one of the most curious features of the history of stability theory in economics, and that is how the development of that theory did not follow the logic of the mathematical theory in which it eventually was to be embedded. That is, in all modern historical reconstructions of general equilibrium theory, it is argued that there are three 'problems' whose solution defined the creation of modern general equilibrium theory: first, there is the problem of the existence of a competitive equilibrium; second, there is the problem of the efficiency or optimality of the competitive equilibrium; and third, there is the problem of the stability of the competitive equilibrium.[3]

The formal logic suggests that, first, one must develop a model, then characterize the equilibrium (the efficiency problem), then establish the existence of such an equilibrium (the existence problem), and then establish the robustness of that equilibrium (the stability problem). Looking at the dates usually provided for the successful solution of those problems we see that Arrow and Debreu separately demonstrated efficiency in 1951. They jointly, and McKenzie independently, solved the existence problem in its modern form (modulo Wald and von Neumann) in 1954. Finally Arrow and Hurwicz established the stability results in 1958. This sequence apparently confirms the formal logic and suggests that the problematic of the mathematized analysis drove the community's work.

The difficulty, however, is that the concern and attention to stability, and the robustness of the equilibrium over time, predated the concern with either existence or efficiency of the competitive equilibrium. The literature associated with Frisch, Tinbergen, Hicks and finally Samuelson was associated with understanding the conditions under which an equilibrium would be stable, so as to permit the conjunction of equilibrium theorizing and unemployment analysis. Such analyses led Hicks to distinguish among equilibria on the basis of their intertemporal linkages and thus to locate 'Keynesian' concerns not in Part I of *Value and Capital* (1939) which concerned static equilibrium and stability analysis, but rather in Part II with its analysis of inter-temporal equilibrium in the sense of expectations and temporary equilibrium. Samuelson solved the linkage problem by showing that, if there were multiple equilibria, stable and unstable equilibria would alternate, and thus the presence of more than one equilibrium would allow scope for policy to move the economy from one to another, for the economy would not necessarily move of its own rules of dynamic adjustment. Lange (1944) allowed equilibria to exist, but showed how instability could appear when or if monetary authorities behaved in perverse ways. And finally Patinkin (1957), the true architect of the theoretical structure we have been calling the neo-classical synthesis, assumed that existence was not problematic, but rather argued that Keynesian concerns could be located in the disequilibrium in the labour market; it was Patinkin who presented the lengthy analysis of the nature and meaning of Walras's *tâtonnements*, the dynamic adjustment mechanism at the centre of the mathematical theory which was coming to represent stability theory in economics.

5 CONVERGENCE AND DIVERGENCE

The issues I have broached can be given an alternative twist if we recognize that the 'facts' of the economy's being stable or not, and the labour market's being in equilibrium or not, are actually constructions. The fact is that controversies are possible when there are alternative constructions, or when the meanings of the artifacts created in the particular communities are not, or have not yet been, stabilized in their meanings. What constitutes the claim that the economy is not in equilibrium when there is a high level of unemployment? Socially the meaning of this claim is jointly negotiated by the economists concerned with macroeconomic issues and by those concerned with the conceptualization of the economy as a coordinated system. Out of that negotiation, a process of argument, written and oral, the presentation and development of evidence of one sort or another and so on, there is a re-conceptualization of the system: the meanings of equilibrium, the economy, employment levels and unemployment levels are stabilized in the sense that individuals use these phrases and ideas in mutually understandable and agreeable ways. As Latour and Woolgar (1979, pp. 176–7) point out:

> Facts and artifacts do not correspond respectively to true and false statements. Rather, statements lie along a continuum according to the extent to which they refer to the conditions of their construction. . . . Our argument is not just that facts are socially constructed. We also wish to show that the process of construction involves the use of certain devices whereby all traces of production are made extremely difficult to detect.
>
> Once the statement begins to stabilise, however, an important change takes place. *The statement itself becomes a split entity*. On the one hand, it is a set of words which represents a statement about an object. On the other hand, it corresponds to an object in itself which takes on a life of its own. . . . At the point of stabilisation, however, there appear to be both objects and statements about those objects. Before long, more and more reality is attributed to the object and less and less to the statement about the object. Consequently, an inversion takes place: the object becomes the reason why the statement was formulated in the first place. . . . The history of its construction is also transformed from this new vantage point: the process of construction is turned into the pursuit of a single path which led inevitably to the 'actual' structure. Only through the skill and efforts of the great scientists could the setbacks and red herrings and blind alleys be overcome and the real structure revealed for what it was.

With respect to the stability literature, what we see is that, by the end of the 1940s or the early 1950s, the economy itself had changed in the only meaningful sense in which that claim can be sustained: that is, discursive practice about the economy had been altered to allow the simultaneous maintenance of the two claims that the economy was in equilibrium and that there were socially unacceptable levels of unemployment associated with either systemic market failures or specific failures in the labour market. The content of the neo-classical synthesis was precisely that particular re-conceptualization, that change in discursive practice.

The mathematization of equilibrium and stability, the papers from

Samuelson's on through Arrow and Hurwicz's, stabilized that discourse and re-negotiated the meaning of the economy-text. The restriction of 'dynamics' to 'dynamical system', and the constriction of 'stable' to 'locally stable equilibrium motion of a dissipative dynamical system' permitted concurrence, initially within the small community of mathematical economists, on the meaning of the claim that unemployment was a disequilibrium position associated with a 'usually' stable competitive equilibrium. The neo-classical synthesis was literally unthinkable before the availability of the mathematization of equilibrium and stability; as consensual meaning was extended to wider and wider communities by the increased understanding of the mathematized framework in which those ideas were made manifest, the neo-classical synthesis too was more and more widely spread. In consequence, for example, Post-Keynesian attacks on that position could not receive a real hearing because they appeared to reject the generally stabilized meanings of the community in favour of meanings introduced by Keynes in the 1930s to modify discursive practice about unemployment (for example, Keynes's introduction of the distinction between voluntary and involuntary unemployment). Post-Keynesians were increasingly isolated as the linguistic practices they engaged in were more and more marginalized by the larger mathematically literate community. Their writings, on Keynes's essential meaning, remind us of those about whom C. Vann Woodward (1986, p. 26) wrote:

> Lost causes, especially those that foster loyalties and nostalgic memories, are among the most prolific breeders of historiography. If survivors deem the cause not wholly lost and perhaps in some measure retrievable, the search of the past becomes more frantic and the books about it more numerous. Blame must be fixed, villains found, heroes celebrated, old quarrels settled, old dreams restored, and motives vindicated. Amid the ruins controversy thrives and books proliferate.

6 CONSTRUCTING MEANING

There will be, no doubt, objections to the view I am presenting here. Primary among them will be the objection that empirical experience is not so invisible as the above account appears to suggest. Surely, it will be claimed, meanings are not so loosely contrived, so free to differ and be seen as differing by various individual economists. Surely, it will be argued, Patinkin was constrained by the facts of the economic data and he had to take that data, that empirical knowledge, not only into account in his account, but to have his account stand or fall by its accord with those data.

How are meanings negotiated in scientific practice? How do particular proposals, presented as contributions to an ongoing discussion with citations of papers, marshalling of data and so on, come to become knowledge? How is the scientific reality, the reality of the economy, created?

> Thus within the negotiation of meanings that turn individual proposals into intersubjective realities, we find ambient nature passively constraining possible meanings through active experience that is inseparable from the language use. . . . Similar constraining processes occur in all discourse communities. . . . Various discourse communities appeal to various kinds of experience as touchstones for their negotiations of communal meaning. . . . Science, however, has taken empirical experience as its major touchstone, so that in the process of negotiation of meaning, empirical experience not only constrains the range of possible meanings but is actively sought in the attempt to establish stable meanings from the negotiation. (Bazerman, 1988, p. 312)

The idea, so abhorred by the hard-headed positivists among the historians of economics, that meanings are negotiated and constructed, seems to turn on the idea that *if* meaning is negotiated, it is fluid and subjective, and *thus* (!) not real; subjectivism is rejected then because realness is a given, like Dr Johnson's kicked rock. Our not-so-straw man (Walker, 1988, p. 110) has argued that

> Subjectivists intermittently need, it seems, to be shocked by the realities of life and death, work and suffering, into a realization of what is obvious to everyone else in the world, namely that it is real and what has happened in the past is not malleable and cannot be altered to fit our interpretations of it. The same is true of the texts we study.

But the point of course is that the meaning of death, even, is socially negotiated; the death of the Shiite warrior who dies in battle has a different personal meaning from that of the infidel with whom he battles. And their own personal meanings are different from mine. A belief in an after-life changes the meaning of death. And of course a belief in the obligations of work in Protestant tradition changed the meaning of work.

Our economy is no less real because its meaning must become stable through the activities of those who study it, and talk and write about it, and form the community which informs the conceptualization called the economy. To say that economists negotiate the meaning of the economy is not to claim that the economy does not exist: it is not comprehensible to me what such a claim could even mean: we have no language to discuss such silliness. No, it is rather that the activities of economists are precisely concerned with stabilizing the meaning of propositions which express ideas about inflation, say, or equilibration of the balance of payments deficit. Models, and theorems, and evidence of both empirical and formal and definitional natures, are adduced to convince other members of the concerned community that some meanings are preferable for the agreed purposes, where those purposes themselves must be re-negotiated from time to time: are we interested in controlling inflation, or are we interested in controlling unemployment, or the trade balance, or none of these at all but rather in controlling the forces of governmental regulation of the economic sphere?

7 CONCLUSION

My perspective is that noted by Knorr-Cetina in her important 1981 monograph. She asked (p. 137):

> [Can] the practice of natural and technological science be distinguished from the symbolic, interpretive, 'hermeneutic' practice of the social sciences, and of social life itself[?] I hold that it cannot. In fact, my goal is to underline the essential similarity between the two modes of production of knowledge which have become so painstakingly separated.

Based on the history I have constructed, a history of a line of mathematized argumentation about the stability of the competitive equilibrium, I have tried to suggest that the papers in that sequence could be well understood as an attempt to impose order and to create knowledge; I have tried to show that that process was a social process of negotiation and argument. That a rational reconstruction of the sequence of works fails to make good sense of the papers I examined should come as no great surprise once it is clearly seen that *ex post* rationalizations, while they stabilize the previous history, do not themselves present their knowledge contemporaneously with the historical action and actors. We are wise after the fact, where the wisdom is the clarity of reason.

NOTES

1. This chapter is a slightly modified version of Chapter 6 of the author's book, *Stabilizing Dynamics: Constructing Economic Knowledge* (New York: Cambridge University Press, 1991).

2. I have refrained from quoting from the latter sections of Walker's paper wherein he takes on the imaginary dragon he calls 'subjectivism' and, having got himself utterly confused about what and who that monster is, ends up slicing off his big toe with his broadsword: he concludes this breathtaking auto-bloodletting with: 'To accept subjectivism would be to revert to unscientific thought, to abandon the clear-minded and rational approach that has led to decades of improvement of the study of the history of economic thought' (Walker, 1988, p. 111).
3. Sometimes it is suggested that there is a fourth problem, which is referred to as the problem of 'uniqueness' of the competitive equilibrium, but, on actual analysis, this problem turns out to be part of the stability problem.

REFERENCES

Arrow, Kenneth J. and Hahn, Frank (1971), *General Competitive Analysis* (San Francisco: Holden Day).

Bazerman, Charles (1988), *Shaping Written Knowledge* (Madison: University of Wisconsin Press).

Blaug, M. (1978), *Economic Theory in Retrospect*, 3rd edn (New York: Cambridge University Press).

Geertz, Clifford (1988), *Works and Lives* (Stanford: Stanford University Press).

Gutting, Gary (1988), 'Michel Foucault and the History of Reason', in Ernan McMullin (ed.), *Construction and Constraint: The Shaping of Scientific Rationality* (Notre Dame: University of Notre Dame Press).

Hahn, Frank (1970), 'Some Adjustment Problems', *Econometrica*, **38** (1), January, pp. 1–17.

Hicks, J.R. (1939), *Value and Capital* (Oxford: Oxford University Press).

Knorr-Cetina, Karin (1981), *The Manufacture of Knowledge: An Essay on the Constructivist and Contingent Nature of Science* (Oxford: Pergamon Press).

Lakatos, Imre (1976), *Proofs and Refutations* (Cambridge: Cambridge University Press).

Lange, O. (1944), *Price Flexibility and Employment* (Bloomington: Principia Press).

Latour, Bruno (1987), *Science in Action* (Cambridge, Mass.: Harvard University Press).

Latour, Bruno and Woolgar, Steve (1979), *Laboratory Life* (Beverly Hills: Sage).

Leijonhufvud, Axel (1968), *On Keynesian Economics and the Economics of Keynes* (New York: Oxford University Press).

Lucas, Robert (1985), *Studies in Business Cycle Theory* (Cambridge, Mass.: MIT Press).

Patinkin, Don (1957), *Money, Interest, and Prices*, 2nd edn 1965 (New York: Harper & Row).

Samuelson, Paul A. (1947), *Foundations of Economic Analysis* (Cambridge, Mass.: Harvard University Press).

—— (1987), 'Out of the Closet: A Program for the Whig History of Economic Science', *History of Economics Society Bulletin*, IX, **1**, Fall, pp. 51–60.

Smith, Barbara H. (1988), *Contingencies of Value* (Cambridge, Mass.: Harvard University Press).

Walker, Donald A. (1988), 'Ten Major Problems in the Study of the History of Economic Thought', *History of Economics Society Bulletin*, X (**2**), 99–116.

Weintraub, E.R. (1985), *General Equilibrium Analysis: Studies in Appraisal* (New York: Cambridge University Press).
Woodward, C. Vann (1986), 'The Lost Cause: Review of Irving Howe's Socialism and America', *New York Review of Books*, 30 January, p. 26.

COMMENT ON WEINTRAUB

Philip Mirowski

Some individuals at the Capri conference regarded Roy Weintraub's recent work, which does not carry on the genre of Lakatosian analysis which he began in his *General Equilibrium Analysis* (1985), with something approaching existential nausea, fearing that he may have become infected with what they regard as the creeping relativism of our age. I am not one of those and, indeed, rather believe that the work which Roy is now doing on the construction of the idea of economic stability within the neoclassical research program will stand as one of the milestones in the history of economic thought in the twenty-first century. Since I agree that there was nothing inevitable about the notion of 'stability' arrived at *circa* 1960, as there could not be, since it was subsequently deconstructed within the program in the next two decades (Mirowski, 1989b), the narrative of how such a state came into being is indispensable in the understanding of the modern evolution of the neoclassical program. What it does not accomplish, and apparently what some of the conferees desired, was some further vindication of the Lakatosian organon.

Let me begin by saying something nice about Lakatos. I would like to claim that Roy's (and others') recent linguistic or hermeneutic turn, for lack of some better phrase, grew in a reasonably organic way out of his previous concern with Lakatos as a tool for organizing the history of economics. The original fascination with the apparatus of the hard core, protective belt and so on could be traced to the ferment in the history and philosophy of science in the 1960s and early 1970s, where many insightful individuals challenged previous received views of the nature and practices of science. The attraction of Lakatos for historians and methodologists of economics was doubly strong: not only did it seemingly hold out the promise of a criterion of progress and development for an intellectual discipline which could be applied from outside that discipline (for, if anything else, methodologists of economics are outsiders) but, since neoclassical economics was little more than reprocessed nineteenth-century physics (Mirowski, 1989a), historians were tropismatically drawn to the philosophy of *physics* to illuminate their own history. But then the congenital disease of physics envy took over and the invocation of Lakatos became an incantation: if only the physicists or philosophers of physics would tell us how to be a science, then that would confer legitimacy on research program X. To prevent economics from being a messy, multivectored motley of a social progress, we would prostrate ourselves before any idol – 'increasing content', 'rational reconstruction', 'the hardening of the hard core', and so forth.

Hence, in the history of thought community, there was a tendency to reduce Lakatos to a system, or even a checklist, to be applied indifferently to Adam Smith and Paul Samuelson. In many instances it led to interminable quibbles over what was and was not in the 'hard core', and other such dull activities. The question which was never asked was: why must economics be like physics, or like what Lakatos said science was?[1] The key here was the heavily freighted notion of the rational reconstruction of history. What did it take to render history 'rational'? As long as rationality was equated with physics, there could be no further serious discussion, especially given the average economist's image of physics. But, of course, there was another, contradictory notion of rationality, one embedded in the economist's training, which defined it as constrained optimization over a conservative preference field. Could science be described as a social process isomorphic to the neoclassical market? While this would at least impose some consistency in the usage of the term 'rationality' in that particular language community, as well as harmonizing with some of its actual linguistic practices ('he's getting less than his marginal product at University of Podunk'; 'the market for game theorists is hot this year'), it seems to have been resisted by orthodox economists and by methodologists.[2] The reasons for the taboo are not relevant here, although one might suggest that, while pushpin is as good as poetry for the average neoclassical, science has always been the exception to the supposed pervasive structure of self-interest in the economist's pantheon.

Given the *culs-de-sac* presented by these notions of rationality, Roy Weintraub's linguistic turn becomes comprehensible as the breaking of a deadlock in the Lakatosian tradition, the transcendence of the incoherent notions of rationality by means of research into the way linguistic and mathematical practice structures our history. I might go a bit further than Roy in suggesting that we put an end to the practice of looking to the Other to provide us with a pre-packaged 'method' and a ready-made legitimation. The rationality of history is constructed; it is not appropriated and not approximated. This resonates with a certain modern movement in philosophy and literary criticism growing out of Nietzsche, Foucault, Rorty and others, who portray the Strong Methodologist as one who re-describes her own discipline's history, and in the process also re-describes the history of other adjoining disciplines. We need no longer take physics as our paradigm, for, when we understand our own heritage, our story of other intellectual endeavours will diverge from those constructed by physicists, or philosophers of physics, or anthropologists. Then we will live in the real world, the world of many methods, many rationalities.

Notes

1. Which, with the very important exception of his *Proofs and Refutations*, was physics for Lakatos.
2. There have been some attempts to apply neoclassical economics to science, ranging from Garner (1979) to some recent work of Nicholas Rescher and Michael Ghislin, but in my experience they are looked askance upon by both philosophers and economists. One recent attempt to bring this contradiction out into the open can be found in Philip Mirowski and Stephen Sklivas (n.d.), 'Why Econometricians Don't Reproduce (Although They Do Replicate)', Columbia University Economics Department Working Paper.

References

Garner, C. (1979), 'Academic Publication, Market Signalling, and Scientific Research Decisions', *Economic Inquiry*, **17**, pp. 575–84.
Mirowski, P. (1989a), *More Heat Than Light: Economics as Social Physics: Physics as Nature's Economics* (New York: Cambridge University Press).
Mirowski, P. (1989b), 'The Rise and Fall of the Concept of Equilibrium in Economic Analysis', *Recherches Economiques de Louvain*, **55**, pp. 1–22.
Rorty, R. *et al.* (eds) (1984), *Philosophy in History* (New York: Cambridge University Press).
Weintraub, E.R. (1985), *General Equilibrium Analysis* (New York: Cambridge University Press).

9. Alternative Accounts of Equilibrium Unemployment

Rod Cross*

Recent controversies over the nature and causes of unemployment have called into question the type of equilibrium concept which is most appropriate for the understanding of economic phenomena. In particular, the issue of whether equilibria, if they exist, in economic systems are path-independent or not has been raised. The contrast is between the orthodox ahysteretic conception of equilibria which are pinned down by state variables alone and hysteretic equilibria in which history, in the form of the path towards equilibrium, helps shape the equilibrium attained or attainable.

During the course of the 1970s the natural rate hypothesis (NRH) came to dominate thought about what determines, and what can be done about, unemployment. As the 1980s proceeded it became increasingly apparent that major amendments were necessary if the NRH were to be able to explain the substantial increase in unemployment that actually occurred in most countries: actual unemployment rates were substantially higher than implied by the NRH. During this process it became fashionable to invoke hysteresis, or path-dependence, as a means of resolving the empirical difficulties. A distinction emerged between those who saw hysteresis as a means of putting Humpty Dumpty in the form of the NRH back together again and those who saw hysteresis as a distinct hypothesis which implies a fundamental departure from the neo- or new classical analytical systems in which the NRH is embedded.

1 THE CONCEPT OF EQUILIBRIUM

To Friedman, the co-originator of the NRH along with Phelps

* This is a shortened version of a paper prepared for the Conference on Transitions in Recent Economics, Capri, October 1989. The longer version is available from the author on request. I am grateful to Antoni Chawluk and Brian Main for comments on the earlier version, and to Mark Blaug and Neil de Marchi for suggestions as to the format of the present version.

(Friedman, 1968; Phelps, 1967), '. . . an equilibrium position is one that, if attained, will be maintained . . .' (Friedman 1976, p. 19). The Walrasian system of general equilibrium analysis is admired for '. . . its beauty, its grandeur, its architectonic structure . . .' (Friedman, 1955, p. 905), but Friedman uses the Marshallian distinctions between market, short-run and long-run equilibria as instruments to generate specific predictions (see Kevin Hoover, 1988, ch. 9). The natural rate concept is defined in Walrasian terms, and is relevant to a Marshallian long run, the corresponding short run being characterized by unanticipated inflation, and the actual differing from the natural rate of unemployment. In contrast, the new classical conception of equilibrium is based on consistent and successful optimization pursued using rational expectations: this procedure collapses the Friedman–Marshall long run into the short run, involving a form of 'Walrasian globalism' (Hoover, 1988, p. 218). It can be argued that '. . . the difference between Friedman and the new classicals . . . is not over the nature of the economy . . . rather . . . Friedman believes that only the Marshallian method of partitioning problems produces *fruitful* results, while the new classicals believe that only the Walrasian method of fully specifying the optimisation problem that agents face produces *secure* results' (Hoover, 1988, p. 230).

Thus the point at issue here does not concern the type of equilibrium concept, but rather whether the Walrasian equilibrium yielding a natural rate of unemployment is relevant to the short or long run. The 1980s debate about equilibrium unemployment has thrown into contention the issue of whether either type of Walrasian equilibrium concept is appropriate to the understanding of economic phenomena.

A central characteristic of Walrasian equilibrium analysis is path-independence: the equilibrium is pinned down by state or structural variables alone, and is independent of the time path towards equilibrium. This property is indicated on Figure 9.1. The introduction of a contractionary shock $\varepsilon(-ve)$ raises the actual rate of unemployment to $U+$, above the U^* pinned down by state variables. According to the NRH the rate of inflation will fall, stimulating a recovery in real demand until the economy returns to the original U^* equilibrium. Conversely an expansionary shock $\varepsilon(+ve)$ will reduce actual unemployment to $U-$ and stimulate an increase in the rate of inflation; as the level of real demand tends to fall because of effects of the real balance type, the economy will revert to the equilibrium U^*. Thus the time path described as the economy adjusts to shocks has no effect on the equilibrium configuration: the natural rate is independent of the time path taken by actual

Figure 9.1 The ahysteretic natural rate of unemployment

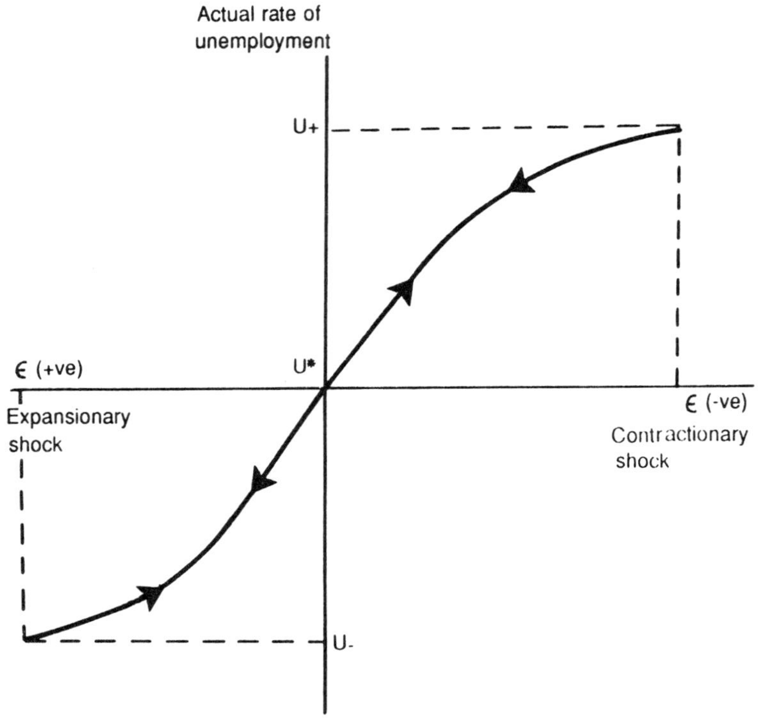

unemployment. It is this type of equilibrium concept which predominates in economics.

Until the 1980s the prominent research programs in economics avoided or excluded hysteresis from the conception of equilibrium employed, and the natural rate hypothesis, at least in its original form, falls squarely into this tradition. Outside the mainstream, notable advocates of the position that it is necessary to invoke hysteresis in order to understand the behaviour of economic systems have included Schumpeter (1934, for example) and his one-time student Georgescu-Roegen (1966). Schumpeter's conception of economic dynamics attached great significance to such effects:

> . . . economic life changes . . . partly because of changes in the data, to which it tends to adapt itself . . . but . . . there is another [source of] changes . . . which arises from within the system, and this kind of change is the cause of so many important phenomena that it seems worthwhile to build a theory for it . . . [this] kind of change . . . so displaces its equilibrium point that the new one cannot be reached from the old one by infinitesimal steps . . .' (Schumpeter, 1934, p. 64)

Even if Schumpeter did not use the term 'hysteresis' in print – this may have been lost in translation or missed by myself – he certainly used the term orally:

> . . . the date is 1946 or 1947 . . . the Graduate Economics Club . . . at Harvard . . . the students like to have Schumpeter introduce the visitor because he always puts on a good show . . . this time the visitor was Roy Harrod . . . Schumpeter gave Harrod one of his typical flowery but slightly tongue-in-cheek introductions, ending with 'Ladies and Gentlemen. I give you now . . . Roy Harrod, who is going to tell us about the very important phenomena of hysteresis' . . . Harrod looked puzzled and flustered, having of course no intention of doing any such thing . . .' (James Tobin, letter to the author, 27 May 1986)

Georgescu-Roegen has consistently argued that in Walrasian general equilibrium systems the auctioneer, or Laplacean demon, will be frustrated by hysteresis:

> . . . an individual who comes to a new economic situation may alter his preferences . . . *ex post* he may discover that the answer he gave to our demon was not right . . . the equilibrium computed by our demon is thus immediately defeated not by the intervention of exogenous factors but by endogenous causes . . . consequently our demon will have to keep on recomputing running-away equilibria, unless by chance he possesses a divine mind capable of writing the whole history of the world before it actually happens. (Georgescu-Roegen, 1971, p. 335)

The analytical differences between ahysteretic and hysteretic equilibria can be illustrated by reference to a swinging pendulum: here it appears to be necessary to invoke knowledge of the past positions of the pendulum as well as the present in order to explain the future motion; the introduction of the present instantaneous velocity as an explanatory state variable, however, gets rid of the problem. Given the reverse nature of derivatives and integrals in calculus, it would appear that, for analytic functions, hysteresis can be removed by introducing time derivatives of a sufficiently high order as explanatory state variables: '. . . if we know the present value of all the temporal derivatives, this is equivalent to full knowledge about the past . . .' (Elster, 1976, p. 376). This procedure, however, does not simplify matters: '. . . there does not seem to be any gain . . . if hysteresis is eliminated by the introduction of infinitely many state variables . . .' (Elster, 1976, p. 376).

In terms of formal models, the contrast between ahysteretic and hysteretic models can be seen in the following equations (see Cross and Allan, 1988):

$$y_t = f(x_t) \tag{9.1}$$

$$y_t = g(\dot{x}_t, x_t) \tag{9.2}$$

$$y_t = b_t + \int_{-\infty}^{t} h_{t-s} x_s e^{-s} ds \tag{9.3}$$

$$y_t = k \begin{array}{l} \dot{x}_{t-1}, \dot{x}_{t-2}, \ldots ; \\ x_{t-1}, x_{t-2}, \ldots \end{array} \tag{9.4}$$

Here the y variables stand for equilibrium values of systems which are explained by the x variables. Equations (9.1) and (9.2) are ahysteretic: state variables only explain the equilibrium, past history being irrelevant except in the influence of the past on the present values of the x variables. Equations (9.3) and (9.4) are hysteretic, history being invoked over and above the traces left by the past in the present. With the ahysteretic equations there will be a unique correspondence between a contemporaneous vector of x variables and the y equilibrium; with the hysteretic equations there will be a potentially infinite set of correspondences between given contemporaneous x vectors and y equilibria, different time paths for the x vectors generating different y equilibria.

An important debate regarding the type of equilibrium analysis appropriate to economics took place in the 1930s. Interestingly enough, given that the natural rate of unemployment concept was coined by analogy to Wicksell's natural rate of interest, the context was also 'natural': '. . . a discussion arose regarding Wicksell's concept of the "natural" interest rate . . . the discussion subsequently extended to the question of what in general was to be understood by a "natural" or "equilibrium" position of a certain set of economic variables . . .' (Frisch, 1936, p. 100). Frisch's celebrated contribution to this debate served to define what emerged to be the standard ahysteretic account of equilibrium in economic systems. An informal awareness was revealed, however, of the alternative hysteretic account of equilibrium: '. . . equilibrium will be determinate . . . even if it is only gradually established, so long as the position of equilibrium is independent of the actual path followed . . . indeterminateness can only arise from the disturbing influence of intermediary situations . . .' (Kaldor, 1933, pp. 126–7).

It is interesting to speculate whether Keynes's 'struggle to escape' from neoclassical analysis would have been eased, and the *General*

Theory made less opaque, if he had been aware of the hysteresis account of equilibria. It is not too difficult to argue that a continuum of equilibria, for any given vector of state variables, corresponding to different historical time paths taken by an economic system, would have provided Keynes with a more coherent vehicle for the exposition of his ideas. Hysteresis models had, by the inter-war period, spread to subjects other than physics, most notably in the form of the Lotka–Volterra model of predator–prey interaction in macrobiology (Lotka, 1925). The irony here is that James Alfred Ewing, who coined the term 'hysteresis', was Professor of Mechanism and Applied Mechanics at Cambridge University from 1890 to 1916 (see Glazebrook, 1935). As far as I am aware, Keynes was not exposed to the concept of hysteresis: the question of why a fruitful cross-fertilization did not occur between Keynes's ideas on involuntary unemployment equilibria and hysteretic models is one worthy of investigation. The interpretation of Keynes's ideas in terms of hysteretic equilibria certainly helps resolve a few difficulties:

> . . . one of Keynes' distinctive contributions to the study of economic fluctuations was his stress on the possibility that they were caused by 'animal spirits' – fluctuations in the expectations of businessmen and financiers about future prosperity which are unrelated to real events . . . his suggestion was that exogenous conditions determine the level of output with a degree of arbitrariness . . . the relevance of animal spirits and of purely nominal changes for the determination of output is difficult to understand in an environment where exogenous conditions sharply determine equilibria . . . were multiple equilibria to be possible, so making the level of output in some sense arbitrary, it would be much easier to understand how extrinsic variables like the money stock or animal spirits could affect the level of output . . . models of multiple equilibria and hysteresis can [help] resolve the problem . . . (Summers, 1988, p. 19)

2 HYSTERESIS AND UNEMPLOYMENT

Edmund Phelps was, as far as I know, the first to apply the term 'hysteresis' to the determination of equilibrium unemployment: '. . . the transition from one equilibrium to the other tends to have long-lingering effects on the labour force, and these effects may be discernible in the equilibrium rate of unemployment for a long time . . . the natural rate of unemployment at any future date will depend upon the course of history in the interim . . . such a property is sometimes called hysteresis . . .' (Phelps, 1972, p. xxiii).

Several economists had previously referred to the effect higher unemployment has on the rate of unemployment consistent with stable prices or inflation, though without using the term 'hysteresis'. Keynes's January 1937 *Times* articles, at a time when unemployment stood at 12 per cent, could be placed in this category (see Peden, 1980, for discussion). Such effects were a major theme in the works of the late Nicholas Kaldor, who knew '. . . nothing about "hysteresis effects" . . . I don't even know what the word means . . . which only goes to show how much new economics there is, the knowledge of which I've never acquired . . . I feel it is too late for me to sit down and learn new theories or concepts' (letter to the author, 24 May 1986). The reaction of James Tobin, whose writings (Tobin, 1965, 1972) are replete with hysteresis effects, is also of interest: '. . . I once again observe the importance of catchy and preferably somewhat mysterious labels in attracting attention in our profession . . . for many years I and others have argued that prolonged actual unemployment will become "natural" . . . but no one paid heed until the label "hysteresis-effect" came into vogue . . .' (letter to the author, 8 April 1986).

Studies of the experience of those suffering long spells of unemployment also pointed to the presence of hysteresis effects without using the terminology:

> . . . unemployed men are not simply units of employability who can be put into cold storage and taken out again immediately they are needed . . . [they experience] a subtle undermining of the constitution through lack of physical exertion and the absence of physical stimuli . . . and the emergence of abnormal psychological conditions characterised by disabling fears, anxiety and sympathetic physical conditions, functional disorders and the like . . .' (Pilgrim Trust, 1938, pp. 67, 137)

Hysteresis effects have been applied in economics to explain the evolution of preferences, the time-inconsistency of optimal plans and international trade adjustment problems as well as unemployment (see Cross and Allan, 1988, for references). The analysis of full economic systems in which equilibria are haunted by hysteresis is still in a state of infancy, hysteresis having only come into vogue in economics during the 1980s. Two examples of the way hysteresis equilibria can arise in general systems analysis will suffice. In the context of search equilibrium models, with correctly perceived, flexible wages and prices, allowing the number of advantageous trades exploited to depend on the levels of stocks held by traders, or a stochastic matching process, generates '. . . multiple steady-state rational expectations equilibria . . . an economy with this type of trade friction does not have a unique natural rate of unemployment' (Diamond, 1982, p. 881; see also Diamond, 1984). In the case of rational expectations equilibria, the history of beliefs about the world can generate many equilibria for any given actual history:

> . . . if you start at a concrete time, with concrete beliefs and information . . . and let agents at each date do the best for themselves . . . and then recalculate what new information this generates and so what new decisions, then you may hope to follow a particular path and if you are lucky it will lead you to one of a multitude of equilibria . . . the explanation of the equilibrium of an economy or of a game is to be sought in the process which got it there . . . the most obvious explanation of the present is to be found in the past . . . the state of the economy which we single out as an equilibrium depends on our theory of the behaviour of agents out of that equilibrium . . . such a theory must turn on the information available to agents and on the manner in which they learn from such information . . . [the implication is] that equilibrium will not be independent of the history of the economy . . . (Hahn, 1987, pp. 321, 324, 325)

There are many channels whereby the equilibrium rate of unemployment can be haunted by hysteresis. During the equilibrium unemployment debate of the 1980s attention has focused on two specific channels: the way the history of an economy changes the balance of *insiders* and *outsiders* in the labour force; and the way actual history shapes *long-term unemployment*. In both cases the history of actual shocks to the economy helps determine the actual unemployment experienced; the latter helps shape the insider–outsider or short- versus long-term unemployed characteristics of the labour force; and changes in such characteristics transform the supply or demand conditions for labour, yielding a change in equilibrium unemployment in sympathy with the initial change in actual unemployment. For detailed accounts of such hysteresis effects see the contributions in Cross (1988).

3 THE MEDIUM-RUN NAIRU

Tracking the evolution of amendments to econometric estimates is not an easy task: new explanatory variables are introduced and existing ones dropped; existing variables are measured in new ways; new time lag structures are introduced; non-linear are substituted for linear specifications; relationships are estimated over different time periods; annual estimates are replaced by quarterly estimates; different restrictions are imposed; test statistics cited in one study are not cited in another; and so on. Apart from creating a headache, these problems suggest that it would be useful to have a common framework inside which to evaluate econometric estimates. NAIRU (non-accelerating inflation rate of unemployment) estimates for the UK are virtually synonymous with the yellow discussion papers of the Centre for Labour Economics at the London School of Economics (LSE). In what follows we will focus on the following sources: Layard and Nickell (1986a) and Nickell (1987); Layard (1986) and Layard and Nickell (1986b) provide summaries of this work. The work cited deals with male unemployment in the UK.

Layard and Nickell (1986a) – LN from now on – present annual estimates of labour demand, prices and wages 1954–83, and quarterly estimates for the same variables 1957(I)–1983(IV). Three models are presented: in the first the unemployment rate for all durations is included in the wage equation; in the second job vacancies is substituted; and, in the third, the short-term unemployment rate, defined as the proportion of the labour force unemployed for less than 26 weeks, is used. The following annual estimates are for the first version of the model, were generated by three-stage least squares, a + indicates variables treated as endogenous, *t*-statistics are in brackets, lower-case letters represent logarithms (we add the log adjective to unemployment to avoid confusion) and Δ indicates a differencing operation. The price and wage equations are as follows (LN, 1986a, Tables 5 and 6):

$$\begin{aligned} p - w = & \underset{(4.2)}{-4.18} + \underset{(5.0)}{0.544}\,(p-w)_{-1} - \underset{(4.2)}{0.336}\,\Delta^2 w^+ \\ & - \underset{(3.8)}{0.242}\,\Delta^2 w_{-1} + \underset{(2.1)}{0.038}\Sigma^+ - 0.486(k-l) \end{aligned} \tag{9.5}$$

S.E. = 0.015; D.W. = 2.27; LM Autocorrelation $\text{Chi}^2(2)$ = 5.37; Parameter Stability, $\text{Chi}^2(5)$, Split 1968 = 1.18.

$$\begin{aligned} w - p = & \underset{(9.0)}{8.41} - \underset{(4.4)}{0.062}\log u + \underset{(3.3)}{0.039}\,MM + \underset{(1.5)}{0.182}\,RR \\ & + \underset{(2.5)}{0.499}v(p_m - \bar{p})^+ + \underset{(2.0)}{0.419}v\Delta(p_m - p)^+ + \underset{(4.1)}{0.085}\,UP^+ \\ & + \underset{(0.9)}{0.179}T_1{}^+ - \underset{(1.7)}{0.021}\,IPD + 1.07\,(k-l) \end{aligned} \tag{9.6}$$

S.E. = 0.015; D.W. = 1.66; LM Autocorrelation $\text{Chi}^2(2)$ = 3.73; Parameter Stability, $\text{Chi}^2(7)$, Split 1968 = 0.92.

The variables are defined as follows: price of value added (p); nominal hourly earnings with employers' labour taxes added (w); capital stock (k); labour force – employees in employment plus unemployment (l); male unemployment rate (u); mismatch – the absolute change in the proportion of these employed in production industries to total employment (MM); replacement ratio – weighted average of unemployment benefits to wages using the proportions 0.35 single person, 0.12 married no children, 0.11 married with one child, two children 0.16 and three 0.12 (RR); import price index (p_m); output price index – where $p = (1 + V)\bar{p} - vp_m$, v being the share of imports in value added – at factor cost (p); union power – measured as the log of the union/non-union wage mark-up estimated by cross-section regression (UP); employers' labour taxes (T_1); incomes policy dummy-value unity in 1976 and 1977, zero elsewhere (IPD); the aggregate demand index (Σ) was estimated as $\Sigma = (p^* - \bar{p}) + 10.76\,AD + 1.028\text{WT}$, where AD is the cyclically adjusted public sector deficit as a percentage of potential GDP, and WT is the deviation of world trade from a quintic time trend.

To identify the natural rate from equations (9.5) and (9.6) it is necessary to eliminate the aggregate demand index (Σ) from (9.5), and open economy influences on UK unemployment are dealt with by conditioning the natural rate on some level of import prices (p_m) in (9.6), or by imposing a zero trade balance condition. This is done by way of the following labour demand and trade balance equations:

$$\begin{aligned} n = {} & \underset{(4.9)}{2.57} + \underset{(8.2)}{1.057}n_{-1} - \underset{(2.6)}{0.361}n_{-2} + 0.304\text{K} \\ & - \underset{(4.9)}{0.285}(w - p)_{-1} + \underset{(3.2)}{0.067}(p^* - \bar{p})^+ + \underset{(3.6)}{0.718}AD^+ + \underset{(1.9)}{0.069}\,WT \qquad (9.7) \end{aligned}$$

S.E. = 0.008; D.W. = 2.23; LM Autocorrelation $\text{Chi}^2(2)$ = 2.20, Parameter Stability, $\text{Chi}^2(7)$, Sample Split 1968 = 5.12.

$$\begin{aligned} B/Y_p = {} & \underset{(2.6)}{41.68} + \underset{(2.7)}{361.03}v\,(p^* - \bar{p})_{-1} + \underset{(1.4)}{135.84}v\,(p_m - p^*)_{-1} - \underset{(2.3)}{39.82}\Sigma_{-1} + \\ & \underset{(1.4)}{24.67}OIL_{-1} \qquad (9.8) \end{aligned}$$

S.E. = 10.46; D.W. = 1.56; LM Autocorrelation ($\text{Chi}^2(2)$ = 4.12; Parameter Stability, $\text{Chi}^2(4)$, Sample Split 1968 = 4.41.

Here B is the nominal value of exports minus imports, Yp is nominal potential GDP and OIL is the real value of North Sea oil production in terms of output prices.

A first problem with using the above estimates to identify a NAIRU is that it was not found possible to pick up a significant effect for unexpected inflation in the wage equation (9.6). This means that the only term capturing unexpected inflation in the system is $\Delta^2 w$ in equation (9.5), this standing as a proxy for $(w - w^e)$. The natural rate equilibrium is identified by setting this term equal to zero.

A second problem in identifying the NAIRU is that of the influence of aggregate demand in equations (9.5) and (9.7). An aggregate demand index is defined as $\Sigma = (p^* - p_m) + 10.76\, AD + 1.028\, WT$, and this relationship is used to 'eliminate' the effect of aggregate demand from equations (9.5) and (9.7).

A third problem is how to deal with open economy influences on the NAIRU. This was achieved – the other method conditions on real import prices – by setting $B = 0$ in equation (9.8), thus identifying the NAIRU as being characterized by a zero trade balance.

Using the above three conditions, equations (9.5)–(9.8) yield a NAIRU:

$$\begin{aligned} 0.44U^* + 0.058 \log U^* = {} & K + 0.029MM + 0.17RR \\ & + 0.08UP + 0.17T_1 \\ & - 0.196IPD + 0.29v(p_m - p^*) \\ & + 0.24\, \Delta v(p_m - p^*) - 0.032OIL \\ & - 0.027OIL \end{aligned} \qquad (9.9)$$

Equation (9.9) is not, as might have been expected, used to derive a time-series for the U^* NAIRU over the 1954–83 period. Instead NAIRUs are estimated for the periods 1967–74 (4.19), 1975–9 (7.63) and 1980–3 (9.07) periods, it being assumed that the actual male unemployment was at the NAIRU value during 1956–66 (1.96). The reason for this procedure relates to the role of aggregate demand:

> . . . in order to see the full contributions to the natural rate increase of the push [structural] factors . . . we must remember that their impact is larger than [the contribution to the change in actual unemployment would suggest] . . . this follows from the fact that when a push factor, such as the benefit replacement ratio, moves adversely, it not only has a direct impact on unemployment, but also serves to reduce the level of demand (Σ) consistent with unchanging inflation . . . (LN, 1986a, p. S159)

Once these effects are taken into account, the influence of the structural or wage pressure variables on the NAIRU appears as shown in Table 9.1 (LN, 1986a, Table 11).

Thus, comparing 1975–9 with 1980–3, for example, structural factors served to raise the NAIRU by 1.44 percentage points to 9.07 per cent,

Table 9.1 Source of changes in the NAIRU and U

NAIRU and its sources	*1956–66 to 1967–74*	*1967–74 to 1975–79*	*1975–79 to 1980–83*
Δ NAIRU	2.23	3.44	1.44
Δ T_1	0.29	0.51	0.69
Δ RR	0.64	−0.12	−0.15
Δ UP	1.40	1.58	1.25
Δ OIL	—	−0.32	−1.73
Δ $(p_m - p^*)$	−0.29	2.02	−0.17
Δ MM	0.19	0.27	0.77
Δ IPD	—	−0.50	0.78
Actual U and demand			
Δ U	1.82	3.01	7.00
Δ Σ	0.12	0.54	6.56

whereas the actual unemployment rate rose by 7 percentage points to 13.79 per cent, 6.56 percentage points of this being attributed to the aggregate demand index (Σ). It is useful to see if the NAIRU estimates over these periods conform to the natural rate predictions that $U > U^* \rightarrow \ddot{P} < 0$, and $U < U^* \rightarrow \ddot{P} > 0$. Over 1956–66, $U = U^* = 1.96$ by assumption, and $\ddot{P} = 0$; from 1967–74, $U = 3.78 < U^* = 4.19$ and $\ddot{P} > 0$; over 1975–9, $U = 6.79 < U^* = 7.63$ though $P < 0$; and over 1979–83, $U = 13.79 > U^* = 9.07$ and $\ddot{P} < 0$. Thus over the three 'free' periods, the natural rate predictions 'work' in two but not in the other. In the problem 1975–9 period, '. . . it is worth noting that, if we exclude 1976 and 1977, when the incomes policy dummy was dramatically successful, then wage inflation rose somewhat over the remainder of the period . . .' (LN, 1986a, p. S159).

The dramatic problem with these NAIRU estimates, however, arises if we ask the model to predict what happened over the period 1983–7. During this period the rate of inflation was steady in the 4–6 per cent range, so $\ddot{P} = 0$. For this to conform to the natural rate predictions we would require $U = U^*$ during this period. The actual rate of unemployment, however, continued to rise during this period, while at the same time virtually all the determinants of the NAIRU indicated in Table 9.1 suggested that U^* was, if anything, falling during this period. Hence the NAIRU estimates for 1983–7 imply that $U > U^*$ by an increasing margin implying $\ddot{P} < 0$, yet the actual course of inflation was characterized by $\ddot{P} = 0$. Thus the original NAIRU estimates of the natural rate imply a quite dramatic conflict between the natural rate hypothesis and actual experience. Hence the natural rate hypothesis would have to be amended substantially in order to avoid the charge of refutation.

Hints as to the way Layard and Nickell were to amend the NAIRU specification were present in the 1986a paper:

> . . . one obvious fact is that since 1981 the whole increase in unemployment has been of people unemployed for over six months . . . there is evidence . . . that long-term unemployed people spend less time and money searching for work than the short-term unemployed . . . they also make fewer job applications . . . it therefore seems quite likely that they exert less downward pressure on wages than the short-term unemployed . . .' (p. S154)

Using S as the proportion of the unemployed who have been so for less than six months, and R for the proportion unemployed for longer than six months, LN estimate (p. S155):

$$\begin{aligned} R = 0.159 + &\underset{(2.5)}{0.466R_{-1}} - \underset{(1.0)}{0.689U} + \underset{(3.9)}{3.89U_{-1}} \\ &- \underset{(2.1)}{2.15U_{-2}} \qquad \qquad OLS\ 1955\text{–}83 \end{aligned} \tag{9.10}$$

which, using $S \equiv 1 - R$ and setting $R = R_{-1}$ and $U = U_{-1} = U_{-2}$, yields

$$S = 0.702U - 1.968U^2. \tag{9.11}$$

In a third specification of the wage equation, (9.6) above, LN substitute S for log U. This version of the model is not used, the results being '. . . very similar, although the general fit is less good . . .' (p. S160). The further argument is that the duration composition effects are captured by the non-linear effect arising from the presence of log U rather than U in the preferred wage equation: '. . . [equation 37] has the concave structure picked up by the log transformation of U . . .' (p. S155). The conclusion on this matter is that '. . . we have some evidence that past unemployment tends to raise unemployment today, but only in our quarterly model . . .' (LN, 1986a, p. S165).

The problem of explaining the fact that UK inflation did not decelerate in the 1983–7 period is addressed in Nickell (1987). The key amendment is to distinguish between a medium- and long-run NAIRU: in the medium run the duration composition of unemployment, itself a function of actual unemployment, helps determine the NAIRU along with the z wage pressure variables; in the long run the duration composition effect washes out, the NAIRU being determined purely by the z variables.

The medium-run NAIRU can be written:

$$U^* = \frac{\alpha_0 + \beta_0 + \beta_4 R + z}{\alpha_2 + \beta_2} \quad (9.12)$$

The corresponding long-run NAIRU is:

$$U^* = \frac{\alpha_0 + \beta_0 + z}{\alpha_2 + \beta_2} \quad (9.13)$$

This long-run NAIRU will be attained only if the proportion of the long-term unemployed in total employment (R) tends to return to a long-run equilibrium value which is independent of the actual rate of unemployment.

Nickell initially simplifies the problem by including unemployment instead of demand in the price equation, hence eliminating the need for a labour demand equation to identify the NAIRU, and by abstracting from open economy considerations. The point of the exercise is to see how the duration composition of unemployment affects the wage equation. This leaves price and wage equations of the form:

$$p - w = \alpha_0 - \alpha_1 (p - p^e) - \alpha_2 U - \alpha_3 x \quad (9.14)$$

and

$$w - p = \beta_0 - \beta_1 (p - p^e) - f(U, U_{-1} \ldots) + \beta_3 x + z \quad (9.15)$$

where x is the trend of productivity. Imposing the $\alpha_3 = -\beta_3$ restriction, and substituting $\Delta^2 p = (p - p^e)$ yields:

$$\alpha^2 U + f(U, U_{-1} \ldots) = (\alpha_0 + \beta_0) - (\alpha_1 + \beta_1)\, \Delta^2 p + z \quad (9.16)$$

The type of NAIRU equilibrium thus depends on the functional form of $f(U, U_{-1} \ldots)$: $f(U, U_{-1} \ldots) = \beta_2 U$ will yield the simple case

$$U^* = \frac{\alpha_0 + \beta_0 + z}{\alpha_2 + \beta_2};$$

$f(U, U_{-1} \ldots) = g\ (log\ U)$ will yield

$$U^* + g\,(log\ U^*) = \frac{\alpha_0 + \beta_0 + z}{\alpha_2 + \beta_2}$$

with $g' > 0$ and $g'' < 0$, so that '. . . as the natural rate gets higher and higher, excess unemployment becomes less and less effective at reducing inflation . . .' (p. 261); and $f\,(U, U_{-1}...) = \beta_4\,\Delta U$ implies

$$U^* = \frac{\alpha_0 + \beta_0 + \beta_4 U_{-1}}{\alpha_2 + \beta_4} + z$$

and so the NAIRU depends also on actual unemployment, and hence on anything that determines actual unemployment, including aggregate demand.

The preferred wage equation, estimated on annual data 1956–83, is (see pp. 268–72 for details of the estimates):

$$w - p = \beta_0 - \beta_1\,(p - p^e) - 0.104\,log\ U + 0.212R + 1.07\,x + z \quad (9.17)$$

The relationship between R and U is given by:

$$\underset{(2.1)}{R = 0.054} + \underset{(3.7)}{0.61R_{-1}} - \underset{(5.6)}{2.41U} + \underset{(6.5)}{5.58U_{-1}} - \underset{(2.4)}{2.18U_{-2}} \quad (9.18)$$

OLS, S.E. = 0.023, $\bar{R}^2 = 0.84$.

Removing the lagged dependent variable from (9.18) and substituting into (9.17) yields:

$$w - p = \beta_0 - \beta_1\,(p - p^e) - 0.104\,log\ U + 0.532U - 1.174\Delta U$$
$$- 0.356\Delta^2 U + 1.07x + z + \text{terms in } \Delta^3 U \quad (9.19)$$

Estimating labour demand and price equations over the same period, and eliminating the aggregate demand variable, yields:

$$p - w = \alpha_0 - \alpha_1\,(p - p^e) - 0.253U + 0.075\Delta U - 0.388\Delta^2 U$$
$$- 1.07x + \text{terms in } \Delta^3 U,\ \Delta i \text{ and } \Delta x \quad (9.20)$$

where i is the inflow rate into unemployment. Adding equations (9.19) and (9.20), and setting $(p - p^e) = 0$, again no satisfactory empirical estimates were found for unanticipated inflation, so it was simply assumed that $(p - p^e) = \Delta^2 P$ – and setting $\Delta^2 P = 0$ yields:

$$0.014 \log U^* - 0.279U^* + 1.10\,\Delta U + 0.693\Delta^2 U = (\alpha + \beta_0) + z + \text{terms in } \Delta^3 U \text{ and } \Delta i \qquad (9.21)$$

This is a NAIRU in that $\Delta^2 P = 0$, but one which does not have NRH properties: U^* depends on the past history of unemployment, this being introduced by way of the influence of the latter on the long-term unemployment proportion R.

The NAIRU expressed in (9.21) occupies a medium-run domain in which $\Delta^3 u$, $\Delta^2 u$, Δu and Δi are non-zero. Setting these expressions equal to zero fields the long-run, or natural rate, NAIRU solution:

$$0.104 \log u^* - 0.279u^* = (\alpha_0 + \beta_0) + z \qquad (9.22)$$

4 HYSTERESIS VERSUS THE NATURAL RATE

A question of fundamental importance is whether the dynamics of the medium-run NAIRU are consistent with convergence to a long-run natural rate equilibrium. Nickell's answer to this question is a guarded yes – 'this work is, of necessity, both tentative and preliminary . . .' (p. 280); '. . . even though increased unemployment is higher than 19.45 per cent, there is no problem about the existence of the natural rate until wage pressure rises to the point where the natural rate reaches 37.1 per cent – any further increase in wage pressure will then generate inflationary pressure which cannot be contained by more deflation . . .' (Nickell, 1987, p. 277).

Given that this view is heavily contingent on a set of tentative empirical estimates, it is interesting to address the question of whether hysteresis effects on the medium-run NAIRU are consistent with convergence to a natural rate equilibrium in a more general context. This is done in Cross (1987), who uses a five-equation model of interaction between prices, expected prices, unemployment and output in which the medium-run natural rate is specified as:

$$U^* = NR + \Pi_1 \dot{U} + \Pi_2 \int^T (U - NR)dt \qquad \Pi_1,\ \Pi_2 > 0 \quad (9.23)$$

where NR is the long-run natural rate.

Solving for P yields:

$$(1 - \alpha\gamma\varepsilon\Pi_1)\dddot{P} + \alpha\gamma\varepsilon(1 - \delta\Pi_1)\ddot{P} + \alpha\gamma\varepsilon(\delta - \Pi_2)\dot{P} - \alpha\gamma\delta\varepsilon\Pi_2 P = -\alpha\gamma\varepsilon_1\dddot{M} + \alpha\gamma\varepsilon(1 - \delta\Pi_1)\ddot{M} + \alpha\gamma\varepsilon(\delta - \Pi_2)\dot{M} - \alpha\gamma\delta\varepsilon\Pi_2 M + \alpha\delta\Pi_2(\bar{U} - NR) \tag{9.24}$$

The Routh-Hurwitz conditions for stability in an equation having a homogeneous form $A\dddot{P} + B\ddot{P} + C\dot{P} + DP = 0$ are $B > 0$, $C > 0$, $D > 0$ and $BC - AD = 0$. In equation (9.24) $D = \alpha\gamma\delta\varepsilon\Pi_2 < 0$, so the system is unstable. Setting $\Pi_1 = \Pi_2 = 0$ yields a stable solution, so the source of instability is clearly the presence of the hysteresis effects on equilibrium unemployment arising from $\dot{U}$ and $\int (U - NR)$. So in this model the introduction of hysteresis effects is inconsistent with the NRH of convergence to a natural rate equilibrium. It is of great interest to know if the amendments to the NAIRU described earlier in this section share this property of ruling out an equilibrium of the form postulated in the natural rate hypothesis.

The Layard and Nickell (LN) models do not test for the existence of a NAIRU equilibrium by checking to see whether a co-integration vector exists between unemployment and the z 'structural variables' which are postulated to pin down this equilibrium: see Granger (1983, 1986), Hendry (1986) and Engle and Granger (1987) for discussion of the co-integration approach to testing for the existence of equilibrium relationships. Nor do their NAIRU estimates include variables which would represent error-correction mechanisms at work in relation to the employment, prices, wages and balance of trade equations used to identify the NAIRU. Using the co-integration framework for econometric appraisal we would expect a satisfactory account of equilibrium unemployment to be able to demonstrate that a co-integration vector exists; describe the disequilibrium processes involved in terms of error correction; and to encompass rival accounts of equilibrium unemployment such as that provided by the hysteresis hypothesis. We will consider two assessments of the co-integration properties of the LN NAIRU models. The first (Jenkinson, 1988) is directed at the original LN model which yields just one NAIRU solution (1986a). The second (Cross, Hutchinson and Yeoward, 1989a and 1989b) is directed at the amended LN model (Nickell, 1987) in which a medium-run NAIRU is distinguished from a long-run NAIRU or natural rate.

Jenkinson tests for co-integration between unemployment and the z 'structural' or wage pressure variables which determine the NAIRU in the original LN model. Table 9.2 reports the results of Jenkinson's tests (pp. 372–3) for the necessary, order of integration, conditions for co-integration.

Table 9.2 Order of integration of NAIRU variables

Variable	*Order of integration I(0)* *DW*	*ADF*	*Order of integration I(1)* *DW*	*ADF*
Unemployment U	0.016	0.37	1.18	−3.26
Mismatch MM	0.463	−2.26	1.97	−6.18
Replacement ratio RR	0.051	1.06	1.52	−4.41
Import prices p_m	0.123	−0.91	2.07	−5.18
Union power UP	0.038	−1.60	1.21	−5.17
Employers' taxes T_1	0.028	2.51	2.65	−4.44

With the possible exception of mismatch, it is not possible to reject the null hypothesis that the levels of the variables have a unit root, but it is possible to reject the null hypothesis that the first differences of the variables have a unit root. These tests are at the 5 per cent level, using the critical values DW* = 0.259 and ADF* = −2.89 (see Sargan and Bhargava, 1983 and Fuller, 1976). Thus the necessary conditions for the existence of a NAIRU equilibrium are satisfied.

The second sufficient condition involves testing for the existence of a co-integration vector (Jenkinson, p. 373):

$$U = -\ 1.452 - 0.420MM + 0.001RR - 0.014p_m + 0.038UP + 0.343T_1 + \varepsilon \qquad (9.25)$$

D.W. = 0.091, A.D.F. = −0.07 (−1.87).

For a co-integration equilibrium to exist it would have to be demonstrated that $\varepsilon \sim I(0)$. The null hypothesis that ε has a unit root, however, cannot be rejected by the D.W. and A.D.F., implying lack of co-integration and non-existence of the NAIRU equilibrium postulated. Mismatch and import prices also have the wrong sign.

Jenkinson proceeds to examine the role played by LN's aggregate demand variable Σ. This is re-defined as $\Sigma \equiv AD + COMP$, where AD is the cyclically adjusted deficit as a proportion of potential GDP and $COMP$ is import prices relative to output prices. After checking that AD and $COMP$ are $I(1)$, the co-integration regression is run excluding the mismatch and employers' labour tax variables:

$$U = -0.270 + 0.003RR + 0.043p_m + 0.043UP - 1.037\ AD$$
$$- 0.235\ COMP + \varepsilon \qquad (9.26)$$

D.W. = 0.334, A.D.F. = −0.26 (−3.53).

In (9.26) the null hypothesis that $\varepsilon \sim I(1)$ can be rejected, suggesting the existence of co-integration. The conclusion is that '. . . the level of demand has an important impact on the equilibrium the economy attains . . . there may exist a number of equilibria which the economy could arrive at . . . government fiscal and monetary policy can influence which equilibrium is actually attained' (Jenkinson, 1988, pp. 374–5).

The response to this criticism turns on the issue of the appropriate functional form for unemployment in LN's wage and price equations. Stephen Nickell (1988) argues that, because of the non-linear, logarithmic relationship between wages and prices and unemployment, the appropriate co-integration regression should contain *log U* rather than *U*. The regression then becomes (Nickell, 1988, p. 383):

$$log\ U = -29.06 + 0.335MM + 0.027RR + 2.32p_m + 0.420UP +$$
$$6.460T_1 \qquad (9.27)$$

D.W. = 1.03.

This can be read as implying that the NAIRU should be renamed LOGNAIRU. The Duhem–Quine problem that hypotheses can usually or always be rescued from refutation by suitable amendments of auxiliary hypothesis arises here. Whether or not it is the critic or proponent of the NAIRU who is responsible for this amendment to the auxiliary background is a matter of frame of reference. In LN's defence it is certainly true that in their original model it is *log U* rather than *U* which affects wages.

The second study, by Cross, Hutchinson and Yeoward (CHY, 1989a) is directed at the amended version of the LN model in which a medium-run NAIRU is distinguished from a long-run NAIRU or natural rate equilibrium. The most succinct summary of this distinction is, see equations (9.12) and (9.13) above, that the long-run NAIRU or natural rate is:

$$U^* = \frac{\alpha_0 + \beta_0 + z}{\alpha_2 + \beta_2} \qquad (9.28)$$

And the medium-run NAIRU is:

$$U^* = \frac{\alpha_0 + \beta_0 + \beta_4 R + z}{\alpha_2 + \beta_2} \qquad (9.29)$$

where z is the vector of 'structural' or wage pressure variables and R is proportion of the unemployed who have been out of work for longer than a year, which is a function of actual unemployment, $R = R(U_t, U_{t-1}, U_{t-2} \ldots)$ For the medium-run NAIRU (9.29) to be consistent with convergence onto a long-run natural rate (9.28) it would have to be demonstrated that R tends to converge onto a long-run equilibrium value R^* corresponding to the long-run natural rate solution U^*. The proportion $R \equiv UL/UT$ where UL is the number of long-term unemployed and UT is total unemployment. Thus for convergence on to R^*, UL would have to be co-integrated with UT.

CHY (1989b) test for co-integration of UL and UT on quarterly UK data, 1948(III)–1987(II). The results of the order of integration tests are reported in Table 9.3, where UL is defined as the number unemployed for longer than a year.

Table 9.3 Order of integration of UL and UT in the UK

	Order of integration I(0)		*Order of integration I(1)*	
Variable	*DW*	*ADF*	*DW*	*ADF*
UL	0.004	−0.004 (−0.886)	0.698	−0.230 (−3.047)
UT	0.008	−0.008 (−1.179)	1.729	−0.432 (−3.604)

The results indicate that the null hypothesis that the levels of the variables have unit roots cannot be rejected, but that the null hypothesis that the first differences have unit roots can be rejected. Thus both UL and UT appear to be $I(1)$.

The co-integration regression estimated (CHY, 1989b, p. 18) is:

$$UL = -115.718 + 0.386\ UT + \varepsilon \qquad (9.30)$$

D.W. = 0.109, D.F. = −0.041 (−1.547).

The null hypothesis that the residual in (9.30) has a unit root cannot be rejected, implying that long-term unemployment is not co-integrated with total unemployment. The implication is that there is no tendency to return to an equilibrium relationship between *UL* and *UT*, or an equilibrium value R^*.

Similar results were obtained by Cross, Hutchinson and Yeoward for the United States (CHY, 1989a). The results shown in Table 9.4 relate to 1959(II)–1987(II).

Table 9.4 Order of integration of UL and UT in the US

	Order of integration I(0)		*Order of integration I(1)*	
Variable	*DW*	*ADF*	*DW*	*ADF*
UL	0.044	−0.032 (−1.683)	0.818	−0.552 (−3.496)
UT	0.071	−0.021 (−1.310)	2.347	−0.586 (−5.311)

The implication again is that *UL* and *UT* are $I(1)$, so the necessary condition for co-integration is satisfied. The co-integration equation is (CHY, 1989a, p. 24):

$$UL = -282.262 + 0.118UT + \varepsilon \qquad (9.31)$$

D.W. = 0.216, A.D.F. = 0.115 (−2.710).

The null hypothesis of a unit root in ε cannot be rejected, so again there is no evidence of a tendency to return to an equilibrium relationship between long-term and total unemployment.

The implication of these results is that the presence of an effect on equilibrium unemployment arising from endogenous (with respect to actual unemployment) changes in the duration composition of unemployment is inconsistent with convergence onto a natural rate equilibrium. The response from proponents of the natural rate hypothesis has been to suggest that *R* might be co-integrated with the *z* variables (Stephen Nickell, private communication). This is an issue which is under investigation: the experience of the period 1981–7 makes co-integration between *R* and *z* appear unlikely, for they have been moving in the opposite directions.

The presence of a unit root in *R* is consistent with the hysteresis hypothesis, and would have the effect of imparting a unit root process to equilibrium unemployment. The Blanchard and Summers model

(1988) provides an example of an hysteresis account of equilibrium unemployment which implies a unit root for unemployment, in the specific form of a random walk. In this case unemployment has the representation:

$$U_t = bU_{t-1} + \varepsilon_t \quad (9.32)$$

If $b = 1$, (9.32) can be re-written:

$$U_t = \sum_{i=1}^{i=n-1} \varepsilon_{t-i} + U_{t-n} \quad (9.33)$$

which implies that the current rate of unemployment depends on all the past shocks to unemployment, and shows no tendency to return to a fixed equilibrium value. Evidence that it is difficult to reject the $b = 1$ null hypothesis for the UK post-1945 has been cited earlier in this section. This is also the case over longer runs of UK data. Cross, Hutchinson and Yeoward (CHY, 1989c) test for a unit root on annual data for UK unemployment over the century 1886–1986: the D.W. and A.D.F. test values are 0.192 and −0.098 (−1.859) respectively, indicating that it is not possible to reject the null hypothesis that U is $I(1)$ (CHY, 1989c, p. 16). Over the same period it is also not possible to reject the existence of a co-integration relationship between $\Delta^2 P$ and ΔU, as implied by hysteresis (CHY, 1989c, p. 21).

$$\Delta^2 P = 0.002 - 0.015\ U + \varepsilon \quad (9.34)$$

D.W. = 2.256, A.D.F. = −1.778 (−5.406).

It is possible to reject the null hypothesis that ε in (9.34) has a unit root, suggesting that $\Delta^2 P$ and ΔU are co-integrated. The implication is that the equilibrium unemployment rate corresponding to $\Delta^2 P = 0$ is characterized simply by $\Delta U = 0$. Given that U has a unit root, the implication is that equilibrium unemployment follows a random walk of the type described in (9.32) and (9.33).

This evidence suggests that there will be a continuum of different possible realizations for unemployment corresponding to different possible histories of an economy: history and 'structural' variables will both determine equilibrium unemployment rather than the 'structural' variables alone specified in the natural rate hypothesis.

Given that unemployment as a percentage is bounded between 0 and 100 per cent, however, it is clear that a pure unit root process, in which unemployment could take any value with non-zero probability, could not be followed by unemployment. The issue here is one of whether the time-series variables can follow pure unit processes. What seems to be required to attempt to resolve these issues is an account of bounded unit root processes.

Subject to these qualifications the evidence of, presumably impure, unit root processes in unemployment certainly creates a problem for the natural rate hypothesis to explain, yet is consistent with the hysteresis account of equilibrium. A way forward in this debate is suggested by the criterion of encompassing. The hysteresis hypothesis (HH) does not deny that the 'structural' variables invoked in the natural rate hypothesis (NRH) affect equilibrium unemployment. The difference is that the HH proposes that the time path taken by an economy also helps determine equilibrium unemployment: the NRH denies this. Seen in this light, an *F* test of the type suggested by Mizon and Richard (1986), in which a regression including the HH and NRH variables is compared with a regression involving the NRH variables alone, would be of great interest. The outcome would, no doubt, not be black or white but some shade of grey, as suggested by the existence of the Duhem–Quine problem. An example of such an encompassing framework is provided in Gordon (1989), which can be re-written:

$$\ddot{P}_t = \alpha(U_t - U^*_t) \tag{9.35}$$

$$U^*_t = NR_t + \beta U_{t-1} \tag{9.36}$$

Equations (9.35) and (9.36) yield:

$$\ddot{P}_t = \alpha(1 - \beta)U_t + \alpha\beta\Delta U_t - \alpha NR_t \tag{9.37}$$

Under the NRH, $\beta = 0$, implying

$$\ddot{P}_t = \alpha(U_t - NR_t) \tag{9.38}$$

whereas under the HH equation (9.37) holds.

5 A METHODOLOGICAL PERSPECTIVE

The approach so far in this chapter has been to look at the 1980s controversy regarding equilibrium unemployment without methodological spectacles. The question then arises as to how the controversies would be perceived from an explicit methodological perspective, such as that offered by the Lakatos theory of the methodology of scientific research programmes (MSRP; Lakatos, 1978, I).

In earlier papers, which assessed the stability of the demand for money controversy (Cross, 1982) and the monetarist research program (Cross, 1984), I argued that the Lakatosian distinction between hard core and protective belt propositions in research programs raised problems of classification and demarcation which could be avoided by identifying research programs by their positive heuristics alone. Seen in this light the natural rate hypothesis (NRH) would be identified by a heuristic of the form: 'explain the equilibrium rate of unemployment consistent with steady inflation by reference to state variables alone, aggregate demand and the actual time path followed by the economy having no effect'. In contrast the hysteresis hypothesis (HH) would be motivated by a heuristic along the lines: 'explain the equilibrium unemployment as being determined by the time path taken by the economy, with both state and aggregate demand variables leaving their marks'. Thus the NRH applies the classical property of monetary neutrality to equilibrium unemployment, whereas the HH denies that this property holds.

As outlined in sections 1 and 2, the notion of hysteresis has been around for a long time, the term having been coined for application to electromagnetic fields over a century ago, and having been argued to be relevant to economic phenomena for half a century or so. The puzzle is why it was only in the 1980s that mainstream research programs in economics came to incorporate hysteresis effects explicitly.

In relation to the NAIRU version of the NRH in Section 3 above, it is reasonably clear that it was the empirical difficulties encountered by the NRH in explaining the sustained rise in unemployment in the 1980s, rather than a Pauline conversion to the theoretical attractions of path dependent equilibria, that sparked the introduction of a medium-run NAIRU bearing the marks of hysteresis. Using the Lakatos appraisal criterion of excess content, the story of how the NAIRU version of the NRH developed in the UK might be as follows. UK unemployment rose from the mid-1960s to late-1970s in a manner that could be explained successfully by reference to the z state variables invoked by the ahysteretic version of the NAIRU. This corroboration of theoretical content served to raise the empirical content of the NAIRU/NRH relative to research programs not specifying an influence for the z state variables. During the course of the 1980s the steady inflation equilibrium rate of unemployment rose sharply, in dramatic conflict with the NRH implication that the NR would fall in response to the downward pressure exerted by the *z* state variables. Unamended, the NRH was exposed to the charge of refutation, there being a decline in corroborated empirical content. The introduction of a medium-run NAIRU dimension to the NRH, in the form of duration composition effects arising from the experience of actual unemployment, provided a successful means of explaining the rise of the NAIRU in the 1980s. This amendment was not ad hoc, being applicable to a general set of instances rather than merely to the anomalous experience of the 1980s. The incorporation of duration composition effects turned out to be consistent both with what happened in the 1980s and with the previous episode, yielding an increase in the empirical content for this modified NAIRU version of the NRH.

The work of Lakatos on the philosophy of mathematics suggested that content was also a suitable appraisal criterion for theoretical or 'quasi-empirical' conjectures, as illustrated in his dialogues regarding Euler's conjecture on polyhedra (Lakatos, 1976). A central point of interest here is whether the presence of hysteresis effects on the medium-run NAIRU is consistent with convergence onto a long-run NR exhibiting no traces of hysteresis. If such convergence does not take place, the medium-run NAIRU amendment would serve to 'save the data' of the 1980s only at the cost of direct contradiction of the NRH and violation of its heuristic. In section 4 above instances where the medium-run NAIRU does not converge onto a long-run NR were outlined, though the Duhem problem of the evidence not being decisive is apparent.

The hysteresis hypothesis (HH) implies that convergence does not take place, the equilibrium rate of employment remaining path-dependent. Path-dependence is also a property of unit root processes, so unemployment following a unit root process is consistent with the HH but is not readily reconcilable with the NRH. The Duhem problem is again relevant here, there being no sure statistical means of rejecting alternative hypotheses of mean reversion. There are also problems with viewing a bounded variable such as unemployment as a pure unit root process, and with comparing logarithmic formulations of the NRH with non-logarithmic versions of the HH. Subject to these caveats, it is possible to see the upsurge of interest in the HH during the 1980s as arising from this hypothesis generating excess empirical content over the NRH alternative. Given the recent and continuing nature of the controversies, however, any such assessment would have to be regarded as tentative.

Does this mean that the Lakatos appraisal criterion of excess content – rather than the full Lakatos SRP typology which was not employed –

in the preceding discussion – explains well the course of the equilibrium unemployment controversies covered in this chapter, with economists voting with their feet for theories with excess empirical content? At the broad brush level of appraisal the answer would be that such tendencies were present, but that it is too early to judge what the outcome of the controversies will be. Given that a similar conclusion emerged from sections 1–4 above without the conscious use of a Lakatosian framework of appraisal, it is clear that the Lakatos framework is at most sufficient but not necessary to raise the issues of empirical content and non-self contradiction which have figured in the controversies discussed in this chapter. It might be the case that Lakatosian ideas have so permeated the economics profession, including the present author, that economists do not bother to invoke the ideas explicitly. The notion of encompassing is interesting here, encapsulating as it does the appraisal criterion that the preferred theory should explain the phenomena explained by other theories, and more. This can be seen as the Lakatos criterion of excess empirical content written in the language of econometrics. The idea that statisticians and econometricians from, say, Cox (1961) through to Mizon and Richard (1986) have been writing econometric analogues of Lakatos, however, is implausible. It is much more plausible to see the development of the encompassing principle as a response to the problem situation of assessing the claims of competing nested and non-nested hypotheses which have both deterministic and stochastic components. The Lakatos excess content criterion suffices to provide a rationale for the encompassing principle, but is not necessary.

The problems involved in appraising controversies of the sort dealt with above were stated with great clarity by Pierre Duhem:

> . . . when certain consequences of a theory are struck by . . . contradiction, we learn that the theory should be modified but we are not told . . . what must be changed . . . no absolute principle directs this inquiry, which different [economists] may conduct in very different ways without having the right to accuse one another of illogicality – [this] does not mean that we cannot properly prefer the work of one [economist] to that of the other . . . but these reasons of good sense do not impose themselves with . . . implacable rigour . . . there is something vague and uncertain about them . . . they do not reveal themselves with the same degree of clarity to all minds . . . hence the possibility of lengthy quarrels between the adherents of an old system and the partisans of a new doctrine. . . (Duhem, 1914, pp. 216–17)

Lakatos argued that it was possible to articulate and justify the 'reasons of good sense' referred to by Duhem: '. . . instead of leaving it to Duhem's inarticulated common sense to judge when a "framework" is to be abandoned . . . this approach injects . . . some hard Popperian standards into appraisal of whether a [theory] progresses or degenerates, or whether one is overtaking another . . .' (Lakatos, 1978, I, p. 122). In relation to the equilibrium unemployment controversies discussed above, the Lakatos criterion of excess empirical content corresponds to a 'reason of good sense' central to the controversy. However, it is not necessary to invoke this criterion to explain the course of the controversy. An alternative 'reason of good sense' would be the desire of the protagonists to avoid embarrassment arising from their theories being contradicted by empirical evidence.

REFERENCES

Bean, C.R., Layard, P.R.G. and Nickell, S.J. (1986) (eds), 'Unemployment', *Economica Supplement*, **53**, p. 210(S).

Blanchard, O.J. and Summers, L.H. (1987), 'Hysteresis in Employment', *European Economic Review*, **31**, 1/2, Feb/March, pp. 288–95.

—— (1988), 'Hysteresis and the European Unemployment Problem', reprinted in R. Cross (ed.), *Unemployment, Hysteresis and the Natural Rate Hypothesis* (Oxford: Basil Blackwell).

Cox, D.R. (1961), 'Tests of Separate Families of Hypotheses', *Proceedings of the Fourth Berkeley Symposium on Mathematical Statistics and Probability*, **1**, pp. 105–23 (Berkeley: University of California Press).

Cross. R. (1982), 'The Duhem–Quine Thesis, Lakatos and Theory Appraisal in Macroeconomics', *Economic Journal*, June, **92**, 366, pp. 320–40.

—— (1984) 'Monetarism and Duhem's Thesis', in P. Wiles and G. Routh (eds), *Economic Theory in Disarray*, pp. 78–99 (Oxford: Basil Blackwell).

—— (1987), 'Hysterersis and Instability in the Natural Rate of Unemployment', *The Scandinavian Journal of Economics*, **89**.1, pp. 77–89.

—— (ed.) (1988), *Unemployment, Hysteresis and the Natural Rate Hypothesis* (Oxford: Basil Blackwell).

Cross, R. and Allan, A. (1988), 'On the History of Hysteresis', in R. Cross (ed.), *Unemployment Hysteresis and the Nature Rate Hypothesis* (Oxford: Basil Blackwell).

Cross, R., Hutchinson H. and Yeoward, S. (1989a), 'The Natural Rate, Hysteresis and the Duration Composition of Unemployment in the US', *Quarterly Journal of Business and Economics*.

—— (1989b), 'Does the Natural Rate Exist?: Long Term Unemployment and Hysteresis in the UK, 1948–1987', University of St Andrews, mimeo.

—— (1989c), 'The Relationship Between Prices and Unemployment Cointegration Tests on the Keynesian Supply Curve, Phillips Curve, Natural Rate and Hysteresis Hypotheses in Britain 1886–1986', University of St Andrews, mimeo.

Diamond, P. (1982), 'Aggregate Demand Management in Search Equilibrium', *Journal of Political Economy*, **90**, 5, pp. 881–94.

—— (1984), *A Search Equilibrium Approach to the Micro Foundations of Macroeconomics* (Cambridge, Mass.: MIT Press).

Duhem, P. (1914, translated 1954), *The Aim and Structure of Physical Theory* (Princeton, NJ: Princeton University Press).
Elster, J. (1976), 'A Note on Hysteresis in the Social Sciences', *Synthese*, **33**, pp. 371–91.
Engle, R.F. and Granger, C.W.J. (1987), 'Dynamic Model Specification and Equilibrium Constraints: Cointegration and Error Correction', *Econometrica*, **55**, pp. 251–76.
Friedman, M. (1955), 'Leon Walras and His Economic System', *American Economic Review*, **45**, 5, 900–909.
—— (1968), 'The Role of Monetary Policy', *American Economic Review*, **58**, 1, March, pp. 1–17.
—— (1976), *Price Theory* (Chicago: Aldine).
—— (1977), 'Nobel Lecture: Inflation and Unemployment', *Journal of Political Economy*, **85**, 3, June, pp. 451–72.
Frisch, R. (1936), 'On the Notion of Equilibrium and Disequilibrium', *Review of Economic Studies*, V, 100–105.
Fuller, W.A. (1976), *Introduction to Statistical Time Series* (New York: John Wiley).
Georgescu–Roegen (1966), *Analytical Economics* (Cambridge, Mass.: Harvard University Press).
—— (1971), *The Entropy Law and the Economic Process* (Cambridge, Mass.: Harvard University Press).
Glazebrook, R.T. (1935), 'James Alfred Ewing, 1855–1935', *Obituary Notices of Fellows of the Royal Society of London*, **1**, pp. 475–92.
Gordon, R.J. (1989), 'Hysteresis and the Natural Rate: Findings for the Past Century in Five Industrial Nations', *Northwestern University mimeo*, May.
Granger, C.W.J. (1983), 'Cointegrating Variables and Error Correcting Models', *UCSD Discussion Paper*.
—— (1986), 'Developments in the Study of Cointegrated Economic Variables', *Oxford Bulletin of Economics and Statistics*, **48**, pp. 213–28.
Granger, C.W.J. and Lee, T-H (1988), 'Multicointegration', *UCSD Discussion Paper*.
Granger, C.W.J. and Newbold, P. (1977), *Forecasting Economic Time Series* (New York: Academic Press).
Hahn, F. (1987), 'Information, Dynamics and Equilibrium', *Scottish Journal of Political Economy*, **34**, 4, November, pp. 321–34.
Hendry, D. (1983), 'Econometric Modelling: the "Consumption Function" in Retrospect', *Scottish Journal of Political Economy*, **30**, 3, November, pp. 193–220.
—— (1986), 'Econometric Modelling with Cointegrated Variables', *Oxford Bulletin of Economics and Statistics*, **48**, 3, August, pp. 213–28.
Hendry, D.F. and Richard, J.-F (1983), 'The Econometric Analysis of Economic Time Series', *International Statistical Review*, **51**, pp. 111–63.
Hoover, K.D. (1988), *The New Classical Macroeconomics* (Oxford: Basil Blackwell).
Jenkinson, T.J. (1988), 'The NAIRU: Statistical Fact or Theoretical Strait-jacket?', in R. Cross (ed.), *Unemployment, Hysteresis and the Natural Rate Hypothesis* (Oxford: Basil Blackwell).
Kaldor, N. (1983), 'A Classifictory Note on the Determinateness of Equilibrium', *Review of Economic Studies*, II, pp. 122–36.

Keynes, J.M. (1936), *The General Theory of Employment, Interest and Money* (London: Macmillan).

Lakatos, I. (1971), 'Replies to Critics', in R.C. Buck and R.S. Cohen (eds), *Boston Studies in the Philosophy of Science* (Dordrecht: Reidel).

—— (1976), *Proofs and Refutations* Cambridge: Cambridge University Press).

—— (1978), *Philosophical Papers, Vol. I: The Methodology of Scientific Research Programmes. Vol. II: Mathematics, Science and Epistemology* (eds. J. Worrall and G. Currie) (Cambridge: Cambridge University Press).

Layard, R. (1986), *How to Beat Unemployment* (Oxford: Oxford University Press).

Layard, R. and Nickell, S. (1986a), 'Unemployment in Britain', *Economica*, **53**, 210, pp. S121–S169.

—— (1986b), 'The Performance of the British Labour Market', CLE discussion paper no. 249, LSE. Lindbeck, A. and Snower, D.J. (1988), 'Union Activity, Unemployment Persistence and Wage-Employment Ratchets', reprinted in R. Cross (ed.) *Unemployment, Hysteresis and the Natural Rate Hypothesis* (Oxford: Basil Blackwell).

Lötka, A.J. (1925), *Elements of Mathematical Biology* (Baltimore: William and Wilkin).

Mizon, G.E. and Richard, J.-F (1986), 'The Encompassing Principle and its Application to Non-Nested Hypotheses', *Econometrica*, **54**, pp. 657–78.

Nickell, S.U. (1979), 'Estimating the Probability of Leaving Unemployment', *Econometrica*, **47**, 5, September, pp. 124–66.

—— (1987), 'Why is Wage Inflation in Britain So High?', *Oxford Bulletin of Economics and Statistics*, reprinted in R. Cross (ed.), *Unemployment, Hysteresis and the Natural Rate Hypothesis* (Oxford: Basil Blackwell).

—— (1988), 'The NAIRU: Some Theory and Statistical Facts', in R. Cross (ed.) *Unemployment, Hysteresis and the Natural Rate Hypothesis* (Oxford: Basil Blackwell).

Peden, G.C. (1980), 'Keynes, the Treasury and Unemployment in the Later Nineteen-Thirties', *Oxford Economic Papers*, March, pp. 1–18.

Phelps, E.S. (1967), 'Phillips Curves, Expectations of Inflation and Optimal Unemployment Over Time', *Economica*, **34**, 3, 254–81.

—— (ed.) (1970), *Microeconomic Foundations of Employment and Inflation Theory* (New York: W.W. Norton).

—— (1972), *Inflation Policy and Unemployment Theory* (London: Macmillan).

Phillips, A.W. (1954), 'Stabilisation Policy in a Closed Economy', *Economic Journal*, **64**, pp. 290–323.

—— (1958), 'The Relationship Between Unemployment and the Rate of Change of Money Wage Rates in the U.K. 1861–1957', *Economica*, **25**, pp. 283–99.

Pilgrim Trust (1938), *Men Without Work* (Cambridge, Cambridge University Press).

Popper, K.R. (1934, 1959 translation), *The Logic of Scientific Discovery* (London: Hutchinson).

Samuelson, P.A. (1972), 'Some Notions of Causality and Teleology in Economics' and 'What Classical and Neoclassical Monetary Theory Really Was', in R.C. Merton (ed.), *The Collected Scientific Papers of Paul A. Samuelson Vol III* (Cambridge, Mass.: MIT Press).

Sargan, J.D. (1964), 'Wages and Prices in the United Kingdom: a Study in

Econometric Methodology', in R.E. Hart, G. Mills and J.K. Whitaker (eds), *Econometric Analysis for National Economic Planning* (London: Butterworths).

Sargan, J.D. and Bhargava, A. (1983), 'Testing Residuals from Least Squares Regressions for Being Generated by the Gaussian Random Walk', *Econometrica*, **51**, 1, February, pp. 153–74.

Schumpeter, J.A. (1934), *The Theory of Economic Development* (Cambridge, Mass.: Harvard University Press).

Summers, L.H. (1988), 'Keynesian Economics and the Phillips Curve', in R. Cross (ed.), *Unemployment, Hysteresis and the Natural Rate Hypothesis* (Oxford: Basil Blackwell).

Tobin, J. (1965), 'Money and Economic Growth', *Econometrica*, **33**, pp. 671–84.

—— (1972), 'Inflation and Unemployment', *American Economic Review*, **62**, pp. 1–19.

Weintraub, E.R. (1985), *General Equilibrium Analysis* (Cambridge: Cambridge University Press).

COMMENT ON CROSS

Mark Blaug

Rod Cross has long been engaged in defending an account of unemployment in terms of 'Hysteresis', that is, a state of unemployment equilibrium that is strictly dependent on history or the actual time path taken to reach that equilibrium. Such a time-dependent explanation of unemployment is utterly at variance with any Phelps–Friedman–Lucas notion of a unique, stable Natural Rate of Unemployment, as well as being deeply subversive of a 200-year-old tradition in economics of timeless equilibrium analysis. Apart from a number of plausible explanations of the time-dependent upward drift of structural unemployment, much of the chapter is concerned, surprisingly enough, with a theoretical attack on the natural rate hypothesis (NRH) on the grounds that typical additions to NRH, such as Friedman's medium-run, positively sloped Phillips curve or Layard–Nickell's distinction between the short-term and long-term unemployed, are inconsistent with convergence of the economy to a natural rate equilibrium. Something is said about the empirical track-record of Friedman's and Layard–Nickell's conjectures but on the whole the emphasis in this chapter is on the logical difficulties of NRH conceived as some sort of proposition in Walrasian general equilibrium theory.

Cross closed with the assertion:

> Methodologists are likely to be interested whether standards such as those suggested by Imre Lakatos are an illuminating means of articulating (Duhem's) 'reasons of good sense' when comparing accounts of equilibrium unemployment. I would say yes, but that the illumination does not follow 'with implacable rigour'.

However those Lakatosian standards are fundamentally the ability of a scientific theory to predict 'novel facts', that is, either unsuspected facts or at least facts that are not themselves employed to generate the theory in question. But what were the 'novel facts' predicted by NRH? Milton Friedman knew that there was 'stagflation' or the simultaneous occurrence of unemployment and inflation. He produced NRH to account for stagflation and, apart from that rationalization, the expectations-augmented vertical Phillips curve *à la* Friedman had no empirical content whatsoever.

The Lucas rational expectations version of NRH, however, did have 'excess empirical content' in its policy-neutral implications and the declining fortunes of the New Classical Macroeconomics are precisely due to the failure of that implication to be verified (Maddock, 1984). Similarly the moment NRH was empirically measured in terms of the non-accelerating inflation rate of unemployment (NAIRU), the rate appeared to be highly unstable and incapable of accounting for the inflation experiences of the 1980s without *ad hoc* amendments, such as the division of the unemployed into those of short and long duration. Cross does indeed tell the story of how Layard and Nickell dealt with the anomalies that their measurement of NAIRU soon encountered but my complaint is that Cross misses a golden opportunity to exemplify the power of Lakatos's standards: he writes at times as if he had never heard of Lakatos.

Cross asks at one point how NRH could ever have been swallowed so uncritically by the profession, given the fact that Friedman had provided no demonstration of the existence of one stable rate of unemployment to which the economy always tends to return, and he quotes Bob Solow who speculates that it came to be believed for extra-scientific reasons. But economists had long believed that the level of frictional unemployment was positive and hence that stable prices implied some definite level of unemployment; there is the famous case of how Keynes himself became worried in 1937 by the inflationary implications of unemployment falling below 12 per cent. In short the notion of some vaguely positive non-inflationary level of unemployment as reflective of the structural rigidities of the labour market is as old as the hills and that is precisely why Friedman's NRH in terms of the asymmetrical price expectations of workers and employers caught on immediately: it was no sooner stated than it seemed obvious. Nevertheless NRH would never have survived if Friedman's followers had not succeeded in operationalizing the concept by marrying an adaptive-expectations mechanism to the expectations-augmented Phillips curve.[1] However this empirically formulated version of NRH soon ran into statistical problems (Blaug, 1985, pp. 684–5), thus clearing the way for the Rational Expectations Revolution.

This significant chapter in the history of monetarism is ignored by Cross who turns instead to numerical estimates of NAIRU without, however, underlining the fact that NAIRU is not so much a watered-down version of NRH as a subtly different conception of the relationship between unemployment and inflation. NRH implies that all unemployment is voluntary, that demand management is futile in the long run (the Friedman Mark I version of monetarism) and even in the short run (the Lucas–Sargent Mark II version of monetarism). NAIRU, on the other hand, is entirely an empirical question: given the wage-price setting characteristics of an economy, is there a narrow range of unemployment below which inflation accelerates and can we accurately predict that range for some policy-relevant period of time, say, two or three years? Cross makes light of the distinction between NRH and NAIRU and in so doing misses, it seems to me, much of the role that empirical anomalies have played in the tortured evolution of macroeconomic theory over the last two decades.

Cross quoted Quine's rather trite formulation of the standard criteria for theory choice: conservatism, modesty, simplicity, generality and refutability. If Lakatos adds bite to such a list it is to underline the priority of the last of these five, to insist that refutability can only be judged in terms of the historical evolution of a scientific theory or research program, and then only in comparison with the historical development of at least one other rival program. Much as I learned from Cross's careful examination of alternative accounts of equilibrium unemployment, I would have learned even more had he viewed his material through Lakatosian-coloured glasses.

Note

1. The fact that Friedman advanced NRH on a long-run vertical Phillips curve without any suggestions for measuring it and that his subsequent addition of a medium-run, positively sloped Phillips curve was likewise unaccompanied by any proposals for quantification tells us a great deal about methodological standards in modern economics.

References

Blaug, M. (1985), *Economic Theory in Retrospect* (Cambridge: Cambridge University Press).

Maddock, R. (1984), 'Rational Expectations Macrotheory: A Lakatosian Case Study in Program Adjustment', *History of Political Economy*, **16**, 291–309.

COMMENT ON CROSS

J.A. Kregel

1

I have always harboured a suspicion that Lakatos's methodology of scientific research programs (MSRP) was just another dodge created to rationalize general equilibrium theory. Discourse with Roy Weintraub has accustomed me to the idea that criticism should be directed not against particular models, but research programs, and that this can be best done by appraisal of the positive and negative heuristic of theories that populate the protective belt of research program in terms of their excess content of a theoretical and/or empirical nature. That appraisal should take place by comparing alternative programs has been given less importance, and MSRP has tended to involve predominantly internal or inside appraisal,[1] using the charges of 'profound misunderstanding' and 'categorical mistake' to ward off the criticism of external or outside participants who fail to adhere to the language of MSRP.

Hence my suspicions that the MSRP masks an unwillingness to 'communicate across research communities' with people who do not share common premises or who do not accept your premises. In any event, to avoid being considered a methodological luddite, I shall accept these rules in appraising Rod Cross's analysis of equilibrium employment theory.

2

Given this premise, the first thing I tried to do was to try to classify the Research Program (RP), the Hard Core Propositions (HCP), the positive heuristic (PH), the Protective Belt (PB) and the theories composing them. It seemed clear that Cross's idea was to appraise the progressivity of 'alternatives', not theories or models, but explanations. These seemed best interpreted as models within theories, but he deals with only NAIRU and Natural Rate Hypothesis (NRH) explanations, which seem different theories rather than different models within a theory. And since both theories seem to fit nicely within the neo-Walrasian research program (NWRP), which is what I presume the reference to 'equilibrium' theories is supposed to evoke, it seemed clear that his was an inside or internal appraisal, without reference to alternative RPs. This is rather disconcerting in a session which is supposed to deal with 'communication across research communities' (a subject about which I have some first-hand experience). Unfortunately, I have no experience, or expertise, in internal appraisal of the NWRP!

But my difficulties were just starting, for instead of an appraisal of one 'alternative' against the other, that is, NRH against NAIRU, Cross has instead matched both off against a third: 'hysteresis'. And here my application of MSRP classifications started to founder. What is the methodological status of 'hysteresis'? Is it a criticism of Weintraub's HC6 ('construct only equilibrium theories') proposition, or is it instead a mutant of the NWRP with only one different gene in position HC6? The former would be an attack on the Hard Core, clearly not appraisal of a RP, while the second would represent a change in the specification of the Hard Core which has occurred, not by means of theory appraisal in the PB, but by appraisal via an alternative HC – again, not an accepted MSRP appraisal.

My rapid reading of Cross left two unclear messages: the first is that the econometric concept of 'encompassing' may be used as a measure of empirical progressivity (although it is not clear that it implies excess content); the second is that hysteretic explanation of unemployment encompasses both NRH and NAIRU (theories? models?) of equilibrium unemployment and is thus superior to both on MSRP grounds of progressivity. Hence the conundrum – just exactly how to classify the role of hysteresis in appraisal.

Is hysteresis part of a different, post-Keynesian research program (PKRP?)? Or is it an (unacceptable) attack on a Hard Core proposition (HC6) of the NWRP?

I do not think the first possibility can be seriously maintained for the very definition of unemployment used by Cross is circumscribed by the NWRP HC and PH. But, if this is the case, how can his major results be viewed within the NWRP and how can MSRP encompass them when they are clearly a criticism of an HC proposition within NWRP rather than appraisal?

3

Cross seems surprised that it took so long for the importance of hysteresis to be recognized within the NWRP, noting that it had been introduced earlier (although as part of alternative paradigms). For example, he conjectures that Schumpeter was the first economist to use the word 'hysteresis'.[2] I was not a student of Schumpeter's, and thus when I first ran into the word in the modern literature (in Franklin Fisher's work) it was Joan Robinson (1956, p. 58) that came to mind:

'In most economic reactions the path the market follows, while it is adapting itself to a change, has a long-persisting effect upon the position that it reaches'.

Clearly, it is not for want of people proposing hysteresis that it is absent from the NWRP. Instead I would suggest that those who suggested that such a conception of equilibrium introduced into any of the theories of the PB might wreak havoc were fobbed off with accusations of 'profound misunderstanding of the concept of equilibrium' and methodological ludditism. I may refer the reader to Weintraub (1985a) for the precise form of argument as applied to Joan Robinson and (1985b) for Nicholas Kaldor. It would appear that the discussion and introduction of hysteresis was prevented precisely because it was tarred as an attack on a HCP and thus without merit or consideration, interpreted as a naive and uninformed complaint about 'lack of realism'.

Hence my perplexity at classifying hysteresis in Cross's paper. How is it possible for exactly the same proposition to be considered at one point in time as an attack on the realism of the HCP of a RP and therefore unscientific and reprehensible, and at another as an acceptable means of appraising the progressivity of a theory in the PB when it is clearly not itself either a RP or a PB theory, but rather an alternative HCP? I am just not sure that Weintraub's HC6 can be stretched this far without reducing the NWRP to banality: 'My body exists, therefore it is coordinated and must be discussed with reference to an equilibrium state.' But it surely does make a difference whether this state is homeostasis or complete entropy!

As Cross himself notes, the NWRP that he uses to define 'equilibrium' unemployment is one in which unemployment in general, and involuntary unemployment in particular, cannot exist. The concept of hysteresis is then not a new theory with excess content, but rather exposes an anomaly which renders NWRP degenerative. Indeed, from the point of view of a PKRP, the entire history of the NWRP has been an attempt to explain a concept that does not exist within the RP. When this anomaly was raised by Robinson and Kaldor it was diagnosed as an attack upon the realism of a HCP; in Cross's hands it becomes an example of a degenerative program whose response that unemployment reflects individual free inter-temporal choice between work and anticipated holiday time mirrors that of the degenerative Marxist RP which insists that prices reflect labour values.

4

This brings us back to communication across research communities. Why are ideas put forward in one RP initially rejected as methodologically uninformed attacks on the HC of another, only to reappear some time later as perfectly acceptable propositions, without reference or recognition of their former lives? This is not an abstract problem. A good example is a book written by Sidney Weintraub (1958), which fell outside any defined RP of the time. Robert Solow (1959) first gave it a disparaging review, and then some ten years later, together with Joe Stiglitz (1968), published an article which adopted the same general framework, without any reference to the earlier work![3]

In this respect it is unfortunate that Cross accepts Coddington's interpretation of Keynes's definition of involuntary unemployment as incomprehensible (he makes it unnecessarily difficult by getting the quotation wrong!), for the pains Keynes takes over this definition are due to his concern for the problem of communication across RPs. To this end he states clearly, in Chapter 2, his interpretation of the prevailing (and prior) RP, and warns readers that involuntary unemployment cannot be demonstrated within any of them. He then suggests that his position can be best seen as undertaking the impossible, of making parallel lines meet to produce an equilibrium position in which there are workers who are unable to find work even though they are offering to work at the prevailing wage rates, by the simple substitution of one of the axioms of the prevailing RPs. By analogy with non-Euclidean geometry, which preserves all the axioms and theorems of Euclidean geometry for non-Euclidean space, but provided a revolution in the interpretation of these theorems by simply changing one axiom, Keynes suggests that he can do the same thing by changing the second classical postulate that labour can determine the real wage at which it works.[4] If we are to make sense of Keynes's definition of involuntary unemployment it can only be done by discovering how Keynes attempted to communicate it 'across' RPs. Cross's attempt to insert hysteresis in the NWRP HC certainly appears similar to Keynes's strategy and thus should produce the same conclusion that the NWRP is degenerate.

Notes

1. For those who do not notice, the use of these terms is meant to recall not only the use made of them by Latsis (1976) in his discussion of situational determinism but by Lindbeck and Snower (1988) in their explanation of the impact of unemployment on wages.

2. Although, unlike Schumpeter, they did not all know the secret word – I have a suspicion that it must have been Dick Goodwin who tipped him off.
3. Solow's claim that it dealt with disequilibrium adjustment rather than equilibrium does not take away from the fact that it looks very much like work that might have taken place within the same RP. See Weintraub, 1970.
   More recently, in an article by Greenwald and Stiglitz (1987), we find the rediscovery of the wheel of Kalecki's principle of increasing risk and Eichner's corporate levy.
4. Keynes has to give two definitions precisely because he recognizes that he is speaking to two alternative RPs, the Classics and Pigou. These ideas are presented in more detail in Kregel, 1987.

References

Cross, R. (1989), 'Alternative Accounts of Equilibrium Unemployment', mimeo, St Andrews.

Greenwald, B. and Stiglitz, J. (1987), 'Keynesian, New Keynesian and New Classical Economics', *Oxford Economic Papers*, **39**, pp. 119–32.

Kaldor, N. (1972), 'The Irrelevance of Equilibrium Economics', *Economic Journal*, **82**, pp. 1237–55.

Kregel, J.A. (1987), 'The effective demand approach to employment and inflation analysis', *Journal of Post Keynesian Economics*, **10**, pp. 133–45.

Lakatos, I. (1970), 'Falsification and the Methodology of Scientific Research Programmes', in I. Lakatos and A. Musgrave (eds), *Criticism and the Growth of Knowledge*, pp. 91–195 (Cambridge: Cambridge University Press).

Latsis, S. (1976), 'A research programme in economics', in S. Latsis (ed.), *Method and Appraisal in Economics*, pp. 1–41 (Cambridge: Cambridge University Press).

Lindbeck, A. and Snower, D.J. (1988), 'Union Activity, Unemployment Persistence and Wage-Employment Ratchets', in R. Cross (ed.), *Unemployment, Hysteresis and the Natural Rate Hypothesis* (Oxford: Basil Blackwell).

Robinson, J. (1956), *The Accumulation of Capital* (London: Macmillan).

Solow, R. (1959), 'Review of S. Weintraub: *An Approach to the Theory of Income Distribution*', *Journal of Political Economy*, **67**, pp. 420–21.

Solow, R. and Stiglitz, J. (1968), 'Output, Employment and Wages in the Short Run', *Quarterly Journal of Economics*, **82**, pp. 537–60.

Weintraub, E.R. (1985a), 'Joan Robinson's Critique of Equilibrium: An Appraisal', *American Economic Review*, **75**, pp. 146–9.

—— (1985b), *General Equilibrium Analysis: Studies in Appraisal* (Cambridge: Cambridge University Press).

Weintraub, S. (1958), *An Approach to the Theory of Income Distribution*, (Philadelphia, Chilton).

—— (1970), 'Solow and Stiglitz on Employment and Distribution: A New Romance with an Old Model', *Quarterly Journal of Economics*, **84**, pp. 144–52.

B Delineating Programs

10. The Development of New Classical Macroeconomics: Lessons for Lakatos

Rodney Maddock

1 INTRODUCTION

Lakatos's analysis (1970) of the working of research programs contains a number of clear guides as to how one might implement his ideas. He understands programs to have a number of static characteristics and certain properties which transform the theoretical body in one way or another and convert it into a new version; the sequence of theory variants comprises the program. It is defined however by its invariant, hard core elements. The practical lessons are that from the relevant writings one should try first to identify the invariant elements. These should then be classified to try to separate out the hard core elements which define the program, and the remainder should be assigned temporarily to its protective belt. With this sketch of the commonalities of the program, one then returns to the literature in an attempt to understand the role of the residual features in the development of the program.

In our assessment of the usefulness of Lakatos to our understanding economics I think that the features upon which we should focus are the definition of the program and the rationalization of its transitions.

An alternative evaluation of his contribution would focus on what I see as a quite separate, and separable, element of Lakatos's analysis concerning the interaction of programs. His view that successful theories will be those which survive certain tests in terms of content has an entirely different status from that of the internal dynamics of each program. Even he concedes that his evolutionary principles will be modified to the extent that some programs are better funded than others, and will depend upon the tendency for scholars to remain captives of the programs which they experienced in their younger days and so on. There is in fact little contact between the two elements of his analysis. Activities in other programs may result in problem shifts within a program but that is but one of many possible sources of dynamic change and not necessarily the most important. While his views on the evolutionary success of programs make an interesting contribution, I do not propose to consider them here, preferring to concentrate on the guidance Lakatos has given to the rational reconstruction of programs.

Program competition does not seem a necessary element of the evolution of a research program. While Lakatos believes that the ultimate success of a line of research depends upon its empirical content there is no necessary suggestion that a particular program will not survive all of us. This is not to say that progressiveness is not a central feature of our analysis. Lakatos's basic assumption is that the fundamental motor of science is the continuing search for progressivity within one's research program. Where scientists seem to get distracted from this search, the ancillary concepts play a part, but any problem shift arising from such a distraction will be put to the acid test of progressivity. There does not seem to be any necessary reason, however, to insist upon both progress and competition; for rational reconstruction the search for progress should be sufficient.

This chapter is intimately related to Maddock (1984). That paper attempted a Lakatosian reconstruction of the rational expectations literature. It revealed (1) a major problem shift in the research dated around 1975 wherein the research forms shifted from the natural rate and towards the importance of policy; (2) the paucity of the empirical support it had managed to garner; and (3) the existence of some papers with no clear Lakatosian function. In this chapter I want to highlight the problems I had in forcing the literature into the particular methodological framework. By this I hope to demonstrate the areas in which one might look to *modify* the received methodology of scientific research programs. Clearly difficulties of application of such a methodology could lead one to *abandon* it: the alternative is to try to improve it. This work should be read as providing constructive suggestions for developing the Lakatosian method.

My plan, then, is to analyse the early phases of the evolution of the work on rational expectations by rational reconstruction based on internal analysis and to generate ideas for the further development of Lakatos's work. I concentrate in Section 2 on the problem of identifying just what is the research program with which I am concerned. The program having been identified, Section 3 will then turn to Lucas's search for that program and show the difficulties the poor definition of the program in the early years poses for a Lakatosian reconstruction. This is the most problematic section since Lakatos provides us with little guidance as to just how a program does come into existence. Section 4 explains the process by which the central concept of rationality of expectations was chosen for its core role. Section 5 then considers the original novelty of the program. The following Section tries to find a place for papers whose primary function seems to be to advocate the strengths of the program with a Lakatosian reconstruction. Section 7 explores the status of the general equilibrium pretensions of the rational expectations theorists and Section 8 discusses their devotion to testing and the pursuit of empirical support of their theoretical novelty. This is followed by a conclusion.

2 DIFFICULTIES OF DEFINING THE PROGRAM

The impact of Lucas, Sargent, Wallace, Barro and the other economists who brought rational expectations to the forefront of economic debate in the 1970s has been such that their work has been given its own label, usually now that of 'new classical economics'. The phenomenon of labelling reflects the general acceptance that these scholars were involved in a distinct activity but I want to concentrate for the moment on the particular label used which suggests a continuity between the ideas of Lucas and his collaborators and a long tradition in economics based upon the idea that the macroeconomy tends to self-equilibrate satisfactorily. By contrast I have previously called this program 'rational expectations macrotheory', an expression which conveys the narrower and stronger sense that the economy involved also equilibrates quickly, where by equilibration I mean that it returns to its natural levels.[1] The 'new' in 'new classical' is usually taken as conveying the same meaning.

In terms then of our basic problem of identifying just what is the program in which we are interested, of identifying the hard core propositions which define the program, we obviously have to decide whether we are interested in the rational expectations writers as members of the 'classical economics' program or whether the 'new classical program' in the sense of rapid equilibration is to be our focus. The fundamental difficulty with the application of the Lakatosian methods would thus appear to start from the fact that research programs, such as this one, are also members of a series of ever-broader, containing, programs. 'New classical economics' sits within 'classical economics', which sits within 'economics' and so on.

While not addressing this question directly Lakatos provided a definition of a research program which resolves the issue at one level. He proposed asking whether the new theory had included all the unrefuted content of the earlier ancestor-theories. If it had not, it could fairly be described as a separate program.

The joint rational expectation and natural rate (of unemployment) hypotheses[2] clearly reject some unrefuted content of the pre-existing theory of macroeconomic policy, which program allows a role for active policy strategies. The new theory also rejects some of the unrefuted content of the program of classical macroeconomics – it denies the effectiveness of policy even in the short run. Friedman had argued that government could hold unemployment indefinitely below the natural rate by a policy of accelerating inflation.[3] The rational expectations theorists, however, argue that no policy may be capable of doing that. Some propositions of the two most prominent macroeconomics programs, each of which had attracted some support and had unrefuted content, were denied by this emerging program.

Thus it seems clear that the rational expectations stream of research satisfies the two tests that Lakatos had set up to define new research programs and hence itself can be treated as a distinctive program, whether by the name of 'new classical economics' or some other. It has an identity of its own, distinguished from related theories in its rejection of some of their unrefuted content.

The program pairs two hypotheses.[4] The first is that economic actors have rational expectations about prices – that is, that their subjective distribution of expected prices is equal to the objective distributions (at least in the relevant moments). The second is that the slope of the aggregate supply function in price space depends upon the difference between prices and expected prices. Some economists hold one of these views, some another. The willingness to hold both simultaneously will be taken to define work within the new classical economics program.

An alternative approach[5] would see the Friedman/Phelps/Lucas literature as part of the response of the classical program to an important empirical observation – the occurrence of stagflation in the late 1960s. Lakatosians could then ask whether the response had been of an ad hoc or potentially fruitful kind.

Thus one of the difficulties of operating within the rubric of a Lakatosian reconstruction is that one can analyse the same theoretical phenomenon at a variety of different levels and in the context of encompassing research programs. In a large literature this can clearly lead to confusion; the same contributions will be assessed in quite different ways, depending on whether they are defined as being within program A or program B: one person's hard core will be another's protective belt. However, as long as one starts with a clear definition of the level of program and of its core content, one can apply the standard methods. Whether the analysis is interesting or important will depend upon whether any actual group of scholars is pursuing the positive heuristic identified by the analyst.

I am able to evade this problem since I choose Lucas as the unifying scholar whose underlying heuristic drove the development of the program during the 1970s. He had a program and he knew where it was going: I am thus able to define a clear research program; it was separate from classical economics in the sense of Lakatos's content rule and was unified by a driving scholarly vision.

3 PROBLEMS POSED BY THE HARDENING OF THE HARD CORE

Lakatos noted: 'The actual hard core of a programme does not actually emerge fully armed like Athene from the head of Zeus. It develops slowly by a long, preliminary process of trial and error',[6] but does not go on to describe the process. The description of the hardening of the rational expectations program's hard core will be attempted in this section.[7] Lacking any theory of the phenomenon, the argument may be a little disjointed at times, but does seem to capture the evolution within a Lakatosian spirit.

Friedman,[8] apparently dissatisfied with the implications for aggregate-supply and aggregate-demand theory of a stable Phillips curve, developed one of the conjectures from which the new theories arose. He insisted that there was no long-run, stable trade-off between unemployment and inflation. He did, however, see the possibility of a short-run trade-off. This arose from a discrepancy between actual and anticipated inflation rates. When he used the term 'long run', he meant the stage when the economic process had stabilized, and no distinction between actual and expected inflation was in evidence. He felt that the government was able to create a sequence of disequilibria by causing accelerating inflation wherein expectations would never fully catch prices. In such a case, the trade-off would continue in evidence. Friedman used examples of supply in the labour market in support of his proposition. Similar conclusions arose from a contemporary work by Phelps.

The other essential ingredient of the new classical program was the idea of rational expectations propounded by Muth in 1961: 'I should like to suggest that expectations . . . are essentially the same as the predictions of the relevant economic theory' (p. 316).

While the Friedman/Phelps idea was seized upon immediately and the expectation-augmented Phillips curve adopted almost universally within the profession, the idea of rational expectations had been slower bearing fruit. The reasons for this are not clear and are perhaps simply fortuitous. Certainly Lucas drafted a paper on investment in 1966 with the title, 'Optimal investment with rational expectations' which referred to, and incorporated the idea of, rational expectations, and Arrow had used the concept as well. Perhaps part of the problem arose because Muth failed to clarify the way forward. His 1981 paper was actually written soon after the 1961 classic but he did not publish. This was unfortunate because in it he points the way to a large number of the estimation techniques subsequently used to make the idea of rational expectations operational. He shows how, with appropriate care, one can generally replace an expectations variable with the actual value taken and then use estimation techniques recognizing the 'error-in-variable' which has been introduced. It took economists most of the 1970s to rediscover the procedures mapped out but left unpublished in the early 1960s.

4 GETTING RATIONAL EXPECTATIONS INTO THE CORE

The integrating framework superimposed upon the scaffolding provided by Friedman, Phelps and Muth was derived out of a pair of papers by Lucas and Rapping. One Lucas–Rapping paper (1969a) used a simple two-period household labour-supply model.[9] To evaluate future possibilities, the household needed to calculate a present discounted value of future money wages, and hence of prices. From the 'representative' household function, the authors inferred an aggregate labour supply function. It included as arguments the present value of future money wages and future prices. These future values were then represented by their anticipated values. To make these estimates operational, anticipated entities were replaced by a Koyck lag structure on past levels of the particular thing being anticipated. Inverting the lag function and substituting the results for 'anticipations' terms reduced everything to variables currently known.

Such a model produced the results the authors sought. The labour supply equation was homogeneous in neither current money wages nor current prices. This implied a 'rational' money illusion in labour market responses to monetary shifts. This illusion resulted from the assumption about the way the labour suppliers formed their price expectations – that the suppliers expected a return to normal prices. Subject to the rationality of this belief and its implied adaptive mechanism, all behaviour by the individuals involved was rational. No extra-market wage contracts were introduced. In Friedman's long run, at normal prices, the expectations mechanisms would be 'correct', and the long-run elasticity of labour supply would hold. With all this, the model yielded a short-run supply elasticity. This was the first real step; this labour market model, which combined short-run variability in labour supply with long-run inelasticity, provided the impetus for a genuinely rational expectations approach to the formulation of labour market equilibrium. Quite distinctly from the explanations offered by Lipsey,[10] the Phillips curve could be 'explained' without reference to collective bargaining, or any other non-market decision process.

Lucas and Rapping had said that one of their purposes was 'the rationalization in supply and demand terms of the observed correlation between unemployment rates and inflation, or the Phillips curve'.[11] Patently they succeeded. On the contrast this suggested between the two explanations, the battle was not entered – 'While we offer no crucial test of the two views, we shall show that a competitive market theory is rich in implications and consistent with the U.S. experience.'[12]

Retrospectively it is easy to see the role of this work in the hard core development. All behaviour modelled arose out of optimization in a market context. In the labour market, the short-run elasticity and long-run inelasticity of supply had been explained in a way which produced non-homogeneity of supply in current monetary variables. These were to become important features of the developing literature. The result was achieved by a Koyck-lag (that is, adaptive) representation of the price expectation determining mechanism. Clearly the authors realized that their result turned on this modelling of the formation of expectations. Their introductory comment to the particular specification was: 'Since we know in advance that the problem has no neat illuminating solution, there is little incentive to conduct this analysis. Instead we postulate the adaptive scheme.'[13] Their awareness of the ideational conflict between the optimization of the objective function and arbitrary specification of the expectations mechanism seems to have been intuitive rather than explicit in *this* work:

> . . . our model emphasizes the crucial role of expectations formation while testing only the very crudest expectations models. We have used an adaptive scheme which will clearly hold under reasonably stable rates of price increase. To define what is meant by reasonable stability, and to discover how expectations are revised when stability ceases to obtain, seem to us to be a crucial unresolved question.[14]

The expectations formation process was still seen as a question requiring a behavioural hypothesis logically distinct from the one suggested in the optimization calculation.

The authors were, however, to draw quite general conclusions from their work, and especially as to what represented a legitimate interpretation of it. They wrote: 'One cannot use our estimated structural equations to study the dynamics of labor market response to changes in prices and output . . . this is illegitimate . . . Movements will be determined simultaneously.'[15]

The explicit criticism of Friedman's accelerating inflation proposition came in their next work.[16] The one we have just looked at explored Friedman's suggestion that a short-run Phillips curve correlation would appear as a result of errors in expectations formation. He assumed from this that the government could continue to exploit the relationship by causing an accelerating inflation. Here the authors drew the line. They argued that the price-expectation formation mechanism built into Friedman's analysis (and that built into their own earlier paper) was based on 'the assumption of an unreasonable stubbornness on the part of households: if a sustained inflationary policy is pursued by the government, households following the adaptive rule will continue *forever* to underpredict future prices'.[17] The resolution they achieved was to modify the autoregressive construct to remove this particular weakness. In place of a simple, fixed, Koyck lag they postulated a 'rational distributed lag function'. This was the best fitting lag structure in explaining past values of the variable being predicted. It was not an arbitrary structure imposed a priori, but one that arose (econometrically) from the data. The weights were constrained to sum to unity. In a lag formation of this type, proportional changes in past prices resulted in proportional changes in expected prices.

The sense then was that the earlier model produced its results from rational behaviour and an arbitrary lag function on expectations. The irrationality of the lag function was demonstrated by Friedman's own example of the possibility of its sub-optimal response to an accelerating inflation. A slightly 'smarter' mechanism was proposed in its place. It made greater use of past data, and hence responded more adequately to patterns in past experience.

Lucas and Rapping then formulated and tested an unemployment function. They transformed the aggregate supply equation into an unemployment equation, and then substituted the rational distributed large formulation for price expectations. Working with a 1904–65 dataset for the US, they estimated a relationship between unemployment and current and past values of both prices and wages, and of lagged unemployment. The hypothesis that there was no long-run

Phillips curve was accepted for 1904–29 and 1946–65, but not for the middle period. They found a short-run Phillips curve in each period but it was statistically less obvious for 1946–65.

The conclusion Lucas and Rapping drew from all this was that the existence of a short-run Phillips curve, in the absence of any long run trade-off, had been demonstrated in practice. They had already demonstrated the possibility in theory. Their major inference from the work was that statistical Phillips curves were highly unstable. In the absence of any understanding of causes, they felt that these observed relationships provided a 'weak foundation' for policy.

While Muth was cited amongst the references for the paper above, the idea of rational expectations in his sense was not exploited therein. Expectations of future prices were still being explained by reference to past *price* experience alone. By 1972, however, Lucas had a perfectly clear idea of the questions he meant to ask. The insight was that any attempt to use policy to shift the macroeconomic outcome along the Phillips curve could be frustrated by changes in expectations which shifted the curve itself. The objective of the paper in Lucas's eyes was:

> . . . to consider some of the issues involved in capturing this 'expectations theory' or 'natural rate hypothesis'[1] in an explicit, testable econometric model.
>
> [1] With no pretence to precision, let us define the natural rate hypothesis as the hypothesis that different time paths for the general price level will be associated with time paths of real output that do not differ *on average* . . .

Since Lucas was talking about testing the natural rate hypothesis, it seems that this cannot have been considered a 'hard core' element of the work.[18] He conceded that a negative correlation between unemployment and the inflation rate did exist in US time-series data. His feeling was that:

> . . . these observations raise a dual challenge to proponents of the natural rate hypothesis. The first involves econometric testing: if one rejects the use of the observed correlation . . . as a test of the existence of a usable trade-off, what is the alternative? Or is the natural rate hypothesis to be judged solely on 'theoretical' grounds? The second involves policy evaluation: if one cannot evaluate what alternative economic policies by extrapolating along estimated regression lines, what alternative exists? or is the goal of qualitative policy evaluation to be abandoned?[19]

At this stage it is a little hard to see just what constituted the hard core of the program. Since the natural rate was considered a candidate for testing, it clearly cannot qualify. One obtains the impression that the microeconomic basis offered by Lucas and Rapping might be crucial. The emphasis offered there on developing Phillips curve-type relationships on the basis of a household labour supply decision had some of the characteristics of hard core elements. It was taken as a fundamental principle from which the models were 'deduced', it was not subjected to test and without it the literature makes little sense.

Unfortunately for this tentative conclusion, early in this paper Lucas spoke of the labour supply model as one of a number of possible rationalizations for the Phillips curve trade-off: 'It may be supplemented by consideration of the firm's inventory problem (which involves the same sort of intertemporal substitution as the consumer's supply problem), by considering activities of workers other than work and "leisure" (for example, school, job search, and so forth), and in other ways as well.'[20] If the labour supply decision is merely one of a set of potential bases upon which an appropriate aggregate supply curve can be constructed, it can hardly constitute a hard core element. Lucas would require that whichever basis one used would have to be derivable from the individual maximizing behaviour, but this appears to be a more important element than the *particular* formulation used. The selection criteria for any such rationalization are production of the right type of supply curve and use of individual optimization. This appears to shift the search over to the supply curve itself. We shall see that it does indeed have hard core features – without it the subsequent literature makes no sense. A variety of microeconomic supports can be offered for it, and it is not tested (as we shall see), at least not alone.

Lucas went on to offer a critique of the expectations mechanisms explored in his two papers with Rapping. He cited two deficiencies. The first was that output gains did flow from an inflationary policy over an infinitely long period of adjustment. The other was that there always existed some inflationary policy which could produce sustained gains in real output, in an economy characterized by those expectations mechanisms. In his eyes, these were sufficient reasons to disqualify these formulations. They failed to disallow systematically biased expectations and conceded the chance of both short- and long-run trade-offs between inflation and real output.

The structure of Lucas's positive argument was simple. Take an aggregate supply curve of the type we have discussed. Add various hypotheses concerning expectations. In those cases which fail to produce a long-run natural rate outcome, *the expectational assumptions were to be discarded* (one notices, not the supply curve).

Lucas then found an expectations formulation which did produce the natural rate outcome when paired with his aggregate supply curve. It had been used by Muth,[21] and christened 'rational expectations': it required that price expectations be equal to the objective distribution of prices. To define such price expectations meant consideration of the determination of the distribution of prices and, to specify this distribution, Lucas added an aggregate demand function and policy rule to the aggregate supply function. From these a reduced-form price equation was obtainable which yielded the required distribution. Price expectations then became the mathematical expectation of this equation. With price expectations and prices both expressed as functions of the policy variables, of lagged dependent variables (if any), and of disturbance terms, the only difference between them lay in the absence of the disturbance terms in the expectations equation. The slope of the supply curve depended only on this difference and thus was independent of policy choice. This structure produced Lucas's desired result – the time path of income, on average, was independent of the time path of prices at the theoretical level.

The rationality of expectations formation required that individuals knew the reduced form price equation, or acted as if they did. Lucas did not 'explain' his choice of the rational expectations mechanism in any way, except in terms of the production of the natural rate outcome. At the behavioural level he simply referred the reader back to Muth.[22]

Looking back to that source, one finds that Muth had made three points concerning the hypothesis: (1) that it was potentially fruitful; (2) that, if the expectations were not moderately rational, economists could make a lot of money; and (3) that the appropriate test was to see whether 'rational' models explained data better than other theories. The first two are possible reasons for use of the theory. The criterion of fruitfulness enters the Lakatosian schema disguised as the positive heuristic, and certainly one can choose to work in a program because one feels that it has heuristic power. Unfortunately, before the fact, this is a highly subjective assessment. The second argument concerns the behavioural veracity of the hypothesis. Since Muth wrote this paper (in 1961), a lot of economists have indeed made a lot of money selling information. Before then Keynes and Ricardo (at least) did fairly handily from speculation. Thus, as a description of actual behaviour, the hypothesis appears rather dubious, undermined by Muth's own supportive argument and the evidence of history. Alone, with Lakatos applauding, we arrive at the third point. The rational expectations hypothesis will be judged by the corroborated novel predictions which arise from it in the course of its application.

Having satisfied the test of conformity with the supply curve in the production of the natural rate outcome, the rational expectations hypothesis was enshrined in the hard core. After this, within the literature, it was never questioned by its proponents, and strongly defended under challenge. Protective arguments developed.

5 POLICY RULES AND NOVEL FACTS

It is a little difficult to assess the status of the policy rule within the program. At this stage Lucas merely introduced it casually. He stated: 'By a *policy* we shall mean a (possibly randomized) rule giving the current value of x_t [the policy variable] as a function of the state of the system.'[23] A little later he added the suggestion that his model was capable of supporting quantitative policy evaluation. To this he appended the footnote:

> Provided, of course, that the policy satisfies the regularity conditions set out earlier in this section. Certainly, suppliers following Equation 1 [aggregate supply curve] could be 'gamed' into higher production by an aggregate demand sequence that kept them in continual surprise; the point is that such a sequence could not be generated by a policy rule that responds to the state of the economy in a stationary way.[24]

This clearly has the characteristic of a hard core assumption. Government is restricted to policy rules that respond to the economy in a stationary way.[25] Some futher assumptions become clear as we progress.

Having paired the supply formulation with the rational expectations hypothesis, Lucas had developed a model which produced a short-term positive correlation between income and policy. It also had a built-in, vertical aggregate supply curve. This format had the properties which featured in all subsequent discussions.

The parameters of the income equation (in reduced form) incorporated the parameters of the policy rule – since this policy rule had been introduced with the structural equations.[26] As Lucas argued, this suggested that the usual test of the natural rate, by checking to see whether the sum of the policy parameters in the income equation was zero, was not valid. The sum would differ with every different policy rule. Lucas suggested an alternative test. He said that one could first estimate the parameters of the policy rule. Taking these as given, the parameters of the solution equation in income could be reduced to nonlinear functions of the slope parameter of the aggregate supply equation. This meant that there was a specified relationship between the parameters of the income equation if the Lucas formulation were valid.

Testing to see whether this restriction were useful in reducing the error sum of squares compared with the unrestricted estimate was proposed as a procedure for checking the natural rate proposition.

In Lakatosian terms, the theory predicted a novel fact – the restriction on the parameters of this relation between income and policy variables. It looked as if the program was progressive. A hard core had emerged – the supply curve, rationality of expectations, and the policy rule construct. A novel fact had been predicted and a test of it suggested.

6 ADVERTISING, ADVOCACY AND COMMUNICATION

Lucas had 'explained' in terms of the new program just why alternative tests of the natural rate hypothesis had failed, and could be expected to fail. The 1972 paper, 'Econometric testing of the natural rate hypothesis' was invited, and Lucas saw himself as 'a spokesman for the deviant Friedman–Phelps view',[27] and he put the argument for the weaknesses of standard testing procedures rather as an advocate. This step was not progressive in Lakatosian terms within the program of new classical economics, nor is it degenerative. From that point of view it seems rather superfluous.[28] If people working in other programs use some alternative procedure to test a proposition one chooses to test within one's own program, it is likely that that procedure will appear 'wrong', 'inappropriate', 'inapplicable' or 'invalid'. In all likelihood, so will their conclusion. Each program should be expected to choose a different method, to arrive at its own conclusion.

Lucas's challenge can be interpreted in a number of ways. One is that rational expectations was not really a separate research program, or at this stage did not realize that it was. Alternatively one might suggest that there is an 'attack' function between competing programs that Lakatos did not recognize. Here we have the case where Program A casts doubt on the way Program B draws conclusions from its empirical researches. It was not a corroborated novel fact which the program was challenged to consider, but a challenge to the logic of its procedures. If this had stimulated a progressive problem shift within the other program(s), this attack process may be a creative (progressive) force which has been excluded from the Lakatosian model. Wallis's subsequent development of empirical procedures for escaping the difficulties suggested by Lucas was clearly a positive development for the theory of economic policy paradigm.[29]

This seems to be an avenue where rhetoric is important. Lakatos is concerned with the abstract logic of ideas and tends to treat the movement of particular scholars amongst programs as epiphenomenal although it is ultimately guided by the search for progressivity. However in practice and in the short run conversion is important; it brings additional brainpower to the program and hence accelerates its development, and in a concrete sense it also raises both the funding of the program with pecuniary benefits to its proponents and their professional status. To the extent that Lakatos is not concerned with the sociology of knowledge and restricts himself to its logic, he will not be able to incorporate all of the behaviours and ideas generated within a program into rational reconstruction of the program.

A later example of the same sort of behaviour is provided by the Sargent and Wallace horse-race papers (1975, 1976). These provided examples of conditions where different models would produce different outcomes, and especially of the situations in which different policy rules would have quite distinct macroeconomic implications. The function of these *examples* seems to have been to facilitate the change in focus of the program from the natural rate and onto the impotence of policy.[30]

We thus find two important sets of papers written (by my reconstruction) in order to communicate with other programs, or with scholars *not* in the program. To explain such behaviour we would have to modify the MSRPs to suggest some role for such cross-program communication. The most content-laden modification we can make to incorporate these examples is that communication is important at times of 'crisis'; for example, soon after the program has been formulated or after a problem shift. One might also imagine that the failure of a major experiment in some programs might require rationalization so that this could be another situation where communication would be important to maintain the coherence of a program but becomes crucial in times of major disjuncture in the program's development.

7 GENERAL EQUILIBRIUM

As well as this excursion into communication, into the proclamation of the merits of his program and the weaknesses of others, Lucas made a major foray into general equilibrium analysis in his (1972b) paper. Rather than going on to test his novel fact, which one imagines would have been the next step in a program guided by Imre Lakatos, Lucas took time to develop a different type of theoretical construct; 'an explicitly elaborated example, to my knowledge the first, or an economy in which some of these propositions [the characteristics of the US economy suggested by Friedman] can be formulated rigorously and shown to be valid'.[31]

Lakatos had suggested that a rigorous formulation of the argument of a program was essential. To find the rigorous development of an *example* as important does not seem to fit within his 'methodology of scientific research programmes'. And an example it truly was – people lived for two periods, worked for the first period only, were isolated onto two distinct 'islands' . The only function of government was to issue fiat money, and that only to the older generation. In the example, Lucas showed quite rigorously that a short-run Phillips curve relationship appeared as a result of inadequate local information. The classical neutrality proposition resulted in the absence of the information restriction.

This paper was quoted in virtually every subsequent work produced by the new classical economics in that decade. Fairly clearly, it was seen as important. The longest panegyric was delivered by Sargent and Wallace, and is quite informative about the light in which the work is seen within the program:

> The main ideas we are summarizing are due to Robert E. Lucas, Jr., and were advanced by him most eloquently in the context of a stochastic general equilibrium model. Lucas's paper analyses policy questions in what we regard as the proper way, namely, in the context of a consistent general equilibrium model. This present paper is a popularization that fails to indicate how Lucas's neutrality propositions are derived from a consistent general equilibrium model with optimizing agents. It is easy to overturn the 'neutrality' results that we derive below from an ad hoc structure by making ad hoc changes in the structure. The advantage of Lucas's model is that ad hockeries are given much less of a role and, consequently the neutrality proposition he obtains is seen to be a consequence of individual agents' optimizing behaviour.[32]

The Lucas paper added no novel fact to that known before. Equally it involved no verbal legerdemain to shrug off criticism. Being merely one example amidst a large number of possibilities, it did not provide a sufficient logical base for the program. Its function, especially in the use to which it was put by Sargent and Wallace in the above quotation, was as part of the negative heuristic. Many re-formulations of the underlying relationships could destroy the neutrality outcome. Such modifications were to be considered invalid (that is, not worthy of consideration as criticisms) unless they were based in a general equilibrium model of the type Lucas had used. That rules out a huge amount of what has been, and is being, written in macroeconomics. The frequency with which the work is cited seems to underscore the importance of this particular defensive function.

To understand this work better we have to consider the intellectual journey upon which Lucas had embarked earlier. Looking back to his papers of the late 1960s such as Lucas (1965) and (1966) and Lucas and Prescott (1971), one is impressed by Lucas's determination to provide a sound and rigorous microeconomic justification for investment behaviour. The earliest of these papers focuses upon the investment behaviour of a firm facing given prices while constrained by gestation and depreciation lags, then the feedback effect from prices is allowed for, and eventually stochastic demand effects are incorporated.

Putting this work on the investment side together with the Lucas and Rapping research which attempted to find a sound microeconomic formulation of the labour supply function which could be aggregated to an economy-wide supply function, we obtain a rounder picture of Lucas as a scholar with the broader research program of the 1960s and 1970s in the search for microfoundations of macroeconomics.

If we are to understand Lucas as operating simultaneously within both a broad and a narrow research program, the general equilibrium thrust to his work is more easily explicable. Within macroeconomics research, broadly, the search for a microfoundation for macroeconomics was a fundamental element of the positive heuristic. Great leaps in understanding of consumption functions, in investment behaviour and in modelling the demand for money had arisen from the pursuit of the microeconomic maximizing paradigm. How then could we expect anything more of Lucas, as a member of this broad program, than that he would attempt to incorporate his rational expectations models within this general equilibrium framework?[33]

But, analysed in the narrow sense of the 'new classical economics program' the function of this general equilibrium preoccupation is not clear. It served no clear part of the positive heuristic of the program. Unlike the microfoundations of macroeconomics more generally it generates no testable hypotheses; there is no increase in content. The role played by the general equilibrium method was purely negative; in the eyes of the insiders it served to invalidate specifications of the place of expectations in supply which otherwise would have contradicted the key predictions of the framework. It was by reference to this structure that other research was labelled 'ad hoc' and deemed unworthy of attention.

If we are to accept Lucas's own reconstruction of the influences on him in this period a key role in his conviction about the microfoundations program was played by Phelps in his introduction to Phelps (1970). That author wrote

> There is now emerging a new kind of microeconomics of production, labor supply, wage and price decision – a body of theory that goes beyond neoclassical intertemporal equilibrium. The theory . . . sticks doggedly to the neoclassical postulates of lifetime expected utility maximization and net worth maximization, it makes no appeal to faulty perceptions and it does not fundamentally require that price setters economize on their decision-making time. . . . The theoretical departure that is common to these otherwise neoclassical papers is their removal of the Walrasian postulate of complete information. (p. 4)

To understand Lucas we have to appreciate his work in this broader context.

8 THE COMMITMENT TO TESTING

Lucas made the first attempt at corroboration of the novelty of the program.[34] It looked rather like a test of the natural rate hypothesis, but did in fact incorporate the rational expectations perspective in its specifics. Recall that the natural rate hypothesis was presented as the proposition that the time path of output was independent of the time path of prices on average. Lucas re-expressed this as the conjecture that, according to the hypothesis, changes in the average inflation rate should not increase the average output (relating to its natural rate). Not knowing the natural rate, Lucas could hardly use this null-relationship as a testable proposition. He instead utilized the idea that this relationship in the means implied a relationship in the variances.[35] This provided the fulcrum for the test.

The lever came from the rational expectations hypothesis. Under those conditions, and with the policy rule, Lucas was able to show that the formulation implied an inverse relationship between the variance of nominal income and the slope of the apparent macroeconomic trade-off in the economy under test. 'The greater this variance, the less "favourable" the trade off' became the null hypothesis. It must be ceded the status of a valid test of the novel fact – it was a relationship generated out of the joint hypothesis, but quite distinct from anything offered by alternative theories.

The test was heartening to the theory rather than corroborative of it. The *two* countries with highly variable national income histories had very steep trade-offs, exactly in accordance with the theory. Almost all of the effect of any change in nominal income was taken up by price increases. The *sixteen* examples with more stable records had much gentler slopes to their real income equations.

There were, however, some worrisome features of the test. The complete dichotomization of the sample group leads one to fear that there may have been some other differences between the two groups of countries not captured in the model. This fear was compounded by the *very* low R^2 (=0.018) for the fit of the income equation for Argentina, one of the peculiar set of two. Sargent in his comments on this work referred to problems that Lucas had with the data. All in all, it probably has to be thrown into the 'verdict pending' basket.

Following the partial success of this test procedure, the new classical paradigm persisted with the empirical validation of its novel facts, but with very little success. Sargent was closely involved in most of this research and produced one of the memorable phrases in the literature when he suggested (1976a, p. 233) that his results were 'not obscenely at variance with the data'. This might be the summary comment on the literature. Generally there has been scant evidence in support of the propositions of the new classical economics.

The attitudes of Lucas, Sargent and Barro to testing seems in the very best Lakatosian tradition. Again in the case of Lucas it was a habit which carried over from his work on investment. Even when he was working in a theoretical vein in pursuit of optimal investment policies for a firm, he was sensitive to the needs of testing: 'In order to maintain contact with empirical investment studies, the discussion of each model concludes with the difference equation in gross or net investment which provides the natural discrete time approximation to the continuous optimal plan' (Lucas, 'Distributed Lags', p. 39). The introduction of rational expectations into that literature is justified as 'an uncertain future is introduced into an adjustment-cost type model of the firm, and the optimal response to this undertainty is studied in an attempt to integrate variables . . . into the existing [empirical] theory' (Lucas and Prescott, 'Investment under Uncertainty', p. 659.

Maddock (1984) argues that the failure of the program to produce empirical support, and the necessity in its testing procedures to use ad hoc fixes to skirt the problem of persistence, was the main reason for the problem shift of the mid-1970s. There, under the weight of empirical failures with tests oriented towards the natural rate hypothesis, the program was re-oriented to establish the neutrality of policy as its central hypothesis.

From the very first days of the program, right through the 1970s, the new classical research paradigm sought empirical justification of its 'facts'. The suggestion above that the search for progressiveness and for its empirical support is the essential element of the Lakatosian model of science is confirmed by the behaviour of the scholars involved in this program:

> Obviously there is a large gap between the highly abstract model of 'Expectations and the Neutrality of Money' and an econometric model capable of giving reliable, quantative assessments of the consequences of alternative monetary- and fiscal-policy rules. Much of my work over the past decade [to 1981] has been directed towards trying to narrow this gap

is Lucas's own explanation of his intellectual endeavours.[36] He and his collaborators sought novelty and 'tortured the data in the hope that nature would confess' that they were right. Again in this they belong to a strong empiricist tradition in American economics.

It seems that there is considerable evidence from new classical economics of the Lakatosian assumption that the drive behind the development of a research program is the pursuit of progressiveness and a striving towards empirical validation.

9 CONCLUSIONS

This was the way the program emerged. The hard core had solidified, testing had started, and an important defensive mechanism was in place. While a number of subsequent works can be considered to have increased the robustness of the structure and to have actually modified it somewhat, the first-round hardening process was complete. From this evidence it seems that the Lakatosian model of the development of a research program provides an adequate framework with which to explain the sequence of literature associated with the new classical tradition. There are, however, several weaknesses in the fit of the model.[37]

One arises out of the failure of Lakatos to consider the possibility that scholars would simultaneously belong to more than one research program. The emergence of a new program requires a period during which researchers will be working within an older theory structure and will at some point jump to an incompatible framework. Lucas worked as a standard neo-classical microeconomist on problems of the micro-foundations for macroeconomics who suddenly realized that an idea he had used in a microcontext produced startling results in macro-economics. The power of the novel ideas clearly set him running with them, simultaneously exploring their implications, considering their destructive potential for the standard theories, and trying hard to build a sound theoretical foundation for his arguments.

Lakatos does not prepare us well for this early formative stage of a program. He provides no guidance as to why Lucas should have maintained the supply formulation and modified the expectations structure after the Lucas and Rapping papers. Why was the program born?

A second major weakness of the MSRP lies in its failure to address adequately the social aspects of academic research. Lakatos recognizes that a well-funded research program will persist even if it is not very progressive but ignores the corollary that scientists in pursuit of funding can be expected to market their product aggressively. While value-laden, the term 'rational expectations' was known within the profession from the early 1960s without providing any apparent incentive for all and sundry to use it because it was obviously the right way to model expectations. No, the powerful ability of the ideas to convert awaited the combination of the expectations and supply formulations in a way which produced startling results. What is more, the ideas were accompanied by a telling critique of the alternative program concerned with the theory of policy.

The ability of the program to capture the interest of the generation of economists being trained in the 1970s was crucial to its great popularity in that decade and perhaps to the rapid exhaustion of its potential. The ability to convert was partly explained by the advertising undertaken on its behalf. There is a clear feedback from advertisement to recruitment, and from recruitment to the pace of exploration of the positive heuristic of any program. It is an element of the sociology of knowledge rather than its logic but the two are related in a way that lies outside Lakatos. A simple modification would suggest that communication will be necessary at times of major disjuncture in the development of a program.

Another element which seems deficient in Lakatos concerns the definition of research programs. If we regard Lucas as having originated the new classical research program, and are obliged to interpret his work within that program, then the general equilibrium component seems to belong to its negative heuristic. Its function was to allow researchers to proceed without being distracted by a whole class of macroeconomics-based critics. On the other hand it would be possible to understand the work of Lucas as being part of the search for a new microeconomic foundation for observed macroeconomic phenomena, and his use of rational expectations as simply the attempt to incorporate expectations within that endeavour. The work might also be seen as a standard working out of the positive heuristic of neo-classical economics, of its extension into the modelling of expectations, something which had been on the research agenda since the work of Simon, Muth and others in the 1950s. Others of course will see the new classical economists as part of the classical tradition in macroeconomics, and of course the label used reinforces this suggestion. If Lucas and his co-workers are classical economists, then the general equilibrium component is a standard part of the hard core beliefs of program members and quite unsurprising.

Thus one is led to the possibility that the general equilibrium element to the program is part of

1. the positive heuristic, if the program is part of the microfoundation literature;
2. the hard core, if it is part of the classical economic tradition; and
3. the negative heuristic, if Lucas and the others comprise their own 'rational expectations macrotheory' program.

While there are underlying difficulties with the definition of just which program we are addressing, the empirical focus is quite clear. Lucas and Sargent operated within the Lakatosian guidelines in the way that they developed novel facts and then searched for corrobation. Virtually all of their articles have a commitment to testability. Perhaps the most precise statement of their underlying beliefs is given in their volume (1981):

> Yet how, exactly, does the economist who is persuaded of the usefulness of [an] idea, or at least invested enough to give it an honest test, alter the way he practices his trade? A full answer to this question is, we believe, a central issue on the current research agenda of time-series economics and dynamic economic theory. (p. xi)

There does not seem to be any evidence from the working of this program that the fundamental Lakatosian assumption that science is about the pursuit of progressivity is in any way vitiated.

In the introduction I suggested that a Lakatosian method of rational reconstruction would start from the literature, classify its hard core elements, and then go on to interpret other elements according to the various functions he laid out. It is now clear that such an approach provides a difficult test of the method. By starting with the full body of literature one is starting from what economists actually do, and trying to rationalize it. To the extent that behaviour is not rational such a method will fail to explain academic activity adequately. But even more, to the extent that behaviour is motivated by ends other than progressivity, Lakatos is certain to fail. The nature of those failures provides the raw material from which an 'improved' methodology of scientific research programs can be developed.

NOTES

1. See Maddock (1984) for an analysis which complements this paper. In that other work I traced the workings of the program focusing particularly on the transition of interest from the natural rate of unemployment towards the impotence of policy which occurred around the mid-1970s.
2. Singly, they can be used in a variety of ways and produce a variety of results. Here we are concerned with their use in tandem.
3. Milton Friedman, 'Monetary Policy'.
4. Variously these hypotheses are characterized as the rational expectations hypothesis, the natural rate of unemployment hypothesis, or a combination of the two. The distinction should always be clear from the context.
5. Lucas has subsequently justified his work as being an essential part of an older research program. Lucas says, 'My own research has been concerned almost exclusively with the attempt to discover a useful theoretical explanation of business cycles' (Lucas, *Studies in Business Cycle Theory*, p. 2) and goes on to say: 'Research during the 1970s forced me . . . progressively . . . towards a . . . view that seemed to me essentially the same in substance, however different in method, as the view taken by many pre-Keynesian theorists.'
6. Lakatos, 'Methodology', p. 133, footnote 2.
7. The discussion is mainly concentrated here but flows over into the later sections with the argument summarized in Section 9.
8. Milton Friedman, 'Monetary Policy'.
9. Lucas and Rapping, 'Real Wages'.
10. Lipsey, 'Unemployment and the Change of Money Wages'.
11. Lucas and Rapping, 'Real Wages', p. 748.
12. Ibid., p. 722.
13. Ibid., p. 731.
14. Ibid., p. 754.
15. Ibid., p. 748.
16. Lucas and Rapping, 'Expectations and the Phillips Curve'. Lucas notes (p. 5, *Studies in the Business Cycle*) that Friedman's 1968 paper was given when he and Rapping were writing their prior paper.
17. Ibid., p. 344.
18. The very definition of hard core is usually 'not subject to change within the program' so this point seems obvious.
19. Ibid., p. 51.
20. Ibid., p. 52.
21. Muth, 'Rational Expectations'.
22. Lucas, 'Testing the Natural Rate', p. 55.
23. Ibid.
24. Ibid., p. 56.
25. Definitions of the different classes of rules are given in any systems textbook.
26. The role of the policy rules in the model came to central stage after the problem shift in the program in the mid-1970s but at this stage it seems simply to be necessary to generate the rational expectations solution by closing the system.
27. Lucas, *Studies in Business Cycle Theory*, p. 10.
28. This clearly depends on how one defines programs. An argument by rational expectations theorists can be informational to another program while it has no progressive role in its own. The paper is a perfect example of an attempt at dialogue between competing research paradigms: Lucas was invited as a token, and put his case in the hope of establishing communication.
29. Wallis, 'Econometric Implications', shows that the appropriate testing procedure is one which separates the structure of 'exogenous' processes such as policy from the economic structure and allows the traditional view of econometric policy evaluation

to be maintained. This response can be viewed as a positive development by the theory of economic policy program in response to the Lucas critique.

30. Maddock (1984) argues this case in some detail.
31. Lucas, 'Expectations and Neutrality', p. 104.
32. Sargent and Wallace, 'Theory of Economic Policy', p. 169.
33. In his interview with Klamer, Lucas relates 'this business of microfoundation has been kicking around for years. Rapping's and my paper is pretty conventional; that's what everyone was doing. You take a sector, you get some kind of maximum problem for a household or a firm, you work it out, and then you hope that it suggests some kind of fairly simple regression equation . . . That was a very common enterprise' (p. 36).
34. Lucas, 'Evidence on Trade-Offs'.
35. Various rational expectations arguments are couched in terms of other than first moments. Here the idea is that people are less likely to confuse real and nominal effects in an environment of frequent nominal changes.
36. Lucas, *Studies in Business Cycle Theory*, p. 13.
37. I use the term 'fit' deliberately. I take the MSRP as the theory, and the sequence of papers by Lucas *et al.* as the data it seeks to explain.

REFERENCES

Carter, Michael and Maddock, Rodney (1984), *Rational Expectations: Macroeconomics for the 1980s?* (London: Macmillan).

Friedman, Milton (1966), 'What Price Guideposts?', in George P. Schulz and Robert Z. Aliber (eds), *Guidelines: Informal Controls and the Market Place*, pp. 52–76 (Chicago: Chicago University Press).

—— (1968) 'The Role of Monetary Policy', *American Economic Review*, **58**, March, pp.1–17.

Gordon, Robert J. (1976a), 'Recent Developments in the Theory of Inflation and Unemployment', *Journal of Monetary Economics*, **2**, April, pp. 185–219.

—— (1976b), 'Can Econometric Policy Evaluation be Salvaged? – A Comment', in "The Phillips Curve and Labor Markets', pp. 47–61, supplement to the *Journal of Monetary Economics* **1**, April, ed. by Karl Brunner and Allan Meltzer.

Granger, Clive W.J. (1969), 'Investigating Causal Relationships by Econometric Models and Cross-Spectral Methods', *Econometrica*, **37**, July, pp. 424–38.

Hall, Robert E. (1975), 'The Rigidity of Wages and the Persistence of Unemployment', *Brookings Papers on Economic Activity*, **2**, pp. 301–35.

Klamer, Argo (1984), *Conversations with Economists* (Totawa, New Jersey: Rowman and Allanheld).

Lakatos, Imre (1970a), 'Falsification and the Methodology of Scientific Research Programmes', in Imre Lakatos and Alan Musgrave (eds), *Criticism and the Growth of Knowledge*, pp. 91–195 (Cambridge: Cambridge University Press).

—— (1970b), 'History of Science and its Rational Reconstructions', paper presented at the Biennial Meeting of the Philosophical Association, October.

—— (1976), *Proofs and Refutations*, ed. by John Worrall and Elie Zahar (Cambridge: Cambridge University Press).

Lipsey, R.G. (1960), 'The Relation Between Unemployment and the Rate of Change of Money Wage Rates: A Further Analysis', *Econometrica*, **27**, February, pp. 1–31.

Lucas, Robert E. Jr. (1965), 'Distributed Lags and Optimal Investment Policy' in R. Lucas and T. Sargent (eds), *Rational Expectation and Econometric Practice*, pp. 39–54, previously unpublished.

—— (1966), 'Optimal Investment with Rational Expectations', in R. Lucas and T. Sargent (eds), *Rational Expectation and Econometric Practice*, pp. 55–66, previously unpublished.

—— (1972a), 'Econometric Testing of the Natural Rate Hypothesis', in *Otto Eckstein (ed.), The Economics of Price Determination Conference*, pp. 50–9, Board of Governors of the Federal Reserve System.

—— (1972b), 'Expectations and the Neutrality of Money', *Journal of Economic Theory*, **4**, April, pp. 103–24.

—— 'Some International Evidence on Output Inflation Trade-Offs', *American Economic Review*, **63**, June, pp. 326–34.

—— 'An Equilibrium Model of the Business Cycle', *Journal of Political Economy*, **83**, December, pp. 1113–44.

—— (1976), 'Econometric Policy Evaluation: A Critique', in Karl Brunner and Allan Meltzer (eds), *The Phillips Curve and Labor Markets*, pp. 19–46, supplement to the *Journal of Monetary Economics*, **1**, April.

—— (1981a), *Studies in Business Cycle Theory* (Cambridge, Mass.: MIT Press).

—— (1981b), 'Distributed Lags and Optimal Investment Policy', in R. Lucas and T. Sargent (eds), *Rational Expectations and Econometric Practice*, pp. 39–54.

Lucas, Robert E. Jr. and Prescott, E.C. (1971), 'Investment under Uncertainty', *Econometrica*, **39**, 5, pp. 659–81.

Lucas, Robert E. Jr. and Rapping, Leonard (1969a), 'Price Expectations and the Phillips Curve', *American Economic Review*, **59**, June. pp. 670–80.

—— (1969b), 'Real Wages, Employment and Inflation', *Journal of Political Economy*, September pp. 721–54.

Lucas, Robert E. Jr. and Sargent, Thomas (1981) (eds), *Rational Expectations and Econometric Practice*, vol. 1 and 2 (Minneapolis: University of Minnesota Press).

Maddock, Rodney (1984), 'Rational Expectations Macrotheory: a Lakatosian case study in program adjustment', *History of Political Economy*, **16**, Summer, pp. 291–310.

Muth, John F. (1961), 'Rational Expectations and the Theory of Price Movements', *Econometrica*, **29**, July, pp. 315–35.

—— (1981), 'Optimal Properties of Exponentially Weighted Forecasts', in R. Lucas and T. Sargent (eds), *Rational Expectations and Econometric Practice*, pp. 23–32.

Phelps, Edmund S. (1967), 'Phillips Curves, Expectations of Inflation and Optimal Unemployment over Time', *Economica*, **34**, August, pp. 254–81.

Phelps, Edmund S. *et al.* (1970), *Microeconomic Foundations of Employment and Inflation Theory* (New York: W.W. Norton).

Sargent, Thomas J. (1973), 'Rational Expectations, the Real Rate of Interest and the Natural Rate of Unemployment', *Brookings Papers on Economic Activity*, **2**, pp. 429–72.

—— (1976a), 'A Classical Macroeconomic Model for the United States', *Journal of Political Economy*, **84**, April, pp. 207–37.

—— (1976b), 'The Observational Equivalence of Natural and Unnatural Rate Theories of Macroeconomics', *Journal of Political Economy*, **84**, June, pp. 631–40.

Sargent, Thomas J. and Neftci, Salih (1978), 'A Little Bit of Evidence on the Natural Rate Hypothesis from the U.S.', *Journal of Monetary Economics*, **4** April, pp. 315–19.

Sargent, Thomas J. and Wallace, Neil (1975), 'Rational Expectations, the Optimal Monetary Instrument and the Optimal Money Supply Rule', *Journal of Political Economy*, **83**, April, pp. 241–55.

—— (1976), 'Rational Expectations and the Theory of Economic Policy', *Journal of Monetary Economics*, **2**, April, pp. 169–84.

Wallis, K.F. (1980), 'Econometric Implications of the Rational Expectations Hypothesis', *Econometrica*, **48**, January, pp. 49–73.

COMMENT ON MADDOCK

Alessandro Vercelli

Maddock's discussion is very stimulating and covers a wide range. In order to organize the discussion of its contents I will distinguish two basic issues which are somewhat intermingled in the paper: (1) *lessons from Lakatos*: application of Lakatos's conceptual framework for interpreting the genesis of new classical economics; (2) *lessons for Lakatos*: reflections on the case study to appraise the validity of the Lakatosian model.

The first issue assumes the validity of the Lakatosian framework to find a convincing interpretation of the genesis of new classical macroeconomics, while the second assumes an interpretation of the same genetic process in order to appraise the validity of the Lakatosian model. From a logical point of view the two questions must be kept rigorously separated to avoid circularity: we cannot use an interpretation inspired by the use of the Lakatosian framework for appraising its validity. However we can avoid circularity by basing the appraisal of Lakatos's model upon a comparison between the interpretation inspired by the Lakatosian framework and a different interpretation assumed to be independently valid. This different interpretation is just hinted at by Maddock in purely pre-analytic terms. Circularity is then avoided but only at the risk of giving an impression of arbitrariness (particularly if we abstract from the other works of the author on the same subject: Maddock, 1984; Carter and Maddock, 1984).

Notwithstanding the title, I think that the first issue – *lessons from Lakatos* – occupies most of the chapter and the best of it. I will thus limit myself to discussing this aspect.

The author discusses first the preliminary question as to whether new classical economics can be considered a research program in the sense of Lakatos. Since the new theory rejects some of the unrefuted content of preceding macroeconomic theories it qualifies as a distinct research program and thus as a legitimate object of the Lakatosian model. So far so good.

The author then has to identify the hard core of the new research program. This is the central and most delicate point of the chapter. The choice of the author falls on the two following hypotheses: rational expectations about prices and the new classical aggregate supply function, that is 'the slope of the aggregate supply function in price space depends upon the difference between prices and expected prices'. The hard core of the research program is thus characterized by the acceptance of both these hypotheses: 'The willingness to hold both simultaneously will be taken to define work within the new classical economics program' (p. 339). Although this choice is well argued, I have doubts about it.

The rational expectations hypothesis is considered by Lucas himself as just a 'technical model-building principle'. In addition, he believes that 'recent research utilizing this principle has reinforced many of the policy recommendations of Milton Friedman and other postwar monetarists but has contributed few, if any, original policy proposals (Lucas, 1981, pp. 1–2). Lucas also made clear on different occasions that what he is really committed to is the adoption of a hypothesis on expectations formation fully consistent with the classical principles of optimization and equilibrium. The hypothesis of rational expectations is so far certainly the best existing theory of expectations formation consistent with the classical principles, but he gives the impression of being prepared to abandon it for a better one having the same requisites. While the hypothesis of rational expectations amounts to equating the subjective distribution to the objective distribution for the relevant variables, what is really required is simply an explicit theoretical link between them (see Lucas and Sargent, 1981, p. xvi). Moreover it came to be progressively recognized that the different results of new classical models depend on the market clearing assumption rather than on the hypothesis of rational expectations (see, for example, Tobin, 1980). This assumption has been applied also by authors not belonging to the new classical school, who obtained completely different results (for an application to Keynesian economics see, for example, Begg 1982). Maddock himself maintained in his book on rational expectations that 'there are a variety of models, even Keynesian ones, which assume expectations are formed rationally but which allow for an effective demand management' (Carter and Maddock, 1984, pp. 2–3).

The Lucas aggregate supply hypothesis gets closer to the heart of the new classical research program. However it is just one possible explanation of the observed short-run correlation between prices and quantities consistent with the classical dichotomy principle. In the 1980s different explanations consistent with the classical dichotomy were suggested by members of the school (see, for example, the literature on real business cycles which emphasizes technological surprises rather than price surprises).

The above observations suggest that the two hypotheses considered by Maddock as the hard core of Lucas's research program are nothing but a new specification of the classical research program. What is the *differentia specifica*? It is, in my opinion, essentially methodological. According to Lucas, any macroeconomic proposition, to be scientifically acceptable, must be properly microfounded on Walrasian general equilibrium theory. What is really crucial is a commitment to what I propose to call 'pure-equilibrium method', that is, the two assumptions that agents always optimize and that markets always clear. These assumptions together constitute the hard core of new classical economics. The proof is that only in this case is Lucas not prepared to subject the validity of his assumptions to empirical tests. He considers them conditions of intelligibility which cannot be questioned.

Lucas and his closest collaborators are fully aware that what is *new* in their classical research program is mainly methodological (see, for example, the statement quoted by Maddock in note 5). The classical research program is not necessarily committed to *general* equilibrium. On the contrary, the variety of classical macroeconomics criticized by Keynes (represented, for example, by Pigou) was heavily influenced by Marshallian partial equilibrium. Analogously, Friedmanite macroeconomics is inspired by the Marshallian method rather than by the Walrasian method. Moreover, what is really crucial, neither Marshall nor Walras, nor any other classical economist before Lucas, has ever advocated a pure-equilibrium method.

This suggested interpretation of the hard core of new classical economics' research program puts the 'Lucas critique' in a light completely different from that of Maddock. While according to him the 'Lucas critique' does not fit within the 'new classical research program ', in my opinion it gives what Lucas believes to be the ultimate justification of this research program. Only macroeconomic models properly founded on general equilibrium parameters may offer, according to Lucas, a reliable support for policy-evaluation exercises. Why it is so is explained in great detail by Lucas and Sargent in the introduction to the famous book on rational expectations (1981). Basically the same reasoning is repeated by Lucas in Chapter 2 of his latest book (1987) (the quite sophisticated reasoning is summarized and characterized in Vercelli, 1987).

I would like to end these comments by praising Maddock's paper for its stimulating conceptual framework and for its accurate and enlightening reconstruction of the genesis of the new classical research program.

References

Begg, D.K.H. (1982), 'Rational expectations, wage rigidity, and involuntary unemployment', *Oxford Economic Papers*, pp. 23–47.

Carter, M. and Maddock, R. (1984), *Rational Expectations: Macroeconomics for the 1980s*? (London: Macmillan).
Lucas, R.E. Jr. (1981), *Studies in Business Cycle Theory* (Oxford: Basil Blackwell).
—— (1987);, *Models of Business Cycles* (Oxford: Basil Blackwell).
Lucas, R.E. Jr. and Sargent, T.J. (eds) (1981) *Rational Expectations and Econometric Practice* (London: Allen & Unwin).
Maddock, R. (1984), 'Rational Expectations Macrotheory: a Lakatosian case study in program adjustment', *History of Political Economy*, **16**, pp. 291–310.
Tobin, J. (1980), 'Are New Classical Models Plausible Enough to Guide Policy?', *Journal of Money, Credit and Banking*, **12**, pp. 788–99.
Vercelli, A. (1987), *Keynes dopo Lucas. I fondamenti della macroeconomia* (Rome: NIS).

11. Scientific Research Program or Tribe? A Joint Appraisal of Lakatos and the New Classical Macroeconomics

Kevin D. Hoover[1]

> Our craving for generality has another main source, our preoccupation with the method of science . . . Instead of 'craving for generality' I could also have said 'the contemptuous attitude towards the particular case'. (Ludwig Wittgenstein, *The Blue Book*)

The new classical macroeconomics, sometimes known as the rational-expectations school or, more accurateley, as market-clearing macro-economics, dominates macroeconomic analysis today. This is not to say that most macroeconomists have enlisted in its ranks; rather its troops occupy the high ground.[2] Robert Lucas, Thomas Sargent, Robert Barro and its other leaders set the agenda for modern macroeconomics. With rare exceptions, other macroeconomists are either partisans in a guerilla war against new classicism or collaborators (not committed, but going along, especially on matters of method) or they are raising an opposing army (so far without success) that will emulate the organization and discipline of the new classicals while aiming to achieve opposing ends.

The new classical macroeconomics has been the dominant school for the past decade and has existed in a recognizable form for a decade before that. It is not too early to ask how it is related to alternative approaches, how it achieved its ascendancy and where it is going. When new classicism was on the rise, two views of the history and methodology of science – Thomas Kuhn's (1970) scientific revolutions and Imre Lakatos's (1970) scientific research programs – dominated discussions in philosophical circles. Lakatos's approach largely supplanted Kuhn's and subsequently fell out of favour itself. The fashions of the philosophy of science reach economics only after a long and variable lag: Lakatos retains some currency among economists. My approach will be to ask, should it? Does Lakatos's theory of the history of science shed much light on the emergence of the new classical macroeconomics? Does the new classical macroeconomics constitute a scientific research program?

Using economics, and more particularly the development of the new classical macroeconomics, as a test case, I shall argue that Lakatos's approach does not capture the essential features of scientific progress. In the process, I shall isolate – following hints provided by Kuhn – a better description of scientific progress. And, finally, I shall apply this new approach to the case of the new classical macroeconomics.

1 A NEW CLASSICAL RESEARCH PROGRAM

As is well known, for Lakatos the unit of description and the unit of appraisal of scientific endeavour is the scientific research program, comprising a hard core, a positive heuristic and a negative heuristic.[3]

A scientific research program is theoretically progressive if the positive heuristic generates models with increasing content: that is, models that account for the success of earlier models, while adding novel implications. If these implications are *intermittently* confirmed by empirical observation, or even if apparent anomalies can be reinterpreted retrospectively to support the model, the program is empirically progressive. Anomalies are counted against the program only when it fails to progress theoretically and empirically in these senses.

The methodology of scientific research programs suggests several questions about the new classical macroeconomics: is it a distinct program? If so, what is the program? How did it develop? Is it progressing? To answer these questions in the spirit of Lakatos, one must offer a programmatic interpretation.

The hard core of the new classical macroeconomics is encapsulated in the following propositions:[4]

HC1 The economy consists fundamentally of self-interested individuals (methodological individualism).

HC2 The economy is characterized by complete interdependence (general equilibrium).

HC3 Real economic decisions depend only on real magnitudes and not on nominal or monetary magnitudes (no money illusion).[5]

HC4 The economy is in continuous equilibrium (that is, every agent successfully optimizes up to the limits of his information).

HC5 Agents' expectations are the same as forecasts generated by the true economic model of the economy (rational expectations).[6]

The negative heuristic of the new classical program could be summed up in the simple injunction, 'do not violate any hard core propositions'. The new classicals, however, border on the puritanical in their lust for prohibitions; so it is well to be more specific.

NH1 Avoid underived supply and demand curves (no ad hoc models).
NH2 Avoid irrational expectations.
NH3 Avoid partial equilibrium.
NH4 Avoid non-neutrality.
NH5 Avoid disequilibrium.
NH6 Avoid aggregation.
NH7 Avoid unidentified reduced forms.

The characteristic practices of the new classical macroeconomics can be summarized in the positive heuristic, which includes propositions something like the following:

PH1 Construct general equilibrium, dynamic optimization models.
PH2 Use representative agent models.[7]
PH3 Test over-identifying restrictions.
PH4 Test the ability of models to mimic the variances and covariances of the actual economy.[8]
PH5 Use state-of-the-art mathematical techniques.

2 A TRIBAL VIEW

The new classical program just laid out is typical – neither better nor worse than similar exercises constructed for other areas in economics.[9] The reader may nonetheless get the impression that it is essentially arbitrary. The propositions convey a real sense of the nature of the new classical macroeconomics, but it is difficult to say that there are not other sets of propositions and injunctions that differ in some points of substance and form that would serve equally well as a description of the new classical program. The difficulty arises, I believe, because the Lakatosian framework implies too sharp a distinction between what is in the program and what is outside it. Its borders are too definite and too well patrolled, its customs post too heavily manned. The plausible program that I have set out does not inspire the necessary conviction because, in some loose sense, *the new classical macroeconomics is a research program*; however, in Lakatos's particular sense, *it is not a 'scientific research program'*. What is more, I doubt that anything is a scientific research program. To progress beyond vague doubts, we must now consider in greater detail how Lakatos's scientific research programs are too restrictive as descriptions of the scientific endeavour. We shall then consider an alternative description.

The Problem of Individuation

How many research programs are there in economics? Economists give varied answers. Some see each sub-discipline as representing its own research program. Others believe there are but a few competing programs. Remenyi (1979) regards neoclassical economics as the one successful program, alternative programs such as institutionalism and Keynesianism having been driven off the field. Weintraub (1985, ch. 8 and p. 141) adopts a similar position, identifying Walrasian general equilibrium theory as the hard core. Mirowski (1988, ch. 1, esp. pp. 16, 24) likewise finds neoclassical economics to be the dominant (although he is a partisan for a competing program), but he finds the hard core in 'energetics', the foundational metaphor borrowed from physics.

Two points arise from these varied answers. First, there is real disagreement about what programs are currently active and what their nature is. Second, some commentators take a broad view, others a narrow one: neoclassical economics is one big program or a group of specialized programs not in direct competition.[10] Lakatos (1970, p. 132) gives warrant to switching back and forth between the broad and the narrow view: 'Even science as a whole can be regarded as a huge research programme with Popper's supreme heuristic rule: "devise conjectures which have more empirical content than their predecessors".'

Is the new classical macroeconomics a scientific research program, or is it nested in a larger program? Such questions arise with respect to other sub-disciplines with such regularity that Remenyi (1979) has developed a theory of core/demi-core interaction. In Remenyi's scheme, neoclassical economics is a single program in which the various sub-disciplines are nested. Each sub-discipline has its own core, the *demi-core*, which is hard relative to its own protective belt and the other nested programs, although not hard with respect to the hard core of neoclassical economics. Weintraub (1985, ch. 8) uses the core/demi-core model to place general equilibrium analysis in the centre of neoclassical economics while at the same time recognizing the mutual relative autonomy of its sub-disciplines. A glance at the hard core propositions identified for the new classical macroeconomics above is evidence enough that it could be cast as a sub-program of Walrasian general equilibrium theory with HC1, 2 and 4 overlapping with the Walrasian hard core and HC3 and 5 differentiating the demi-core (HC1–5) from the hard core.

The core/demi-core analysis, however, strikes me as a fairly desperate response to the proliferation of apparently separate programs that nonetheless have common features. It subverts the force of the metaphor of the hard core and the protective belt: the fortress – an impenetrable citadel surrounded by elaborate defences. Instead the protective belts of sub-programs overlap and, although their demi-cores may be directly distinct, they share common elements mediated through the hard core. For the hard core to be truly common it is of necessity denuded of substantial content and is reduced to formal and metaphysical features.

So far we have assumed, as most commentators have, that programs are differentiated by their hard cores. Lakatos (1970, p. 133) warrants this assumption. But Lakatos is not consistent on this point, arguing that different programs may have a common hard core and be differentiated only by their positive heuristics.[11]

If programs are differentiated by their positive heuristics, the project of Lakatosian interpretation of economics is in even deeper water. Compared with most presentations of the positive heuristics of putative programs, propositions PH1–5 above are precise. Still I have intentionally used the phrase that the positive heuristic is 'something like' PH1–5 in order to capture the almost universal vagueness on the details.[12] Lakatos himself expects that the positive heuristic should not only be partially articulated, but also set out in advance of the development of progressively more complex models. The positive heuristics are not even partially articulated in the detail that Lakatos requires because neither the scientist nor the commentator can see how models will develop. There are, of course, counter-examples. Lakatos is impressed by Newton's theory of gravitation:

> Most, if not all, Newtonian 'puzzles', leading to a series of new variants superseding each other, were foreseeable at the time of Newton's first naive model and no doubt Newton and his colleagues did foresee them: Newton must have been fully aware of the blatant falsity of his first variants. Nothing shows the existence of a positive heuristic of a research programme clearer than this fact: this is why one speaks of 'models' in research programmes. (Lakatos, 1970, p. 136)

The closest parallel in the new classical macroeconomics is the sequence of real business cycle models following Kydland and Prescott (1982).[13] Taken as a separate program or sub-program, the hard core of the real-business-cycle program is no different from that of other sub-programs in the new classical macroeconomics. And once Kydland and Prescott's model had been subjected to the data, there emerged a fairly clear blueprint of the type of modifications that might make it mimic the data more accurately. The technical difficulties in executing these plans were formidable and have occupied a generation of Minnesota's graduate students.

What is striking, however, is that it is not easy to point to any similar examples of a sub-program within the new classical economics, one which knew exactly where they were going. Such programs or sub-programs exist, but are rare – and not only in economics. Newton-Smith writes:

> One cannot discern in the work of Newton, Einstein or others who have launched successful [Scientific Research Programs] anything like even 'partial articulation' of the protective responses that are to be made in the case of anomalies. (Newton-Smith, 1981, p. 84)

If distinct hard cores or positive heuristics do not provide a basis for effectively discriminating between programs, perhaps the negative heuristic does. Is there any element of the program that is truly beyond all thought of change? It is hard to imagine in 1989 any new model being called new classical or being acceptable to new classicals that violated any of the hard core propositions noted above. Still, when one considers history, adherence to the five propositions is not universal among new classical models.

I once wrote that Lucas and Rapping's (1969) essay on the Phillips curve is 'surely the first paper to deserve to be called "new classical"' (Hoover, 1988, p. 27). Yet Lucas and Rapping employed adaptive expectations, violating NH2 and contradicting HC5. Lucas says that, although he knew about rational expectations at the time the paper was written, he had not yet appreciated the far-reaching implications that they had for modelling nor how essential they were to the project of modelling a world of optimizing agents (see Klamer, 1984, p. 38). What makes Lucas and Rapping (1969) a 'new classical' paper is its then startling insistence on modelling the labour market as in continuous equilibrium without money illusion and with regard to the micro-economic behaviour of individual workers (that is, its strong allegiance to HC2–4).

The models that brought the new classical macroeconomics to the forefront in the profession were the policy-ineffectiveness models of Sargent and Wallace (1975, 1976). These models incorporated rational expectations but otherwise were standard IS/LM models – aggregate, non-optimizing models, violating NH1 and NH6 and contradicting HC1. Sargent and Wallace understood at the time that these models did not conform to the implicit standards of the program.

Sargent and Wallace's (1982) model of the monetary economy advocates a real bills regime in which nominal money balances affect real consumption choices, apparently violating NH4 and contradicting HC3. There is, however, a range of propositions identified as the 'neutrality of money'.[14] Early new classical models had a fairly strong neutrality proposition: namely, anticipated changes in the stock of money have no real effects. This form is violated in Sargent and Wallace's real bills regime and also in the business cycle models advocated by Lucas (1987, p. 83). Still, Lucas (1987, p. 81) says that every serious monetary model must have a neutrality proposition of a weaker form: namely, real allocations are unaffected by currency reforms.

It might be argued that what is happening here is a 'hardening of the hard core'. Lakatos writes: 'The actual hard core of a programme does not actually emerge fully armed like Athene from the head of Zeus. It develops slowly, by a long, preliminary process of trial and error' (Lakatos, 1970, p. 133, fn. 4).

Lakatos unfortunately never gives a thorough discussion of this process. Weintraub (1985, ch. 7) gives a brilliant account of the hardening of the hard core of the Walrasian general equilibrium program. For the Walrasian program, at least, Weintraub believes: '*The propositions of the core remain fixed but the interpretations of the terms of the core change as the core hardens*' (Weintraub, 1985, p. 141, emphasis in original). While this situation is a possible one, it is not generally true. It works in the new classical macroeconomics for the neutrality proposition already discussed: HC3 is maintained for all new classical models so far; but the interpretation of neutrality shifts over time until only the weak sense of a currency reform is defended against all-comers. Equally the rational expectations hypothesis itself may be subject to this process. Early interpretations stressed the actual behaviour of people. One interpretation was that rational expectations imply that people do the best they can with the information they have. Another was that rational expectations imply that people actually know (implicitly) the structure of the model which truly describes the world and use it to form their expectations. Lucas (1987, p. 14, fn. 4) calls the first interpretation 'vacuous' and the second 'silly'. Instead he interprets the hypothesis as 'a consistency axiom for economic models, [which] can be given precise meaning only in the context of specific models' (Lucas, 1987, p. 14, fn. 4). The tune changes, but the words remain the same. On the other hand, one cannot treat the adoption of rational expectations after Lucas and Rapping (1969) or the use and subsequent banishment of the IS/LM framework from new classical models as simply a reinterpretation of a fixed hard core. Rather, the hard core has changed or, perhaps more to the point, has not been fully articulated.

One might be willing to concede that the process of hardening involves substantive change to the hard core, yet believe that once the hard core has set it cannot change further: the hard core is something like epoxy. But perhaps not; perhaps the hard core is more like Elmer's glue, which is hard enough until it gets wet. It is hard to imagine the new classical macroeconomics giving up the rational expectations hypothesis. It is not, however, inconceivable. The inventor of rational expectations, John Muth, has recently worked on 'implicit expectations'.[15] *Implicit expectations* are unbiased expectations in which the prediction error is uncorrelated with the actual realization. In a parallel form, *rational expectations* are unbiased expectations in which the prediction error is uncorrelated with the predictions. Although implicit expectations and rational expectations are mutually exclusive, Lovell (1986, 112–14) points out that both are unbiased and can be defended as the product of rational choice. Lovell also presents evidence of cases in which implicit expectations dominate rational expectations empirically.[16] It is not inconceivable that models which satisfy HC1–4 might nevertheless employ implicit expectations and still be regarded as new classical.

To take another case, the assumption of continuous equilibrium has been interpreted as involving a Walrasian equilibrium of price-takers. One could easily imagine this being extended to an equilibrium of price-setters. This would be an example of reinterpretation of an unchanged proposition of the hard core. The discussion of policy rules in the new classical macroeconomics after Kydland and Prescott (1977) has, however, become dominated by game-theoretic analysis.[17] A principal characteristic of game theory is the proliferation of equilibrium concepts to the point where 'equilibrium' may have no substantive content at all. It is conceivable that new classical macroeconomics may some day so fully incorporate game theory that HC4 is no longer considered essential.

Tribe and Nation

I have so far tried to undermine the plausibility of Lakatos's methodology of scientific research programs: to suggest that it is difficult to identify the hard core of a program conclusively or to maintain that it is in any sense immutable, that the negative heuristic is after all just a heuristic, not a set of unbreachable injunctions and that the positive heuristic is rarely well-enough defined in practive to be fitted to the theoretical task to which Lakatos sets it. Still I go this far with Lakatos: no program, even a methodological program, falls under its own weight alone; it must be pushed by a more attractive program.

So what is the alternative? Let us recall Kuhn's competing theory of the development of science. Pehaps Kuhn's (1970) most lasting contribution was to elevate 'paradigm' from a relatively obscure grammatical term to a key word in the lexicon of general intellectual discourse.[18]

Kuhn was infamously imprecise in the first edition of *The Structure of Scientific Revolutions* (1962) on the meaning of 'paradigm'. Masterman (1970) finds 21 senses of paradigm in Kuhn's book. These, she believes, can be encapsulated in three primary meanings. Kuhn concedes Masterman's point, although he sees but two principal meanings:

> On the one hand, [paradigm] stands for the entire constellation of beliefs, values, techniques, and so on shared by the members of a given community. On the other, it denotes one sort of element in that constellation, the concrete puzzle-solutions which, employed as models or examples, can replace explicit rules as a basis for the solution of the remaining puzzles of normal science.
>
> . . .
>
> Philosophically, at least, this second sense of 'paradigm' is the deeper of the two . . . (Kuhn, 1970, p. 175)

Most commentators have not followed Kuhn in preferring this second sense, but continue to prefer the first, sociological or Gestalt sense. Appreciating that common usage had hijacked his preferred sense, Kuhn adopts the term 'exemplar' for his second sense (Kuhn, 1970, p. 187).[19] I would like to take Kuhn at his word and concentrate on the second, philosophically deeper, sense of paradigms as concrete exemplars of puzzle-solving.

Sartre's dictum, 'existence precedes essence', has an analogue in scientific practice: *models (or theories) precede programs*. To take one example of many, Lucas (1972b) is an attempt to resolve a particular puzzle: what constitutes a decisive test of the natural rate hypothesis? The natural rate hypothesis predated the new classical macroeconomics; and Lucas introduces rational expectations into the model not to establish a new world-view or to further a nascent program but to make Friedman's original presentation of the natural rate hypothesis more consistent with the general presumption that economic agents optimize. It is only later, only after one of the many messages of this paper has been generalized into the 'Lucas critique', only after the principal authors of new classical models began to write interpretive tracts, that the programmatic force of this paper became clear.[20]

One might conclude from this example that programs can only be written retrospectively. But, in fact, it is more complicated than that. Concrete models are a mixture of the programmatic and the adventitious with no firm boundary between the two. The characteristic feature of the concrete exemplar is its richness. Its power over the imagination arises from the virtually inexhaustible lode of special features. When the model is used as an exemplar for another model, usually by another modeller, not every feature of the exemplar is transferred. Key features or methods or assumptions are transferred, while others are neglected. In choosing which features to borrow, however, the modeller already provides an interpretation of what is important – an interpretation which in turn may be adopted by still other modellers. Or it may be rejected by them, and the mine of the original model reworked once more. More explicitly interpretive works serve the same function. They isolate features from a model or a group of models in order to sell them as an appropriate way forward. Interpretive works, then, serve a prospective as well as a retrospective role in the development of a program or school.

The image of scientific practice that I wish to convey is one of specific models serving as concrete exemplars. Other models may develop merely as elaborations or variants of them. Others again may be quite different in detail or purpose, but nonetheless take over key assumptions or borrow techniques. Still others may borrow only the 'spirit' of the original exemplar. Scientific practice, therefore, consists of groups of related and partly overlapping models and practices.

The picture here differs from Kuhn's (1970) account of scientific revolutions. No model is primary. One model may have preceded the others. Others may have borrowed different elements from it. The model may continue to have life or it may become moribund with later models supplanting it as an exemplar. When many variants on a model exist, any one may, for many purposes at least, serve as the exemplar. Kuhn's account of revolution producing a dominant paradigm, which becomes the exemplar for a period of normal science is then too simple, too linear, to capture the multifariousness of scientific practice.

If this account is correct, however, one might ask in what sense there could be a new classical school or, even in a loose sense, a new classical research program. Where is the *essence* of new classicism in the sea of overlapping but not universal features or models? My point is that there is no such essence, yet there still is a new classical macroeconomics. The models that form new classicism bear a *family resemblance* one with another. The philosopher Ludwig Wittgenstein writes:

> The tendency to look for something common to all the entities which we commonly subsume under a general term. – We are inclined to think that there must be something in common to all games, say, and that this common property is the justification for applying the general term 'game' to the various games; whereas games form a *family* the members of which have family likenesses. Some of them have the same nose, others the same eyebrows and others again the same way of walking; and these likenesses overlap. The idea of a general concept being a common property of its particular instances connects up with other primitive, too simple, ideas of the structure of languages. (Wittgenstein, 1975, p. 17)[21]

In a similar vein, he writes:

> We find what connects all the cases of comparing is a vast number of overlapping similarities, and as soon as we can see this, we feel no longer compelled to say that there must be some one feature common to them all. What ties the ship to the wharf is a rope, and the rope consists of fibres, but it does not get its strength from any fibre which runs through it from one end to the other, but from the fact that there is a vast number of fibres overlapping. (Wittgenstein, 1975, p. 87)

There are two points here. One is that the concrete cases or entities are primary and that they do not 'participate' in some sort of pre-existing essence but constitute the multifarious essences that interpretation finds in them. The second is that, despite this lack of essence, these cases or entities nevertheless form families: ropes have no fibres that run their entire lengths, but there really are ropes and they really do tie up ships; the models of the new classical microeconomics do not all have an identical hard core or protective belt, but there really is a family of models that deserves to be called 'new classical'.

Lakatos is not unaware of nor completely unsympathetic to the view I advocate here. He writes:

> Some eminent philosophers, however, ridicule the idea of statute law, the possibility of any valid demarcation [between science and non-science]. According to Oakeshott and Polanyi there must be – and can be – no statute law at all: only case law. They may also argue that even if one mistakenly allowed for statute law, statute law too would need authoritative interpreters. I think that Oakeshott's and Polanyi's position has a great deal of truth in it. After all, one must admit (*pace* Popper) that until now all the 'laws' proposed by the apriorist philosophers of science have turned out to be wrong in the light of the verdicts of the best scientists. (Lakatos, 1978, pp. 136, 137)

To give up statute law is not to give up general principles; rather it is to acknowledge that one must discover the general principles in the particular cases. The complexities and the highly particular features of individual cases do not rule out a rational approach to the law. Nor do they rule out the individuation of tort law from contract law, contract law from criminal law and so forth: the borders are not strict, but there are distinct subjects. The same is true of alternative programs in economics.

Lakatos seems aware of some of this. Still there is far more of Popper than of Oakeshott, Polanyi or Wittgenstein in Lakatos. Lakatos's methodology of scientific research programs sees science as a collection of nation-states. Each program is defined by its hard core and protective belt – a constitution, and police and military. The negative heuristic defines its borders with a surveyor's precision, while the positive heuristic stands guard ready to protect the nation from unwanted anomalies or adversarial nation-states.

In contrast, the view I advocate sees science as a collection of tribes. Models and theories are united by ties of kinship and consanguinity. Each program or school stakes out its ground. Occasionally boundaries are sharp, as when tribes are divided by a river or mountain range, yet one country usually imperceptibly blends into the other. Even a tribe's sense of self-identity may show the same blending. Economists on the borders of new classical economics may sometimes identify themselves as new classical and sometimes as something else. Still, for all the blurring of the edges, when one is in the heart of Cherokee country or the heart of Chicasaw country, one knows it. Where the Lakatosian map of the scientific world delineates the borders of nations, occasional border disputes to the contrary notwithstanding, my map shows the names of the various scientific tribes scattered indefinitely (but not inaccurately) across the known world and with the *terra incognita* and the uncharted seas marked clearly with the cartographer's warning: 'There be monsters and dragons'.

3 THE ETHNOGRAPHY OF THE NEW CLASSICAL MACROECONOMICS

A Table of Exemplars

My suggestion that an anthropological metaphor captures the scientific endeavour – and economics in particular – has been buttressed with essentially anecdotal evidence. It should be possible, however, to investigate systematically the relations of kinship and consanguinity among the concrete exemplars of the new classical economics. Figure 11. 1 is a tentative step towards such an investigation. It is a sort of family tree of the new classical economics. For the most part its entries are particular papers that were important in the development of new classical doctrine. I did not intend to list every new classical paper; rather, following the logic of my earlier argument, the papers serve as exemplars of the main lines of new classical thinking. Just as many Latin nouns once declined serve equally well as grammatical paradigms, so too many of the papers on the list could be replaced with a related paper.

The table was constructed backwards from current research to its antecedents. My aim was to indicate which concrete exemplars influenced which other ones. Arrows indicate direction of influence. Sometimes this influence is direct, sometimes indirect.[22] I have not attempted to reproduce the full and complex interrelationships between the exemplars listed.[23] Papers or topics in solid rectangles indicate influences from outside the new classical macroeconomics. Papers in broken rectangles indicate cases in which new classical influences have moved outside the new classical macroeconomics.

The table is divided into a grid for ease of reference. The bottom cells of the column indicate seven families of currently active research within the tribe of new classical macroeconomics: monetary models of business cycles, finance-based models of money, real models of business cycles, the analysis of policy rules, structural estimation of market-clearing rational expectations models, vector autoregression for policy analysis and overlapping-generations models of money.[24] Even when the papers listed are several years old, there is other derivative work currently being done in these areas. I have intentionally omitted some topics. Recent work on growth theory with increasing returns is omitted because of my own ignorance of the literature, and work on the consumption function under rational expectations (following Hall, 1978) is omitted because of its equivocal place in new classical macroeconomics. Other possibly eligible areas may also have been omitted. Including the omitted topics would not alter the general conclusions I shall draw about methodology.

The rows of the table indicate roughly the generations of new classical models. The story told by the table goes roughly as follows. The two principal influences on the earliest distinctively new classical papers are Friedman's and Phelps's natural rate hypothesis (IA) which influenced Lucas and Rapping (1969) and which, together with Muth's now famous paper on rational expectations, form the core of Lucas's papers on the

Figure 11.1 A table of kinship and consanguinity for the new classical macroeconomics

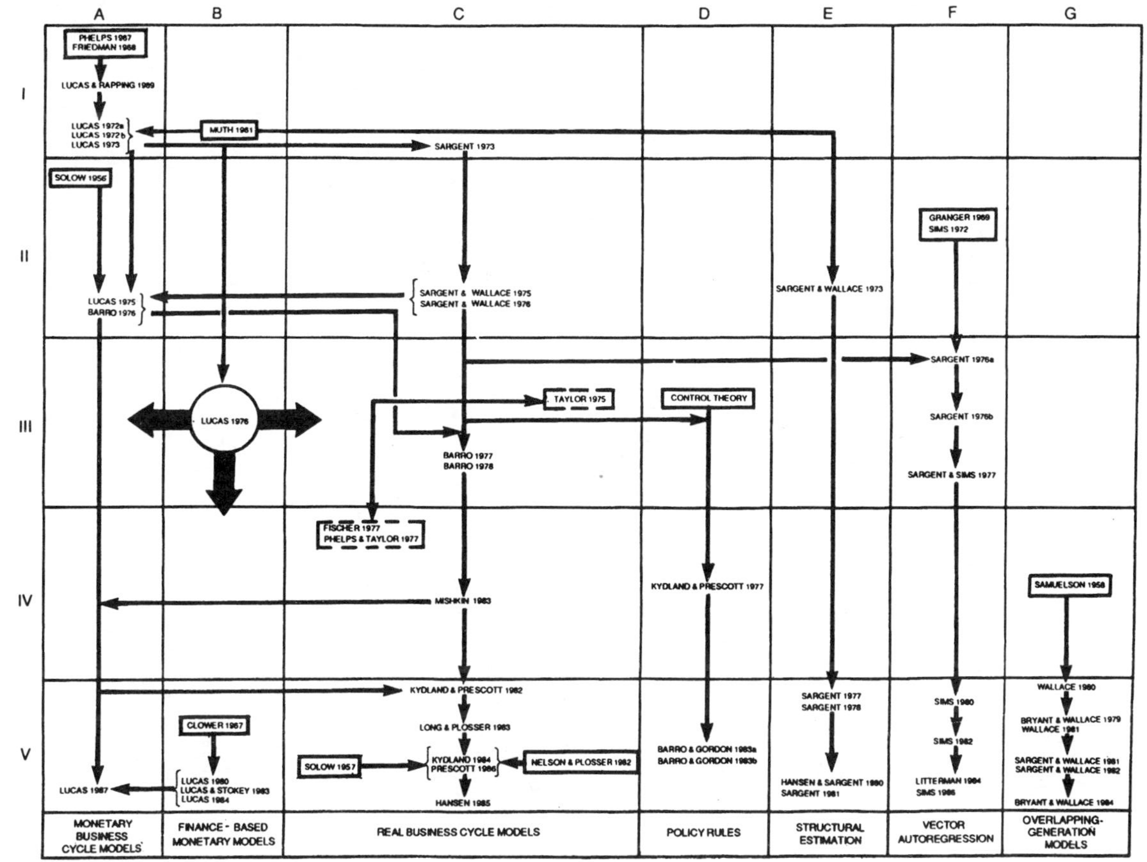

natural rate hypothesis and the Phillips curve in the early 1970s. Lucas's surprise-only aggregate-supply function suggested to him an explanation for business cycles, so that these papers form the direct ancestors of all monetary equilibrium theories of the business cycle.

Lucas's early papers are tremendously important for their other influences as well. Sargent's extension of Lucas's work to the consideration of interest rates (IC) became the basis for his work with Wallace on the ineffectiveness of monetary policy (IIC). This is part of the second generation of new classical models. The first generation aimed largely at discovering whether the insistence on general equilibrium and rational expectations made much difference to theoretical models and to the interpretation of pre-existing debates. It had little influence on the larger profession. The second generation began staking out novel and controversial ground. The policy-ineffectiveness papers sought to undercut the very possibility of policy, which had animated macroeconomics since its inception. The early business cycle papers (IIA) similarly sought to overturn the general presumption that business cycles must be disequilibria.

The third and fourth generations worked at exploring and systematizing the implications of the second-generation models. In this generation, we find the attempts to isolate which assumption are critical to the policy-ineffectiveness conclusions. One result is that contract or sticky-price models are developed which, while not new classical, nonetheless use the rational expectations hypothesis (for example, Fischer, 1977 and Phelps and Taylor, 1977: IVC). Similarly this debate produced models of the process of learning and convergence to rational expectations (for example, Taylor, 1975: IIIC). The first real empirical investigations of new classical macroeconomics occur in these generations (for example, Barro, 1977, 1978: IIIC) and Sargent's classical macromodel (IIIF).

What distinguishes generation III from generation IV in the table is Lucas's (1976) policy invariance paper – the famous 'Lucas critique' (IIIB). Lucas's paper is the most important synthesis of new classical ideas ever written. In the table it is circled to indicate its special place. Bold arrows are drawn pointing generally to exemplars in its own and later generations. To draw in any detail all of the necessary arrows would clutter the table too much. Lucas's paper is the Ibn Saud of the new classical macroeconomics. Ibn Saud, the first king of a united Saudi Arabia, married the daughters of important and often warring tribes, gave them sons and then divorced them, leaving them with a generous pension and much goodwill. As a consequence Saudi Arabia has an enormous number of royal princes, and formerly fractious tribes are united by ties of kinship and loyalty to the royal family. Lucas's paper serves a similar function, inseminating *every* new classical model in generation IV and often at once with concrete examples of how ignoring new classical principles can lead modellers astray and with concrete suggestions about how to proceed (for example, beware of free parameters; reduce everything to the bedrock of optimization with only tastes and technology given).[25] Even the distant family of the overlapping-generations models of money (G), which has no other direct connection with the other six families, is clearly part of the new classical tribe because of the virile influence of Lucas (1976).[26]

Some Anthropological Questions

Having set out a table of kinship for the new classical tribe, it is – with sincere apologies to any serious anthropologists – time to pursue some further anthropological investigations.

Foundation myths

Every culture has some account of its own beginnings – some are folk tales, some are literary fabrications. The ancient Greeks are an example of the former, believing themselves to be autochthonous. The ancient Romans, however, looked to the poet Virgil to teach them that they had descended from Aeneas, who had fled from the ruins of his native Troy. In economics, neoclassical economics follows the Greek example. Economics is the consequence of the inexorable logic of choice, a product of the human condition rather than of history. New classical macroeconomics is more like the Romans. The new classicals look back to an earlier age, to the classics (as Keynes defined them). When the classical citadels crumbled after Keynes slipped in his Trojan horse, the *General Theory*, a few weary survivors (Friedman *inter alia*) made their way to Chicago to refound a Republic of Virtue on virgin soil. Lucas, who from our table of kinship, is clearly Octavius, the perfected product of Roman virtue, is also Virgil himself, the fabricator of the myth (see especially Lucas, 1977, 1980b).

Like most myths, this one has a germ of truth. We have already seen the critical role played by Milton Friedman in the formation of the new classical tribe, and there is no doubt that Friedman provides a link to pre-Keynesian traditions. Still, the new classical myth is not real history.[27] It nevertheless has its uses. Lucas's interpretive papers serve to underscore certain new classical values with enough rhetorical force for the younger generation of new classical economists to know what is expected of them, how to behave, how to model – not in technical detail (for that they have other exemplars) but in broad spirit.[28]

Scope and range

Any tribe occupies some particular places for some particular times. The table of kinship reveals chronological development of the new classical macroeconomics, vertical development from generation to generation, as well as horizontal development, a range of topics from theoretical monetary models to policy issues to technical empirical applications. One might ask why I have drawn these particular papers together as 'new classical' rather than a much narrower or much broader collection.

The case for the much broader grouping is indicated by the important exemplars that I have chosen to box in as outside the tribe: should not all the relatives be included? Unfortunately the end of that road is complete lack of discrimination. After all, in some sense, every person is related to every other person.[29] Yet, even where I come from, in Franklin County, Virginia, a place overrun with Perdues, Hodges's and Scruggs's, no Perdue, Hodges or Scruggs 'claims kin' with all of the other Perdues, Hodges's or Scruggs's.

Gordon (1989) takes the new classical macroeconomics to be much narrower: the close descendants of Lucas's original work on the natural rate hypothesis and the Phillips curve – including IA, IIA, IC, IIC, IIIC, IVC and IIIB on Figure 11.1, but excluding just about everything else. New classical macroeconomics died for Gordon at a conference in 1979 when Barro presented an empirical paper that failed to support the Lucas surprise-only aggregate-supply function. Gordon has apparently identified new classical macroeconomics with its most prominent policy conclusion: the policy-ineffectiveness propositions after Sargent and Wallace (1975, 1976).

Now something like Gordon's death of new classicism occurred. It is represented in Figure 11.1 by the exemplar of Mishkin (1983) – an empirical investigation critical of the surprise-only proposition. This was a key event in the life of the new classical tribe – but not its death. Lucas's recent monetary model of the business cycle (VA) as well as the entire real business cycle literature (VC) is a reaction to the empirical research in IIIC and IVC. Gordon recognizes the real business cycle models as somehow being new classical, but dismisses them as arid, technical exercises. What really tells against Gordon's narrow identification of the new classical economics is the strength of the influences from those papers that he admits are centrally new classical to the papers in columns D, E, F and G that he ignores.

I have argued that it is family resemblance that links the exemplars of research programs together. Resemblance is clearly in the eyes of the beholder, but the point of tables of kinship is that some of the links of family are objective: there is little room for reasonable people to disagree on the existence of the influence. The reason to reject the narrow view of what is new classical is twofold: genetic linkages exist between exemplars and the resemblances among exemplars are strong. Although it is hard to be sure where to draw the borders, which wayward daughters to exclude or which prodigal sons to include, there is no real doubt about the members in the centre of the family.

Anthropologists and linguists distinguish between *diachronic* analysis, which concentrates on a particular time, and *synchronic* analysis, which concentrates on change over time. Looked at synchronically, it is easier to see the argument for a narrow conception of what constitutes new classical macroeconomics – although not so narrow a conception as Gordon's. The current research in VA–E on Table 11.1 is central to most conceptions of the new classical macroeconomics. Financed-based models of money (VB) are direct competitors with overlapping-generations models. Similarly the strategies of structural estimation (VE) and vector autoregression are usually seen as incompatible.[30] One might then simply say that the program of vector autoregressions and overlapping-generations models should be excluded from new classicism altogether. But that would be a superficial judgement. Financed-based models employing cash-in-advance constraints and overlapping-generations models both enthusiastically endorse the principle of Lucas (1976) that everything should be derived from tastes and technology, and they both aim at providing a secure microfoundation for policy analysis. The differ over the substantive point – what is ad hoc. To Sargent and Wallace the cash-in-advance constraint has no deep justification, whereas to Lucas, who places it in a search framework, it arises from the fact that there are 24 hours in the day and the earth goes around the sun. Similarly the advocates of vector autoregressions agree with the advocates of structural estimation that well-founded theoretical restrictions should be used to identify econometric models; they disagree on what is well founded.[31]

Such disagreements are the sort that Lakatos might see as arising from different hard cores and hence as defining separate programs. Looked at diachronically, however, we can appreciate the common genesis of these alternative approaches. We can see them as cousins under the skin – what they share in roots outweighing the vastly differing circumstances in which they live. It is possible for cousins to 'claim kin', and still not care for each other very much. It also helps explain what would otherwise be paradoxical: that Sargent and Wallace, who are key players in the central new classical story, are also key players in the overlapping-generations program; that Sargent, who is the principal advocate of structural estimation, played an important part in the establishemnt of the program of vector autoregressions, and has not renounced it even though he no longer works within it.[32]

Social structure

The table of kinship alone does not tell us all that we might wish to know about the social structure of the new classical tribe. I would like to concentrate on one aspect of social structure often stressed by anthropologists and economists alike – the division of labour. One might think of each of the current families of research (VA–F) as Hindu castes with specialized occupations. Or, if we take a bolder division of occupations into just two – theory and empirics – we might think of these families as like the 12 tribes of Israel, which were divided into priests and everyone else.

It is evident in considering the papers that make up each family that they are not as radically separated as the table might suggest. In particular there is a close interplay between theory and empirics. The econometric techniques developed in the structural estimation program, for instance, are almost wholly a response to the theoretical implications of the Lucas critique.[33] This relationship would not surprise Lakatos: new theory leads to appropriate new empirical methods. Lakatos (1970, p. 137), however, believes that the methodology of scientific research programs accounts for the fact that theoretical science is relatively autonomous. He writes:

> If a scientist (or mathematician) has a positive heuristic, he refuses to be drawn into observation. He will 'lie down on his couch, shut his eyes and forget about data' . . . Occasionally, of course, he will ask Nature a shrewd question: he will then be encouraged by Nature's YES, but not discouraged by its NO. (Lakatos, 1970, p. 135, fn. 1)

The case of the new classical macroeconomics suggests that this is not quite correct. First, two of the new classical families we have identified are families of empirical methods (VE and F). Although these families reveal their own programmatic tendencies, their provenance is the difficulties inherent in the correct empirical implementation of new classical theory. New classicals have not been content to lie on their couches, but in some degree have felt compelled to confront data.

Second, although our diachronic analysis of the new classical macroeconomics does not reveal any 'crucial experiments', it does provide examples in which empirical results fundamentally re-directed theoretical research. The most obvious case is the series of tests of the surprise-only aggregate-supply function (IIIC and IVC). The theoretician in the thrall of a positive heuristic asked Nature a shrewd question and Nature answered, MAYBE NOT.[34] Contrary to Lakatos, the advocates of monetary business cycle models were discouraged. They did not renounce their models, but interest shifted almost entirely to real-business-cycle models. And, even when interest in monetary models has been revived, as in Lucas (1987), the monetary source of aggregate fluctuations is no longer shocks to monetary policy.

Less obviously, the program of real-business-cycle models within that program is supported by empirical results. Nature's less-than-decisive suggestion that GNP is non-stationary (Nelson and Plosser, 1982: VC) is thought by new classicals to favour real models of the business cycle over monetary models. Monetary cycles, they argue, must be cycles about a trend, whereas the time-series evidence suggests that movements in the trend itself dominates cyclical behaviour.[35] Similar evidence from the program of vector autoregressions suggested that monetary policy had little effect on output. Again this was taken to favour real-business-cycle models.

Particular developments within the program of real-business-cycle models also responded to empirical results. Proponents of real-business-cycle models have taken the appropriate test of their models to be the ability of the model to reproduce the variances/covariances of the actual post-war data for the US. Kydland and Prescott's (1982) model did not do this very well. The precise manner of its failure helped determine the details of the modifications represented by the four exemplars listed below it in Figure 11.1 (VC).

At a cruder level, the observation that money is dominated in rate of return by other financial assets explains not only the progressive development of the overlapping-generations models (G) from simple store of value models such as Wallace (1980) to models with legal restrictions such as Sargent and Wallace (1982) and Bryant and Wallace (1984), but also the introduction of the cash-in-advance constraint, borrowed from Clower (1967), into financed-based models of money (VB).

There is a division of labour in scientific research between theory and empirics with influence running in both directions. And, as any economist would expect, there are gains from trade.

Insiders and outsiders

I have argued that what makes a particular model new classical is partly its genesis – where it fits in the family tree – and partly its family resemblance to exemplars that are clearly part of the new classical tribe. Anthropologists, however, understand that such relationships are not enough to forge and maintain tribal identity. The borders of a tribe need to be at least loosely patrolled if its identity is not be submerged into surrounding tribes. The ancient Israelites had their shibboleth. 'Shibboleth' is the ancient Hebrew word for an ear of corn. Non-Hebrews could be distinguished from Hebrews by their difficulty in pronouncing this word correctly. Likewise the dietary laws of many religions and cultures function in part to distinguish them from surrounding groups.[36] Those propositions and injunctions identified as the hard core (HC1–5) and negative heuristic (NH1–7) in the tentative Lakatosian new classical program in section 1 above serve less as rigid guides to research than as shibboleths and dietary laws. I have myself had the experience of people at certain conferences inching a little bit further away from me at dinner simply for having expressed healthy scepticism about one or more of these propositions and injunctions.

On the other hand, tribes are not autarkic; they trade and communicate with other tribes or link up with them through marriage. Such intercourse is often vital. The table of kinship imperfectly, but strikingly, reveals the importance of influences from outside the new classical economics. There is probably not a single technique or basic model that originated within the new classical tribe. Many were adapted and modified, but their connections with outside sources remain clear.

Similarly the new classical tribe has itself influenced outsiders. The cases indicated on Figure 11.1 are cases of largely negative influence. The papers in the boxes in IIIC and IVC are reactions to the unpalatable conclusions of Sargent and Wallace (1975, 1976). The new classical macroeconomics has, however, had positive influences as well. The drive for microfoundations and for technical rigour, which is characteristic of the new classical tribe, has infused much of the macroeconomic profession.[37] This is seen very clearly in Blanchard and Fischer's (1989) graduate textbook, which is Keynesian in 'spirit' but stresses microfoundations and aspires to technical rigour no less than that found in Sargent (1979, 1987) – the key new classical textbooks.[38]

Although trade outside the tribe is crucial, we are not really somehow one big family. The role of the shibboleth is important. This is most strikingly illustrated by the overlapping-generations models of money (G). As I observed above, this family is less tightly linked through direct bloodlines to the other families in the new classical tribe. What is more, there is a large literature on overlapping-generations models that could not be considered to be remotely new classical. In the final analysis, what makes the exemplars listed in G 'new classical' is the motivations that their authors have in formulating them – their ritual incantation of new classical principles, their obedience to the dietary laws, as it were.[39] Wallace (1980, p. 51), for example, justifies his interest in overlapping-generations models by his hope that they will provide a structural explanation for time-series correlations (that is, that they will offer a way around the Lucas critique).

Even though the new classical macroeconomics has, and must have, its shibboleths and dietary laws, its commerce with other tribes demonstrates that fruitful communication is possible. Contrary to Lakatos, who rules out discussion of hard core propositions, and contrary to Kuhn, at his most radical, or to Feyerabend, both of whom find competing approaches to be actually incommensurable, communication is both possible and useful. It is true that different schools of economic thought often fail to understand one another. The new classicals often do not understand the Keynesians and do not usually even attempt to understand the post-Keynesians, but this lack of communication cannot be blamed on incommensurability, and a conventional decision to opt for ignorance should not be endorsed.[40] Semantic disputes, equivocations and confusions are commonplace; they nonetheless should not be raised into methodological principles.

4 CONCLUSION

Lakatos writes:

> *All* methodologies, *all* rational reconstructions can be historiographically 'falsified': science *is* rational, but its rationality cannot be subsumed under the general laws of any methodology. (Lakatos, 1978, p. 130)

The historiography of the new classical macroeconomics shows that Lakatos's own methodology is falsified like all the others. Lakatos, of course, was not claiming any special dispensation. He would argue that the best methodology is not that which is truest, but that which rationalizes science the most thoroughly.

My principal criticism of Lakatos's method is that its unit of appraisal, the scientific research program, cannot be individuated in a commonly acceptable way. Because it cannot be individuated it cannot have normative force for working scientists and economists. What does have normative force is the concrete model, the exemplar of how to solve a particular sort of problem. I do not, however, wish to raise the exemplar to the status of a Lakatosian 'unit of appraisal'. Exemplars resonate on many levels: theory, technique, world-view, metaphysics. The development of the new classical economics, and no doubt other areas of economics and other sciences, shows that science develops on all of these levels. Scientific practice cannot be split into well-defined atoms to be judged on formal criteria as Lakatos's negative heuristic attempts to do. Rather alternative scientific models must be judged according to which gives the best explanation, and they must be allowed to communicate and inform one another.[41] The only iron-clad methodological rule is C.S. Peirce's (1931, para. 135): 'Do not block the way of inquiry'.

For Lakatos, the history of science is important because one cannot assess a research program unless one knows its past: is it progressing or degenerating? But if scientific practice is to be judged according to how good an explanation it provides relative to the alternatives, it would seem that only the present counts. Still the tribal view of science presented in section 3 above suggests that history is important.

The problem of judging scientific achievement is that we have no bird's-eye view. Modern mariners or adventurers have the benefit of maps and devices to locate themselves on the maps. In contrast, the scientist, like the early explorers, has no place to stand to look down upon his own progress. The scientist must construct his maps as he goes. Before the eighteenth century, when the sextant and chronometer permitted sailors to determine their longitudes precisely, navigators relied on *rutters*, log books that recorded the directions of currents, the changing colours of the sea, the characteristic features of important bits of land, and so forth. The more experienced the navigator on a route, the better his rutter. The rutter represented accumulated knowledge to be passed on to other navigators, a record of the past. It could be useful in only a general way in truly untravelled waters. But if, in sailing such waters, the navigator reached an impasse, the rutter not only told the way back, it also provided the best hints about which alternative routes might be worth a try. The history of economics, like the history of other sciences, is a rutter: a record of the roads taken and also a record of the forks, of the roads not taken that lead who knows where.

In Hoover (1988), I attempt to assess the successes and failures of the new classical macroeconomics. Starting with strong exemplars, it has been a programmatic success. Lucas, Sargent and Wallace in effect forged a trail that was easy for their followers to walk along. No other approach seemed to move ahead so far or so fast. Still, on balance, I feel that the new classical macroeconomics has built a fine, paved road into a valley surrounded on three sides by impassable mountains. The message of my methodological ruminations is partly that there is no reason for other schools of thought not to learn from new classical efforts. If nothing else, we know a lot more about road-building. But now I think we must back-track if we are to find a way forward. The traditional concerns of Keynesians with disequilibrium, especially with involuntary unemployment, uncertainty and macroeconomic policy, are not to be dismissed using the clean, simple devices of perfect competition, Walrasian general equilibrium, representative agents and (nearly) perfect knowledge.

NOTES

1. I am grateful to Thomas Mayer, Steven Sheffrin, Julie Nelson, Nancy Wulwick, Wing Woo and the participants in the Conference on Alternative Research Programmes in Recent Economics, Capri, Italy, 16–19 October 1989, for comments on earlier drafts.
2. Gordon (1989) goes to great lengths to document that its following is highly limited.
3. Lakatos (1970). For an excellent account of Lakatos's methodology, see Newton-Smith (1981) ch. 4.
4. It would be possible, but tedious, to present detailed citations from new classical literature justifying the hard-core propositions listed here as well as the negative and positive heuristics listed below. Instead, the reader is referred to Hoover (1988), especially chs 1, 9 and 10, to the interpretive literature of the new classical economists themselves – particularly, Lucas (1977), (1980b), Lucas and Sargent (1979) and Sargent (1982, 1986) – and to Klamer (1984) especially chs 1–4.
5. This proposition is not to be confused with the usual assumption of rationality in microeconomics, which merely requires complete, transitive preferences. This proposition goes further and place restrictions on the *content* of utility functions (for example, that nominal money balances may not be a source of utility) rather than on their *form*.
6. This might be seen as an implication of HCI–4; but for a contrary view see Hahn (1986) p. 281.
7. A tragic flaw in the new classical macroeconomics is the inconsistency between PH2 and NH6; see Hoover (1988) pp. 242–4.
8. PH3 and PH4 are not really compatible. Yet both are found among new classical economists and sometimes in the same economist.
9. See, for example, Latsis (1976) p. 22 on the program of situational determinism, Coats (1976) pp. 53, 54 on demand analysis, Weintraub (1985) p. 109 on general equilibrium theory and Remenyi (1979) pp. 55–61 on neoclassical economics.
10. The point was made splendidly at the Capri conference in the papers presented in the same session as this one (and published in this volume). Rodney Maddock interprets the new classical macroeconomics as a narrow Lakatosian program, the hard core of which is (1) the Lucas supply function, (2) rational expectations and (3) policy characterized by fixed rules. In contrast, Roger Backhouse characterizes the new classical macroeconomics as a sub-program of a fully specified neo-Walrasian program. My characterization in section 1 above falls neatly between these extremes.
11. 'But one should not forget that *two specific theories, while being mathematically (and observationally) equivalent, may still be embedded into different rival research programmes, and the power of the positive heuristic of these programmes may well be different*. The point has been overlooked by proposers of equivalence proofs (a good example is the equivalence proof between Schrödinger's and Heisenberg's approach to quantum physics)' (Lakatos, 1970, p. 164, fn. 3, italics in the original).

12. Such vagueness is by no means unique to applications of Lakatos to economics; cf. Newton-Smith (1981) ch. 2, section 2.
13. See Hoover (1988) ch. 3.
14. Fisher and Seater (1988) gives an exhaustive theoretical and empirical account of the alternatives.
15. See the citation in Lovell (1986).
16. Lovell (1986) pp. 121, 122, observes that Muth's recent empirical work uses implicit not rational expectations.
17. See Hoover (1988) ch. 4, section 4.3 for a discussion and references.
18. Having even made the list, 'What Literate Americans Know', in Hirsch's (1987) *Cultural Literacy*.
19. Most commentators are so impressed by the proliferation of senses identified by Masterman that they neglect the degree to which she and Kuhn pare them down.
20. See in particular Lucas (1976), Lucas and Sargent (1979), Sargent (1982) and, above all perhaps, Sargent's (1979) textbook, which literally made a school out of new classical models.
21. See also Wittgenstein (1953) pp. 31 ff.
22. Sometimes influence shown as mediated through various papers was actually more direct than shown. I have not always indicated the direct influences when it would have overly cluttered the diagram.
23. A careful examination of the patterns of citations of the various papers would provide a more complete analysis of patterns of influence. This task, however, awaits a more dedicated historiographer than I profess to be.
24. These topics are critically surveyed in Hoover (1988).
25. Maddock, who tries to place the new macroeconomics into a narrow Lakatosian framework (see n. 10 above) is puzzled by the role of Lucas (1976). He sees it finally as a paper 'written to detract from the credibility of alternative research programs'. The straitjacket of Lakatos's categories forces this view and makes Lucas's most cited paper appear peripheral. Yet to those inside the new classical macroeconomics and to most outsiders it is crucially important. Maddock is left with a puzzle, while the view expounded here explains the importance of Lucas's paper naturally.
26. Of course one should also note that Sargent and Wallace are the principal authors in this literature. That alone would no doubt forge the link.
27. Hoover (1988) chs 9 and 10 seeks to correct two aspects of the new classical foundation myth.
28. Although I have not tried to map them onto Figure 11.1, there of course exist *interpretive* exemplars as well as substantive ones.
29. Traditionally, of course, we all descended from Adam and Eve. Recent analysis of chromosomes from people all over the world indicates that we probably all have at least one common human female ancestor. And of course logical analysis suggests that this must be so: each person has two parents, four grandparents, eight great-grandparents, etc. Carrying this back, say, 35 generations, implies that, if they were all distinct, each of us would have 34 billion ancestors. This exceeds the number of people who have ever lived. We must share a large number of ancestors with others; and, taken far enough back, it is highly improbable that any two of us do not have a common ancestor. This insight forms the basis for Bernheim and Bagwell's (1988) criticism of proofs of Ricardian equivalence that typically assume that families are unrelated dynasties.
30. Cooley and LeRoy (1985); but cf. Hoover (1988) ch. 8, sec. 8.4.
31. Sims (1980) and esp. (1986b) p. 15.
32. Pure time-series econometrics is important in Sargent's (1979) textbook. Also see his comments on the 'atheoretical' approach in Klamer (1984) p. 75.
33. See Hoover (1989).
34. Gordon (1989) regards Barro and Rush (1980) as nature saying, NO!, emphatically – as a decisive crucial experiment. Gordon, however, seems to have been the only one who heard nature quite so clearly.

35. This reasoning has been questioned, see Hoover (1988) pp. 42–8.
36. See Levi-Strauss (1978).
37. I am sympathetic with the view that rigour is often bought at the price of relevance and sound analysis.
38. Lucas tends to see a revolution of rigour rather than a competition between schools; see Lucas (1980b) p. 286 and (1987) pp. 35, 46, 47, 107, 108. This picks up on a genuine similarity between neo-Keynesians and new classicals, but badly underplays the differences.
39. In this, they are like the Falashas, the black Jews of Ethiopia – isolated, but faithful.
40. In interviews with Klamer (1984) both Lucas (p. 35) and Sargent (p. 76) admit ignorance of and lack of serious concern for the work of Marxists, post-Keynesians and other non-conventional economists.
41. An extended discussion and defence of this moderate realist view of science is found in Newton-Smith (1981).

REFERENCES

Barro, Robert J. (1976), 'Rational Expectations and the Role of Monetary Policy', in Lucas and Sargent (1981), pp. 229-259. Reprinted from *Journal of Political Economy*, **59** (2), pp. 93–116.

—— (1977), 'Unanticipated Money Growth and Unemployment in the United States', in Lucas and Sargent (1981) pp. 563–84. Reprinted from *American Economic Review*, **67** (2).

—— (1978), 'Unanticipated Money, Output, and the Price Level in the United States', in Lucas and Sargent (1981) pp. 585–616.

Barro, Robert J. and Gordon, David B. (1983a) 'A Positive Theory of Monetary Policy in a Natural Rate Model', *Journal of Political Economy*, **91** (4), pp. 589–610.

—— (1983b), 'Rules, Discretion and Reputation in a Model of Monetary Policy', *Journal of Monetary Economics*, **12** (2), pp. 101–21.

Barro, Robert J. and Rush, Mark (1980), 'Unanticipated Money and Economic Activity', in Stanley Fischer (ed.), *Rational Expectations and Economic Policy* (Chicago: University of Chicago Press).

Bernheim, B. Douglas and Bagwell, Kyle (1988), 'Is Everything Neutral?', *Journal of Political Economy*, **96** (2), pp. 308–38.

Blanchard, Olivier Jean and Fischer, Stanley (1989), *Lectures on Macroeconomics* (Cambridge, Mass.: MIT Press).

Bryant, John and Wallace, Neil, (1979), 'The Inefficiency of Interest-bearing National Debt', *Journal of Political Economy*, **87** (2), pp. 365–81.

—— (1984), 'A Price Discrimination Analysis of Monetary Policy', *Review of Economic Studies*, **51** (2), pp. 279–88.

Clower, Robert (1967), 'A Reconsideration of the Microfoundations of Monetary Theory', *Western Economic Journal*, **6** (1), pp. 1–8.

Coats, A.W. (1976), 'Economics and Psychology: The Death and Resurrection of a Research Programme', in Latsis (1976) pp. 43–62.

Cooley, Thomas F. and LeRoy, Stephen F. (1985), 'Atheoretical Macroeconometrics: A Critique', *Journal of Monetary Economics*, **16** (3), pp. 283–308.

Fischer, Stanley (1977), 'Long-Term Contracts, Rational Expectations, and the Optimal Money Supply Rule', in Lucas and Sargent (eds) pp. 261–84. Reprinted from *Journal of Political Economy*, **85** (1), pp. 191–206.

Fisher, Mark and Seater, John J. (1988), 'Neutralities of Money', unpublished typescript, North Carolina State University and University of Pennsylvania, October.

Friedman, Milton (1968), 'The Role of Monetary Policy', *American Economic Review*, **58** (1), pp. 1–17.

Gordon, Robert J. (1989), 'Fresh Water, Salt Water and Other Macroeconomic Elixirs', *Economic Record*, **65** (189), pp. 177–84.

Granger, C.W.J. (1969), 'Investigating Causal Relations by Econometric Models and Cross-spectral Methods', in Lucas and Sargent (1981) pp. 371–86. Reprinted from *Econometrica,* **37** (3).

Hahn, Frank H. (1986), 'Review of Arjo Klamer, *Conversations with Economists: New Classical Economists and Opponents Speak Out on the Current Controversy in Macroeconomics*', *Economics and Philosophy*, **2** (2), pp. 275–82.

Hall, Robert E. (1978), 'Stochastic Implications of the Life Cycle-Permanent Income Hypothesis: Theory and Evidence', in Lucas and Sargent (1981) pp. 501–20. Reprinted from *Journal of Political Economy* **86** (6).

Hansen, Gary D. (1985), 'Indivisible Labor and the Business Cycle, *Journal of Monetary Economics* **16** (3), pp. 309–28.

Hansen, Lars Peter and Sargent, Thomas J. (1980), 'Estimating and Formulating Dynamic Linear Rational Expectations Models', in Lucas and Sargent (1981) pp. 91–125. Reprinted from *Journal of Economic Dynamics and Control*, **2** (1).

Hirsch, E.D., Jr. (1987), *Cultural Literacy: What Every American Needs to Know* (Boston: Houghton Mifflin).

Hoover, Kevin D. (1988), *The New Classical Macroeconomics: A Sceptical Inquiry* (Oxford: Basil Blackwell).

—— (1989), 'Econometrics as Observation: The Lucas Critique and the Nature of Econometric Inference', paper presented at the History of Economics Society meetings, 10–13 June 1989, Richmond, VA.

Kareken, John H. and Wallace, Neil (eds) (1980), *Models of Monetary Economies* (Minneapolis: Federal Reserve Bank of Minneapolis).

Klamer, Arjo (ed.) (1984), *The New Classical Macroeconomics: Conversations with New Classical Economists and Their Opponents* (Brighton, Sussex: Wheatsheaf Books).

Kuhn, Thomas S. (1970), *The Structure of Scientific Revolutions*, 2nd edn; (1st edition 1962) (Chicago: University of Chicago Press).

Kydland, Finn E. (1984), 'Labor-Force Heterogeneity and the Business Cycle', in Karl Brunner and Allan H. Meltzer (eds), *Essays on Macroeconomics Implications of Financial and Labor Markets and the Political Process*, Carnegie-Rochester Conference Series on Public Policy, vol. 21, Autumn (Amsterdam: North-Holland).

Kydland, Finn E. and Prescott, Edward C. (1977), 'Rules Rather than Discretion: The Inconsistency of Optimal Plans', in Lucas and Sargent (1981); pp. 619–38. Reprinted from *Journal of Political Economy*, **85** (3).

—— (1982), 'Time to Build and Aggregate Fluctuations', *Econometrica*, **50** (6), 1345–69.

Lakatos, Imre (1970), 'Falsification and the Methodology of Scientific Research Programmes', in Lakatos and Musgrave (1970) pp. 91–196.
—— (1978), 'History of Science and its Rational Reconstructions' in Worrall, John and Currie, Gregory (eds), *The Methodology of Scientific Research Programmes: Philosophical Papers, volume 1* (Cambridge: Cambridge University Press), pp. 102–38.
Lakatos, Imre and Musgrave, Alan (eds) (1970), *Criticism and the Growth of Knowledge* (Cambridge: Cambridge University Press).
Latsis, Spiro (1976), *Method and Appraisal in Economics* (Cambridge: Cambridge University Press).
Levi-Strauss, Claude (1978), *The Origin of Table Manners*, translated by John and Doreen Weightman (London: Jonathan Cape).
Litterman, Robert B. (1984), 'Forecasting and Policy Analysis with Bayesian Vector Autoregression Models', *Federal Reserve Bank of Minneapolis Quarterly Review*, **8** (4), pp. 30–41.
Long, John B. and Plosser, Charles I. (1983), 'Real Business Cycles', *Journal of Political Economy*, **91** (1), pp. 39–69.
Lovell, Michael C. (1986), 'Tests of the Rational Expectations Hypothesis', *American Economic Review*, **76** (1), pp. 110–24.
Lucas, Robert E., Jr. (1972a), 'Expectations and the Neutrality of Money', reprinted in Lucas (1981) pp. 66–89.
—— (1972b), 'Econometric Testing of the Natural Rate Hypothesis', in Lucas (1981) pp. 90–103. Reprinted from pp. 50–9 of Otto Eckstein (ed.), *The Econometrics of Price Determination Conference* (Washington, D.C.: Board of Governors of the Federal Reserve System).
—— (1973), 'Some International Evidence on Output–Inflation Tradeoffs', in Lucas (1981) pp. 131–45. Reprinted from *American Economic Review*, **63** (3), pp. 326–34.
—— (1975), 'An Equilibrium Model of the Business Cycle', in Lucas (1981) pp. 179–214. Reprinted from *Journal of Political Economy*, **86** (6), pp. 1113–44.
—— (1976), 'Econometric Policy Evaluation: A Critique', in Lucas (1981) pp. 104–30. Reprinted from pp. 19–46 of Karl Brunner and Allan H. Meltzer (eds), *The Phillips Curve and Labor Markets*, Carnegie-Rochester Conference Series on Public Policy, vol. 1 (Amsterdam: North-Holland).
—— (1977), 'Understanding Business Cycles', in Lucas (1981) pp. 215–39. Reprinted from Karl Brunner and Allan H. Meltzer (eds), *Stabilization of the Domestic and International Economy*, Carnegie-Rochester Conference Series on Public Policy, vol. 5, Spring (Amsterdam: North-Holland).
—— (1980a). 'Equilibrium in a Pure Currency Economy', in Kareken and Wallace (1980) pp. 131–46.
—— (1980b), 'Methods and Problems in Business Cycle Theory', in Lucas (1981) pp. 271–96. Reprinted from *Journal of Money, Credit and Banking*, **12** (4, part 2).
—— (1981), *Studies in Business Cycle Theory* (Oxford: Basil Blackwell).
—— (1984), 'Money in a Theory of Finance', in Karl Brunner and Allan H. Meltzer (eds) *Essays on Macroeconomic Implications of Financial and Labor Markets and the Political Process*, Carnegie-Rochester Conference Series on Public Policy, vol. 21 (Amsterdam: North-Holland).

—— (1987), *Models of Business Cycles* (Oxford: Basil Blackwell).
Lucas, Robert E. Jr. and Rapping, Leonard A. (1969), 'Real Wages, Employment and Inflation', in Lucas (1981) pp 19–58. Reprinted from *Journal of Political Economy* **77** (5), pp. 721–54.
Lucas, Robert E. Jr. and Sargent, Thomas J. (1979), 'After Keynesian Macroeconomics, reprinted in Lucas and Sargent (1981) pp. 295–320.
—— (1981), *Rational Expectations and Econometric Practice* (London: George Allen & Unwin).
Lucas, Robert E. Jr. and Stokey, Nancy L. (1983), 'Optimal Fiscal and Monetary Policy in a Cash-in-Advance Economy', *Journal of Monetary Economics*, **12** (1), pp. 55–93.
Masterman, Margaret (1970), 'The Nature of a Paradigm', in Lakatos and Musgrave (1970) pp. 59–90.
Mirowski, Philip (1988), *Against Mechanism: Protecting Economics from Science* (Totowa, NJ: Rowman & Littlefield).
Mishkin, Frederic S. (1983), *A Rational Expectations Approach to Macroeconomics: Testing Policy Effectiveness and Efficient Market Models* (Chicago: University of Chicago Press).
Muth, John F. (1961), 'Rational Expectations and the Theory of Price Movements', in Lucas and Sargent (1981) pp. 3–22. Reprinted from *Econometrica*, **29** (6).
Nelson, Charles R. and Plosser, Charles I. (1982), 'Trends and Random Walks in Macroeconomic Time Series: Some Evidence and Implications', *Journal of Monetary Economics*, **10** (2), pp. 139–62.
Newton-Smith, W.H. (1981), *The Rationality of Science* (London: Routledge & Kegan Paul).
Peirce, Charles S. (1931), *Collected Papers*, vol. 1 (Cambridge, Mass.: Belknap Press).
Phelps, Edmund (1967), 'Phillips Curves, Expectations of Inflation and Optimal Unemployment Over Time', *Economica* NS, **34** (3), pp. 254–81.
Phelps, Edmund and Taylor, John B. (1977), 'Stabilizing Powers of Monetary Policy Under Rational Expectations', *Journal of Political Economy*, **85** (1), pp. 163–90.
Prescott, Edward C. (1986), 'Theory Ahead of Measurement', *Federal Reserve Bank of Minneapolis Quarterly Review* **10** (4), pp. 9–22. Reprinted from Karl Brunner and Allan H. Meltzer (eds), *Real Business Cycles, Real Exchange Rates and Actual Policies*, Carnegie-Rochester Conference Series on Public Policy, vol. 25, Autumn (Amsterdam: North-Holland).
Remenyi, Joseph V. (1979), 'Core Demi-core Interaction: Toward a General Theory of Disciplinary and Subdisciplinary Growth', *History of Political Economy*, **11** (1), pp. 30–63.
Samuelson, Paul A. (1958), 'An Exact Consumption-Loan Model of Interest with or without the Social Contrivance of Money', *Journal of Political Economy*, **56** (6), pp. 467–82.
Sargent, Thomas J. (1973), 'Rational Expectations, the Real Rate of Interest and the Natural Rate of Unemployment', *Brookings Papers on Economic Activity*, no. 2, pp. 429–72.
—— (1976a), 'A Classical Macroeconometric Model for the United States', in Lucas and Sargent (1981) pp. 521–51. Reprinted from *Journal of Political Economy*, **84** (2).

—— (1976b), 'The Observational Equivalence of Natural and Unnatural Rate Theories of Macroeconomics', in Lucas and Sargent (1981) ppl 553–62. Reprinted from *Journal of Political Economy*, **84** (3).
—— (1977), 'The Demand for Money during Hyperinflations under Rational Expectations', in Lucas and Sargent (1981) pp. 429–52. Reprinted from *International Economic Review*, **18** (1).
—— (1978), 'Estimation of Dynamic Labor Demand Schedules under Rational Expectations', in Lucas and Sargent (1981) pp. 463–500. Reprinted from *Journal of Polititical Economy*, **86** (6).
—— (1979), *Macroeconomic Theory* (New York: Academic Press).
—— (1981), 'Interpreting Economic Time Series', *Journal of Political Economy*, **89** (2), pp. 213–48.
—— (1982), 'Beyond Demand and Supply Curves in Macroeconomics', *American Economic Review*, **72** (2), pp. 382–9.
—— (1986), *Rational Expectations and Inflation* (New York: Harper & Row).
—— (1987), *Dynamic Macroeconomic Theory* (Cambridge, Mass.: Harvard University Press).
—— (1975), ' "Rational Expectations", the Optimal Monetary Instrument and the Optimal Money Supply Rule', in Lucas and Sargent (1981) pp. 215–28. Reprinted from *Journal of Political Economy*, **83** (2), pp. 241–54.
—— (1976), 'Rational Expectations and the Theory of Economic Policy', in Lucas and Sargent (1981) pp. 199–213. Reprinted from *Journal of Monetary Economics*, **2** (2), pp. 169–83.
—— (1981), 'Some Unpleasant Monetarist Arithmetic', *Federal Reserve Bank of Minneapolis Quarterly Review*, **5** (3), pp. 1–17. Reprinted in Sargent (1986).
—— (1982), 'The Real-Bills Doctrine versus the Quantity Theory: A Reconsideration', *Journal of Political Economy*, **90** (6), pp. 1212–36.
Sargent, Thomas J. and Sims, Christopher A. (1977), 'Business Cycle Modeling without Pretending to Have Too Much *A Priori* Theory', in *New Methods in Business Cycle Research: Proceedings from a Conference* (Minneapolis: Federal Reserve Bank of Minneapolis), pp. 45–110.
Sargent, Thomas J. and Wallace, Neil (1973), 'Rational Expectations and Dynamics of Hyperinflation', in Lucas and Sargent (1981) pp. 405–28.
Sims, Christopher A. (1972), 'Money, Income and Causality', in Lucas and Sargent (1981) pp. 387–403. Reprinted from *American Economic Review*, **62** (4), pp. 540–52.
—— (1980), 'Macroeconomics and Reality', *Econometrica*, **48** (1), pp. 1–48.
—— (1982), 'Policy Analysis with Econometric Models', *Brookings Papers on Economic Activity*, no. 1, pp. 107–52.
—— (1986a), 'A Rational Expectations Framework for Short Run Policy Analysis', in William A. Barnett and Kenneth J. Singleton (eds), *New Approaches to Monetary Economics: Proceedings from the Second International Symposium in Economic Theory and Econometrics* (Cambridge: Cambridge University Press).
—— (1986b), 'Are Forecasting Models Usable for Policy Analysis?, *Federal Reserve Bank of Minneapolis Quarterly Review*, Winter, pp. 2–15.
Solow, Robert M. (1956), 'A Contribution to the Theory of Economic Growth', *Quarterly Journal of Economics*, **70** (1), pp. 65–94.

—— (1957), 'Technical Change and the Aggregate Production Function', *Review of Economics and Statistics,* **39** (3), pp. 312–20.

Taylor, John B. (1975), 'Monetary Policy during the Transition to Rational Expectations', *Journal of Political Economy*, **83** (6), pp. 1009–21.

Wallace, Neil (1980), 'The Overlapping Generations Model of Fiat Money', in Kareken and Wallace (1980) pp. 49–82.

—— (1981), 'A Modigliani–Miller Theorem for Open-Market Operations', *American Economic Review*, **71** (3), pp. 267–74.

Weintraub, E. Roy (1985), *General Equilibrium Analysis: Studies in Appraisal* (Cambridge: Cambridge University Press).

Wittgenstein, Ludwig (1953), *Philosophical Investigations* (Oxford: Basil Blackwell).

—— (1975), *The Blue and Brown Books* (Oxford: Basil Blackwell).

COMMENT ON HOOVER

Nancy J. Wulwick

The essay by Kevin Hoover is flashy, brilliant. In a discipline replete with mathematics, the convenient subterfuge for poverty of expression, that Hoover so powerfully wields literary metaphor in making his arguments is indeed remarkable.

The key metaphor of Kevin's essay is that economics is a region occupied by tribes. Leijonhufvud (1973) too wrote about life among the econ, as a tribal nation.[1] Since Kevin by original training is a philosopher, it is not surprising that his metaphor is a familiar one in the philosophy of science. Wittgenstein, whom he quotes, saw that concepts may have 'family resemblances' and Toulmin saw related concepts as regions on a map.[2] Hoover, the author of *New Classical Macroeconomics* (1988), encyclopaedically traces the historical development of the new classical tribe. His essay is undoubtedly a *tour de force*.

Yet, I find, in my capacity as an historian of economic thought, that his anthropological analogy gives an unexceptional, yet insufficient rationale for the new classical economic story. The organization of the material that comes before the historian of economics goes beyond a mere familial classification. The historian of economics analyses the *dynamic* that led economic concepts to appear to be grouped as they are.

Lakatos offered historians of science specific guidelines on the way to approach their subject-matter. I amongst others have told a convincing story about modern economics by applying the Lakatos methodology (Wulwick, 1987).[3]

Kevin, however, has not understood the historiographical problem that Lakatos perceived or the way that he attempted to solve this problem. In gist, Lakatos tried to demarcate science from non-science, while recognizing that scientific practice in fact was often unscientific. This by nature was a complex problem. Moreover Lakatos, as is the wont of many creative thinkers, presented the answer in a haphazard, messy way. By focusing on singular quotes drawn from Lakatos's 1970 essay, it seems to me that Kevin has adopted the genre of setting up a straw man in order to develop his own line of argument.

It would have been inappropriate for me at the conference, peopled as it was by the *cognoscenti* of methodology, to give an exegesis of what Lakatos said. Thus I have adopted the familiar strategy in Comments such as these of giving a counter-example to reveal the weakness in my colleague's argument. This counter example is about new classical economic growth theory, which Kevin has not discussed.

The Comment touches upon three topics: (1) the importance of competition, (2) the validity of the notion of the positive heuristic, and (3) the role of empirical progress, in the Lakatos methodology of scientific research programs. In concluding, the Comment pinpoints a problem within the Lakatos methodology itself that requires further thought.

In the new graduate textbook of the day, Blanchard and Fischer (1989) begin by stating an established fact about economic growth.[4] They call this the Solow-Kaldor fact of growth, which states that the rate of productivity growth is positive and shows no tendency to fall. Chapter 2 of the textbook explains this fact by means of a dynamic utility-maximizing model. Subject to the national income accounting identity and the production function, the calculus of variations gives the rate of increase of capital that maximizes the utility integrand. Traditionally the terminal condition of this so-called Ramsey–Solow model was steady state growth (Ramsay, 1928; Solow, 1956).[5] Rebelo (1987), Romer (1986, 1989) and Lucas (1988) have amended the production function to produce increasing returns.[6] With this change in the technological constraint, the solution to the maximization problem yields productivity growth. Thus Blanchard and Fischer conclude that the new models reproduce the Solow–Kaldor fact of growth.

Three questions arise in trying to make sense of the new growth models. First, what sort of economics have the growth models adopted? Romer, who recently received his PhD at Chicago, came under Lucas's sway. Rebelo, who has just received his PhD at Rochester, was a student of King, a new classical macroeconomist, and of Romer. Given his new classical pedigree, it was with some initial dismay that I discovered considerable diversity in the Lucas/Rebelo/Romer models. Robelo arrived at productivity growth by setting the elasticity of output in respect to capital to one, as if capital did not work with a fixed factor. Romer treated specialized capital inputs as if these were technological externalities. Lucas added a variable of human capital that accounts for the statistical residual previously attributed to exogenous technical progress. These different models have contrasting policy implications. Rebelo and Romer have permitted taxation to encourage growth, Lucas has ruled out policy interventions.

However all the models have assumed (1) that agents attempt to maximize utility; (2) the existence of a competitive equilibrium, if only Pareto sub-optimal; and (3) perfect foresight of all relevant prices, whether on the part of the social planner or the private people. Looking at Weintraub's (1985) list of 'hard core' assumptions of the neo-Walrasian research program, it seems to me that these new classical economic growth models belong to the protective belt of that research program.[7] In other words, the new classical economics constitutes one 'tribe' within the neo-Walrasian 'nation'.

However such bald classification of economic ideas as Kevin has pointed out smacks of arbitrariness. The classification works only to the extent that my story is compelling. Let us continue.

Second, what does the new growth theory do? The new growth economists admit that they are merely explaining a well-known fact. Their contribution as they see it is to do so by means of the best mathematical technique. Though many of the models really are not so technically sophisticated, the authors adhere to the ethos that, as Lakatos remarked, the engineer will, as a matter of fact, prefer the predictions of the most advanced theory of the day'.[8] In the minds of the new classical theorists, appropriate modelling ensures the understanding of the fact of economic growth that the neoclassical and the post-Keynesian theories failed to provide.

The neoclassical growth model, introduced by Solow (1957), produced productivity growth by adding a multiplicative factor of technical progress to the constant returns to scale production function.[9] This growth model was a partial equilibrium model that ignored utility maximization and took into account the fact that the labour market may fail to clear. Moreover, in making technical progress exogenous, so the new classical economists have contended, the neoclassical model cannot show the effects of government intervention on the potential rate of growth. This indeed is the case for the neoclassical growth model based on the conventional production function, which presented a problem for Solow, who was involved in growth policy. His 1962 paper on the lagging US growth rate was written when he was a staff member of the Council of Economic Advisers and his 1959 paper on long run growth was an input to the 1962 *Economic Report of the President*, which proposed expansionary policies to promote capital investment and thus accelerate the growth of potential output.[10] Solow solved his modelling problem by maintaining the constant returns to scale production function, while redefining capital as vintage capital, with the result that investment was needed to put the newest techniques into effect. His mathematical models, though, failed to explain the source of the technical progress embodied in investment.

Countering the neoclassical model, the post-Keynesian Kaldor constructed demand-led growth models in which technical progress depended on the amount of capital investment (Kaldor 1957, 1958)[11]

But Kaldor did not think that agents optimized. And he knew too little and disliked mathematics too much to model formally non-convexities. There is little difference between the outcome of the Kaldor and the Romer demand-led growth models. Both, for instance, generate a stable growth path with a rising capital–labour ratio. Yet, as Romer has pointed out, he unlike Kaldor has arrived at the right result the 'right' (mathematical) way.

In sum, the new classical growth models arose as formal devices to compete with the neoclassical and post-Keynesian models and advance economic modelling by explaining the ultimate source of economic growth.

Third, why has the growth theory appeared now? Macroeconomics is pre-eminently a policy-oriented subject. Thus 'external' factors have entered into its development more than in the natural sciences.[12] Krugman's work on the phenomenal growth of the 'Gang of Four' promoted interest in growth. Weitzman's popularization of increasing returns (in the context of profit sharing) provided another impetus. De Long (1988) showed that the growth rates of rich countries in the mid-1800s have diverged since, which conflicted with the predictions of neoclassical theory and invited some notion of increasing returns.[13] Ostensibly the new growth theory shows the new classical economists to be as pragmatic and policy-oriented as the next (neoclassical) guy.

Let us now consider the 'internal' factors. By the 1980s, new classical econometrics developed to that point where growth theory became a timely research topic. The new classical econometric techniques integrated the 'business cycle' with the 'growth trend'. As a result, growth itself became a non-stationary trend. (In contrast, the old, neo-classical models made the cycle deviate from a stationary trend.) The new growth theory has complemented the new classical econometric model. In particular, the mathematics of the new theory can model the jumps of the optimal growth path due to exogenous shocks.

The new classical theory evinces the solution to an old mathematical problem. From 1930 to 1960, neo-Walrasian theorists focused on mathematical proofs of Walras's proposition that the perfectly competitive market produces a stable general equilibrium. The Ramsey (1928) problem, how to model the path of this general equilibrium, was put on the 'back burner'. In 1956, Samuelson and Solow clumsily solved the Ramsey problem by using the calculus of variations, with which most economists of the time were unfamiliar. In the 1960s, the calculus of variations received a boost. The prize-winning book by Pontryagin *et al.* (1962) showed how to control the optimal trajectory of space vehicles even when inequalities, boundary maxima and discontinuities (or 'jumps') were involved.[14] The Pontryagin 'maximum principle' generalized dynamic maximization in the same way that the Kuhn–Tucker theorem generalized the static case. Neo-Walrasian growth theory, interpreting the solution to the missile-optimizing problem in terms of prices (in itself a quantum jump), henceforth became a variant of optimal control theory, despite the conspicuous absence of a suitable controller.[15] Within the abstract context in which the new classical economists work, the modern calculus of variations promises a substantive pay-off.

The conclusion to this story about new classical growth theory can go two ways. As Lakatos stated,

> [a] '*model*' is a set of initial conditions . . . which one knows is *bound* to be replaced during the further development of the programme, and one even knows, more or less, how . . . [I]f the positive heuristic is clearly spelt out, the difficulties of the programme are mathematical rather than empirical. (1978, I, p. 51)

Accordingly we might conclude that neo-Walrasian general equilibrium theory, by solving the problem of the optimal general equilibrium path, has achieved heuristic success. However, as Lakatos continued. 'We may appraise research programmes . . . for their *heuristic power*: how many new facts did they produce . . .?' (p. 52). In this light, the development of the new classical growth theory, in merely accommodating a known fact, signifies the degeneration of the neo-Walrasian research program.[16]

The moral of this story is that economists who admire Lakatos need to clarify the connection between the concept of heuristic power and the criterion of empirical progress. Without this connection, the methodology of scientific research programs, while useful in historiography, is limited as a tool of appraisal.

Notes

1. Leijonhufvud, A. (1973), 'Life Among the Econ', *Western Economic Journal*, **11**, pp. 327–37;
2. *Wittgenstein*, D. Bloor (1983) p. 30; *The Philosophy of Science*, S. Toulmin (1952) pp. 113–14.
3. 'The Phillips Curve: Which? Whose? To Do What? How?', *Southern Economic Journal*, 1987.
4. *Lectures on Macroeconomics*, MIT, p. 81 and ch. 1.
5. F.P. Ramsey (1928) 'A Mathematical Theory of Saving', *Economic Journal*, pp. 543–59; Solow, R.M. (1956), 'A Contribution to the Theory of Economic Growth', *Quarterly Journal of Economics*, pp. 65–94.
6. S. Rebelo (1987), 'Long Run Policy Analysis and Long Run Growth', unpublished paper; R.E. Lucas (1988), 'On the Mechanics of Economic Development', *Journal*

of Monetary Economics, pp. 3–42; P. Romer (1986), 'Increasing Returns and Long-Run Growth', *Journal of Political Economy*, pp. 1002–37; P. Romer (1989), 'Capital Accumulation in the Theory of Long-Run Growth', in *Modern Business Cycle Theory* (Harvard University Press).

7. *General Equilibrium Analysis: Studies in Appraisal*, E.R. Weintraub, p. 109.
8. 'History of Science and its Rational Reconstructions', in (1978), *The Methodology of Scientific Research Programmes, Philosophical Papers, Volume I, Imre Lakatos* edited by John Worrall and Gregory Currie (Cambridge: Cambridge University Press), p. 192.
9. Solow, R.M. (1957), 'Technical Change and the Aggregate Production Function', *Review of Economics and Statistics*, **23**, pp. 101–8.
10. R.M. Solow (1959), 'Investment and Technical Progress', in *Mathematical Methods in the Social Sciences*, edited by K.J. Arrow *et al.*, (Stanford University Press); (1962), 'Technical Progress, Capital Formation, and Economic Growth', *American Economic Review*, **52**, pp. 76–86 (p. 81); *Economic Report of the President, Hearing before the JEC, 87th Congress, March 1961*, pp. 335–41, 372.
11. N. Kaldor (1957), 'A Model of Economic Growth', *Economic Journal*, pp. 591–624; (1958) 'Capital Accumulation and Economic Growth', printed in (1963) *The Theory of Capital, Proceedings of a Conference held by the International Economic Association*, edited by F.A. Lutz and D.C. Hague, Macmillan.
12. 'History of Science and its Rational Reconstructions', in *Philosophical Papers, Volume 1, Imre Lakatos* (1978), p. 138.
13. J.B. de Long (1988), 'Productivity Growth, Convergence, and Welfare,' *American Economic Review*, **78**, pp. 1138–54.
14. Pontryagin, L.S., *et al.*, *The Mathematical Theory of Optimal Processes.*
15. *Mathematical Theories of Economic Growth*, E. Burmeister and A.R. Dobell (1970), 12.
16. Lakatos, 'History of Science', p. 112.

REPLY TO WULWICK

Kevin D. Hoover

Nancy Wulwick has a sharp eye for the chinks in one's armour. I pointedly omitted consideration of the recent new classical literature on growth with increasing returns because I am largely ignorant of it. I therefore found her comment instructive and useful, if somewhat beside the point of my paper. She tells the tale well; but her telling leaves me with no doubt that it fits better into the positive framework of my paper than into Lakatos's methodology of scientific research programs.

Wulwick accuses me of practising the venerable fallacy of erecting a straw man for the pleasure of knocking it over. It is never made explicit, however, for which of Lakatos's features I have substituted straw for flesh, bone and blood. The bulk of Wulwick's comment is not devoted to substantiating this charge – making it, of course, especially difficult to answer. Rather it concentrates on her own tale about growth theory. As far as this is pertinent to my argument at all, it commits the fallacy of *ignoratio elenchi*.

New classical growth theory is held up as a counter-example to my analysis. The story that Wulwick tells goes back to Ramsey, Kaldor, Samuelson and Solow. It is a story of diverse models, which nonetheless have common threads, responding to newly acquired technical capacities on the part of economists and to concrete empirical puzzles – for example, the 'Kaldor fact' and the non-convergence of growth rates. Her portrayal of me to the contrary notwithstanding, I never shared her initial dismay at the diversity of the models nor am I now so greatly impressed by their common features – for both are precisely what my analysis of other cases suggests that one should expect.

Wulwick's conclusion attempts to establish something I never denied. There are research programs; the historian may use the notion if she finds it useful. Wulwick's story is not a counter-example; for I have never given an example that conflicts with it. Instead it is a story of borrowing, adaptation and development in which the facts that Ramsey was a pre-Keynesian, Kaldor a post-Keynesian (of sorts), Samuelson and Solow neoclassical synthesizers and Lucas, Romer *et al.* new classicals seem to have no purchase whatever. Indeed Wulwick seems to subsume them all into a neo-Walrasian research program. This last move requires exactly the sort of loose usage about what it is to be a research program against which I argued at length.

New classical macroeconomics, including its recent forays into growth theory, can be beaten into the likeness of a Lakatosian scientific research program. But the Lakatosian program, however specified, does not exert any normative force over the practitioners within the program. Some will argue (and Lakatos himself argues) that his methodology is not meant to do this. But Lakatos is not consistent on this point; and, in any case, I do not believe that he is entitled to make it once he begins to use words like 'appraisal', 'progressive' and 'degenerating', which carry normative baggage under every reasonable interpretation, and once he begins to give advice such as cutting the funding of degenerating research programs. In contrast, it seems to me that the concrete exemplars of the new classical economics (that is, the models and the examples of successful empirical investigation and interpretation) do exert normative force. Wulwick's story, I believe, gives further support to this view.

12. The Neo-Walrasian Research Program in Macroeconomics

Roger E. Backhouse*

1 THE PROBLEM

The notion that contemporary macroeconomics can be viewed as part of a 'neo-Walrasian' research program or something very similar is hardly novel or, perhaps, very controversial. The desire of contemporary macroeconomists to ground their theories in individual optimizing behaviour and to have a coherent microeconomic foundation for what they do, the main characteristic of neo-Walrasian economics, is almost too obvious to require comment. The issue of how far contemporary macroeconomics can legitimately be viewed as part of such a Lakatosian scientific research program and the process whereby this came about have, however, never been properly investigated. The purpose of this chapter is to make a first attempt at filling this gap.[1]

The thesis put forward here[2] is that mainstream macroeconomics since Keynes can be viewed in terms of the extension of the neo-Walrasian research program to encompass theories which previously lay outside its domain and to explain an increasing range of macroeconomic phenomena.[3] The starting-point (in section 2) is the definition of the hard core and heuristics of the neo-Walrasian research program, together with an explanation of what it means to talk about a research program's being extended to encompass theories developed outside the program.[4] We then go on (in section 3) to provide a rational reconstruction of the history of macroeconomics since Keynes. After considering, in section 4, some of the issues involved, we discuss, in section 5, some of the novel facts predicted by the neo-Walrasian research program.

* This chapter is a greatly revised version of part of a paper presented to a seminar on 'Post War Economic Thinking and its Relevance for Policy' at the Katholieke Universiteit, Leuven, in May 1988. I am indebted to the participants in this seminar, and to Mark Blaug, Tony Brewer and Neil de Marchi, for helpful comments on various drafts of the paper. Special thanks are due to Roy Weintraub, whose extensive criticisms and invaluable advice led me to modify the original draft substantially. Needless to say, none of them should be held responsible for the use I have made of their ideas.

Section 6 tackles the all-important issue of whether or not the research program is progressive. Conclusions are drawn in the final section.

2 THE NEO-WALRASIAN RESEARCH PROGRAM

The best starting-point is Weintraub's definition of the neo-Walrasian research program (Weintraub, 1985, p. 109). He defines six hard-core propositions.

HC1 There exist economic agents.
HC2 Agents have preferences over outcomes.
HC3 Agents independently optimize, subject to constraints.
HC4 Choices are made in interrelated markets.
HC5 Agents have full relevant knowledge.
HC6 Observable economic outcomes are coordinated, so they must be discussed with reference to equilibrium states.

There are also positive and negative heuristics, such as the following:

PH1 Go forth and construct theories in which agents optimize.
PH2 Construct theories that make predictions about equilibrium states.
NH1 Do not construct theories in which irrational behaviour plays any role.
NH2 Do not construct theories in which equilibrium has no meaning.
NH3 Do not test hard core propositions.

This definition of a neo-Walrasian research program was designed for analysing the evolution of general equilibrium theory, something Weintraub manages to do very successfully. If we are to analyse the progress of macroeconomics since Keynes in terms of the neo-Walrasian research program, however, we need to define the program a little more broadly. In particular, propositions HC5 and HC6 need to be changed. In addition certain other heuristics, not stated by Weintraub, need to be made explicit.

The need to drop the assumption of 'full relevant knowledge' is obvious, for limited knowledge is a key factor in many present-day macroeconomic models.[5] Even models which assume rational expectations are not assuming perfect foresight. We could replace HC5 with a weaker hard-core proposition, but it seems better to replace it with an additional positive heuristic:

PH3 Construct theories in which agents have a well-defined set of information about relevant phenomena.[6]

Proposition HC6 is more difficult, for a number of reasons. In the literature Weintraub was concerned with, equilibrium was a clearly defined concept. In macroeconomics, on the other hand, there are two problems with the concept of equilibrium. One is that the term 'equilibrium' is used in a number of different ways. The other is that much macroeconomics has been concerned with disequilibrium, and with the failure of the market to coordinate economic activities. It would, of course, be possible to define the terms 'equilibrium' and 'coordination' in such a way as to render HC6 a hard core proposition for mainstream macroeconomics, but it seems preferable to replace it with something less misleading. Finding an acceptable alternative is difficult, for proposition HC6 covers two aspects of neo-Walrasian economics: the notion that markets coordinate the actions of different individuals and the idea that we should, in our theories, allow for the effects of market interactions working themselves through. The best solution is simply to drop HC6. The first aspect of HC6 is already covered by HC4. The second aspect can be picked up by modifying PH2 (which has to be modified anyway for the same reasons as we have to drop HC6). A suitable modification is to replace HC6 with the following:

PH2* Specify the model-specific meanings of equilibrium and disequilibrium and analyse the model in terms of these.

One of the characteristics of neo-Walrasian economics, which distinguishes it from much earlier economic writing, is that formal models are used. In his appraisal of general equilibrium theory it was not necessary for Weintraub to make this explicit: the whole literature took this for granted. In macroeconomics, however, this is not the case, many economists having worked with much more rough and ready methods. To define the neo-Walrasian research program properly, therefore, we need to add to the above list of positive heuristics.

PH4 Construct fully-specified, consistent models, simplifying where necessary in order to be able to do this, and draw only those conclusions which can be proved to be implied by the models.

PH5 Specify the rules governing the interaction of agents (in terms of game theory, make the game explicit).

In many cases PH5 implies competition, but it is of course more general. Some equilibrium element is obviously implied by the assumption that agents optimize: in this limited sense, therefore, equilibrium is implied by HC2 and PH1.

If we accept these modifications to Weintraub's definition of the neo-Walrasian research program we have a program with the following hard core and positive heuristics (the negative heuristics are exactly the same as for Weintraub). Note that the positive heuristics have been placed in a more sensible order and have been re-numbered (subsequent references all refer to this new list).

HC1 There exist economic agents.
HC2 Agents have preferences over outcomes.
HC3 Agents independently optimize, subject to constraints.
HC4 Choices are made in interrelated markets.

PH1′ (PH4) Construct fully-specified, consistent models, simplifying where necessary in order to be able to do this, and draw only those conclusions which can be proved to be implied by the models.
PH2′ (PH2*) Specify the model-specific meanings of equilibrium and disequilibrium and analyse the model in terms of these.
PH3′ (PH1) Construct theories in which agents optimize subject to constraints.
PH4′ (PH5) Specify the rules governing the interaction of agents (in terms of game theory, make the game explicit).
PH5′ (PH3) Construct theories in which agents have a well-defined set of information about relevant phenomena.

This is slightly but significantly broader than the research program suggested by Weintraub and it can be used to make sense of the main developments in mainstream macroeconomics since Keynes. General equilibrium theory, as analysed by Weintraub, can easily be seen as a part of this research program. Overall the research program presented here has a smaller hard core and a longer list of positive heuristics than Weintraub's: in other words, we are placing a greater emphasis on the neo-Walrasian research program as a research strategy rather than a set of assumptions about the world. It has to be said, however, that the differences are very slight. Whether we use the term neo-Walrasian to denote the broader program suggested here, or the 'sub-program' described by Weintraub, is essentially arbitrary and is of no importance.

Finally, before going on to consider the history of macroeconomics, we need to consider the notion that a scientific research program may be extended to encompass *theories* that previously lay outside its domain, for this is not the same as that of a research program dealing with anomalies. The idea is that, possibly quite apart from any anomalies, theories may have been developed outside the research program (they may have been developed within another program) which can be used and developed in accordance with the program's positive heuristics. If this happens it is quite possible that theories may be taken over before economists[7] have been able to establish whether they are or are not consistent with the program's hard core. The theories concerned may contain anomalies, the hard core being protected from these in the usual way, or it may be that the question of consistency with the hard core has, temporarily, been left open. The work needed to do this may be postponed for several reasons: (a) a desire to tackle problems one at a time; (b) an absence of suitable techniques for tackling certain problems; (c) a desire to try out theories before being convinced that it is worth finding out whether or not they can be integrated into the research program.

3 A RATIONAL RECONSTRUCTION OF MACROECONOMICS SINCE KEYNES

Phase I: The Establishment of the Neo-Walrasian Research Program

Keynes's *General Theory* was certainly not part of any neo-Walrasian research program. In particular his theory was based on certain 'psychological laws' which had no grounding in optimizing behaviour. Assumptions HC2 and HC3 were not a part of Keynesian economics. Similarly Keynes did not follow the heuristics detailed above. On the other hand, although Keynes himself was reluctant to use his theory in this way, it was only a short step from the *General Theory* to constructing a formal model of the economy as a whole, for it contained all the necessary simplifications. In addition he defined a new concept of equilibrium appropriate to his model. This achievement was succinctly summed up by J.M. Clark, who wrote, in a letter to Keynes,

> It has seemed to me that what I call the 'income-flow analysis', of which yours is the most noted presentation, has done something which has not been done in comparable degree since Ricardo and Marx: namely, constructed a coherent logical theoretical system or formula having the quality of a mechanism, growing directly out of current conditions and problems which are of paramount importance and furnishing a key to working out definite answers in terms of policy. (Keynes, 1971–83, XXIII, p. 191)

The first stage in the extension of the neo-Walrasian research program to cover macroeconomics was to take Keynes's simplifications and, following PH1′ and PH2′, to construct from them a coherent, formal model of the economy. This was the achievement of Champernowne (1936), Harrod (1937), Meade (1937) and Hicks (1937). In the process of doing this they re-defined the notion of equilibrium, expressing it in terms of simultaneous equations (absent from the *General Theory*).[8] The remaining positive heuristics were, at this stage, ignored. The main reason for this was that the most important task was to show that, assuming it could eventually be reconciled with the program's hard core, the new theory could be used to solve interesting problems: that it constituted a progressive problem shift. This is one of the reasons why Hicks's contribution was so important: although all four worked with what was essentially the same set of equations, it was he who showed, in a way that Champernowne, Meade and Harrod did not, how the new mathematical apparatus could be used to solve the riddle of how Keynes's theory related to that of the classics.

The next stage in establishing the neo-Walrasian research program was to follow up PH3′ and to replace Keynes's somewhat arbitrary (by neo-Walrasian standards) behavioural functions with ones securely based on optimizing behaviour. This took place in the 1940s and 1950s. The main work involved the two most novel aspects of then *General Theory* – the consumption function and the demand for money – and includes the well-known contributions of Friedman, Modigliani, Baumol, Tobin *et al.*[9] The third major component of Keynes's theory, his marginal efficiency of capital, also received attention, though this presented less of a problem as it was believed to correspond fairly closely to traditional concepts thought quite consistent with optimizing behaviour.

At the same time as detailed work was being carried out on the component parts of the Keynesian system, work was also being undertaken on the explicit integration of such optimizing models into a formal model of the economy as a whole, the most important work here being Patinkin's *Money, Interest and Prices* (1957).[10] Earlier writers (for example, Modigliani, 1944) had contributed to this process by putting Keynesian/Hicksian equation systems forward as aggregative versions of Walrasian models, but the link between micro- and macro-systems was far clearer and more explicit in Patinkin's work than in previous contributions. In addition the major technical problems concerning the compatibility of Keynesian theory, the quantity theory and Walrasian excess demand functions had by then been solved (or were thought to have been solved).[11] The theory, popularized by Samuelson (1955) as 'the neoclassical synthesis'[12] and of which *Money, Interest and Prices* is the outstanding example, was consistent with the neo-Walrasian hard core and in addition all the positive heuristics bar one[13] had been followed. By the mid-1950s, therefore, the neo-Walrasian research program in macroeconomics had been securely established.[14] There was still much work to do, but subsequent work can be seen as developing and extending the program rather than as establishing it.

Phase III: The Development of the Neo-Walrasian Research Program

The first major challenge to the neoclassical synthesis, as it is reasonable to call the macroeconomic theory that had emerged by the end of the 1950s, was posed by Clower (1965).[15] The neo-classical synthesis explained unemployment in terms of wage rigidity: the labour market was not in equilibrium. Clower's argument was that if the labour market were not in equilibrium the conventional model of consumer decisions would be mis-specified. It was necessary to re-write the consumer's maximization problem such that demands for goods depended not only on endowments and prices but also on realized sales of labour (or any other good the consumer is trying to sell). More generally, if an agent faces a constraint in one market his or her demands or supplies in all other markets will typically be affected. Clower presented these arguments as a challenge to the prevailing theory, but it is important to note that, though Clower saw them as presenting a fundamental challenge to orthodox ideas, they did not constitute any challenge to the neo-Walrasian research program *as it is defined here*: indeed his work could be construed as following its heuristics very closely. He observed an inconsistency in the existing theories and modified the theory in such a way as to protect the hard core.

Clower's ideas were soon taken up by several economists (for example, Solow and Stiglitz, 1968; Barro and Grossman, 1971; Malinvaud, 1977)[16] who used them as the basis for new models of macroeconomic equilibrium. The assumption of wage inflexibility made in the neoclassical synthesis models was generalized to the assumption that all prices took time to move,[17] the new 'rationing models' describing the equilibria that would result as long as prices were out of equilibrium. These models were formal optimizing models, specifying a new set of rules governing the interaction between agents. They defined a new equilibrium concept (fixed price equilibrium) in terms of which the economy was analysed. This was all in accordance with the positive heuristics of the neo-Walrasian research program.

For a few years this extension to the neo-Walrasian research program appeared both theoretically and empirically progressive. Focusing on the failure of prices to adjust instantaneously rather than on wage inflexibility seemed to remove an anomaly in explanations of unemployment. In addition the use of rationing models led to further successful predictions, some of which are discussed in section 5 below. These new insights, however, proved limited. More important than this, by the mid-1970s the assumption of price stickiness came to be seen as a major anomaly, and attempts were made to solve it through what turned out to be a progressive extension of the research program.

The problem with existing theories was that variations in the level of output and employment could be explained only by assuming that prices were inflexible, an assumption which seemed inconsistent with the hard-core postulate of optimizing behaviour: if a market is out of equilibrium it is in the interests of both buyers and sellers to change the price. This hard-core assumption had to be protected by assuming that it was costly for firms to change prices, that changing prices took time and other assumptions which were ad hoc in the sense that they had nothing to do with either the hard core or the positive heuristics of the research program. The response to this came in papers by Phelps (1967) and Friedman (1968) who showed how limited information could be used to explain why changes in the level of demand frequently affected output and employment. Phelps explained this using his famous 'island' parable (later taken up by Lucas). The economy consists of a number of islands and, whilst workers are fully informed about prices and wages on their own island, information flows between islands are costly. If wages on one island fall, workers will not know whether this reflects an economy-wide fall in wages or whether it is specific to their own island. Some workers will thus choose to become unemployed in order to search for better wages elsewhere. A fall in wages will, therefore, even if prices fall in the same proportion, lead to a fall in employment.

It is with the work of Phelps and Friedman that PH5′ becomes important to the neo-Walrasian research program: prior to this economists had not given much attention to the information available to agents. The assumption that workers have incomplete information made it possible to reconcile unemployment with the hard-core postulate of maximizing behaviour (Phelps described himself as sticking 'doggedly' to this assumption) and turned the 'anomaly' of the Phillips curve into corroborating evidence for the neo-Walrasian program. In addition, when economists began to examine the implications of imperfect and asymmetric information and to allow for different attitudes towards risk, they started to explain previously unexplained phenomena: for example, the existence of long-term labour contracts (for example, Baily, 1974; Azariadis, 1975; Calvo and Phelps, 1977; Hall, 1980) and why employers may pay more than the market-clearing wage rate (Weiss, 1980). Anomalies have been turned into corroborating evidence for the program.

The most widely known extension to the neo-Walrasian program has been its extension to the formation of expectations: the theory of rational expectations. As with price stickiness, the assumption that expectations adjusted slowly in response to changes was ad hoc: it was part of the protective belt, required to protect the hard core. The theory of rational expectations, developed by Muth (1961) and applied to macroeconomics by Lucas (1972) showed how this anomaly could be eliminated. More important than this, however, the assumption of rational expectations opened up a new set of macroeconomic models capable of generating new predictions. Such models included not only the 'new classical macroeconomics', associated with Lucas, Sargent, Wallace, Barro and their followers, but also work such as that of Dornbusch (1976). The introduction of rational expectations was undoubtedly *theoretically* progressive. Whether or not it was *empirically* progressive is considered below.

4 EVALUATING THE NEO-WALRASIAN RESEARCH PROGRAM

Novel Facts[18]

There seems little doubt that the neo-Walrasian program in macroeconomics has been *theoretically* progressive. It has managed to explain an increasing range of economic phenomena without resorting to an increasing number of ad hoc auxiliary assumptions. The critical question, however, is whether or not it has also been *empirically* progressive. This is important for two reasons. The obvious one is that we are interested not only in explanation but also in appraisal: we want to know whether the subject is developing in a satisfactory manner. The other reason is related to this. If Lakatos's methodology of scientific research programs were an appropriate model of the way scientists (including economists) behaved, we would expect economists to support progressive research programs. Therefore, if we could show that the neo-Walrasian research program were empirically progressive, we would have shown those economists working within the program (the vast majority of post-war macroeconomists, if the rational reconstruction given here is appropriate) to have been behaving in a rational manner.

We would thus have corroborating evidence for the adequacy of the rational reconstruction contained in section 3. As Lakatos put it, 'In the light of better rational reconstructions of science one can always reconstruct more of actual great science as rational' (Lakatos, 1971, p. 132).

The fundamental notion here is that a theoretical change is progressive if it is content-increasing: if theories explain not only the facts that they were designed to explain, but also some novel facts. It is the prediction of such novel facts that distinguishes progressive research programs from series of ad hoc rationalizations. The key issue here is what constitutes a novel fact. The most clear-cut examples of novel facts are, of course, facts not known when the theory is proposed: genuine predictions which turn out to be successful. Such predictions clearly provide corroborating evidence for a research program. It is, however, necessary to broaden the definition of novel facts to include new interpretations of already-known facts and facts which were not previously explained within the research program (Lakatos, 1970, pp. 32, 70–1). If a new theory explains the phenomena it was designed to explain and in addition explains what had previously been an anomaly, an unexplained fact or fact explicable only some ad hoc auxiliary hypothesis, this can be interpreted as corroboration of the program. When it comes to comparing two research programs, a program can also be corroborated if it explains facts which played no essential role in the competing program (they may have been explained only with the aid of ad hoc hypotheses, or they may have been ignored as being unimportant).[19]

To show that the neo-Walrasian research program in macroeconomics has been progressive we must, therefore, find examples of where it has successfully predicted novel facts. To do this we must do three things: (1) We must find examples of novel facts, which can be (i) predictions before the event, (ii) facts that were not previously explained, (iii) new interpretations of old facts or (iv) facts which played no role in competing research programs. These facts must all be facts that the theory was not specifically designed to explain. (2) We must show that these novel facts follow from the hard core and heuristics of the neo-Walrasian program. (3) We must show that these were corroborated. Note that it is not necessary that all, or even most of, the predictions made within the neo-Walrasian program be confirmed: rather, to quote Lakatos, 'what matters is a few dramatic signs of empirical progress' (Lakatos and Zahar, 1976, p. 179).

Alternative Programs

In appraising the neo-Walrasian research program we must not forget the existence of alternative research programs. In particular it is important that any 'novel facts' we use as evidence for the program's success do not follow equally well from the heuristics of some competing program. A program which is especially important here is what can best be called the 'Chicago' program. This is important because there is such a large overlap between the two programs. Though they overlap, however, they are not the same.[20]

The main distinguishing feature of Chicago economics is what Reder has termed 'Tight Prior Equilibrium' theory, based on the hypothesis of Pareto-optimality; namely that

> decision-makers so allocate the resources under their control that there is no alternative allocation such that any one decision maker could have his expected utility increased without a reduction occurring in the expected utility of at least one other decision maker. (Reder, 1982, p. 11)

Imperfect competition, market failure and government intervention are taken to be sufficiently infrequent and have a sufficiently limited impact for the hypothesis of perfect competition to provide a good approximation to the way in which markets work (Reder, 1982, p. 15).

A further difference between Chicago and neo-Walrasian economics concerns the role of formal model building. Although many Chicago economists do construct formal mathematical models, and although much of Chicago economics could be seen as also lying within neo-Walrasian economics, the construction and use of formal models do not receive the same emphasis. There is a strong tradition in Chicago economics, of which Friedman is undoubtedly the main representative, which favours simple models. Models which would be quite respectable Chicago economics (such as are found in most of Friedman's work) would not be seen as 'fully specified' in the sense of heuristic PH1′.[21]

5 SOME NOVEL FACTS GENERATED BY THE NEO-WALRASIAN RESEARCH PROGRAM

The Consumption Function

One of the earliest examples of successful prediction in post-war macroeconomics is the life-circle/permanent income theory of consumption, of which Friedman's *The Theory of the Consumption Function*

(1957) is the outstanding example. Note that, although there are substantial differences between the approaches of Chicago economists (Friedman) and non-Chicago ones (Ando and Modigliani), with the latter providing a much more formal treatment of the maximizing hypothesis, we are not attempting here to distinguish between them, accepting the generally-held view that the two theories yield substantially the same empirical predictions.

The basic facts the life-cycle theory was designed to explain were:

> (a) the rough constancy of the average propensity to consume in the United States over the past half-century, as measured by time series data, despite a substantial rise in real income; (b) the rough similarity of the average propensity to consume in budget studies for widely separated dates, despite substantial differences in average real income; (c) the sharply lower savings ratio in the United States in the period after World War II than would have been consistent with the relation between income and savings computed from data for the interwar period. (Friedman, 1957, p. 38)

Friedman managed to explain not only these broad generalizations, but his theory also predicted several additional 'novel facts' concerning things such as shifts in the consumption function over time, the differences between farm and non-farm savings behaviour, inter-country differences and so on. He confronted these predictions with detailed evidence, in all cases coming to the conclusion that the data either supported his theory or were not inconsistent with it (the data were often inconclusive). Friedman claimed:

> Perhaps the two most striking pieces of evidence for the hypothesis are, first, its success in predicting in quantitative detail the effect of classifying consumer units by the change in their measured income from one year to another; and, second, its consistency with a body of data that *have not heretofore been used in analyzing consumption behaviour* or, indeed, *even regarded as relevant to consumption behaviour*, namely, data on the measured income of individual consumer units in successive years. (Friedman, 1957, p. 225, emphasis in original)

The theory was developed to explain one set of data and was then used to make predictions concerning other things. Friedman and many other economists considered that these predictions were mostly confirmed. Though there are now signs of a possible movement away from the permanent income-life cycle theory, and it is conceivable that it might at some stage be abandoned (see Gilbert, this volume), the theory was thought for many years to have been important in predicting a broad range of facts about the behaviour of consumption and income.

Inflation and Unemployment

The expectations-augmented Phillips curve as developed by Phelps and Friedman led to a number of predictions concerning the relationship between the level of aggregate demand, inflation and unemployment. The main ones were that: (1) the level of unemployment consistent with a constant inflation rate is independent of the inflation rate; (2) persistent low unemployment will lead to accelerating inflation; and (3) increasing the growth rate of demand produces a short-term rise in unemployment, but in the long run produces only a rise in inflation.

The first of these predictions is difficult, if not impossible, to test conclusively because, as Friedman admitted, the 'natural' rate of unemployment is not constant. There have been numerous attempts to estimate the natural rate, but the problems are sufficiently great for it to be hard to regard such work as being anything like a satisfactory test of the theory. The best we can say is that the hypothesis has not been refuted by empirical evidence. The other two, related, predictions, on the other hand, could be regarded as having been corroborated by the experience of the 1970s. The predictions were first made in 1967,[22] when inflation had started to rise, but had not yet reached levels which suggested anything substantially different from earlier experience: there was little evidence that inflation was accelerating or that the 'conventional' Phillips curve had broken down (see Figure 12.1).

During the late 1960s there was a large expansion of aggregate demand, due first to Kennedy's application of Keynesian policies and later to the cost of the Vietnam war. The sharp rise in inflation, without much change in unemployment, in 1968–9 could be explained in terms of a non-linear Phillips curve, but once this high inflation rate began to feed into expectations, the economy moved off the 1960s Phillips curve. Rising unemployment was needed in 1970–1 simply to stop inflation rising still further: even with unemployment rates comparable with those of the early 1960s inflation remained over 3 per cent. Friedman and Phelps could well have argued that these events vindicated their predictions, and that their predictions were made well in advance of events.[23]

Models of Price Stickiness

One of the problems with the consumption function and the expectations-augmented Phillips curve as examples of the neo-Walrasian research program generating novel facts is that they do not discriminate between the neo-Walrasian and Chicago research programs. In order to

Figure 12.1 The US Phillips curve, 1960–72

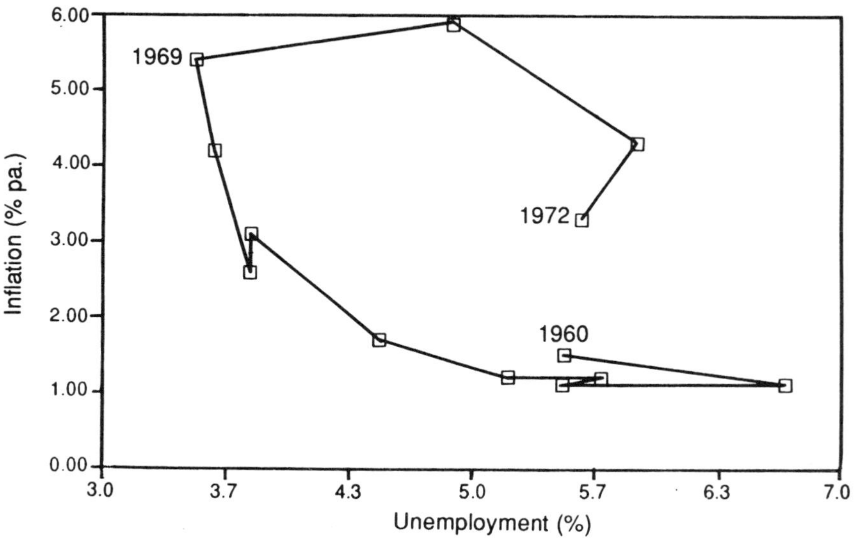

do this, therefore, we turn now to examples of predictions made by models which lie squarely within the neo-Walrasian research program but which are clearly outside the Chicago program. Start with rationing models. These were designed to explain the problem of Keynesian unemployment, but the logic of the simple two-market models initially discussed led naturally to a threefold classification of Keynesian unemployment, classical unemployment and repressed inflation (a logically possible fourth category was dismissed as economically uninteresting). Though these models are notoriously difficult to estimate, let alone to test, disequilibrium phenomena causing severe econometric problems, it could be argued that they were corroborated by the response of different economies to OPEC I.

Labour market institutions were very different in Europe and the US, with real wage rigidity in Europe and nominal wage rigidity in the US. This should, if rationing models are correct, result in classical unemployment in the US and Keynesian unemployment in Europe. Econometric evidence on real wage gaps is too tenuous to provide any firm evidence that the theory was confirmed, but it is reinforced by evidence that European governments responded as though the problem was one of classical unemployment (they tried to reduce real wages) whilst the US tried to deflate demand. If we assume that governments were acting rationally, this suggests that these economies were behaving in conformity with rationing theory. What makes this significant is that this was happening in circumstances that had not previously been observed, the oil shock with the simultaneous fall in productivity and deflation of aggregate demand being unlike anything that had happened before.

A more dramatic and much more conclusive example is the 'Dornbusch model' (Dornbusch, 1976). This combined the assumption of perfect foresight in financial markets (equivalent to rational expectations in the deterministic model Dornbusch was using) with sluggish price-adjustment in goods markets. His prediction was that a monetary expansion (contraction) would produce a depreciation (appreciation) of the exchange rate, which might overshoot its long-run equilibrium. The characteristic feature of Dornbusch's model, distinguishing it from previous exchange-rate models, was that flexibility and rational, forward-looking behaviour in financial markets contributed to instability, rather than reducing it.

As dramatic a test of this theory as one might reasonably expect to see came in the UK in 1979–80 when the newly-elected Conservative government introduced an exceptionally tight monetary policy at the same time as financial markets were becoming much more flexible. From the third quarter of 1979 (the election was in October 1979) the growth rate of both broad and narrow monetary aggregates fell sharply: after being positive in the first half of 1979 growth rates of the real money supply fell to *minus* 10 per cent per annum in the first half of 1980.[24] Real interest rates rose very sharply. The result, as the Dornbusch model predicts, was a massive appreciation of sterling. Relative unit labour costs, perhaps the best measure of the real exchange rate, rose by an unprecedented 54 per cent in two years.

There are, as always, other factors to take into account. North Sea oil was coming on stream and this would account for part of the appreciation, especially after OPEC II. However most calculations of the 'oil premium' suggest that it was substantially below the appreciation that was observed. In addition, oil exploration had been under way since the mid-1970s and the results, though obviously subject to uncertainty, must to a substantial extent have been anticipated. Furthermore the severity of the recession, due to a massive de-stocking as firms failed to export goods, suggests that the exchange rate had risen well above the level compatible with international competitiveness. It could be argued, therefore, that the 'Thatcher experiment' corroborated the predictions of the Dornbusch model.

The New Classical Macroeconomics

The new classical macroeconomics produces such strong predictions, with such dramatic implications for government policy and presenting suitable econometric challenges, that there have been numerous attempts to test them. The predictions resulting from the new classical macroeconomics include: (1) anticipated changes in aggregate demand will have no effect on real output (structural neutrality), with the corollary that only unpredictable movements in aggregate demand will affect real variables; (2) the more unpredictable is aggregate demand, the smaller is the effect on real output of any given unpredictable movement in aggregate demand. Lucas (1973) produced empirical evidence in support of the latter whilst Barro (1977, 1978; Barro and Rush, 1980) produced evidence for the former.

These predictions and the empirical evidence which seemed to corroborate them have stimulated much econometric work, with many economists coming to the conclusion that the new classical theories were not consistent with the data. For example, Gordon (1982) found that anticipated changes in aggregate demand *did* have a significant effect on real output. He reconciled this with Barro's evidence, according to which anticipated changes in the money supply had no such effects, by suggesting that the link between monetary growth and the growth rate of demand was weak. The reason for Barro's results was the traditional Keynesian notion that money had only a limited effect on aggregate demand. Other economists criticized Barro and Lucas on more technical grounds (lag lengths, the type of statistical tests they performed and so on).

The new classical assumptions have also been applied to generate other predictions. One of the most dramatic predictions concerned the consumption function, where Hall claimed that 'no variable apart from current consumption should be of any value in predicting future consumption' (Hall, 1978, p. 971). As with Lucas's and Barro's results, subsequent empirical evidence has suggested that this is not so: that other variables do affect consumption.

Finally it is worth pointing out that the logic of the new classical theory is that there should be no business cycle. According to the new classical theory it is only unanticipated, hence unpredictable changes in aggregate demand that cause departures from full employment.

Fluctuations in real output about full-employment output should, therefore, be uncorrelated with any information available to decision makers, a prediction which is inconsistent with the existence of a business cycle (that is, with deviations from full-employment output exhibiting positive serial correlation). Had there been no business cycle we can be sure that this would have been cited as corroborating evidence for the new classical program (a part of the Chicago program) so it seems reasonable to cite the existence of a business cycle as evidence against it.[25] Lucas and others have, of course, attempted to explain why there is a business cycle, but the assumptions they introduce to do this are essentially ad hoc.

6 IS THE NEO-WALRASIAN PROGRAM IN MACROECONOMICS PROGRESSIVE?

The first thing to look for is predictions before the event, for, although it is not necessary that predictions be of this type, there can be no doubt that these constitute corroborating evidence. Owing to the nature of economics such predictions are inevitably hard to obtain – until a new circumstance has arisen economists often have no incentive to construct a theory capable of generating predictions. Furthermore, once a prediction has been made, behaviour may change in response to this prediction so as to ensure that it is never tested.

Two predictions before the event have been cited above: the Friedman–Phelps prediction of the consequences of sustained high aggregate demand in the late 1960s, and Dornbusch's prediction of the consequences of a severe monetary shock in a world of floating exchange rates, mobile capital and rational expectations. Doubts have been expressed about both, but it can nonetheless be argued that these have been dramatically corroborated.

Broadening our use of the term 'prediction' to include predictions of anything that the theories concerned were not designed to predict, we have the example of Friedman's theory of the consumption function, designed to explain a few basic facts, but which explained a large number of related facts. To this could be added numerous instances of neo-Walrasian theories explaining other phenomena they were not designed to explain. Indeed it could be argued that the main feature of neo-Walrasian economics, too obvious to need documenting, is its ability to generate and explain apparently disparate phenomena in terms of maximizing behaviour.

There is, however, a serious problem here, connected with the question of what constitutes the relevant theory. Take an example. Dixit (1978) uses a rationing model, of the type used by Barro, Grossman, Malinvaud *et al.* to analyse the problem of the balance of trade. He managed to explain in terms of this theory 'facts' about the relationship between the government deficit and the balance of trade which were essentially ad hoc assumptions (believed to be empirically justified) in another research program (the so-called 'New Cambridge' theory).[26] The issue here is whether this constitutes an example of disequilibrium macroeconomics, designed to explain the problem of Keynesian unemployment in a closed economy, successfully generating predictions in an area that it was not intended to cover; or whether we have to regard Dixit's model as a new model designed to explain the balance of trade. At another level, could the whole of neo-Walrasian *macro*economics be regarded as generating predictions from a theory aimed at explaining something very different (whatever neo-Walrasian *micro*economics is about)? We might wish to examine assumptions used in different neo-Walrasian models in detail to determine when we have a 'new' theory and when we have simply an application of an old theory, but we are in the end faced with a subjective decision about what constitutes a new model.[27] We thus have to make a subjective decision as to whether a prediction has been generated from a model designed to explain something else, or whether it has been generated by a purpose-built one. To criticize neo-Walrasian economics we focus on theoretical novelties; to defend it we focus on the fact that many theories are 'essentially' the same.

There is also the issue of how neo-Walrasian economics compares with other competing, and possibly overlapping programs – in particular, of what can be claimed *vis-à-vis* the Chicago program. The overlap between these two programs is so large that to a certain extent they stand or fall together. The examples cited in section 5, however, suggest that there is a strong case for claiming that neo-Walrasian macroeconomics remains progressive in a way that Chicago *macro*-economics (we are making no comment on Chicago microeconomics) does not. There are two sides to this. On the one hand, important predictions from the non-Chicago part of neo-Walrasian economics have been successful. On the other hand, the dramatic predictions made within the new classical macroeconomics have not been confirmed.

7 CONCLUDING REMARKS

In this chapter I have viewed contemporary macroeconomics from a

Lakatosian perspective, for two reasons. The first is to provide another case study which can be used in evaluating the relevance of Lakatosian ideas for economics. This is one reason why Lakatosian ideas have been applied relatively rigidly: we need to see how far we can push them before they cease to work. Here the main conclusion to emerge from the chapter is that the rational reconstruction of macroeconomics since Keynes provided in section 3 fits the facts very well. There are the problems of pre-test bias and of having fewer observations than we would like. In addition, we have not explored the alternatives to the neo-Walrasian program adequately. On the other hand, the fact that we can reconstruct the period's 'great (macroeconomic) science' as rational can be taken as corroborating the Lakatosian perspective. Furthermore the key feature of the neo-Walrasian program as described here is its stress on rational behaviour. This is something that most of the theorists concerned would immediately acknowledge as a key assumption underlying their work and underlying post-war economic theory. In addition possibly the most common defence of neo-Walrasian economics (from practitioners, not methodologists) is that 'it works'. By this economists usually have in mind something akin to the Lakatosian criterion for a progressive research program: that their theories provide a source of new predictions, a significant number of which turn out to be correct. The Lakatosian perspective can thus be defended on the grounds that it is in accordance with the way economists see their work.[28]

The second reason for adopting a Lakatosian perspective is to appraise contemporary economics. I am assuming that the superstructure of economic theory needs an empirical justification, and that Lakatos's methodology provides a possible way of doing this. Here the conclusion to emerge from the chapter is that the neo-Walrasian research program appears to be both theoretically and empirically progressive.

By way of a postscript it is worth noting a corollary to the argument advanced here. This concerns 'monetarism' and 'Keynesianism'. These are often presented as two rival research programs. According to our interpretation of post-war macroeconomics, however, much of the debate between monetarism and Keynesianism emerges as a debate within the neo-Walrasian program.[29] This would explain why Keynesian and monetarist theories have developed in such similar ways during the post-war period.[30] The very great changes which have taken place in macroeconomics since 1970 should, according to this interpretation, be seen not in terms of the replacement of one research program with another but in terms of a shift of attention within a larger research program.

NOTES

1. Most accounts of macroeconomics since Keynes either discuss only a part of the story (for example, Leijonhufvud, 1976; Weintraub, 1979; Gerrard, 1988) or discuss it in terms of monetarism and Keynesianism (for example, Blaug, 1980, 1985; Backhouse, 1985). As I argue elsewhere (Backhouse, 1988b), such approaches are legitimate but they play down important aspects of the way macroeconomic theory, both Keynesian and monetarist, has evolved.
2. Both post-Keynesian and 'Austrian' economics, for example, fall outside the scope of this chapter.
3. In addition to the particular research programs with which he was concerned, Lakatos recognized that science as a whole could be seen as one huge research program (1970, p. 47). The neo-Walrasian program proposed here clearly comes in between these two levels.
4. The conventional way to view such issues is to see them in terms of the 'victory' of one scientific research program over another. Though it might be possible to adopt such an approach it is not followed here: the difficult task of defining a 'Marshallian' research program (or whatever research program Keynes was working within) would, even if it were successfully pursued, distract us from the main task.
5. It can be retained, but only at the cost of reinterpreting 'relevant' in such a way as to deprive it of any meaning. Such a strategy fails to capture the two crucial characteristics concerning assumptions about knowledge in neo-Walrasian models: that agents must be in a position to be able to act rationally; and that assumptions must be such as to render formal mathematical analysis possible.
6. It could be argued that HC5 used to belong to the hard core of the neo-Walrasian research program, but that it was dropped, being replaced with PH3. This change represented a progressive problem shift. It is discussed further below.
7. The question of whether the same thing happens in other disciplines is left open.
8. This process is discussed in detail in Young (1987).
9. These are too well-known for exact references to be required.
10. There is a problem in knowing how to fit *Value and Capital* (1939) into this story. On the one hand Hicks has claimed that his IS-LM paper and *Value and Capital* grew out of the same earlier work (for references see Young, 1987, p. 46). On the other hand, *Value and Capital*, surprisingly, contains no reference to the IS-LM paper. It is worth noting the observation made by Maes (1988) that Hicks, although he had developed a portfolio theory of money in the 1930s, failed to use it as the foundation for his macroeconomic writing on money; instead, like most of his contemporaries, he adopted the cruder characterization of the monetary sector derived from Keynes's *General Theory*. This suggests that, when telling the story of macroeconomics in the 1940s, it may be right to leave *Value and Capital* out. Patinkin acknowledges the influence of *Value and Capital* only on the microeconomic part of *Money, Interest and Prices*: the macroeconomic section refers to IS-LM but not *Value and Capital*.
11. I have in mind the literature associated with the real balance effect and the determinacy of the price level, and the question of whether wage rigidity was necessary or sufficient for an unemployment equilibrium to emerge.
12. The third edition of his textbook, published in 1955, was the first to use this term.
13. HC5′ will be considered later.
14. Samuelson (1955) claimed that the neoclassical synthesis had the support of 90 per cent of American economists.
15. There were also important elements of disequilibrium in Patinkin (1957) but these were not presented as undermining the neoclassical synthesis. Clower's (and later Leijonhufvud's) rhetoric was very important.
16. This list includes only authors of macroeconomic theories. Microeconomic general equilibrium theory was also affected, economists such as Arrow, Hahn, Benassy,

Dreze and many others working on such models. For a survey see Drazen, 1980. I have not included Leijonhufvud, whose name is frequently bracketed with Clower's in this context, for though his book (1968) did much to stimulate interest in this type of theory, he did not construct formal models in the way required by the neo-Walrasian research program. Whilst his 1968 book was definitely Walrasian in its approach, his later work took him outside this research program.

17. This was explained by Clower as being the consequence of removing the artificial device of the Walrasian auctioneer.
18. The ideas in this section are all taken from Lakatos. It is included because when I presented early drafts of this chapter I was criticized both for paying too much attention to predictions and for not paying enough attention to them. I concluded that it was necessary to explain in more detail what I was trying to do.
19. Lakatos and Zahar (1976), p. 185; c.f. Zahar (1973). They argue that it was only this category of novel facts that, for many years, provided any corroborating evidence in favour of Copernicus's research program *vis-à-vis* Ptolemy's.
20. It would clearly be desirable to discuss the hard core and heuristics of competing research programs in the same detail as we have discussed those of the neo-Walrasian program. However, because this is too large a task to perform here, Reder's characterization of Chicago economics is taken as defining the program adequately for the purposes of this chapter.
21. In section 5 below we consider the consumption function and the expectations-augmented Phillips curve. In both cases Friedman's contribution exemplifies the Chicago, non-neo-Walrasian approach, with the work of Ando and Modigliani (on consumption) and Phelps (the Phillips curve) representing the neo-Walrasian approach.
22. This is when the results were first published, Friedman's 'The role of monetary policy' (1968) having been delivered as his Presidential Address to the AEA the previous year.
23. We have provided data only for the years up to 1972 in order to leave aside the complications caused by the oil-price rise of 1973–4 and the productivity slow-down, confining our attention to the period when the main cause of inflation was high aggregate demand.
24. The one exception to this pattern was sterling M3, the aggregate to which the government was paying most attention. Monetary base, M1 and the aggregates broader than sterling M3 all behaved as described here. The errant behaviour of sterling M3 may explain why the government effected such a severe recession despite policy statements which appeared to imply a 'gradualist' outlook. The severity of the monetary policy, and the mechanism whereby it affected the economy, are clearly documented in Buiter and Miller (1981).
25. See Okun (1980) for a discussion of new classical theories of the cycle and the evidence against them.
26. The thesis was that a change in the government deficit would, in the short run, cause the balance of trade to change by an equal and opposite amount. The New Cambridge explanation used the accounting identity that the sum of sectoral deficits must be zero together with the assumption that the private sector deficit was approximately constant. The latter assumption was believed to have empirical support, but there was no theoretical rationale for it.
27. A related point is made, in a very different context, in Backhouse (1988a).
28. I am grateful to Harry Collins for drawing my attention to this issue.
29. It is not, of course, entirely within neo-Walrasian economics. We might wish, for example, a 'National Bureau' research program, dominated by Wesley Clair Mitchell, having heuristics that are very different from those of the neo-Walrasian program. Friedman's work would fit into such a program much better than into the neo-Walrasian program.
30. This is argued in more detail in Backhouse (1988b).

REFERENCES

Azariadis, C. (1975), 'Implicit contracts and underemployment equilibria,' *Journal of Political Economy,* **83**, pp. 1183–1202.

Backhouse, R.E. (1985), *A History of Modern Economic Analysis* (Oxford: Basil Blackwell).

—— (1988a), 'Perspectives on the history of economic thought', *Scottish Journal of Political Economy*, **35** (1), pp. 97–104.

—— (1988b), 'Post-war macroeconomics', (mimeo).

Bailey, M.N. (1974), 'Wages and employment under uncertain demand', *Review of Economic Studies*, **41**, pp. 37–50.

Barro, R.J. (1977), 'Unanticipated money growth and unemployment in the United States', *American Economic Review*, **67**, pp. 101–15.

—— (1978), 'Unanticipated money, output and the price level in the United States', *Journal of Political Economy*, **86**, pp. 549–80.

Barro, R.J. and Grossman, H.I. (1971), 'A general disequilibrium model of income and employment', *American Economic Review*, **61**, pp. 82–93.

Barro, R.J. and Rush, M. (1980), 'Unanticipated money and economic activity', in S. Fischer (ed.), *Rational Expectations and Economic Policy*, National Bureau of Economic Research (Chicago: Chicago University Press).

Blaug, M. (1980), *The Methodology of Economics* (Cambridge: Cambridge University Press).

—— (1985), *Economic Theory in Retrospect*, 4th edn (Cambridge: Cambridge University Press).

Buiter, W. and Miller, M. (1981), 'The Thatcher experiment: the first two years', *Brookings Papers on Economic Activity*, pp. 315–79.

Calvo, G. and Phelps, E.S. (1977), 'Employment-contingent wage contracts', in K. Brunner and A. Meltzer (eds), *Stabilization of the Domestic and International Economy*, Carnegie-Rochester Series on Public Policy pp. 160–68 (Amsterdam: North-Holland).

Champernowne, D. (1936), 'Unemployment, basic and monetary: the classical analysis and the Keynesian', *Review of Economic Studies*, **3**, pp. 201–16.

Clower, R.W. (1965), 'The Keynesian Counter-Revolution: A Theoretical Appraisal' in F.H. Hann and F. Brechling (eds), *The Theory of Interest Rates* (London and Basingstoke: Macmillan).

Dixit, A.K. (1978), 'The balance of trade in a model of temporary equilibrium with rationing', *Review of Economic Studies*, **45**, pp. 393–404.

Dornbusch, R. (1976), 'Expectations and exchange rate dynamics', *Journal of Political Economy*, **84**, pp. 1161–76.

Drazen, A. (1980), 'Recent developments in macroeconomic disequilibrium theory', *Econometrica*, **48**, pp. 283–306.

Flemming, J.S. (1973), 'The consumption function when capital markets are imperfect', *Oxford Economic Papers*, **25**, pp. 160–72.

Friedman, M. (1957), *The Theory of the Consumption Function* (Princeton: Princeton University Press).

—— (1968), 'The role of monetary policy', *American Economic Review*, **58**.

Gerrard, B. (1988), 'Keynesian economics: the road to nowhere?' in J. Hillard (ed.), *J.M. Keynes in Retrospect* (Aldershot: Edward Elgar).

Gilbert, C. (1990), 'Do economists test theories? – demand analysis and consumption analysis as tests of theories of economic methodology', this volume.

Gordon, R.J. (1982), 'Price inertia and policy ineffectiveness in the United States, 1890–1980', *Journal of Political Economy*, **86**, pp. 971–87.

Hall, R.E. (1978), 'Stochastic implications of the life cycle–permanent income hypothesis: theory and evidence', *Journal of Political Economy*.

—— (1980), 'Employment fluctuations and wage rigidities', *Brookings Papers on Economic Activity*, **1**, pp. 91–124.

Harrod, R.F. (1937), 'Mr Keynes and traditional theory', *Economica*, **5**.

Hicks, J.R. (1937), 'Mr Keynes and the "classics": a suggested interpretation', *Econometrica*, **5**, pp. 147–59.

—— (1939), *Value and Capital* (Oxford: Oxford University Press).

Keynes, J.M. (1971–83), *The Collected Writings of John Maynard Keynes* (London: Macmillan).

Lakatos, I. (1970), 'Falsification and the methodology of scientific research programmes', in I. Lakatos and A. Musgrave (eds), *Criticism and the Growth of Knowledge* (Cambridge: Cambridge University Press). Reprinted in Lakatos (1978).

—— (1971), 'History of science and its rational reconstructions', in R.C. Buck and R.S. Cohen (eds), P.S.A. 1970, *Boston Studies in the Philosophy of Science*, 8 (Dordrecht: Reidel). Reprinted in Lakatos (1978) pp. 102–38.

—— (1978), *The Methodology of Scientific Research Programmes: Philosophical Papers, Volume I* (Cambridge: Cambridge University Press).

Lakatos, I. and Zahar, E.G. (1976), 'Why did Copernicus's programme supersede Ptolomy's?', in R. Westman (ed.), *The Copernical Achievement* (Los Angeles: University of California Press). Reprinted in Lakatos (1978), pp. 168–92.

Leijonhufvud, A. (1968), *On Keynesian Economics and the Economics of Keynes* (Oxford: Oxford University Press).

—— (1976), 'Schools, "revolutions" and research programmes in economic theory', in S.J. Latsis (ed.), *Method and Appraisal in Economics* (Cambridge: Cambridge University Press).

Lucas, R.E. (1972), 'Expectations and the neutrality of money', *Journal of Economic Theory*, **4**, pp. 103–24.

—— (1973), 'Some international evidence on output–inflation trade offs', *American Economic Review*, **63**, pp. 326–34.

McCloskey, D.M. (1986), *The Rhetoric of Economics* (Brighton: Wheatsheaf Books).

Maes, I. (1988), 'Did the Keynesian revolution retard the development of portfolio theory?', *Banca Nazionale del Lavoro Quarterly Review*.

Malinvaud, E. (1977), *The Theory of Unemployment Reconsidered* (Oxford: Basil Blackwell).

Meade, J.E. (1937), 'A simplified model of Mr Keynes's system', *Review of Economic Studies*, **4**, pp. 98–107.

Modigliani, F. (1944), 'Liquidity preference and the theory of interest of money', *Econometrica*, **12**, pp. 45–88.

Muth, J.F. (1961), 'Rational expectations and the theory of price movements', *Econometrica*, **29**, pp. 315ff.

Okun, A.M. (1980), 'Rational-expectations-with-misperceptions as a theory of the business cycle', *Journal of Money, Credit and Banking*, **12**, pp. 817–25.

Patinkin, D. (1957), *Money, Interest and Prices* (Evanston, Ill: Row, Peterson and Co).

Phelps, E.S. (1967), 'Phillips curves, expectations of inflation and optimal unemployment over time', *Economica*, **34**, pp. 254–81.
Reder, M.W. (1982), 'Chicago economics: permanence and change', *Journal of Economic Literature*, **20** (1), pp. 1–38.
Sachs, J.D. (1979), 'Wages, profits and macroeconomic adjustment', *Brookings Papers on Economic Activity*, **2**, pp. 269–319.
Samuelson, P.A. (1955), *Economics*, 3rd edn (New York and London: McGraw Hill).
Solow, R.M. and Stiglitz, J.E. (1968), 'Output, employment and wages in the short run', *Quarterly Journal of Economics*, **82**, pp. 537–60.
Weintraub, E.R. (1979), *Microfoundations* (Cambridge: Cambridge University Press).
—— (1985), *General Equilibrium Analysis: Studies in Appraisal* (Cambridge: Cambridge University Press).
Weiss, A. (1980), 'Job queues and layoffs in labor markets with flexible wages', *Journal of Political Economy*, **88**, pp. 526–38.
Young, W. (1987), *Interpreting Mr Keynes: The IS-LM Enigma* (Cambridge: Polity Press).
Zahar, E. (1973), 'Why did Einstein's programme supersede Lorentz's (I), *British Journal for the Philosophy of Science*, **24**, pp. 95–123.

COMMENT ON BACKHOUSE

Maarten C.W. Janssen[1]

Backhouse's chapter starts with the observation that contemporary macroeconomics is part of a neo-Walrasian research program, and is subsequently devoted to the question of how this current state of affairs came about. The main thesis of the chapter is that 'mainstream macroeconomics since Keynes can be viewed in terms of the extension of the neo-Walrasian program to encompass theories which previously lay outside its domain' (p. 403). In this comment I will, by way of contrast, provide some elements of an alternative account of the history of macroeconomics of the last 50 years.[2] The alternative account is consistent with Backhouse's initial observation, but differs from his main thesis. At the end of the comment I briefly compare the advantages of both approaches.

1 Two Programs of Research in Macroeconomics[3]

I will take seriously the idea that in present-day economics the neo-Walrasian program has encompassed (sequences of) theories that were previously regarded as being outside its domain. In my view this means that we have to consider the notion that the theories that fall outside the neo-Walrasian program share one or more programs of their own. I will claim that there are (were) such programs in the field of mainstream macroeconomics.

The general conception of the economy that gradually emerged in macroeconomic textbooks of the 1950s and 1960s was one in which the economy is described in terms of disembodied and homogeneous flows and the relation between these flows. Such an approach is of course only fruitful if the aggregate relations are stable over time. Strongly associated with this view is the idea that the economy can be (temporarily) regulated on the basis of knowledge that is provided by these estimated aggregate relations.

This view on the method of macroeconomics was shared by a large number of macroeconomists. Nevertheless there were important differences in opinion with respect to the question of how an economy is supposed to function. Two schools were dominant in this period: Monetarism and Keynesianism. The basic idea of *Keynesian*-type models is that employment is related to aggregate output, which in turn is determined by consumption and investment demand. Unemployment results when demand deficiencies exist. From time to time such deficiencies in aggregate demand exist, because the economic system is thought to be not self-stabilizing in the short run. In cases of demand deficiencies the government is in a position to stimulate aggregate demand, thereby increasing the level of employment. In the *Monetarists'* view there exists a short-term relationship between the level of aggregate output and the quantity of money. In their view this does not mean, however, that the monetary authorities should increase the quantity of money if there is unemployment in the economy. On the contrary, the lag with which money affects output is difficult to predict, so that an active monetary policy could easily be pro-cyclical rather than counter-cyclical. Moreover monetarism supposes that the economy is self-regulating in the sense that a so-called natural rate of unemployment will be attained 'in the long run'. Thus monetarism is a particular species of the classical doctrine in economics, which in its crudest form states that the real part of the economy is independent of the monetary part. The monetarists believe that this so-called classical dichotomy holds in the long run.

From this sketch of a part of the history of macroeconomics it is possible to distil some elements that are shared by what I will call the macroeconomic approach.

MA1 The economy can be described in terms of models consisting of a few regularities between aggregate quantities.
MA2 The aggregate regularities are stable over (some) time.
MA3 The aggregate regularities can be estimated by means of econometric methods.

The Keynesian program of research is further characterized by the idea that unemployment is a consequence of deficiencies in aggregate demand and that government policies can stimulate demand. The six propositions (MA1–3 plus K4–6 below) together contribute the defining characteristics of the Keynesian program.

K4 A market economy does not automatically produce at an efficient level.
K5 Unemployment is a consequence of deficiencies in aggregate demand.
K6 Government policies can push the economy towards more efficient levels of production.

The *monetarist* (classical) program of research is further characterized by the following three views. MA1–3 and M4–6 are regarded as constituting the defining characteristics of this program.

M4 In the short run, the level of economic activity depends on the quantity of money.
M5 In the long run, the economy will produce at an efficient level and the classical dichotomy holds.
M6 There is no scope for discretionary policies.

2 A Program of Research in Microeconomics

Most Lakatosian appraisals in economics have Weintraub's (1985) reconstruction of what he called 'neo-Walrasian economics' as a starting-point.[4] Backhouse is no exception to this rule. The reader is referred to his chapter for a re-statement of the lists of hard-core propositions and heuristics. In this section I will confine myself to two sorts of observations with respect to this program.

First, Weintraub's formulation of the hard-core propositions is subtle, but also rather vague. Different interpretations of the propositions are possible and needed if they are to be applied to the field of macroeconomics. This will be illustrated by concentrating on two hard-core propositions. Comparing HC1 and HC4 reveals that there is no such statement as 'there exist markets'. The theory of missing markets is becoming one of the major branches in modern Keynesian economics (see, for example, Hahn, 1989). If a particular interpretation of the hard-core propositions is chosen, this literature is a part of the program. HC6 poses that equilibrium states reflect some form of coordination. It does *not* say that economic activities are perfectly coordinated. It is, however, well-known that there is a wide variety of equilibrium notions in the profession, each of which assumes a different degree of coordination. Pareto optimality is an essential element of some equilibrium notions (such as market clearing in a perfectly competitive economy) while other equilibrium notions such as the Nash equilibrium are in general not Pareto-optimal. There is even the possibility that different Nash equilibria in a model are Pareto-ranked. A branch in modern Keynesian macroeconomics studies is so-called 'coordination failures', which are formally represented by multiple Pareto-ranked Nash equilibria (see, for example, Cooper and John, 1988). In order to restrict the analysis to Nash equilibria some form of coordination mechanism has to be assumed, but in these models there is no perfect coordination because the outcomes are socially inefficient.

The second observation concerns the heuristics of the program. Roughly speaking, the positive heuristics is a partially articulated set of suggestions for further research. In Lakatos's view the hard core constitutes the program, but the positive heuristic ensures that the program is going in some direction. Looking at Weintraub's formulation of the positive heuristic of the neo-Walrasian program reveals that it is a simple restatement of the content of the hard core propositions. Accordingly it is difficult to regard it as a set of instructions on how to modify the program. Because of the difficulties of providing a reasonable statement of the positive heuristic I prefer the term 'program of research'.

3 Guide and Supply Programs

In this section I provide some hints on how the microeconomic neo-Walrasian program has interacted with the two macroeconomic programs of research. Before so doing I introduce a model of scientific development by Zandvoort (1986). Zandvoort is of the opinion that recent developments in the physical sciences can only be understood in terms of asymmetric cooperation between research programs. He distinguishes a *guide program* that determines the issues which have to be discussed and a *supply program* that provides the language and methods by means of which the issues have to be tackled. The nature of the two programs differs considerably, hence the asymmetric cooperation. Roughly speaking, the guide program has a well-defined domain of issues with which it is concerned, but it does not have a method of its own. The reverse holds true for the supply program, which is characterized by a clear-cut method and a rather vague domain of intended applications.

In my opinion this model of scientific development fits the history of macroeconomics since the 1960s quite well. I propose that the two traditional macroeconomic programs act as two guide programs, whereas the neo-Walrasian research program functions as the supply program. It is as if macroeconomics guides the neo-Walrasian program of research by providing the issues that have to be discussed. The differences in opinion between the two macroeconomic programs of the 1950s and 1960s largely carry over to the modern literature. The new Keynesian program tries to establish the Keynesian position from within the neo-Walrasian program of research. The same holds true for the new classical program with respect to the classical (monetarist) position.[5] In fact the so-called microfoundations debate is the continuation of an old debate in a new language. The microfoundations literature can thus be understood in terms of two competing macroeconomic guide programs that cooperate with one and the same supply program.

4 Comparative Advantages

In order to show that the above sketch is a potentially fruitful way to discuss the history of macroeconomics I will briefly indicate some troublesome questions for a strict Lakatosian interpretation and some answers that are suggested by the above interaction model.

The first question to be considered is why the literature Backhouse considers in his paper is part of macroeconomics. How are we able to talk about microeconomics and macroeconomics if both are part of one and the same neo-Walrasian program? The interactive model sketched in the previous section suggests that we can make the distinction because modern macroeconomics (the microfoundations approach) discusses the 'same' issues as the old monetarists and Keynesians, *but in another language*. The study of aggregate relations is replaced by the general equilibrium method. Our model gives a natural account of the fact that in the 1950s and 1960s most macroeconomic studies employ aggregate relations and in our account there is no need to say that 'it may be that the question of consistency with the hard core has, temporarily, been left open' (p. 407).

An important second question is why the differences between more Keynesian and more classical (monetarist) opinions still exist. Section 3 of Backhouse's paper suggests that the Keynesian view of the 1950s and 1960s is replaced by the classical view on the functioning of a market economy. I doubt that this is the case. The Keynesian view has never been far from centre stage and has recently been engaged in a revival. General equilibrium models with imperfect competition (see, for example, Hart, 1982) and the use of game theory in a macroeconomic context (see, for example, Cooper and John, 1988) give an alternative formulation of such Keynesian concepts as underemployment, the multiplier and the effectiveness of government policies. This state of affairs neatly fits in with the interaction model, while the coexistence of Keynesian and Classical views cannot easily be captured in a strict Lakatosian interpretation.

A final question concerns the adequacy of the Lakatosian formulation itself. Lakatos (1970) makes a clear and fundamental distinction between hard-core propositions and the positive heuristics. By adapting some of Weintraub's hard-core propositions and subsuming them in the positive heuristics, Backhouse (1989) in fact shows that there is hardly such a distinction in his formulation of the Lakatosian elements. In my opinion the neo-Walrasian program *does not have an internal positive heuristic*. It is a toolbox waiting to be used in a creative way.[6] *One* of the ways it can be used is by macroeconomics in order to deal with specific macroeconomic issues. The interaction model suggests that the guide program may play the role of a positive heuristic *external* to the neo-Walrasian program.

Notes

1. This research has been financially supported by the Netherlands Organization for Scientific Research. I thank Neil de Marchi and other participants in the conference for helpful comments.
2. An elaboration of the remarks in this comment can be found in Janssen (1989).
3. In what follows I will employ the term 'program of research' instead of 'research programs' in order to avoid Lakatosian connotations of the term. I try to show that in order to understand the history of macroeconomics an unconventional look at the way different programs of research interact is more fruitful than a dogmatic Lakatosian interpretation.
4. The term 'neo-Walrasian program' may be misleading, because several papers in a so-called '*non*-Walrasian' tradition fulfil all hard-core propositions.
5. Lucas's monetary model of the business cycle can be regarded as a re-formulation of the monetarist view, while the more recent real business cycle models adhere to the more narrow view that the classical dichotomy holds even in the short run.
6. A with all toolboxes, it cannot be used for all kinds of purposes; that is, the toolbox also has a selective role, choosing the issues it is able to handle.

References

Backhouse, R. (1991), 'The Neo-Walrasian research program in Macro-economics', this volume.
Cooper, R. and John, A. (1988), 'Coordinating Keynesian Coordination Failures', *Quarterly Journal of Economics*, **103**, pp. 441–63.
Hahn, F.H. (ed.) (1989), *The Economics of Missing Markets, Information and Games* (Oxford: Clarendon Press).
Hart, O. (1982), 'A Model of Imperfect Competition with Keynesian Features', *Quarterly Journal of Economics*, **97**, pp. 109–38.
Janssen, M. (1989), 'The Alleged Necessity of Microfoundations', University of Groningen, mimeo.
Lakatos, I. (1970), 'Falsification and the Methodology of Scientific Research Programs', in I. Lakatos and A. Musgrave (eds), *Criticism and the Growth of Knowledge* (Cambridge: Cambridge University Press).
Weintraub, E.R. (1985), *General Equilibrium Theory: Studies in Appraisal* (Cambridge: Cambridge University Press).
Zandvoort, H. (1986), *Models of Scientific Development and the Case of NMR* (Dordrecht: Reidel).

C Assessing Sraffian and Austrian Economics

13. Negative and Positive Contributions: Appraising Sraffa and Lakatos

Ian Steedman

> It is the fashion of the present time to disparage negative logic – that which points out weaknesses in theory or errors in practice without establishing positive truths. Such negative criticism would indeed be poor enough as an ultimate result; but as a means to attaining any positive knowledge or convictions worthy the name, it cannot be valued too highly . . . If there are any persons who contest a received opinion . . . let us thank them for it, open our minds to listen to them, and rejoice that there is someone to do for us what we otherwise ought, if we have any regard for either the certainty or the vitality of our convicitions, to do with much greater labour for ourselves. (J.S. Mill, *On Liberty*, 1859)

In one of the letters which kindly invited me to the Capri conference, I was asked to provide 'an assessment of just what the Sraffian Research Program had given us, after three decades and more', it being understood that the 'main purpose is to assess the usefulness of the ideas of Imre Lakatos to our understanding of recent developments in economics: but we shall not be limited by him'. In another such letter, it was suggested that ideally my 'evaluation of Sraffian economics should employ the Lakatosian apparatus, amending it along the way if necessary'. I hope that what follows does lie somewhere in the space spanned by these slightly divergent signposts. I shall take it that 'three decades and more' is a generous way of saying 29 years and that 'The Sraffian Research Program' – if it exists – was launched explicitly only in 1960 with the publication of *Production of Commodities by Means of Commodities*. Nothing will be said here of either Sraffa's 1925–26 contributions or his contribution to Ricardo scholarship and the lively debate in historiography that it has generated, but it should be noted that these omissions will perhaps distort our account of Sraffa's overall achievement. In Section 1, with little or no reference to Lakatos, I shall draw attention to the *negative* contribution made by Sraffa and by other theorists influenced by him. Section 2 will move on to consider whether any more positive Sraffian research program(s) has (have) emerged, some limited attention being paid to Lakatos. Section 3 will present a discussion of what light the Lakatosian methodology and the Sraffian contribution can throw upon each other, before a brief conclusion.

1 NEGATIVE LOGIC

It need hardly be recalled that *Production of Commodities* carries the sub-title 'Prelude to a Critique of Economic Theory', or that, in his Preface, Sraffa observed that, 'It is . . . a peculiar feature of the set of propositions now published that, although they do not enter into any discussion of the marginal theory of value and distribution, they have nevertheless been designed to serve as the basis for a critique of that theory' (1960, p. vi). It is not in the least forced, then, to begin by considering Sraffa's 1960 contribution to 'negative logic', as Mill put it. I take it that there will be no need here to rehearse any of the details of Sraffa's arguments in *Production of Commodities*. Rather it should suffice simply to mention the following results:

1. Standard assumptions in economic theory do not rule out the possibility of the re-switching of techniques. It follows that neither the period of production nor *any* other 'physical, technical' measure of the 'capital-intensity' of a technique is necessary inversely related to the interest rate.
2. The value of a 'park' of machines of different ages is not independent of income distribution; more specifically, it increases with the interest rate. When combined with the re-switching result, this teeters on the brink of stating what came to be known as the possibility of capital-reversing. While Sraffa did not refer overtly to this possibility while discussing the choice of technique, he did make it clear early in the book (Section 7) that 'one of the aims of this work' was to 'achieve freedom' from such ideas as that the 'cost of production' or '"capital" in its quantitative connotation' could be 'measured independently of, and prior to, the determination of the prices of the products' (1960, p. 9). *Production of Commodities* indeed succeeds in showing that such independent measurement is impossible. Sraffa refers in this context to 'the "quantity of capital" which is implied in the marginal productivity theory' (ibid.), which helps to explain which kind of 'marginal theory of value and distribution' he sought to promote the criticism of. (With respect

to 'achieving freedom', recall that Feyerabend (1988, p. 117) cites Francis Bacon's Aphorisms, from the *Novum Organum*, to the effect that preconceived notions, opinions, even the most common words 'must be abjured and renounced with firm and solemn resolution'.) It may be noted here that, the logical possibility of reswitching and of capital-reversing having been established, it is for those who would ignore such possibilities to justify themselves empirically. 'Sraffian' economists have no obligation to show that either reswitching or capital-reversing is empirically common.

3. 'If *n* different qualities of land are in use . . . [their] order of fertility . . . is not defined independently of the rents; that order, as well as the magnitude of the rents themselves, may vary with the variation' of wages and profits (1960, pp. 74–5).
4. In the presence of joint production, a *negative* amount of a primary input may be imputed to the (direct and indirect) production of a commodity. Consequently it is not guaranteed that real returns to primary inputs are always inversely related to the interest rate.

Although the above examples of 'negative' results from *Production of Commodities* have been given only briefly, no economic theorist will miss the point that they are of wide-ranging significance for some quite fundamental parts of economic theory. To demonstrate the presence of flaws in widely used theoretical constructions *is to make a major contribution*. If, with Mill, we should thank those who contest received opinion, how much more should we thank those who destroy false received opinion? There is no need to read any irony into Samuelson's suggestion (following Lange on von Mises) that, 'One can insist, seriously, that a neoclassical Hall of Fame deserves Sraffa's statue' (1987, vol. IV, p. 457). (How 'negative contributions' fit into the Lakatosian scheme and whether Sraffa's negative results belong to a marginalist or Sraffa's research programme – or both, or neither – will be considered below.)

The negative aspect of Sraffa's *Production of Commodities* has, of course, been reflected and extended in much subsequent work. We need not, presumably, inflict on ourselves yet another potted history of the so-called 'capital controversies', for the story is so familiar. (Why were they *called* 'controversies'? After all, one side was simply correct, so what was controversial? Levhari's (1965) error?) It need only be recalled here, for the sake of clarity, that capital-reversing does not require re-switching, that homogeneous labour and a uniform interest rate were only assumed for simplicity (never being essential), that output aggregation is relevant just as is capital aggregation, that capital aggregation raises just the same difficulties at the industry level as it does at the economy level and that Samuelson was right to remark that, 'If all this causes headaches for those nostalgic for the old time parables of neoclassical writing, we must remind ourselves that scholars are not born to live an easy existence. We must respect, and appraise, the facts of life' (1966, p. 583). The 'negative contribution' of Sraffian authors did not, of course, end with the (narrowly interpreted) re-switching and capital-reversing demonstrations. The use of the 'rate of return' concept by Irving Fisher and by Solow was criticized. The 2 × 2 'general equilibrium' model – with labour and 'capital' endowments and food and clothing outputs – was found wanting and it was shown that, with a positive rate of interest, the land–labour ratio might be *positively* related to the rent–wage ratio. Hence, not surprisingly, certain familiar results in H-O-S trade theory and in general equilibrium tax theory were demonstrated to be invalid. It has also been shown, along Sraffian lines, that Hicks-neutral technical progress is virtually impossible in an inter-industry system and that, even in a land and labour only system with joint products, Hicks-neutral *progress* may shift the real wage-real rent frontier *towards* the origin. On the macro front, a Sraffian critique of the 'neoclassical synthesis' has been provided. (I take it that it would be excessive to provide a long bibliography here: a large collection of 'Sraffian' papers can be found in Steedman (1988)).

Critical Sraffians have not, it need hardly be said, been obsessively anti-marginalist; perish the thought. Thus Sraffa's framework has been applied to the sharp criticism of what might be called traditional Anglo-Saxon Marxist economic theory and many notions concerning 'values', prices of production, 'surplus value', 'exploitation', the falling rate of profits, the intensity of labour and so on have been demonstrated to be unsustainable. Details, presumably, need not be entered into here; see Steedman (1977).

To expound in full all the results of Sraffian 'negative logic' which have been hinted at above would require at least a very long chapter, perhaps more. *Many* 'negative' contributions have been made – and negative contributions *are* contributions. With Mill, we should 'open our minds to listen to them'. Passinetti had no hesitation in referring to such work when praising Sraffa. He concluded his IESS biographical entry on Sraffa by saying that, 'it is curious that Sraffa's analysis should emerge as the basis for a critique and discarding of well-established concepts both in marginal economic theory and in Marxian economic theory. Yet it is clearly in relation to developments of this kind that the significance of Sraffa's book will eventually have to be assessed' (1979, p. 738). In a revised Italian version this became ' "Molto probabilmente" it will be in relation . . .' (1985, p. 32). Be that as it may, we must now turn to consider the 'positive' Sraffian contribution.

2 POSITIVE CONTRIBUTIONS

That Sraffa intended his *Production of Commodities* to make a significant 'negative contribution' is hardly open to serious doubt. It has also been suggested that Sraffa's second objective in that work was to re-launch the classical economists' approach to political economy (Roncaglia, n.d., p. 13). In similar vein, Garegnani has written of Sraffa's project of attempting to rectify the course taken by political economy after its post-Ricardo deviation and of a first step in this project being that of bringing back to light the classical point of view with respect to value and distribution (1985, p. 322). Again, more recently, Garegnani has written of 'the continuity between the work of the classical economists and the contemporary work of Sraffa and other authors working along the same lines' (1987, p. 573). Schefold (1989, p. 313) is perhaps less sure about this 'second objective', writing, 'To the extent that Sraffa's theory is at all suitable for "positive" economics (which, given its subtitle, is not clear from the outset) . . .'. Certainly, direct textual evidence of such a second objective is limited in *Production of Commodities*. In his Preface, Sraffa refers to the standpoint of the work as being 'that of the old classical economists from Adam Smith to Ricardo' (1960, p.v); in the text there is a favourable reference to 'Such classical terms as "necessary price," "natural price" or "price of production" ' (p. 9); and Appendix D, 'References to the Literature', refers only to Quesnay, Smith, Ricardo, Torrens, Malthus and Marx (pp. 93–5). Other than that, Sraffa offers only silence: which does not, of course, show that he did not have the second objective referred to. His devoted work on Ricardo could be, and has been, seen as further evidence of the project of restoring a 'classical approach'. Moreover *Production of Commodities* itself can be said to provide a definitive solution to the problem, left unresolved by both Ricardo and Marx, of determining prices of production and the profit rate, despite their interdependence – an interdependence which baffled Ricardo and Marx (but not Dmitriev and Bortkiewicz). Both Roncaglia (n.d.) and Garegnani (1985, 1987) point to this positive contribution of Sraffa's as being part of his constructive project. Certainly *Production of Commodities* provides great insight into the explanation of relative price movements in the face of changes in the profit rate (*passim*) and – a separate point this – the Standard Commodity may be seen either as the solution to (one aspect of) Ricardo's tortuous problem of an invariable standard or, less positively, as showing definitively that no actual commodity could ever be expected to provide such a standard. Moreover Sraffa's distinction between basics and non-basics has been seen (for example, by Roncaglia, 1978, pp. 52–6; Pasinetti, 1979, pp. 737–8) as an improvement of the classical distinction between wage goods and luxury goods.

Let us suppose, then, that *Production of Commodities* provided the basis not only for a critique of economic theory but also for the revivification of classical polical economy and, moreover, made certain positive contributions to such a revival. A single short work, presumably, cannot constitute a scientific research program, even if it can institute one. Where might we turn to find the other members of a 'Sraffian Scientific Research Program'? Deferring any direct reply for the moment, we note that Roncaglia (n.d.) has distinguished – cautiously – *three* Sraffian Schools. What matters here is not the question whether Roncaglia has made 'the correct' distinctions and allocations but the mere fact that a well-informed observer of the 'Sraffian scene' can already propose a tripartite division – a fact of obvious relevance for any attempt to provide a Lakatosian account of the Sraffian SRP(s). *Very* briefly, Roncaglia's three Schools may be epitomized as the (Ricardian) approach of Pasinetti, the (Marxian) approach of Garegnani and the (Smithian) approach of Sylos Labini. (The parenthetical labels are Roncaglia's.) Pasinetti's development of Sraffa is characterized as extending the formal analysis, often in terms of vertically-integrated sectors (sub-systems), to incorporate technical change, income elasticities of demand, aspects of 'Cambridge' theories of full employment growth and income distribution and so on, the emphasis throughout being laid on the reproducibility of (most) commodities. For Garegnani, in Roncaglia's account, the focus of attention is the concept of a 'surplus' and Sraffa's work pointed to a return to Marx. In this approach, the *deliberately* limited analysis of value and distribution constitutes the 'core', dealing with questions to which precise answers can be given. (Garegnani's 'core' is not a Lakatosian 'hard core'; it includes questions, problems and solutions.) Using short chains of reasoning, as recommended by Marshall, all the surrounding (and perhaps more interesting and important) questions relating to activity levels, growth, technical change, distribution and so on are to be studied with due attention to history and institutions. The Sylos Labini approach (to which Roncaglia himself is perhaps closest) is characterized as still making the concept of 'surplus' central but as being more 'open' methodologically and emphasizing the development of the division of labour, accumulation and different market forms and types of barriers to entry. Sraffa's work, it is said, is an essential contribution to a 'modern classicism' but by no means a *sufficient* basis for such a project of reconstruction.

We shall return to Roncaglia's 'Sraffian Schools' but it will be useful first to recall, with desperate brevity, a number of more specific areas in which 'Sraffian' economists might be said to have made 'positive contributions'. There is no space for details and no claim is implied that the following is an exhaustive list. More importantly, perhaps, there is *no* implication that the findings to be referred to should be of interest and of use only to economists with a 'Sraffian' background.

1. Sraffa's important conceptual distinction between basic and non-basic commodities has been further clarified in certain respects, not least with respect to the pricing of non-basics and to the role of these latter in determining Sraffa's 'maximum rate of profit, R'. (It may be of interest here that a major contribution was made by E. Zaghini, not often described as a 'Sraffian economist'.)
2. As was mentioned above in passing, Sraffa's concept of a 'sub-system' (1960, Appendix A) has received considerable elaboration in the hands of Pasinetti, in his fascinating work on vertical integration. These ideas have been used in empirical studies.
3. The theory of choice of technique in joint production systems has gone way beyond Sraffa's treatment (1960, Section 96) which has, indeed, been shown to be unacceptable. In the course of the relevant discussions, light has been shed on the question of what determines the relation between the number of activated processes and the number of positively-priced commodities. (It is *not* the case that 'Sraffian' economists all simply assume square systems, ignoring the contribution of von Neumann, the significance of weak inequality price/cost relations and so on.)
4. No serious economic theorist should be satisfied with the very common 'radioactive decay' treatment of fixed capital. Building on Sraffa's treatment (1960, Chapter X) a number of writers have developed extensive (often rather long!) analyses of the choice of technique, of truncation, of the correct pricing of used machines and so on.
5. Sraffa's brief discussion of the theory of rent (1960, Chapter XI) has been amplified and extended by a number of authors into a detailed analysis of the complex inter-relationships between commodity prices, land use, extensive and intensive rent and wages and profits.

6. Whilst the roots of the five above-mentioned topics are perfectly explicit in *Production of Commodities*, the three topics still to be referred to are, at most, only hinted at in that work. Sraffa considered only 'prices of production' and noted that his book 'contains no reference to market prices' (1960, p. 9). In the works of Smith, Ricardo and Marx, of course, a reference to market prices often raises the question of their 'gravitation' towards 'natural prices' and there is by now quite a large 'Sraffian' literature on the conditions under which such 'gravitation' can or cannot plausibly be supposed to occur. (This literature naturally has a formal overlap with many 'neoclassical' stability analyses, so it should perhaps be remarked that the former is always based on allowing transactions to take place at 'current' prices in a 'real time' process.)
7. In recent years a number of 'Sraffian' writers have been much exercised in trying to develop a theory of effective demand, capacity utilization and the determination of 'long period' output levels. (If my description appears more tentative in this case, that may be because I have not fully understood this particular branch of the Sraffian tree.)
8. Prompted perhaps by a hint from Sraffa (1960, Section 44), work has been developing on the interrelationships between the rate of profits and the rate of interest – work which may come to provide a useful link between the more formal Sraffian analyses of value and distribution theory and the much wider questions of money and, more generally, economic policy.

3 SRAFFA AND LAKATOS

Could a Lakatosian appraisal of Sraffian economics amount to little more than an abuse of Lakatos's MSRPs to dress up, in recently fashionable clothes, a view (favourable or unfavourable) of such economics which had, in fact, been arrived at already, quite independently of Lakatos's conceptions? I ask the question only to register the fact that I do not think that it should be airily waved aside as 'obviously' a non-serious question. At the very least, raising the question openly might serve to keep us alert to the alleged danger. In similar vein, we might note that appraisal needs to be based on the *fullest* knowledge and understanding of a body of work but that such knowledge and understanding may often be possessed only by the 'insider', who might be expected to be lenient in his appraisal. Conversely someone who suspects, on whatever grounds, that a body of work is not that valuable, may not be motivated to acquire the knowledge and understanding necessary for adequate appraisal. (Cp. Lakatos's own observation: 'But the sociology of knowledge frequently serves as a successful cover for illiteracy', 1972, p. 174, n. 1.) The 'insider' might be tempted to abuse Lakatos's work to glorify his own scientific allegiance, the 'critic' to abuse it to cover his own illiteracy. But enough of preliminary remarks.

First, I should like to ask a question about 'negative contributions', which, like Mill, I value highly: the elimination of error is desirable, I should say, whether or not it does (ever can) lead to truth. The kind of 'negative contributions' referred to in Section 1 above presumably do not constitute empirical progress or empirical refutation in any SRP. Do they constitute theoretical progress and, if so, within which SRP? Does a demonstration of the non-validity of some familiar piece of theorizing count as theoretical progress in the Lakatosian schema? I am unclear about this. If the answer is 'No', then my response is that that is an inadequacy within the schema: it fails to recognize a class of valuable contributions. If the answer is 'Yes', then I ask within *which* SRP this theoretical progress is to be said to take place. In our case, are the 'negative' Sraffian results to be regarded as theoretical progress within some Sraffian SRP(s) or within some marginalist or marxian SRP(s)? Recall Samuelson's remark about Sraffa's statue in the 'neoclassical Hall of Fame', which might seem to encourage the second answer. Suppose that this second answer is the approved Lakatosian response. Are we then to infer that, since Sraffa and others have made theoretical progress within the marginalist SRP (*ex hypothesi*), they must have been sharing the presuppositions, or the hard-core propositions, or the positive or negative heuristics of that SRP? If not, why not and just what are we to infer? That in fact the presuppositions and so on are *not*, after all, always a vital part of a SRP? Suppose, alternatively, that Sraffa and others are said to have made (negative) theoretical progress within some Sraffian SRP(s). *Prima facie*, that would seem an odd thing to say, when they are simply demolishing other people's theoretical constructions. Perhaps the conclusion is simply that the Sraffian 'negative contribution' to economic theory also provides, unintentionally, a 'negative contribution' to the Lakatosian MSRP *as applied to economics*? (I risk no broader conclusion.) I thus lightheartedly propose a (mild) MSRP dilemma; if the Sraffian negative contribution is not recognized as theoretical progress, then that is a weakness of the MSRP; if it is so recognized, then the MSRP may have difficulty in accommodating it within some SRP without resort to ad-hocery. (Or could one 'sidestep' the supposed dilemma by not locating this negative contribution within either SRP and by seeing it rather as an aspect of the rivalry between two (or more) SRPs?) In presenting these questions and this dilemma to the Capri conference, I supposed that the experts on Lakatosian methodology would provide immediate and agreed answers to the questions and a resolution of the dilemma; my expectation was not fulfilled.

Let us now shut our eyes to the above and consider how the Lakatosian MSRP and the 'positive contributions' of the Sraffians might illuminate one another, whether to their advantage or their disadvantage. We know that the appropriate units of appraisal are said to be SRPs, not single hypotheses or theories. We also know, however, that Fulton (1984) has urged rather firmly that it is neither helpful nor in the spirit of Lakatos's own work on physics to interpret a SRP too broadly. Fulton was too polite to suggest that one might be moved to laughter on comparing some of the different 'hard cores' which have been proposed as characterizing 'neoclassical economics', an animal we are all supposed to know intimately – but I am not sure that he needed to be. If we cannot agree 'reasonably' closely and easily in identifying the hard core of something we know so well, the lesson is probably that the attempt is misconceived. Fulton displays admirable sense, it seems to me, in suggesting that it is more appropriate to speak of, say, the neoclassical human capital SRP, or the H-O-S trade theory SRP (1984, pp. 202–3). As he puts it, neo-classical economics consists of 'a large number of interrelated research programs' (p. 203). Fulton's conclusion, of course, is that the MSRP may be of some use in economics *if* interpreted and used with *modesty* (pp. 202–4). How do things stand with respect to Sraffian economics?

I shall assume, without further discussion, that it would certainly be a waste of everyone's time to speak of, for example, the 'scientific research program of a modernized classical study of the laws of motion of capitalism' (I deliberately make things easy for myself here) and most probably be a waste of time to speak of '*the* Sraffian SRP'. Let us begin, then, by jumping to the other extreme and considering, for example, 'the SRP of providing a complete characterization of the choice of technique in square joint production systems subject to constant returns to scale'. We could easily identify a fairly clearly delimited body of work in this area and, if we thought it worthwhile, we could probably specify fairly readily a common set of presuppositions and of never-questioned assumptions. Common 'rules of discussion' would emerge, I think, and we should find that there has been quite definite and impressive theoretical progress made since Sraffa's contribution (1960, Section 96). Unsettled disputes remain. I am not aware that any empirical progressiveness could be established to date. I say that we probably *could* set out the history of this narrowly defined body of work in terms of a hard core, positive and negative heuristics and so on – but what would we *gain* by so doing? As a first approximation to the answer, I cautiously suggest 'Nothing'.

The example of the last paragraph might perhaps be thought too narrow, too contrived, so let us try a more ambitious project as the possible subject of a Lakatosian account – Garegnani's 'surplus approach' as outlined, for example, in his recent *New Palgrave* entry (1987, vol. IV, pp. 560–74). As was mentioned in section 2, Garegnani sets out a research project which *starts* from an analytical 'core' of 'Sraffian' value and distribution theory in which the real wage, the social product and the conditions of production are *provisionally* treated as data. Using short chains of reasoning, paying full attention to historical and institutional considerations and recognizing that there may be 'feedbacks' between intra- and extra-core variables, one is then, step by step, to construct a modern 'classical' political economy. There is no suggestion that the relationships considered within the 'core' are of greater interest or importance than others (1987, p. 562). It would not be at all difficult, I think, to provide a Lakatosian *description* of the 'surplus approach' research program. Whether a Lakatosian appraisal is yet possible is perhaps less clear. The forces engaged in the development of this program are, numerically, but small and not all of its protagonists believe in publishing too quickly. There is thus no adverse criticism implied in saying that the program has yet to be implemented sufficiently for an 'appraisal' of its results to be appropriate. We must wait to see. (If anyone asks 'How long?', I ask, 'Does the MSRP give any useful advice on how to answer that?') But we can note even now that the *aim* of such work is to produce empirical propositions. It is thus quite wrong to say – as was said at the Capri conference – that 'Sraffian economics' is entirely about matters of logic and is thus not be be considered in terms of the MSRPs.

Consider now the possibility of taking Roncaglia's two other 'Sraffian Schools' as embodying two SRPs. The position here would not be very different, I suggest, from that outlined with respect to the 'surplus approach' (although it might be less straightforward to identify a clear-cut and explicit programmatic statement in these other two cases). Again we must wait to see, for it would presumably be merely pretentious to dress up an assessment of, say, Pasinetti's achievement in *Structural Change and Economic Growth* as a 'Lakatosian appraisal of the Pasinetti Scientific Research Program'. To do that might be unfair to Pasinetti and would be unfair both to Lakatos and to one's readers.

Suppose that we now stipulate, purely for the sake of the argument, that Roncaglia's three Sraffian Schools do in fact correspond to three 'Sraffian SRPs'. We *might well* decide that they share certain presuppositions, a respect for classical political economy, a respect for Sraffa's work and an inclination not to accept every aspect of marginalist economic theory. We *might* be able to set out certain common 'hard-core' propositions and positive and negative heuristics – but I do not think we ought to be surprised if we find that these common elements, if any, are not very numerous. (They might still be important, of course.) This suggests, then, that (to misquote Fulton), if Sraffian economics is to be described and appraised *à la* Lakatos, it must be seen as a 'number of interrelated research programs'. (This conclusion could conceivably be premature if 'The actual hard core of a program . . . develops slowly, by a long, preliminary process of trial and error' (Lakatos, 1972, p. 133, n. 4). *How* could Weintraub write, 'This hardening process was ignored by Lakatos' (1985, p. 140) – and after quoting Lakatos, as I have just done, on p. 112)?

Deciding 'how many' SRPs Sraffian economics embodies is probably a task best left undone. But in the hope of providing yet another possible candidate for SRP status, I now return to my earlier list of eight areas in which positive Sraffian contributions have arguably been made. As noted before, in section 2, the first five (basics/non-basics; vertical integration; joint production; fixed capital; rent) all derive quite directly from *Production of Commodities*. Within reasonably close limits all the work referred to here starts from assumptions found in Sraffa's book. Moreover, although the topics investigated are quite distinct, this body of work not only shares a rather precise set of common assumptions but is developed by uniformly mathematical methods. And, indeed, the same *types* of mathematical argument are used repeatedly in the production of theoretical progress in these different subject areas. Could this body of work usefully be described as an SRP? Since I have worked within it, I had better propose a fairly deflating label for it, such as the 'Derivatively Sraffian SRP'. This DSSRP could quite readily be displayed in Lakatosian style, with an already-hardcore, clear heuristics, rapid theoretical progress but no empirical progress. What would one learn from setting out such a display which one did not know already and which is worth knowing? Little or nothing? Of course, one *could* say, quite truthfully, that working within the DSSRP does remind one of Lakatos's remarks that Newton was not concerned with the evidence but just developed his research program (1972, pp. 1135–6); that 'If a scientist (or mathematician) has a positive heuristic, he refuses to be drawn into observation' (p. 135, n. 1); that 'the positive heuristic forges ahead with almost complete disregard of "refutations" ' (p. 137). That is just how it is within the DSSRP. But what would be the *point* of saying this, if not to glorify (or ridicule) the DSSRP, by appearing to compare it with Newton's wonderful achievement?

How might one criticize 'Sraffian economics' in terms of the MSRPs? Certainly not in terms of lack of theoretical results – both negative and positive – and certainly not in terms of persistent, flagrant ad-hocery in response to empirical refutation. There has not been any empirical refutation to respond to! More likely, presumably, is the allegation that the Sraffian SRPs do not 'display an *intermittently progressive empirical shift*' (Lakatos, 1972, p. 134, emphasis in original). It would be only too easy at this point to launch into a song-and-dance routine in which the 'Lakatosian' pro-Sraffian reminds us that 'Our term "intermittently" gives sufficient *rational* scope for dogmatic adherence to a programme in face of *prima facie* "refutations" ' (ibid. emphasis in original) and that budding SRPs should not be discarded too readily (p. 157), while the 'Lakatosian' anti-Sraffian asks, over and over, 'But where *is* the progressive empirical shift?' So I won't launch into it. The point is that our pro- and anti-Sraffian ideologues could harangue each other just as efficiently (and fruitlessly) *without* abusing the memory of Imre Lakatos. His studies of the history and philosophy of physics and mathematics need not be plundered and abused to dress up (it is no more) an old argument in economics. Indeed one should consider seriously Zamagni's (1982) warnings that each science may need its proper (different) methodology, that methodology follows science rather than leads it, and that it is indeed undesirable that methodologists be permitted to prescribe what is good procedure in science.

The question still stands, of course, as to whether 'Sraffian economics' can properly be criticized for not yet having produced interesting and (in principle) testable propositions. A useful preliminary step at this point would be to produce examples of *other* research programs in economics, which lie outside the mainstream and thus have limited 'background intellectual and theoretical resources' to call on, which are pursued by a *very* small number of people, which have been directed in the first 15 or 20 years of their pursuit largely to 'negative' or critical work – and to see how many interesting and testable propositions they have produced after a *total* life (including the 15–20 years of critical work) of 29 years. Against the benchmark of such examples, one could then appraise the Sraffian case. If all the other cases show notable empirical achievements, the Sraffian 'defence counsel' will have something to answer, if such achievements are a necessary condition of value in an economic theory. If none of them shows empirical results, the

Sraffian 'prosecutor' may have to think twice. *Et cetera*. One should not simply *assume*, of course, that impressive empirical progress is in any way the norm in economics; indeed it was argued at the Capri conference (by Kurt Klappholz) that economics in general has exhibited *little* empirical progress. (See, further, the paper by Shearmur and the comment by Klappholz in this volume.)

4 CONCLUDING ASSERTIONS AND QUESTIONS

1. Sraffa and 'Sraffian' authors have made a number of indefeasible contributions to 'negative logic', to the *elimination of theoretical error* in economics. To give anything less than ungrudging recognition to these contributions would be plain silly. (According to Feyerabend, 1988, pp. 156–7, 'the standards of rationality defended by the Popperian school . . . are standards of *criticism*: rational discussion consists in the attempt to criticize, and not in the attempt to prove or to make probable . . . Develop your ideas so that they can be criticized; attack them relentlessly; do not try to protect them but exhibit their weak spots; eliminate them as soon as such weak spots have become manifest.' Presumably, then, no economists declaring themselves Popperians could *ever* appear to brush aside or seek to diminish the value of Sraffian 'negative contributions'. Could they?)

2. How do negative theoretical contributions feature in the MSRPs? Are they registered as theoretical progress? If they do not feature at all, or feature and are not valued, that is a weakness in the MSRPs.

3. If 'Sraffian negative contributions' can be given their proper place in a Lakatosian appraisal, will they appear within some Sraffian SRP, or in marginalist SRPs and the Anglo-Saxon Marxist SRP? *If* this question causes any embarrassment, that signals a problem within the MSRPs.

4. Any talk of *the* Sraffian SRP is almost certainly a waste of time, at best. If Sraffian economics is to be discussed in Lakatosian terms, one should follow Fulton's example and attempt to distinguish a number of well-defined Sraffian SRPs. The links between them, the things that make these SRPs members of the same family, may be fairly sparse.

5. With respect to positive contributions to date, some Sraffian candidate SRPs exhibit rapid theoretical progress, some limited theoretical progress. Predictions about the future theoretical progress to be made within these SRPs probably tell one more about the predictor's current prejudices than they do about future progress.

6. It is not clear to me that any Sraffian SRP has yet produced

valuable empirical progress. I have proposed above a useful preliminary to any *serious* (unprejudiced) appraisal of how much this matters.

7. A number of contributors to an earlier conference (see Latsis, 1976) were less than fully convinced that the MSRPs add greatly to our understanding of economics. I cannot comment on Imre Lakatos's contributions to the study of physics or mathematics but I share the scepticism to be found in parts of Latsis (1976) with respect to the supposed application or misapplication of Lakatos's work to the study of economics. To remove such scepticism, it is *not enough* to point to studies of economics in which intelligent and imaginative people have employed the MSRPs and have come up with some interesting observations about episodes in economics. Were those interesting observations produced *by the use* of the MSRPs? Or were they produced by the intelligence and imagination of the authors? More precisely, which valuable insights into the development of economics have been arrived at which could not have been arrived at as easily *without* the employment of the MSRPs? In which valuable studies have the MSRPs contributed significantly to the *content* of the findings, as opposed to providing a *form* in which they could be set out? I readily acknowledge that it may not always be simple to make the decisions required by these questions.

REFERENCES

As was mentioned in the text, this list does not include the many, many works referred to only by implication.

Feyerabend, P. (1988), *Against Method* (revised edition) (London: Verso/New Left Books).

Fulton, G. (1984), 'Research programmes in economics', *History of Political Economy*, **16**(2), pp. 187–205.

Garegnani, P. (1985), 'Ricordo di Piero Sraffa', in *I Limiti della politica economica* (Società italiana degli economisti) Giuffrè editore.

—— (1987), 'Surplus approach to value and distribution', in *New Palgrave Dictionary of Economics*, vol. IV (London: Macmillan).

Lakatos, I (1972), 'Falsification and the methodology of scientific research programmes', in I. Lakatos and A. Musgrave (eds), *Criticism and the Growth of Knowledge* (reprinted with corrections) (Cambridge: Cambridge University Press).

Latsis, S. (ed.) (1976), *Method and Appraisal in Economics* (Cambridge: Cambridge University Press).

Levhari, D. (1965), 'A nonsubstitution theorem and switching of techniques', *Quarterly Journal of Economics*, **79**, pp. 98–105.

Pasinetti, L.L. (1979), 'Sraffa, Piero', in D.L. Sills (ed.), *International Encyclopedia of the Social Sciences*, biographical supplement, vol. 18 (New York: Free Press).

—— (1981), *Structural Change and Economic Growth* (Cambridge: Cambridge Unviersity Press).
—— (1985), 'Piero Sraffa (1898–1983). Breve saggio bio-bibliografico', in *Due scritti bio-bibliografici su Piero Sraffa,* Temi di discussione 50, Servizio studi della Banca d'Italia, Rome.
Roncaglia, A. (1978), *Sraffa and the Theory of Prices* (New York: Wiley).
—— (n.d.[1985?]), 'The Sraffian schools', mimeo, Rome.
Samuelson, P.A. (1966), 'A summing up', *Quarterly Journal of Economics*, **80**, pp. 568–83.
—— (1987), 'Sraffian economics', in *New Palgrave Dictionary of Economics*, vol. IV (London: Macmillan).
Schefold, B. (1989), *Mr. Sraffa on Joint Production and Other Essays* (London: Unwin Hyman).
Sraffa, P. (1960), *Production of Commodities by Means of Commodities* (Cambridge: Cambridge University Press).
Steedman, I. (1977), *Marx after Sraffa* (London: New Left Books).
—— (ed.) (1988), *Sraffian Economics* (vols I and II) (Aldershot: Edward Elgar).
Weintraub, E.R. (1985), *General Equilibrium Analysis. Studies in Appraisal* (Cambridge: Cambridge University Press).
Zamagni, S. (1982), 'Introduzione', *Saggi di filosofia della scienza economica* (à cura di Stefano Zamagni) Rome, Nuova Italia Scientifica.

COMMENT ON STEEDMAN

Stefano Zamagni

Steedman's brilliant paper has a double purpose: to appraise Lakatos through Sraffa and to appraise Sraffa through Lakatos. While I am basically with him in his evaluation of Lakatos's methodology of scientific research programs (MSRP), I have some remarks about his way of appraising Sraffa.

1. In the past 15 years, our ability to evaluate Lakatos's MSRP has improved considerably in view of the many attempts to provide a number of Lakatosian rational reconstructions in the history of economic thought. As far as I know, the work of Steedman is the first attempt to apply, in a most creative way, the MSRP to Sraffian economics. What are the advantages of viewing Sraffian economics from the perspective of the Lakatosian program? How do Lakatosian categories allow us to see Sraffian theory in a more informative way than other metascientific views? In what ways does Sraffian economics fit the Lakatosian view of theories? These are the questions which Steedman poses in his paper and the overall conclusion he achieves – which I share with him – is substantially negative.

Needless to say, an assessment of this sort is not decisive by itself. First, one should check whether or not the Lakatosian methodology has been properly applied to the particular field under scrutiny. For instance, Fulton claims that too many people have applied this scheme over too large an area of economic theory;[1] the suggestion being that the Lakatos methodology should be applied to a specific set of theories within a school of thought. Secondly, one should keep in mind that following Lakatos himself, a negative appraisal is not enough to reject a methodology in the same way that it is not enough to reject a scientific theory. All this must be acknowledged and deserves attention.

However it also seems proper to recall what Schumpeter said in his first Tokyo lecture when he referred to the German *Methodenstreit* as 'one of the greatest misfortunes: they started to squabble about methods. Hundreds of books about methods appeared in Germany and out of a hundred articles on economics in periodicals I have counted 36 of a methodological nature. That is dreadful . . . a waste of energy . . . If epistemology provides for our needs, why go out of the way to enter a region not our own and deal with questions we are just as well without?'.[2] The message is clear. It is the practice of science which makes the method, not vice versa. Hence the priority of the single research with respect to discipline: researches are not engendered predetermined by disciplines, but indeed the latter are forged on researches.

2. I move now to Steedman's appraisal of Sraffian economics. Is the conceptualization of a market economy on which Sraffa's construction rests adequate? Is Sraffa's approach really the best place to set up the base camp to climb the peak representing the rehabilitation of the classical approach? How to account for the limited theoretical progress of the Sraffian program? To attempt an answer it is necessary to keep in mind what lies at the core of classical thought: the idea of a link between division of labour, growth of markets and productivity increases. So much so that even the classical interest in distribution stemmed from an interest in accumulation and not in distribution *per se*. This implies that a primary aim of a theory designed to re-launch the classical approach should be the understanding of processes of change. Now it is a fact that Sraffa himself was exclusively concerned with such properties of an economic system as do not depend on changes in the scale of production or in the proportions of factors. However this does not mean that the system is invariant under those changes, and in fact Sraffa had no intention of affirming this. In view of his particular targets, Sraffa was justified in taking an observed system of relations as given.

What happened after the publication of *Production of Commodities* was that the economists following Sraffa's program, instead of pushing it ahead in the direction of studying change over time, chose to refine, extend and generalize the results already achieved by Sraffa – the only notable exception being the work of Pasinetti on structural change and disproportional growth. The result has been that this research program is unable to say something of significance about fundamental issues such as the analysis of the turbulent phases accompanying a structural change. In fact, after a structural change, a new long-run position defined with respect to the particular composition of the capital stock and compatible with the composition of demand can only be achieved, if ever, when the transmutation of the capital stock to the proportions required by the new situation has been completed. In turn this might require a modification of the mode of behaviour of the agents, especially of the capitalists who do not simply adapt themselves, but react to the new situation.

Clearly the study of these turbulent, not-so-short periods poses interesting problems. For example, suppose that, owing to a change in the composition of output, the input coefficient matrix changes. How can we conceive the market process to establish the new centres of gravity? What should we assume for the existence and proper working of such a process? For sure, if such an economic adjustment process does not exist, this will not allow the new production coefficients to determine the new long-run prices. Now it should be obvious that the problem of transition from an 'old' to a 'new' long-run position has nothing to do with the problem either of stability or of gravitation. Indeed the 'new' position is history-dependent, in the sense that its features depend on the path followed by the economy during the transition, which – as a consequence – cannot be conceived of as a process of gravitation considered as 'an adaptation to quantities already fixed, i.e. determined in another part of the theory'.[3]

To sum up. My account of the unprogressiveness in the Lakatosian sense of the Sraffian research program rests on the following three points: (1) the *positive* contribution of this program is explicitly directed at the revivification of the classical approach; (2) the main thrust of the classical approach is the study of processes of change over time; and (3) the route taken by Sraffian economics has *de facto* prevented the elaboration of a suitable dynamic method of analysis.

This is not the place to try an explanation of why that happened. Let me simply suggest that a not unimportant reason is to be found in the circumstance that a good deal of Sraffian economics has ended up by unconsciously accepting the task of dealing with classical themes within the prevalent mode of doing theory. Of course this is not surprising. When a theoretical mode becomes dominant it also establishes a standard for correct theorizing in the sense that it fixes the canons of rational validation for any theoretical enquiry. This produces a dangerous distortive effect, since one starts formulating his metatheory of a given domain with an already formed model of valid reasoning. This model then makes us quite incapable of seeing how reason does and can really function in the domain to the degree that it does not fit the Procrustean bed of that model of validation.

3. A methodological aporia which, present in Sraffa's work, seems to have escaped the attention of those workng within this research program deserves to be briefly considered. In *Production of Commodities* (Section 35) we find the proposition that non-basic commodities do not enter the standard commodity in a single product system and in Appendix B the statement that it may be impossible to equalize profit rates throughout the economy. To my knowledge, these two assertions are shared, in various ways, by all Sraffian authors.

However, quite some time ago, Zaghini showed both that the standard commodity may contain non-basics and that the equalization of the profit rate in all sectors is always possible.[4] The condition for the standard commodity to contain all the non-basics in positive proportions, as well as the basics, is that the largest positive eigen-value of the submatrix composed of non-basics only be greater than the largest positive eigen-value of the submatrix composed of basics only. In symbols: $\lambda\ (A_{22}) > \lambda(A_{11})$. On the other hand, the condition for the existence of a uniform profit rate (and strictly positive prices) is that the profit rate be restricted in the interval

$$\left[0,\ \min\left(\frac{1}{\lambda(A_{11})} - 1, \frac{1}{\lambda(A_{22})} - 1\right)\right] \text{ with } \lambda(A_{11}) < 1 \text{ and } \lambda\ (A_{22}) < 1.$$

Now, since at the *theoretical* level the possibility that $\lambda(A_{22}) > \lambda(A_{11})$ cannot be excluded, the only way to assure the validity of the above-mentioned assertions is to jump to the *empirical* level. Indeed this is the move made by Sraffa himself in his correspondence with P. Newman: 'In a real system there is not one but a large number of basic products and the ratio resulting from the system which they form is *practically certain* to be much smaller than the own ratio of any one separate non-basic'.[5] So we happen to know that $\lambda(A_{22}) < \lambda(A_{11})$ from practice, not from theory. As should be evident, the methodological aporia is to take for granted something which the model ought to be able to explain. Indeed one cannot invoke factual realism to exclude something which is logically legitimate and this is all the more striking in a theoretical enterprise which is considered to be the quintessence of abstract reasoning. After all, is it not the case that, on the famous re-switching of techniques debate, the Sraffian authors have always – and correctly – insisted that the issue of the practical relevance of the re-switching phenomenon should be kept separate from the issue of its theoretical significance?

But why has Sraffian economics always rejected the case $\lambda(A_{22}) > \lambda(A_{11})$ as unrealistic? Essentially because it jeopardizes the predominance of the basic sector over the non-basic one, to the effect that it is the non-basic sector which determines the range of the profit rate and, in consequence, the range of all other magnitudes. Indeed, under the above condition, the physical own rate of reproduction of basics exceeds that of non-basics and such a state of affairs is certainly not the one envisaged by the classical economists. It is therefore understandable why a research program designated to rehabilitate the classical vision might not be insensitive to the case. However there is an important difference. The classics used to speak of wage-goods and luxury goods, a distinction which bears in itself an empirical connotation. On the other hand, Sraffa's distinction between basics and non-basics is a purely theoretical one, so much so that the definition of basics can be formulated only *after* the productive system has been set up.[6] In conclusion, it is certainly true that – as Steedman correctly says – Sraffa's distinction is clearly a generalization of the classical one, but it is achieved at a very high price in terms of methodological coherence.

Notes

1. G. Fulton, 'Research Programmes in Economics', *History of Political Economy*, **16**, 1984, pp. 187–205.
2. J. Schumpeter. 'The Present State of Economics', *Kokumin Keizai Zasshi*, **50**, 1931, p. 16; now in L. Allan (ed.), *Journal of Economic Literature*, **20**, 1982.
3. P. Garegnani, 'On a Change in the Notion of Equilibrium in Recent Work on Value and Distribution', in M. Brown, K. Sato and P. Zarembka (eds), *Essays in Modern Capital Theory*, (Amsterdam: North-Holland, 1976) p. 132.
4. E. Zaghini, 'On Non-Basic Commodities', *Revue Suisse d'Economie Politique et de Statistique*, **103**, 1967, pp. 257–66.
5. P. Sraffa, 'Letter to Peter Newman, dated 4/6/1962' in K. Bharadwaj, 'On the Maximum Number of Switches between Two Production Systems', *Revue Suisse d'Economie Politique et de Statistique*, **106**, 1970, pp. 425–6. Note that the *R* used by Sraffa corresponds, in terms of the above notation, to $(1/\lambda(A_{11}) - 1)$.
6. Moreover a pure wage-good (in the classical sense) takes the character of a basic or of a non-basic according to the way the wage rate is specified. See A. Salanti, 'Sraffa's Views about Non-Basics and Ricardo's Corn Model', *Economic Notes*, **12**, 1983, pp. 145–9.

COMMENT ON STEEDMAN

Edwin Burmeister*

1 Introduction

Almost as an aside, Ian Steedman has raised the following important questions regarding the so-called 'capital theory controversies' that raged in the mid-1960s and early 1970s:[1]

1. 'Why were they *called* 'controversies'?'
2. 'After all, one side was simply correct, so what was controversial?'
3. '[Was the controversy about] Levhari's (1965) error?'

We will answer these three questions after first demonstrating that they involve issues of considerable substance.

The two sides Steedman refers to are identified with Cambridge, US (primarily MIT); and Cambridge, UK though of course economists from elsewhere have been involved in the debate. Despite my strong identification with MIT (I was a graduate student there in 1965 when Cambridge, UK claimed victory), 25 years has been sufficient time for my passion about the subject to wane, and I return to it now with the hope that a more mature view and my own special knowledge of historical events will help both to answer Steedman's questions and to open up new areas of research for economic historians. More importantly, I will discuss – though only superficially here – a closely related problem that is not sufficiently well-understood: the proper role of assumptions and approximations in economic science.

2 A Brief Review

A little background material will be helpful. I date the start of my brief review with the publication of Joan Robinson's *Essays in the Theory of Economic Growth* in 1962 and *The Accumulation of Capital* in 1966 (both were published by St Martin's Press), which elaborated a theme first put forward in 1953.[2] Her basic message in these works was that the existence of heterogeneous capital goods – the fact that there are many physically different types of machines used for production – has important and complex implications for economic theory. My personal

*I am grateful to Neil de Marchi for his helpful comments on an earlier draft of this paper. This research was supported by the National Science Foundation (SES-86-18403).

interpretation of how this message was received at MIT *before* August 1965 (see below for the importance of this date) is, 'Yes, there are technical complications that arise because of heterogeneous capital goods, but none of them really matter for any important economic implication.' I leave it for economic historians to make or break the case for this personal interpretation, but warn that there is a voluminous technical literature that should be scrutinized.[3]

Nevertheless the non-technical evidence I now turn to is compelling: the tale of the *neoclassical parable* as developed in Cambridge, US and as told by Samuelson in the sixth edition of his famous principles text.[4] To avoid misunderstandings that so easily arise by quoting out of context, the relevant first part of the Appendix to Chapter 28 is reproduced here:

APPENDIX: THEORETICAL ASPECTS OF INTEREST, MONEY, AND POLICY

Here, very briefly, can be mentioned some elaborations and qualifications of this chapter's discussion.

Productivity or Impatience?

Some people like to find a single cause for everything, and such people ask: "Is interest caused by the productivity of capital? Or by the fact that savers must be paid for the unpleasant task of 'abstinence' or 'waiting'? Which is more important: opportunity to invest or impatience to spend?"

Our previous argument shows this is a false antithesis. *Both* factors operate to determine the time path of interest: the impatience to spend, or the tendency to prefer the present to the future, limits the growth rate and attained size of capital; and the productivity factor tells us what is the interest or net productivity that can be earned as we have various [594] amounts of diverse capital goods. Just as both blades of a scissors are needed to cut – so that you cannot say that one blade rather than the other is doing the actual work – similarly, both factors, impatience *and* productivity, interact to determine the behavior of interest rates.

Determination of the Interest Rate

Can our account of interest determination avoid the use of Fig. 1's simplifying concept of a stock of homogeneous capital? Yes, in a number of ways, some of which are too complex to explain in an introductory work. Thus, we may work with a variety of different physical capital goods and processes, being careful never to add their heterogeneous units together, noting that the sum of their capitalized market values does depend (in a virtuously, and not viciously, circular way) on the market interest rate, and never forgetting that it is machines and not hunks of dollars which enter into physical production functions. If the realistic problem of uncertainty about the future and the risks thereby implied could be ignored, advanced treatises can show rigorously how an equilibrium interest-rate pattern can be defined in such a heterogeneous model.

This is clearly not the place for such refinements. But it is desirable to show that the diminishing-returns phenomenon, depicted by the downward-sloping *DD* curve of Fig. 1, is a truth quite independent of using the simplified homogeneous capital stock of Fig. 1. The key to a simple approach comes from Fisher's diagram in the footnote below, which states the fundamental fact about the whole theory of interest: Society can exchange present consumption goods for future consumption goods at a trade-off rate depicted by the rate of interest.

Diminishing returns again. Figure 5 depicts the foregoing basic fact and also shows the basic technical fact of diminishing returns. During the first three years, society is shown with level consumption of 100 and zero net investment. Then, in 1972, we sacrifice 10 units of present consumption goods. What does this bring us in the next year? Exactly 10 + 2 units of extra consumption: the 10 is return of our principal, the 2 represents the [595] basic fact of a 2⁄10, or 20 per cent per year, interest rate (the "net productivity of capital").

Figure 5 Present vs. future consumption at diminishing returns

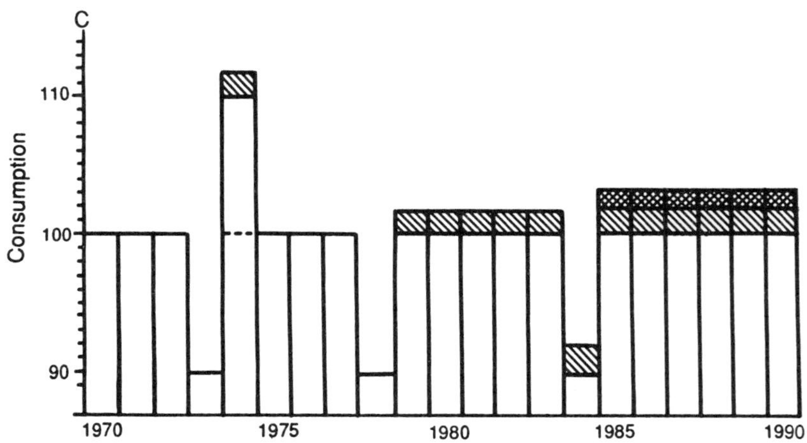

Society can continue thereafter consuming all its NNP. It could get 20 per cent interest in the market place, but does not choose to make any net investments. In this equilibrium, land sells at 5-year purchase; each tool is just replaced and must be earning a net yield of 20 per cent so that the present discounted value of its future rental receipts will just equal its initial cost of production.

In 1978, however, people decide that they do not have a 20 per cent subjective time preference for present consuming over future consuming. So again they sacrifice 10 units of current consumption. But this time they do not decide to take all their fruits in the following year. Instead, they decide to enjoy the extra fruits in a new higher *plateau* of *C*. How much *perpetual* *C* can they get? The diagram verifies what the 20 per cent interest rate has already suggested. Sacrifice of 10 C today has given them a perpetual extra C of 2 per year, equal to 20 per cent of 10.

That could be the end of the story. But we want to investigate diminishing returns. So in 1984, after enjoying steady C at 102 for several years, they decide once again to sacrifice 10 of present C in return for a perpetual higher plateau of C. If they are ignorant of the law of diminishing returns, they may be naive enough to expect an increment of 20 per cent again. Nature will teach them otherwise: she will now give them the smaller dark blocks of extra level of C: to exaggerate the phenomenon of diminishing returns. Fig. 5 makes the interest rate fall all the way down to 10 per cent.

Now land will sell at 10 years' purchase; now all tools will have become so numerous as to bring down their per annum yield to 10 per cent, where again their present discounted value is equal to their initial costs of production. Now longer-lived species of pine trees will pay: mellower wine; more roundabout processes of production generally; more durable (even though costlier) razor blades. Now consumption loans among persons will be at a pure interest rate of 10 per cent.

Long-run equilibrium. How long could this accumulation process of sacrificing current C [596] go on? Just as Fig. 1 suggested, it can go on until the interest rate is zero, or until people want to do no net saving. At the zero rate of interest, if we could ever quite reach this point on the horizon, the plateau of consumption would be as high as is technically possible with the given labor, land, and primary resources. It is a kind of "golden age."[1]

In real life three or more things keep us from reaching the golden age:

1. People may be so impatient that at some interest rate like 3 per cent, they will not want to do net saving.

2. Inventions will come along and offset diminishing returns by shifting upward all curves *like DD* in Fig. 1.

3. There is always riskiness in a dynamic society: long before the pure interest rate reaches zero, the profit-rate-inclusive-of-premium-for-risk may have hit a floor below which investment lags. We must examine this important matter.

3 What Was the Appendix Error?

Samuelson's sixth edition Appendix to Chapter 28 contains an error that is different from but closely related to 'Levhari's error' – Steedman's question (3). We will discuss 'Levhari error' in the next section.

The Appendix error is that Figure 5 is, in general, wrong. Likewise

[1] Advanced books show that this golden rule must be modified if primary resources such as labor are all growing at 3 or 5 per cent per year. Then the golden age of maximal per capita consumption comes when the interest rate has been brought down also to 3 or 5 per cent: then the young earners in society, who are saving for their old age, are just enough more numerous than the retired earners, who are eating up what they had earlier saved: and then there is just enough net saving and investing to keep all capital goods growing in full proportion to the growth in primary labor. Then we have an equilibrium, a nice moving equilibrium with balanced growth. (If land will not grow at all, Malthus reminds us that this Eden must come to an end in the absence of inventions.)[597]

the discussion of Figure 5 in the subsection entitled 'Diminishing returns again', beginning on page 595 and ending on 596, also contains errors. However, it is important to recognize that Samuelson's Figure 5 depicting the trade-off between consumption today and consumption tomorrow is correct. Similarly most of his discussion in the Appendix is correct. The error is that, when there is more than one capital good, the situation shown in my Figure 1 can occur, as simple numerical examples prove. Thus, even though the steady-state equilibria labelled A and B have lower interest rates than the steady-state equilibrium C, consumption is higher at C than at A or B.

Figure 1 Failure of 'the neoclassical parable'

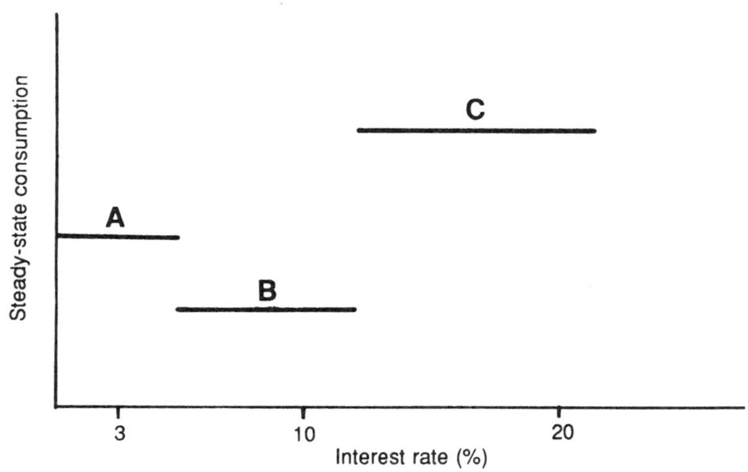

I have stressed the 'paradoxical behaviour' of per capita consumption across steady-state equilibria, but it is evident that the behaviour illustrated in Figure 1 implies that there cannot exist any well-behaved 'aggregate production function' that produces net output (consumption) from labour and 'the aggregate capital stock'. This conclusion follows immediately since, across steady-state equilibria, larger quantities of 'aggregate capital' should be associated with smaller interest rates; but if this is so, then the steady state labelled C in Figure 1 must have a smaller stock of 'aggregate capital' than either steady states A or B, and so it should produce less, not more, net output.

4 What Was Levhari's Error?

I do not believe that Samuelson ever thought that the parable he told in his sixth edition was literally true – that is why he called it a parable. Nevertheless it is fair to say that the belief among Cambridge, US economists (myself included) was that the parable contained enough economic truth to be called a principle: *Across steady-state equilibria, larger quantities of 'aggregate capital' are associated with lower interest rates and higher consumption.*

The basis of this belief was mainly the one-capital-good models of Irving Fisher and Robert Solow, as well as the literature already cited in note 3. It was thought that one simply needed to impose some mild technical regularity condition(s) on a technology with heterogeneous capital goods to render the parable true as a theorem. One conjecture that circulated in the early 1960s was that a sufficient regularity condition would be the assumption that the technology was *indecomposable* – that every capital good and labour be required, either directly or indirectly, as an input to produce output of any other good. With this or some other technical assumptions, it was thought, the problems caused by the existence of heterogeneous capital goods – in particular, the type of problems discussed by Joan Robinson – could be circumvented. Then all the economic results that come from a world with only one type of capital good could be trusted to yield correct insights about behaviour in the more complex world of many capital goods.

To understand Levhari's error, we first must define *re-switching of techniques*. The reader interested in details is referred to my 1980 book or to other references,[5] and here I give only the essentials.

Let a particular list of the quantities of inputs and outputs that are technologically feasible be called a *technique of production*. If a particular production technique, call it A, represents a steady-state equilibrium at an interest rate r_1, and if another technique represents a steady-state equilibrium at a higher interest rate $r_2 > r_1$, then technique A is said to recur and re-switching of techniques is said to exist if it is possible for technique A to again represent a steady-state equilibrium at some higher interest rate $r_3 > r_2$.

Thus, *if* re-switching exists, the behaviour illustrated in Figure 2 also exists. Note that it entails all of the problems already revealed by Figure 1.

In one chapter of his MIT PhD dissertation, David Levhari put forward the proposition that if the technology was indecomposable – that is, if *every* technique of production was itself indecomposable – then the re-switching of techniques could not occur. From what we have said here, it is now evident that this proposition was not very interesting: even if it were true, it would only rule out the behaviour in Figure 2, not the behaviour in Figure 1. Indeed this is precisely the conclusion that was also reached by Joan Robinson.[6]

Figure 2 The re-switching of techniques

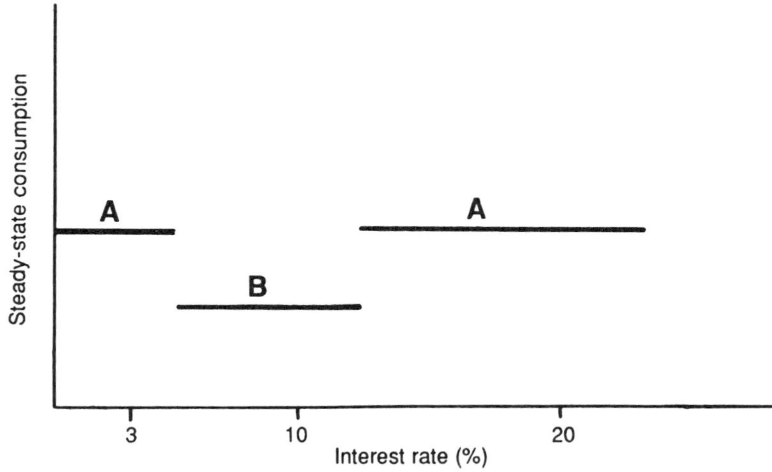

Levhari's 'proof' misused an inequality result from linear programming and was wrong. However the error was sufficiently subtle for it to escape the scrutiny of everyone at MIT, as well as the referees at *The Quarterly Journal of Economics*, where this chapter of his dissertation was published; see the reference in note 5.

There are two points that deserve emphasis. First, Levhari's claim for a proof did not generate great excitement at MIT because everyone *believed* the result to be true, and hence the details of the proof never received proper scrutiny. Second, this particular proposition was a very small part of Levhari's otherwise outstanding dissertation. Indeed even the published paper with the famous error contains an ingenious (correct) proof of a more important proposition: namely, in a technology with alternative techniques of production, a sequence of production decisions that maximize profits at given prices will lead to the unique (except for ties) cost-minimizing equilibrium.

Unfortunately for Levhari and Cambridge, US economists, not only was the proof wrong, but so was the proposition. A counter-example was given by Luigi Pasinetti at the First World Congress of the Econometric Society held in Rome in August, 1965. This involved a high degree polynomial and was unnecessarily complex, but the result was clear: *re-switching was possible even with an indecomposable technology*.

5 Cambridge, UK Claims (Too Much?) Victory

Shortly thereafter, simple numerical examples were produced which showed that the behaviour illustrated in Figure 1 was also possible: the neoclassical parable could be wrong even in models that did not exhibit re-switching. The first reference I know of is Bruno, Burmeister and Sheshinski, cited above in note 5, but in the autumn of 1965 both false and true claims started to circulate so fast that it was almost impossible to keep track. The issues were judged to be of sufficient importance for *The Quarterly Journal of Economics* to publish a special *Symposium* issue in November 1966.

Cambridge, US economists were very candid in admitting their errors. For example, the Levhari-Samuelson paper cited in note 5 begins: 'We wish to make clear for the record that the nonswitching theorem associated with us is definitely false. We are grateful to Dr. Pasinetti . . .' Likewise the seventh edition of Samuelson's *Economics*, published in 1967, is purged of all errors; see the Appendix to Chapter 30 in that edition, pages 585–90.

Meanwhile Cambridge, UK economists claimed victory: Levhari was wrong, Samuelson was wrong, Solow was wrong, MIT was wrong, neoclassical economics was wrong. However the fact that Levhari's proposition was wrong, and the fact that this led to the discovery that the neoclassical parable as embodied in Figure 1 was wrong, are not sufficient reasons for concluding that *all* of neoclassical economics was wrong! Indeed a careful comparison of the relevant Appendices in Samuelson's sixth and seventh editions reveals how very little hinged on the mistakes that had been made. We will turn to the question, 'What *is* correct?' after first discussing a late entry into the debate: Austrian economists.

6 The Austrians Claim They Know Better (but Don't)

Many Austrian economists believed that capital theory was one of their strong points, and they certainly paid little attention to the 'technical work' done by either Cambridge, US economists or Cambridge, UK economists (as exemplified by Joan Robinson). After all, Boehm-Bawerk had taught them that roundabout production processes (that take more time to produce output) are technologically superior, and so one only needed an index of roundaboutness to replace the faulty concept of an aggregate capital stock: *time* itself would provide the key to aggregation.

This view was summarized in a paper by Leland Yeager,[7] which was awarded a prize by *Economic Enquiry* for the 'best paper published that year'. My own work, however, showed that an Austrian approach to capital theory was merely a special case of the Leontief–von Neumann methods and could solve *none* of the re-switching-related problems. Essentially, if one replaces the interest rate in Figures 1 or 2 with some index of roundaboutness, a well-behaved Austrian model should have *increasing* steady-state consumption because more roundabout processes are technologically superior and hence can produce output. I proved that there does not exist *any* index of 'roundaboutness' that rules out the behaviour in Figures 1 or 2. This result appeared in 1974,[8] though I had discovered it many years before; I did not consider it by itself to be of sufficient importance for publication.

When in 1976 I moved from the University of Pennsylvania to the Center for Advanced Studies at the University of Virginia, Leland Yeager became my colleague and discussions about capital theory ensued. Like Levhari and Samuelson, Yeager readily admitted his mistake, and we jointly published a note on the issue.[9] It is ironic that Yeager won a prize, while Levhari has become known for his 'famous error' – yet both made mistakes of essentially the same magnitudes: the kind 'anyone could make', in my opinion.

7 What *Is* Theoretically Correct?

As already noted, the fundamental neoclassical proposition that there is a negative sloped, concave trade-off between consumption today and consumption tomorrow – a basic result of Irving Fisher in a one-capital-good world – remains valid despite the existence of heterogeneous capital goods. Moreover, though all of the re-switching debate was concerned with non-joint production technologies having only one primary factor (labour), these assumptions can be weakened without altering the truth of this inter-temporal consumption trade-off. (Even with only one capital good, however, the situation depicted in Figure 1 can arise in joint production economies). This correct inter-temporal trade-off is illustrated in Samuelson's Figure 1. These results generalize easily to many time periods.

The results that follow from a one-capital-good model without production, where the behaviour shown in Figures 1 and 2 is impossible and in Samuelson's Figure 4 is correct, are very, very special. If we restrict our attention to a comparison of steady-state equilibria – which were part of the ground rules for the capital controversies – then a necessary and sufficient condition for the one-capital-good results to obtain can be derived by evaluating the change in the capital stock at *switch points*. A switch point in Figure 1 is an interest at which both techniques A and B, say, generate the same equilibrium prices and hence are both viable. That is, at a switch point rate of interest, either A, B, or any linear combination of them can represent a competitive equilibrium. The actual physical stock of capital – both the types and the quantities – depend on which technique is employed. Let k_{iA} denote the equilibrium stock of the i-th type capital good when technique A is employed, and similarly for technique B. Also suppose the r' is a switch point, with technique A being the unique choice for values of r slightly less than r' and technique B being the unique choice for values of r slightly greater than r'. A *necessary and sufficient* condition to exclude the behaviour in Figure 1 and 2 is that

$$\text{(Condition)} \quad \sum_{i=1}^{n} p_i(k_{iA} - k_{iB}) < 0 \quad \text{at} \quad r = r'$$

for *all* switch points and all pairs of techniques. These results were proved by me for several different models.[10]

What about the elusive 'aggregate production function?' Again restricting our attention to comparisons of steady-state equilibria, one can define an index of per capita 'capital' K and an 'aggregate production function' $F(K)$ giving net output (per capita consumption) *if, and only if* the above Condition holds. This result, though it seemed important to me, has received almost no attention.[11] Incidentally, the function F has the neo-classical properties $F'(K) = r$ (the 'marginal product of capital' is equal to the steady-state interest rate) and $F''(K) < 0$ (diminishing returns).

Be this as it may, more recently my view has been that the comparison of alternative steady-state equilibria is fundamentally the wrong economic exercise. As I have already stated, different techniques such as A, B and C entail *different stocks of capital goods*, both different types and quantities. It is obvious, therefore, that in general one cannot move from B to A or C in one time period; it may take longer for the capital stocks to adjust to the types and levels of goods appropriate for the new production technique. Thus when one compares infeasible alternatives – say the 'choice' of whether or not, starting at the steady-state equilibrium using technique B, to stay there or to be at the steady-state equilibrium using technique C in Figure 1 – it is not so surprising that 'paradoxical' results emerge.

The economically relevant choices are either to stay at B, or to follow any one of the feasible dynamic paths that start from B. Some of these feasible paths may lead to a new steady-state equilibrium using technique C, but these will be a small subset. Now it is true that the above Condition is relevant for some of the properties exhibited by these dynamic paths, but it only serves as one of many possible restrictions on the set of feasible paths.[12] When one does study the dynamic properties of feasible paths, no paradoxes arise and the intuition of neoclassical economics is left intact.[13]

8 Has It Made Any Difference?

After all the smoke has cleared, it is both interesting and somewhat disturbing to answer the question, 'Has it made any difference?' By 'make a difference' here I mean make a difference either about the way economists think or about the way they do empirical work.

There are groups of economists in Europe – especially in Germany and Italy – for whom all this has made a big difference. Many of them have abandoned neoclassical economics for their own refinements of classical economics. This line of research is exemplified by the recent book edited by Bharadwaj and Schefold[14].

In the US, on the other hand, business goes on as if the controversy of the mid-1960s and 1970s had never happened. For example, every macroeconomics textbook that I have seen talks about 'capital' as though it were a well-defined concept – which we have seen it is not, except in a very special one-capital-good world.[15] Similarly all of 'the rational expectations revolution' and virtually all of the economic work in macroeconomics ignore the problems of heterogeneous capital goods.

Whether or not this methodology can lead to serious mistakes – either by way of faulty explanations or by way of bad policy implications – is unknown. The only study I know of that sheds any light on this question is by Frank Fisher, who concluded that the old methods of relying on an index of the capital stock, treating it as if it measured the quantity of a single capital good, and then estimating a Cobb-Douglas 'aggregate production function' work surprisingly well, at least whenever (for whatever reason) labour's share is approximately constant.[16]

The problem, of course, is that those interested in empirical work really have no available alternatives. Even if appropriate data were available on the stocks of different types of capital goods over time – and they are not – the econometric problems associated with estimation of macroeconomic models with heterogeneous capital goods are severe. These statistical problems probably could be surmounted, but there is no point in even trying if the data are not available.

Meanwhile those taking the classical route have contributed

essentially *no* empirical results either to support or to help understand their case.

9 Models, Approximations and Questions

It is probably the ambition of every scientist to discover a general theory that explains (almost) everything of interest. Einstein, for example, moved from his special theory of relativity to his much more influential general theory of relativity, and he died working on an even more general unified field theory. The work in economics by David Hendry on encompassing shares this view that 'bigger and more general theories are better'.

But is this really always true at the empirical and policy level? I think not. *All* theories are distortions of reality – otherwise they would not be theories. The practical issue is not whether or not the assumptions we make to build a model distort reality; they must. Rather the practical issue is whether or not these distortions are sufficiently small for us to take the implications of the model as approximately true and therefore to use them.

Moreover, while a particular model may yield approximate but acceptable answers for some sets of questions, it might simultaneously give awful answers to other questions. For example, by ignoring friction Newton was able to provide very accurate (though approximate) answers to questions such as, 'How long will it take a sphere to roll down a smooth inclined plane?' Obviously this same model that distorts reality by ignoring friction is totally inappropriate for studying the effects of how long it takes an automobile to stop when the brakes are applied.

And so it is with economics. There are full-employment models that may give perfectly acceptable answers to questions about the effect of money supply growth on inflation, but such models obviously cannot answer questions about the costs of alternative unemployment insurance plans. In economics it take both wisdom and the art of convincing others to sell a particular model as 'interesting and relevant'. But in all cases, whether or not a particular model is 'a good one' *cannot* be answered independently of what questions it is intended to answer; and even then the suitability of approximate answers cannot be evaluated without knowing to what purpose those answers are going to be put.

In this less-than-idealistic but operational spirit, perhaps the approximate answers provided by these theoretical and empirical one-capital-good models are not so bad after all. Until there is clear evidence to the contrary, it is certain that they will prevail in our profession.

10 The Answers to Steedman's Three Questions At Last

I now rapidly conclude with my answer to Steedman's three questions:

1. 'Why were they *called* 'controversies'?'
2. 'After all, one side was simply correct, so what was controversial?'
3. '[Was the controversy about] Levhari's (1965) error?'

Answers

1. The controversy – which has still not been settled – centres on whether or not the behaviour revealed to be possible by the existence of re-switching was (i) devastating to neoclassical economics or (ii) unimportant to the central core of neoclassical economics.
2. Once the truth was known, there was *no* controversy about the facts, and many Cambridge, US economists contributed to uncovering the far-reaching consequences of re-switching. Most of these findings constitute 'negative results'.
3. No.

Notes

1. Ian Steedman this volume, page 437.
2. Joan Robinson, 'The Production Function and the Theory of Capital', *Review of Economic Studies*, XXI (1953–4) pp. 312–20.
3. One can argue the case both on theoretical and empirical grounds. Some of the essential references include: Paul A. Samuelson, 'Parable and Realism in Capital Theory: The Surrogate Production Function', *Review of Economic Studies*, XXIX, **80** (June 1962) pp. 193–206; Robert M. Solow and Paul A. Samuelson, 'Balanced Growth under Constant Returns to Scale', *Econometrica*, **21**, 3 (July 1953) pp. 412–24; Robert M. Solow, 'The Production Function and the Theory of Capital', *Review of Economic Studies*, XXIII, **15** (1955–6), pp. 101–8; Robert M. Solow, 'Technical Change and the Aggregate Production Function', *Review of Economics and Statistics*. XXXIX, **3** (August 1957) pp. 312–20; H. Uzawa, 'On a Two-Sector Model of Economic Growth', *Review of Economic Studies*, XXIX, **78** (October 1961) pp. 40–7; Robert M. Solow, 'Note on Uzawa's Two-Sector Model of Economic Growth', *Review of Economic Studies*, XXIX, **78** (October 1961) pp. 48–50; L.R. Klein and A.S. Goldberger, *An Econometric Model of the United States, 1929–1952* (Amsterdam: North-Holland, 1955).
4. Paul A. Samuelson, *Economics: An Introductory Analysis*, 6 edn, Appendix to Chapter 28, 'Interest and Capital', pp. 594–600 (New York: McGraw-Hill, 1964).
5. Edwin Burmeister, *Capital Theory and Dynamics* (New York: Cambridge University Press, 1980). Definitions can also be found in the original Levhari paper and in the Bruno, Burmeister and Sheshinski paper: David Levhari, 'A Non-substitution Theorem and Switching of Techniques', *The Quarterly Journal of Economics*, LXXIX, **1** (February 1965) pp. 98–105; Michael Bruno, Edwin Burmeister and Eytan Sheshinski, 'The Nature and Implications of the Reswitching of Techniques', *The Quarterly Journal of Economics*, LXXX, **4** (November 1966) pp. 526–53. Also see: David Levhari and Paul A. Samuelson, 'The Nonswitching

Theorem is False', *The Quarterly Journal of Economics*, LXXX, **4** (November 1966) pp. 518–9; LXXX, **4** (November 1966) pp. 568–83.

The terms 'switching', non-switching', and 're-switching' were probably used earlier by Joan Robinson, but I do not have accurate references.

6. Joan Robinson 'The Unimportance of Reswitching', *The Quarterly Journal of Economics*, LXXXIX, **1** (February 1975) pp. 32–9.
7. Leland B. Yeager, 'Toward Understanding Some Paradoxes in Capital Theory, *Economic Inquiry*, September 1976, pp. 313–46.
8. Edwin Burmeister, 'Synthesizing the Neo-Austrian and Alternative Approaches to Capital Theory: A Survey', *Journal of Economic Literature*, June 1974.
9. Edwin Burmeister and Leland B. Yeager, 'Continuity and Capital Reversal: Reply', *Economic Inquiry*, January 1978.
10. See, for example: Edwin Burmeister, 'Real Wicksell Effects and Regular Economies', in M. Brown, K. Sato and P. Zarembka, eds, *Essays in Modern Capital Theory* (Amsterdam: North-Holland, 1976); Edwin Burmeister, 'Comments on Capital Aggregation', in Dan Usher (ed.), *The Measurement of Capital* (Chicago: The University of Chicago Press, 1980); Edwin Burmeister and Stephen J. Turnovsky, 'Capital Deepening Response in a Model with Many Capital Goods', *American Economic Review*, December 1972.
11. Edwin Burmeister, 'Professor Pasinettis's "Unobtrusive Postulate", Regular Economies, and the Existence of a Well-Behaved Aggregate Production Function', *Revue d'Economie Politique*, September – October 1979.
12. Edwin Burmeister, 'On the Uniqueness of Dynamically Efficient Steady States', *International Economic Review*, February 1981; Edwin Burmeister and Peter J. Hammond, 'Maximin Heterogeneous Capital Accumulation and the Instability of Paradoxical Steady States', *Econometrica*, May 1977.
13. Edwin Burmeister, 'Sraffa, Labor Theories of Value, and the Economics of Real Wage Determination', *Journal of Political Economy*, June 1984.
14. *Essays on Piero Sraffa: Critical Perspectives on the Revival of Classical Theory*, Krishna Bharadwaj and Bertram Schefold (eds), (London: Unwin Hyman Limited, 1989).
15. A typical treatment is contained in Chapters 9 and 10 of Barro's leading textbook: Robert J. Barro, *Macroeconomics*, 3rd edn. (New York: John Wiley, 1990.)
16. Franklin M. Fisher, 'Aggregate Production Functions and the Explanation of Wages: A Simulation Experiment', *Review of Economics and Statistics*, LIII, **4**, (November 1971) pp. 305–25.

14. The Progress of Subjectivism

Don Lavoie

Both the successes and the failures of the Austrian research program can be attributed to its central and most cherished idea, subjectivism. The point of this chapter is to re-interpret critically the school's traditional writings on subjectivism in order to separate what is 'progressive' about the idea from what is not.

1 INTRODUCTION

> All this stands out most clearly in that among the social sciences whose theory has been most highly developed, economics. And it is probably no exaggeration to say that every important advance in economic theory during the last hundred years was a further step in the consistent application of subjectivism. That the objects of economic activity cannot be defined in objective terms but only with reference to a human purpose goes without saying. Neither a 'commodity' or an 'economic good', nor 'food' or 'money', can be defined in physical terms but only in terms of views people hold about things. Economic theory has nothing to say about little round disks of metal as which an objective or materialist view might try to define money. . . . Nor could we distinguish in physical terms whether two men barter or exchange or whether they are playing some game or performing some religious ritual. Unless we can understand what the acting people mean by their actions any attempt to explain them, i.e., to subsume them under rules which connect similar situations with similar actions, are bound to fail. (F.A. Hayek, 1955, p. 31)

The principle of subjectivism can be put briefly as the idea that what matters is not things themselves, but what things *mean* to people, and the way this leads them to act and interact. It is significant that the word 'subjectivism' in Austrian literature stands for both a central idea within Austrian economics and for the school itself. The specific principle of subjectivity is not merely one among many basic ideas in the Austrian theoretical toolkit; it is the principle that defines the standard by which all the theoretical tools are judged.

From its very inception with Carl Menger's participation in the marginalist revolution, the Austrian school has marked its own 'progress' by the degree to which it applied the subjectivist principle consistently. This is not to say that members of the school have always meant exactly the same thing by the principle. Some of the most important differences among such leading Austrian economists as Ludwig von Mises, Friedrich Hayek, Ludwig Lachmann and Israel Kirzner involve different nuances in their interpretations of the idea.[1] Yet there is more unity to the school than first meets the eye, and the unity stems, I believe, primarily from the fact that they all consider their chief contribution to be a matter of extending Menger's subjective value theory to other areas of economics. The subjectivist approach is thought to apply a 'better' theory not only of value and prices, but of interest, cost, the value of money, the process of economic development, the nature and structure of capital, the causes of cyclical fluctuations, and other matters. I will not attempt to summarize all these applications of subjectivism; this has been done well by others.[2] What I would like to do here is consider what exactly is meant by 'better' in this context. What is it that makes this principle so attractive to Austrian economists that they use it to define their own scientific progress?

To speak of the progress of the Austrian school is already to invite controversy. To many observers what we have here is a spectacular failure. The Austrian school shot into prominence roughly a century ago, as a more or less equal partner with Walrasian and Marshallian versions of the neoclassical revolution against classical economics. It did enjoy a golden age for several decades alongside the other two branches, but some 50 years ago went into severe decline. By now it is scarcely remembered that there once was such a school. The few scattered outposts around today like to call themselves a 'resurgence', but there is a long way to go before the school recovers the reputation it had in its golden age.

Part of what follows will suggest a few possible reasons why the school went into decline, but I want to treat the story not primarily as a tragedy, but as a story which may yet have a happy ending.[3] My point will be not so much to explain its undeniably severe fall as to explain what successes the school has enjoyed. When it first arose it did so on the issue of subjectivism. Its golden age involved a series of expanding applications of the subjectivist perspective. When it was 'rejuvenated' in the 1970s it was again over the issue of subjectivism. It was the arrival at New York University of Ludwig Lachmann, and his challenge that the Austrian school was not radically subjectivist enough, that seems to have provoked the school back onto the road to progress. There is something about this idea of subjectivism that seems to fuel the Austrian theoretical imagination.

After identifying what I think is the progressive aspect of subjectivism, I will mention some other aspects of the concept which may have contributed to the school's decline. The weaknesses as well as the strengths of the school's notion of subjectivism may be largely due to the same historical influence, that of the *Verstehen* or understanding school in German social thought.[4] The successes consist primarily in a sharpened ability, in a certain sense, to 'see things as the agents do'. The weaknesses of the school, on the other hand, derive from what is misleading about this very way of putting it.

One contemporary branch of the *Verstehen* tradition, hermeneutics, especially as articulated by Hans-Georg Gadamer, offers some important correctives to the ways of talking about 'understanding' that dominated the *Verstehen* tradition when, early in this century, the Austrian school was borrowing from it. Seeing things from the agent's point of view appears to demand a mysterious sort of empathic ability, and drags the *Verstehen* tradition into historicism. Fear of letting economic theory get tangled up in such difficulties provoked the Austrians into some of their more dubious efforts to separate theory from history, and to construct an objectivist, aprioristic, ahistorical foundation for economic theory. The school may be starting to find a way out of that tangle in its recent turn, under Lachmann's influence, towards hermeneutics.

Difficulties for the school have arisen from the fact that the particular packaging of connotations in these terms, 'objective' and 'subjective', excludes the specific combination of connotations the Austrians were trying to uphold in their economics.[5] 'Subjective' is taken to refer to meaning, and to be tied to a specific, historical context, which the Austrians wanted for their economics, but also implies the more questionable idea that this meaning is 'internal' to a single mind, that it is essentially arbitrary and that it is inaccessible to, and independent of, other minds. 'Objective' is taken to refer to things that are non-arbitrary, universal and open to public scrutiny, which the Austrians wanted for their economics, but also to imply detachment from the subject-matter and some sort of freedom from all prejudices, which they should not have wanted. The Austrians were trying to develop an economics that was both 'subjective' and 'objective', but only in the 'good' sense of the terms.

The title is intended to suggest the Lakatosian issue of assessing the progress of research programs, although I am not sure to what extent I will be adhering to Lakatos's methods.[6] I do think that the general approach he recommended, of trying to piece together creatively a 'rational reconstruction' of the progress of a research program, is highly illuminating in all scholarly endeavours. The history of thought is more productive of insight than our official philosophies seem to allow, and Lakatos's most valuable influence may simply be the impetus he gave to intellectual history. The judgement of whether a research program is progressive can only be made retrospectively, after it has had a chance to try itself out. There is a special vantage-point conferred by historical distance that allows us to make more reasonable judgements about whether a research program was progressive or not, and about exactly what its progress consisted in.[7] The assessment of rival research programs can proceed on the basis of which one explains, in some sense, what the other cannot.

This chapter will be, at least to that extent, in the Lakatosian spirit. It will present subjectivism as an idea that progressed because it helped Austrians explain – or perhaps the word should be 'understand' – economic phenomena better. It does not aim at recovering what the Austrian authors originally intended, but at offering a sort of rational reconstruction of what was true in what they were saying.[8] Like Lakatos's approach, it does not shy away from taking some liberties with the author's intention in order to focus more centrally on what can, retrospectively, be discerned to be the progressive aspect of the contribution. It aims at taking a reading – from my own particular vantage-point – of the Austrian school's most important principle.

2 THE MEANING OF SUBJECTIVISM

> For a long time men failed to realize that the transition from the classical theory of value to the subjective theory of value was much more than the substitution of a more satisfactory theory of market exchange for a less satisfactory one. The general theory of choice and preference goes far beyond the horizon which encompassed the scope of economic problems as circumscribed by the economists from Cantillon, Hume, and Adam Smith down to John Stuart Mill. It is much more than merely a theory of the 'economic side' of human endeavors and of man's striving for commodities and an improvement in his material well-being. It is the science of every kind of human action. (Ludwig von Mises [1949] 1966, p. 3)

To Austrian economists, subjectivism is the principle that economics is fundamentally about meaning. It began as a narrow issue within value theory and gradually evolved into a broader and more philosophical principle about the nature of the human sciences. As a technical point in value theory, it is widely endorsed by mainstream neoclassical economists. It is because for contemporary Austrian economists the principle represents a whole perspective on the fundamental nature of human society, and no longer merely a point in value theory, that they see so much more significance in it than mainstream economists do. Subjectivism stands for a way to keep the human in the human sciences. It is not some sort of detached universal principle, but the battle-cry of a specific resistance movement. It resists what Austrian economists consider the dominant mentality of modern times, a mentality we may be well label objectivism, which aims at the removal of human purpose from the human sciences.

Objectivism, at one time, was itself a progressive move. Before the rise of objectivism, pre-scientific world-views had treated everything, whether natural or social, as the result of human or godly purposes. This anthropocentric perspective did leave room for an economics of meaning, but it left no room for what Austrian economists consider an equally fundamental notion, unintended consequences. It attributed the meaning it discerned to the deliberate purposes of kings or gods rather than to the consequences of the process of interplay among the diverse purposes of the participants.

The replacement of such anthropocentric approaches by 'objective' ones was crucial in enabling natural science to achieve its spectacular progress over the past three centuries. Naturally enough, the idea arose of applying this move to the human sciences, and even here it led to progress. It was probably this attempted eschewal of kings' and gods' purposes from explanations that enabled the systematic human sciences like economics to get started. Objectivism forced the recognition that all action, even that of kings and gods, is constrained by systematic forces beyond our control. Reality, as we like to say, impinges. Kings whose policies conflicted most with economic principles, for example, generally found economic circumstances worse than their policies intended.

But this removal of anthropocentrism cannot be taken to its logical conclusion without making complete nonsense of the whole enterprise of economics and other human sciences. While the systematic phenomena we study are not the deliberate product of an all-powerful will, they are nonetheless products of intentions. The phenomena, the prices, money, credit system and so on under study are only recognizable as such by reference to the purposes of the individual human beings who make up an economy.

Classical economics sought to explain markets 'objectively' in the sense that economic phenomena were to be understood as obeying definite laws whose workings could be externally observed, recorded and systematized. The laws of political economy were characteristics of economic phenomena themselves and not the reflection of the purposes of any political or supernatural beings. By 'objectifying' price phenomena in this way the great classical economists were able to show why intelligent policy making requires a systematic study of political economy. The significance of this accomplishment for mankind can hardly be overestimated.

The objectification of economic phenomena was mainly accomplished through the formulation of a systematic theory of value. Value theory was thought to constitute a device for measuring something like a substance that can be thought of as underlying the surface phenomena of prices. Value represented a kind of centre of gravity around which prices fluctuated. By invoking this idea of an underlying value, one could show that prices bear a systematic relationship to one another in a manner which a superficial observation of prices could not discern.

But introducing this new underlying level raised a difficult problem for classical economics. The units of surface prices were obvious enough, but these money units were unsuitable as the unit of value. If value is a kind of substance whose relative quantities underlie and help to explain prices, then what are the units in which such quantities might be measured? Hints in Adam Smith that labour hours might be considered the measure of value were elaborated by David Ricardo into an impressively systematic theory. There were several complex difficulties of explanation, especially concerning rent, interest and profit, which remained to be cleared up, but the basic thrust of classical economics was clear. Value is not some arbitrary thing which a king could declare to be different from what it is. It is determined by specific economic circumstances and can no more be overturned by legal decree than could the law of gravity.

Yet there was something wrong with this objectification of value. It failed to disclose how economic phenomena are resultants of purposeful activity. Even though it was true that the value of, say, a bushel of wheat, was no arbitrary thing, nevertheless it seemed inadequate to treat value as a quantity of some substance that was somehow 'inside' that bushel of wheat. The bushel's physical characteristics, its colour, weight, chemical composition and so on, are objective in a sense that its value is not. For after all, in a society that has no regular market for wheat, this bushel would lack the value it 'has' in our society.[9]

Carl Menger's critique of the objectivism of classical value theory forms the conventional starting-point of the Austrian strand of neoclassical economics. As Menger put it, value 'is nothing inherent in the good itself' ([1871] 1981, p. 58) but is entirely dependent on the way the good is perceived by acting subjects. What gives economic value to a good is not its own objective characteristics, but simply the fact that it is thought to be valuable. This move in value theory has gradually come to have broader significance, applying to the whole of economics. It is not directly the way the world is which matters to economics, but rather the way it appears to acting agents.

Menger was struggling to see value as a manifestation of the *meaning* individual subjects attach to objects under definite socioeconomic, institutional arrangements. What value theory is for in economics is to connect observable and superficially 'objective' price phenomena to their true sources of meaning in the 'subjective' purposes of individual human beings in society. Alternative theories of value are different ways of seeing the 'inner' meaning of the outwardly meaningless regularities of market phenomena, of tracing them to the human purposes that underlie them. Value phenomena are not external things like cloud patterns but consequences of meaningful action. Value needs not only to be explained as a regularity that is observable 'from without', but also must be intepreted and understood 'from within'.

Menger's discussion of the relationships among the different 'orders' of production can be understood as an account of the transmission of meaning from lower-order consumer decisions up into the higher orders. A factory in itself is not valuable to anybody; it gains value only by its perceived ability to contribute to the production of consumer goods in the future. If their supporting demand ceases in the lower orders, then once-valuable capital goods can instantly become worthless. In other words prices carry meaning from consumers to producers, informing choices that are situated at points economically remote from consumption.

With Menger's critique, the traditional search for a 'measure of value' and all the intricate difficulties in which classical economics thereby got entangled could be ended. A significant turning-point in economics, perhaps the single most important step of progress in the discipline so far, was here achieved. Quantitative price relationships in the economy could be understood without recourse to some mysterious underlying substance called value, but by reference to qualitative evaluations on the margin of definite amounts of the goods by acting subjects. Cardinal value theory was replaced by ordinal value theory. Cost of production approaches seem Ptolemaic after this Copernican change in value theory.

The success of the Mengerian critique of 'objectivism' within value theory launched the Austrian school, which has ever since been extending the critique to the rest of economics. Böhm-Bawerk wrote a masterful critique of the objectivist, cost-of-production theories of interest and, when he slipped into objectivistic notions himself, Mises and Fetter radicalized the theory further. Interest represents a time-discount of the future as seen from the forward-looking agent's point of view. Wieser showed why cost is itself subjective, based as it is on the value of forgone opportunities considered by the agent himself at the moment of choice. Mises applied subjectivism to the issue of the value of money, stressing the meaning money balances have to individual agents. Lachmann's work on capital further extends subjectivism to the issue of the capital structure.

The whole emphasis on knowledge and discovery in the contemporary school can be seen as further effort to come to grips with the way phenomena are understood by the agents themselves. Further progress has been achieved by the close examination of the phenomenological situation of the real-world actor, embedded in time, facing uncertainty, but capable of creativity.[10]

From early on many Austrians had sensed that the point they called subjectivism was not only broader than value theory, but broader than economics. With Ludwig von Mises's methodological contributions the point was explicitly developed as a general principle of the human sciences. Mises drew for this argument upon the *Verstehen* tradition, directly from Max Weber and Alfred Schütz, and indirectly from Wilhelm Dilthey and J.G. Droysen.[11] From the *Verstehen* tradition Mises borrowed his methodological dualism, the idea of knowledge-from-within to describe this level of meaning, as distinguished from the external kind of knowledge thought to be relevant to the natural sciences.[12]

What Lachmann (1977, pp. 48–9) calls 'an economic theory designed to interpret meaning' tries to see economic phonemena as intelligible, even though unintended, products of human purposes. It thereby transcends the extremes of the anthropocentrism of pre-scientific thinking and the anthropomorphism of objectivism. It represents a radical critique of the reduction of the subject-matter of the human sciences to 'objects' that happen to be functionally related to one another. It sees the economist's task as having a greater affinity with that of a humanist scholar discerning the meaning of a text than with a chemist examining the causes of a chemical reaction.

The point is not to abandon the study of causation, but to recognize the fact that many of the relevant causes we are looking for in economics are themselves meanings. The modern split of the natural sciences and the humanities has tended to have the unfortunate consequence of confining causation to the former and meaning to the latter, thereby leaving no philosophical room for the Austrian position. Dilthey's notorious comment that the natural sciences explain while the human sciences understand is partly responsible for this problem.[13] Although the Austrians adopted Dilthey's notion of understanding for empirical economics, they never doubted that economics has explanatory ambitions.

Motivated by the aspiration for pure objectivity, many try to explain human activity exclusively 'from without', as if we were biologists observing an ant hill. There is no reason why we should not take advantage of the fact that we are already living in the phenomena we study. We do not need to believe the agents' own accounts of their situation to realize that their beliefs need to be accounted for in ours. We need, in some sense, to get 'inside' their perspective, in order to see how it contributed to, and was shaped by, the overall course of events.

It is important to realize that subjectivism is not only taken in a negative sense, as a limit to our knowledge, a denial of the capacity to attain what would always be preferable, objectivity. The notion of knowledge-from-within is intended to stress precisely that there is a source of knowledge here that the human sciences can take advantage of. As Hayek (1955, p. 26) put the point,

> The social sciences . . . are concerned with man's conscious or reflected action. . . . The external stimulus which may be said to cause or occasion such actions can of course . . . be defined in purely physical terms. But if we tried to do so for the purposes of explaining human action, we would confine ourselves to less than we know about the situation.

This, then, is why I think subjectivism has led to progress in the Austrian school. In the philosophical atmosphere of objectivism, it made it permissible for the school to put meaning at the centre of economics. The strengths of the school were due to its use of the *Verstehen* tradition to defend economics from encroachment by objectivistic methodologies.

3 WHAT SUBJECTIVISM NEED NOT MEAN

> If to us post-Kuhnians today it seems quaintly old-fashioned to speak of the basic concepts of any social science as 'universally valid prior to all experience' (Schütz, 1967, p. 242), given the ideological dimensions of modern culture, it was quite otherwise in Schütz's circle, wherein defense of this tenet was a criterion of membership. (Christopher Prendergast, 1986, p. 2)

The principle of subjectivism, understood as an economics of meaning, has served as an engine of theoretical progress for the Austrian school. But there are certain peculiarities of the principle's typical formulations that may be inhibiting further progress. So far I have emphasized the aspects of what the Austrian school has traditionally meant by subjectivism which I believe they should have meant. I would like to turn now to some aspects that they seemed to mean, but need not have, and perhaps should not have. I will not be able to provide a critique of each of them, but only to distinguish them from the point about meaning. I do happen to find these aspects much more open to challenge and suspect they might constitute excess baggage that interferes with the Austrians' ability to persuade other economists of the virtues of the meaning-oriented notion of subjectivism.

It Does Not Have to be Presented as an Objective Science of Subjective Phenomena

It is common for Austrians to contrast the clarity and certainty they thought was attainable in science, including economic theory, with the ambiguities and uncertainties that agents in the economy face. Choices of agents are described as subjective, whereas choices of economic theorists are described as objective. Though the Austrians placed 'subjectivism' at the very centre of their theorizing, their language often exhibits an underlying fear of threatening science by letting subjectivism 'go too far'. The subjectivity of the phenomena observed, one often finds the Austrian insisting, need not 'contaminate' the objectivity of the observation.[14]

The traditional Austrian school was situated in a philosophical milieu where the commitment to objectivity, in the sense of detachment from the subject-matter, was obligatory. Science was thought to be a kind of perspective-less perspective, unbiased, untainted by the person, the historical situation, the linguistic mode of presentation and so on. The natural sciences were thought to have made their success by securing a formal separation from their subject-matter. The social sciences were seen as having been poisoned by ideological bias. To gain respect the human sciences needed to rid themselves of all elements of personal belief and attain this lofty standpoint of scientific detachment.

This attitude lies behind the traditional Austrian insistence on the 'value-free' character of science. In their different ways, each of the leading Austrian economists, even as they insisted that the subject-matter of economics was subjective, tried to make the science of economics objective, and insulate it from that subjectivity. The insulation was achieved, in effect, by driving a wedge between theory and history.

Mises's aprioristic methodology can be seen as an awkward move, forced by the need for a declaration of scientific objectivity.[15] Although in an interesting passage he admits the arbitrariness of the move, his move is to treat economic concept formation, that is, theorizing, as a different kind of thing altogether from understanding.[16] History was inevitably 'tainted' with the subjectivity of the historian and his time, but theory could lay claim to a special sort of objectivity, taking it out of history. We need theory to read the historical record, but we can develop theory itself deductively and prior to all historical experience.[17]

Both sides of this formula, 'an objective science of subjective phenomena', are misleading, and taken together they might be dangerous. Science, whether social or natural, is not objective in the sense of being ahistorical and perspective-less, nor is the subject-matter of the human sciences subjective in the sense of being private and inaccessible. The attempt to supply a firm foundation for economic theory leads the Austrians to drive another unfortunate wedge, this time between the school's conceptions of scientific and practical knowledge. If the sort of understanding taking place among scientists is something different in kind from that taking place among agents in the economy, then the connection between science and everyday life may become problematic. Austrians like to remark that scientists are human actors too, so that if economics is the general science of action it should apply to scientists' actions too. But they seem to have felt the need to put science on a categorically different footing from the life-world in order to secure its objectivity.

I see no need for the school to make such concessions to the Cartesian conception of object and subject, a conception that has been undermined from all sides of contemporary philosophy. The *Verstehen* tradition, at the time the Austrian school was borrowing from it, was already beginning to see its way beyond these false alternatives, by introducing the ideas of the 'life-world' and the 'inter-subjective'. The inter-subjective refers to meaning, but treats this as 'internal', not to a single mind, but to a linguistic and cultural tradition, a discourse. All human understanding, both everyday and scientific, is rooted, not in the individual brain, but in culture. It is made up of elements of shared understandings which are passed down to us as traditions. The inter-subjective is what makes the mutual communication among scientists possible. Yet is is also descriptive of what Austrians have called subjective choices of agents in the economy. Scientists simply have an extended, specialized and, it is hoped, critical discourse as the basis for their inter-subjective choices, but there is no difference in kind between scientists and people.

It Does Not Need to be Taken as an Excuse for Formalism

In the same places where Mises and Hayek suggest the sense of subjectivism as the need to deal with the level of meaning, they add comments which seem to imply that economic theory, as opposed to history, need not deal with that level much, after all. If the level of meaning is something that is internal to an individual mind, it lies beyond economic science to explain and needs to be taken as given. The economist declares himself neutral on the validity or ethics of the subject's perspective, and needs only to 'plug these in' to his science to clarify the objective consequences of the subjective givens.

One consequence of this way of describing subjectivism may be a permissive attitude towards abstract theorizing that stays aloof from empirical work. The common opinion of subjectivism is that its importance is strictly theoretical, that if one were to take it seriously in empirical work one would become mired in the problem of how to read people's minds.[18] Since the subjective preferences that our theory deems so important happen to lie buried inside minds, someone might argue, we may as well treat them formally, rather than as a matter of empirical research. We can at least construct a formal theoretical image of choice, even if it turns out that we have no way of knowing what peoples' subjective preferences really are. We can theoretically conceive of choice *as if* it were based on a consistent, pre-existing, ordinal ranking of all known alternatives. As Mises ([1949] 1966, p. 3) puts it, 'All ends and all means, both material and ideal issues, the sublime and the base, the noble and the ignoble, are ranged in a single row and subjected to a decision which picks out one thing and sets aside another.'

This move to formalism does not appear to follow directly from subjectivism in the sense of an economics of meaning. Indeed it seems to run against the whole spirit of that sense of subjectivism. Arranging alternatives in a single row is not the only way of conceiving choice and, if empirical psychology can show us that actual human choice is done in a more complex way, then why should not economic theory pay attention? Such declarations of firm disciplinary borders have obvious dangers for science and do not derive from the basic point of subjectivism. Subjectivism would do better without them.

It Does Not Have to be Identified with Introspection

Perhaps the main reason for the anti-empirical interpretation of subjectivism is to be traced back to the tendency to identify the investigation of meaning with introspection. Subjectivism says that the level of meaning is where all the action is, in the sense that the driving force of the economy is what things mean to the participating agents. But some renderings of the idea seem to depict this driving force as itself utterly private and inaccessible, taking place deep inside the private consciousness of individual agents. Since the level of meaning is 'within the mind', individual economists need to rely on introspection to gain certain knowledge of the way their own minds work. They then need to confront what philosophers call the problem of 'Other Minds'. Considering the activities of other human beings as meaningful is taken to be an extension of a prior and more certain, strictly internal source of knowledge. We only know for sure that our own mind works as we internally observe it, and we need to make the pragmatic assumption that other minds exist and work like ours.[19]

It seems to me that this view, if taken to its logical conclusion, would make empirical work impossible. After all, penetrating very far into the relevant empirical reality, the thought processes of numerous other human individuals, sounds almost absurdly difficult. What the theory considers the most important thing to study, what is inside human minds, cannot be got at empirically, except indirectly, by analogy with our own introspectively examined mind.

I see no reason to interpret subjectivism in this way. Meaning does not have to be taken in Cartesian fashion as something that is buried deep inside separate skulls, access to which can only be directly gained internally. through introspection. Introspection itself is not primary, but completely depends on language, which comes from the inter-subjective.[20] Meaning can be viewed as something that resides 'within' the inter-subjective, and thus is taking place out in the open all the time and all around us. If we still want to talk about knowledge-from-within, we should recognize that what it is inside is not an isolated, individual mind, but a communicative process, a discourse.

The approach of starting from introspection and extrapolating out to Other Minds gets things backwards. As contemporary versions of the *Verstehen* approach have shown, we only understand our world, and ourselves, because we understand one another. We only understand each other, in turn, because we all spent some substantial part of our lives being encultured into the life-world.[21]

The way in which contemporary versions of the *Verstehen* approach have improved upon such misleading formulations of 'knowledge-from-within' offers hope, I think, for the Austrian school to progress further. Just as past progress has been attributed to successive radicalizations of the principle, I think that further progress requires yet another step of radicalization. But radicalization requires getting to the roots of the matter, which is to say, in this case, achieving more clarity about just what we mean by subjectivism in the first place.

NOTES

1. For examples of their approach to subjectivism, see Mises ([1949] 1966); Hayek (1955); Lachmann (1971) and Kirzner (1986a).
2. See the recent paper, 'Why Subjectivism?' by Leland Yeager (1987, p. 21). Austrian economists are so fond of the subjectivist principle that, to otherwise sympathetic observers, such as Professor Yeager, they may appear utterly preoccupied with it. Yeager comments that the famous passage from F.A. Hayek which leads off this paper has been 'quoted ad nauseam' by Austrians. Yeager is understandably concerned that the idea sometimes plays the role of a mere slogan for the faithful, a purity test to show that 'I Am More Subjectivist Than Thou', as he entitled one section of his paper. Without denying that such dogmatism can be found in the Austrian school (and every other) I would like to pay exclusive attention here to the views of the major contributors to the school, scholars of the stature of Menger, Mises and Hayek, undoubtedly among the great names in modern economics. I suspect that they had some good reasons for attributing such importance to the principle of subjectivism.
3. The fact that the school fell into obscurity cannot be blamed entirely on the Austrians themselves. Some events, such as the great depression and Hitler's seizure of Austria, were certainly undeserved external blows to the school. Shortcomings in their own formulations, however, might have had something to do with some of the other blows the Austrians sustained in the 1930s. The Austrians' do-nothing response to the great depression, their apparent defeat at the hands of Keynes and Sraffa in macroeconomics and at the hands of the market-socialists, Lange and Lerner, in the calculation debate might have been averted had the Austrian research program overcome its own internal difficulties. And the gradual rise of methodological formalism, which favoured the other two branches of neo-classical economics, might have been challenged more effectively had the Austrian school held a more adequate philosophical self-understanding.
4. By the *Verstehen* tradition I will mean a broad range of scholars, including such classic figures as J.G. Droysen, Wilhelm Dilthey, Heinrich Rickert, Max Weber and Alfred Schütz, who have already influenced the Austrian school, as well as such contemporary thinkers as Hans-Georg Gadamer and Paul Ricoeur, who have only begun to influence it.
5. Although both the words, 'objective' and 'subjective', have specific meanings in economics, stemming from their use in value theory, I think the connotations the words have to philosophers are highly suggestive of the difficulties faced by economists.
6. For one thing, Lakatos studied this question almost exclusively in the context of the natural sciences and mathematics, and it seems to me there are distinctive problems in the philosopohy of the human sciences which his work says nothing about. My view is not that of strict methodological dualism, as advocated by the older *Verstehen* approach and Mises, but of a position derived from Hayek and Michael Polanyi that could be called methodological dualism by degree. I discuss the similarities and differences between the human and natural sciences in (1987).
7. Gadamer's version of the *Verstehen* tradition attaches great importance to this productivity of historical distance. 'Time,' he writes, 'is not a chasm which we could bridge over in order to recover the past; in reality it is the ground which supports the arrival of the past and where the present takes its roots.' Instead of considering

temporal distance an obstacle, he suggest we should think of it 'as a fundament of positive and productive possibilities for understanding. It is not a distance to be overcome, but a living continuity of elements which cumulatively become a tradition, a tradition which is the light wherein all that we carry with us from our past, everything transmitted to us, makes its appearance' ([1963] 1987, p. 136).

8. The topic before us is more the spirit rather than the letter of the Austrian texts, the direction in which I think they point, rather than the position they actually occupied. For a useful discussion of this perspective on the issue of authorial intention, see Chapter 2 of Warnke's book on Gadamer's hermeneutics (1987, pp. 42–72).
9. Readers might notice that the way I am wording the Austrian critique of classical economics makes it sound similar to the Marxian critique of commodity fetishism. It seems to me that Menger's value theory solves the problem Marx had identified in classical value theory better than Marx's own rather convoluted value theory can.
10. See especially the work by O'Driscoll and Rizzo (1985).
11. See in this regard the comment Mises makes (in private correspondence, published in Rothbard, 1989, p. 31) about the origin of what I am calling the essential issue of subjectivism, which he describes there as 'the proposition that the reaction depends on the meaning the actor ascribes to the stimulus'. Referring to his essay 'Begreifen und Verstehen' ([1933] 1981, pp. 130–45) Mises says he made this point 'in order to refute the crude behavioristic stimulus-response scheme'. He points out that he and Max Weber never claimed authorship for the idea and that 'Perhaps one has to credit Droysen or Dilthey.'
12. Friedrich Wieser had made extensive use of the notion of 'knowledge from within', and it is likely that the whole school, from Menger on, were significantly influenced by the various parts of the *Verstehen* tradition. It is with Mises's work in the 1930s that the Austrian school aligns most closely and explicitly with the *Verstehen* tradition.
13. To be fair to Dilthey, he never took so simplified a view as this famous comment seems to imply, and always thought the human sciences needed to deploy a different type of causal analysis. See Ermarth (1978).
14. For example, the stir Lachmann created that rejuvenated the Austrian school in the 1970s was due, I think, to his provoking this underlying fear. The American Austrian school had thought of itself as having already taken the idea to its extreme conclusions, until it met Lachmann. A heated debate began and continues between more 'moderate' and more 'radical' interpretations of subjectivism. The fear the moderate camp has of Lachmann and his radical followers is that their position leads to nihilism, to the abandonment of science, to historicism. In my view all this alarm only shows how many Austrians had not yet worked out the implications of their own principle of subjectivism.
15. I have argued (1986) that Mises was not entirely consistent in what he said about apriorism, and that there is room for an alternative reading of his message.
16. Mises ([1933] 1981, p. 133) writes:

> In and of itself, it would have been possible to include in the definition of understanding every procedure that is directed toward the comprehension of meaning. However, as things stand today, we must accommodate ourselves to the prevailing usage. Therefore, within the procedures employed by the sciences of human action for the comprehension of meaning we shall differentiate between conception and understanding. Conception seeks to grasp the meaning of action through discursive reasoning. Understanding seeks the meaning of action in empathic intuition of a whole.

As things stand today, it could be argued, the prevailing usage in the *Verstehen* tradition permits and even insists on this wider notion of understanding. Understanding includes discursive reasoning, logical argumentation, causal explanation, and any other 'procedure that is directed toward the comprehension of meaning'.

17. Since Mises admits that theory needs to be applied to history to be useful, and that the topics theory decides to take up are shaped by history, his position is not quite as extreme as it sometimes sounds.
18. Often those who make this argument refer to the famous Lester/Machlup debate, which they interpret as showing why subjectivist empirical research is impracticable. In another paper (1990a) I argue that the lesson of that debate is on the contrary that we need to get more 'close-up' to the subjects' point of view in order to do satisfactory empirical work.
19. Austrian economists have often encouraged this reading of subjectivism as a matter of introspection. The whole language, deployed, for example, by Wieser and Mises, of gaining access to 'knowledge-from-within', which the Austrians got from the *Verstehen* tradition, is highly misleading. Hayek (1955, p. 26) seems to proceed in this fashion when he says that we know certain things 'solely from our own subjective experience' and that we have to 'take it for granted that other men treat various things as alike or unlike just as we do'.
20. In fact as children we learn to understand others before we develop the notion of self. And in general we do not come to self-understanding by treating the self as an object for private examination, but by interacting with other selves.
21. I have elaborated elsewhere (1990b) on the way the difference between a Cartesian and a cultural notion of 'subjectivism' has implications for the theory of entrepreneurship.

REFERENCES

Ermarth, Michael (1978), *Wilhelm Dilthey: The Critique of Historical Reason* (Chicago: University of Chicago Press).

Gadamer, Hans-Georg [1960] (1989), *Truth and Method*, revised translation by J. Weinsheimer and D. Marshall (New York: Crossroad).

—— [1963] (1987), 'The Problem of Historical Consciousness', reprinted in Paul Rabinow and William M. Sullivan, *Interpretive Social Science: A Second Look* (Berkeley: University of California Press).

Hayek, Friedrich, A. (1955), *The Counter-Revolution of Science* (London: Free Press of Glencoe).

Kirzner, Israel M. (1986a), 'Another Look at the Subjectivism of Costs', in Kirzner (1986b).

—— (ed.), (1986b), *Subjectivism, Intelligibility, and Economic Understanding: Essays in Honor of Ludwig M. Lachmann on his Eightieth Birthday* (New York: New York University Press).

Lachmann, Ludwig M. (1971), *The Legacy of Max Weber* (Berkeley: The Glendessary Press).

—— (1977), *Capital, Expectations, and the Market Process: Essays on the Theory of the Market Economy* (Kansas City: Sheed, Andrews and McMeel).

Lavoie, Don (1986), 'Euclideanism Versus Hermeneutics: A Re-interpretation of Misesian Apriorism', in Kirzner (1986b).

—— (1987), 'The Accounting of Interpretations and the Interpretation of Accounts: The Communicative Function of "The Language of Business" ', *Accounting, Organizations and Society*, **12**, pp. 579–604.

—— (1990a), 'Hermeneutics, Subjectivity, and the Lester/Machlup Debate: Toward a More Anthropological Approach to Empirical Economics', in Warren Samuels (ed.), *Economics As Discourse* (Boston: Kluwer Academic Publishing).

—— (1990b), 'The Discovery and Interpretation of Profit Opportunities: Culture and the Kirznerian Entrepreneur', paper prepared for the conference on '*The Culture of Entrepreneurship*', sponsored by the Institute for the Study of Economic Culture, held in Indianapolis, Indiana, 26–7 January 1990.

Menger, Carl [1871] (1981), *Principles of Economics* (New York: New York University Press).

Mises, Ludwig von [1933] (1981), *Epistemological Problems of Economics* (New York: New York University Press).

—— [1949] (1966), *Human Action* (Chicago: Henry Regnery Company).

O'Driscoll, Gerald P. and Mario J. Rizzo (1985), *The Economics of Time and Ignorance* (Oxford: Basil Blackwell).

Prendergast, Christopher (1986), 'Alfred Schütz and the Austrian School of Economics', *American Journal of Sociology*, **92** (1), (July), pp. 1–26.

Ricouer, Paul (1981), 'The Model of the Text: Meaningful Action Considered as a Text' in *Hermeneutics and the Human Sciences*, edited and translated by J.B. Thompson (New York: Cambridge University Press).

Rothbard, Murray (1989), 'My Break With Branden and the Rand Cult', *Liberty*, **3** (1), (September), pp. 27–32.

Warnke, Georgia (1987), *Gadamer: Hermeneutics, Tradition and Reason* (Oxford: Polity Press).

Yeager, Leland (1987), 'Why Subjectivism?', *The Review of Austrian Economics*, **1**, pp. 5–31.

COMMENT ON LAVOIE

Bruce J. Caldwell

Don Lavoie mentions but does not employ Lakatos's MSRP in describing the progress of subjectivism, and I will not use it in my discussion either. Though one of the purposes of the Capri conference was to establish the following claim as true or false, my strong prior is that the Lakatosian framework is inadequate as a general vehicle for appraising the progress or decline of research programs in economics.

It is not that Lakatos was bereft of insights. The early Lakatos had a number of valuable things to say, and even the later Lakatos got a few things right. For example, every science has a hard core and a protective belt, and all offer advice in the form of positive and negative heuristics. (Can we imagine a program in economics or any other field which did not direct us to look at some problems rather than at others, or one which did not at the outset of an analysis take certain propositions as given?) It is the Lakatosian emphasis on novel facts and progressive problem-shifts that does not wash in the dismal science. Hard cores are ubiquitous, but novel facts are hard to come by, as I suspect this conference will demonstrate.

Since Lakatos is an interpreter of Popper, I will add that there are other interpretations of Popper's philosophy of science which seem to me to make good sense. The Popper I like is Popper the evolutionary epistemologist, whose ideas have been trumpeted by his student and biographer, Bill Bartley. (See, for example, Radnitzky and Bartley, 1987.) It is the Socratic Popper whom we meet on the pages of Larry Boland's *Foundations of Economic Method* (1982), the Popper who is best labelled a critical rationalist or a critical pluralist. It is the Popper revealed 30 years ago in Klappholz and Agassi (1959), perhaps the least appreciated statement of Popperian principles in the methodological literature in economics. And finally, it is the Popper whose ideas sometimes creep into the writings of Lakatos, as when he claims that falsifications should not kill hypotheses too quickly, or that there is no instant rationality, or that all tests are always three-cornered affairs.

The Popper I am thinking about, then, emphasizes criticism and the critical attitude, but does not lay out in minute detail specific criteria of appraisal which must be met by scientific research programs. The weakness and strength of this broader approach is its paucity of specific methodological content, its absence of decision rules. In my opinion, this is as it should be: *there simply is not much content to be had at the meta-methodological level*. One can try to foster the critical attitude and to engage in critical discourse, but the content of the criticism does not emerge until the act of criticism has begun. All of the Popperians mentioned above (with the exception of Lakatos) recognize and accept this. Lakatos wanted to have it both ways and ended up having it neither way.

Let us turn to Don Lavoie's contribution. Don has chosen a fascinating topic, the role of subjectivism within Austrian economics. Among certain contemporary Austrians (for example, O'Driscoll and Rizzo, 1985) subjectivism is viewed as a (or even *the*) defining characteristic of Austrian analysis. With some qualifications, Lavoie seems to share this position. What does *not* come out in his chapter is that, although all Austrians might accept the label 'subjectivist', considerable disagreement exists among them over what the label implies.

This has been true throughout the history of the movement. The founder of Austrian economics, Carl Menger, had some very unsubjectivist things to say about the biological bases of needs and about the progress of wants as societies develop. In their later years, both Menger and Friedrich Wieser became interested in the psychological underpinnings of economics. (See, for example, Runde, 1988; Endres, 1989; Shearmur, 1990.) Ludwig von Mises castigated his predecessors for their concern with psychology and did so on subjectivist grounds. He insisted on founding economics on a *logic* of choice, one which would be forever independent of the latest empirical (and thereby contingent) findings of psychologists. When he argues at the end of his chapter that Austrians should lift the ban against the empirical investigation of thought processes, Lavoie is in a sense rehabilitating the views of Menger and Wieser on the importance of psychology.

If we move to the contemporary scene, divisions over the appropriate role of subjectivism continue to be evident. Now it is Mises and his followers who are accused of being insufficiently subjectivist. The critics are followers of Ludwig Lachmann, whose eclectic position takes considerable inspiration from the work of the English economist George Shackle. Lachmann earned the ire of many fellow-Austrians when he claimed that Mises and Hayek dropped the ball in the 1930s by failing to apply the subjectivist program to the question of expectations formation. If this were not bad enough, Lachmann argued further that the mantle of subjectivism was actually carried forward by Keynes (whom Lachmann portrays as a subjectivist) and by subjectivist Post-Keynesians like Shackle.

Shackle's affiliation with the Post-Keynesians, whose policy views are anathema to the Austrians, was not lost on Lachmann's critics. And there have been many critics of what has come to be called 'radical subjectivism'. Don mentions the polite dissent of Leland Yeager. He could also have mentioned the attacks by Murray Rothbard and his followers, which have been notable for their viciousness. Even among more thoughtful Austrians concern has been expressed: one need only recall Stephen Littlechild's suggestively titled comment, 'Radical Subjectivism or Radical Subversion?' (1979).

Thus outside observers should be alerted to the fact that Don's views are not uncontroversial. It is for this reason that I was somewhat disappointed with his chapter. Don's approach is perhaps best described as programmatic. He offers a definition of subjectivism, one which is very much in line with his recent emphasis on hermeneutical interpretation. In concluding, he also tells us what subjectivism should not include. This manner of presentation obscures the myriad debates over the proper definition and role of subjectivism which have engaged Austrians for so many years. Why did Mises find Menger to be insufficiently subjectivist, and why did Lachmann find Mises guilty of the same crime? Why is it now legitimate to blend subjectivism with empirical psychology, when it was so expressly forbidden in the 1920s? A familiarity with the old debates is crucial to an understanding of the development of Austrian thought. But, more important for present purposes, knowledge about them is necessary if one is to make an informed judgement on the issues. The historical account which Don provides shows that all Austrians are well described as subjectivists. But it does little to advance the very live debate within the Austrian camp as to what it *means* to be a subjectivist. Until these matters are clarified, the claims and counter-claims of various Austrian subjectivists will be extremely difficult to adjudicate.

There is an intriguing methodological question that such a study might help to answer: Why are the groups like the Austrians and Post-Keynesians so enamoured of subjectivism? The answer one gets will change according to which historical episode is investigated, of course: Menger's usage of subjectivism was different from Mises's. Matters are simpler in more recent years. For contemporary Austrians and Post-Keynesians, subjectivism is a weapon for attacking the enemy of mathematical formalism. The most frequent target of both groups is usually described as general equilibrium theory.

It is here that things get interesting, especially for a methodologist. The two groups, Austrians and Post-Keynesians, see different things when they look at general equilibrium theory. The Austrian attack began back in the days of the socialist calculation debate. Market socialists had used general equilibrium models to assert the formal structural identity of free market and socialist economies. The Austrian response emphasized the inability of such models to capture the dispersion and subjectivity of knowledge, problems which necessitated the existence of a system of markets if the coordination of agents' plans was ever to occur. Post-Keynesians took general equilibrium analysis to be integral to the defence of the market system. For them the notions of kaleidic change and the emergence of novelty were arguments against the prospect that markets provide a stable equilibrating mechanism. Perhaps it is not surprising to find that some subjectivists believe that subjectivism establishes the veracity of markets while others think the opposite. After all, the same division holds true among general equilibrium theorists: market advocates focus on the Pareto efficiency of competition, while detractors zero in on the stringency of the marginal conditions.

Anyway I think it is safe to assert that so far neither subjectivist group can claim victory. Post-Keynesians have not established that forces of kaleidic change must always dominate the coordinating effects of markets and, even if they did, nothing in their argument provides grounds for the belief that the government could or should try to do anything about it. For their part, some of Lachmann's followers have already admitted that there is no guarantee that a market process coordinates agents' plans. Some have turned instead to the invisible hand metaphor for locating forces which might lead to the stabilization of social processes. But there is no guarantee that such forces will always be operative, nor that their outcomes will always be beneficent. In addition it seems clear that one *can* design institutions (in contrast to awaiting their eventual emergence) which allow the free play of human action to structure other institutions: how else to describe what constitutions do?

For what it is worth, I do not think that the question of whether free markets are best is answerable in the large by subjectivists, general equilibrium theorists, or anyone else. Such questions are only answerable in the small, where specific cases are investigated in all their institutional messiness. Even then answers are not always forthcoming and, when they are, they are always contingent.

This is not to say that the analyses of either general equilibrium theorists or subjectivists are worthless, for both provide an important service. And, to close on a provocative note, I think that subjectivists and general equilibrium theorists provide the *same* service. Both are in the business of supplying metaphors or descriptions or models of the way the economy operates. These metaphors are obviously very different from many of the models which economists build. They are probably best described as metaphysical research programs, for they are not testable in any significant sense, nor is it clear what purpose testing them would serve. It is because these metaphysical programs operate at such a high level of generality that both sympathizers and opponents of free markets are able to make use of them. And although such programs are not testable, progress within them can take place as a result of debates between opposing camps. What I mean is this: though neither subjectivists nor general equilibrium theorists will be able to answer the question of whether free markets are best, their disagreements will shed light on the strengths and limitations of the models they employ.

This permits me to end with a question. If what I have just suggested is true, that both general equilibrium theory and subjectivism play the role of metaphysical research programs, why is it that most economists consider general equilibrium theory to be science and subjectivist analysis to be something less?

References

Boland, Lawrence A. (1982), *The Foundations of Economic Method* (London: Allen & Unwin).

Endres, A.M. (1989), 'Menger, Wieser, Böhm-Bawerk and the Analysis of Economizing Behavior: Surpassing the Logic of Choice', manuscript.

Klappholz, K. and Agassi, J. (1959), 'Methodological Prescriptions in Economics', *Economica* (February), pp. 60–74.

Littlechild, Stephen (1979), 'Comment: Radical Subjectivism or Radical Subversion?', in Mario Rizzo (ed.), *Time, Uncertainty, and Disequilibrium* (Lexington, Mass.: Lexington Books).

O'Driscoll, Gerald and Rizzo, Mario (1985), *The Economics of Time and Ignorance* (Oxford, Basil Blackwell).

Radnitzky, Gerard and Bartley, W.W. III (eds), (1987), *Evolutionary Epistemology, Theory of Rationality, and the Sociology of Knowledge* (La Salle, IL: Open Court).

Runde, Jochen (1988), 'Subjectivism, Psychology, and the Modern Austrians', in Peter Earl (ed.), *Psychological Economics: Development, Tensions, Prospects* (Boston: Kluwer Academic).

Shearmur, Jeremy (1990), 'From Hayek to Menger: Biology, Subjectivism, and Welfare', in Bruce Caldwell (ed.), *Carl Menger and his Legacy in Economics* (Durham, N.C.: Duke University Press).

15. History and Sociology of Science and History and Methodology of Economics

H.M. Collins

HISTORY AND SOCIOLOGY OF SCIENCE

Imagine a space whose dimensions are time and sociometric distance. Science takes place in the middle – in the here and now. There is a time leading up to an experiment, there is the experiment, and time elapses after the experiment is done. In the other dimension sociometric space stretches away from the location of the experiment in all directions. Time is measured in days and years while sociometric space can be measured in *relations*, though there are no universal units. For example, in terms of the unit, 'handshaking relation', I am about three units away from the current Prime Minister of Britain, Mrs Margaret Thatcher; I have shaken hands with the Vice-Chancellor of my university and he, I am sure, has shaken hands with someone who has shaken hands with Mrs Thatcher. In terms of units of a more intimate nature I am delighted to say that I am much further from Mrs Thatcher sociometrically. Getting scientific value out of measuring sociometric distances is difficult both conceptually and practically but it is a perennially useful idea at the level of metaphor. For example, it shows why you may know much less about what is going on in another department of your own university than about what is going on in, say, an economics department on the other side of the world. Sociometrically you may be very close to the department on the other side of the world, while you are sociometrically distant from the lab next door.

Sociologists, being quintessentially aware of the methodological shortcomings of social science, are rather reluctant to talk about their 'findings', but if there is a finding belonging to the sociology of scientific knowledge it is that 'distance lends enchantment'. For example, sociometric distance from another laboratory tends to make the work of that laboratory seem more properly scientific. This is recognized in the 'war stories' of sociologists of science: if you go to a laboratory and ask scientists to tell you about their work so that you can understand science better, they will nearly always advise you that the real science is being done elsewhere. However high the reputation of the laboratory in which you locate your fieldwork, the natives will always tell you that you are still in the foothills; the true summit is always just over the next horizon. Scientists know about their own fudges and uncertainties but they do not think the same happens elsewhere, because all they know of other labs is the cleaned-up accounts found in the journals. The journals conspire to maintain the myth of a clear and determinate scientific method operating everywhere but here.

On the time dimension one sees that experiments seem well-designed and determinate in outcome *before* they are done and *after* the dust has settled. Only while they are being performed and interpreted do they seem messy and unclear. Experiments are well designed recipes for discovering truth everywhere except for here and now.[1]

Historians and sociologists of science have discovered that the canonical version of scientific method cannot be found at the workface of science. For example, something as straightforward as the idea that results are replicable turns out to be ambiguous in application because scientists involved in real-time controversies cannot agree about what counts as a replicated result. They cannot even agree about what counts as a result and what counts as an artifact. To take a glaring example, there is a whole science called parapsychology that is replicable for the practitioners (I am referring to the couple of dozen serious and respected researchers who work in universities and similar institutions), while for most of the scientific community there is nothing there at all.[2] In this case there are no clear facts or findings and methodological principles do not seem to help.

Once this characteristic of science was noticed, history and sociology of scientific knowledge moved away from inventing universal models, instead describing science in the way it is experienced by scientists. This does not mean that microscopic description is the end point, but more general theories of science are expected to be at least *compatible* with laboratory experience. These modern studies seem more 'realistic'. (The irony is, of course, that many of the people who do such studies confess to not knowing what being more realistic would mean.)

This is certainly not the only way to do history and sociology of science. There are teleological, hidden-hand traditions in the history of science, and there is the Mertonian tradition in sociology, neither of which takes cognizance of what scientists do. There is nothing incoherent in these ways of talking about science; they just seem a lot less interesting than the ways that do involve finding out what scientists do.[3]

Of course having to know what scientists do creates new difficulties in at least one respect. The problem is getting near enough to the science to see what it is really like; contemporary historians and sociologists must minimize their social and temporal distance from science so that they are not enchanted by the distant perspective. In terms of Figure 15.1, the problem is to get into the middle.

Figure 15.1 Science located in time and sociometric space

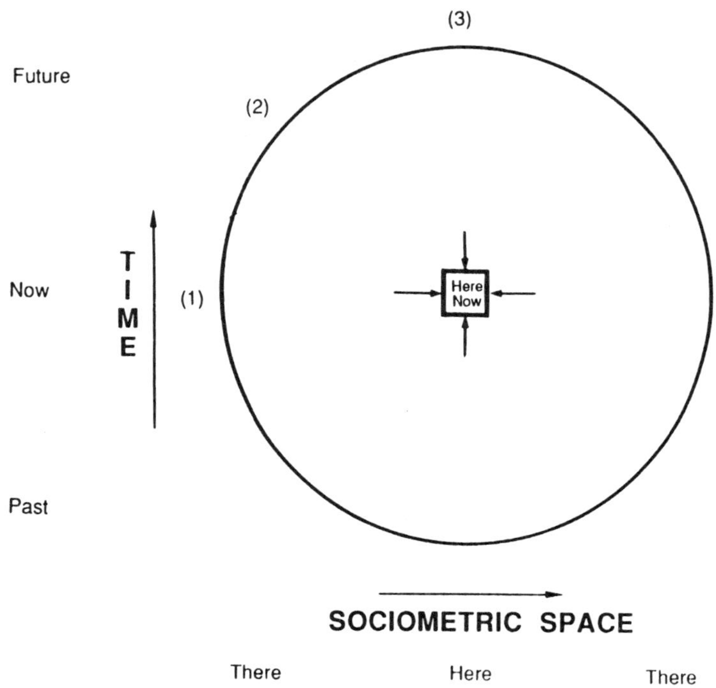

The method preferred by sociologists is participation in the work itself.[4] This involves a difficult trip in sociometric space which takes one from a position like that marked as (1) to the middle of the diagram. Later one might re-emerge with one's newly-acquired native competence and try to fit it together with some more sociological thinking. The historian has to make a still more remarkable journey, crossing not only space but time. The historian starts from some position like that marked as (2). I do not know how historians do the journey – it ought to be impossible – but they do. They have managed remarkable things in the history of science in recent years.[5]

PRESCRIPTIVE METHODOLOGY OF ECONOMICS

Why should historians of economics concern themselves with what is going on in the history and sociology of the natural sciences? Historians of economics may have quite different aims. There is, however, at least one group who *ought* to be practising their craft in the new way – the methodologists. Normative methodologies have to be followed by economists themselves. To understand what economists might reasonably be advised to do one must first understand how economists actually work. This can only be done from the here and now of economics. An example will make this more clear.

Consider the Lakatosian prescription 'seek novel empirical content'. That sounds like a usable prescription and it may well have guided the actions of economists from time to time.[6] But, in seeking novel empirical content, can these economists have been doing what Lakatos had in mind? I think the answer must be 'no' because Lakatos judged what counted as novel empirical content by rational reconstruction from a great distance in time and space whence scientific work looks very different from the way it looks in the here and now. What looks like a clear piece of novel empirical content from the temporal and sociometric distance might look much more disreputable here and now. Likewise what might look like a clear piece of novel empirical content *now* might look like a mistake in a decade; what looks like a piece of novel empirical content *here* might look like a mistake from over there.[7] Thus someone who changes their research strategy because they are seeking novel empirical content here and now might not be involved in a progressive problem-shift. The only sure common ground between what Lakatos had in mind and what scientists seeking novel empirical content have in mind is the *words* 'novel empirical content'. The *content* of 'novel empirical content' need not correspond at all.

For 'Seek novel empirical content!' to be a usable prescription the Lakatosian scheme would have to be extended. It would have to be able to give rise to advice such as: 'Seek novel empirical content for a period of two years, and then give up if you don't find it!' or 'Finding novel empirical content is finding it to your satisfaction and the satisfaction of groups in at least two other research centres, even if everyone else says what you have found is artifact!' The choices that face researchers in the here and now are not about big questions but about how big answers are to be applied in practice. Only local prescriptions are usable. As it happens, there is no reason to suppose that the examples I have given would guarantee scientific progress. The challenge for the determined prescriptivist is to find locally applicable advice that would do the scientific trick.[8]

What I have argued is that, even if one's aims are normative and prescriptive, one still needs to start with the *descriptive* practices of modern history and sociology of scientific knowledge if one is to come up with advice that can be used.

HISTORY OF ECONOMICS

I have described the methods of historians and sociologists of science. I have said these methods require the researcher's consciousness to be shifted to the location of the scientist. For most historians and sociologists this is difficult. For historians of economics, on the other hand, it ought to be very easy. It seems from casual observation that, unlike historians and sociologists of natural science, most historians of economics already practise the subject that they want to describe.[9] They work in university departments of economics as economists while their history takes only part of their time. This should put them in a remarkably advantageous position *vis-à-vis*, say, historians of physics or sociologists of parapsychology, who have to make a great intellectual journey before they can get started. And yet many historians of economics seem to want to throw away these advantages, preferring to do the sort of history of economics which does not require any special *understanding* of the subject.[10] With a few exceptions, historians of economics adopt the distanced viewpoint of rational reconstruction as their perspective. While physically located in the centre of the diagram they are mentally located in the vicinity of the point marked as (3) in Figure 15.1.

Part of the reason for this must be the very institutional location of historians of economics which confers upon them such a potential advantage. The professional reference-group for historians of economics is not historians of science but other economists. The judges of good work in the history of economics are likewise economists, rather than historians of science in general. That, I suppose, is why only a few historians of economics have been caught up with the changes that have happened in the history of science over the last two decades. In addition, being on the outside of these debates, perhaps they remain enchanted with the idea of science and disenchanted with their own economics. Like the scientists in the war stories, they may still believe that what they do is not real scientific economics; the real economics can be found on the next hilltop. Perhaps, even if they have never seen the canonical model of economic science at work, they believe it is just over the horizon.

CONCLUSION

The practice of history and sociology of natural science no longer uses the method of rational reconstruction. It has turned to understanding the world of scientists themselves – not necessarily as an end-point, but certainly as a starting-point.[11] Most historians of economics have not followed this route. Of course, *as* historians of economics, they do not have to follow trends in the history of the other sciences. But those who are serious about giving methodological advice as a result of their studies must.

Because of their location within departments, it is peculiarly easy for historians of economics to overcome the methodological problems which beset the followers of the new trend. If they follow this course, however, their identification as economists first and historians second is likely to cause problems of academic status and academic allegiance. There is also the danger that their institutional colleagues, fellow-economists who are more attuned to economics' image of itself than the view from the history of science, will find peer review and the allocation of professional rewards difficult.

NOTES

1. For a discussion of distance lending enchantment and many other arguments and examples concerning the detailed nature of science in the here and now, see H.M. Collins, *Changing Order: Replication and Induction in Scientific Practice* (London: Sage, 1985).

   I try to analyse the passage of an experiment through time in my paper 'Certainty and the Public Understanding of Science: Science on Television', *Social Studies of Science*, **17** (1987) pp. 684–713. This deals with experiments on the dating of the Shroud of Turin.
2. In the case of parapsychology, distance may seem to lead to disenchantment but this is to confuse scientific method and scientific truth. Anti-parapsychologists believe that parapsychologists' claims are based on cheating and carelessness. That is, they believe that positive findings in parapsychology are the result of failure to follow scientific method; positive findings in other areas are thought to be obtained by following scientific method. The notion of a clear scientific method is therefore preserved. Those who know the work of serious parapsychologists in detail will know that, as far as care, honesty and assiduous experimental design is concerned, parapsychology is an exemplary science. It is just that the application of scientific method can nowhere guarantee to produce what comes to be counted as truth.
3. For an argument about different ways of doing history and sociology of science see H.M. Collins, 'What is TRASP: The Radical Programme as a Methodological Imperative', *Philosophy of the Social Sciences*. **11**, (1981) pp. 215–24.

4. I say 'preferred' because participation cannot always be achieved. Sometimes the sociologist is reduced to conducting a series of interviews. Nevertheless, even under these circumstances it is participation rather than observation that informs the work. This makes the interview quite different from, say, oral history or survey work. It is not a matter of asking scientists what their methods are or privileging oral accounts, it is a matter of understanding.

   My favourite example of the difference goes as follows: Imagine you are watching a couple dancing the tango in a Birmingham ballroom. You ask your native informants, 'What are those people doing?' Imagine the informants giving three answers:
   (i) 'They are trying to win a medal for ballroom dancing.'
   (ii)'They are engaged in surreptitious sexual dalliance.'
   (iii)'They are trying to bring on rain.'

   For the fieldworker gathing *information*, these answers consist of one which is true and two which are lies. The fieldworker will have to work out which is which. For the fieldworker who is trying to *understand* the conduct of social life in Birmingham the answers consist of one joke and two possibilities, all of which improve the fieldworker's understanding of what counts as a legitimate thing to be doing when you are dancing the tango in that society. (That is, one might try to win a medal or get some surreptitious physical pleasure but one would *not* try to bring on rain.) Obviously the fieldworker who is trying to understand has to be enough of a participant to recognize what is a joke and what is not.

   For a longer analysis fo the nature of participant observation see, for example, H.M. Collins, 'Concepts and Methods of Participatory Fieldwork', in C. Bell and H. Roberts (eds), *Social Researching*, (London: Routledge, 1984) pp. 54–69.
5. My favourite example is S. Shapin and S. Schaffer, *Leviathan and the Air-Pump: Hobbes, Boyle and the Experimental Life* (Princeton: Princeton University Press, 1985).
6. Rod Maddock confesses that it has guided his actions.
7. In parapsychology what looks like nothing empirical at all might turn out, in a couple of centuries, to have been of crucial importance. While I would not advise anyone to become a parapsychologist, I am grateful that there are parapsychologists just in case what they are doing turns out to be valuable. If we did not have them we would have to invent them.
8. The headache is similar to that brought on by introducing a bit of dogmatism into Popper's falsificationism. One man's dogmatism is another man's unfalsifiability.
9. My casual observations, I'm afraid, are restricted to those historians and methodologists invited to the delightful Capri conference.
10. *Understanding* is used here not to mean technical grasp – though this is certainly necessary – but empathy with the day-to-day experience of being an economist. It is the phenomenological sense of understanding for which the German word *verstehen* is often used.
11. Ironically Lakatos's brilliant work of rational reconstruction – *Proofs and Refutations* – has been one of the major inspirations in the development of the new history and sociology of science because it revealed the locally contingent nature of arguments about what constitutes a proof in mathematics and helped to pull us away from the grip of transcendental thinking.

16. Afterword

Mark Blaug

Neil de Marchi and I have been interested and to some extent even fascinated by Imre Lakatos's philosopohy of science since before we attended the Nafplion Colloquium on Research Programs in Physics and Economics in 1974. At that colloquium he produced a most illuminating early case study in the application of Lakatos's MSRP (de Marchi, 1976) and I followed on shortly thereafter with a somewhat jejune exposition of the differences between Popper, Kuhn and Lakatos (Blaug, 1976a). Over the years, many others contributed Lakatosian appraisals of particular research programs in economics and in 1985, during conversations at a methodological symposium in Amsterdam (de Marchi, 1988), we decided that it might be time to hold a second Lakatos conference to see where we stood in regard to the applicability of MSRP to economics. We put together a list of like-minded economists and approached Spiro Latsis, himself responsible for the very first exploration of how Lakatos can shed light on what economists do (Latsis, 1972), for financial support. Thanks to the generosity of the Latsis Foundation under the chairmanship of Spiro Latsis, we were able to convene that conference in Capri in October 1989.

I say that 'we put together a list of like-minded economists', but that conjures up a closed shop of committed Lakatosians. However, right from the outset, we were determined to kill three birds with one stone: (1) to promote the writing of further case studies in the application of Lakatos's MSRP, particularly to such apparently intractable fields as game theory, and Sraffian economics; (2) to re-examine the coherence of Lakatos's MSRP both in purely philosophical terms and in terms of its cogency for a subject like economics; and (3) to follow the spirit of the Nafplion conference by adding to a meeting of economists a sprinkling of physicists, philosophers and sociologists of science. Hence we invited some whom we knew to be deeply sympathetic to the Popper–Lakatos tradition but also some who had long declared their antipathy to all that; by letter and by word of mouth we encouraged an open-minded attitude both to MSRP and its relevance to economics – the last thing we wanted was the sort of veneration of Lakatos that

Popper has received in some circles (though thankfully not in economic circles). At most we suggested that there were potentially positive elements in Lakatos's approach that had not yet been fully exploited and, therefore, that all participants should make an earnest effort to take Lakatos seriously.

No one could possibly have predicted how the mixture of people collected at Capri would react to our instructions but I was personally taken aback by what can only be described as a generally dismissive, if not hostile, reaction to Lakatos's MSRP. Of the 37 participants, I estimate that only 12 were willing to give Lakatos a further run for his money and of the 17 papers delivered at the conference not more than five were unambiguously positive about the value of MSRP. The objections to Lakatos ran along many lines but there were two notes that were struck repeatedly. The first was the recognition that there is no way of writing down once and for all the precise content of the hard core of any SRP in economics that would command the universal assent of all the protagonists of that program. The relative arbitrariness of any such specification was somehow regarded as a serious shortcoming of Lakatos's methodology. Misgivings on that score were often associated with a sense of irritation that Lakatos nowhere provides any criteria for attributing a particular theory to a particular SRP; in short, Lakatos is too vague about how to get started with a Lakatosian appraisal of an economic theory. But all such objections were only preludes to a deeper one, namely that of measuring scientific 'progress' by an empirical yardstick. Lakatos's insistence on the importance of 'novel facts' in the appraisal of rival SRPs struck most participants as inappropriate to a social science like economics. Speaker after speaker railed against what Wade Hands called 'novel fact fetishism' and complained that Lakatos's methodology lacked a way of capturing gains in understanding that do not directly issue in testable predictions about hitherto unsuspected or previously regarded as irrelevant and even forbidden 'novel facts'.

The first of these objections to MSRP is not, I think, a serious one but the second is deeply troubling as symptomatic of a general attitude not just to methodology but also to economics as a whole. Let me explain.

The distinction between the 'hard core' and the 'protective belt' of a research program is at bottom a purely logical one. Once we have accepted the notion that individual scientific theories are necessarily linked together in a network of ideas called an SRP and that, being a program of promising work to be carried out in the future rather than a perfectly finished product, such an SRP must change and evolve in time, it follows that there is some core in the SRP that changes much less than the rest of it. If this were not the case, how would we know that we were talking about the same SRP? Similarly, to the extent that the SRP is a *program*, it must provide its protagonists with some list of dos and don'ts in research practices. Consequently it must be possible in principle to specify the hard core, the positive and negative heuristics and the protective belt of theories in any SRP. But that is not to say that such a specification is set in concrete for all time, nor that everyone will agree on the precise outlines of that specification. I have been a classic 'liberal' all my life (well, ever since the age of 21) but I am not the liberal today that I was 40 years ago and, there are certain notions which I have held on to all these years even though I am not sure that I could write down precisely what they are and even though I know that my list would probably not agree with those of Friedrich Hayek or Milton Friedman or George Stigler. But, surely, that is not an argument against the proposition that 'liberalism' is a well-defined *program* for thinking about the nature of power and the role of the state? Likewise we economists do not agree on the 'essence' of Keynesian economics and we are not absolutely sure that we can set down in so many words the characteristic ideas of a Keynesian economist and yet we have no difficulty in labelling Paul Samuelson and James Tobin and Paul Davidson and James Meade as Keynesians, even though volumes could be written on what separates each from the other in their interpretation of Keynes.

The task of delineating the structure of an SRP in terms of its hard core and protective belt is, I do believe, immensely clarifying in attempting to assess its value but the notion that this is a simple and unambiguous exercise is, surely, naive.

That brings us to 'novel fact fetishism', the Lakatosian thesis that progress of knowledge is ultimately to be judged in terms of the 'excess empirical content' of successive amendments of a program. This, as I said earlier, is the great bugbear of the anti-Lakatos camp. Wade Hands (1990, p. 78) expressed the point in these words:

> Why would we want to accept the position that the sole necessary condition for scientific progress is predicting novel facts not used in the construction of the theory? Surely humankind's greatest scientific accomplishments have amounted to more than this. We in economics and those in every other branch of science choose theories because they are deeper, simpler, more general, more operational, explain known facts better, are more corroborated, are more consistent with what we consider to be deeper theories: and for many other reasons. Even if we can find a few novel facts here and there in the history of economics, and even if those novel facts seem to provide an occasional 'clincher', the history of great economics is so much more than a list of these novel facts. Smith's invisible hand, the Ricardian

> Law of comparative advantage, Walrasian notions of multimarket interdependency, Marshallian welfare economics and the basic Keynesian notion of output and employment being determined by aggregate demand: these things constitute *great* economics; such theoretical developments have given us insight and *progress*, not an occasional novel fact.

This is an argument that deserves careful dissection. There is a subtle distinction in Lakatos between MSRP, the methodology of scientific research programs, and MHRP, the methodology of historiographical research programs, that is, between the notion of an SRP, made up of a hard core and a protective belt, plus the proposition that the evolution of an SRP *should* be appraised in terms of excess empirical content, and the quite distinct historical thesis that scientists in fact adopt and reject SRPs in accordance with that appraisal criterion. MSRP is defended in the first instance *à la* Popper on purely normative grounds: 'scientific progress' is progress in achieving 'objective knowledge' of a world that exists independently of our wishes and the only way we can be sure that we have achieved objective knowledge of reality is to commit ourself to the prediction of novel facts.[1] Of course even then we cannot be *sure* that we have achieved objective knowledge. The case for placing so much emphasis on the importance of making accurate predictions is basically what Hands calls the 'no miracles argument': a theory that successfully predicts out-of-sample data from sample data is likely to have captured some aspect of objective reality because otherwise its record of predictive success is simply miraculous. Theories may also be simple, elegant, general and fruitful but none of these desirable properties in any way guarantees verisimilitude, that is, nearness to truth about an objective world.

It is perfectly true that Popper failed to provide any quantitative measure of the verisimilitude of a theory: when faced with competing theories A and B, we never can say unambiguously that theory A is better than theory B because it is nearer to the truth. Indeed the quest for a numerical measure of verisimilitude stands condemned on a priori grounds. When we consider the complexity of scientific theories and the fact that their domains rarely overlap perfectly, the notion of being able to compare them in terms of a single metric seems almost absurd. But that does not imply that we are left without any epistemological basis for appraising competing theories. We may continue to rank theories in terms of their predictive success, indeed we must do so if we care about verisimilitude, but we cannot defend our rankings as anything but qualitative and necessarily questionable judgements.

All this is familiar Popperian territory in which we lay down methodological standards by drawing solely on logical and epistemological considerations. But Lakatos went beyond Popper in arguing that MSRP may also be defensible on positive grounds in terms of the history of science. In other words, it is one thing to define an SRP as 'progressive' because it accurately predicts novel facts and quite another to assert that scientists actually subscribe to the progressive SRPs that can be found in the history of a science. Lakatos conjectured that both propositions hold but he invited us to study the history of science to bear him out, holding out the possibility of course that this fundamental conjecture might be refuted. There is, therefore, no inherent connection between MSRP and MHRP and it may well be that the former is true and the latter is false. Thus, in my *Methodology of Economics* (1980), I argued that modern economists preach the methodology of falsificationism but rarely practise it: they are 'innocuous falsificationists'.[2] This thesis may be expressed by saying that in economics MHRP is largely false; however that in no way denies the force of MSRP: the normative case for falsificationism might stand up even if the positive one fell to the ground.

To give one more example of the separability of MSRP and MHRP, I argue in Blaug (1991a) that Keynesian economics was a 'progressive' RP in the 1930s and 1940s because it successfully predicted a number of novel facts, in particular that the numerical value of the expenditure multiplier is greater than unity, lying somewhere between 1·5 and 3. This fact was not novel in the sense of being totally unknown before the publication of *The General Theory* because Richard Kahn and Jens Warming had both hit on the idea apparently independently. However the multiplier remained a more or less isolated idea in both of these expositions and, in so far as it was embedded in a wider theoretical structure, it was that of Keynes's *Treatise on Money* rather than *The General Theory*. What made the multiplier argument so telling in *The General Theory* was that it was derived from a more fundamental idea about economic behaviour, namely, the consumption function, and that the particular form which Keynes adopted for the consumption function turned out to imply other novel facts about saving behaviour and the relationship between saving and investment, which in turn were corroborated by empirical studies almost as soon as they were announced. In addition Keynes developed a monetary theory of interest to complement his theory of effective demand, according to which variations in output and not variations in the rate of interest bring saving and investment into equilibrium. In short, Keynes's multiplier 'explained' the fact of the more than proportionate impact of investment on income whereas Kahn's multiplier merely calculated its value (in terms of employment).

This is a different argument from the standard account of the Keynesian Revolution according to which the merit of Keynes was that he 'explained' the existence of protracted unemployment which the orthodox theory of the day ruled out as impossible. But I contend that pre-Keynesian orthodox economists had no difficulty whatsoever in 'explaining' mass unemployment. To 'explain' anything is to relate the unfamiliar to the familiar and there was nothing more familiar to orthodox economics than the idea that imperfections of competition, such as trade unions, the growth of monopoly and the constant interference of governments in the setting of prices and wages, not to mention erroneous monetary policies, might cause a breakdown in the natural recuperative powers of the capitalist system. In other words, Keynesian economics was unnecessary if all that was wanted was an explanation of mass unemployment.

Now this may or may not be a valid contention but the point is that it does not by itself begin to account for the Keynesian Revolution, that is, the unprecedented speed with which Keynes conquered the minds of his fellow economists. That is a question in MHRP rather than MSRP and it is possible to argue that Keynesian economics was a progressive SRP in its day and age because it predicted the novel fact of the positive multiplier but economists joined the camp of Keynesian economics for other reasons, say, because they wanted to believe in a kind of economics – any kind of economics – that made it easy to recommend active policies to combat the depression.

So, if we are going to attack 'novel fact fetishism', we ought to make it clear whether we are attacking it on normative or on positive grounds: the methodology of science is not reducible to the history of science; neither is the history of science reducible to the methodology of science.

I would insist that Lakatos was quite right to highlight the prediction of novel facts. Nevertheless there is no warrant for the apparently common belief (see the chapters by Shearmur and Steedman, above) that Lakatos never recognized anything like 'theoretical progress' or the pure refinement of ideas and techniques as an end in itself. Here again we are threatened by a Babel of tongues: Lakatos called the process of predicting novel facts 'theoretical progress' and the corroboration of these predictions 'empirical progress'. What is usually called 'theoretical progress', Lakatos labelled 'heuristic progress' and, as de Marchi shows in his introduction to this volume and in his commentary on Kim's essay, Lakatos certainly did *not* lose sight of the role of advances in problem-solving techniques; he was perfectly willing to recognize model improvement as a sign of progress and only regarded excess empirical content as *desirable* in each model improvement. As a historian of mathematics, it is hardly likely that Lakatos would have failed to notice that some proofs are better than others, that an increase in analytical rigor is not to be despised, and that a simpler, more elegant demonstration of a proposition is a matter for genuine congratulation. However neither he nor anyone else has ever succeeded in quantifying this notion of what we shall now continue to call 'theoretical progress', meaning Lakatosian heuristic progress. This is a point worth remembering for those who make much of Popper's failure to solve the problem of verisimilitude. Never mind! There is such a thing as theoretical progress even though we can do little to compel a sceptic to agree that it has taken place.

Although we can make much or little of Lakatos's observations on the role of the problem-solving abilities of scientific theories – and I do think that de Marchi makes too much of it – there is every reason in a subject like economics to insist again and again on the ultimate litmus paper test of excess empirical content: Lakatosian methodologists may suffer from 'novel fact fetishism' but modern economists suffer from 'novel fact deprivation'.

As de Marchi notes in his introduction, the self-image of economists is extraordinarily close to the idea portrayed in MSRP: they see themselves to a considerable extent as Lakatosian methodology would imply. However, when pressed, they consistently minimize the importance of empirical progress as against theoretical progress. John Hicks had doubts all his life about the need to submit economic theory to an empirical test and had little use for Lakatos and all that; nevertheless he also believed that economic theory must serve as a handmaiden of economic policy, a position which clearly contradicts his apparent rejection of verisimilitude as a criterion for better or worse economics (Blaug, 1988). Similarly, Kenneth Arrow, when asked by George Feiwel: 'What criteria would you use to evaluate the soundness of an alternative theory?', replied:

> Persuasiveness. Does it correspond to our understanding of the economic world? I think it is foolish to say that we rely on hard empirical evidence completely. A very important part of it is just *our* perception of the economic world. If you find a new concept, the question is, does it illuminate your perception? Do you feel you understand what is going on in everyday life? Of course, whether it fits empirical and other tests is also important. (Feiwel, 1987, p. 242)

Both Hicks and Arrow shared the Nobel Prize for their contributions to the development of general equilibrium (GE) theory and it does not require more than a nodding acquaintance with GE theory to realize that its advocates are very likely to play down the role of testing and empirical evidence. GE theory simply has no empirical content whatsoever. But what about input–output analysis or computable GE models or IS-LM, which was, after all, the first operational, albeit highly simplified, GE model of the entire economy (Patinkin, 1990). Alas, here once again we must distinguish between radically different theoretical conceptions travelling under the same label.[3] We can speak of GE theory in at least two senses. The first is the Walrasian notion of the problem of multimarket equilibrium – does it exist; is it unique; is it stable? Let us agree from now on to call this the Walras/Arrow/Debreu GE theory or Walrasian GE theory for short. The second is the more general notion of an economic model expressed as a set of simultaneous equations in which two or more but typically a large number of endogenous variables are simultaneously solved in terms of one or more exogenous variables. Let us agree to call this the GE *model* as distinct from the Walrasian GE *theory*.

Now, clearly, the GE model is rich in empirical content. Indeed, its only *raison d'être* is to demonstrate the difference it makes to assume that everything else remains constant in a partial equilibrium treatment of an economic problem. At the same time we need constantly to remind ourselves that there is nothing obvious or commonplace about a GE view of a problem: all-round multimarket equilibrium is a feature of certain *models* of the economy and not necessarily a reflection of how that economy is constituted. Thus we assume too readily after studying GE theory that prices are actually determined simultaneously in the real world, but a sequential process of price determination – first the price of coal, then the price of steel, and then the price of automobiles – is perhaps a more plausible representation of how prices come to be set in the course of real-world competitive rivalry. In any case, the superiority of general over partial equilibrium models is fundamentally an empirical question: taking account of all interdependencies is obviously better than ignoring them, but it is also much harder work and the pay-off in predictability may not warrant the extra effort.

The Walrasian GE *theory*, on the other hand, rests on totally different foundations. Walras's masterstroke was not just to seize on multimarket equilibrium as *the* central economic problem – a thought that had not truly occurred to any economist before him – but to pose its solution as *analogous* to the algebraic problem of solving a set of simultaneous equations. Walras's procedure, as we all know, was to write down a set of abstract demand and supply equations and then to 'prove' the existence of a solution for this set of simultaneous equations by counting the number of equations and unknowns. This strictly static picture of the determination of multimarket equilibria was then followed up by a quasi-realistic explanation of how the competitive mechanism might establish such an equilibrium in practice, namely by automatic price adjustments in response to the appearance of excess demand and supply. He struggled to provide a realistic account of this process of *tâtonnement* in successive editions of his *Elements of Pure Economics* but in the end virtually admitted it himself to be a failure.

Walrasian GE theory went into a decline almost as soon as Walras had formulated it and for over 60 years remained the prerogative of a small number of mathematically inclined economists here and there in Europe and the United States. Then, in the 1930s, largely as a result of the writings of Hicks, Samuelson and Lange, Walrasian GE theory began its long climb from relative obscurity to the very forefront of economic theorizing in the famous Arrow/Debreu articles of the 1950s. It is a story brilliantly told by Weintraub (1985) in a style recalling Lakatos's own in *Proofs and Refutations*. In the course of that telling Weintraub fails to notice that attitudes to Walrasian GE theory have gone through a 180-degree revolution since Walras's own times. Walras himself seems to have conceived of his model as an admittedly abstract but not misleading representation of the manner in which competition drives prices to their equilibrium values in a capitalist regime. Similarly in the 1930s it was common to regard it as a reasonable approximation to the description of an actual capitalist economy. Thus, in the great Socialist Calculation Debate, Oskar Lange argued that socialism could employ a procedure for equilibrating prices that would mimic the one ostensibly employed under capitalism, namely a Walrasian *tâtonnement* (Kowalik, 1987; Lavoie, 1985, chap 4). However nowadays the Walrasian schema is defended as a purely formal statement of the concept of general equilibrium, telling us what we *mean* by a logically consistent equilibrium model; not even the most enthusiastic advocates of GE theory pretend for one moment that it provides any kind of description of, or prescription for, a capitalist economy, preferring indeed to speak of GE as a 'framework' or 'paradigm' rather than a 'theory' (Hahn, 1984, p. 45–6).[4]

Roy Weintraub has argued that GE theory must be construed as the hard core of the neoclassical SRP and his account of the long upward struggle of GE theory from the 1920s to the 1950s is presented as a critical case study in the 'hardening' of that hard core. But there was neoclassical economics before the revival of GE theory; surely we are not denying that Marshallian economics is neo-classical economics and yet Marshall relegated GE to a brief appendix to his *Principles*. Similarly, modern economics is full of partial equilibrium theories that draw little even on GE models and certainly nothing at all on Walrasian

GE theory. In short, there is something wrong with Weintraub's story. What seems to have happened historically is that GE theory invaded neoclassical economics and in the process transformed it into an increasingly technical, highly formal apparatus for talking about an economy as if that talk corresponds to a real economy. We can establish the existence, stability and determinacy of general equilibrium with a rigor that would have amazed Walras but we cannot even begin to describe how competition actually operates in real markets. As Frank Fisher (1987) has said: 'the very power and elegance of [general] equilibrium analysis often obscures the fact that it rests on very uncertain foundations. We have no similarly elegant theory of what happens *out* of equilibrium, of how agents behave when their plans are frustrated. As a result we have no rigorous basis for believing that equilibrium can be achieved or maintained if disturbed.'

Modern Austrian economists go so far as to suggest that the Walrasian approach to the problem of multimarket equilibrium is a *cul de sac*: if we want to understand the *process* of competition, rather than the equilibrium *end-state* achieved by competition, we must begin by discarding such static reasoning as is implied by Walrasian GE theory. I have come slowly and extremely reluctantly to the view that they are right and that we have all been wrong. To imagine, as do Arrow and Hahn (1971, pp. vi–vii) that Walrasian GE theory makes precise an economic tradition that is as old as Adam Smith is to commit a category mistake: Adam Smith's 'invisible hand' referred to the dynamic process of competition and not to the static, end-state conception of perfect competition that came into economics with Cournot (see Backhouse, 1990). The fact is that modern economics comes equipped with an elegant analysis of the nature of equilibrium as the final outcome of the workings of the competitive mechanism and yet is virtually silent on the precise means by which buyers and sellers resolve their differences on the way to final equilibrium. This lacuna in modern microeconomics is deeply embarrassing because most of the acclaimed virtues of competition in the public utterances of economists derive from the dynamic characteristics of competition in fostering technical dynamism and cost-cutting innovations. But these are the disequilibrium features of the process of competition that have disappeared by the time we come to consider the final equilibrium outcome. In short, whatever the analytical virtues of GE theory, it is of little help and is perhaps a positive hindrance in explaining the true merits of competition.

But so what? We are not all doing GE theory, so why decry the work of Arrow, Debreu, McKenzie, Hurwicz, Sonnenschein, etcetera? It is only one kind of economics after all. On the contrary: it is the most prestigious economics of all and it has absorbed an entire generation of some of the finest minds in modern economics. And yet despite the enormous intellectual resources that have been invested in the endless elaboration of GE theory – with and without money, with and without increasing returns, and the rest – it is extremely questionable, to say the least, whether these efforts have thrown any light at all on the way economic systems function in practice.

Worse still, it has fostered an attitude to economics as a purely intellectual game in which we model economic processes that bear a vague resemblance to real-world processes and then comfort ourselves that their constant technical improvement will one day bear surprising fruit in generating substantive hypotheses about economic behaviour. When I read in Ian Steedman's paper to the Capri conference that Sraffian economists, having established the logical possibility of re-switching and capital-reversing, have no obligation to demonstrate its empirical importance, I could almost weep. What he seems to be saying, as did Joan Robinson who invented this stance (Blaug, 1980, pp. 206–7), is that Sraffians care more about economic theory than about the economy: they would rather score a nice logical point against neoclassical economics than advance our understanding of how the economy actually works. But they have learned this attitude to economic theory as a purely intellectual game from their orthodox colleagues working on GE theory.

Can Sraffian economics be criticized for not yet having produced interesting testable propositions, Steedman asks. No, he replies, because Sraffians are few in number and 30 years is too soon and, anway, is empirical progress really the norm in economics? There we have it! His defence might carry some conviction if lack of empirical thrust in Sraffian economics, its total preoccupation with what Steedman rightly calls 'negative logic', were regarded as a worrying problem by Sraffians. But an exhaustive survey of the Sraffian literature reveals not a single discussion of the empirical emptiness of Sraffian economics before that of Steedman. Some Sraffians see their efforts as rehabilitating classical political economy, but, as Zamagni points out in his commentary on Steedman, the Sraffian model is a curiously misplaced starting-point for a revival of the economics of Smith, Ricardo and Marx. Theirs was fundamentally a dynamic economics, whereas Sraffa is essentially a particular species of the Walrasian genus and hence condemned as a static, end-state theory. Note too that Steedman appraises Sraffa implicitly on grounds of mathematical consistency, while rejecting Lakatos's MSRP. However he fails utterly to justify *his* methodology, which seems to be that of theory improvement as an end in itself: economists can safely do economics in an arm-chair.[5]

After this diatribe against the 'noxious influence' of Walras on modern economics, I return to the fundamental role of novel facts and empirical progress in appraising the evolution of a SRP. I have tried to make a normative case for 'novel fact fetishism' in terms of the philosophy of Realism but, despite all that I have said about Walrasian GE theory, there is also a positive case to be made for it. After all, if economists *never* paid attention to empirical evidence and *never* rejected a theory that had been repeatedly refuted by the evidence, I would be prepared to abandon both MHRP and MSRP. But there is much Chicago-style neoclassical microeconomics that is deeply imbued with the spirit of empirical testing and there is little doubt that the pursuit of empirical validation has driven the old Monetarism as well as the New Classical Macroeconomics (as Maddock makes clear in his chapter above). Kurt Klappholz in discussions at Capri asked how many examples there are in economics of even low-level regularities being decisively refuted, and he cited the Phillips curve as the only example that came to mind. But in fact there are many more examples: Marshall's conjecture that there are Giffen goods and hence positively sloped demand curves; Bowley's 'law' of constant relative shares; Smith–Ricardo–Marx–Keynes's 'law' of the downward trend in the profit rate; Keynes–Hansen's thesis of secular stagnation; the permanent-income hypothesis; and even the quantity theory of money as a proposition about the stability of velocity and the 'neutrality' of money. Of course much depends on what is meant by a *decisive* refutation of an economic generalization and, needless to say, I agree that economists generally lack 'universal laws' in the natural science sense of the term. Still I find it difficult to imagine how one can account for the rise and decline of Keynesian economics, the rise and decline of monetarism (in the Friedman sense of fighting inflation by means of money supply targets) and the rise and virtual decline of the New Classical Macroeconomics in entirely theoretical terms. These research programs began to fail either because they contradicted some patently observable facts about the world – stagflation in the case of Keynesian economics; the failure to control inflation by controlling the money supply alone in the case of monetarism – or because they implied predicted relationships that were not borne out by the evidence collected expressly to support the program – as in the case of Lucas and company (see Blaug, 1985, pp. 678–92). In other words, economists may be 'innocuous falsificationists' but they *are* falsificationists and Lakatos's MHRP is far from refuted.

Despite the jaundiced reaction to Lakatos of many of the Capri participants, I remain convinced that Lakatos is still capable of inspiring fruitful work in methodology. Vernon Smith *et al.*, Roger Backhouse and particularly Neil de Marchi summarize what is valuable in Lakatos and I do not need therefore to labour the point. In retrospect, I wish that we had succeeded in obtaining Lakatosian appraisals of such SRPs as behavioural economics, post-Keynesian economics and both the old and new Institutionalism, each of which might have taught us lessons of their own. But perhaps that is an agenda for a third Lakatos conference in another five or ten years.

NOTES

1. Economics is not poetry or music or art and in economics we do have to ask whether the theories we espouse 'correspond' to a world that we may wish to change – this is why, McCloskey, Mirowski and Weintraub notwithstanding, we do better to model a methodology of economics on the philosophy of science than on literary criticism.
2. It is not always clear what is meant by the label of 'falsificationism'. I defend it as 'a methodological standpoint that regards theories and hypotheses as scientific if and only if their predictions are, at least in principle, empirically falsifiable'. Bruce Caldwell (1982), in attacking my argument, introduced the distinction between 'confirmationism' and 'falsificationism'. He noted that modern economists believe 'that theories should be testable; that a useful means of testing is to compare the predictions of a theory with reality; that predictive accuracy is often the most important characteristic a theory can possess; and that the relative ordering of theories should be determined by the strength of confirmation, or corroboration, of those being compared' (Caldwell, 1982, p. 124). These four principles, he declared, define the methodology of 'confirmationism'. 'Falsificationism', he alleged, is a tougher doctrine. In its simplest form it implies that 'scientists should not only empirically test their hypotheses, they should construct hypotheses which make bold predictions, and they should try to refute these hypotheses in their tests. Equally important, scientists should tentatively accept only confirmed hypotheses, and reject those which have been disconfirmed. Testing, then, should make a difference' (Caldwell, 1982, p. 125). Clearly the difference between confirmationism and falsificationism is a difference of degree; my notion of 'innocuous falsificationism' is virtually identical to Caldwell's confirmationism, in which case it is difficult to see in what sense he is really objecting to my argument (see Blaug, 1984).
3. The following pages draw heavily on my pamphlet (Blaug, 1988).
4. See also Arrow's highly ambiguous defence of GE theory in interviews with George Feiwel (1987, pp. 196ff), during which he continually conflates the GE model and the Walrasian GE theory.
5. Zamagni shows that even Sraffa himself sometimes appealed to facts to justify some of his very abstract assumptions. But once we begin to appeal to facts, where do we stop? These are methodological questions which Sraffians have not even begun to ask.

REFERENCES

Arrow, K.J. and Hahn F.H. (1971), *General Competitive Analysis* (Edinburgh: Oliver & Boyd).

Backhouse, R. (1990), 'Competition', in J. Creedy (ed.), *Foundations of Economic Thought* (Oxford: Basil Blackwell).

Blaug, M. (1980), *The Methodology of Economics* (Cambridge: Cambridge University Press).
—— (1984), 'Comment 2', in P. Wiles and G. Routh (eds), *Economics in Disarray* (Oxford: Basil Blackwell).
—— (1985) *Economic Theory in Retrospect* (Cambridge, Cambridge University Press) 4th edn.
—— (1988), *Economics Through the Looking Glass* (London: Institute of Economic Affairs).
Caldwell, B. (1982), *Beyond Positivism: Economic Methodology in the Twentieth Century* (London: Allen & Unwin).
Eatwell, J., Milgate, M. and Newman, P. (1987), *The New Palgrave. A Dictionary of Economics* (London: Macmillan) 4 vols.
Feiwel, G.R. (1987), *Arrow and the Ascent of Modern Economic Theory* (London, Macmillan).
Fisher, F. (1987), 'Adjustment Processes and Stability', *The New Palgrave*, I (London: Macmillan).
Hahn, F. (1984), *Equilibrium and Macroeconomics* (Oxford: Basil Blackwell).
Kowalik, T. (1987), 'Lange–Lerner Mechanism', *The New Palgrave*, III (London: Macmillan).
Lavoie, D. (1985), *Rivalry and Central Planning: The Socialist Calculation Debate Reconsidered* (Cambridge: Cambridge University Press).
de Marchi, N. (ed.) (1988), *The Popperian Legacy in Economics* (Cambridge: Cambridge University Press).
Patinkin, D. (1990), 'In Defense of IS-LM', *Banco Nazionale del Lavoro Quarterly Review*, No. 172, March, pp. 119–34.

Bibliography

Agassi, J. (1966), 'Sensationalism', *Mind*, **75**, pp. 1–24.

—— (1988), *The Gentle Art of Philosophical Polemics* (LaSalle, IL: Open Court).

Ahonen, Guy (1989), 'On the empirical content of Keynes' *General Theory', Ricerche Economiche*, **43**, pp. 256–67.

—— (1990), 'Commentary on Hands' "Second Thoughts on 'Second Thoughts' " on the Lakatosian progress of *The General Theory', Review of Political Economy*, **2**, pp. 94–101.

Akerman, J. (1955), discussion of a paper in 'Report of Uppsala Meeting', by Bent Hansen, *Econometrica*, **23**, p. 201.

Aigner, J.A. and Zellner, A. (1988), *Journal of Econometrics*, **39** (Special issues on 'Causality'), pp. 1–234.

Aldrich, J. (1989), 'Autonomy', *Oxford Economic Papers*, **41**, pp. 15–34.

Anderson, G.J. and Blundell, R.W. (1983), 'Testing restrictions in a dynamic model of consumers' expenditure', *Review of Economic Studies*, **50**, pp. 397–410.

—— (1984), 'Consumer non-durables in the U.K.: a dynamic demand system', *Economic Journal*, **94**, Supp., pp. 35–44.

Ando, Albert (1989), 'Comments' [on Campbell and Mankiw, 'Consumption, Income, and Interest Rates: Reinterpreting the Time Series Evidence'], in Olivier Jean Blanchard and Stanley Fischer (eds), *NBER Macroeconomics Annual 1989*, pp. 234–44 (The MIT Press: Cambridge, Mass.).

Archibald, G.C. (1959), 'The state of economic science', *British Journal for the Philosophy of Science*, **10**, pp. 58–69.

—— (1966), Refutation or Comparison?', *British Journal for the Philosophy of Science*, **17**, pp. 279–96.

—— (1979), 'Method and Appraisal in Economics', *Philosophy of the Social Sciences*, **9**, pp. 304–15.

Arouh, Albert (1987), 'The mumpsimus of economists and uncertainty in the progress of economic knowledge', *Journal of Post-Keynesian Economics*, **9**, pp. 395-423.

Arrow, K.J. (1951), *Social Choice and Individual Values* (New Haven, Conn.: Yale University Press).

Arrow, Kenneth J. and Hahn, Frank (1971), *General Competitive Analysis* (Edinburgh: Oliver and Boyd and San Francisco: Holden Day).

Attfield, C.L.F. (1985), 'Homogeneity and endogeneity in systems of demand equations', *Journal of Econometrics*, **27**, pp. 197–209.

Attfield, C.L.F. and Browning, M.J. (1985), 'A differential demand system, rational expectations and the life cycle hypothesis', *Econometrica*, **53**, pp. 31–48.

Aumann, R.J. (1987), 'Correlated Equilibrium as an Expression of Bayesian Rationality', *Econometrica*, **55**, pp. 1–18.

—— (1987), 'Game Theory', in J. Eatwell, M. Milgate and P. Newman (eds), *The New Palgrave*, vol. 2, pp. 460–79.

—— (1988), 'Preliminary Notes on Irrationality in Game Theory', IMSSS Summer Seminar on Economic Theory, Stanford.

Axelrod, R. (1980), 'The Emergence of Cooperation Among Egoists', *The American Political Science Review*, **75**, pp. 306–18.

—— (1986), 'An Evolutionary Approach to Norms', *American Political Science Review*, **80** (Dec), pp. 1095–1111.

Azariadis, C. (1975), 'Implicit contracts and underemployment equilibria', *Journal of Poltical Economy*, **83**, pp. 1183–1202.

Backhouse, Roger (1985), *A History of Modern Economic Analysis* (Oxford: Basil Blackwell).

—— (1988), 'Perspectives on the history of economic thought', *Scottish Journal of Political Economy*, **35** (1), pp. 97–104.

—— (1988), 'Post-war macroeconomics' (mimeo).

—— (1990), 'Competition', in J. Creedy (ed.), *Foundations of Economic Thought* (Oxford: Basil Blackwell).

—— (1990), 'Lakatos and Economics', paper presented at the History of Economics Society Conference, Lexington, Virginia, June (mimeo).

Baily, M.N, (1974), 'Wages and employment under uncertain demand', *Review of Economic Studies*, **41**, pp. 37–50.

Bannerjee, A. and Dolado, J. (1988), 'Tests of the Life Cycle-Permanent Income Hypothesis in the presence of random walks: asymptotic theory and small sample interpretations', *Oxford Economic Papers*, **40**, pp. 610–33.

Barnett, William A., Geweke, John and Yue, Piyu (1988), 'Semi-parametric Bayesian Estimation of the Asymptotically Ideal Model: the AIM Demand System', unpublished manuscript, University of Texas at Austin.

Barro, Robert J. (1976), 'Rational Expectations and the Role of

Monetary Policy', in Lucas and Sargent (1981). Reprinted from *Journal of Political Economy*, **59** (2), pp. 93–116.
—— (1977), 'Unanticipated Money Growth and Unemployment in the United States', in Lucas and Sargent (1981), pp. 563–84. Reprinted from *American Economic Review*, **67** (2), pp. 101–15.
—— (1978), 'Unanticipated Money, Output, and the Price Level in the United States', in Lucas and Sargent (1981), pp. 585-616. Reprinted from *Journal of Political Economy*, **86**, pp. 549–80.
Barro, Robert J. and Gordon, David B. (1983), 'A Positive Theory of Monetary Policy in a Natural Rate Model', *Journal of Political Economy*, **91** (4), pp. 589–610.
—— (1983), 'Rules, Discretion and Reputation in a Model of Monetary Policy', *Journal of Monetary Economics*, **12** (2), pp. 101–21.
Barro, R.J. and Grossman, H.I. (1971), 'A general disequilibrium model of income and employment', *American Economic Review*, **61**, pp. 82–93.
Barro, Robert J. and Rush, Mark (1980), 'Unanticipated Money and Economic Activity', in Stanley Fischer (ed.), *Rational Expectations and Economic Policy* (Chicago: University of Chicago Press).
Barten, A.P. (1969), 'Maximum likelihood estimation of a complete system of demand equations', *European Economic Review*, **1**, pp. 7–73.
Bartley, W.W. III (1984), *The Retreat to Commitment*, 2nd enlarged edn (LaSalle, IL: Open Court).
—— (1987), 'Theories of Rationality', in G. Radnitzky and W.W. Bartley III (eds), *Evolutionary Epistemology, Rationality, and the Sociology of Knowledge*, pp. 205–14 (LaSalle, IL: Open Court).
Basmann, R. (1963), 'The Causal Interpretation of Non-Triangular Systems of Economic Relations', *Econometrica*, **31**, pp. 439–54 and 'A Rejoinder', same volume, pp. 451–6.
—— (1965), 'A Note on the Statistical Testability of "Explicit Causal Chains" against the Class of "interdependent" Models, *Journal of the American Statistical Association*, **60**, pp. 1080–93.
Baumol, W. (1951), *Economic Dynamics* (New York: Macmillan).
Bazerman, Charles (1988), *Shaping Written Knowledge* (Madison: University of Wisconsin Press).
Bean, C.R., Layard, P.R.G. and Nickell, S.J. (1986) (eds), 'Unemployment', *Economica Supplement*, **53**, p. 210(S).
Beardsley, Timothy M. (1989), 'Chilling Out', *Scientific American*, September **261**, p. 20.
Begg, D.K.H. (1982), 'Rational expectations, wage rigidity, and involuntary unemployment', *Oxford Economics Papers*, pp. 23–47.

Bentzel, R. and Hansen, B. (1954), 'On Recursiveness and Interdependency in Economic Models', *Review of Economic Studies*, **22**, pp. 153–68.

Bentzel, R. and Wold, H. (1946), 'On Statistical Demand Analysis from the Viewpoint of Simultaneous Equations', *Skandinavisk Aktuarietidskrift*, **29**, pp. 95–113.

Bergstrom, A.R. (1988), 'The History of Continuous-Time Econometric Models', *Econometric Theory*, **4**, pp. 365–83.

Bernheim, B. Douglas and Bagwell, Kyle (1988), 'Is Everything Neutral?', *Journal of Political Economy*, **96** (2), pp. 308–38.

Beveridge, S. and Nelson, C.R. (1981), 'A new approach to decomposition of economic time series data into permanent and transitory components with particular attention to measurement of the business cycle', *Journal of Monetary Economics*, **7**, pp. 151–74.

Bicchieri, Cristina (1988), 'Strategic Behavior and Counterfactuals', *Synthese*, **76**, pp. 135–69.

—— (1989), 'Progress without growth? The case of the "marginalist revolution" in economics', *Ricerche Economiche*, **43**, pp. 236–54.

Binmore, K. (1987), 'Modeling Rational Players', *Economics and Philosophy*, Part 6, I and II.

Birner, Jack (1988), 'Comment' on Weintraub's 'The neo-Walrasian program is empirically progressive', in de Marchi (ed.), *The Popperian Legacy in Economics* (Cambridge: Cambridge University Press), pp. 47–51.

—— (1990), *Strategies and Programmes in Capital Theory. A Contribution to the Methodology of Theory Development*, PhD thesis, University of Amsterdam (privately printed).

Blanchard, Olivier Jean and Fischer, Stanley (1989), *Lectures on Macroeconomics* (Cambridge, Mass.: MIT Press).

Blanchard, O.J. and Summers, L.H. (1987), 'Hysteresis in Employment', *European Economic Review*, **31** 1/2, Feb/March, pp. 288–95.

—— (1988), 'Hysteresis and the European Unemployment Problem', reprinted in R. Cross (ed.), *Unemployment, Hysteresis and the Natual Rate Hypothesis* (Oxford: Basil Blackwell).

Blaug, Mark (1976), 'Kuhn versus Lakatos, *or* paradigms versus programmes in the history of economics', in Spiro Latsis (ed.), *Method and Appraisal in Economics* (Cambridge: Cambridge University Press), pp. 149–80.

—— (1976), 'The empirical status of human capital theory: a slightly jaundiced survey', *Journal of Economic Literature*, **14**, pp. 827–55.

—— (1978), *Economic Theory in Retrospect*, 3rd edn (New York: Cambridge University Press).

—— (1980), *A Methodological Appraisal of Marxian Economics* (Amsterdam: North-Holland), partly reprinted in Blaug, *Economic Theories*, pp. 17–56.

—— (1980), *The Methodology of Economics. Or, How Economists Explain* (Cambridge: Cambridge University Press).

—— (1983), 'A methodological appraisal of radical economics', in A.W. Coats (ed.), *Methodological controversy in economics: historical essays in honor of T.W. Hutchison'*, pp. 211–45, reprinted in Blaug, *Economic Theories*, pp. 57–87.

—— (1984), 'Comment 2', in P. Wiles and G. Routh (eds), *Economics in Disarray* (Oxford: Basil Blackwell).

—— (1985), *Economic Theory in Retrospect*, 4th edn (Cambridge: Cambridge University Press).

—— (1988), *Economics Through the Looking Glass* (London: Institute of Economic Affairs).

—— (1990), 'Second thoughts on second thoughts: reconsidering the Lakatosian progress of *The General Theory*. Reply to Hands', *Review of Political Economy*, **2**, pp. 101–3.

—— (1990), *Economic Theories, True or False? Essays in the History and Methodology of Economics*, Aldershot: Edward Elgar.

—— (1991), 'Second Thoughts on the Keynesian Revolution', *History of Political Economy* (forthcoming) and Blaug, *Economic Theories*, pp. 88–106.

Blinder, A.S. (1987), 'Keynes, Lucas and Scientific Progress', *American Economic Review*, **77**, 2, May, pp. 130–36.

Blundell, R.W. (1988), 'Consumer behaviour: theory and empirical evidence', *Economic Journal*, **98**, pp. 16–65.

Blundell, R.W. Pashardes, P. and Weber, G. (1988), 'What do we learn about consumer demand patterns from micro-data?', Institute for Fiscal Studies, Working Paper No. W88/10.

—— (1989), 'What do we learn about consumer demand patterns from micro-data?', paper given to IFS-LBS conference 'Aggregation in Economic Modelling', October 1989.

Bodkin, R. (1963), 'Windfall income and consumption: a comment', *American Economic Review*, **52**, pp. 445–7.

Boland, Lawrence A. (1982), *The Foundations of Economic Method* (London: Allen & Unwin).

Braithwaite, R.B. (1960), *Scientific Explanation* (Cambridge: Cambridge University Press).

Brams, S. (1975), *Game Theory and Politics* (London: Macmillan).

Brams, S. and Fishburn, P. (1978), 'Approval Voting', *American Political Science review*, **72**, pp. 831–47.

Brandon, Robert N. (1990), *Adaptation and Environment* (Princeton: Princeton University Press).
Bridgman, P. (1927), *The Logic of Modern Physics* (New York: Macmillan).
Brook, William (1974), 'Money and Growth: The Case of Long-run Perfect Farsight', *International Economic Review*, October, **15**, pp. 750–70.
—— (1982), 'Asset Prices in a Production Economy, in J.J. McCall (ed.), *Economics of Information and Uncertainty*, pp. 1–43 (Chicago: University of Chicago Press).
Brown, Elba K. (1978), 'The Keynesian and neo-classical research programs: a comparison', PhD thesis, Duke University.
—— (1981), 'The Neo-classical and Post-Keynesian Research Programs: The Methodological Issues', *Review of Social Economy*, **39**, pp. 111–32.
Brown, T.M. (1952), 'Habit persistence and lags in consumer behavior', *Econometrica*, **29**, pp. 355–71.
Browning, M.J., Deaton, A.S. and Irish, M. (1985), 'A profitable approach to labor supply and commodity demands over the life cycle', *Econometrica*, **53**, pp. 503–43.
Bryant, John and Wallace, Neil (1979), 'The Inefficiency of Interest-bearing National Debt', *Journal of Political Economy*, **87** (2), pp. 365–81.
—— (1984), 'A Price Discrimination Analysis of Monetary Policy', *Review of Economic Studies*, **51** (2), pp. 279–88.
Buchanan, J.M. and Tullock, G. (1962), *The Calculus of Consent* (Ann Arbor: The University of Michigan Press).
Buiter, W. and Miller, M. (1981), 'The Thatcher experiment: the first two years', *Brookings Papers on Economic Activity*, pp. 315–79.
Burdett, K. (1978), 'A theory of employee search and quit rates', *American Economic Review*, **68**, 1, pp. 212–20.
Byron, R.P. (1970), 'A simple method for estimating demand systems under separable utility assumptions', *Review of Economic Studies*, **37**, pp. 261–74.
Cagan, P. (1956), 'The monetary dynamics of hyperinflation', in M. Friedman (ed.), *Studies in the Quantity Theory of Money* (Chicago: University of Chicago Press).
Caldwell, B. (1982), *Beyond Positivism: Economic Methodology in the Twentieth Century* (London: Allen & Unwin).
Calvo, G. and Phelps, E.S. (1977), 'Employment-contingent wage contracts', in K. Brunner and A. Meltzer (eds), *Stabilization of the*

Domestic and International Economy, Carnegie-Rochester Series on Public Policy, 1977, pp. 160–68.

Campbell, J.Y. and Deaton, A.S. (1989), 'Why is consumption so smooth?', *Review of Economic Studies*, **56**, pp. 357-74.

Campbell, J.Y. and Mankiw, N.G. (1987), 'Permanent income, current income, and consumption', NBER Working Paper, 2436.

Campbell, J.Y and Mankiw, Gregory N. (1989), 'Consumption, Income, and Interest Rates: Reinterpreting the Time Series Evidence', in Olivier Jean Blanchard and Stanley Fischer (eds), *NBER Macroeconomics Annual 1989*, pp. 185–215 (Cambridge, Mass.: The MIT Press).

Campbell, Richmond and Vinci, Thomas (1983), 'Novel confirmation', *The British Journal for the Philosophy of Science*, **34**, pp. 315–41.

Carrier, M. (1988), 'On novel facts: a discussion of criteria for non-ad-hocness in the methodology of scientific research programmes', *Zeitschrift für Allegmeine Wissenschaftstheorie*, **19**, pp. 205–31.

Carter, M. and Maddock R. (1984), *Rational Expectations: Macro-economics for the 1980s?* (London: Macmillan).

Champernowne, D. (1936), 'Unemployment, basic and monetary: the classical analysis and the Keynesian', *Review of Economic Studies*, **3**, pp. 201–16.

Chesher, A. and Lancaster, T. (1983), 'The estimation of models of labour market behavior', *Review of Economic Studies*, **50**, 4, pp. 609–24.

Christ, C. (1951), 'A Test of an econometric Model for the United States, 1921–1947, in *Conference on Business Cycles*, Universities-National Bureau Committee for Economic Research, New York: National Bureau of Economic Research, pp. 35–107; and Comments by M. Friedman, pp. 107–14.

Christ, C. *et al.* (1960), 'A Symposium on Simultaneous Equation Estimation', *Econometrica*, **28**, pp. 835–71.

Christensen, L.R., Jorgenson, D.W. and Lau, L.J. (1975), 'Trans-cendental logarithmic utility functions', *American Economic Review*, **65**, pp. 367–83.

Christiano, Lawrence J. (1989), 'Comments' [on Campbell and Mankiw, 'Consumption, Income and Interest Rates: Reinterpreting the Time Series Evidence'], in Olivier Jean Blanchard and Stanley Rischer (eds), *NBER Macroeconomics Annual 1989*, pp. 216–33 (Cambridge, Mass.: The MIT Press).

Classen, K.P. (1979), 'Unemployment insurance and job search', in

S.A. Lippman and J.J. McCall (eds), *Studies in the Economics of Search* (Amsterdam, North-Holland), pp. 191–219.

Clower, R.W. (1965), 'The Keynesian Counter-Revolution: A Theoretical Appraisal' in F.H. Hahn and F. Brechling (eds), *The Theory of Interest Rates* (London and Basingstoke: Macmillan).

Clower, Robert (1967), 'A Reconsideration of the Microfoundations of Monetary Theory', *Western Economic Journal*, **6** (1), pp. 1–8.

Coats, A.W. (1974), 'Situational determinism in economics: The implications of Latsis' argument for the historian of economics', *The British Journal for the Philosophy of Science*, **25**, pp. 285–8.

—— (1976), 'Economics and Psychology: the death and resurrection of a research programme', in Latsis (ed.), *Method and Appraisal*, pp. 43–64.

—— (1983), *Methodological controversy in economics: historical essays in honor of T.W. Hutchison* (Greenwich, Conn.: JAI Press).

Coddington, A. (1983), *Keynesian Economics* (London: Allen & Unwin).

Cohen, L. Jonathan (1980), 'What has science to do with truth?', *Synthese*, **45**, pp. 489–510.

Cooley, Thomas F. and LeRoy, Stephen F. (1985) 'Atheoretical Macroeconometrics: A Critique', *Journal of Monetary Economics*, **16** (3), pp. 283–308.

Cooper, R. and John, A. (1988), 'Coordinating Keynesian Coordination Failures', *Quarterly Journal of Economics*, **103**.

Coppinger, Vicki, Smith, Vernon L. and Titus, Jon A. (1980), 'Incentives and Behavior in English, Dutch and Sealed-Bid Auctions', *Economic Inquiry*, **18**, January, pp. 1–22.

Cowles Commission, Monograph 10 (1950), *Statistical Inference in Dynamic Economic Models*, ed T.C. Koopmans (New York: Wiley).

—— Monograph 11 (1950), *Economic Fluctuations in the United States 1921–1941*, L.R. Klein (New York: Wiley).

—— Monograph 14 (1953), *Studies in Econometric Method*, ed. W.C. Hood and T.C. Koopmans (New York: Wiley).

Cox, D.R. (1961), 'Tests of Separate Families of Hypotheses', *Proceedings of the Fourth Berkeley Symposium on Mathematical Statistics and Probability*, **1**, pp. 105–23 (Berkeley: University of California Press).

Cox, James C. and Oaxaca, Ronald (1989), 'Laboratory Experiments with a Finite Horizon Job Search Model', *Journal of Risk and Uncertainty*, **3**, September, pp. 301–29.

Cox, James, C., Roberson, Bruce and Smith, Vernon L. (1980), 'Theory and Behavior of Single Object Auctions', in *Research in Experimental Economics*, vol. 2, pp. 1–43. (Greenwich, CT: JAI Press).

Cox, James, C., Smith, Vernon L. and Walker, James M. (1988), 'Theory and Individual Behavior of First-Price Auctions', *Journal of Risk and Uncertainty*, March **1**, pp. 61–99.

Cross, Rod (1982), 'The Duhem–Quine Thesis, Lakatos and the appraisal of theories in macroeconomics', *The Economic Journal*, **92**, 366, pp. 320–40.

—— (1984) 'Monetarism and Duhem's Thesis', in P. Wiles and G. Routh (eds), *Economic Theory in Disarray*, pp. 78–99 (Oxford: Basil Blackwell).

—— (1987), 'Hysteresis and Instability in the Natural Rate of Unemployment', *The Scandinavian Journal of Economics*, **89**, 1, pp. 71–89.

—— (ed.) (1988), *Unemployment, Hysteresis and the Natural Rate Hypothesis* (Oxford: Basil Blackwell).

—— (1989), 'Alternative Accounts of Equilibrium Unemployment', mimeo, St Andrews.

Cross, R. and Allan, A. (1988), 'On the History of Hysteresis', in R. Cross (ed.), *Unemployment, Hysteresis and the Natural Rate Hypothesis* (Oxford: Basil Blackwell).

Cross, R. Hutchinson H. and Yeoward, S. (1989), 'The Natural Rate, Hysteresis and the Duration Composition of Unemployment in the U.S.', *Quarterly Journal of Business and Economics*.

—— (1989), 'Does the Natural Rate Exist?: Long Term Unemployment and Hysteresis in the U.K., 1948–1987', University of St Andrews, mimeo.

—— (1989), 'The Relationship Between Prices and Unemployment: Cointegration Tests on the Keynesian Supply Curve, Phillips Curve, Natural Rate and Hysteresis Hypotheses in Britain 1886–1986', University of St Andrews, mimeo.

van Damme, E. (1983), *Refinements of the Nash Equilibrium Concept* (Berlin: Springer Verlag).

Davidson, J.E.H. and Hendry, D.F. (1981), 'Interpreting econometric evidence: the behaviour of consumers' expenditure in the U.K.', *European Economic Review*, **16**, pp. 177–92.

Davidson, J.E.H., Hendry, D.F., Srba, F. and Yeo, S. (1978), 'Econometric Modelling of the Aggregate Time Series Relationship Between Consumers' Expenditure and Income in the U.K.', *Economic Journal*, **88**, pp. 661–92.

Deaton, A.S. (1974), 'The analysis of consumer demand in the United Kingdom, 1900–1970', *Econometrica*, **42**, pp. 341–67.

—— (1974), 'A reconsideration of the empirical implications of additive preferences', *Economic Journal*, **84**, pp. 338–48.

—— (1977), 'Equity, efficiency and the structure of indirect taxation', *Journal of Public Economics*, **8**, pp. 299–312.

—— (1987), 'Life-cycle models of consumption: Is the evidence consistent with the theory?' in T.F. Bewley (ed.), *Advances in Econometrics*, **II**, pp. 121–48, (Cambridge: Cambridge University Press).

—— (1989), 'Saving and liquidity constraints', Fisher-Schultz Lecture, European Meeting of the Econometric Society, Munich, September 1989.

Deaton, A.S. and Muellbauer, J. (1980), 'An Almost Ideal Demand System', *American Economic Review*, **70**, pp. 312–32.

—— (1980), *Economics and Consumer Behaviour* (Cambridge: Cambridge University Press).

Desai, Megnad :1975), 'The Phillips Curve: A Revisionist Interpretation', *Economica*, **42**, (175), pp. 1–19.

—— (1981), *Testing Monetarism* (London: Pinter).

—— (1984), 'Wages, Prices and Unemployment a Quarter Century After the Phillips Curve', in D.F. Hendry and K.F. Wallis (eds), *Econometrics and Quantitative Economics* (Oxford: Basil Blackwell).

Diamond, P. (1982), 'Aggregate Demand Management in Search Equilibrium', *Journal of Political Economy*, **90**, 5, pp. 881–94.

—— (1984), *A Search Equilibrium Approach to the Micro Foundations of Macroeconomics* (Cambridge, Mass.: MIT Press).

Dickey, D.A. and Fuller, W.A. (1979), 'The Distribution of Estimators for Autoregressive Time Series with a Unit Root', *Journal of the American Statistical Association*, **74** (366), June, pp. 427–31.

—— (1981), 'Likelihood Ratio Statistics for Autoregressive Time Series with a Unit Root', *Econometrica*, **49**, 4, July, pp. 1057–72.

Dickey, D.A., Bell, W.R. and Miller, R.B. (1986), 'Unit Roots in Time Series Models: Test and Implications', *The American Statistician*, **40** (1), pp. 12–26.

Dixit, A.K. (1978), 'The balance of trade in a model of temporary equilibrium with rationing', *Review of Economic Studies*, **45**, pp. 393–404.

Dixon, H. (1988), 'A Simple Model of Imperfect Competition with Walrasian Features', in R. Cross (ed.), *Unemployment, Hysteresis and the Natural rate Hypothesis* (Oxford: Basil Blackwell).

Dornbusch, R. (1976), 'Expectations and exchange rate dynamics', *Journal of Political Economy*, **84**, pp. 1161–76.

Drazen, A. (1980), 'Recent developments in macroeconomic disequilibrium theory', *Econometrica*, **48**, pp. 283–306.

Duesenberry, J.S. (1949), *Income, Saving, and the Theory of Consumer Behaviour* (Cambridge, Mass.: Harvard University Press).

Duhem, P. (1914, translated 1954), *The Aim and Structure of Physical Theory* (Princeton, NJ: Princeton University Press).

Eatwell, J., Milgate, M. and Newman, P. (eds) (1987), *The New Palgrave, A Dictionary of Economics* (London: Macmillan).

Ehrenberg, R.G. and Oaxaca, R. (1976), 'Unemployment insurance, duration of unemployment and subsequent wage gain', *American Economic Review*, **66** (5), pp. 754–66.

Elster, J. (1976), 'A Note on Hysteresis in the Social Sciences', *Synthese*, **33**, pp. 371–91.

Endres, A.M. (1989), 'Menger, Wieser, Bohm-Bawerk and the Analysis of Economizing Behavior: Surpassing the Logic of Choice', manuscript.

Engle, R.F. and Granger, C.W.J. (1987), 'Dynamic Model Specification and Equilibrium Constraints: Cointegration and Error Correction', *Econometrica*, **55**, pp. 251–76.

Epstein, R. (1987), *A History of Econometrics* (Amsterdam: North-Holland).

Ermarth, Michael (1978), *Wilhelm Dilthey: The Critique of Historical Reason* (Chicago: University of Chicago Press).

Feiwel, G.R. (1987), *Arrow and the Ascent of Modern Economic Theory* (London: Macmillan).

Feyerabend, P. (1988), *Against Method* (revised edn) (London: Verso new Left Books).

Fischer, Stanley (1977), 'Long-Term Contracts, Rational Expectations, and the Optimal Money Supply Rule', in Lucas and Sargent (eds), pp. 261–84 reprinted from *Journal of Political Economy*, **85** (1), pp. 191–206.

Fisher, F. (1987), 'Adjustment Processes and Stability', *The New Palgrave*, I (London: Macmillan).

Fisher, I. (1926), 'A Statistical Relation Betwen Unemployment and Price Changes', *International Labour Review*, **13** (6), pp. 785–92. Reprinted in *Journal of Political Economy*, **81** (2), March/April, pp. 496–502.

Fisher, Mark and John J. Seater (1988), 'Neutralities of Money', unpublished typescript, North Carolina State University and University of Pennsylvania, October.

Fisher, Robert M. (1982), 'The Marginalist Revolution Reconsidered: The Birth of an Economic Research Program', PhD thesis, Duke University.

—— (1986), *The logic of economic discovery. Neo-classical economics and the marginal revolution* (New York: New York University Press).

Fisk, M. (1973), *Nature and Necessity: An Essay in Physical Ontology* (Bloomington, IN: Indiana University Press).

Flavin, M. (1981), 'The adjustment of consumption to changing expectations about future income', *Journal of Political Economy*, **89**, pp. 974–1009.

Flemming, J.S. (1973), 'The consumption function when capital markets are imperfect', *Oxford Economic Papers*, **25**, pp. 160–72.

Flinn, C. and Heckman, J. (1982), 'New method for analyzing structural models of labor force dynamics', *Journal of Econometrics*, **82**, pp. 115–68.

Folks, J.L. (1981), *Ideas of Statistics* (New York: John Wiley & Sons).

Fouraker, L.E. and Siegel, Sidney (1963) *Bargaining Behavior* (New York: McGraw-Hill).

Friedman, J. (1977), *Oligopoly and the Theory of Games* (Amsterdam: North-Holland).

Friedman, M. (1953), *Essays in Positive Economics* (Chicago: University of Chicago Press).

—— (1953) 'The methodology of positive economics', in M. Friedman, *Essays in Positive Economics* (Chicago: Chicago University Press).

—— (1955), 'Leon Walras and His Economic System', *American Economic Review*. **45** (5), pp. 900–909.

—— (1957), *A Theory of the Consumption Function* (Princeton: Princeton University Press).

—— (1966), 'What Price Guideposts?' in George P. Schulz and Robert Z. Aliber (eds), *Guidelines: Informal Controls and the Market Place*, pp. 52–76 (Chicago: Chicago University Press).

—— (1968), 'The Role of Monetary Policy', *American Economic Review*, **58** (1), March, pp. 1–17.

—— (1976), *Price Theory* (Chicago: Aldine).

—— (1977), 'Nobel Lecture: Inflation and Unemployment', *Journal of Political Economy*, **85** (3), June, pp. 451–72.

Frisch,R. (1933), 'Propagation Problems and Impulse Problems in Dynamic Economics', in *Economic Essays in Honour of Gustav Cassel* (London: Allen & Unwin).

—— (1936), 'On the Notion of Equilibrium and Disequilibrium', *Review of Economic Studies*, V, pp. 100–105.

Fudenberg, D. and Kreps, D.M. (1988), 'A Theory of Learning, Experimentation, and Equilibrium in Games', mimeo, Stanford University.

Fuller, W.A. (1976), *Introduction to Statistical Time Series* (New York: John Wiley).

Fulton, G. (1979), 'Aggregate production functions: an appraisal via the methodology of scientific research programmes', MSc (Econ.) thesis, The Queen's University, Belfast.

—— (1984), 'Research programmes in economics', *History of Political Economy*, **16**, pp. 187–206.

Gadamer, Hans-Georg [1960](1989), *Truth and Method*, revised translation by J. Weinsheimer and D. Marshall (New York: Crossroad).

—— [1963](1987), 'The Problem of Historical Consciousness', reprinted in Paul Ribanow and William M. Sullivan, *Interpretive Social Science: A Second Look* (Berkeley: University of California Press).

Gallant, A. Ronald (1984), 'The Fourier Flexible Form', *American Journal of Agricultural Economics*, **66**, pp. 204–8.

Gardner, Michael R. (1982), 'Predicting Novel Facts', *The British Journal for the Philosophy of Science*, **33**, pp. 1–15.

Garegnani, P. (1985), 'Ricordo di Piero Sraffa', in *I limiti della politica economica* (Societa italiana degli economisti) Giuffre editorie.

—— (1987), 'Surplus approach to value and distribution', in *New Palgrave Dictionary of Economics*, vol. IV (London: Macmillan).

Garner, C. (1979), 'Academic Publication, Market Signalling, and Scientific Research Decisions', *Economic Inquiry*, **17**, pp. 575–84.

Garraty, J.A. (1979), *Unemployment in History* (New York: Harper and Row).

Gavroglu, K., Goridaroulis, Y. and Nicolacopalis, P. (eds) (1989), *Imre Lakatos and Theories of Scientific Change* (Boston: Kluwer/Nijhoff).

Geertz, Clifford (1988), *Works and Lives* (Stanford: Stanford University Press).

Gerrard, B. (1988), 'Keynesian economics: the road to nowhere?', in J. Hillard (ed.), *J.M. Keynes in Retrospect* (Aldershot: Edward Elgar).

Georgescu-Roegen (1966), *Analytical Economics* (Cambridge, Mass.: Harvard University Press).

—— (1971), *The Entropy Law and the Economic Process* (Cambridge, Mass.: Harvard University Press).

Giere, R.N. (1983), 'Testing Theoretical Hypotheses', in J. Earman (ed.), *Testing Scientific Theories* (Minneapolis: University of Minnesota Press).

Gilbert, Christopher L. (1976), 'The Original Phillips Curve Estimates', *Economica*, **43**, pp. 51–7.

—— (1986), 'Professor Hendry's econometric methodology', *Oxford Bulletin of Economics and Statistics*, **48**, pp. 283–307.

—— (1988), 'The Development of Econometrics in Britain since 1945', PhD thesis, Oxford.

—— (1988), 'Richard Stone and the emergence of modern econometrics', Institute of Economics and Statistics, Oxford, processed.

—— (1989), 'Economic theory and econometric models' *Economic and Social Review*, **21**, pp. 1–25.

—— (1989), 'LSE and the British approach to time series econometrics', *Oxford Economic Papers*, **41** (1), pp. 102–30.

Gilbert, C.L. and Jalilian, H. (1989), 'The demand for travel and the demand for travelcards on the London Regional Transport network', Institute of Economics and Statistics, Oxford, Applied Economics Discussion Paper 83.

Gillies, D. (1959), 'Solutions to General Non-Zero Sum Games', in *Contributions to the Theory of Games*, **4**, Princeton University Press.

Glass, J.C. and Johnson, W. (1988), 'Metaphysics, MSRP and economics', *The British Journal for the Philosophy of Science*, **39**, pp. 313–29.

—— (1989), *Economics: Progression, Stagnation or Degeneration?* (Hemel Hempstead: Harvester Wheatsheaf).

Glazebrook, R.T. (1935), 'James Alfred Ewing, 1855–1935', *Obituary Notices of Fellows of the Royal Society of London*, **1**, pp. 475–92.

Gordon, R.J. (1976), 'Can Econometric Policy Evaluation be Salvaged? – A Comment', in 'The Phillips Curve and Labor Markets', Supplement to the *Journal of Monetary Economics*, **1**, April, pp. 47–61, edited by Karl Brunner and Allan Meltzer.

—— (1976), 'Recent Developments in the Theory of Inflation and Unemployment', *Journal of Monetary Economics*, **2**, April, pp. 185–219.

—— (1982), 'Price inertia and policy ineffectiveness in the United States, 1890–1980', *Journal of Political Economy*, **86**.

—— (1989), 'Fresh Water, Salt Water and Other Macroeconomic Elixirs', *Economic Record*, **65** (189), pp. 177–84.

—— (1989), 'Hysteresis and the Natural Rate: Findings for the Past Century in Five Industrial Nations', *Northwestern University mimeo*, May.

Gorman, W.M. (1981), 'Some Engel curves', in A.S. Deaton (ed.), *Essays in the Theory and Measurement of Consumer Behaviour* (Cambridge: Cambridge University Press).

Gronau, R. (1971), 'Information and frictional unemployment', *American Economic Review*, **61** (2), pp. 290–301.

Granger, C.W.J. (1969), 'Investigating Causal Relations by Econometric Models and Cross-Spectral Methods', in Lucas and Sargent (1981), pp. 371-86. Reprinted from *Econometrica*, **37**, July, pp. 424–38.
—— (1983), 'Cointegrating Variables and Error Correcting Models', *UCSD Discussion Paper*.
—— (1986), 'Developments in the Study of Cointegrated Economic Variables', *Oxford Bulletin of Economics and Statistics*, **48**, pp. 213–28.
—— (1987), 'Implications of aggregation with common factors', *Econometric Theory*, **3**, pp. 208–22.
—— (1988), 'Aggregation of time series – a survey', Federal Bank of Minneapolis, Institute for Empirical Macroeconomics, Discussion Paper 1.
Granger, C.W.J. and Lee, T-H. (1988), 'Multicointegration', *UCSD Discussion Paper*.
Granger, C.W.J. and Newbold, P. (1977), *Forecasting Economic Time Series* (New York: Academic Press).
Greenwald, B. and Stiglitz, J. (1987), 'Keynesian, New Keynesian and New Classical Economics,' *Oxford Economic Papers*, **39**, pp. 119–32.
Gutting, Gary (1988), 'Michel Foucault and the History of Reason', in Ernan McMullin (ed.), *Construction and Constraints: The Shaping of Scientific Rationality* (Notre Dame: University of Notre Dame Press).
Haavelmo, T. (1943), 'The Statistical Implications of a System of Simultaneous Equations', *Econometrica*, **11**, pp. 1–12.
—— (1944), *The Probability Approach to Econometrics*, Supplement to *Econometrica*, **12**.
—— (1947), 'Methods of Measuring the Marginal Propensity to Consume', *Journal of the American Statistical Association*, **42**, pp. 105–22.
—— (1954), *A Study in the Theory of Economic Evolution* (Amsterdam: North-Holland).
—— (1956), 'Ligninger vs. Identiteter i Okonomist Makroteori', in *25 Essays in Honour of Erik Lindahl* (Stockholm: Ekonomist Tidskrift).
—— (1958), 'Hva Kan Statiske Likevektsmodeller Fortelle Oss?', *Festskrift til Frederik Zeuthen* (Copenhagen: Nationalokonomisk Forening) (Supplement to *Nationalokonomisk Tidsskrift*, 96) published in English: 'What Can Static Equilibrium Models tell Us?', *Economic Inquiry*, **12** (1974), pp. 27–34.
—— (1958), 'The Role of the Econometrician in the Advancement of Economic Theory', *Econometrica*, **26**, pp. 351–7.

Hacking, Ian (1979), 'Imre Lakatos's Philosophy of Science', *British Journal for the Philosophy of Science*, **30**, pp. 381–410.

—— (1981), 'Lakatos's Philosophy of Science', in Hacking (ed.), *Scientific Revolutions*, pp. 128–43 (Oxford: Oxford University Press).

—— (1983), *Representing and Intervening* (Cambridge: Cambridge University Press).

Hahn, F. (1970), 'Some Adjustment Problems', *Econometrica*, **38** (1), January, pp. 1–17.

—— (1984), *Equilibrium and Macroeconomics* (Oxford: Basil Blackwell).

—— (1986), 'Review of Arjo Klamer, *Conversations with Economists: New Classical Economists and Opponents Speak Out on the Current Controversy in Macroeconomics, Economics and Philosophy*, **2** (2), pp. 275–82.

—— (1987), 'Information, Dynamics and Equilibrium', *Scottish Journal of Political Economy*, **34** (4), November, pp. 321–34.

—— (ed.) (1989), *The Economics of Missing Markets, Information and Games* (Oxford: Clarendon Press).

Hall, R.E. (1975), 'The Rigidity of Wages and the Persistence of Unemployment', *Brookings Papers on Economic Activity*, **2**, pp. 301–35.

—— (1978), 'Stochastic implications of the Life Cycle–Permanent Income Hypothesis: theory and evidence' in Lucas and Sargent (1981), pp. 501–20. Reprinted from *Journal of Political Economy*, **86**, pp. 971–87.

—— (1980), 'Employment fluctuations and wage rigidities', *Brookings Papers on Economic Activity*, 1980, **1**, pp. 91–124.

Hamminga, B. (1983), *Neoclassical Theory Structure and Theory Development* (New York: Springer).

—— (1984), 'Possible approaches to reduction in economic theory', in W. Balzer *et al.* (eds), *Reduction in Science*, pp. 295–317 (Dordrecht: Reidel).

—— (1990), 'Learning economic method from the invention of vintage models', in N.B. de Marchi (ed.), *Methodological Reflection in Economics* (forthcoming).

Hammond, Claire Holton (1987), *The Benefits of Subsidized Housing Programmes: An Intertemporal Approach* (Cambridge: Cambridge University Press).

Hands, D. Wade (1979), 'The methodology of economic research programmes', *Philosophy of the Social Sciences*, **9**, pp. 293–303.

—— (1984), 'The role of crucial counterexamples in the growth of

economic knowledge: Two cases in the recent history of economic thought', *History of Political Economy*, **16**, pp. 59–67.
—— (1985), 'Karl Popper and Economic Methodology', *Economics and Philosophy*, **1**, pp. 83–99.
—— (1985), 'Second Thoughts on Lakatos', *History of Political Economy*, **17**, pp. 1–16.
—— (1988), 'Ad Hocness in Economics and the Popperian Tradition', in N. de Marchi (ed.), *The Popperian Legacy in Economics*, pp. 121–37 (Cambridge: Cambridge University Press).
—— (1990), 'Second Thoughts on "Second Thoughts": Reconsidering the Lakatosian Progress of *The General Theory*', *Review of Political Economy*, **2**, pp. 69–81.
—— (1991), 'Falsification, situational analysis and scientific research programs: the Popperian tradition in economic methodology', mimeo 1989; forthcoming in Neil de Marchi (ed.), *Methodological Reflection in Economics* (Boston: Kluwer/Nijhoff).
Hansen, B. (1955), 'Report of the Uppsala Meeting', *Econometrica*, **23**, pp. 198–216.
Hansen, Gary D. (1985), 'Indivisible Labor and the Business Cycle', *Journal of Monetary Economics*, **16** (3), pp. 309–28.
Hansen, Lars Peter and Sargent, Thomas J. (1980), 'Estimating and Formulating Dynamic Linear Rational Expectations Models' in Lucas and Sargent (1981), pp. 91–125. Reprinted from *Journal of Economic Dynamics and Control*, **2** (1).
Hansson, B.A. (1982), *The Stockholm School and the development of Dynamic Method* (London: Croom Helm).
Harrison, Glenn and McCabe, Kevin A. (1989), 'The Role of Experience in Testing Non Cooperative Bargaining Theory in Experiments', working paper.
Harrod, R.F. (1937), 'Mr Keynes and Traditional Theory, *Econometrica*, **5**, pp. 74–86.
Harsanyi, T. (1967–8), 'Games with incomplete information played by Bayesian players', Parts I, II and III, *Management Science*, **14**, pp. 159–82, 320–34, 486–502.
—— (1977), *Rational Behaviour and Bargaining Equilibrium in Games and Social Situations* (Cambridge: Cambridge University Press).
Hart, O. (1982), 'A Model of Imperfect Competition with Keynesian Features', *Quarterly Journal of Economics*, **97**.
Harvey, A.C. (1981), *The Econometric Analysis of Time Series* (Deddington: Philip Allan).
Harvey-Phillips, M.B. (1983), 'T.R. Malthus on the "Metaphysics of

Political Economy": Ricardo's critical ally', in A.W. Coats (ed.), *Methodological Controversy in Economics*, pp. 185–210.
Hausman, Daniel M. (1991), *The Inexact and Separate Science of Economics*, forthcoming.
Hayek, Friedrich A. (1955), *The Counter-Revolution of Science* (London: Free Press of Glencoe).
Hendry, D. (1983), 'Econometric Modelling: the "Consumption Function" in Retrospect', *Scottish Journal of Political Economy*, **30** (3), November, pp. 193–220.
—— (1986), 'Econometric Modelling with Cointregrated Variables', *Oxford Bulletin of Economics and Statistics*, **48** (3), August, pp. 213–28.
Hendry, D.F. and Ericsson, N.R. (1989), 'An Econometric Analysis of U.K. Money Demand', discussion paper No. 41, Nuffield College, Oxford.
Hendry, D.F. and Richard, J.-F. (1983), 'The Econometric Analysis of Economic Time Series', *International Statistical Review*, **51**, pp. 111–63.
Hicks, J.R. (1937), 'Mr Keynes and the "classics": a suggested interpretation', *Econometrica*, **5**, pp. 147–59.
—— (1939), *Value and Capital* (Oxford: Clarendon Press).
—— (1956), *A Revision of Demand Theory* (Oxford: Clarendon Press).
—— (1976), '"Revolutions" in economics', in Latsis (ed.), *Method and Appraisal*, pp. 207–18.
Hill, B.M. (1986), 'Some subjective Bayesian considerations in the selection of models', *Econometric Reviews*, **4**, pp. 191–246.
Hirsch, E.D., Jr. (1987), *Cultural Literacy: What Every American Needs to Know* (Boston: Houghton Mifflin).
Hobson, J.A. (1985), 'The Meaning and Measure of Unemployment', *Contemporary Review*, March, pp. 415–32.
Holt, Charles A. (1980), 'Competitive Bidding for contracts under alternative auction procedures', *Journal of Political Economy*, **88**, pp. 433–45.
Hoover, Kevin, D. (1988), *The New Classical Macroeconomics* (Oxford: Basil Blackwell).
—— (1989), 'Econometrics as Observation: The Lucas Critique and the Nature of Econometric Inference', paper presented at the History of Economics Society meetings, 10-13 June 1989, Richmond, VA.
Hume, D. (1758), 'Of Money', reprinted in P.C. Newman *et al.* (eds), *Soure Readings in Economic Thought* (New York: W.W. Norton, 1954).
Hutchison, T.W. (1976), 'On the History and Philosophy of Science

and Economics' in Latsis, *Method and Appraisal in Economics*, pp. 181–206.

Jalladeau, J. (1978), 'Research Program versus Paradigm in the Development of Economics', *Journal of Economic Issues*, **12**, pp. 583–608.

Janssen, Maarten (1989), 'The alleged necessity of microfoundations', University of Groningen, mimeo.

—— (1990), *Micro and Macro in Economics: An Inquiry into their Relation* (Groningen: Walters-Noordhoff).

—— (1992), 'What is this thing called microfoundations?', *History of Political Economy* (forthcoming).

Jenkinson, T.J. (1988), 'The NAIRU: Statistical Fact or Theoretical Straitjacket?', in R. Cross (ed.), *Unemployment, Hysteresis and the Natural Rate Hypothesis* (Oxford: Basil Blackwell).

Jovanovic, B. (1979), 'Job matching and the theory of turnover', *Journal of Political Economy*, **87** (5), pp. 972–90.

Kahn, R.F. (1976), 'Unemployment as Seen by the Keynesians', in G.D. Worsick (ed.), *The Concept and Measurement of Involuntary Unemployment* (London: Allen & Unwin).

Kalai, E. and Stanford, W. (1988), 'Finite Rationality and Interpersonal Complexity in Repeated Games', *Econometrica*, **56**, pp. 397-410.

Kaldor, N. (1933), 'A Classificatory Note on the Determinateness of Equilibrium', *Review of Economic Studies*, **II**, pp. 122–36.

—— (1972), 'The Irrelevance of Equilibrium Economics', *Economic Journal*, **82**, pp. 1237–55.

Kareken, John H. and Wallace, Neil (eds), (1980), *Models of Monetary Economies* (Minneapolis: Federal Reserve Bank of Minneapolis).

Keynes, J.M. (1930), *Treatise on Money* (London: Macmillan).

—— (1936), *The General Theory of Employment, Interest and Money* (London: Macmillan).

—— (1973), *The Collected Works of John Maynard Keynes*, vol. **XIV**. (ed.) D. Moggridge (London: Macmillan).

—— (1971–83), *The Collected Writings of John Maynard Keynes* (London: Macmillan).

Khalil, Elias (1987), 'Kuhn, Lakatos, and the history of economic thought', *International Journal of Social Economics*, **14**, pp. 118–31.

Kiefer, N.M. and Neumann, G.R. (1979), 'An empirical job search model with a test of the constant reservation wage hypothesis', *Journal of Political Economy*, **87** (1), pp. 89–107.

—— (1979), 'Estimation of wage offer distributions and reservation wage', in S.A. Lippman and J.J. McCall, (eds), *Studies in the economics of search* (Amsterdam: North-Holland) pp. 171–90.

—— (1981), 'Individual effects in a non-linear model: explicit treatment of heterogeneity in the empirical job search model', *Econometrica*, **49** (4), pp. 965–79.

Kim, J. (1988), 'The development of job search theory: a methodological essay', unpublished paper, Duke University.

—— (1989), 'Testing in Modern Economics: The Case of Job Search Theory', paper prepared for the conference on Transitions in Recent Economics: Studies in Alternative Research Programmes, Capri, Italy, October 1989.

—— (1990), 'Discovery and Testing in Economics: The Case of Job Search Theory', PhD thesis, Duke University.

King, Ronald R., Smith, Vernon L., and Williams, Arlington, W. (1989), 'The Robustness of Bubbles and Crashes in Experimental Stock Markets', Department of Economics, University of Arizona.

Kirzner, Israel M. (1986), 'Another Look at the Subjectivism of Costs', in Kirzner (ed.) (1986).

—— (ed.) (1986), *Subjectivism, Intelligibility, and Economic Understanding: Essays in Honor of Ludwig M. Lachmann on his Eightieth Birthday* (New York: New York University Press).

Klamer, Argo (1984), *Conversations with Economists* (Totawa, New Jersey: Rowman and Allanheld).

—— (1984), 'Levels of discourse in new classical economics', *History of Political Economy*, **16**, pp. 263–90.

—— (1984), *The New Classical Macroeconomics: Conversations with New Classical Economists and Their Opponents* (Brighton, Sussex: Wheatsheaf Books).

Klappholz, K. (1989), 'Rent Control' in J. Eatwell, M. Milgate, and P. Newman (eds) *Social Economics* (Macmillan: London).

Klappholz, K. and Agassi, J. (1959), 'Methodological Prescriptions in Economics', *Economica*, N.S. vol. 26 (February), pp. 60–74.

Kleidon, Allan W. (1986), 'Anomalies in Financial Economics: Blueprint for Change?' in R.M. Hogarth and M.W. Reder, (eds), *Rational Choice*, (Chicago: University of Chicago Press).

Klein, L.R. (1950), *Economic Fluctuations in the United States 1921–1941*, Cowles Commission Monograph No. 11 (New York: Wiley).

—— (1962), *An Introduction to Econometrics* (New York: Prentice-Hall).

Knorr-Cetina, Karin (1981), *The Manufacture of Knowledge: An Essay on the Constructivist and Contingent Nature of Science* (Oxford: Pergamon Press).

Koertge, N. (1974), 'On Popper's Philosophy of Social Science', in

K.F. Schaffner and R.S. Cohen (eds), *PSA 1972*, pp. 195-207 (Dordrecht: D. Reidel).

—— (1975), 'Popper's Metaphysical Research Program for the Human Sciences', *Inquiry*, **19**, pp. 437–62.

—— (1979), 'The Problem of Appraising Scientific Theories', in P.D. Asquith and H.E. Kyburg, Jr (eds), *Current Research in Philosophy of Science*, pp. 228–51 (East Lansing, MI: Philosophy of Science Association).

Koopmans, T.C. (1945), 'Statistical Estimation of Simultaneous Economic Relations', *Journal of the American Statistical Association*, **40**, pp. 448–66.

Kowalik, T. (1987), 'Lange-Lerner Mechanism', *The New Palgrave*, 3 (London: Macmillan).

Koyck, L.M. (1954), *Distributed Lags and Investment Analysis* (Amsterdam: North-Holland).

Krajewski, W. (1977), *Growth of Knowledge and the Correspondence Principle* (Dordrecht: Reidel).

Kregel, J.A. (1987), 'The effective demand approach to employment and inflation analysis,' *Journal of Post Keynesian Economics*, **10**, pp. 133–45.

Kreinin, M. (1961), 'Windfall income and consumption: additional evidence', *American Economic Review*, **51**, pp. 388–90.

Kreps, D.M. (1987), 'Nash Equilibrium' in Eatwell, Milgate and Newman, *The New Palgrave*, pp. 167–77.

Kreps, David, Milgrom, Paul, Roberts, John and Wilson, Robert (1982), 'Rational Cooperation in the Finitely Repeated Prisoners' Dilemma', *Journal of Economic Theory*, **27**, pp. 245–52.

Kreps, D.M. and Wilson, R. (1982), 'Reputation and Imperfect Information', *Journal of Economic Theory*, **27**, pp. 253-79.

—— (1982), 'Sequential Equilibria', *Econometrica*, **50**, pp. 863–94.

Kuhn, Thomas S. (1970), *The Structure of Scientific Revolutions*, 2nd edn (1st edn 1962) (Chicago: University of Chicago Press).

Kuipers, Th.A.F. (1982), 'Approaching Descriptive and Theoretical Truth', *Erkenntnis*, **18**, pp. 343–78.

—— (1987), 'A Structuralist Approach to Truthlikeness', in Th.A.F. Kuipers, *What is Closer to the Truth?* (Amsterdam: Rodopi).

Kydland, Finn E. (1984), 'Labor-Force Heterogeneity and the Business Cycle', in Karl Brunner and Allan H. Meltzer (eds), *Essays on Macroeconomics Implications of Financial and Labor Markets and the Political Process*, Carnegie-Rochester Conference Series on Public Policy, vol. 21, Autumn (Amsterdam: North-Holland).

Kydland, Finn E. and Prescott, Edward C. (1977), 'Rules Rather than

Discretion; The Inconsistency of Optimal Plans', in Lucas and Sargent (1981), pp. 619–38. Reprinted from *Journal of Political Economy*, **85** (3).

—— (1982), 'Time to Build and Aggregate Fluctuations', *Econometrica*, **50** (6), pp. 1345-69.

Lachmann, Ludwig M. (1971), *The Legacy of Max Weber* (Berkeley: The Glendessary Press).

—— (1977), *Capital, Expectations, and the Market Process: Essays on the Theory of the Market Economy* (Kansas City: Sheed, Andrews and McMeel).

Lakatos, Imre (1968), 'Changes in the Problem of Inductive Logic', in I. Lakatos (ed.), *The Problem of Inductive Logic*, pp. 315–417 (Amsterdam: North-Holland).

—— (1970), 'Falsification and the Methodology of Scientific Research Programmes', in Lakatos and Musgrave, *Criticism and the Growth of Knowledge*, pp. 91–196.

—— (1971), 'History of Science and its Rational Reconstructions', (paper presented at the Biennial Meeting of the Philosophical Association, October 1970) in R.C. Buck and K.S. Cohen, (eds), *Boston Studies in the Philosophy of Science*, vol. 8, pp. 91–136 (Dordrecht: Reidel). Reprinted in Lakatos (1978), pp. 102–38.

—— (1971), 'Replies to Critics' in R.C. Buck and K.S. Cohen (eds), *Boston Studies in the Philosophy of Science* (Dordrecht: Reidel).

—— (1976), *Proofs and Refutations*, edited by John Worrall and Elie Zahar (Cambridge and New York: Cambridge University Press).

—— (1978), *Philosophical Papers, Vol. I: The Methodology of Scientific Research Programmes. Vol. II: Mathematics, Science and Epistemology*, J. Worrall and G. Currie (eds), (Cambridge: Cambridge University Press).

Lakatos, Imre and Musgrave, Alan (eds) (1970), *Criticism and the Growth of Knowledge* (Cambridge: Cambridge University Press).

Lakatos, I. and Zahar, E.G. (1976), 'Why did Copernicus's programme supersede Ptolomy's?', in R. Westman (ed.), *The Copernical Achievement* (Los Angeles: University of California Press). Reprinted in Lakatos (1978), pp. 168–92.

Lancaster, T. (1979), 'Econometric methods for the duration of unemployment', *Econometrica*, **47** (4).

Lancaster, T. and Chesher, A. (1982), 'An econometric analysis of reservation wage', *Econometrica*, **49** (4).

Lancaster, T. and Nickell, S. (1980), 'The analysis of reemployment for the unemployed', *Journal of the Royal Statistical Society*, **143** (2), pp. 141–65.

Lange, O. (1944), *Price Flexibility and Employment* (Bloomington: Principia Press).

Landsberger, M. (1979), 'Restitution receipts, household savings and consumption behavior in Israel', Jerusalem, Research Department, Bank of Israel.

Langlois, Richard N. (1982), 'Austrian Economics as Affirmative Science: Comment on Rizzo', in Israel M. Kirzner (ed.), *Method, Process and Austrian Economics*, pp. 75–84 (Lexington, Mass.: Lexington Books).

Latour, Bruno (1987), *Science in Action* (Cambridge, Mass.: Harvard University Press).

Latour, Bruno and Woolgar, Steve (1979), *Laboratory Life* (Beverly Hills: Sage).

Latsis, S.J. (1972), 'Situational Determinism in Economics', *The British Journal for the Philosophy of Science*, **23**, pp. 207–45.

—— (1976), 'The limitations of single-exit models: reply to Machlup', *The British Journal for the Philosophy of Science*, **27**, pp. 51–60.

—— (ed.) (1976), *Method and Appraisal in Economics* (Cambridge: Cambridge University Press).

—— (1976), 'A research programme in economics', in *Method and Appraisal*, pp. 1–41.

Lau, L.J. (1982), 'A note on the fundamental theorem of exact aggregation', *Economic Letters*, **9**, pp. 119–26.

Lavoie, D. (1985), *Rivalry and Central Planning: The Socialist Calculation Debate Reconsidered* (Cambridge: Cambridge University Press).

—— (1986), 'Euclideanism Versus Hermeneutics: A Reinterpretation of Misesian Apriorism', in Kirzner (1986).

—— (1987), 'The Accounting of Interpretations and the Interpretation of Accounts: The Communicative Function of "The Language of Business" ', *Accounting, Organizations and Society*, **12**, pp. 579–604.

—— (1990), 'Hermeneutics, Subjectivity, and the Lester/Machlup Debate: Toward a More Anthropological Approach to Empirical Economics' in Warren Samuels (ed.), *Economics as Discourse* (Boston: Kluwer Academic Publishing).

—— (1990), 'The Discovery and Interpretation of Profit Opportunities: Culture and the Kirznerian Entrepreneur', paper, prepared for the conference on *The Culture of Entrepreneurship*, sponsored by the Institute for the Study of Economic Culture, held in Indianapolis, Indiana, 26–7 January 1990.

Lawson, T. (1985), 'The Context of Prediction and the Paradox of Confirmation', *British Journal for the Philosophy of Science*, **36**, pp. 393–407.

Layard, R. (1986), *How to Beat Unemployment* (Oxford: Oxford University Press).
Layard, R. and Nickell, S. (1986), 'Unemployment in Britain', *Economica*, **53** (210), pp. S121–S169.
—— (1986), 'The Performance of the British Labour Market', CLE discussion paper No. 249, LSE.
Leamer, E.E. (1983), 'Let's take the con out of econometrics', *American Economic Review*, **73**, pp. 31–43.
Lee, Lung-Fei, and Mark M. Pitt (1986), 'MIcroeconometric Demand Systems with Binding Nonnegativity Constraints: The Dual Approach', *Econometrica*, **54**, pp. 1237–42.
Leijonhufvud, A. (1968), *On Keynesian Economics and the Economics of Keynes* (New York: Oxford University Press).
—— (1976), '"Schools", "revolutions", and research programmes in economic theory', in Latsis (ed.), *Method and Appraisal*, pp. 65–108.
Leong, Siew Meng (1985), 'Metatheory and metamethodology in marketing: A Lakatosian reconstruction', *Journal of Marketing*, **49**, pp. 23–40.
Leser, C.E.V. (1963), 'Forms of Engel functions', *Econometrica*, **31**, pp. 694-703.
L'Esperance, W.L. (1964), 'A Case Study in Prediction: the Market for Watermelons', *Econometrica*, **32**, pp. 163–73.
Levhari, D. (1965), 'A nonsubstitution theorem and switching of techniques', *Quarterly Journal of Economics*, **79**, pp. 98–105.
Levi-Stauss, Claude (1978), *The Origin of Table Manners*, translated by John and Doreen Weightman (London: Jonathan Cape).
Lewbel, A. (1989), 'A demand system rank theorem', *Econometrica*, **57**, pp. 701–6.
Lewis, D.K. (1969), *Convention* (Cambridge, Mass.: Harvard University Press).
Lindbeck, A. and Snower, D.J. (1988), 'Union Activity, Unemployment Persistence and Wage-Employment Ratchets', reprinted in R. Cross (ed.), *Unemployment, Hysteresis and the Natural Rate Hypothesis* (Oxford: Basil Blackwell).
Lippman, S.A. and McCall, J.J. (1976), 'The economics of job search: a survey, I', *Economic Inquiry*, **14** (2), pp. 155–89.
Lipsey, R.G. (1960), 'The Relation Between Unemployment and the Rate of Change of Money Wage Rates: A Further Analysis', *Econometrica*, **27**, February, pp. 1–31.
—— (1963), *Introduction to Positive Economics* (London: Weidenfeld & Nicolson).
—— (1968), 'Structural and Demand Deficient Unemployment Recon-

sidered', in B.J. McCormick and E. Owen Smith (eds), *The Labour Market* (Harmondsworth: Penguin).

Litterman, Robert B. (1984), 'Forecasting and Policy Analysis with Bayesian Vector Autoregression Models', Federal Reserve Bank of Minneapolis Quarterly Review, **8** (4), pp. 30–41.

Littlechild, Stephen (1979), 'Comment: Radical Subjectivism or Radical Subversion?', in Mario Rizzo (ed.), *Time, Uncertainty, and Disequilibrium* (Lexington, Mass.: Lexington Books).

Liviatan, N. (1963), 'Tests of the Permanent-Income Hypothesis based on a reinterview savings survey', in C.F. Christ *et al.*, *Measurement in Economics* (Stanford: Stanford University Press).

Long, John B. and Plosser, Charles I. (1983), 'Real Business Cycles', *Journal of Political Economy*, **91** (1), pp. 39–69.

Lötka, A.J. (1925), *Elements of Mathematical Biology* (Baltimore: William and Wilkins).

Lovell, Michael, C. (1986), 'Tests of the Rational Expectations Hypothesis', *American Economic Review*, **76** (1), pp. 110–24.

Lucas, Peter E. Jr. (1981), 'Distributed Lags and Optimal Investment Policy', in R. Lucas and T. Sargent (eds), *Rational Expectations and Econometric Practice.*

Lucas, Robert (1985), *Studies in Business Cycle Theory* (Cambridge, Mass.: MIT Press).

Lucas, R.E. Jr. (1965), 'Distributed Lags and Optimal Investment Policy' in R. Lucas and T. Sargent (eds), *Rational Expectations and Econometric Practice*, pp. 39–54, previously unpublished.

—— (1966), 'Optimal Investment with Rational Expectations', in R. Lucas and T. Sargent (eds), *Rational Expectations and Econometric Practice*, pp. 55–66, previously unpublished.

—— (1972), 'Econometric Testing of the Natural Rate Hypothesis', in Otto Eckstein (ed.), *The Economics of Price Determination Conference*, pp. 50–59, Board of Governors of the Federal Reserve System, and in Lucas (1981), pp. 96–103.

—— (1972), 'Expectations and the Neutrality of Money', *Journal of Economic Theory*, **42**, April, pp. 103–24. Reprinted in Lucas (1981), pp. 66–89.

—— (1973), 'Some International Evidence on Output Inflation Trade-Offs', in Lucas (1981), pp. 131–45. Reprinted from *American Economic Review*, **63**, June, pp. 326–34.

—— (1975), 'An Equilibrium Model of the Business Cycle' in Lucas (1981), pp. 179–214. Reprinted from *Journal of Political Economy*, **83**, December, pp. 1113–44.

—— (1976), 'Econometric Policy Evaluation: a Critique', in K. Brunner and A.H. Meltzer (eds), *The Phillips Curve and Labor Markets*, pp. 19–46 (Amsterdam: North-Holland). Supplement to the *Journal of Monetary Economics*, **1**, April. Also in Lucas (1981), pp. 104–30.

—— (1977), 'Understanding Business Cycles', in Lucas (1981). Reprinted from Karl Brunner and Allan H. Meltzer (eds), *Stabilization of the Domestic and International Economy*, Carnegie-Rochester Conference Series on Public Policy, vol. 5, Spring (Amsterdam: North-Holland).

—— (1978), 'Unemployment Policy', *American Economic Review*, **68** 2, May, pp. 353–7.

—— (1980), 'Equilibrium in a Pure Currency Economy', in Kareken and Wallace (1980), pp. 131–46.

—— (1980), 'Methods and Problems in Business Cycle Theory', in Lucas (1981), pp. 271–96. Reprinted from *Journal of Money, Credit and Banking*, **12** (4, part 2).

—— (1981), 'Distributed Lags and Optimal Investment Policy', in R. Lucas and T. Sargent (eds), *Rational Expectations and Economic Practice*, pp. 39–54.

—— (1981), *Studies in Business-Cycle Theory* (Oxford: Basil Blackwell and Cambridge, Mass.: MIT Press).

—— (1984), 'Money in a Theory of Finance', in Karl Brunner and Allan H. Meltzer (eds), *Essays on Macroeconomic Implications of Financial and Labor Markets and the Political Process*, Carnegie-Rochester Conference Series on Public Policy, vol. 21 (Amsterdam: North-Holland).

—— (1987), *Models of Business Cycles* (Oxford: Basil Blackwell).

Lucas, Robert E. Jr. and Prescott, E.C. (1971), 'Investment Under Uncertainty', *Econometrica*, **39** (5), pp. 659–81.

Lucas, Robert E. Jr. and Rapping, Leonard A. (1969), 'Price Expectations and the Phillips Curve', *American Economic Review*, **59**, June, pp. 670–80.

—— (1969), 'Real Wages, Employment and Inflation', in Lucas (1981). Reprinted from *Journal of Political Economy*, **77** (5), pp. 721–54.

Lucas, Robert E. Jr. and Sargent, Thomas (1979), 'After Keynesian Macroeconomics', reprinted in Lucas and Sargent (1981), pp. 295–320.

—— (eds) (1981), *Rational Expectations and Econometric Practice*, Vols 1 and 2 (London: Allen & Unwin and Minneapolis: University of Minnesota Press).

Lynch, L.M. (1983), 'Job search and youth unemployment', *Oxford Economic Papers*, **35**, (Supplement), pp. 271–82.

McCabe, Kevin A. (1989), 'Fiat Money as a Store of Value in an

Experimental Market', *Journal of Economic Behavior and Organization*, **12**.

McCall, J.J. (1970), 'Economics of information and job search', *Quarterly Journal of Economics*, **84** (1), pp. 113–26.

McCarthy, M. (1987), 'Econometrics after the Cowles Commission Work and the Brookings Project: Successes, Mistakes and Possible New Directions', unpublished paper.

McCloskey, Donald (1983), 'The Rhetoric of Economics', *Journal of Economic Literature*, June, **21**, pp. 481–517.

—— (1985), *The Rhetoric of Economics* (Madison: University of Wisconsin Press).

—— (1986), *The Rhetoric of Economics* (Brighton: Wheatsheaf Books).

—— (1988), 'Thick and thin methodologies in the history of economic thought', in de Marchi (ed.), *Popperian Legacy*, pp. 245–57.

McElroy, Marjorie B. (1981), 'Duality and the Error Structure in Demand Systems', National Opinion Research Center, University of Chicago working paper no. 81–2.

—— (1988), 'Additive General Error Models for Production, Cost, and Derived Demand or Factor Share Systems', *Journal of Political Economy*, **95**, pp. 737–55.

McMahon, Michael R. (1984), 'An appraisal of the new classical macroeconomics', *Journal of Macroeconomics*, **6**, pp. 335–46.

Machlup, Fritz (1974), 'Situational determinism in economics', *The British Journal for the Philosophy of Science*, **25**, pp. 271–84.

Mack, R.P. (1948), 'The direction of change in income and the consumption function', *Review of Economics and Statistics*, **30**, pp. 239–58.

Maddock, Rodney (1984), 'Rational expectations macrotheory: a Lakatosian case study in programme adjustment', *History of Political Economy*, **16**, pp. 291–310.

Maes, I. (1988), 'Did the Keynesian revolution retard the development of portfolio theory?, *Banca Nazionale del Lavoro Quartley Review*.

Mäki, Uskali (1986), 'Scientific Realism and Austrian Explanation', unpublished.

—— (1989), 'Mengerian Economics in realist Perspective', paper presented at a conference on 'Carl Menger and His Legacy in Economics', Duke University, April 1989.

—— (1989), 'On the Problem of Realism in Economics', *Ricerche Economiche*, **43**, pp. 176–98.

—— (1990), 'Methodology of economics: complaints and guidelines', *Finnish Economic Papers*, **3**, pp. 77–84.

—— (1990), 'Friedman and realism', *Research in the History of Economic Thought and Methodology*, **10**.

Malinvaud, E. (1977), *The Theory of Unemployment Reconsidered*, (Oxford: Basil Blackwell).

de Marchi, Neil (1976), 'Anomaly and the development of economics: the case of the Leontief paradox', in Latsis (ed.), *Method and Appraisal*, pp. 109–27.

—— (1987), 'The Cambridge Didactic Style and Keynesian Macro-economics', paper given at the History of Science Meeting, Raleigh, October 1987.

—— (1987), 'Paradoxes and anomalies', in John Eatwell, Murray Milgate and Peter Newman (eds), *The New Palgrave Dictionary of Economics*, pp. 796–9 (New York: Stockton Press, vol. 3).

—— (1988), 'Popper and the LSE economists', in N. de Marchi (ed.), *The Popperian Legacy in Economics* (Cambridge: Cambridge University Press).

—— (1990), ' "Discovery" and the unimportance of Lucas' test of the natural rate hypothesis', mimeo.

de Marchi, Neil and Gilbert, Christopher J. (1989), Introduction, in de Marchi and Gilbert (eds), *History and Methodology of Econometrics*, pp. 1–12 (Oxford: Oxford University Press).

—— (1989), *History and Methodology of Econometrics* (Oxford: Economic Pappers Issue) vol. **41**, 1, January.

de Marchi, Neil and Kim, Jinbang (1989), 'Ceteris Paribus as prior knowledge: a view from economics', *PSA 1988* (2), pp. 317–25.

Marschak, J. (1942), 'Identity and Stability in Economics: A Survey', *Econometrica*, **10**, pp. 61–74.

—— (1949), 'Statistical Inference from Non-Experimental Observation: An Economic Example', *Proceedings of the International Statistical Conferences*, 1947, III (A), pp. 289–301.

—— (1968), 'Economics of Inquiring, Communicating, Deciding', *American Economic Review Proceedings*, May, **58**, pp.1–18.

Marshall, A. (1980), *Principles of Economics* (London).

Masterman, Margaret (1970), 'The Nature of a Paradigm', in Lakatos and Musgrave (1970), pp. 59–60.

Mayer, T. (1972), *Permanent Income, Wealth and Consumption* (Berkeley: University of California Press).

—— (1980), 'Economics as hard science: realistic goal for wishful thinking', *Economic Inquiry*, **18**.

Maynard Smith, J. (1982), *Evolution and the Theory of Games* (Cambridge: Cambridge University Press).

Meade, J.E. (1936), *An Introduction to Economic Analysis and Policy* (Oxford: The Clarendon Press).
—— (1937), 'A Simplified model of Mr. Keynes's system', *Review of Economic Studies*, **4**, pp. 98–107.
—— (1948), *Planning and the Price Mechanism* (London: George Allen & Unwin).
Meinhold, R.J. and Singpurwal, N.D. (1983), 'Understanding the Kalman Filter', *American Statistician*.
Menger, Carl [1871](1981), *Principles of Economics* (New York: New York University Press).
Mertens, Jean-François (1987), 'Supergames', in J. Eatwell, M. Milgate and P. Newman (eds), *The New Palgrave*, vol. 4, pp. 551–2.
Miller, D.W. (1974), 'Popper's Qualitative Theory of Verisimilitude', *British Journal for the Philosophy of Science*, **25**, pp. 166–77.
Mirowski, Philip (1988), *Against Mechanism: Protecting Economics from Science* (Totowa, NJ: Rowman & Littlefield).
—— (1989), *More Heat Than Light: Economics as Social Physics: Physics as Nature's Economics* (New York: Cambridge University Press).
—— (1989), 'The Rise and Fall of the Concept of Equilibrium in Economic Analysis', *Recherches Economiques de Louvain*, **55**, pp. 1–22.
Mises, Ludwig von [1933](1981), *Epistemological Problems of Economics* (New York: New York University Press).
—— [1949](1966), *Human Action* (Chicago: Henry Regnery Company).
Mishkin, Frederic S. (1983), *A Rational Expectations Approach to Macroeconomics: Testing Policy Effectiveness and Efficient Market Models* (Chicago: University of Chicago Press).
Mizon, G.E. (1984), 'The encompassing principle in econometrics', in D.F. Hendry and K.F. Wallis (eds), *Econometrics and Quantitative Economics* (Oxford: Blackwell).
Mizon, G.E. and Richard, J.-F. (1986), 'The encompassing principle and its application to non-nested hypotheses', *Econometrica*, **54**, pp. 657–78.
Modigliani, F. (1944), 'Liquidity preference and the theory of interest of money', *Econometrica*, **12**, pp. 45–88.
Modigliani, F. and Brumberg, R. (1953), 'Utility analysis and the consumption function: an interpretation of the cross-section data', in K.K. Kurihara (ed.), *Post Keynesian Economics* (London: George Allen & Unwin).

—— (1955), 'Utility Analysis and Aggregate Consumption Functions: An Attempt at Integration', mimeo.

—— (1955), 'Utility Analysis and the Consumption Function: An Interpretation of Cross-Section Data', in K.K. Kurihari (ed.), *Post Keynesian Economics* (London: Geroge Allen & Unwin).

Morgan, M.S. (1987), 'Statistics without Probability and Haavelmo's Revolution in Econometrics', in Kruger, G. Gigerenzer and M.S. Morgan (eds), *The Probabilistic Revolution Vol 2: Ideas in the Sciences* (Cambridge, Mass.: MIT Press).

—— (1988), 'Finding a satisfactory empirical model', in N. de Marchi (ed.), *The Popperian Legacy in Economics* (Cambridge: Cambridge University Press).

—— (1990), *The History of Econometric Ideas* (Cambridge: Cambridge University Press).

—— (1990), 'Perspectives in the History of Econometrics', *Econometric Theory*, **6**, pp. 151–64.

Mortensen, D.T. (1970), 'A theory of wage and employment dynamics', in E.S. Phelps *et al.*, *Economic Foundation of Employment and Inflation Theory*, pp. 167–211, (New York: Norton).

Moulin, H. (1986), *Game Theory for the Social Sciences*, 2nd edn, (New York: New York University Press).

Muellbauer, J. (1983), 'Surprises in the consumption function', *Economic Journal*, **93**, Supplement, pp. 34–50.

Muellbauer, J. and Pashardes, P. (1988), 'Tests of dynamic specification and homogeneity in demand systems', Institute for Fiscal Studies, Discussion paper 88/6.

Musgrave, Alan (1974), 'Logical Versus Historical Theories of Confirmation', *British Journal for the Philosophy of Science*, **25**, pp. 1–23.

—— (1976), 'Method or Madness?' in R.S. Cohen, P.K. Feyerbend and M.W. Wartofsky (eds), *Essays in Memory of Imre Lakatos*, pp. 457–91 (Dordrecht: Reidel).

—— (1989), 'Deductive heuristics', in Gavrogulu *et al.* (eds), *Imre Lakatos and Theories of Scientific Change*, pp. 15–32.

Muth, J.F. (1961), 'Rational expectations and the theory of price movements', in Lucas and Sargent (1981), pp. 3–22. Reprinted from *Econometrica*, **29**, July, pp. 315–35.

—— (1981), 'Optimal Properties of Exponentially Weighted Forecasts', in R. Lucas and T. Sargent (eds), *Rational Expectations and Econometric Practice*.

Nash, J. (1950), 'Equilibrium Points in N-person games', *Proceedings of the National Academy of Sciences*, USA, **36**, pp. 48–9.

—— (1953), 'Two-person Cooperative Games', *Econometrica*, **21**, pp. 129–40.

Nelson, C.R. and Plosser, C.I. (1982), 'Trends and Random Walks in Macroeconomic Time Series: Some Evidence and Implications', *Journal of Monetary Economics*, **10** (2), pp. 139–62.

von Neumann, J. and Morgenstern, O. (1943), *Theory of Games and Economic Behavior* (Princeton: Princeton University Press).

Newton-Smith, W.H. (1981), *The Rationality of Science* (London: Routledge & Kegan Paul).

Nickell, S.U. (1979), 'The effect of unemployment and related benefits on the duration of unemployment', *Economic Journal*, **89**, pp. 34–49.

—— (1979), 'Estimating the probability of leaving unemployment', *Econometrica*, **47**, 5, September, pp. 1247–66.

—— (1985), 'Error correction, partial adjustment and all that: an expository note', *Oxford Bulletin of Economics and Statistics*, **47**, pp. 119–31.

—— (1987), 'Why is Wage Inflation in Britain So High?', *Oxford Bulletin of Economics and Statistics*, reprinted in R. Cross (ed.), *Unemployment, Hysteresis and the Natural Rate Hypothesis* (Oxford: Basil Blackwell).

—— (1988), 'The NAIRU: Some Theory and Statistical Facts', in R. Cross (ed.), *Unemployment, Hysteresis and the Natural Rate Hypothesis* (Oxford: Basil Blackwell).

Nickles, Thomas (1987), 'Methodology, Heuristics and Rationality', in Joseph C. Pitt and Marcello Pera (eds), *Rational Change in Science*, pp. 103–32 (Dordrecht: Reidel).

Nola, R. (1987), 'The Status of Popper's Theory of Scientific Method', *British Journal for the Philosophy of Science*, **38**, pp. 441–80.

Nunan, R. (1984), 'Novel Facts: Bayesian Rationality, and the History of Continental Drift', *Studies in the History and Philosophy of Science*, **15**, pp. 267–307.

O'Brien, D.P. (1976/1983), 'The longevity of Adam Smith's vision: Paradigms, research programmes and falsifiability in the history of economic thought', *Scottish Journal of Political Economy*, **23**, pp. 133–51. Revised version in A.W. Coats (ed.), *Methodological controversy in economics*, pp. 89–124.

Oddie, G. (1986), 'The Poverty of the Popperian Program for Truthlikeness', *Philosophy of Science*, **53**, pp. 163–78.

O'Driscoll, Gerald P. and Mario J. Rizzo (1985), *The Economics of Time and Ignorance* (Oxford: Basil Blackwell).

Ohlin, B. (1937), 'Some Notes on the Stockholm Theory of Savings and Investment', *Economic Journal*, **47**, pp. 53–69 and 221–40.

Okun, A.M. (1980), 'Rational-expectations-with-misperceptions as a theory of the business cycle', *Journal of Money, Credit and Banking*, **12**, pp. 817–25.

Orcutt, G.H. and Cochrane, D. (1949), 'A Sampling Study of the Merits of Autoregressive and Reduced Form Transformations in Regression Analysis', *Journal of the American Statistical Association*, **44**, pp. 356–72.

Pasinetti, L.L. (1979), 'Sraffa, Piero' in D.L. Sills (ed.), *International Encyclopedia of the Social Sciences*, biographical supplement, vol. 18 (New York: Free Press).

—— (1981), *Structural Change and Economic Growth* (Cambridge: Cambridge University Press).

—— (1985), 'Piero Sraffa (1898–1983). Breve saggio bio-bibliografico', in *Due scritti bio-bibliografici su Piero Sraffa*, Temi di discussione 50, Servizio studi della Banca d'Italia, Rome.

Patinkin, Don (1957), *Money, Interest and Prices* (Evanston, Ill.: Row, Peterson and Co).

—— (1965), *Money, Interest and Prices*, 2nd end (New York: Harper & Row).

—— (1990), 'In Defense of IS-LM', *Banco Nazionale del Lavoro Quarterly Review*, No. 172, March, pp. 119–34.

Peden, G.C. (1980), 'Keynes, the Treasury and Unemployment in the Later Nineteen-Thirties', *Oxford Economic Papers*, March, pp. 1–18.

Peirce, Charles S. (1931), *Collected Papers*, vol. 1 (Cambridge, Mass.: Belknap Press).

Pera, Marcello (1987), 'The Rationality of Discovery: Galvani's Animal Electricity', in Pitt and Pera (eds), *Rational Changes in Science*, pp. 177–201.

—— (1989), 'Methodological Sophisticationism: A Degenerating Project', in Gavrogul *et al.* (eds), *Imre Lakatos and Theories of Scientific Change*, pp. 169–81.

Phelps, E.S. (1967), 'Phillips Curves, Expectations of Inflation and Optimal Unemployment Over Time', *Economica*, **34**, 3, pp. 254–81.

—— (ed.) (1970), *Microeconomic Foundations of Employment and Inflation Theory* (New York: W.W. Norton).

—— (1972), *Inflation Policy and Unemployment Theory* (London: Macmillan).

Phelps, Edmund and Taylor, John B. (1977), 'Stabilizing Powers of Monetary Policy Under Rational Expectations', *Journal of Political Economy*, **85** (1), pp. 163–90.

Phillips, A.W. (1954), 'Stabilisation Policy in a Closed Economy', *Economic Journal*, **64**, pp. 296–323.

—— (1958), 'The Relationship Between Unemployment and the Rate of Change of Money Wage Rates in the U.K. 1861–1957', *Economica*, **25**, pp. 283–99.

Pilgrim Trust, (1983), *Men Without Work* (Cambridge: Cambridge University Press).

Pitt, J.C. and Pera, M. (eds), (1977), *Rational Changes in Science* (Dordrecht: Reidel).

Plosser, C.I. and Schwert, G.W. (1978), 'Money, Income and Sunspots: Measuring Economic Relations and the Effects of Differencing', *Journal of Monetary Economics*, **4**, pp. 637–60.

Pool, Robert (1989), 'Skepticism Grows Over Cold Fusion', *Science*, 21 April, **244**, pp. 284–5.

Popper, K.R. (1934), *The Logic of Scientific Discovery* (London: Hutchinson).

—— (1963), *Conjectures and Refutations* (London: Routledge).

—— (1965), *Conjectures and Refutations* (New York: Harper & Row).

—— (1968), *The Logic of Scientific Discovery* (New York: Harper & Row).

—— (1972), *Objective Knowledge: An Evolutionary Approach* (London: Oxford University Press).

—— (1973), *Objective Knowledge* (Oxford: Clarendon Press).

—— (1976), 'The Logic of the Social Sciences', in T.W. Adorno *et al.* (eds), *The Positivist Dispute in German Sociology*, pp. 87–122 (New York: Harper & Row).

—— (1976), *Unended Quest: An Intellectual Autobiography*, (LaSalle, IL: Open Court).

—— (1983), *The Open Universe* (London: Hutchinson).

—— (1983), Quantum Theory and the Schism in Physics (London: Hutchinson).

—— (1983), *Realism and the Aim of Science* (London: Hutchinson and Totowa, NJ: Rowman and Littlefield).

—— (1985), 'The Rationality Principle', in D. Miller (eds), *Popper Selections*, pp. 357–65 (Princeton: Princeton University Press).

Porter, David and Smith, Vernon, L. (1989), 'The Scope of Bubbles in Experimental Asset Markets', Department of Economics, University of Arizona.

Prendergast, Christopher (1986), 'Alfred Schütz and the Austrian School of Economics', *American Journal of Sociology*, **92** (1), July, pp. 1–26.

Prescott, Edward C. (1986), 'Theory Ahead of Measurement', *Federal*

Reserve Bank of Minneapolis Quarterly Review, **10** (4). Reprinted from Karl Brunner and Allan H. Meltzer (eds), *Real Business Cycles, Real Exchange Rates and Actual Policies*, Carnegie–Rochester conference Series on Public Policy, vol. 25, Autumn (Amsterdam: North-Holland).

Qin, D. (1989), 'The History of Econometric Thought: The Formation of Econometrics (1930–1969), DPhil thesis, Oxford.

Quine, W. Van O. (1951), 'Two Dogmas of Empiricism', *Philosophical Review*, reprinted in Quine (1980).

—— (1980), *From a Logical Point of View*, 2nd edn rev. (Cambridge, Mass.: Harvard University Press).

Quine, W. Van O. and Ullian, J.S. (1988), 'Hypothesis' from *The Web of Belief*, reprinted in Klemke E.D. *et al.* (eds) (1988), *Philosophy of Science* (Amherst, NY: Prometheus Books).

Radnitzky, Gerard and Bartley, W.W. III (eds) (1987), *Evolutionary Epistemology, Theory of Rationality, and the Sociology of Knowledge* (LaSalle, IL: Open Court).

Raiffa, H. (1982), *The Art and Science of Negotiation* (Cambridge, Mass.: Harvard University Press).

Rapoport, A. (1987), 'Prisoner's Dilemma', in Eatwell, Milgate and Newman (eds), *The New Palgrave*, pp. 199–204.

Rapoport, A. and Chammak (1965), *Prisoner's Dilemma* (Wisconsin: University of Michigan Press).

Reder, M.W. (1982), 'Chicago economics: Permanence and change', *Journal of Economic Literature*, **20** (1), pp. 1–38.

Remenyi, J.V. (1976), 'Core–demi-core interaction in economics', PhD thesis, Duke University.

—— (1979), 'Core–demi-core interaction: towards a general theory of disciplinary and subdisciplinary growth', *History of Political Economy*, **11**, pp. 30–63.

Reny, P. (1985), 'Rationality, Common Knowledge and the Theory of Games', mimeo, Princeton University.

Ricouer, Paul (1981), 'The Model of the Text: Meaningful Action Considered as a Text' in *Hermeneutics and the Human Sciences*, edited and translated by J.B. Thompson (New York: Cambridge University Press).

Rizzo, M.J. (1982), 'Mises and Lakatos: a reformulation of Austrian methodology', in I.M. Kirzner (ed.), *Method, Process and Austrian Economics*, pp. 53–73, (Lexington, Mass.: D.C. Heath Lexington Books).

Robins, Philip K. (1990), 'Child Care Policy and Research: An Economist's Perspective', paper prepared for the Carolina Public

Policy conference on The economics of Child Care, University of North Carolina, Chapel Hill, May 1990.
Robinson, J. (1956), *The Accumulation of Capital* (London: Macmillan).
Roncaglia, A. (1978), *Sraffa and the Theory of Prices* (New York: Wiley).
—— (n.d., 1985?), 'The Sraffian schools', mimeo, Rome.
Rorty, R. (1979), *Philosophy and the Mirror of Nature* (Princeton: Princeton University Press).
Rorty, R. *et al.* (eds) (1984), *Philosophy in History* (New York: Cambridge University Press).
Rosenberg, A. (1981), *Sociobiology and the Preemption of Social Science* (Baltimore, MD: Johns Hopkins University Press).
—— (1986), 'Lakatosian consolations for economics', *Economics and Philosophy*, **2**, pp. 172–89.
—— (1988), *Philosophy of Social Science* (Boulder, CO: Westview Press).
Rosenthal, R. (1981), 'Games of Perfect Information, Predatory Pricing, and the Chain Store Paradox', *Journal of Economic Theory*, **25**, pp. 92–1000.
Roth, A. (1988), 'Laboratory Experiments in Economics', *The Economic Journal*, **98**, pp. 974–1032.
Rothbard, Murray (1989), 'My Break with Branden and the Rand Cult', *Liberty*, **3** (1) (September), pp. 27–32.
Rubenstein, A. (1989), 'The Electronic Mail Game: Strategic Behaviour Under "Almost Common Knowledge" ', *American Economic Review*, forthcoming.
Runde, Jochen (1988), 'Subjectivism, Psychology, and the Modern Austrians', in Peter Earl (ed.), *Psychological Economics: Development, Tensions, Prospects* (Boston: Kluwer Academic).
Sachs, J.D. (1979), 'Wages, profits and macroeconomic adjustment', *Brookings Papers on Economic Activity*, **2**, pp. 269–319.
Salanti, Andrea (1990), 'On the Lakatosian Apple of Discord Between Historians and Methodologists', University of Bergamo, mimeo.
Salmon, M. (1982), 'Error Correction Mechanisms', *Economic Journal*, **92**, pp. 615–29.
Samuelson, P.A. (1947), *Foundations of Economic Analysis* (Cambridge, Mass: Harvard University Press).
—— (1955), *Economics*, 3rd edn (New York and London: McGraw Hill).
—— (1958), 'An Exact Consumption-Loan Model of Interest with or

without the Social Contrivance of Money', *Journal of Political Economy*, **56** (6), pp. 467–82.
—— (1966), 'A summing up', *Quarterly Journal of Economics*, **80**, pp. 568–83.
—— (1972), 'Some Notions of Causality and Teleology in Economics' and 'What Classical and Neoclassical Monetary Theory Really Was', in R.C. Merton (ed.), *The Collected Scientific Papers of Paul A. Samuelson Vol. III* (Cambridge, Mass.: MIT Press).
—— (1987), 'Out of the Closet: A Program for the Whig History of Economic Science', *History of Economics Society Bulletin*, IX, **1**, Fall, pp. 51–60.
—— (1987), 'Sraffian economics', in *New Palgrave Dictionary of Economics*, vol. IV (London: Macmillan).
Sargan, J.D. (1964), 'Wages and Prices in the United Kingdom: a Study in Econometric Methodology', in R.E. Hart, G. Mills and J.K. Whitaker (eds), *Econometric Analysis for National Economic Planning* (London: Butterworths).
Sargan, J.D. and Bhargava, A. (1983), 'Testing Residuals from Least Squares Regressions for Being Generated by The Gaussian Random Walk', *Econometrica*, **51** (1), February, pp. 153–74.
Sargent, T.J. (1973), 'Rational Expectations, the Real Rate of Interest and the Natural Rate of Unemployment', *Brookings Papers on Economic Activity*, **2**, pp. 429–72.
—— (1976), 'A Classical Macroeconometric Model for the United States', in Lucas and Sargent (1981), pp. 521–51. Reprinted from *Journal of Political Economy*, **84**, April, pp. 207–37.
—— (1976), 'The Observational Equivalence of Natural and Unnatural Rate Theories of Macroeconomics', in Lucas and Sargent (1981), pp. 553–62. Reprinted from *Journal of Political Economy*, **84**, June, pp. 631–40.
—— (1977), 'The Demand for Money during Hyperinflations under Rational Expectations', in Lucas and Sargent (1981), pp. 429–52. Reprinted from *International Economic Review*, **18** (1).
—— (1977), 'Observations on improper methods of simulating and teaching Friedman's time-series consumption model', *International Economic Review*, **18**, pp. 445–62.
—— (1978), 'Estimation of Dynamic Labor Demand Schedules under Rational Expectations', in Lucas and Sargent (1981), pp. 463–500. Reprinted from *Journal of Political Economy*, **86** (6).
—— (1979), *Macroeconomic Theory* (New York: Academic Press).
—— (1981), 'Interpreting Economic Time Series', *Journal of Political Economy*, **89** (2), pp. 213–48.

—— (1982), 'Beyond Demand and Supply Curves in Macroeconomics', *American Economic Review*, **72** (2), pp. 382–9.
—— (1986), *Rational Expectations and Inflation*, (New York: Harper & Row).
—— (1987), *Dynamic Macroeconomic Theory* (Cambridge, Mass.: Harvard University Press).
Sargent, Thomas J. and Neftci, Salih (1978), 'A Little Bit of Evidence on the Natural Rate Hypothesis from the US', *Journal of Monetary Economics*, **4**, April, pp. 315–19.
Sargent, Thomas J. and Sims, Christopher A. (1977), 'Business Cycle Modeling without Pretending to Have Too Much *A Priori* Theory', in *New Methods in Business Cycle Research: Proceedings from a Conference*, pp. 45–110 (Minneapolis: Federal Reserve Bank of Minneapolis).
Sargent, Thomas J. and Wallace, Neil (1973), 'Rational Expectations and the dynamics of Hyperinflation', in Lucas and Sargent (1981), pp. 405–28.
—— (1975), 'Rational Expectations, the Optimal Monetary Instrument and the Optimal Money Supply Rule', in Lucas and Sargent (1981), pp. 215–28. Reprinted from *Journal of Political Economy*, **83**, April, pp. 241–55.
—— (1976), 'Rational Expectations and the Theory of Economic Policy', in Lucas and Sargent (1981), pp. 199–213. Reprinted from *Journal of Monetary Economics*, **2**, April, pp. 169–84.
—— (1981), 'Some Unpleasant Monetarist Arithmetic', *Federal Reserve Bank of Minneapolis Quarterly Review*, **5** (3), pp. 1–17. Reprinted in Sargent (1986).
—— (1982), 'The Real-Bills Doctrine versus the Quantity Theory: A Reconsideration', *Journal of Political Economy*, **90** (6), pp. 1212–36.
Schefold, B. (1989), *Mr. Sraffa on Joint Production and Other Essays* (London: Unwin Hyman).
Schelling, T. (1971), *The Strategy of Conflict* (Cambridge, Mass.: Harvard University Press).
Schmidt, Reinhard H. (1982), 'Methodology and Finance', *Theory and Decision*, **14**, pp. 391–413.
Schultz, H. (1938), *The Theory and Measurement of Demand* (Chicago: University of Chicago Press).
Schumpeter, J.A. (1934), *The Theory of Economic Development* (Cambridge, Mass.: Harvard University Press).
Shearmur, Jeremy (1990), 'From Hayek to Menger: Biology, Subjectivism, and Welfare', in Bruce Caldwell, (ed.), *Carl Menger and his Legacy in Economics* (Durham, N.C.: Duke University Press).

Shiller, R.J. (1981), 'Do Stock Prices Move Too Much to be Justified by Subsequent Changes in Dividends?', *American Economic Review*, **7**, pp. 421–36.

Siegel, Sidney and Fouraker, L.E. (1960), *Bargaining and Group Decision Making* (New York: McGraw-Hill).

Simon Herbert A. (1953), 'Causal Ordering and Identifiability' in W. Hood and T. Koopmans (eds), *Studies in Econometric Method*, Cowles Commission Monograph 14 (New York: Wiley).

—— (1976), 'From substantive to procedural rationality', in Latsis (ed.), *Method and Appraisal*, pp. 129–48.

Simon, H.A. and Wold, H. (1955), 'Causality and Econometrics: Comment' and 'Causality and Econometrics: Reply', *Econometrica*, **23**, pp. 193–7.

Sims, Christopher A. (1972), 'Money, Income and Causality', in Lucas and Sargent (1981), pp. 387–403. Reprinted from *American Economic Review*, **62** (4), pp. 540–52.

—— (1982), 'Policy Analysis with Econometric Models', *Brookings Papers on Economic Activity*, no. 1, pp. 107–52.

—— (1986), 'A Rational Expectations Framework for Short Run Policy Analysis', in William A. Barnett and Kenneth J. Singleton (eds), *New Approaches to Monetary Economics: Proceedings from the Second International Symposium in Economic Theory and Econometrics* (Cambridge: Cambridge University Press).

—— (1986), 'Are Forecasting Models Usable for Policy Analysis?', *Federal Reserve Bank of Minneapolis Quarterly Review*, Winter, pp. 2–15.

—— (1989), 'Macroeconomics and Reality', *Econometrica*, **48** (1), pp. 1–48.

Smith, Barbara H. (1988), *Contingencies of Value* (Cambridge, Mass.: Harvard University Press).

Smith, Vernon L. (1987), 'Experimental Methods in Economics', in J. Eatwell, M. Milgate and P. Newman (eds), *The New Palgrave*, vol. 2.

—— (1989), 'Theory, experiment, and economics', *Journal of Economic Perspectives*, **3**, pp. 151–69.

Smith, Vernon L., Suchanek, Gerry L. and Williams, Arlington W. (1988), 'Bubbles, Crashes, and Endogenous Expectations in Experimental Markets', *Econometrica*, September **56**, pp. 1119–51.

Solow, R.M. (1956), 'A Contribution to the Theory of Economic Growth', *Quarterly Journal of Economics*, **70** (1), pp. 65–94.

—— (1957), 'Technical Change and the Aggregate Production Function', *Review of Economics and Statistics*, **39** (3), pp. 312–30.

—— (1959), 'Review of S. Weintraub: *An Approach to the Theory of Income Distribution*', *Journal of Political Economy*, **67**, pp. 420–21.
—— (1980), 'On Theories of Unemployment', *American Economic Review*, **70** (1), pp. 1–11.
—— (1986), 'Unemployment: Getting the Questions Right', *Economica*, **53**, 210S, pp. S23–34.
—— (1987), 'Discussion', *Economic Policy*, **5**, October, pp. 181–5.
Solow, R. and Stiglitz, J. (1968), 'Output, Employment and Wages in the Short Run, *Quarterly Journal of Economics*, **82**, pp. 537–60.
Sonnenschein, Hugo (1983), *The Economics of Incentives: An Introductory Account*, Nancy L. Schwartz Memorial Lecture, Evanston: J.L. Kellogg Graduate School of Management, Northwestern University.
Spanos, A. (1986), *Statistical Foundations of Econometric Modelling* (Cambridge: Cambridge University Press).
Spinnewyn, F. (1979), 'The cost of consumption and wealth in a model with habit formation', *Economics Letters*, **2**, pp. 145–8.
—— (1981), 'Rational habit formation', *European Economic Review*, **15**, pp. 91–109.
Sraffa, P. (1969), *Production of Commodities by Means of Commodities* (Cambridge: Cambridge University Press).
Steedman, Ian (1977), *Marx after Sraffa* (London: New Left Books).
—— (ed.) (1988), *Sraffian Economics* (Vols I and II) (Aldershot: Edward Elgar).
Stigler, G.J. (1961), 'The economics of information', *Journal of Political Economy*, **69** (3), pp. 213–25.
—— (1962), 'Information in the labor market', *Journal of Political Economy*, **70** (5), pp. 594–S105.
Stiglitz, J.E. and Weiss, A. (1981), 'Credit rationing in markets with imperfect information', *American Economic Review*, **73**, pp. 393–411.
Stoker, T.M. (1986), 'Simple tests of distributional effects on macroeconomic equations', *Journal of Political Economy*, **94**, pp. 763–95.
Stone, J.R.N. (1945), 'The analysis of market demand', *Journal of the Royal Statistical Society*, **108**, pp. 286–382.
—— (1954), 'Linear expenditure systems and demand analysis: and application to the pattern of British demand', *Economic Journal*, **64**, pp. 511–27.
—— (1954), *The measurement of Consumers' Expenditure and Behaviour in the United Kingdom, 1920–38*, vol. 1 (Cambridge: Cambridge University Press).

Strotz, R.H. (1960), 'Interdependence as a Specification Error', *Econometrica*, **28**, pp.428–42.

Strotz, R.H. and Wold, H. (1960), 'Recursive versus Nonrecursive Systems: An attempt at Synthesis', *Econometrica*, **28**, pp. 417–27.

—— (1963), 'The Causal Interpretability of Structural Parameters: A Reply', *Econometrica*, **31**, pp. 449–50.

Suits, D. (1955), 'An Econometric Model of the Watermelon Market', *Journal of Farm Economics*, **37**, pp. 237–51.

Summers, L.H. (1988), 'Keynesian Economics and the Phillips Curve', in R. Cross (ed.), *Unemployment, Hysteresis and the Natural Rate Hypothesis* (Oxford: Basil Blackwell).

Taylor, John B. (1975), 'Monetary Policy during the Transition to Rational Expectations', *Journal of Political Economy*, **83** (6), pp. 1009–21.

Theil, H. (1955), *Linear Aggregation of Economic Relations* (Amsterdam: North-Holland).

—— (1967), *Economics and Inforamtion Theory* (Amsterdam, North-Holland).

Thornton, H. (1802), *An Inquiry into the Nature and Effects of the Paper Credit of Great Britain* (London).

Tichy, P. (1974), 'On Popper's Definitions of Verisimilitude', *British Journal of the Philosophy of Science*, **25**, pp. 155–60.

Tinbergen, J. (1935), 'Annual Survey: Suggestions on Quantitative Business Cycle Theory', *Econometrica*, **3**, pp. 241–308.

—— (1937), *An Econometric Approach to Business Cycle Problems* (Paris: Hermann & Cie).

—— (1939), *Statistical Testing of Business Cycle Theories*, vols I and II (Geneva: League of Nations).

—— (1949), 'Comments in discussion on Marschak's paper (1949)', *Proceedings of the International Statistical Conferences*, 1947, III (A).

Tirole, Jean (1982), 'On the Possibility of Speculation Under Rational Expectations', *Econometrica*, pp. 1163–81.

Tobin, J. (1965), 'Money and Economic Growth', *Econometrica*, **33**, pp. 671–84.

—— (1972), 'Inflation and Unemployment', *American Economic Review*, **62**, 1–19.

—— (1980), 'Are New Classical Models Plausible Enough to Guide Policy?', *Journal of Money, Credit and Banking*, **12**, pp. 788–99.

Tooke, T. (1838), *A History of Prices* (London: Longman, Orme, Brown, Greene and Longmans).

Toruno, Mayo C. (1988), 'Appraisals and rational reconstructions of general competitive equilibrium theory', *Journal of Economic Issues*, **22**, pp. 127–55.

Tötsch, I. (1988), 'Screening in Labour Markets with Heterogeneous Workers' in R. Cross (ed.), *Unemployment, Hysteresis and the Natural Rate Hypothesis* (Oxford: Basil Blackwell).

Van Fraassen, B. (1980), *The Scientific Image* (Oxford: Clarendon Press).

Vercelli, A. (1987), *Keynes dopo Lucas. I fondamenti della macroeconomia* (Rome: NIS).

Verstegen, B.H.J. (1984), 'Aspprirations, reference groups, and the consumer', *De Economist*, **132**, pp. 300–325.

Vickrey, William (1961), 'Counterspeculation, Auctions and Competitive Sealed Tenders', *Journal of Finance*, May, **16**, pp. 8–37.

Vint, John (1990), 'Thornton and Mill on the Supply and Demand of Commodities: A Lakatosian View', Manchester Polytechnic, mimeo.

Walker, Donald A. (1988), 'Ten Major Problems in the Study of the History of Economic Thought', *History of Economics Society Bulletin*, **X** (2), pp. 99–116.

Walker, James M., Smith, Vernon L. and Cox, James C. (1990), 'Inducing Risk Neutral Preferences: An Examination in a Controlled Market Environment', *Journal of Risk and Uncertainty*, **2**, September, pp. 219–35.

Wallace, Neil (1980), 'The Overlapping Generations Model of Fiat Money', in Kareken and Wallace (1980), pp. 49–82.

—— (1981), 'A Modigliani–Miller Theorem for Open-Market Operations', *American Economic Review*, **71** (3), pp. 267–74.

Wallis, K.F. (1969), 'Some recent developments in applied econometrics; dynamic models and simultaneous equation systems', *Journal of Economic Literature*, **7**, pp. 771–96.

—— (1973), *Topics in Applied Econometrics* (London: Gray–Mills).

—— (1980), 'Econometric Implications of the Rational Expectations Hypothesis', *Econometrica*, **48**, January, pp. 49–73.

Warnke, Georgia (1987), *Gadamer: Hermeneutics, Tradition and Reason* (Oxford: Polity Press).

Watkins, J. (1970), 'Imperfect Rationality', in R. Borger and F. Cioffi (eds), *Explanation in the Behavioural Sciences*, pp. 91–121 (Cambridge: Cambridge Univeristy Press).

—— (1978), 'The Popperian Approach to Scientific Knowledge', in G. Radnitzky and G. Anderson (eds), *Progress and Rationality in Science*, pp. 23–43 (Dordrecht: Reidel).

—— (1984), *Science and Scepticism* (Princeton, NJ: Princeton University Press).

Weber, Robert J. (1987), 'Games with Incomplete Information', in J. Eatwell, M. Milgate and P. Newman (eds), *The New Palgrave*, vol. 2.

Weintraub, E. Roy (1979), *Microfoundations. The Compatibility of Microeconomics and Macroeconomics* (Cambridge: Cambridge University Press).

—— (1982–3), 'Substantive mountains and methodological molehills', *Journal of Post-Keynesian Economics*, **5**, pp. 295–303.

—— (1985), 'Appraising general equilibrium analysis', *Economics and Philosophy*, **1**, pp. 23–37.

—— (1985), *General Equilibrium Analysis: Studies in Appraisal* (Cambridge: Cambridge University Press).

—— (1985), 'Joan Robinson's Critique of Equilibrium: An Appraisal' *American Economic Review*, **75**, pp. 146–9.

—— (1987), 'Rosenberg's "Lakatosian consolations for economics": comment', *Economics and Philosophy*, **3**, pp. 139–42.

—— (1988), 'The neo-Walrasian program is empirically progressive', in de Marchi (ed.), *Popperian Legacy*, pp. 213–27.

—— (forthcoming), *Stabilizing Dynamics* (Cambridge: Cambridge University Press).

Weintraub, S. (1958), *An Approach to the Theory of Income Distribution* (Philadelphia: Chilton).

—— (1970), 'Solow and Stiglitz on Employment and Distribution: A New Romance with an Old Model', *Quarterly Journal of Economics*, **84**, pp. 144–52.

Weiss, A. (1980), 'Job queues and layoffs in labor markets with flexible wages', *Journal of Political Economy*, **88**, pp. 526–38.

Weitzman, M. (1979), 'Optimal search for the best alternative', *Econometrica*, **47** (2), pp. 641–54.

Wittgenstein, Ludwig (1953), *Philosophical Investigations* (Oxford: Basil Blackwell).

—— (1975), *The Blue and Brown Books* (Oxford: Basil Blackwell).

Wold, H. (1938), *A Study in the Analysis of Stationary Time Series* (Uppsala: Almqvist & Wiksell).

—— (1949), 'Statistical Estimation of Economic Relationships', *Proceedings of the International Statistical Conferences*, 1947 (V), pp. 1–22.

—— (1954), 'Causality and Econometrics', *Econometrica*, **22**, pp. 162–77.

—— (1955), 'Possibilités et Limitations des Systèmes à Chaîne Causale', *Cahiers du Séminaire d'Econométrie*, **3**, pp. 81–101.

—— (1956), 'Causal Inferences from Observational Data: A Review of

Ends and Means', *Journal of the Royal Statistical Society*, Series A, pp. 28–50.
—— (1958), 'A Case Study of Interdependent Versus Causal Chain Systems', *Revue de l'Institut International de Statistique*, **26**.
—— (1959), 'Ends and Means in Econometric Model Building', in U. Grenender (ed.), *Probability and Statistics: The Harald Cramer Volume* (Stockholm: Almqvist & Wiksell).
—— (1960), 'A Generation of Causal Chain Models', *Econometrica*, **28**, pp. 443–63.
—— (1982), 'Models for Knowledge', in J. Gani (ed.), *The Making of Statisticians* (New York: Springer–Verlag).
Wold, H. and Juréen, L. (1953), *Demand Analysis* (Stockholm: Almqvist & Wiksell).
Wong, Stanley (1978), *The Foundations of Paul Samuelson's Revealed Preference Theory* (London: Routledge & Kegan Paul).
Woodward, C. Vann (1986), 'The Lost Cause: Review of Irving Howe's Socialism and America', *New York Review of Books*, 30 January, p. 26.
Worrall, J. (1978), 'The Ways in Which the Methodology of Scientific Research Programmes Improves on Popper's Methodology', in G. Radnitzky and G. Anderson (eds), *Progress and Rationality in Science*, pp. 45–70 (Dordrecht: Reidel).
—— (1982), 'Scientific Realism and Scientific Change', *Philosophical Quarterly*, **32**, pp. 201–31.
—— (1989), 'Structural Realism: The Best of Both Worlds?', *Dialectica*, **43**, pp. 99–124.
Wulwick, Nancy J. (1987), 'The Phillips Curve: Which? Whose? To do What? How?', *Southern Economic Journal*, **53**, pp. 834–57.
—— (1989), 'Phillips' Aporoximate Regression', *Oxford Economic Papers*, **41** (speical issue), pp. 170–88; reprinted in de Marchi and Gilbert (eds), *History and Methodology of Econometrics*.
Yeager, Leland (1987), 'Why Subjectivism?', *The Review of Austrian Economics*, **1**, pp. 5–31.
Young, H.P. (ed.) (1985), *Cost Allocation: Methods, Principles, Applications* (Amsterdam: North-Holland).
Young, W. (1987), *Interpreting Mr. Keynes: The IS-LM Enigma* (Cambridge: Polity Press).
Zahar, Elie (1973), 'Why Did Einstein's Programme Supersede Lorentz's? (I)', *British Journal for the Philosophy of Science*, **24**, p. 95–123.
—— (1982), 'The Popper–Lakatos Controversy', *Fundamenta Scientiae*, **3**, pp. 21–54.

—— (1983), 'The Popper–Lakatos Controversy in the Light of "Die Beiden Grundprobleme der Erkenntnistheorie" ', *British Journal for the Philosophy of Science*, **34**, pp. 149–71.

—— (1983), 'Logic of Discovery of Psychology of Invention?', *The British Journal for the Philosophy of Science*, **34**, pp. 243–61.

Zandvoort, H. (1986), *Models of Scientific Development and the Case of NMR* (Dordrecht: Reidel).

Zamagni, S. (1982), 'Introduzione', *Saggi di filosofia della scienza economica* (a cura di Stefano Zamagni) Rome, Nouva Italia Scientifica.

Zellner, A. (1988), 'Bayesian analysis in econometrics', *Journal of Econometrics*, **37**, pp. 27–50.

Name Index

Agassi, J. 35, 36, 39, 50–53, 67, 140, 487
Ahonen, G. 13
Aigner, J. 260
Åkerman, J. 271
Aldrich, J. 270, 271
Allen, A. 297, 300
Anderson, G. 145
Anderson, R. 230
Ando, R. 173, 414, 423
Archibald, C. 30, 140
Arrow, K. 273, 275, 280, 283–4, 286, 340, 422, 505, 507–8, 511
Attfield, C. 142, 145
Auman, R. 184, 187–8, 190–91, 194, 202, 206, 214
Axelrod, R. 91
Azariadis, C. 411

Bachelard, G. 279
Backhouse, R. 7, 21, 24, 387, 422–3, 427–32, 508, 510
Bacon, F. 437
Bagwell, K. 388
Bailey, M. 411
Bannerjee, A. 157
Barnett, W. 170
Barro, R. 337, 352, 364, 378, 380, 388, 409, 411, 418, 420, 469
Barten, A. 144–6, 150
Bartley, W. 36, 50, 68, 92, 100, 487
Bassmann, R. 254, 259
Baumol, W. 260, 408
Bazerman, C. 287
Beardsley, T. 199
Becker, G. 194
Begg, D. 361
Bentzel, R. 242–6, 259, 264
Bergstrom, A. 259
Bernheim, B. 388
Beveridge, S. 157
Bharadwaj, K. 466
Bhargava, A. 310
Bianchi, M. 20, 28
Bicchieri, C. 7, 192
Binmore, K. 192
Birner, J. 12, 16, 20
Blanchard, O. 314–15, 384, 396
Blaug, M. 7, 13, 21, 23, 27, 29, 30, 49, 50, 52, 85, 137–9, 162, 164, 279, 325, 422, 499, 503, 505, 510–11
Blundell, R. 145–7, 152, 163
Bodkin, R. 163
Böhm-Bawerk, E. von 463, 476
Boland, L. 487
Bowley, A. 205, 207, 510
Brams, S. 182, 187
Brandon, R. 25
Bridgman, P. 140
Brown, E. 30
Brown, T. 155
Browning, M. 142
Brumberg, R. 155
Bruno, M. 463
Bryant, J. 383
Buchanan, J. 55
Buiter, W. 423
Burdett, K. 129
Burmeister, E. 463, 468–9
Byron, R. 150, 163

Cagan, P. 154
Caldwell, B. 511
Calvo, G. 411
Campbell, J. 157–8, 164
Carrier, M. 73, 100
Carter, M. 360–61
Cartwright, N. 230
Chammack, A. 185
Champernowne, D. 408
Christ, C. 246
Christensen, L. 146
Christiano, L. 172–3
Classen, K. 117

Clower, R. 383, 409, 422–3
Coates, A.W. 387
Cochrane, D. 245
Coddington, A. 330
Cohen, L. 89
Collins, H. 22, 47, 50, 423, 497–8
Coppinger, V. 219
Cooley, T. 388
Cooper, R. 429, 431
Cox, D. 319
Cox, J. 218–20, 222
Cournot, A. 206–7
Cramer, H. 239
Cross, R. 8, 22–3, 30, 297, 300–301, 309–10, 312–15, 317, 324–30

Damme, E. van 188
Davidson, J. 162
Davidson, P. 143–8, 501
Deaton, A. 150–51, 157–8, 160, 162–4, 172–3
Debreu, G. 182, 283, 507–8
Derrida, J. 277
Desai, M. 8
Descartes, R. 41–2, 51
Dewald, W. 230
Diamond, P. 300
Dilthey, W. 477–8, 483–4
Dixit, A. 420
Dolado, J. 157
Dornbusch, R. 411, 417–19
Drazen, A. 423
Droysen, J. 477, 483
Duesenberry, J. 145, 155, 163
Duhem, P. 319

Edgeworth, F. 182
Ehrenberg, R.G. 117, 119
Einstein, A. 83, 467
Elster, J. 297
Endres, A. 488
Engle, R. 310
Epstein, R. 249, 254, 259–60
Ermarth, M. 484

Feiwel, G. 505
Fetter, F. 477
Feyerabend, P. 37, 385, 437, 448
Fischer, S. 384, 388, 396
Fish, S. 277
Fishburn, P. 187
Fisher, F. 466, 509
Fisher, I. 438, 461, 464
Fisher, M. 378
Fisher, R. 14, 30
Fisk, M. 100
Flavin, M. 157
Folks, J. 129
Foucault, M. 279–80, 292
Friedman, J. 182
Friedman, M. 6, 40, 53, 71, 86, 140, 153–8, 160, 163, 171–2, 231, 246, 278, 294–5, 324–6, 338–42, 347, 349, 356, 361, 372, 376, 379, 408, 410, 413–14, 419, 423, 501
Frisch, R. 238–40, 243, 253, 255, 258, 271, 284, 298
Fuller, W. 311
Fulton, G. 7, 8, 12, 29, 444, 446, 451

Gadamer, H-G. 472, 483–4
Gale, D. 274, 275–6
Gallant, A. 170
Gardner, M. 64, 73, 96, 99
Garegnani, P. 439–40, 445
Garner, C. 293
Geertz, C. 278
Georgescu-Roegen, N. 296–7
Gerrard, B. 422
Gilbert, C. 20, 138, 139, 141–2, 147, 150, 163, 169, 174, 260, 414
Gillies, D. 182
Glass, J. 8, 29, 30
Glazebrook, R. 299
Goldberger, A. 468
Gordon, R. 316, 380–81, 387–8, 418
Gorman, T. 146
Granger, C. 141, 163, 310
Greenwald, B. 331
Gronau, R. 106, 129
Grossman, H. 409, 420
Gutting, G. 279

Haavelmo, T. 141–2, 239–46, 251–2, 259, 266, 270–72
Habermas, J. 50, 52, 277
Hacking, I. 20, 26, 67, 139
Hahn, F. 273, 275, 301, 387, 422, 429, 507–8

Hall, R. 156–7, 164, 172–3, 376, 411, 418
Hamminga, B. 7, 13, 28, 83, 94–100
Hammond, C. 170
Hammond, P. 469
Hands, W. 4, 7, 13, 14,1 6, 19, 26–8, 36, 50–51, 72–3, 76, 81, 85, 99, 500–502
Hansen, A. 510
Hansen, B. 250–51, 259
Hansson, B. 238–9, 260
Harrison, G. 217–18
Harrod, R. 260, 297, 408
Harsanyi, T. 184, 186, 202–3, 224
Hart, O. 431
Harvey, A. 138
Harvey-Phillips, M. 8, 30
Hausman, D. 26
Hayek, F. 51, 470–71, 478, 481, 483, 485, 488, 501
Hecksher, E. 16
Hegel, G. 52
Hendry, D. 13, 253, 259, 310, 467
Hicks, J. 5, 148–9, 162, 274, 284, 408, 422, 438, 505, 507
Hill, B. 162
Hirsch, E. 388
Holt, C. 220
Hoover, K. 23, 271, 295, 369, 386–9, 395–9
Hurwicz, L. 274, 276, 280, 284, 286, 508
Hutchinson, H. 310, 312–15
Hutchison, T. 5, 29

Jalilian, H. 147, 163
Janssen, M. 12, 13, 20, 432
Jenkinson, T. 310–12
John, A. 429, 431
Johnson, W. 8, 29, 30
Jovanovic, B. 129
Juréen, L. 252–3, 260

Kahn, R. 503
Kalai, E. 192
Kaldor, N. 298, 300, 329, 397–8, 401
Keynes, J. 164, 256, 260, 278, 281, 286, 298–300, 325, 330–31, 345, 362, 379, 403–4, 406–8, 422, 483, 488, 510
Kiefer, N. 123–4
Kim, J. 8, 15, 20, 129, 132–6, 169–70
King, R. 216–18
Kirzner, I. 471
Klamer, A. 8, 14, 30, 369, 387–8
Klappholz, K. 19, 53–4, 140, 448, 487, 510
Kleidon, A. 214
Klein, L. 255, 256–7, 259–60, 468
Knorr-Cetina, K. 22, 278, 288
Koertge, N. 6, 72–3
Koopmans, T. 241, 244–5, 259
Kowalik, T. 507
Koyck, L. 155, 340–41
Krajenski, W. 88
Kregel, J. 331
Kreinin, M. 163
Kreps, D. 192–3, 206
Kuhn, T. 2, 21, 24, 42, 63, 139, 364–5, 372–3, 385
Kuipers, T. 83, 89
Kydland, F. 368–9, 371, 383

Lachmann, L. 471–2, 477, 484, 488–90
Lakatos, I. 1, 3, 5–9, 11, 14, 16–26, 35–49, 51, 53, 56, 58–72, 76, 79, 81–3, 96, 98–9, 100, 105, 127–8, 132–6, 1139, 291–2, 317, 318–20, 325–6, 335–9, 348–9, 353–6, 360, 364, 367–8, 370, 372, 374–5, 381–3, 385–7, 397, 399, 412, 422–3, 431, 446–7, 451, 483, 487–8, 495, 498–503
Lancaster, T. 120–21
Landsberger, M. 163
Lange, O. 55, 284, 437, 483, 507
Langlois, R. 30
Latour, B. 277, 285
Latsis, S. 6, 11, 14, 17, 30, 40, 51, 330, 387, 449, 499
Lau, L. 146
Laudon, L. 41, 43, 51–2
Lavoie, D. 25, 484–5, 487–9, 507
Lawson, T. 100
Layard, R. 302–6, 324–5
Leamer, E. 138, 200
Lee, L-F, 174
Leibniz, G. 42
Leijonhufvud, A. 5, 283, 395, 422–3
Leon, S. 30

Leontief, W. 16
Lerner, A. 483
Leroy, S. 388
Leser, C. 148
L'Esperance, W. 160
Levhari, D. 437, 456, 459–63, 468
Levy-Strauss, C. 389
Lewbel, A. 146
Lewis, D. 203
Lindbeck, A. 330
Lippman, S. 129
Lipsey, R. 140, 341
Littlechild, S. 489
Liviatan, N. 154, 158
Long, J.B. de 398
Lotka, A. 280, 299
Lovell, M. 371, 388
Lucas, R. 23, 282, 324, 336–57, 361–2, 364, 369–72, 376–81, 383, 386–9, 396, 410–11, 418–19, 432, 510
Lundberg, E. 239, 259

Machlup, F. 86
Mack, R. 155
Maddock, R. 8, 14, 23, 30, 325, 336, 352, 356, 360–62, 387–8, 498
Maes, I. 422
Mäki, U. 9, 28, 73, 85–6, 91–4
Malinvaud, E. 409–20
Mankiw, N. 164, 172–3
Marchi, N. de 8, 12, 14, 27, 30, 50, 85, 140, 142, 256, 499, 504–5, 511
Marschak, J. 251, 259
Marshall, A. 362, 440
Marx, K. 439, 442, 484, 510
Masterman, M. 372
Mayer, T. 138, 154, 156, 163
Maynard Smith, J. 190
McCabe, K. 217–18
McCall, J. 106, 129
McCarthy, M. 254
McCloskey, D. 137, 200, 269, 511
McElroy, M. 174
McKenzie, L. 283, 508
McMahon, M. 30
Meade, J. 55, 408, 501
Meinhold, R. 164
Menger, C. 71, 470–71, 475–6, 483, 488–9
Mertens, J-F. 202, 206
Milgrom, P. 206
Mill, J.S. 3, 436–7
Miller, A. 6
Miller, M. 423
Millikan, R. 227–8, 230
Mirowski, P. 10, 26, 28, 293, 367, 511
Mises, L. von 86, 437, 471, 473, 476–7, 480–81, 483–5, 488–9
Mishkin, F. 380
Mitchell, W. 423
Mizon, G. 139, 316, 319
Modigliani, F. 155, 408, 414, 423
Morgan, M. 8, 21, 22–3, 241, 253, 259, 266–9, 270
Morgenstern, O. 182, 183, 185
Mortensen, G. 106
Moulin, H. 20, 28, 184, 188
Muellbauer, J. 143–5, 148, 150, 160, 162–4
Murphy, K. 173
Musgrave, A. 6, 12, 16, 26–7, 51, 73, 96–100
Muth, J. 156, 269, 339–40, 343, 345, 354, 371, 376, 411

Nash, J. 181–2, 207
Nelson, C. 157, 383
Neumann, G. 123–4
Neumann, J. von 181, 183, 185, 284, 441
Newton, I. 11, 38, 50, 368, 446, 467
Newton-Smith, W. 369, 387–9
Nickell, S. 120–21, 157, 302–14, 324–5
Nola, R. 73
Nordhaus, W. 173
Nowak, L. 88
Nunan, R. 100
Nüniluoto, I. 85, 89

Oakeshott, M. 375
Oaxa, R. 117, 119, 218
O'Brien, D. 3, 17, 30
Oddie, G. 67, 85
O'Driscoll, G. 484, 488
Ohlin, B. 16, 260
Okun, A. 423
Orcutt, G. 245

Pashardes, P. 145, 163

Pasinetti, L. 438, 440–41, 445, 452, 462
Patinkin, D. 282, 284, 286, 408, 422, 506
Peden, G. 300
Pera, M. 6, 17, 26, 27
Phelps, E. 294, 299, 324, 338–9, 340, 347, 350–51, 376, 378, 410–11, 415, 419, 423
Pierce, C.S. 386
Pitt, M. 174
Pizon, A. 362
Plosser, C. 383
Polyanyi, M. 375, 483
Pool, R. 199
Pontryagin, L. 398–9
Popper, K. 2, 7, 11, 16, 18–21, 27, 35–50, 51–3, 56, 58–72, 76, 79, 81, 83, 85–6, 88, 89, 91, 93, 99–100, 128, 133–4, 139, 162, 367, 375, 487, 499–500, 502, 505
Porter, D. 216, 218
Prendergast, C. 478
Prescott, E. 350, 352, 368–9, 371, 383

Quin, R. 254, 259, 270
Quine, W. 326

Raiffa, H. 188
Ramsey, F. 396, 401
Rapoport, A. 185, 189–90
Rapping, L. 340–44, 350, 354, 369, 371, 376
Rebel, S. 396
Reder, M. 16, 413
Remenyi, J. 7, 13, 29, 367, 387
Reny, P. 192
Ricardo, D. 345, 439–40, 442, 475, 510
Richard, J. 139, 319
Rickert, H. 483
Ricoeur, P. 483
Rizzo, M. 30, 484, 488
Robbins, L. 85
Roberson, B. 219–20
Roberts, J. 206
Robins, P. 170
Robinson, J. 328, 329, 456, 461, 463, 469, 509
Romer, P. 396, 398
Roncaglia, A. 439–40, 445–6
Rorty, R. 26, 277, 292–3
Rosenberg, A. 6, 70
Rosenthal, R. 190, 230
Roth, A. 187
Rothbart, M. 484, 489
Rubenstein, A. 190
Runde, J. 488
Rush, M. 388, 418

Salanti, A. 26, 28, 455
Samuelson, P. 16, 78–9, 83, 94, 149, 169–70, 256, 260, 269, 273–4, 279–80, 284, 286, 292, 398, 401, 408, 422, 437–8, 443, 457–61, 463–4, 468
Sargan, D. 309
Sargent, T. 164, 337, 348–9, 352, 355, 361–2, 364, 369–70, 378, 380–84, 386–9, 411, 501, 507
Scarf, H. 183, 274–6
Schefold, B. 439, 466
Schelling, T. 188
Schmidt, R. 30
Schultz, H. 140, 149, 162–3
Schumpeter, J. 296–7, 328, 331, 451
Schutz, A. 477–8, 483
Seater, J. 388
Selten, R. 184
Shackle, G. 488
Shapin, S. 498
Shearmur, J. 19, 25, 448, 488, 504
Sheshinski, E. 463
Shiller, R. 214
Shubik, M. 182
Siegel, S. 203–4, 206–7
Simon, H. 30, 248, 354
Sims, C. 388
Singpurwalla, N. 164
Sklivas, S. 293
Smith, A. 292, 439, 442, 475, 508, 510
Smith, B. 277, 280
Smith, C. 231
Smith, V. 14, 21, 129, 185, 197, 216, 218–20, 222, 227
Snower, D. 330
Solow, R. 325, 330–31, 396–8, 401, 409, 438, 461, 468
Sonnenschein, H. 201, 508
Spanos, A. 140
Spinnewyn, F. 163
Sraffa, P. 435–55, 483

Stanford, W. 192
Steedman, I. 25, 42, 438, 451–2, 455, 456, 459, 504, 509
Stigler, G. 106, 194, 501
Stiglitz, J. 160, 330–31, 409
Stoker, T. 145, 147
Stone, R. 149–50, 170
Strotz, R. 247, 249, 255, 259
Suchanek, G. 216–18
Suits, D. 246–7, 265
Summers, L. 299, 314–15

Tarski, A. 59
Taylor, J. 378
Theil, H. 144, 250
Thursby, J. 230
Tichy, P. 67
Tinbergen, J. 237–9, 241-3, 249, 253, 255–8, 259–60, 271, 284
Tirole, J. 214
Titus, J. 219
Tobin, J. 300, 361, 408, 501
Torino, M. 29
Toulmin, S. 395
Tullock, G. 55
Turnovsky, S. 469

Uzawa, H. 468

Van Fraassen, B. 152
Vann Woodward, C. 286
Vercelli, A. 362
Verstegen, B. 29
Vickrey, W. 186, 202, 219–23
Vint, J. 14

Wald, A. 284
Walker, D. 280, 287
Walker, J. 220, 222
Wallace, N. 337, 348–9, 369–70, 378, 380–84, 385–6, 388, 411
Wallis, K. 163, 347, 356
Walras, L. 506–9
Warming, J. 503
Warnke, G. 484
Watkins, J. 6, 35, 39, 52, 67–8, 72–3, 85, 92, 98–9, 100
Weber, M. 477, 483–4
Weber, R. 206
Weintraub, R. 8, 12, 14, 16, 22, 24, 29–30, 109, 256, 260, 267, 274, 291–2, 327, 329, 331, 370, 387, 397, 404–6, 422, 429, 430–31, 446, 507, 511
Weintraub, S. 330
Weiss, A. 160, 411
White, S. 52
Wicksell, K. 240, 298
Wieser, F. 477, 484–5, 488
Williams, A. 216–18
Wilson, E. 280
Wilson, R. 192, 206
Wittgenstein, L. 364, 374–5, 388, 395
Wold, H. 239, 242–58, 259–60, 264–7, 269–72
Wong, S. 11
Woolgar, S. 277, 285
Worrall, J. 6, 50, 73, 92–3, 96, 100
Wulwick, N. 8, 15, 30, 395, 401–2

Yeagr, L. 463–4, 483, 489
Yeoward, S. 310, 312–4, 315
Young, H. 186
Young, W. 422

Zaghini, E. 441, 453
Zahar, E. 6, 65, 68, 96, 100, 412, 423
Zamagni, S. 447, 509, 511
Zandvoort, 4, 13, 430
Zellner, A. 162, 260

Subject Index

adaptive expectations *see* expectations
ad hoc strategems 2, 4, 72, 100, 139, 145, 201, 223, 318, 325, 350, 410–12, 419–20
aggregation 141, 144–6, 437–8
anomalies 10, 411
auctions 186, 197–213, 218–23
Austrian economics 25, 463–4, 470–85, 508
auxiliary assumptions 20, 126–7, 154

bargaining, bilateral 204–6, 217
basics and non-basics, in Sraffa 440–41, 453–5
business cycles 240–51, 256, 258, 356, 361, 368–9, 378, 383, 398, 418–19

capital controversies 437, 509
capital markets, perfect 160, 162
capital reversing 436, 437–8, 460–66
Centre for labour economics, LSE 302
ceteris paribus clauses 110, 113, 140–41
Chicago economics 16, 194, 413, 415–16, 419–20, 510
classical economics 452–5, 474–5, 509
cobweb model 238
competition, perfect and imperfect 413, 508
co-integration 310–12
consumer behaviour *see* demand theory
consumption theory 138, 153–61
conventionalism 36, 38
co-operation 181–2, 184, 189, 206
core, in game theory 182
corroboration, in Popper 95–6

deconstructing the history of economics 276–9
demand theory 20, 29, 82, 138, 139–40, 142–53, 159, 161, 169–71, 174
depreciation, in Sraffa 441
disequilibrium *see* dynamics
Duhem–Quine thesis 105, 116, 128, 312, 316, 318
duopoly *see* oligopoly
dynamics 273–88

econometrics 138, 237–58, 269, 382
economics of law 55
efficient markets, theory of 54
encompassing 13, 139, 319, 328
essentialism 71–2, 86–90, 92–3, 99
equilibrium, concepts of 21, 180, 183–5, 187, 194, 238–9, 243, 251, 281–3, 285, 294–8, 301, 337, 362, 371, 405, 408–9, 429, 507
evolutive games 189–90
excess content *see* novel facts
exemplars 372–3, 375–6
expectations, adaptive 154, 163–4, 324–5, 341–2, 369
  rational 23, 156, 174, 214–18, 295, 300–301, 324, 338, 340–41, 345–6, 354, 365, 370–71, 411, 417, 466
experimental economics 14, 21, 197–224

facts, status of 285–8
falsification 37, 61, 69, 127–9, 200, 510–11
futures markets 218

game theory 20–21, 179–95, 201–24, 371
  empirical content of, 185–7
general equilibrium theory 24, 29–30, 159, 180, 257, 268, 269, 274–5, 281, 283, 295, 324, 327, 349–50, 355, 362, 367–8, 370, 397–8, 403–32, 438, 489–91, 505–9
Giffen goods 510

hard core, in MSRP 9, 12, 16–19, 23, 88, 267, 270, 274–5, 292, 328, 337, 339, 343–4, 347, 355, 360, 365–6, 368, 370–72, 384, 404–6, 410, 429, 487, 500–501
hermeneutics 278, 472, 489
heuristics, in MSRP 9, 11–12, 16–18, 21, 24, 27–37, 270, 274–5, 317, 327, 345, 349–50, 354–5, 366, 372, 379, 384, 399, 404–6, 429–30, 446–7, 487, 501
history of science 4–5, 22, 35, 43–7, 279, 492–8, 504
homogeneity, of demand functions 144–5, 170
hysteresis 22, 294–301, 317–18, 324, 328–30

immunizing strategems *see* ad hoc stratagems
indecomposability 461–2
inflation, theories of 415
information, complete and incomplete 182–3, 202–3, 206–7, 351, 404, 410
instrumentalism 71, 86, 99
interdependence, of utilities 180
international trade theory 16, 30, 82, 438
introspection, in Austrian economics 481–2

job search theory 20, 82, 105–25
joint production 441

Keynesian economics 13, 14, 96, 256–8, 281, 286, 421, 427–8, 430–31, 501, 503–4, 510
Keynesian revolution 503–4

laboratory experiments 197–9, 227–30, 492–8
labour contracts 410–11
life cycle hypothesis 155, 171, 414
linear programming 181
Lucas critique 372–3, 378, 382

marginal productivity theory 436
market failure 54–5
market socialism *see* socialist calculation debate
Marshallian methods 352, 422
Marxian economics 438
mathematical politics 182
mathematics, history of 38–9, 40
measurement, in economics 147–8
metaphysics 18, 37, 39
methodology 6, 162, 447
methodology of scientific research programs (MSRP) 1–18, 23–4, 26–8, 63–4, 127–8, 193, 200–201, 266, 269, 271, 276–7, 291–2, 317–20, 327, 335–6, 353–5, 360, 364–6, 382, 385–6, 395, 401–2, 411–12, 421, 435, 442–4, 446–9, 451, 472–3, 487, 495, 499–502, 504
*see also*hard core, in MSRP; heuristics, in MSRP; novel facts; research programs
models and modelling 139–42, 154
monetarism 421, 428–9, 510
multiplier, in Keynes 268, 503

NAIRU *see* natural rate hypothesis
Nash equilibrium 182–3, 193, 201–3, 205–6, 219, 429
natural rate of interest 298
natural rate hypothesis 22–3, 294–318, 324–30, 338, 343, 351, 372, 415, 428
natural rate of interest 298
neoclassical synthesis 283–4, 285–6, 409
neo-Walrasian research programme *see* general equilibrium theory
new Cambridge theory 420, 423
new classical growth theory 396–9, 401
new classical macroeconomics 14, 23–4, 282, 324, 337–53, 364–87, 418–20, 430, 510
Neyman–Pearson testing 139, 252
non-empirical criticism 54–5
novel facts 4–5, 7, 13–14, 16, 18–19, 26–8, 58–73, 76–83, 94–100, 128, 132–6, 266, 317–19, 324, 347, 411–12, 414, 419–21, 423, 487, 500–503, 505, 510

oligopoly 206–13

operationally meaningful theorems 78–9
optimal control theory 399
overlapping – generations model 381–5

paradigm 372–3
parapsychology 497–8
Pareto optimality 54–5
path-dependence of equilibrium *see* hysteresis
permanent income hypothesis 137, 142, 153–61, 171–4, 413–14, 419
Phillips curve 140, 227, 324, 339, 341–4, 349, 410, 415, 510
physics envy 291
policy ineffectiveness 346–7, 349, 352, 369, 378
Pontryagin maximum principle 399
Poppers World Three 3, 136
Post-Keynesian economics 282, 286, 397, 488–9
predictive success, in economics 93–4
prisoner's dilemma game 180, 185, 189–90, 206
problem situation, in Popper 11, 19
problem solving 11, 12, 18, 20, 27, 41, 43
process analysis 237–58, 266–72
productivity growth 396
program rivalry 21, 22, 336
progress of knowledge 3–4, 5, 8, 37, 87–8, 279, 505
public choice theory 55

quantity theory of money 510

rational reconstructions 22–7, 274–9, 288, 292, 385, 421, 473, 496–7
rationality, principle of 21, 54, 68–9, 180–81, 183–4, 187, 190–92, 194, 387, 421
realism 85–90, 91–2, 287, 510
reality gap, between history and methodology of sciences 6, 10–18, 193, 276-9
relative shares, constancy of 510
relativism 291
rent control 54
rent theory in Sraffa 437, 441
replication, in science 493
research programs 4, 266–7, 327, 366–8, 430
reservation wage 108–9, 110, 111, 113, 117, 123
reswitching of techniques 436–8, 454, 461–9
returns to scale, constant and increasing 396–8
rhetoric 99, 347

sequence analysis *see* process analysis
Shapley value 186
simultaneous equations model 239–53, 264
situational analysis, in Popper 68–9, 70
socialist calculation debate 56, 507
sociology of science 35–6, 99, 348, 354, 492–8
Sraffian economics 25, 435–55, 509
  empirical content of 446–9
stability analysis 22, 274–88, 291, 442
stagflation 338, 510
standard commodity 439–40
statistical demand curves 3
stock market bubbles 214–18
subjectivist economics *see* Austrian economics

technical progress 397, 438
testing 8, 9, 15, 16–21, 23, 41, 47–9, 105, 110–11, 114, 116, 126–7, 129, 132, 137–8, 142, 152, 161–2, 174, 194, 245, 252–3, 351–3, 355, 447–8
theories, role of 4–5
theory choice 8, 9
tragedy of the commons 190
truth, search for 59

uncertainty 143
unemployment, theories of 22, 106, 294–318, 415–17
  concepts of 301, 329–30, 416
unobservables 113–15

value-free science 479–80
value theory 475–6
vector autoregressions 381–3

verisimilitude, in Popper 7, 19, 26, 58, 59–63, 76–83, 85, 88, 90, 91–2, 502
verstehen doctrine 472, 477–8, 480, 482–4, 498
Vickrey's auction 186

wage dispersion 106, 108